PERSIAN GULF COMMAND

PERSIAN GULF COMMAND

A HISTORY OF THE
SECOND WORLD WAR
IN IRAN AND IRAQ

ASHLEY JACKSON

YALE UNIVERSITY PRESS
NEW HAVEN AND LONDON

For information about this and other Yale University Press publications, please contact:
U.S. Office: sales.press@yale.edu   yalebooks.com
Europe Office: sales@yaleup.co.uk   yalebooks.co.uk

Set in Minion Pro by IDSUK (DataConnection) Ltd
Printed in Great Britain by Gomer Press Ltd, Llandysul, Ceredigion, Wales

Library of Congress Control Number: 2018936161

ISBN 978-0-300-22196-1

A catalogue record for this book is available from the British Library.

10 9 8 7 6 5 4 3 2 1

This book is dedicated to Sabre, an Australian kelpie, without whose gentle attentions it might have appeared a year ago. Also, to Andrew Stewart, for his friendship, wisdom and generosity.

CONTENTS

ILLUSTRATIONS

1. A firing party of British infantrymen provides cover for Royal Engineers building a temporary bridge near Ramadi, 1 June 1941. © Imperial War Museum (E3318).
2. Blenheim Mark Is of 84 Squadron flying in formations of three over the Iraqi desert. © Imperial War Museum (CM109).
3. The fort at Rutbah, Iraq, under attack from Bristol Blenheim Mark IVs of 84 Squadron on 9 May 1941. © Imperial War Museum (CM822).
4. A crew of No. 2 Armoured Car Company service a .303 Browning machine gun beside their GMC Mark I Otter light reconnaissance car at RAF Habbaniya. © Imperial War Museum (CM5698).
5. British troops look out across the Tigris from the roof of the British Embassy in Baghdad, 11 June 1941. © Imperial War Museum (E3464).
6. The commanding officer of 84 Squadron briefs his aircrew before a training sortie at Shaibah, Iraq. © Imperial War Museum (CM107).
7. Recruits for the RAF Iraq Levies at drill. © Imperial War Museum (E11584).
8. A wooden painted plaque of the British 10th Army insignia: a golden *lamassu*. British Army artist.
9. A map showing the extent of America's base infrastructure spread along the Iranian lines of communication.
10. A patient being treated for heatstroke, Iraq, 20 September 1943. © Imperial War Museum (E26027).

PREFACE AND ACKNOWLEDGEMENTS

This project began when I convened a workshop at Mansfield College, Oxford on research into unusual aspects of the British Empire's war experience (the summary papers of which were subsequently published in the journal *Global War Studies*). Captivated by material on Iran and Iraq, hastily consulted in order to offer insights from a relatively unheralded sphere of wartime activity, I decided to try to write a book on the subject, combining some of the excellent published work on disparate facets of the war in the region with new material gleaned from the archives. In the light of the workshop, Yasmin Khan and I successfully applied for a grant from the Arts and Humanities Research Council to look at the war in both India and the Iran–Iraq region. Our shared desire was to examine military affairs and grand strategy, while also investigating the war from the perspective of local politics and socioeconomic change. Thus, in the wake of Yasmin's acclaimed *The Raj at War*, published in 2015, comes *Persian Gulf Command*.[1]

Now, at the culmination of the project, the first reflection that comes to mind is that I bit off more than I could chew, but that I'm rather glad I did. I wanted to produce a pioneering synthesis of the surprisingly large body of published work on the two countries' wartime experience, at the same time introducing as much archival material as possible. While in more immodest moments I like to think that such a work – of synthesis and thematic collection – has been the result, the fact is that there are so many pools of highly developed specialist literature that I could not hope to plumb them all. The book covers numerous different disciplines and fields of expertise, including international politics, the national and local politics of Iran and Iraq, diplomatic, imperial and military history, and more general history, social and economic. It means that this is something of a jack-of-all-trades work, but a faithful one nonetheless, and one that may spur others to add further to the subject's study.

This is clearly a book written by a British historian, focusing on the British war effort, using primarily British sources (with a significant American archival component too). Having looked at tens of thousands of document pages, the surface has been scratched but not always very deeply penetrated – and that's just to speak of the British side of the archival equation. It's difficult to make a genuine apology for this: as most historians know only too well, time and money can only be made to go so far. While I could have taken another year or three in researching and writing the book, there's a limit to how much one can view, how much one can process, as well as how much one can fit within the covers of a single volume – at least, one that people are able to lift.

There's another factor, too, one that afflicts many historical studies: monolingualism. The fact is that I can't easily use archives written in foreign languages. In order to do so, I must work with people who can access them, assess what's available and what's worth consulting, and then translate them. And these are very time-consuming and specialist tasks that cost an awful lot of money, particularly if one wants anything more than a soupçon of the material, a dash of colour, from the archive in question. But enough of caveats and excuses. The time has come to echo Churchill's words, addressed to his wife as he dispatched the proofs of the early volumes of *The World Crisis*: 'We have reached the moment when one must say "As the tree falls, so shall it lie".'

Readers will find that the book is weighted towards the period 1939–43. This is because I have found this to be the most interesting period from the perspective of the key decisions affecting the Iran–Iraq region. It is in these years, particularly 1940–42, that the drama lies because no one then knew which way the war would go. In the period between September 1939 and June 1941, Britain and the leaders of Iran and Iraq watched a range of situations unfolding, and pondered fighting each other as well as the Soviets and the Germans – or, in some cases, whether to ally with them. The spring and summer of 1941 saw extensive military action across the region. There then followed an intensive period of readying the region to face invasion, peaking in 1942 and then dropping off dramatically in early 1943 when allied victories elsewhere all but removed the threat. The focus then became the development of the supply line from the Persian Gulf across Iran and Iraq to the Soviet Union, and America joined the story in force. The last years of the war were years of virtually no strategic threat to the region. The situation inside Iran and Iraq, politically and in terms of food supply, stabilized, though secessionist movements prospered. This later period's main feature was the drawing up of battle lines between and among the 'Big Three' allies, with the opening shots fired in America's contest with British imperialism and the West-versus-East struggle that would come to be known as the Cold War. Due to the focus on the earlier years of the war, 'allies' is used rather than 'Allies' throughout the text to avoid confusion when speaking of allied powers before and after the 1 January 1942 United Nations declaration.

Finally, a note on the title. I felt that *Persian Gulf Command* captured the sweep that I hoped the book would encompass; it is not a direct reference to the US Army's Persian Gulf Command that was formed during the war (though it plays a key part in the story). For a long time my working title was *The Pink Elephant and the Peacock Throne*, the former referring to the shoulder flash worn by the troops of Britain's Persia and Iraq Command, whose red elephant on its blue background rapidly faded to pink in the sun, and the latter to the famous throne of the kings of Persia. But I always knew that it would be considered too obscure to actually make the front cover.

The Arts and Humanities Research Council deserve special thanks. I am particularly indebted to Andrew Stewart for his extraordinary generosity with source material and numerous discussions on the subject matter and the broader war context. It is important to acknowledge the specialist scholars without whose work a book of synthesis such as this would be quite impossible to prepare. Covering several distinct fields of scholarship means that one depends on such experts, and must deal with the constant sinking feeling that inevitably brief treatments of their work have not done them justice. They are too numerous to list, but one might mention the work of Mohammad Gholi Majd, who offers unique perspectives on wartime Iran; Richard Stewart's book on Iran's invasion; Daniel Silverfarb, who wrote a splendid history of British–Iraqi relations; Simon Davis, whose take on intra-allied relations in the Persian Gulf region in the 1940s challenges some monumental received wisdoms, and whose erudition and knowledge of both primary and secondary material appears to be unrivalled; and Adrian O'Sullivan, whose extraordinary body of work on espionage and counter-espionage in Iran and Iraq is a wonder to behold. In terms of specialist journals, *Middle Eastern Studies* without doubt contains the greatest concentration of material relevant to this subject. Honourable mention must also be made of the raft of marvellous work published by contemporaries, often bearing titles such as 'A Year of Battle', 'Eastern Epic', 'Middle East Diary' 'Near East' or 'Eastern Approaches', and eyewitness accounts appearing in specialist institutional journals such as the *Household Cavalry Magazine*. Finally, there are the astonishingly useful websites that one occasionally happens upon, such as that maintained by the RAF Habbaniya Association, Christopher Chant's gargantuan 'Codenames: Operations of World War Two' web resource and James Dunford Wood's precious website containing 612 diary entries written by his father, an RAF airman who fought in Iraq and elsewhere in the Middle East.

Thanks are also due to Jacob Blandy for gracing the text with his copy-editing skills; Dr Ali Gheissari, visiting fellow at the Middle East Centre, St Antony's College, Oxford; Dr Chris Tripodi, King's College London; Professor Robert Service, St Antony's College, Oxford; Dr David Priestland, St Edmund Hall, Oxford; Farang Jophur; Dr Homa Katouzian, St Antony's College, Oxford; Francis Gotto, Mike Harkness, Richard Higgins, Jane Hogan and Danielle McAloon of Durham University Special Collections; Dr Simon Davis of City University New York; Allen Packwood and the staff at the Churchill Archives Centre, Churchill College, Cambridge; Shire PA for digitization work; Aysha al-Fekaiki for her time with me as a King's undergraduate research fellow; Dr Oliver Haller for his excellent German research and translations; and Dr Suzanne Bardgett, Director of Research at the Imperial War Museum, for involving me in the IWM–AHRC–BBC Monitoring Service project, which allowed me access to the BBC Monitoring collection, at the time not open to the public. I am also indebted to the members of my operational studies classes on the Advanced Command and Staff Course in 2016 and 2017 at the Defence Academy of the United Kingdom; Jonathan Marley of the Irish Staff College for inviting me to lecture on the Iran–Iraq case study in 2017; Cole Horton for his insights on Kurdish history; Dr Francis Grice for research in the American national archives; Chris Snelling for permission to use excerpts from notes on his father-in-law Jim Hancock's experiences with the Royal Engineers in wartime Iraq; and Geoffrey Spender at the Imperial War Museum for assistance with images. Lastly, thanks to the wonderful team at Yale University Press, especially Rachael Lonsdale, Marika Lysandrou and Heather McCallum.

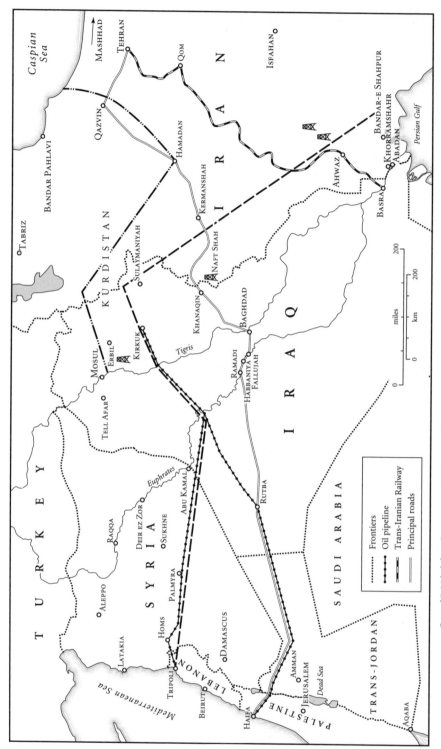

Caspian Sea

MASHHAD

TEHRAN

QOM

ISFAHAN

BANDAR-E SHAHPUR

KHORRAMSHAHR

ABADAN

Persian Gulf

QAZVIN

HAMADAN

AHWAZ

I R A N

BANDAR PAHLAVI

KERMANSHAH

NAFT SHAH

BASRA

TABRIZ

K U R D I S T A N

SULAYMANIYAH

KHANAQIN

BAGHDAD

Tigris

MOSUL

ERBIL

KIRKUK

RAMADI

HABBANIYA
FALLUJAH

I R A Q

200

200

miles

km

0

TELL AFAR

RUTBA

Euphrates

T U R K E Y

RAQQA

DEIR EZ ZOR

SUKHNE

ABU KAMAL

S A U D I   A R A B I A

Frontiers

Oil pipeline

Trans-Iranian Railway

Principal roads

ALEPPO

S Y R I A

PALMYRA

HOMS

DAMASCUS

L E B A N O N

T R A N S - J O R D A N

LATAKIA

TRIPOLI

BEIRUT

AMMAN

JERUSALEM

Dead Sea

Mediterranean Sea

HAIFA

P A L E S T I N E

AQABA

General British defence line, envisaged 25 February 1942,
against simultaneous German invasion of Turkey and Iran

General British defence line, envisaged 19 May
1942, in event of German breakthrough into Iran

General British defence line, envisaged 19 May 1942, in event of German breakthrough into Iran

INTRODUCTION

Early in the Second World War, men who had fought in the 1914–18 Mesopotamia campaign found themselves, once again, sailing up the Persian Gulf towards Basra and the Shatt al-Arab river:

> In these desolate and thirsty lands hundreds of thousands of Indian and British troops were destined to live for many months, and some to die. This, once again, was to be a test of British power to survive, to organize and labour, in conditions as disheartening as any the world could offer. Here, when the British Commonwealth faced alone the most destructive power in history, when German guns commanded Dover, when the spreading fires of war increased incessantly the need for men and material, an army was to be born, to remain and grow gigantic, hundreds of miles from any major battle ... The finest in men and material that the Commonwealth could create or discover, was to be poured out in the vast and empty lands between the Caspian and the Persian Gulf. Was this immense expenditure of labour and living wasted?[1]

The following pages answer this question, and others relating to the politics of the great powers, the war's grand strategy and the impact of the conflict on the people of Iran and Iraq. Histories of the war in the 'Middle East' – a problematic appellation – focus overwhelmingly on the campaigns in North Africa. As this book explains, however, the 'proper' Middle East, located farther eastwards, witnessed extensive wartime activity and was a focal point for the ambitions of each of the 'Big Three' allied powers.[2] Furthermore, it might be argued that the focus on the British Empire's defence of Egypt rather misses the point that this was primarily intended to protect what lay beyond it – the oil of Iran and Iraq – as well as the vital Suez Canal, which itself was prized not just as the 'Clapham Junction' of imperial sea communications, but as an artery through which Iranian oil could flow.[3] Britain sought to use the war to round off its historic position in the Iran–Iraq region, as did the Soviet Union, while America entered the region in force for the first time, laying the foundations of its puissant post-war presence. Meanwhile, years of German political, economic and ideological penetration of Iran and Iraq had cultivated close links. During the war, Berlin aimed to incite anti-allied nationalists and, through the employment of saboteurs, spies and military assets, to prepare the way for the entry of a victorious Wehrmacht once its enemies had been crushed elsewhere.

Though a theatre of extensive activity, the region has not made its way into popular memory of the war and has had minimal impact on the historical record. Reflecting this, Colonel George Heaney, a Survey of India officer sent to the region to map possible invasion routes, wrote that the 'Allied Forces in Persia and Iraq were singularly unsuccessful at catching and holding the limelight'.[4] American servicemen dispatched there in their tens of thousands put it more bluntly, referring to themselves as the 'FBI' – the 'forgotten bastards of Iran'.[5] Despite its minor billing in subsequent histories, at the time the region was considered vital by the British because of its oil. It was ranked second only to the British Isles themselves by Winston Churchill and the Chiefs of Staff during the crucial months of 1941–42, when the war hung in the balance. Iran attracted the attention of Franklin D. Roosevelt and Joseph Stalin too, because of its potential as a 'land bridge' over which military aid could flow from the Anglo-American powers to their Soviet ally.

The war brought numerous conflicts across the region to a dramatic head. Arab nationalists saw an opportunity to rise up and depose their European masters, and Britain and Iraq, erstwhile allies, turned their guns on each other. Iranian and Iraqi elites vied for power within their states, states that faced uprisings from regional ethno-nationalists wishing to secede. Britain and the Soviet Union prepared for war with each other, before becoming allies and jointly invading Iran; and allied forces fought their Axis foes, including the Vichy French, through both covert and overt means. For the British, the region had to be defended because of its oil, and through the fog of war London descried a new moment in the Middle East, an historic opportunity to flesh out its territorial claims across the great arc from Suez to the headwaters of the Persian Gulf. What transpired was an impressive last hurrah of British imperialism before its precipitate post-war decline.[6]

As well as heralding a new era of Soviet assertiveness, the war brought American political, economic and military power to the region in an unprecedented manner. Though the arrival of American troops and Lend-Lease largesse indicated the potency of the Grand Alliance, it also meant that American–Soviet competition was grafted onto pre-existing Anglo-Soviet tensions – and that Anglo-American disagreements regarding the region's future would become manifest. Thus, while the region became a unique arena of allied cooperation, it simultaneously became a debut stage for the Cold War and a point of contention between competing Anglo-American visions of the post-war world.

In addition to the strategies and military endeavours of these external great powers, the following chapters chronicle the encounters between the people of Iran and Iraq and the American, British, German, Indian, Polish, Nepalese and Soviet civilians and military personnel deposited there by the tides of global conflict. The sheer weight of allied activity, and the wider ramifications of a deeply penetrative global conflict, sucked ordinary people into the maelstrom of war, harming their economic wellbeing and transforming the political landscape of their countries. What is more, the war profoundly shaped the political trajectory of both countries, laying the foundations for the rise of the Baathist state in Iraq and heralding the reign of Shah Mohammad Reza Pahlavi in Iran following his father's dramatic abdication in the wake of an Anglo-Soviet invasion.

Persian Gulf Command tells of the travails of state development in Iran and Iraq, of diplomacy, strategy and the age-old contest between imperialism and nationalism. It is a story of invasions, coups d'état, logistics, scorched earth, covert operations and warfare on land and in the air, set against the backdrop of societies blighted by the effects of war. These included runaway inflation, food shortages, rationing, friction between occupying forces and civilians and the migration of refugees. The story begins with the inter-war evolution of the Iranian and Iraqi states, the former under the Qajar dynasty, the latter under the Hashemites, a process shaped dramatically by the proximity of great powers, and by the presence of oil.

CHAPTER 1

Iran, Iraq and the great powers

With a land mass of 636,000 square miles, Iran is bigger than Britain, France, Germany and Spain combined, a rugged and arid land that, except for two lowland regions, is dominated by mountains and deserts. At over 169,000 square miles, neighbouring Iraq is a little larger than Germany. Mountainous in the north, it consists mainly of desert and the alluvial plains of two great rivers, the Euphrates and the Tigris. The sheer size of the two countries informed their wartime experience, for if nothing else, the conflict revolved around the movement of things across vast distances, be they troops, armoured cars, aircraft, boots or sacks of wheat. Or, indeed, oil, which pulsed through pipelines stretching for hundreds of miles across the Iraqi desert to the Mediterranean coast, and sailed down the Shatt al-Arab in tankers, fuelling British engines around the world.

Those living and working in the region grew blasé about the distances and terrain that they encountered. General Sir Archibald Wavell, returning to Cairo after a conference in Basra, dozed and read Trollope as his aircraft crossed the desert, one engine malfunctioning and Messerschmitts reported to the north.[1] From British headquarters in Baghdad, Lieutenant-General Arthur Smith was sent to attend a conference in Jerusalem. 'My driver asked the way and was told: "Go along the Habbaniya road and take the first turn on the left. You can't mistake it, it's macadam." "How far?", asked the driver. "Oh, about 400 miles",' was the nonchalant reply.[2] On furlough in India, Freya Stark, employed at the British Embassy in Iraq, matter-of-factly described how she purchased a car, drove through the Punjab to the Indus and, via Quetta, 'entered eastern Persia by skirting Afghanistan'.[3]

The region's strategic prominence in the Second World War was determined both by geography and resources. Iraq lay athwart the old overland route to the east, prized by the British because troops and military resources could move along it between Basra and Palestine via Iraq, thereby connecting the Indian Ocean to the Mediterranean and linking east with west. This was a particularly important line of communication in the imperial defence system because it offered an invaluable alternative should the Suez Canal sea route ever be closed. In addition, Iraq's RAF bases and flying-boat facilities at Basra, Habbaniya and Shaibah were key staging posts on the British Empire's civil and military air routes.[4] During the war, Shaibah served as one of four transit routes feeding the Desert Air Force and also the Soviet Union.[5] Iran, meanwhile, was the British Empire's main source of oil, and its transport network was to gain significance as a junction connecting Anglo-American military supplies to Soviet forces fighting the Germans following the launch of Adolf Hitler's Barbarossa offensive.

In the early twentieth century the Iran–Iraq region had assumed cardinal importance to Britain because of its oil. In 1909 the Glasgow-based Burmah Oil Company had formed the Anglo-Persian Oil Company; three years later the world's largest refinery was constructed at Abadan in Iran, 38 miles south-east of Basra on the Shatt al-Arab river. As First Lord of the Admiralty, in 1913 Winston Churchill oversaw the Royal Navy's conversion from coal- to oil-powered ships and negotiated a deal which saw the British government acquire a controlling stake in the company. Anglo-Persian's Abadan refinery became Britain's most valuable piece of overseas real estate, and under a 1933 agreement the company held a sixty-year concession on over 100,000 square miles of oil-rich south-west Iran.

By the late 1930s the Iranian oilfields were producing over 10 million tons of crude annually, and from this source the Abadan facility could refine sufficient fuel to meet a year's war needs for the Royal Navy. Abadan's oil was transported in tankers down the Shatt al-Arab into the Gulf, from where it entered the Indian Ocean via the Strait of Hormuz for distribution across the British Empire. From the more recently exploited oilfields of Kirkuk and Mosul, first proved in 1927, Britain drew a further 4 million tons a year, and oil from both countries was pumped to the eastern Mediterranean along two parallel pipelines, each 12 inches in diameter. With pumping stations positioned at intervals – the flatness of the land meant that the oil had to be pushed through the pipes – the pipeline went first to Haditha on the Euphrates, where it forked off to Haifa in Palestine (620 miles away) and Tripoli in Lebanon (532 miles away). Between Kirkuk and Haditha, the pumping stations were numbered in sequence, K1, K2 and so on. After Haditha, they were numbered according to terminus – T1, T2 et cetera for those going to Tripoli, H1, H2 et cetera for those going to Haifa.[6]

Each pumping station was a small town occupying over 100 acres. Surrounded by wire fencing, each contained a fort, pumping machinery, accommodation, power generators and an ice plant. Dwelling in each station were about 500 employees, a population that, with wives, children, police and hangers-on, swelled to around 2,000 souls. 'They were small townships which we had created deep into absolute desert,' wrote George Tod, a liaison officer employed to keep the peace with the tribes who resided in the environs of the pipeline and its twelve pumping stations.[7] A refinery was completed at Haifa in Palestine in 1939, to which oil was piped from Iran. Like the Abadan facility, it was primarily for Royal Navy supply, though its output of white products – the highest value petroleum products, which included aviation fuel – was to gain greatly in strategic importance during the war.

Simply put, the 'oil of Persia and Iraq was a *sine quâ non* to Britain in a time of war'.[8] Without it, Britain's capacity to wage war would be severely degraded, and its rivals knew this. Though Britain was the incumbent power, other external powers coveted the region's resources. The Russo-Persian Treaty of Friendship of 1921 had repudiated Moscow's historic claims in northern Iran, yet its ambitions were dormant, not extinguished, and were to be revived by war and an appetite for oil and other strategic benefits, such as access to the Persian Gulf's warm-water ports. German political and economic links with Iran and Iraq were well established, and American commercial interests had been sprouting here and in other Gulf countries for some decades.

German influence in Iran and Iraq

A major stimulus of the tension and unrest that afflicted Iran and Iraq during the Second World War was the German influence that flourished there. German interests had been assiduously cultivated through trade, political exchanges, personal relationships and copious, sophisticated propaganda aimed at the Arab world and Middle East in general, as well as specifically at countries such as Egypt, Iran, Iraq and Syria. Since the nineteenth century, it had also been an area of targeted German foreign policy initiatives aimed at supporting German ambitions for European expansion by challenging the interests of the British and French. On the ground, men such as Wilhelm Wassmuss, the First World War-era diplomat and spy, and Fritz Grobba, envoy to Iraq from 1932 and German Foreign Office Plenipotentiary for the Arab Countries and head of the Arab Committee from 1942, forwarded German interests, though they were not always effectively supported from Berlin.[9]

Extensive German activity meant that Britain and its allies could not isolate the region from the effects of war. Pre-existing German influence was bolstered by battlefield success as the war got under way, and the sense that the Third Reich's military power was creeping ever closer to the region, a prospect welcomed by many. During the inter-war years a resurgent Germany had been courted by politicians and military leaders in both countries, viewed as a lever in the struggle to remove or at least circumscribe the influence of Britain and the Soviet Union and pursue the dream of genuine independence.[10] The Shah of Iran, Reza Pahlavi, looked to Germany as a counterweight to British and Soviet influence, while politicians and military leaders in Iraq admired Nazi achievements and saw German support as a means of ridding their country, and the wider Middle East, of British and French colonialism. In Iraq and the wider Arab world, Germany's anti-Jewish stance was admired, especially given the situation in Mandatory Palestine, to which Jews were being granted rights of settlement under British auspices.

Germany's central pitch throughout the Middle East was that it was the friend of all those opposing colonialism and imperialism, an enthusiastic sponsor of nationalism and the scourge of the Jews. This message was broadcast in Iran and Iraq by diplomats, undercover agents and the media, and amplified by the Third Reich's military prestige and economic power. Bespoke Arabic- and Persian-language propaganda was beamed into both countries as European powers jockeyed for position and peddled their ideologies. Radio Bari began broadcasting to the region in 1934, Radio Berlin in 1939. In response, the BBC Arabic Service and dedicated Persian language broadcasts had also taken to the airwaves by the time war broke out.[11]

Iran had reached out to German advisers since the nineteenth century, and at the time of the First World War German foreign policy had sought to stir anti-British sentiment, presenting a psychological challenge to the habitually paranoid imperial mind, and seeking to ally with khans willing to rise against the British and their local allies. By the time of the Second World War, German officials were well aware of the region's strategic importance and the benefits accruing to the external power that commanded its resources, and they coveted its oil. Senior Nazis such as Reinhard Heydrich, Foreign Office officials like Ernst Woermann, and diplomats like Fritz Grobba, Berlin's representative in Baghdad, understood that Arab nationalism could be marshalled to undermine Britain's position in the Middle East.[12] They also knew how big a blow it would be to the British Empire if Germany could seize control of the oilfields, or at least degrade Britain's ability to access them. In Berlin, documents such as 'The necessity for action in the Arabian south-east and Iran', a Foreign Office product, did the rounds.[13]

Germany's long-established connections with Iran and Iraq meant that various government ministries and state-linked agencies had developed an intimate knowledge of the two countries. Intelligence and information was collected and digested, with a view to eventual German dominance, while a large expatriate community was 'organized on National Socialist principles': there were nearly 1,000 registered Nazi Party members, tightly organized in area groups, spread across Iran.[14] A screening of the film Victory in the West in early 1941 attracted 1,300 Germans from across the country.[15] Detailed country studies were prepared by a number of organizations including the Wirtschafts- und Rüstungsamt (War Economy and Armaments Department) of Oberkommando der Wehrmacht (OKW), the high command of the armed forces. Other interested organizations included the Auswärtiges Amt – the Foreign Ministry – and firms such as Rheinmetall-Alkett-Borsig, a major manufacturer of armoured vehicles. Their files and publications variously analysed natural resources, trade policy, weapons exports and the activities of the British and the Soviets in the region.[16]

Yet while Grobba and other German Middle East experts liked to speak of an 'almost instinctive' friendship between Germany and the Arabs – and the Iranians – this friendliness was stimulated as much by anti-British, anti-French and anti-Soviet sentiment as by pro-German inclinations. Furthermore, and to the chagrin of men such as Grobba and Heydrich, German 'friendship' had its limits, and there was always an ambivalence to Germany's commitment to the region. Hitler, famously, was transfixed by the prospect of invading the Soviet Union. The extent to which Middle East specialists and on-the-ground actors could get Berlin's ear, and link their knowledge and activity to military operations and Hitler's grand strategy, was consistently problematic. Though German forces and agents would become embroiled there, North Africa and the Middle East were peripheral to the Führer's vision.

Germany's interests and activities in the region were to suffer from the fragmented manner in which strategy was formulated under Hitler, characterized by competing power centres and the perennial challenge of capturing and then holding the Führer's attention. Illustrating the ambivalence of German policy in the Middle East, although the views of many Germans and Iraqis aligned when it came to Jews, the German government sponsored the very migration of Jews into Palestine that so incensed Arab nationalists, as a way of shrinking Germany's own Jewish population while earning revenue for the state as it did so. Further hampering German policy, the Rome–Berlin Axis of 1936 had acknowledged Italian primacy in the Middle East, ceding to it the role of 'lead power' in exchange for a free German hand in eastern Europe. Though German popularity was unbridled in certain quarters, Italy was viewed with suspicion, its recent violent conquest of Abyssinia demonstrating Mussolini's imperial proclivities and outweighing his efforts to portray himself as the defender of Islam.

Iran, Reza Shah's regime and the great powers

For generations, Iran had provided a backdrop to the glacial collision of British and Russian interests emanating on the one hand from the expansionist and defensive impulses of the Raj, and on the other from Russia's – later the Soviet Union's – position in Transcaucasia (Armenia, Azerbaijan and Georgia) and its southward march through Central Asia. The oil of Iran and Transcaucasia increased the value of the region in the eyes of both powers, and reinvigorated the likelihood of war between them. For Britain and the Soviet Union, Iran was familiar territory, a borderland to their respective Asian empires, the gateway to India, and a bone of contention at the heart of their geostrategic aspirations. Along with neighbouring Afghanistan and India's fabled North-West Frontier, it was the playing field of 'the Great Game'.[17]

The British and Indian governments were keen to sponsor a strong and British-influenced regime in Tehran – viewed as a crucial buffer against Soviet expansion – while the Persian Gulf was a waterway they were determined to control, a feature of Britain's maritime dominance of the Indian Ocean region. A war was fought against Iran for control of the city of Herat in 1856–57, and in an act of détente diplomacy half a century later, Britain and Russia deflated strategic tension by agreeing to divide Iran into two informal spheres of influence, Russian in the north, British in the south. With a 'truce' declared, it became easier for the British to consolidate their grip on southern Iran, while the Russians made good their claims in Transcaucasia, a region over which several Russo-Persian wars had been fought between the seventeenth and nineteenth centuries.

British and Russian encroachment meant that Iran was seriously affected by the military and socioeconomic ramifications of the First World War, becoming a major battlefield between the Ottoman Empire on the one hand, and the British and Russian empires on the other.[18] The armies of foreign powers occupied Iran and 'turned vast swaths of the countryside into a wasteland of contagious disease, famine, and tribal insurrection'.[19] Involvement in the war cost Iran dear, and in the post-war years British influence in Iranian affairs waxed strong given the temporary enervation of its Russian (now Soviet) rival in the aftermath of the 1917 Russian Revolution. The idea took hold that the British were to blame for almost anything bad that happened to the country, even to individuals within it.[20]

By the time of the Second World War, Iran existed in a state of precarious independence, with two great-power neighbours looking over the borders, active within them, and ready to compromise that independence should circumstances so dictate. Given this, it is no surprise that many elite Iranians, the shah included, sought opportunities to reduce British and Soviet influence. The rise of Nazi Germany, and the shah's drive for regime centralization and modernization, offered an opportunity to achieve this. So, too, did the growing presence of American interests, both commercial and private. By tempting Americans in, the Iranians hoped to snare the government in Washington and rope it into the political affairs of the country as a counterweight to the overbearing imperial neighbours.

Though 'at the beginning of the twentieth century Iranian society bore few apparent signs of having emerged from the Middle Ages', by the 1930s things were changing under the modernizing drive of Reza Shah Pahlavi, the officer in the Persian Cossack Brigade who had usurped power in the early 1920s, overthrowing the Qajar dynasty and ascending to the peacock throne.[21] Under the new shah's rule, the 'entire paraphernalia of the state primarily served the interests of the elite and, more generally, the upper class at the expense of the subordinate classes'.[22] While the majority of people lived in rural poverty, new state structures emerged, including a powerful army and bureaucracy, and a new state railway. These instruments were used to centralize power, bringing the regime into conflict with regional potentates and powerful tribal confederacies such as the Kurds and Qashqai. Tribal lands were confiscated, great families reduced, nomads forced into sedentary existence and political opponents such as Mohammad Mossadegh locked away. Taking a top-down approach to 'progress', areas of Tehran were westernized and traditional practices, including in matters of dress, were modernized by decree, causing anguish and resentment. The power of Islamic courts and priests was curtailed. With varying degrees of condescension, and influenced by romanticized visions of 'the East', visitors such as the Arabist Gerald de Gaury noted how 'modern' Iranians sought to show off 'school knowledge of European civilization and pretended to a culture excluding everything old and traditional': 'By the Shah's orders, travellers were forbidden to photograph camels, donkeys, beggars and so on ... Tehran had been ruthlessly changed by pulling down old houses, bazaars, mosques and baths, their replacements being drearily straight and parallel streets of similar houses and glass-fronted shops.'[23] The Belgian diplomat Harold Eeman wrote that the shah 'meant to modernize his country as Kemal Ataturk had modernized Turkey', modernization bringing 'interference and exactions' to the poor. The shah wished to rid Iran 'of all reminders of a discredited past. Unable to detect beauty in old buildings, he did not hesitate to have them pulled down.'[24] The French traveller and journalist Eve Curie found on her visit to Tehran in 1941 that the city conformed to what guidebooks called a 'modern capital' in that 'everything picturesque had been severely banned from it and that impressive new buildings had been erected, which suffered from the "modernistic" ideas of the 1920s'. In building these new structures, however, the shah had neglected to provide his capital with an adequate sewerage system or clean drinking water.[25]

Though the British had sponsored his rise to power, the shah's nationalist, centralizing proclivities caused him to resent Britain's extraordinary influence in his country, including its stranglehold over the oil industry and its revenues. As a report to the British Foreign Office succinctly put it, from the beginning of his reign the new shah 'hated HMG [His Majesty's Government]'.[26] At his behest, the British-owned and managed Imperial Bank of Persia lost its function as a state bank, the Royal Navy's Gulf coaling stations on Hengam and Qeshm islands were closed, the Indo-European Telegraph line was absorbed into the Iranian system, the Imperial Airways route to India was transferred from the Iranian to the Arabian side of the Gulf, and the Anglo-Persian Oil Company's concession was revised in Iran's favour. All of this amounted, in the words of Clarmont Skrine, a member of the British consular service, to the 'progressive weakening of British influence and prestige'.[27]

Yet despite all this, on the eve of the Second World War Britain remained a powerful actor in Iranian affairs, exercising what amounted to a semi-colonial hold on the south of the country. Relying on political and economic influence rather than a military presence to secure its vital interests, Britain coaxed and cajoled Iran. Jock Colville was working in the Eastern Department at the Foreign Office when war broke out:

> My parish, with of course a senior First Secretary in charge, was Turkey and Persia. Persia was just a little tiresome, as the Shah, Reza Pahlevi, was a temperamental despot. We had to be particularly polite to him because of the enormous interests of the Anglo-Persian Oil Company (now British Petroleum) in the country ... the most interesting work I had was to assess the claims of Persia to receive support in armaments and flying instruction as compared with other countries. Persia has every intention of remaining neutral, but her goodwill is essential to us both on account of imperial communications and because of the Anglo-Persian Oil Company, on which the navy to a large extent depend for their oil supplies. It is therefore important to please the Shah by supplying him with aeroplanes and instructors, even if our effort in so doing will be wasted on incorrigibly neutral soil.[28]

Iran and the coming of war

Ann Lambton, a British orientalist employed in the Tehran legation, wrote that the shah's regime was 'profoundly unpopular'. Unfortunately for the British, almost 'the entire responsibility for the dictatorship was laid by educated and uneducated alike at the doors of the British government, upon whom fell the odium for its actions'.[29] The Soviet Union, meanwhile, was 'hated and feared', an old enemy and invader that had only disgorged a swath of Iranian territory in the aftermath of its own implosion following the 1917 revolution. In contrast, many Iranians were impressed by the manner in which the National Socialists had reversed Germany's economic fortunes and restored national pride.

Strong pro-German sentiment among Iranian nationalists dated from the First World War, and many Iranians had been deeply impressed by new theories of European nationalism, especially given their emphasis upon Aryan superiority. Hitler's rise to power and Germany's rapid militarization and industrialization were viewed admiringly. 'The two factors – pro-German feeling and Aryan nationalism – later became embodied in an almost completely emotional commitment to Nazi Germany, the rising power which was both anti-Russian and anti-British.'[30] There were more-concrete links too. When Arthur Millspaugh and his American financial advisory team left Iran in 1927, Reza Shah 'gravitated towards Weimar Germany in the hope of restructuring Iran's military and economy and curbing British and Soviet influence'.[31] Germans were invited to assist in the shah's modernization programme. A German directed the national bank, Junkers aircraft company was contracted to develop the postal service, agents such as the Škoda representative worked under commercial cover, and the Third Reich's economic minister visited Tehran in 1935. Germany helped Iran by lending technical skills, building infrastructure and sending advisers to the government and teachers to the schools. Iranian students went to Germany to study, and German technology played 'by far the most important role in the construction of the Trans-Iranian Railway'. Neatly symbolizing Germany's concrete yet discrete influence upon the country, 'the ceiling of Tehran railway station's great hall was even decorated – though with some subtlety – with large swastikas'.[32] Germany's senior representative in the country was an SS brigadier, Erwin Ettel, described by his British counterpart, Sir Reader Bullard, as 'a tremendous Nazi'.[33]

The supposed ethnic link was one of Germany's bridges to political and cultural cooperation. Germany made an exception in the Nuremberg Racial Laws for Iranians, defining them as 'pure Aryans'. Indicative of these blossoming links, in 1935 the country's name was changed from Persia to Iran, meaning 'Aryan' or 'land of the Aryans':

> The suggestion for the change is said to have come from the Iranian ambassador to Germany, who came under the influence of the Nazis ... It is said that some German friends of the ambassador persuaded him that, as with the advent of Reza Shah, Persia had turned a new leaf in its history and had freed itself from the pernicious influences of Britain and the Soviet Union ... it was only fitting that the country be called by its own name, 'Iran'. This would not only signal a new beginning and bring home to the world the new era in Iranian history, but would also signify the Aryan race of its population, as 'Iran' is a cognate of 'Aryan' and derived from it.[34]

By 1939 Germany was Iran's dominant economic partner and most-favoured trading nation, accounting for 41 per cent of its foreign trade.[35] Thousands of Germans lived and worked in Iran, and by the time of the war a well-coordinated fifth-column organization had been formed from among them and Germany's Iranian friends. Their aim was variously to support uprisings intended to tie down British and Soviet forces, prevent the movement of troops across Iraq from India, and to conduct sabotage operations in the Soviet Union's rear. There was an active Abwehr (German military intelligence) element, its mission being to gather information about Soviet oil installations and military activities in the Caucasus and to infiltrate labour and government circles in order to incite sabotage against British oil interests.[36]

Ahmed Asadi, a wealthy Armenian-born Iranian nationalist working gratis for the German secret service as 'a Persian patriot', explained his country's predicament to Berthold Schulze-Holthus, an Abwehr agent deployed to Iran in 1941:

'You must understand the situation in this land properly. For decades we have been living in a high-tension field of international politics between Russia and England. The Russians have exploited our earlier weakness and have taken the Caucasus from us. Azerbaijan, on the other side of the frontier, for a Nationalist Persian, corresponds to Alsace-Lorraine for a German. The British!' He took a deep breath and a scowl appeared on his placid features. 'Have you ever watched how they strut about here in their khaki uniforms? And even when they're in mufti, in their pith helmets ... The sahibs, the white lords who look upon us as colonials and treat us with unbearable arrogance. What remains to us then, except to play the one off against the other? The Russians against the British and vice versa. But today we are expecting a great deal from a third power, which can be either Germany or the USA. In any case, a power which is ready to treat us fairly on an equal basis.'[37]

The start of war brought consternation to the royal family in Tehran, for it was clear that no good could come of it for their country. To start with, Britain's blockade of Germany severed trade relations. Reza Shah was in a particularly difficult position. Though the old autocrat yearned for a British withdrawal from his land, he feared the Soviets much more, and knew that any diminution of British influence would cause a commensurate rise in Soviet encroachment. The Soviet threat was much more direct, amounting to the desire to annex Iran's northern provinces. Things were made far worse by the Nazi–Soviet Pact, concluded days before the outbreak of war. The pact was borne of Stalin's conviction that Britain and France could not be relied upon to deter German expansion and that, therefore, conciliating Hitler was the only viable course of action. Signed by Vyacheslav Molotov, People's Commissar for Foreign Affairs, and Joachim von Ribbentrop, Hitler's Foreign Minister, the agreement promised non-aggression between the two states, and divided Europe into spheres of influence. In the Middle East, the Iran–Iraq region was marked as a Soviet zone. Moscow greedily eyed Iranian land and oil and access to the Persian Gulf, and Stalin demanded that 'the area south of Batum and Baku in the general direction of the Persian Gulf' be recognized as 'the centre of the aspirations of the Soviet Union'.[38] The Nazi–Soviet Pact reinvigorated Iranian fears of invasion, as it made it much more likely that the Soviets would behave avariciously and begin once again to pursue their ambitions for Iranian territory and resources.

While watching Soviet activities with concern, the British came to interpret the shah's reluctance to clamp down on German activities within his country as both pro-German and anti-British. But though the Germans did indeed collect intelligence, promote anti-British sentiment and prepare to welcome German forces, British perceptions of the shah's sympathies were 'fearful distortions of the cautious ruler's steps to maintain Iran's neutrality'.[39] The fact was that anti-British and anti-Soviet sentiment probably outweighed pro-Nazi sentiment, and pre-existing friendship with Germany based upon trade and diplomacy had as much to do with this as it had with any innate value attached to Nazism.

Taking advantage of the Nazi–Soviet Pact, Moscow flexed its muscles.[40] In March 1940 Soviet forces amounting to five infantry divisions, a cavalry division and three tank divisions moved into the Baku region of Azerbaijan. A formidable new army group was being created to intimidate Iran and bolster Soviet claims. As an earnest of ill intent, in May 1940 the Soviets demanded that Iran grant them the use of seven airfields, and Stalin called for the release of detained Iranian communists along with exclusive rights to Iranian oil. While Germany welcomed this discord, there was cause for concern, too, because Britain, with its back to the wall and its main ally France close to defeat, made plans to move into Iran to either occupy or destroy its oilfields and refineries.

'German and Soviet diplomacy has been bending every effort to under-mine Iran's morale and weaken her will to resist blandishments and threats from Berlin and Moscow,' wrote Cornelius Engert, American chargé d'affaires in Tehran. Observing Soviet moves in the Baltic states, Iran feared that Moscow would look to the Black Sea and the Caspian Sea and attempt to press 'special rights' in the north-western provinces of Iranian Azerbaijan and Gilan, and would possibly send in troops to protect such 'rights'.[41] The American diplomat reported that the shah was 'showing increasing irrita-tion at the hollowness and hypocrisy of both German and Russian propa-ganda', though was constrained in his actions by the strong pro-German element in the army. As Engert wrote, the shah would much rather 'go his own way and not get entangled in a European war, but must walk the tightrope between Britain and Russia . . . He is above all intent on avoiding if possible the recurrence of the unfortunate experience during the last war'. As news of the Soviet Union's war with Finland reached Tehran, and Turkey manoeuvred uncomfortably between Britain and Germany, the shah became increasingly concerned about the fate of smaller powers in wartime.[42] While he was deeply impressed by Finnish resistance to Soviet forces, he did not wish to attempt to emulate it.[43]

The principal objective of German propaganda, wrote Engert, was 'to create discord between Britain and Iran and between Britain and the Soviet Union'. In January 1940, for example, the Germans reacted to the Iranian government's decree that all German and Soviet nationals should leave the province of Khuzestan where the Anglo-Iranian oilfields were situated. German propaganda 'seized upon the measure to start a whispering campaign in the bazaars that England will now soon order Iran to decree a general mobilization and that the Soviets will have just cause to accuse Iran of playing the game of her "British masters"'.[44]

Fearing a Soviet invasion, the Iranian government tried to get Britain to provide arms and enter into a formal commitment for joint defence. Britain's unwillingness to supply arms intensified the Iranian regime's inse-curity and frustration, causing it to look elsewhere for succour. Feeling extremely vulnerable in the light of the Nazi–Soviet Pact, the shah turned naturally to Britain, with Foreign Secretary Lord Halifax reporting that he was putting 'out feelers to find out what assistance he might expect from us'.[45] He asked to buy military aircraft; thirty Blenheim bombers, thirty Wellingtons, thirty-five Hurricanes and thirty Curtiss fighters. 'The Iranian Minister for War,' the Chiefs of Staff told the War Cabinet, 'had approached our Military Attaché unofficially with a request for certain British aircraft to be supplied by spring and to suggest that the time had come for Iran and Britain to coordinate offensive plans for war against Russia.'[46] But while British officials on the ground argued in favour of the proposition, the War Cabinet concluded that Iran was too low on the 'priority list' for Britain to be able to supply it with weapons. 'Preference' went 'presently to Turkish and Finnish demands, which are the most urgent', and there was little realistic prospect in 1940 of Britain being in a position to furnish the shah with scores of bombers and fighters.[47] Even though Britain was also concerned about Soviet ambitions in Iran, it did not trust the Iranian government or the capacity of the Iranian military to resist invasion, whether supplied with British weapons or not.

Meeting with little success in his attempts to procure British weapons, the shah turned to America, requesting the purchase of fifty heavy bombers and thirty pursuit aircraft.[48] But the Americans were reluctant to act in Iran, especially in the face of an increasingly assertive and hostile Soviet Union. In January 1940, the American minister in Tehran reported a conversation with the Iranian Minister of Finance: the Soviets had warned the Iranian government that it would not permit the granting of an oil concession to an American company. 'When I asked whether he meant in the northern provinces he said "No, anywhere in Iran".'[49] This summarized what was to become a sustained Soviet objection to America's presence in the region, which was to have far-reaching consequences as the war progressed. Besides this, when it came to arms exports Washington observed a strict order of priority. American forces had first call, Britain second. Iran was not even on the list. Halifax, when serving later as British ambassador in Washington, met with Under Secretary of State Sumner Welles to request that the Americans refuse Iranian requests. The main reason was the fear that weapons would fall into German hands and be used against the British. In his reply, Welles pointed out that refusals to consider Iranian requests for American goods were causing resentment. Halifax said that in order to keep the shah 'sweet' some British aircraft – perhaps a dozen Hurricanes – might be shipped out for assembly in a factory run by British workers near Tehran. But the British remained loath to provide this kind of inducement: they did not think the Iranian regime worthy of such investment, did not trust it, and had better things to do with their scant resources.

The shah reacted to Soviet troop movements on the border between Iranian and Soviet Azerbaijan by accelerating defensive preparations.

Foreigners were banned from travelling in Mazandaran province on the Caspian coastline, 'because it is rumoured that fortifications and field defences are being constructed'.[50] The British looked on anxiously, contemplating a pre-emptive occupation of Iran, or at least the destruction of its oil wells, fretting lest the Soviets make the first move. Fearing pre-emptive British intervention, Stalin relaxed the pressure on Iran in August 1940. The Germans now spotted an opportunity. Seeing Iran menaced by the Soviet Union yet unable to prise adequate assistance from America or Britain, it offered Iran an alliance.

Britain, Arab nationalism and the Iraqi state

Like its neighbour, Iraq had been the scene of an extended campaign during the First World War as the British endeavoured to oust the Ottomans and nullify German initiatives and intrigues.[51] British by right of conquest by the time of the armistice in November 1918, in the subsequent peace negotiations Iraq entered the rolls of the British Empire as a League of Nations mandate. Based in the new capital city of Baghdad, buttressed by RAF biplanes and a powerful British embassy, local power devolved to a narrow elite and the newly created Hashemite monarchy.[52] Though maligned as an alien ruler imposed by a colonial power – King Faisal had never visited Iraq before his arrival in Basra aboard a British warship in 1921 – the king's role was essential in gluing together a composite, fledgling state.[53] Nevertheless, his position was inherently ambivalent; while dependent on the British, the king's loyalty to them was inevitably tempered by his own and his government's ambitions for greater independence and greater Arab unity. 'Without the Nationalists there could be no hope of independence and without the British the State could not exist.' The king was obliged, therefore, to 'run with the hare and hunt with the hounds'.[54] Described as a dynasty of realists by Gerald de Gaury, friend and adviser to the royal family, Iraq's kings 'served and used Islamic traditions, the Ottoman, British and American empires and Arab nationalism', according to the needs of the moment.[55] Reflecting Iraq's unusual fabrication and Britain's imperial shadow, Leo Amery, Secretary of State for India during the war and a former Colonial Secretary, remarked that 'if the writ of King Faisal runs effectively throughout his kingdom it is entirely due to British aeroplanes. If the aeroplanes were removed tomorrow, the whole structure would inevitably fall to pieces.'[56]

The renowned Baghdad-born British historian of the Middle East, Elie Kedourie, has claimed that the Iraqi state was a fraud from its inception; there was no Arab nation, nor any coherent political unities after the end of Ottoman rule.[57] It was politically fragile and liable to frequent changes of government as elite factions vied for power and the rewards of office. In terms of foreign policy, Iraqi leaders were always looking beyond the borders of their state, 'seeking to rule over a Greater Syria or a Fertile Crescent. Iraq's foreign policy was thus a restless quest for prestige and position in the middle eastern cockpit.'[58] Its military was partial to coups d'état, a handful of which had already occurred by the time war broke out.[59] Of particular importance in Iraqi politics by the time of the Second World War were four extremely influential, militantly pan-Arabist and very anti-British Army officers. They were Salah al-Din al-Sabbagh, commander of the 3rd Division stationed in and around Baghdad; Kamil Shabib, commander of the 1st Division; Fahmi Sa'id, commander mechanized forces; and Mahmud Salman, commander of the air force. Between them they commanded two of the Iraqi army's four divisions, its single mechanized brigade and the entire air force. Known to the British as the Golden Square and to Iraqi historians as the Four Colonels, they dominated the military establishment: 'neither the regent nor any of the politicians could defy them without great political and personal risk.'[60]

Because of the artificiality of the Iraqi state and the fractious nature of its political system – and the fact that members of the political elite were clearly out for their own interests, not the wellbeing of the Iraqi people – its governments had little popular support. National politics obtruded less and less into the lives of people the farther one travelled from Baghdad – unless, of course, a community was being actively persecuted by the regime. The separatism of communities such as the Assyrians, the Kurds and the Yazidis, and the state's attempts to tame them, created major rifts in the fabric of the young nation. Then there were religious differences, both within Islam and without. Tribal sheikhs had little love for the Baghdad government and often looked to the British for support. As independence approached in the late 1920s most of the Shiite community, more than half the population, were said to have wanted the British to stay on as rulers, as did other minority communities. Many of the great landlords and merchants evinced little interest in national politics beyond that required to protect their own affairs, and 'wished the politicians at the bottom of the sea.'[61] David Fieldhouse claims that the majority of the great landowners regarded the British as protectors of their interests, and were viewed by the monarchy as allies against hostile urban politicians and a politically active army.[62]

In 1930, the Anglo-Iraqi Treaty granted Iraq its independence upon the expiry of the mandate two years later. But it was to be a heavily circumscribed independence, for the terms of the treaty permitted the British to retain large forces in the country and to transit troops across it, Iraq fulfilling the function of a strategic 'land bridge' connecting the Mediterranean and the Persian Gulf. The trans-desert line of communication and the port of Basra, key to the ingress and egress of troops and located in a commanding position vis-à-vis the Iranian oilfields and refineries, were crucial features of the system of imperial defence. Protecting the Mosul and Kirkuk oilfields, and the pipelines carrying Iranian and Iraqi oil to the Mediterranean, was another primary British concern. Too valuable to be granted real independence, Iraq remained an integral part of the British world system. The treaty, in particular the RAF bases that it permitted, was deeply resented, viewed by Iraqi nationalists as an infringement of sovereignty and an unwelcome source of continued British interference in Iraqi affairs. It was accepted as an unavoidable condition of independence, a 'half the loaf is better than none' solution. But seeking to change it or tear it up altogether became the main focus of Iraqi nationalists, an ambition that friendship with Germany might further.

As well as dispensing military power locally in a good old-fashioned 'colonial policing' role, the British airbases, one at Habbaniya west of Baghdad, the other at Shaibah near Basra, were important links in the chain of air stations connecting Britain to key destinations across the Empire. Flying-boats routinely landed next to the British Overseas Airways Corporation terminal on the shore of Lake Habbaniya, and the runways allowed for the movement of resources between Egypt and India in emergencies, and as part of the peacetime business of moving people and aircraft around the Empire.[63] They also afforded facilities close to areas of the Soviet Union that Britain might one day have to attack if the two rivals went to war, and to the oilfields of both Iraq and south-west Iran that it might have to defend. Ground defence for the airbases was provided by British-officered RAF Levies drawn from Iraq's Arab, Assyrian and Kurdish communities. Summarizing Iraq's importance shortly before the outbreak of war, Sir Thomas Inskip, Minister for Co-ordination of Defence, outlined the importance of Iraq and the British forces stationed there:[64]

The air forces in this country serve the double purpose of maintaining our air communications, strategical and civil, with India and the Far East and of protecting our most important oil interests in Iraq and Iran. At Habbaniyah and Basra fully equipped airbases have been established which are remote from air attack by our potential enemies. In addition, the overland route from Basra to Palestine and Egypt, to which we attach considerable importance, runs through Iraq.[65]

Britain also enjoyed significant purchase on the country's economy. It controlled the Iraq Petroleum Company consortium and was able to employ Iraqi oil for its own purposes, and the Iraqi dinar was tied to sterling. The Iraq Currency Board, headquartered in London, determined the volume of bank notes in circulation and two of the three most influential commercial banks were British. Almost all foreign business houses were British, a large amount of Iraq's overseas trade was carried in British vessels and most foreign capital invested in the country was British too.[66] Further cementing Britain's grip, it enjoyed an unofficial though potent voice in the formulation of Iraqi foreign policy. The British ambassador in Baghdad was arguably the most powerful man in the country, a British major-general acted as inspector-general of the Iraqi army and the Iraqi military was tethered to Britain through training and the procurement of weapons.[67] Hallmarks of Iraq's dependent status, all these aspects of the Anglo-Iraqi relationship were widely resented by Iraq's leading political figures. Though at the outbreak of war the government was led by the relatively pro-British Nuri as-Said, and the regent Prince Abdulillah remained friendly, tensions simmered just below the surface.

Britain's position in Iraq was further undermined by the cancerous effect of its stewardship of the Palestine mandate. The festering 'Palestine problem' was a fly in Britain's ointment throughout the Arab world, a visceral matter impervious to white papers, immigration quotas or diplomatic solutions. Sir Basil Newton, Britain's ambassador in Baghdad from 1939, put his finger on the problem: 'The British had created an impossible situation for themselves in the Middle East with their Zionist project in Palestine ... Why would anyone in the region welcome the implanting of a colony of European Jews in the midst of over a million Christian and Muslim Palestinians?'[68] Criticism of Britain's Palestine policy, wrote Freya Stark of the Baghdad embassy's Public Relations Section, was 'absolutely *universal* from both friends and enemies', and clearly 'lies at the root of all our troubles'.[69]

Along with the enmity caused by the terms of the Anglo-Iraqi Treaty, the Palestine situation created fertile ground for the growth of German influence. Fritz Grobba had become German consul in Baghdad on Iraq's independence. 'Fair, plump of face ... [with] shrewd blue eyes', Grobba told Iraqis, humiliated by the mandate system and then the treaty, and by broken promises regarding a greater Arabian state, that Germany was the one great power capable of helping them rid their country of the British. It was, furthermore, a power harbouring no designs on territory in the Middle East, a veritable innocent in a world marred by colonialism.[70] This stirred anti-British and anti-French sentiment. In the years preceding the war Grobba's house in Baghdad was a central meeting place for Iraqi nationalists.[71] *Mein Kampf* was serialized in Iraqi newspapers, Nazi-inspired clubs gained popularity among 'modern', educated young men and Hitler Youth-style organizations competed with the British-influenced Boy Scouts. The leader of the Hitler Youth, Baldur von Schirach, stopped off in Baghdad in 1937 on a return journey from Tehran. An Arab Scout group was formed, the 'general trainer' of which was Salah al-Din al-Sabbagh, leader of the Golden Square. A May 1939 law made military training mandatory in schools and small Nazi groups were established, such as the Youth Troops, the Iron Guard and the Sabawi National Force, all headed by Yunis al-Sabawi, translator of *Mein Kampf* and an extreme nationalist.[72] These and other organizations were vigorously sponsored by Grobba.

The weakness of the Iraqi regime meant that Nazi propaganda easily influenced young Iraqis. Refugees from Palestine and Syria also played an important part in the formation of nationalist and anti-Jewish clubs and societies. But although there were 'proper' Nazi organizations, such as al-Futuwwa, directly inspired by the Hitler Youth, many Arab intellectuals were drawn more to German military power and defiance of the 'dictates of Versailles' than to Nazi ideology itself.[73]

Paul Knabenshue, head of the American legation in Baghdad, told the State Department in Washington that Iraqi students who went to Germany returned 'violently pro-German'; pro-German officials in the Ministry of Education promoted a youth movement developed along Nazi lines; junior officers in the army were German-leaning; and Axis propaganda was widespread and effective.[74] Most senior Iraqi officers had been trained by the Germans as part of the Ottoman army, lending an historical, even a nostalgic, dimension to the Arab–German nexus. The attitude of many Iraqi officers had been shaped at school and at the military college where instructors 'taught that military action was the only way to improve Iraq's political status and free it from foreign control, and imbued a spirit of political action' in their students.[75] Animosity towards Britain was stoked by the vehemently anti-British and anti-Jewish Grand Mufti of Jerusalem, Haj Amin al-Husseini, exiled from Palestine to Iraq in 1937 and again in October 1939 when he moved from Beirut to Baghdad following the Arab revolt. He was voted a salary by the Iraqi parliament, though Prime Minister Nuri as-Said optimistically promised the British that he would get him to declare support for Britain and suppress his political activity. But the Grand Mufti was not so easily muffled, and was greeted by the Iraqi media as a hero of the struggle against Zionism and Britain's Palestine policy.[76] Along with the Golden Square, he was a prime mover of Iraqi government policy from this point onwards.

The Grand Mufti condemned Britain's pro-Zionism and preached pan-Arabism and anti-colonialism. His presence in Iraq did much to increase both anti-British and pro-German sentiments. Along with his associates he fused 'Islamist Jew-hatred with the modern conspiracy theories of Nazi and European anti-Semitism', and his doctrine 'permeated the consciousness of millions within the Arab world'.[77] The Grand Mufti aligned himself with the Nazis and, splendidly uncensored despite Nuri's pledge to the British, appealed to Arabs to cast off the colonial yoke. The British authorities compiled a thick dossier on the man, considered the region's main anti-British activist. The file contained details of his fundraising activities and contacts with the Axis along with plans for his removal, which included a propaganda campaign aimed at undermining his political reputation and pan-Arabist credentials.[78] Senior British politicians suggested kidnapping him and taking him to Cyprus, employing Britain's tried-and-tested method of political exile; Jewish activists, meanwhile, offered to assassinate him.[79]

America in Iran

While Britain and the Soviet Union were old hands in the region, the Middle East was an obscure and remote corner of the world as far as Washington was concerned: 'Intelligence operatives in the War Department knew virtually nothing about the region. In fact, when questions first arose about possible operations in Iran, the best source of information proved to be the Library of Congress, where consultants on Islamic archaeology provided maps and information on roads and other transportation routes.'[80] What limited contact the American government had had with its Iranian counterpart was ruptured in 1935 following the arrest of the former Iranian ambassador to Washington, Ghaffar Jalal, following a road accident in Elkton, Maryland.[81] The American press reported the incident as a typical example of an arrogant foreigner disregarding the country's laws; back in Tehran, the shah was furious because Jalal's still-valid diplomatic immunity had been ignored. Taking the arrest as a national insult, he recalled Jalal, broke off diplomatic relations, and closed all consular offices.[82]

Despite this break in formal political relations, non-governmental contact between America and Iran stretched back to the nineteenth century. It revolved around the activities of Presbyterian missionaries and administrative and financial experts hired by the Iranian state, ostensibly to help modernize aspects of the country's economy and governance but actually intended to involve America in Iranian affairs as a counterweight to British and Soviet influence. Arthur Millspaugh served as administrator-general of Iranian state finances in the 1920s, at Iran's request, and American commercial and oil interests were growing. In contrast to its post-war image as 'an unwelcome imperialist interloper', before the war America was viewed in an overwhelmingly positive light.[83] It was seen as a benefactor that could help deepen and protect Iran's independence and bolster its capacity to resist the imperial encroachments of other powers, through a strategy known as 'positive equilibrium'. Inevitably, Iranian attempts to involve America in the country's political affairs were viewed frostily in London and Moscow, and the American government was not at all interested in making itself unpopular in a distant region, regarded as Britain's bailiwick. Undeterred, attempts to embroil America in Iranian affairs continued. American investment, not least in the oil industry, was actively encouraged. The seeds of future entanglement had been sown, and from them would grow competition and rivalry with both Britain and the Soviet Union, and a changing dynamic in American–Iranian relations.

Britain and the challenges of imperial overstretch

Britain's presence in the Iran–Iraq region rested on a rickety agglomeration of military force (both present and latent), economic power, diplomatic swagger and political alliances with those who could be persuaded to follow Britain's lead, often doing so because their position depended on Britain's continued pre-eminence. But these alliances grew shaky as Britain's grip on the region became less secure and the prestige of the Axis rose. With the coming of war, the British craved strong, friendly regimes in Iran and Iraq along with acquiescent populations. But relations with the governments in Baghdad and Tehran were marred by historic differences and the taint of imperialism, further complicated by the blandishments of Germany and, as the war unfolded, eroded by the prospect of British defeat. Unlike the Germans, who enjoyed the lustre of novelty, Britain's presence in Iran and Iraq was familiar and decidedly tarnished. For all Britain's influence within them, these were independent nation-states, not colonies, and their political elites had cause to wish the British gone, or at least to have the terms of their presence fundamentally modified. Furthermore, while it could exert influence, Britain could not dictate who the Iranian and Iraqi governments talked to, had diplomatic and economic relations with and permitted to enter their countries. Though Britain was powerfully positioned in the Middle East, its forces were spread thin and it lacked sufficient local support in its contest with Germany and Italy, with many people judiciously deciding to sit on the fence and see which way the winds of war would blow.

The British, understandably, were inclined to construe what were fundamentally anti-British opinions and actions as pro-German ones, conflating cause and effect. But while they routinely overemphasized pro-German inspiration behind the opposition they encountered, their fears were by no means groundless. The European situation stood as eloquent testament to the effects of political penetration and the power of fifth-column movements. German commercial and political agencies had extensive interests in the region, and Nazi propaganda aimed at the Middle East was both copious and sophisticated. Britain was blamed for traumas in the recent history of both countries, notably the famine that swept Iran as a consequence of its hapless involvement in the First World War, killing millions, and the violence that followed Iraq's accession to the British Empire, which resulted in the deaths of thousands.

Britain's unpopularity was illustrated by reactions to the untimely demise of King Ghazi of Iraq in April 1939. A staunch pan-Arabist, Ghazi had opposed the presence of Britain in his country while also being obliged to work with it.[84] He had hated his time as a pupil at Harrow School, threatening to return one day with his army and burn it down.[85] A heavy-drinking womanizer who adored wild parties and fast cars, Ghazi became a 'nationalist idol'.[86] Most Iraqis 'forgave his faults and admired his support for Palestinian rights and Arab unity, and for plans to counter British dominance with

German help'. Young Iraqis carried his photograph in their wallets and cheered him wherever he went.[87] On the day of his death, Ghazi had invited friends to the Zuhur Palace for dinner and drinks. Afterwards he wanted to show a film, which he had left in a royal cottage on the banks of the Tigris. With two attendants he leapt into his open-topped Buick and, passing along a narrow track near the stables, came off the road after speeding over a hump-backed bridge. The car hit a telegraph pole, which collapsed, striking the king on the head and fracturing his skull. He died soon after. Dr Harry Sinderson, the king's physician, and his colleague Dr Noel Barham attended the dying king. They insisted that Dr Saib Shawkat also attend, and all three signed the death certificate. The British also left the car on display, to try to convince the people that their king had died in an accident.[88]

However, many Iraqis refused to believe that Ghazi's death was accidental. Grobba and his pro-German friends put it about that the British secret service had arranged the death of the Arabs' 'hero king', handing out pamphlets indicting London;[89] one accused the British of objecting to Ghazi's work towards greater Arab unity. There were demonstrations on the streets: in Mosul, oil capital of the north, a crowd of mourners surrounded the British consulate. Consul George Monck-Mason appeared on the balcony and attempted to reason with the people in Arabic, explaining that there had been no British-backed plot. But the crowd broke in to the consulate, killed Monck-Mason and looted the building before setting it ablaze. Grobba's agents in Mosul had 'whipped up a crowd of coolies working on the railway to a fanatical fury'.[90] The event was reported across the Empire. The headline in the *Sydney Morning Herald* read: 'British consul's murder: felled with pickaxe.' The article reported Prime Minister Neville Chamberlain's statement to the Commons regarding 'Iraqi reparations' for damage to British property, and the Iraqi government's pledge to pay a grant to Monck-Mason's dependants, hold a full enquiry and to conduct a public funeral with full honours.[91] The *Ottawa Evening Journal* ran the story as its second headline: 'British consul at Mosul murdered after King killed.'[92]

As was their wont throughout the colonial and semi-colonial world, the British blamed 'agitators' for Monck-Mason's murder, a standard appellation for anyone who opposed their presence and their policies: 'That Iraqis themselves might bear grievances against their colonial master is continually denied in the Foreign Office documents ... Although the crisis passed, the British Embassy increasingly viewed all manifestations of Arab nationalism as a challenge to imperial interests.'[93] Ghazi was replaced by a regent, Prince Abdulillah, because his successor, Faisal II, was only three years old. Abdulillah was more pro-British than Ghazi, proud to have British friends such as Winston Churchill and Lady Cunard and fond of Bond Street shops.[94] But he still had to deal with the ambiguity at the heart of the monarchy's, and the nation's, existence – the irreconcilable struggle of Arab and Iraqi nationalism against British imperialism.

Though pro-British, Prime Minister Nuri as-Said was also an Iraqi nationalist, and had to walk a political tightrope given the power of anti-British factions and the need to fend off accusations of being a British stooge. An Iraqi-born former Ottoman officer present from the foundation of the state in 1921, he believed that any Iraqi administration's ability to rule the fractious, artificial state was tenuous, and that this rendered British support essential. On the outbreak of hostilities, the British government had requested that Iraq sever diplomatic relations with Germany, in line with the terms of the Anglo-Iraqi Treaty, intern German nationals and provide all possible assistance. Nuri complied, breaking off diplomatic relations and expelling Grobba and his diplomatic team. Nuri also halted trade with Germany, arrested German adult males and handed them to the British, expelled others and prohibited German broadcasts.[95] He introduced curfews, censorship, rationing and powers to rule by decree and by administrative regulation. But he stopped short of declaring war on Germany. Attempting to bargain, Nuri said that he would declare war if Britain offered financial and diplomatic rewards.

In the conflict's early months, this situation was acceptable to the British, if not ideal. But there was discord within governing circles. Nuri's political opponents thought new wartime powers would be used against them, and tried to cultivate rival factions in the army while criticizing the government's pro-British stance. Pro-German military leaders were angered that Nuri had not used Britain's request to sever relations with Germany as a bargaining chip in order to seek a revision of the Palestine White Paper, and his rivals portrayed him as excessively pro-British.

British officials were frustrated by their own unpopularity and the contrasting appeal of all things German. The Public Relations Section of the Baghdad Embassy cast the challenges faced by Britain in the following terms: 'The prevailing motto in this part of the world is "better the Devil we don't know than the Devil we do." During the last war we were the unknown devil; now we are the known one! Here in Iraq our basic difficulty is really that we have given them everything, politically speaking, and have got nothing more even to promise.'[96] Foreign Secretary Halifax told his Cabinet colleagues that the Iraqi government itself was worried about the effect of the Palestine situation on public opinion. He urged propaganda and other measures to assuage Iraqi concerns, and quoted a communication from Nuri as-Said:

> As a complement to the measures which are being taken by the Iraqi Government themselves to defeat enemy trickery, His Majesty's Government, and, if possible, the French Government as well, should issue a clear and unambiguous pronouncement guaranteeing immediately, or at least at the end of the war, the execution of promises already given for the organization of the self-government of Palestine and Syria.[97]

Regent Abdulillah expressed regret that the 1939 Palestine White Paper had not gone further in guaranteeing Palestinian rights.[98] C.H. Summerhayes, Monck-Mason's replacement as consul in Mosul, wrote that the issue of Palestine was the main one 'whereby nationalists and religious extremists and their "foreign supporters" excite general opposition to British interests'.[99] Pan-Arabist protagonists had renewed pressure on Ambassador Newton, demanding that the British take concrete action favourable to the Arab cause in Palestine and Syria. Paul Knabenshue told his State Department masters that from 'an international point of view anti-British feeling in Iraq has recently been the outstanding feature of the political situation here'. There were various reasons for it, he continued, but the 'basic cause is the Palestine problem'.[100] So, with deep rifts in the Iraqi ruling elite over how to position the country in the light of the war, and the golden opportunity presented by the likelihood of German success, the situation was unenviable for the British. The governments in Baghdad and Tehran were untrustworthy, and both Germany and the Soviet Union threatened Britain's position in the region. Given all of this, it was imperative that adequate military preparations be made to secure a part of the world considered vital to the survival of the British Empire and its capacity to wage war.

CHAPTER 2

Defending Iran and Iraq

Iran and Iraq were geese that laid golden eggs, and so had to be defended at almost any cost. The British needed unfettered access to the region's oil, and to its lines of communication. In defending Iran and Iraq, control of the port of Basra was key to British strategy, a vital point of access and a base area capable of being built up in order to allow the ingress and egress of troops and war material, by land or by sea. There were then the overland lines of communication via which troops could enter the region for its defence, or be moved across it to support other theatres of operations. The region was threatened externally by Germany and the Soviet Union, and the British believed that there was also a possibility that Iran might be induced to attack Iraq. In meeting these threats, the British planned on the assumption that they would defend Iraq and if necessary the British zone in Iran with the assistance of the Iraqi military. But the suspect loyalty of the Iraqi government and the power of anti-British politicians and officers meant that the Iraqi military itself posed an internal threat.

Meeting these internal and external challenges demanded an enormous amount of planning and logistical preparation. The coming of war required wide-ranging defensive initiatives, the identification of threats, calculation of risk, and acceptance of contingency. It is useful to understand exactly what all of this meant, and to comprehend how prosaic matters such as railway rolling stock and desert supply dumps were the crucial cogs that kept the wheels of imperial defence turning. Often overlooked, logistical preparations and advanced planning for the movement of military resources around the world and the sustainment of forces in distant theatres were the indispensable hand-maidens of successful strategy. Preparation for a range of possible war-time eventualities – through activities such as developing logistical infrastructure, conducting war games and exercises, surveying routes, stockpiling fuel and ammunition, and making plans to deploy troops – allowed Britain a degree of operational flexibility. The plans and preparations that it made could be re-rolled as the nature of the threat changed, and the infrastructure that the British developed was on hand and ready for use when required. Alliances with countries such Iraq were a crucial variable in plans to defend a far-flung imperial estate, though war had a habit of rearranging the roster of allies and enemies. Early in the war, for example, Britain expected to be fighting the Soviets in the Iran–Iraq region, and when the Italian declaration of war opened North Africa and the Middle East to combat, the Germans were added to the list, coming a step closer when Hitler attacked the Soviet Union. But Britain did not expect to be fighting Frenchmen and Iraqis in this theatre, as was actually to occur, and at the start of the war could not have anticipated the arrival of American forces that the course of the war was to bring.

Although Iran and Iraq were acknowledged to be of great strategic value as war approached, they presented a command headache for Whitehall and the Chiefs of Staff. This was because they fell between the two pillars of Britain's imperial land and air power, represented by Middle East Command, founded in June 1939 to coordinate the three armed services in defending Egypt and its environs, and India Command, historic guardian of imperial interests in Arabia and the Persian Gulf. Hard-pressed commanders in Cairo and Delhi found it difficult to devote due attention to Iran and Iraq given their distance, and the fact that major theatres of combat operations were to develop elsewhere within their respective fiefs. Middle East Command understandably fixated on events unfolding in North Africa and southern Europe, and was also responsible for the campaign that developed in East Africa. India Command, though more sensitive to Iran and Iraq's strategic importance, had the subcontinent's defence to worry about, especially given the Japanese threat, and in the early years of the war was racing to expand, train and equip the Indian Army. As a result of this situation, Iran and Iraq flip-flopped between the two commands, the situation remaining unresolved until a bold Churchillian initiative reorganized the entire command structure through the creation of a dedicated Persia and Iraq Command.

Streamlining the command structure, however, could not alter the fundamental problem facing the British early in the war – that there were simply too many vital interests to be protected, too many actual and potential points of enemy attack and too few resources with which to meet them. Imperial overstretch was the issue, compounded by widely dispersed enemies and the Empire's need to operate on exterior, rather than interior, lines of communication. Like many other senior military men, Major-General Sir John Kennedy, Director of Military Operations at the War Office, had cause to remark upon Winston Churchill's constant pressure to send more troops to the Middle East. Churchill, by now prime minister, 'fretted at the delays which are inseparable from the preparation of modern fighting forces, and he pressed us incessantly to "grapple with the enemy"'. But despite his fulminations, the pugnacious prime minister understood the root of the problem. As he put it to Kennedy during a conference on the allocation of military equipment to Britain's allies, 'there were too many little pigs and not enough teats on the old sow'.[1]

The War Cabinet and Chiefs of Staff constantly returned to this theme. In September 1940, for example, they considered a sweeping strategic appraisal, the 'main thrust' of which was an examination of 'the factors affecting our ability to defeat Germany'.[2] The access of both sides to oil was high on the list, and the main short-term threats to British interests included possible attacks on Britain itself, mounting shipping losses, the security of the Middle East and the security of Britain's West African colonies, which contained vital resources and ports deemed 'essential to the control of our sea communications'. Continuing its global panorama, the document noted that Malaya was 'by no means secure', and that Iraq and Palestine were threatened and required reinforcement as soon as possible. It was here that the British Empire's grand strategy began to hit the buffers:

> The necessity for making provision for our security overseas thus postpones the time when we can hope to undertake major offensive operations ... While it is obviously desirable to secure every part of the British Empire against enemy aggression, it is clear that, with the forces at our disposal, the allocation of defence resources to different areas must be directly related to the extent that each will contribute to the defeat of Germany.[3]

This was the real-life game of *Risk* played by policymakers, planners and regional commanders as they wrestled with the complexity created by the coincidence of global war and global empire.

Nevertheless, centuries of campaigning and the operation of a coherent system of imperial defence meant that the British were not without experience when it came to coordinating war on a global scale. Resident in so many parts of the world courtesy of a sprawling empire, and possessed of the world's most widely dispersed armed forces, Britain could call upon a global military infrastructure. This placed it in an advantageous position in terms of ready access to local knowledge and resources, enabling it to plan for the logistical nitty-gritty that was essential if activity on the ground was to be translated into strategic success. But the disadvantage brought by global empire was the need to defend all parts of it, creating manifold vulnerabilities and the challenge of dispersing resources to meet anticipated threats.

The system of imperial defence relied upon British sea power guaranteeing Britain's ability to move troops and military resources around the world to be deposited wherever they were needed, assuming, of course, that there were sufficient to go round. The movement of troops from India to reinforce British positions in the Mediterranean and the Middle East was a tried-and-tested aspect of Britain's global military planning as part of the system of imperial defence. There were also plans to reinforce Iran and Iraq, should they be threatened, with troops coming in the opposite direction, striking eastwards from Palestine. Central to all plans was the ability to transit troops across Iraq, entering either from the British mandates of Palestine and Trans-Jordan, or landing at Basra having been transported by sea from India or elsewhere. The overarching system, of which such plans were but component parts, could be relied upon to beef up Britain's military presence if necessary; troops could be inserted into Iraq so long as Britain retained control of the sea lanes of the Indian Ocean and the Persian Gulf, and access to Basra and the Shatt al-Arab. Courtesy of the Iraqi lines of communication, it could also reinforce overland from Egypt and Palestine.

The threat to the region came from three distinct directions in the early stages of the war. As the Chiefs of Staff instructed the War Cabinet, it 'might develop either through deterioration of internal security, Russian aggression, or a German advance through Syria.'[4] Defensive plans were well in hand. Plans Heron, Herring, Lobster and Sabine were designed to buttress the region's defences in order to meet internal or external threats by loading troops into Iraq from the west or the east, or by using Iraq as a conduit to rush troops to Egypt and destinations to the west. Plan Heron envisaged the deployment of a brigade from India to Egypt, either via the Suez Canal or, if it had been closed by enemy action, via the Iraqi land bridge extending from Basra to Baghdad and then across the desert to Trans-Jordan and Palestine.[5] The British moved the Force Heron brigade to Egypt by sea just before war broke out, intended as a shot across the bows of the Germans, the Italians and those Egyptians who might favour the Axis cause. But although Heron Force was lifted by sea, Whitehall assured Ambassador Newton in Baghdad that this 'in no way' encroached on arrangements made for the movement of forces via Iraq, a plan 'which may still have to be implemented if further reinforcements were sent from India to Egypt in an emergency.'[6] 'In war,' Lacy Baggallay of the Foreign Office's Eastern Department told Newton, 'the route will be a most useful channel for reinforcements, certainly from India, and possibly even from home' should the Mediterranean be shut to shipping.[7]

Plan Sabine, meanwhile, anticipated the build-up of three Indian divisions for the defence of Iran and Iraq, primarily with the Soviet Union in mind. It envisaged an initial division (codenamed Trout) securing Basra and establishing it as a base for a larger force. It would arrive prepared for an opposed landing and would immediately set about ensuring the safety of the Basra bridgehead, Abadan and the Shatt al-Arab.[8] The two follow-on Sabine divisions would assist the Iraqi army in repelling Soviet invasion forces in the Kirkuk–Khanaqin area on the border with Iran. Highlighting the manner in which responsibility for Iran and Iraq's security fell awkwardly between India Command and Middle East Command, Force Sabine was to be controlled by the latter even though the troops involved would be furnished and sustained by the former.

Plan Lobster envisaged reinforcement from the west provided by an infantry brigade group dispatched from Palestine. It would travel towards Baghdad via the desert route, and was intended to bolster the Iraqi army in the event of an invasion threat and reassure the Iraqi population by visible displays of force in urban and rural areas. If Britain needed to defend Iraq, British authorities wanted troops, military vehicles and aircraft to be seen as widely as possible so that people could behold the British acting in Iraqi interests, honouring the 1930 treaty. Details of Plan Lobster were discussed when representatives of Air Headquarters Iraq and the British Advisory Military Mission to Baghdad visited Headquarters British Forces Palestine in May 1940. A reconnaissance of the route and the desert staging posts from Palestine to Ramadi and Musayyib was conducted by officers of the Royal Engineers at the end of the month. The warning order 'Genghis Khan' from Headquarters Middle East would trigger the operation, and the order 'Marco Polo' would send the troops on their way.[9]

Thus the British undertook extensive preparations to facilitate the movement of troops across the Iraqi land bridge in case they needed to fend off a Soviet advance, move troops between the eastern and western hemispheres, or suppress local uprisings. Even if the Suez Canal were lost, as long as Britain remained in control of the waters of the Gulf and the eastern Mediterranean, the roads and railways of Iraq, Trans-Jordan and Palestine would form a conveyor belt along which imperial forces could be passed. In order to make it so, there was lots of work to be done, by both British and imperial servicemen and locally recruited labourers. Crucial to all these plans was the port of Basra, the load-bearing capacity of the railway between Basra and Baghdad, and the road across the desert. In the light of this, the War Office had approved the acquisition of an additional twenty-five flat-bed transportation trucks for the Baghdad–Basra railway line.[10] In terms of logistical uplift, their procurement allowed for an extra 'vehicle type train' to be dispatched across the desert – meaning a train loaded with both soldiers and their vehicles. The current capacity was three: three trains could leave Basra each day, and it took two and a half days to reach Baghdad and return. For the next stage of the journey, troops alighting at Baghdad would be moved across the desert in motor transport echelons following each other at one-day intervals.

The onward movement of troops and their baggage by road on the second leg required a considerable number of vehicles. In a special report, Squadron Leader H.D. Jackman advocated the organization of a permanent convoy for the desert crossing to and from RAF Habbaniya west of Baghdad to Haifa in Palestine. 'It is of greatest importance that a regular and reliable service be instituted for transport of material' between them, he wrote. There were at the time a number of new Crossley 3-ton lorries in Iraq, and he recommended that they be used to form a 'Desert Convoy'.[11] Illustrating the kind of figures involved, if the Lobster brigade group was dispatched from Palestine, 200 buses would be assembled at RAF Habbaniya to move the troops to Baghdad. Other vehicles would convey their baggage and equipment. In order to fuel these troop convoys as they crossed the desert, petrol was stockpiled at desert staging post H3, Landing Ground 5 (LG5), and Habbaniya. When the land bridge was in use, RAF armoured cars based at the staging posts would escort the convoys along what was known as the 'Trans-desert Line of Communication'.[12]

To bring the Iraqi line of communication up to optimal standard, work was undertaken to improve it as well as to amass the resources required for its effective utilization. New desert staging posts were established; early in the war, Lieutenant R.D. Anderson of RAF Habbaniya's No. 1 Armoured Car Company led a convoy of two Hillman Tourers and an RRWT Rover to Musayyib, with orders to establish a new one as the network was extended. John Frost, later to find fame as a paratrooper at Arnhem, was on secondment to the RAF Iraq Levies when war broke out, commanding Landing Ground Number 5 and in charge of half a platoon of Assyrian Levies, a section of RAF armoured cars, a signals unit and thirty Arab labourers.[13] The landing ground was stuffed full of petrol and water supplies for convoys travelling across the desert. With its military bases in Egypt under threat, Britain had decided to move RAF training establishments to Iraq, while Iraq's operational bomber squadrons moved in the other direction, ground crew and equipment going by land. Most of the bomber echelons had already made the move to Egypt, and the training formations were now arriving in Iraq.[14] The convoys that thundered through LG5, Frost wrote, 'looked formidable when approaching or leaving, surrounded by great clouds of dust'.[15] In this manner, young British servicemen, many miles from home and the momentous events taking place in Europe, worked in the heat of the desert to develop the Empire's defences. The desert line of communication that they manned was to see plenty more military traffic in the coming months as imperial forces careered across Iraq and into Iran and Syria.[16]

No army could simply pitch up in land as inhospitable as the Iraqi desert and expect to move men and the hundreds of vehicles that accompanied modern warriors without planning and preparation. An extensive network of bases, hospitals and supply dumps was required, along with maps and guides to prevent units getting lost or following tracks that ended in quagmires, and to ensure that people were fed and watered. 'How,' as the subaltern John Masters incredulously put it as he moved around Iraq with his Gurkha battalion, 'did exactly 843 rations arrive at a map reference in this empty desert just when we needed it', along with supplies of chlorinated water?[17] All necessary material for fighting and sustaining life was delivered by sea for onward movement overland. While in Basra, Masters witnessed three supply ships arriving at once, one containing forty Bren gun carriers, one a heavy anti-aircraft battery, the third a 500-bed base hospital. Meticulous planning in the movement of equipment and investment in infrastructure was the name of the game.

As well as transport, provision had to be made to shelter, feed and care for large numbers of men in transit. The chief engineer at RAF Habbaniya reported that emergency measures for camps and water supplies for Heron Force were based on an assumed passage of one brigade from India per week. Tented rest camps were strung along the route, Middle East Command decreeing that each be capable of accommodating 1,600 soldiers. Tentage for the Lobster brigade group was to be supplied by Palestine, and India Command was to provide 20,000 maps of the route. In order to feed in-transit soldiers, cold storage provision had to be made for food delivered by sea to Haifa and then transported overland and stored at the preposi-tioned rest camps extending across Trans-Jordan and Iraq.[18] RAF Hospital Makina at Basra was expanded to provide 100 beds for line of communica-tion casualties, and RAF Hospital Habbaniya 50.

In light of the German and Soviet threat to Iran and Iraq, senior British officers in the region reassessed matters, as did politicians and defence chiefs back in London. Not only did they need to prepare for attacks on Iran and Iraq, but also to use the region as a base for launching strikes on the Soviet Union, either pre-emptively or reactively, should the two nations go to war. This appeared more likely with the signing of the Nazi–Soviet Pact. The conclusion of the agreement had sent shock waves across eastern Europe and the Middle East, escalating the chances of war with the Soviet Union in both regions; the governments of Britain, Iran and Iraq were all alive to the threat. The War Cabinet urged propaganda penetration in addi-tion to defensive preparations. Iran was considered 'particularly susceptible to propaganda' and its military forces assessed to be of 'a very low category'. The threat to the Iraqi lines of communication and the region's oil was emphasized.[19] The Chiefs of Staff recommended that at the 'first sign of Russian aggression against Iran we would have to provide for internal secu-rity and air defence of Anglo-Iranian oilfields and the port of Basra'. Soviet aggression might take the form of an advance on Tabriz with five or six divisions, or a seaborne expedition across the Caspian with Tehran as the objective.[20] Air Vice-Marshal Harry George 'Reggie' Smart, commanding British Forces in Iraq and Britain's senior officer on the spot, conducted an assessment of the Iraqi forces alongside which the British expected to fight. The possibility of Soviet bombers operating against British targets from Iranian bases was also taken into account and he provided an analysis of defensive dispositions in Iran, including distances, routes, bridges and lines of communication.[21] Special maps detailing these features were produced so that commanders on the ground could study invasion routes and work out how to interdict them.

If Stalin invaded Iran, the British identified two passable routes that they could employ, and noted that the only 'feasible line of advance on S. IRAQ would be from Tehran area'. The climatic conditions were such that between November and March the routes through the mountains 'may be rendered impassable by snow or rain for 4 to 6 days. In early summer, communications in the plains area are liable to interruption by flood for indefinite periods ... To meet any Russian threat against North Iraq including Kirkuk oilfields it is estimated that 2 divisions ... would be required to support the Iraqi divisions at present in Mosul-Kirkuk area'. To meet a threat against southern Iraq, 'one division based on Basra and operating in AIOC [Anglo-Iranian Oil Company] area of Iran is considered sufficient'.[22]

Back in London, Lord Chatfield, Minister for Co-ordination of Defence in Neville Chamberlain's government, addressed the Cabinet, outlining proposals from the Chiefs of Staff for the defence of Iran and Iraq. He reported that Britain needed 'to be administratively prepared to operate a force amounting to some 12 divisions and 39 squadrons' in the Iran–Iraq region, a very significant force projection indeed, which would comprise something in the region of 100,000 men and hundreds of aircraft.[23]

In May 1940 RAF Headquarters Middle East, based in Cairo and the Middle East's highest air force command, discussed a 'Joint Plan for the Defence of Iraq and the British Lines of Communication between the Persian Gulf and Trans-Jordan' with its subordinate formation, Reggie Smart's Air Headquarters Iraq. In the same month, the Iraqi Ministry of Defence chaired a British–Iraqi conference to consider joint defence planning against the Soviet Union.[24] Among other things, the delegates at these meetings in Baghdad and Cairo pored over the latest intelligence regarding the strength and location of Soviet forces in Transcaucasia, which were regularly monitored. The 'first line strength' of Soviet air forces stationed there stood at 180 obsolescent fighters, 12 bombers and 65 reconnaissance/army cooperation aircraft, mostly stationed at Baku.[25] From the RAF's point of view, it was estimated that resisting a Soviet invasion would require five bomber squadrons, two fighter squadrons and three army cooperation squadrons, units dedicated to interacting with ground forces and providing close air support, tactical reconnaissance and artillery spotting. Three additional bomber squadrons and a fighter squadron would be required for the destruction of the Caucasus oilfields, if this was required.

While Stalin's forces might invade Iran, the Joint Planning Staff concluded that

> RUSSIA is unlikely to invade N. IRAQ solely for the purpose of securing the KIRKUK oilfields as there would be no means for exporting the oil. It is possible, though unlikely that RUSSIA may seek to cut off this source of our oil supplies at the instigation of GERMANY . . . In view of the recent disclosure to RUSSIA of our designs on BAKU, it is conceivable that she may hope, by seizing N. IRAQ, to remove the threat by denying to our air forces those air bases in N. IRAQ which are within effective bombing range.[26]

Baku, on the Caspian, was the capital of the Soviet republic of Azerbaijan, and of vital importance to the Soviet Union because of its oilfields. Britain's 'designs on Baku' were its plans for a strategic bombing offensive to destroy the Soviet oil industry, collapse the Soviet economy and deny Germany access to its resources.

The Chiefs of Staff told the War Cabinet that reliance on Caucasian oil was 'a fundamental weakness in the Russian economy' and that the Caucasus, from a British point of view, was 'the one area in which Russia is really vulnerable'. If it came to war, the British would exploit this vulnerability by dropping large amounts of high explosives on the area. Plans were developed to strike the Soviet Union from Iraq in conjunction with French forces operating from Syria. Western Air Plan 106, or Operation Pike as it was known, targeted Batum, Baku and Grozny. In March and April 1940 an RAF photo reconnaissance unit flying Lockheed Super Electras surveyed the ground, flying from RAF Habbaniya. The aircraft flew over Iranian Kurdistan and the Caspian Sea before circling over the target areas and taking reels of pictures.[27]

The Soviets, of course, were aware of the British threat. To counter it, the Chiefs of Staff believed that Moscow might order a pre-emptive attack 'aimed at adding depth in front of the Baku defences' that would facilitate operations against Anglo-Iranian oilfields and objectives in Iraq. It was impossible to predict. If Soviet bombers penetrated so far south, the Chiefs of Staff averred, the imperial infantry division allocated for the protection of Basra and the Iranian oilfields might also face 'scenes of serious disorder resulting from Russian air attacks and tribal uprisings'.[28] In the event of invasion and significant subversive activity, 'we would have to move troops to the oilfields region with or without Iranian consent . . . in either event we see no reason to coordinate plans with the Iranian Government in advance.[29] With war already being waged against Germany and war with the Soviet Union in the offing, nothing could be left to chance, as the region's oil was a strategic 'must have' for the British.

To help facilitate strikes against Soviet targets, the British examined the possibility of opening an airbase in the Tehran region. Discussions on the subject revealed British thinking on the shah's regime, and their concerns that he might seek to trade base rights for British military support in defending the country against Soviet invasion. Feeling desperate, the shah wished for a formal alliance with the British for the defence of his country. The Chiefs of Staff wrote:

> We fully appreciate the Foreign Office view that the price of Iranian assistance would probably be heavy, both at the time of the request and also after the war. We fear that, whatever the Shah asked for the future, he might at the time demand the assistance of a British force for the defence of northern Iran . . . The future is still too uncertain to justify us in mortgaging force to help the Shah by embarking on coordinated war plans, as suggested by the Iranian Minister. In any case we are averse to employing British forces alongside so unreliable an ally as the Iranians, if it can be avoided. For this reason we would prefer to operate against Russia with long-range aircraft based on Mosul.[30]

Lacy Baggallay of the Foreign Office's Eastern Department endorsed this approach: 'The Persians are likely to prove the most difficult and possibly even the most treacherous of allies. We must avoid putting ourselves in their hands more than we can possibly help . . . There will be no question of gratitude . . . by and large the Persians will resent the fact that they were obliged to rely upon us in their hour of need and hold it against us.'[31] Mistrust of the locals, along with the need to second-guess a potential foe and decide whether to strike the first blow, were all part and parcel of the planning and decision-making process, and there were always divergent views. In response to Baggallay, and expressing an alternative point of view, H.J. Seymour minuted: 'We shouldn't be too discouraging lest the Persians see it as cause to do a deal with the Russians.' On 23 May 1940 the Iraqi Ministry of Defence agreed that certain airbases, including Mosul, could be expanded to accommodate long-range RAF bombers and modern aircraft if Britain needed to strike at Soviet industrial and military targets, and this reduced the need for bases in northern Iran.[32]

To bolster Britain's position, non-military countermeasures were also pursued: propaganda to exploit 'the inherent antipathy between Islam and Bolshevism' was proposed, though it was acknowledged that the 'main counter would be Russian propaganda alleging that their object was to free IRAQ from Democratic domination', an interesting term for British imperialism. Dispensing large amounts of money to secure 'loyalty' was also advised, cash being viewed as 'a potent factor both in dealing with Pan-Arab extremists who might otherwise support the enemy on this pretext, and in influencing in our favour various tribes and factions in IRAN and IRAQ ... Since we are dealing with Eastern Countries and people, the power of gold applied personally, should not be forgotten,' it was said, reflecting contemporary stereotypes and the supposed efficacy of political bribery.[33] If it came to war, the British believed that Palestine, Saudi Arabia and Trans-Jordan 'could be relied upon to support British efforts to protect IRAQ against an attack from RUSSIA', and it was noted that 'Kurdish feeling is very anti-Russian and could be kept so by propaganda and subsidies.'[34]

As if the Soviet Union was not enough to worry about, there was also the German threat to consider. A key concern with this in mind was the stance adopted by Turkey, through which, if given permission, German forces could move towards Iran and Iraq. The Middle East, according to the War Cabinet, was 'key to our strategy', and a central aspect of the plans to defend it involved keeping Turkey neutral – as Britain had been unable to do in the First World War, bringing years of bloody fighting to the Balkans, Egypt, Iran, Iraq and Palestine. The War Cabinet feared that 'unless adequately supported, Turkey might be driven to accept temporary German protection. With a view to assisting Turkey in meeting a German threat through Syria on Iran, it is most desirable that reserves are built up.' The prospect of an attack through Syria was made all the more likely by the fall of France in June 1940. The capitulation of its main ally was a disaster for Britain, both at home and in the Mediterranean and Middle East. It removed at a single stroke France's considerable military resources, brought the Italians into the war and presented the dispiriting prospect of a supine Vichy regime granting Germany the right to pass troops and aircraft through Syria in order to strike eastwards. An insecure or hostile Syria was a dagger pointed at the heart of Britain's strategic position in Iran and Iraq. Dill told Wavell that from here Axis aircraft 'could easily deliver air attacks on the refinery at Abadan'. He urged him to rush anti-aircraft guns from Egypt to Abadan, a classic case of robbing Peter to pay Paul as commanders moved their pieces across a global chessboard. Britain could hardly spare such weapons given the dire threat posed by the Luftwaffe, Dill remarked, and guns that were to be sent to Iran from Hong Kong and Singapore were now to remain in place due to the effect the news of the fall of France had had in Japan.[35]

The conjunction of German and Soviet threats only added to the importance of plans to reinforce the region with imperial soldiers. 'Worst-case scenario' plans were drawn up in the event that all else failed. In extremis, Britain planned a methodical scorched-earth retreat involving the destruction of the northern oilfields, refineries, supply dumps, airbases and railways so that no conqueror would be able to enjoy their benefits, and a comprehensive programme of flooding to render large areas of Iraq impassable. In tandem with this scorched-earth campaign, British forces would hold a line of no retreat around Basra and the south-western Iranian oilfields and refineries. 'At the worst we must damage the oil organization in Iraq, destroy the pipe-line and pumping stations, withdraw to the head of the Persian Gulf and deny to the enemy access to the Gulf and the use of the Iranian oil, while retaining the use of that oil for ourselves.'[36] Exploring worst-case scenarios, the Chiefs of Staff concluded that if the Royal Navy lost control of the Mediterranean, 'our position in Egypt and Palestine might become untenable. We might be forced to withdraw towards Iraq and East Africa, but our policy in such an event must be to delay as long as possible an enemy advance to the southward by blocking the Suez Canal ... and to hold as a last resort the head of the Persian Gulf, Aden, and Kenya.'[37] War with the Soviet Union was assessed as likely, and preparations made for a strategic retreat to the Gulf and Iran and Iraq. This was to be the final fall-back line; were an enemy to appear in Iran and Iraq, the British would burn and flood the north and throw a ring around the oilfields of south-west Iran, the Abadan refinery and the port of Basra. This would allow them to continue to access oil, to export it in tankers and, in due course, hopefully, to pump troops into the region in order to reclaim the north.

The British envisaged the Iraqi army operating in a static defence, as opposed to a combat, role. Major-General George Waterhouse, head of the British Military Advisory Mission in Baghdad and inspector-general of the Iraqi army, had been 'selling' the Iraqis the idea of the Shatt al-Arab as the 'windpipe' of Iraq. Grooming the Iraqi army as a proxy force for British purposes, he reported that the 'Iraqis are now thoroughly convinced and contemplate the location of one Division in the South (instead of one Brigade only) ready to advance on Mohammerah (Khorramshahr) and then on to ABADAN when war is declared'.[38] While Waterhouse was keen to stress that the main role of Iraqi forces in the south was the protection of the Shatt al-Arab, there was no question of asking them to fight on behalf of the British outside of Iraq, even if they were employed for static defence at Abadan. This was because Britain 'had a low opinion of the Iraqi military', and did not want Iraq subsequently to claim a right of quid pro quo, seeking territorial aggrandizement in return for having helped Britain.[39] This referred to Iraq's territorial designs on the province of Khuzestan in south-west Iran, known to Iraqis as Arabistan.

In the north of the country, two of Iraq's four divisions stood ready to fight alongside British troops in the event of an attack. 'Most Secret Defensive Measures' for the protection or denial of the Kirkuk oilfields had been enacted by the British and Iraqi authorities. To guard against sabotage, important installations were surrounded with wire fencing and patrolled at night by Iraqi troops and police guards. Plans for the demolition of bridges and key strategic sites were in place. British and Iraqi air assets were available in the region, and to guard against attack by airborne troops, lorries were placed on aerodromes at Baghdad, Rashid airbase, Kirkuk, Mosul and the K1 pumping station, spaced along the runways each evening so as to prevent surprise enemy landings. Airbases were also defended by machine-guns, Bren gun carriers and armoured cars.

But while the British and Iraqi militaries were honing their defensive plans, relations between the two governments were increasingly strained. Britain grew more and more suspicious of the Iraqi government, and questioned its friendship. An additional bone of contention between the two governments revolved around arms supply. A provision of the 1930 treaty was that Britain would equip the Iraqi military. This meant that Iraqi forces would be largely kitted out with British-manufactured weapons systems and, therefore, trained by British officers, helping keep Iraq and its military in Britain's orbit and benefiting Britain's arms industry. Though the British government had reservations about the manner in which the Iraqi government chose to employ those weapons – often in oppressing its own people – they wanted to honour the treaty and prevent Iraq from turning to alternative suppliers.

But when, early in the war, the British government was pressed to satisfy Iraq's requirements for light anti-aircraft guns, Bren gun carriers, anti-tank rifles, mortars and medium artillery, it refused. Given its concerns about Iraq's loyalty to the British cause, London was reluctant to continue supplying weapons. Baghdad's requests were supported by the British ambassador in Baghdad, but Newton had cause to lament the War Office and War Cabinet's unhelpful attitude in this regard, which had a bad effect on the Iraqi government, fuelling anger about the constricting nature of the British 'alliance' and augmenting resentment.[40] As well as denoting mistrust, London's refusal was a reflection of Iraq's lowly position in the wartime pecking order when it came to allocating scarce British resources: the simple fact was that Britain now needed all the production of its armaments industries for itself, its colonies and dominions, and beleaguered European allies considered to be in greater peril. Nevertheless, supplying the weapons might have led to friendlier relations with the Iraqi government, which the British greatly desired, and the Iraqis logically argued that they needed the arms in order to stand shoulder to shoulder with the British in the defence of the region. With this in mind, Foreign Secretary Lord Halifax urged his colleagues to consider Iraqi requests sympathetically as a means of strengthening the pro-British elements in Iraqi governing circles. 'It is against this background that an appeal which has now been received from General Nuri-as-Said, the Iraqi Minister for Foreign Affairs and one who may be regarded as sincerely deploring the growing anti-British feeling, must be considered,' Halifax said.[41] Unfortunately, as 1940 progressed and Britain's military position became more precarious, relations between the two governments suffered correspondingly. Iraqi nationalists saw an opportunity to relieve themselves of Britain's stifling presence once and for all.

CHAPTER 3

Towards the Iraqi coup

The twists and turns of Iraq's complex politics at the time of the Second World War, fascinating or tedious depending on one's interests, have been well documented.[1] Of relevance here is the fact that throughout 1940 the political merry-go-round, in which members of a narrow elite tussled for office and senior military leaders sought to shape national policy, produced a succession of prime ministers but failed to fix upon an effective policy given the proximity of war. On occasion troops were stood to arms in support of rival factions, the regent Prince Abdulillah prudently leaving Baghdad to be close to loyal troops until things blew over. Deeply internal matters of contention, sometimes revolving around the Sunni–Shia divide, were refracted through the extraordinary politics of a world war. The main actors in this drama were Nuri as-Said, the prime minister, and Rashid Ali al-Gailani, the head of the king's executive office, the Royal Diwan, along with the Golden Square officer cabal. While all protagonists desired genuine independence for Iraq and nurtured ardent ambitions for greater Arab unity, they differed in the extent to which they saw Britain retaining a role in developments. Some, like Nuri, considered Britain essential to Iraq's existence and too powerful to be cast off. Others, like Rashid Ali and the Golden Square, saw Britain as an insurmountable obstacle to the pursuit of their goals for Arab and Iraqi independence – and viewed a triumphant Germany as the perfect vehicle to which to hitch their ambitions.

The Golden Square resented Nuri's attempts to curb the power of the military, and in March 1940 Prince Abdulillah, supported by Nuri, turned to Rashid Ali to form a 'national coalition' which included Nuri as Foreign Minister and Taha al-Hashimi as Defence Minister. Rashid Ali, a former member of the Ottoman judiciary and a professor at the Baghdad school of law, had first served as a government minister in 1924. He was anti-British and bent on overturning the Anglo-Iraqi Treaty, and did not share Nuri's conviction that Iraq's best interests were served by alliance with Britain. By bringing most senior politicians into a single government which implicitly accepted the 1930 treaty, however, Nuri and the regent 'believed they could deprive the increasingly vociferous members of the Golden Square of significant political allies'.[2] But a united front failed to emerge given the polarization of opinion; while Nuri made speeches advocating the strengthening of democracy and championing a pro-British form of Arab union, Rashid Ali and the Golden Square stoked pro-Axis sympathies and dared to hope that the time had come to reckon with the British.

Throughout 1940, the main problem from a British point of view was the prospect of Soviet military action in the region and the danger of agitated, anti-British Iraqis threatening British interests and reaching out to the Germans. Major-General Waterhouse wrote that relations with Iraqi officers had been 'universally friendly' until 1940, but from that point onwards 'Salahud-Din [Salah al-Din al-Sabbagh] and his gang laid themselves out to make things extremely difficult for us'.[3] This was compounded by the 'great force of Axis propaganda being concentrated on every Iraqi soldier regardless of rank'.[4] As prime minister, Rashid Ali steered Iraq away from its cautiously pro-British stance. He resumed telegraphic communications with the Axis powers, retained diplomatic relations with Italy and tolerated vociferous pro-German and anti-British press commentary. His government attempted to re-establish diplomatic ties with Germany and to abrogate the treaty. Though he did not initially envisage active cooperation with the Germans, he envied the neutral path being trodden by neighbouring Turkey and was desperate to reduce or eradicate British influence.

Britain's terrible military and diplomatic reverses in the spring of 1940, which included the Dunkirk evacuations, made things far worse. Much if not most of the Iraqi ruling elite thought that Britain would lose the war, creating an atmosphere conducive to crisis. In an attempt to de-escalate the situation, the British were actively 'encouraging' the French to take a liberal line over the future of Syria in order to appease nationalists throughout the region – this a mere week before a triumphant Adolf Hitler visited Compiègne for the armistice negotiations that put the seal on France's abject defeat.

The fall of France dramatically altered the strategic balance in the Middle East, and British vulnerability soared. News of the armistice was received with consternation by British communities around the world. The British diplomat Gerald de Gaury, dining at the summer legation in Isfahan with the British counsellor, his wife and the Apostolic Delegate, recalled the moment: 'After dinner we went out to sit on the terrace facing the tall moonlit trees and long narrow *bassins d'eau*. The moon struck glimmers from the cross and ring of the Apostolic Delegate. A radio placed ready was turned on for the news, news we fearfully half expected. It was of the fall of France. We sat in silence, too moved to speak.'[5]

Iranian and Iraqi nationalists observed Britain standing alone as Germany flattened its neighbours, while to the north, the Nazi–Soviet Pact heralded an intensification of the Soviet threat. London watched the situation with growing concern. 'The adherence of Iraq to the cause of the Allies is in considerable danger,' the Chiefs of Staff told Churchill's War Cabinet: 'Anti-British feeling runs high, particularly among the younger army officers. There are doubts as to the loyalty of the army in an emergency and German exploits do more than merely evoke admiration. There are reports of a Fifth Column organization, though these reports do not give precise information.'[6] Iraqi politicians, including Nuri, did nothing to discourage British alarm about fifth-column activity, believing that such fears strengthened their hand. Until recently, the Chiefs of Staff continued, the Iraqi government had given the impression that it 'faces these difficulties with a measure of impotence, or possibly connivance ... certain repressive measures against public demonstrations, and the press, were taken', and these measures were backed with 'possibly a genuine effort' to keep the young officers under control.[7] But the British were highly sceptical, and did not think the measures went nearly far enough. The importance of more pro-British radio propaganda was strongly emphasized, and it was suggested that the Iraqi government be induced to broadcast British propaganda from Baghdad. But propaganda, sometimes presented as something of a panacea, was no substitute for political and military muscle.

Britain and France's lack of battlefield success, and corresponding German victories, took their toll; 'few people in Iraq really thought that we would win the war,' wrote Halifax.[8] On 12 June 1940 he told the War Cabinet that the situation in Iraq and the wider Middle East 'had grown much worse as a result of constant German successes, culminating in the drive to the Channel ports'; on the same day the 51st Highland Division surrendered at

Saint-Valery-en-Caux, and two days later came the Italian declaration of war, a terrible blow for Britain's position in North Africa and the Middle East. German and Italian propaganda had 'for a long time past been actively exploiting Arab sentiment about Syria and Palestine,' Halifax continued, and 'German success has made this propaganda effective. What is more, it has made it matter, for the Arabs have largely lost confidence in the ability of the Allies to protect them and wish above all to be on the winning side.'[9] Six days earlier, Churchill had expressed to Anthony Eden, Secretary of State for War, his desire for a stream of Indian Army brigades to be sent to Iraq and other locations in the Middle East in order to shore up Britain's position.[10] But infantry brigades did not grow on trees.

People throughout the region looked on agog as France fell, Mussolini showed his hand and the Battle of Britain commenced. Iraqis were 'stunned by the European situation and the plight of the Allied armies stuck in northern France' ahead of the Dunkirk evacuations, wrote Paul Knabenshue, America's consul-general in Baghdad. The situation had 'sobered' those who feared a German occupation of Iraq in the event of Britain losing the war. 'Aside from the relatively few Iraqis who are distinctly pro-German,' the American diplomat continued, 'the other Iraqis are not basically pro-German and are only anti-British because of the latter's alleged treatment of the Arabs in Palestine.' The people were 'keenly but calmly following through radio and press the progress of the Battle of Britain as well as developments in the Balkans and North Africa.'[11]

Attempting to bargain with the British, Rashid Ali said that he would be more cooperative if there was significant movement on the Palestine question; the British said there would be no movement on this front for the duration of hostilities. Britain's decision not to enact the constitutional recommendations of the 1939 Palestine White Paper, which included appointing Palestinians to head government departments inside the mandate and advancing the self-government agenda, stoked Iraqi anger. In July Nuri pushed Britain to at least establish a halfway house, semi-independent government headed by the Iraqi regent.[12] But the British remained unmoved.

Knabenshue reported that Rashid Ali, 'following the oriental custom of using a third party intermediary', communicated to Ambassador Newton that if Britain wanted 'Iraq to state her position more clearly and to act in accordance with British ideas', the following conditions needed to be met: Syria to be given complete independence; the immediate implementation of the terms of the White Paper; and the provision of British arms for the Iraqi military in sufficient quantities and not 'in driblets'. The request for arms imports from Britain was made on the basis that if Iraq were to declare war on Germany – even though its government had no intention of doing so – its security would be endangered.[13] But as we have seen, to the detriment of Anglo-Iraqi relations at this important juncture, the British government, despite the urgings of Ambassador Newton, refused to oblige. This was hardly surprising; the new government's pro-Axis tack was more than enough to set alarm bells ringing.

Beyond elite circles and the political maelstrom of Baghdad, there was mounting nervousness in rural districts. People feared that the war, which seemed to be moving closer, would lead to military conscription. Addressing the Secretary of State in Washington, Knabenshue summarized the situation.[14] There was a possibility that Baghdad and other Iraqi towns would be bombed and that fifth-column elements would coordinate activity with the arrival of German paratroops. Though by now expelled from the country, the former German consul, Fritz Grobba, remained active on the propaganda front, and it was 'widely acknowledged that most of the junior officers in the Iraqi Army are both pro-German and anti-British'. Furthermore, the American diplomat continued, the 'residence in Iraq of the Mufti of Jerusalem and 400–500 of his Palestinian and Syrian followers, all of whom are at least anti-British and who are believed by some to be in German pay, constitute a potential section of a fifth column'. There were rumours that the Grand Mufti planned to lead an attack on Baghdad's British community. Jews and native Christians also feared attack, as did British subjects and other foreigners. America's man in Baghdad believed that expatriates were in danger – there was a clear threat to American citizens and evacuation might be required if the war expanded. At worst, Knabenshue believed, mechanized German forces would invade from the north.

By the summer of 1940 British officials were very alarmed by the decline of British influence in Iraq. A War Cabinet meeting in early July discussed Iraq as well as the evacuation of children from Britain and a possible 'date of invasion' of Britain itself. Such was the gravity of the war situation, and such the vastness of the British Empire and the military dispositions and strategic permutations that its defence entailed. Leo Amery, Secretary of State for India, favoured the dispatch of troops to Iraq as proposed by the Chiefs of Staff, and promised that no difficulty would arise as far as the Government of India was concerned, Plan Sabine already being on the table with its provision of over 20,000 troops for the defence of the region. The initial Trout brigade could reach Iraq before September if shipping was available, and eight more brigades could be there by the following spring.[15]

Britain's security headaches in the region were compounded by the internal threat posed by the Iraqi military. As the war progressed, it became clear that it might not play the part of an ally after all, and might actually become an enemy. At the very least, Britain had to watch its back. Iraq's strategic importance was more starkly revealed the more precarious Britain's position became. Churchill had understood this full well when he replaced Chamberlain as prime minister, as did his War Cabinet colleagues. Italy's declaration of war in June, for example, severely threatened 'our communications through the Red Sea', causing the value of the overland route across Iraq to rocket:

> Although our recent successes have reduced the threat from submarines, the Italians are now free to increase their air forces in East Africa. Air threat to shipping at the southern end of the Red Sea is in consequence likely to increase. The overland route through Iraq from Basra to Palestine becomes, therefore, increasingly important for the transportation of personnel and material. The Iraq Army is responsible for the protection of the railway from Basra to Baghdad but in present circumstances its reliability is doubtful.[16]

At any moment it might be necessary to maintain internal security in Iraq and 'to move rapidly to protect the Abadan refinery against sabotage'. In Whitehall, however, it was argued that to move forces from elsewhere in the Middle East to Iraq would be considered weakness by governments throughout the Arab region. But if 'the troops came from the East they will be a clear addition to our strength and possibly suggest they are intended as an earnest of our intention to fulfil our treaty with Iraq'. For these reasons, the Chiefs of Staff continued, 'the presence of British forces in Iraq are [sic] necessary to safeguard our military interests, to show that we intend to honour our treaty obligations and to make it clear to the Iraqis that the British Empire is a force to be reckoned with'.[17] India therefore prepared to dispatch an infantry division intended 'to stiffen the morale of the Iraqi Government and induce it to take action against the supporters of our enemies'. The force would 'establish a bridgehead at Basra and be ready to send a detachment to protect Abadan'.

The situation, then, looked far from ideal as the British studied the region's security situation in the first year of the Second World War. It seemed as if Britain might need to load troops inwards to protect the oil against Soviet aggression, or to deter an Iraqi uprising – perhaps both. Contingency planning continued along both potential courses of action. British planning assumptions had the Iraqi army operating alongside British forces to defend all-important strategic locations such as Basra and the oilfields and refineries of northern Iraq and south-west Iran. Nevertheless, while planning went ahead, powerful Iraqi politicians and military officers were doing all that they could to terminate cooperation with Britain and make overtures towards Germany. While the British and Iraqis maintained the appearance of allies, cooperating in the region's defence, the long-standing enmity between them was coming to a head.[18]

But the July 1940 decision to send troops to Iraq, taken in London, was reversed in the face of objections coming from elements within Middle East Command, the Government of India and India Command. They expressed reluctance to deploy troops; given the clamant calls of other theatres of operations, there were few to spare and a non-military solution was preferred. The worst possible outcome would be to send insufficient troops for the task in hand. Furthermore, the military option was a last resort in the minds of some of those involved in the decision-making process, as Iran and Iraq, whatever British power and interests within them might be, were independent sovereign states, the former a declared neutral and the latter still not formally at war with Germany. Possibly, the deployment of a division at this juncture would have headed off all of the trouble that was to come. As it was, ineffective non-military measures were again urged; the 'economic weapon' could be wielded through oil and the date trade, and an increase in the volume of propaganda of all kinds was advocated yet again, including better use of radio broadcasts. So too was the use of financial inducements, especially, as Colonial Secretary Lord Lloyd put it, as the Germans 'had bought up all the newspapers'.[19]

It was a catch-22 situation. Too much pressure, and the Iraqi government might crumble and if that occurred, Britain would have to send troops to restore order. As the July 1940 Joint Planning Staff paper put it, 'Under present conditions the most probable cause of hostile attitude on part of Iraqi government would be the movement of British troops into Iraq against their [the Iraqi government's] will'.[20] But on the other hand, if Britain did not get troops to Iraq quickly, their enemies might steal a march and irrevocably weaken Britain's strategic position. Although Britain had stepped away from the decision to send troops, calls for regime change in both Iran and Iraq grew as threats proliferated. 'It should be demanded of the Iraqi government,' declared an Air Ministry document, 'that they should play their responsible part in implementing not merely the letter but the spirit of the Treaty and that public declarations by Iraqi statesmen are essential.'[21]

Also in July 1940, the British Arabist Colonel S.F. Newcombe toured the Middle East under the aegis of the British Council, on a mission to improve Arab opinion about Britain. Stopping in Baghdad, he tried, with Nuri as-Said's assistance, to get the Grand Mufti to approve the Palestine White Paper. It has been claimed that the Grand Mufti would have accepted, providing its constitutional provisions were implemented immediately as part of a deal whereby Iraq would declare war on Germany and place two divisions at Britain's disposal.[22] The Foreign Office was furious with Newcombe's apparent willingness (this was not an official visit) to give the Arabs pretty much all they demanded. It mattered little, because Newcombe failed; the Grand Mufti had already committed himself to the Nazi cause, convinced that the Germans were going to win the war.[23]

British authorities in Baghdad and London knew that the Iraqis were doing what they could to reach out to the Germans. Intelligence revealed that in July, Iraqi Minister of Justice Naji Shawkat had travelled to Ankara on a medical pretext to visit German officials. In addition to the Italian legation in Baghdad, Ankara was the main conduit of communication between Germany and Iraq, given that direct diplomatic relations had been cut. Shawkat returned to Baghdad bearing three German 'desiderata' for the consideration of his government, proposed by Franz von Papen, the German ambassador to Ankara. These were the resumption of telegraphic communications with Berlin, the enactment of German anti-Jewish legislation and the resumption of normal diplomatic relations with the Axis powers.[24] Later, the Grand Mufti's personal secretary visited Berlin for talks with the Foreign Ministry, and a joint German–Italian declaration was issued offering sympathy and support for 'independent Arab peoples'.[25]

By the autumn of 1940, the British had come to view Rashid Ali as 'hopelessly committed to the Axis powers'.[26] Their long-standing ally, Nuri as-Said, was in a weakened position. His stock was low, remarked Sir Robert Brooke-Popham, on a stop-off at Habbaniya en route to Singapore to take over as Commander-in-Chief Far East, 'partly owing to the fact that he has been adopting a pro-British attitude and prophesying a British victory and his opponents have been asking where it is'.[27] At the beginning of November, the British made a determined effort to oust Rashid Ali, employing economic measures such as restricting access to oil and British-controlled shipping, and reducing the export of dates.[28] But Rashid Ali's military backers, the men of the Golden Square, were implacable. As prime minister he had to walk a tightrope in order to survive: whatever the future might hold, Britain was still the primary power in Iraq, but it was becoming difficult to comply with its demands, and the possibility of Britain losing the war had to be taken into account. Rashid Ali understood that the British wanted him out but did not want to be forced out, and British pressure evoked powerful feelings of resentment. He 'successfully tapped into these sentiments ... as the figurehead or symbol of the anti-British (and in the context of the war pro-Axis) movement'.[29]

In the autumn/winter of 1940, with the fall of France and alliance with the Soviet Union, opportunity knocked for the Germans in the Mediterranean and Middle East. It looked as if it might be possible to clear Britain out of the region, and the Mufti, in September 1940, had made proposals to both Axis governments on behalf of the Iraqi government. The Wehrmacht contemplated a pincer movement on the Suez Canal, which would inevitably include the Suez Canal Base Zone, fount of Britain's military power in the region; in October 1940 Lieutenant-General Friedrich Paulus, commander of the Sixth Army and at the time Deputy Chief of the General Staff, estimated that two motorized corps could take the position, moving in to converge on the canal from the Western Desert and the Palestine–Syria region.

In a document entitled 'An advance by the enemy through the Balkans and Syria to the Middle East', the Chiefs of Staff advised the War Cabinet that replacing Rashid Ali with a more pliant prime minister would have a salutary effect, not just in Iraq but also in Turkey and Vichy Syria, making opponents think twice before declaring themselves for Germany and against Britain by word or deed. The Foreign Office was particularly concerned that German activity in Iraq and Syria would see Turkey's precious neutrality disintegrate – and that if the Germans won hold of these countries, Turkey would almost inevitably join the Nazi cause. But Britain needed to proceed with caution, performing a balancing act of its own, securing its interests while at the same time trying not to cause too much upheaval – and painfully aware of the fact that it did not have military resources to spare. Though no large forces were 'at present available for Iraq,' the Chiefs of Staff mused, 'it might be useful to open the desert route as a line of communication in order to show that we intend to exercise our rights under the treaty and that we are not afraid of Iraqi reactions or of the pro-Axis sympathies of the Iraqi Government'.[30] This was to become a major sticking point between Baghdad and London: what, precisely, under the terms of the 1930 treaty, was Britain allowed to move into the country and along its lines of communication? Like most treaties, imprecise language left it open to interpretation. As a precautionary measure, the Chiefs of Staff reported on plans for the destruction of the Iraqi oil wells and the pipelines in Iraq, Palestine and Syria, though emphasized how important it was 'to keep these plans secret from the Iraqi Government ... The weakness of our forces in the Middle East is a serious limitation on our ability to ensure Turkish resistance and a proper attitude on the part of the other countries affected.' Ideally, by the spring of 1941 Britain should have forces positioned in the Middle East for the direct assistance of Turkey, the occupation of Syria in conjunction with Turkey and the occupation of Iraq.[31] But now, in the final days of 1940, forces were not available.

Washington was unsympathetic towards the Iraqi government's stance and discouraged its diplomatic gamesmanship. Secretary of State Cordell Hull instructed Paul Knabenshue to impress upon Rashid Ali that American policy was to give Britain all aid possible, short of actually declaring war. Therefore, 'any decision or action of the Iraq Government which might result in a less cooperative attitude in its relations with Great Britain could not fail to create a most painful impression in the United States'.[32] 'According to our information,' Hull continued, making America's position crystal-clear, British defeat 'would endanger the independent existence of Iraq as well as all other States in the Near and Middle East'.[33] President Roosevelt's representative William J. Donovan visited Iraq to reinforce the message. He asked to see the Grand Mufti and his supporters, who gathered at the American legation. He explained to them in no uncertain terms that America backed Britain, 'and would resent the activities of persons working against her'.[34]

On 6 January 1941 the British Embassy in Washington contacted the State Department to report that Bond Brothers and Company of San Francisco were offering to sell 'miscellaneous war materials to the Iraqi government, much of which was of types specially suited for "gangster" warfare or fifth column activities'.[35] In addition, 'the Iraq Minister of Defence had stated that he had placed orders in the US for 500 Johnson .303 automatic rifles and raw materials for the manufacture of 15 million rounds of small arms ammunition'. The Iraqis were also seeking anti-aircraft guns, and were contemplating procurement from Japan if they failed to obtain them elsewhere. Given its currency control powers, Britain was able to deny Iraq access to American dollars meaning, for example, that it was unable to purchase Douglas aircraft and other war materials it had ordered.[36] Knabenshue believed that it was 'inconsistent with our aid to Britain policy for such permits to be issued at this juncture when it is still uncertain whether this war material may not be used to assist Germany'. Responding on 1 March, Cordell Hull informed Knabenshue that 'for your strictly confidential information, licenses for export to Iraq of war materials are currently being denied'.

Heeding the advice of the Chiefs of Staff, the British government demanded Rashid Ali's removal, aggravating Iraqi mistrust of Britain and emboldening the nationalists. The regent, Prince Abdulillah, pressed hard by the British and Americans, attempted in January 1941 to force him to resign. Knowing the Golden Square supported him and that the regent could not dismiss him, Ali refused. He enlisted the help of a section of the army, and threatened the regent with military action. Nuri, now out of the cabinet, mobilized his parliamentary followers, leading Ali to demand parliament's dissolution. The regent did not sign the dissolution order and, fearing for his life, left for Diwaniyah, where he could rely on loyal army units. This obliged Ali to resign at the end of January, as the Golden Square made it known that it was not prepared to risk civil war to keep him in power. Taha al-Hashimi formed a new government on 1 February 1941, a few days before Lieutenant-General Erwin Rommel was appointed commander of a new German army formation known as the Afrika Korps. The subsequent appearance of German forces in North Africa, intended to bolster the recently routed Italians, encouraged the Iraqis.[37]

It was at this juncture that the wheels of British military planning began, finally, to turn in earnest. Plan Sabine was about to be put into operation. General Sir Claude Auchinleck, Commander-in-Chief India from January 1941, looked with fresh eyes at the situation, and was alarmed. After discussions with General Sir Archibald Wavell, Commander-in-Chief Middle East, and General Sir John Dill, Chief of the Imperial General Staff, it was agreed that India Command would take charge of both the planning and execution of Plan Sabine. But there was friction between the two commands. Auchinleck was convinced that the build-up and defence of Basra was of vital strategic importance for the British war effort, and thought that

Wavell's Middle East Command was too insouciant, believing that a friendly government in Baghdad would be sufficient to secure British interests. In contrast, Auchinleck argued that military muscle was the only way to guarantee the Empire's position in a region where, if it was not careful, Britain might sleepwalk to catastrophe.[38]

The Iraqis were repeatedly told by American and British diplomats that in order to get the British to behave in a friendlier manner, they needed to make some very clear pronouncements about whose side they were on. It was up to them, the War Cabinet declared, to make the first move 'if good relations with this country were to be resumed. We expected them, in the first place, to break off diplomatic relations with Italy.'[39] Through February and March 1941 Britain pressed Prime Minister Taha al-Hashimi to break relations with Italy and curb the influence of the Golden Square. Britain's recent triumphs over Italian forces in East Africa provided positive context for British demands, as did the passage of the Lend-Lease bill in March, promising vast amounts of war material to Britain.[40] All of this put pressure on Rashid Ali and the Golden Square to take action: they believed that the Germans were waiting for them to take the initiative and move unequivocally to kick the British out. True to the schizophrenic nature of Anglo-Iraqi relations at this time, it looked as if Iraq might decide to go to war with Britain, but it simultaneously continued to plan with it as an ally for the region's defence – all while the Soviet general staff studied invasion routes into both Iran and Iraq. Joint Anglo-Iraqi defence planning continued as per the terms of the treaty, and in March 1941 the Chief of the Iraqi General Staff, Major-General Amin Zaki, wrote to Waterhouse, head of the British Military Mission, regarding joint Anglo-Iraqi operations in the event of war with Iran and the Soviet Union. While the 'defence of Iraq will primarily depend on the extent of the anticipated British reinforcements and, especially, on the time of the arrival of such forces,' he wrote, Iraqi forces could gain valuable time for British ground troops to arrive and deploy.[41]

Rashid Ali's coup

The Golden Square, in contact with the Germans, prepared for action. Led by Salah al-Din al-Sabbagh and the Grand Mufti, and 'gilded with Axis gold', it plotted to install a new puppet administration led once again by Ali.[42] Pressure mounted on the British community and its sympathizers inside

Iraq. Organizers of a war charities fête, including the Mayor of Baghdad, received threatening letters, and rumours suggested that the Iraqi air force would bomb the event if it went ahead.[43] Arabic broadcasts from Berlin threatened German bomber attacks too.

Prime Minister al-Hashimi was caught between the Scylla and Charybdis of Britain and the Golden Square. In order to comply with British pressure, he realized that he would have to break the power of the Golden Square, and attempted to transfer its members to less influential military posts, which was robustly resisted. On 28 February there was a secret meeting at the Mufti's house on Zahawi Street. Three members of the Golden Square, as well as Yunis al-Sabawi and Naji Shawkat, swore on the Qur'an to give no more concessions to the British, to refuse to break diplomatic relations with Italy, to expel the most pro-British politicians and to depose Taha if he did not agree.[44] It was not long before the regent learned that his palace was surrounded by troops and decided to leave when the palace cook brought him a copy of his own death certificate, signed and dated for that night.[45] He drove immediately to the house of an aunt, passing troops on the way, and she called a trusted British friend, the royal surgeon, Dr Harry Sinderson.

It was considered too dangerous to take the regent to the British Embassy. Instead, disguised in women's clothes, he fled to the American legation. Abdulillah's aide-de-camp drove in another direction in one of two RAF staff cars sent by the British Embassy, dressed as an RAF officer wearing dark glasses and carrying a copy of *The Times* in the hope of fooling Iraqi roadblocks. Meanwhile the British air liaison officer, Squadron Leader P. Domvile, took Nuri as-Said to Habbaniya so that he could be evacuated too. 'This morning 8:45,' Knabenshue reported to Washington on 2 April,

the Regent came to me in native woman's dress covering dressing gown and pajamas to seek refuge in Legation, having been forewarned of attempt by the four army leaders to force resignation of Prime Minister and rein-statement of Rashid Ali Gailani as Prime Minister ... In consequence of consultation at Legation between the Regent, British Ambassador and myself I took Regent, accompanied by my wife as camouflage, to the British airbase at Habbaniya in my car with the Regent lying on the floor at the back covered by a rug.[46]

Conveniently, Knabenshue was due to visit the airbase anyway in order to meet the incoming British ambassador, Sir Kinahan Cornwallis, an old Iraq hand, who was to replace Newton. Foreign Secretary Anthony Eden told Churchill that though not a diplomat, he had been sent out 'as being the man who knows the country best'.[47]

Rashid Ali was made prime minister on 3–4 April, as the Golden Square seized power, bringing troops into the capital. This differed from previous coups in that it 'was no longer simply aimed at replacing one prime minister with another. Instead, it was directed against the monarch' – in the shape of the regent, Abdulillah – 'whose authority was constitutionally necessary to legitimize the actions of the armed forces and their civilian allies'.[48] Abdulillah was flown from Habbaniya to Basra, from where he would 'attempt to form a new constitutional government and by proclamation call upon the people for support'. Knabenshue reported to Washington that it was not 'yet clear whether Regent to be deposed and Gailani given power of Fuehrer'.[49] As things transpired the regent did not tarry in Basra, instead boarding HMS *Cockchafer* and thereby gaining diplomatic immunity and British protection. The vintage 'Insect'-class gunboat was soon under sail for Trans-Jordan, where the regent was to be a guest of King Abdullah bin al-Hussein in Amman.

Arriving in Baghdad the day after the coup, Ambassador Cornwallis said that he would have no relations with Rashid Ali's ministry.[50] Britain immediately proclaimed the coup unconstitutional, and distributed thousands of copies of a special broadcast made by Prince Abdulillah appealing for resistance. The danger to the port of Basra, to the oilfields and to the overland line of communication 'was instantly obvious to London', a perspective reinforced by Ultra decrypts.[51] Bletchley Park code-breakers intercepted a report from the Italian minister in Tehran stating that he and his German colleagues had agreed on Syria as the best channel through which to send arms to the Golden Square. It was also revealed that Rashid Ali had been given an ultimatum by the Golden Square – 'delete the British military presence and seal a relationship with Germany: otherwise the Army would take over from the junta'.[52]

On 6 April, the day that the Germans invaded Greece, the Iraqis prevented British military personnel from travelling between Baghdad and Habbaniya, and removed radio transmitters from the British Military Mission. On the same day, an increasingly isolated Air Vice-Marshal Smart at Habbaniya asked Cairo for reinforcements. But General Wavell and Air Marshal Sir Arthur Longmore, Air Officer Commanding Middle East, considered Iraq a low priority and rejected the request. Their caution, given the situation in North Africa and southern Europe, was understandable though unhelpful, and Churchill was distinctly unimpressed.

The regent's escape was more than a trifling annoyance for the plotters, because they needed his signature to put a legal and constitutional stamp upon their actions. In the absence of such a facility, Rashid Ali formed a temporary 'Government of National Defence', which the Germans immediately recognized. Moscow quickly followed suit; terrified of German attack, the Soviet government had been making gestures to placate Hitler, easing its pressure on Finland, withdrawing diplomatic recognition of the Greek, Norwegian and Yugoslav governments in exile and, now, acknowledging the legitimacy of Rashid Ali's coup. On 10 April the Iraqi parliament voted for Prince Abdulillah's dismissal. He was indicted in absentia 'for trying to undermine the army, for harming national unity and for flouting the constitution'.[53] He was replaced by Sharif Sharaf bin Rajeh, a distant relative of the king, who called on Rashid Ali to form a government. The new regent's imprimatur, as far as Rashid Ali was concerned, ended the temporary government of national defence and made his regime a legitimate one.

British recognition was not so easily won, however, though Rashid Ali craved it because without the approval of the region's major external power, his position would remain insecure. The new prime minister attempted to persuade Britain that nothing fundamental had changed. In a speech to the senate on 10 April he declared that the national movement was entirely internal and that he intended to carry out the terms of the treaty both to the letter and in spirit.[54] For its part, the British government was 'deeply alarmed' at Rashid Ali's return to power and the 'strongly nationalist colour of his new cabinet'.[55] Britain decided to activate its plans for deploying troops to Basra. The intent was to protect British oil and line of communication interests and show Rashid Ali's government that they would not be pushed around.

The War Office asked Wavell what he could provide if military intervention became necessary, having in mind the pre-existing Plan Lobster for the dispatch of a brigade from Palestine. Wavell replied that all he had to spare was a single British battalion; 'any other action is impossible with existing resources'.[56] Fortunately, India Command was much keener on Iraq than Wavell's Middle East Command. General Auchinleck was afraid that failure to take robust action would lead to the loss of the country, with disastrous consequences for India. On 8 April 1941 Churchill asked India for troops to defend Basra in a 'most immediate' communication to the viceroy. Lord

Linlithgow 'replied that after consultation with the Commander-in-Chief[,] India could send an infantry brigade and a field regiment with ancillary troops' immediately, and quickly follow it with two more in order to make up the full division, 'which India believed was the minimum required for effective strength'.[57] These troops were at the time embarking at Karachi for Singapore. Further, India pledged the immediate dispatch of 364 men of the 1st Battalion the King's Own Royal Regiment by air to Shaibah in a pioneering strategic airlift operation.

The Government of India's largesse was based on what it assessed to be the urgent need for action, not a surfeit of troops. 'When the forces sent to rescue Iraq were despatched India was left with four infantry divisions in the process of being raised and an incomplete armoured division ... all starved of vital equipment.'[58] In contrast to India Command's words and deeds, Wavell remained non-committal and sceptical, telling Auchinleck that the force being dispatched from India 'might suffice to swing the scales in Iraq. I am fully committed in Cyrenaica and can spare nothing.'[59] But he did offer to lend a squadron of Wellington bombers to support the Basra landings. Middle East Command was simply too over-extended and too consumed with the German threat *west* of its Cairo headquarters to be able to see the bigger picture – one that still featured the Soviets. As Compton Mackenzie reminds us, in the spring of 1941, 'the intervention of Russia only seemed a more remote possibility to Cairo because Cairo was naturally preoccupied with the immediacy of the German threat in the Near East'.[60]

The force sent to Iraq by General Auchinleck was commanded by Major-General W.A.K. Fraser. Sailing in convoy on 12 April, Fraser's troops were ordered to occupy the Basra–Shaibah area to ensure future disembarkations, establish a base and prepare to extinguish any Iraqi resistance. Ambassador Cornwallis, however, argued that before landing troops, Britain should invoke its treaty right to transit troops across Iraq, giving the Iraqi government the reason that the situation in the Western Desert required rapid reinforcement. In the light of Rashid Ali's senate speech, Cornwallis reasoned, Britain should at least test whether what he had said about honouring the treaty was true. If rejected, Britain would have the legal right to intervene forcibly. Cornwallis's advice stemmed partly from his concern that unheralded troop landings would be used by Rashid Ali to raise the country against the British.[61] The Chiefs of Staff concurred, so the airborne troops were held back and the troop convoy was ordered to wait at Bahrain.

Auchinleck viewed this cat-and-mouse game with anxiety: all he was interested in was hastening to Basra and securing it for whatever military moves might be necessary, for the sake of Britain's position in Iran and Iraq, and the defence of India. Furthermore, he wasn't really interested in moving troops *through* Iraq, but in keeping them there. There was no time to dally. What, asked Auchinleck, if Rashid Ali used this breathing space to bring in German forces? 'I am convinced that if we are to prevent the general deterioration of the situation in Asia . . . we must show now that we are prepared to maintain our position by force'.[62] Viceroy Linlithgow agreed, and telegraphed Leo Amery, Secretary of State for India, on 13 April, urging him to action. This communication galvanized the Chiefs of Staff, who immediately signalled permission for the convoy to proceed. On 14 April Cornwallis was instructed to serve notice to Rashid Ali of Britain's intention to land troops.[63]

The extent of Rashid Ali's dialogue with the Axis was now clear to Britain. On 9 April a joint statement of support had been sent by the Axis, promising military and financial assistance, though it was vague on specifics but encouraging of armed resistance. A statement offering support in the event of war with Britain arrived a week later, and together these communications convinced Iraqi nationalists that German assistance would be forthcoming. The Iraqi government asked specifically for £1 million, ten squadrons of aircraft and fifty tanks.[64] Neither did Rashid Ali believe that Britain possessed the will or the wherewithal to fight. German prestige, already high, had been further buoyed by recent victories in Greece and Yugoslavia (the latter surrendering on 17 April), leading many to believe that German victory was inevitable. In the last week of April, intelligence led Churchill, the Chiefs of Staff and General Wavell to think that the imminent German invasion of Crete was a decoy, and that the real target was Syria and Iraq. Furthermore, with recent defeats in Greece and Libya, the British were preparing for the potential loss of Egypt and the Suez Canal – 'worst-case scenario' planning that infuriated Churchill when he learned of it.[65]

Landing troops to secure British interests in Iran and Iraq and bring the Iraqi government to heel was entirely prudent. Rashid Ali was taken by surprise when Cornwallis told him on 16 April that, in accordance with the terms of the treaty, imperial troops would soon arrive. In doing so, the British were not honest with the new Iraqi prime minister; they forebore to tell him of their ambitions for Basra, and tried to deceive him as to the purpose of the troops about to land. The ambassador told Rashid Ali that the troops were coming to open the trans-Iraq line of communication, and hinted that if he cooperated, Britain would enter into informal relations with his government and probably grant it recognition. This pleased Rashid Ali, who allowed them to land. But the Golden Square was not pleased, and forced a change of tack. Nevertheless, on 17 April the lead brigade of 10th Indian Division landed. An advance party of headquarters staff from the division's 20th Indian Infantry Brigade had already flown in aboard Douglas DC-2 and Vickers Valentia transport aircraft of 31 (India) Squadron. Two days later the promised troops of the King's Own Royal Regiment flew from Karachi to Shaibah via Sharjah in the Trucial Oman and Bahrain, 'the first ever strategic airlift by British forces in war'.[66] They were transported in five British Overseas Airways Corporation Whitworth Atalanta aircraft lent to the RAF by Imperial Airways, and a dozen 31 Squadron Valentias. Lieutenant-General Edward Quinan was appointed to command British Forces Iraq, the name given to the troops now building up in Basra (until this point, the only British forces in Iraq had been RAF personnel, in line with the terms of the treaty).

Despite the deployment of imperial troops, even at this eleventh hour in Anglo-Iraqi relations, the British were not intent on overthrowing Rashid Ali's government, and might not have sought to do so had it behaved in a less bellicose manner. British policy in early to mid-April 1941 was simply to get a division to Basra as quickly as possible. Bolstered by Auchinleck's stentorian demands, the British government wanted to secure the city and its large British-built port as a major base area – to be able to use it in order to access the Iraqi desert convoy route, and to develop a strategic aircraft assembly plant for fighters and bombers shipped direct from America for onward distribution to the fighting fronts of Asia and the Middle East. Most of all, the objective was to have Basra as a base from which to protect vital British interests, not least oil supplies, in the midst of an increasingly volatile situation. Secondary benefits to the Basra build-up would be the capacity it would allow for supplies to be transported overland to Turkey, as part of attempts to keep it neutral, now that the Aegean was German-dominated. British strength in Basra would also encourage pro-allied sentiment in neighbouring Iran.

On 18 and 21 April Rashid Ali demanded of Cornwallis that no more troops land, that those present move along the desert convoy route and depart Iraq, that all movements be in small contingents and that never more than a brigade be in Iraq at any one time. But more troopships docked on 18 April, escorted by the Australian sloop HMAS *Yarra*. They disgorged further elements of the 20th Indian Infantry Brigade, the 3rd Field Regiment Royal Artillery and the headquarters of the 10th Indian Division. Commanding the division's lead elements as commander 20th Indian Infantry Brigade, Brigadier Donald Powell was prepared for an opposed landing. But the troops disembarked without incident and measures were immediately taken to secure the Basra area. A Gurkha battalion was first to land, and by the evening had seized the docks. The atmosphere was 'sullen and uncooperative. The dock labourers went on strike, forcing the soldiers to unload their own ships before labourers could be brought in from India.'[67] Gurkhas also took control of RAF Quay (the flying-boat facility granted under the 1930 treaty), the RAF hospital, the wireless station and the civil airfield and quays in the Maqil area of the city.

On 20 April Churchill instructed Foreign Secretary Anthony Eden to make it clear to Cornwallis that:

> our chief interest in sending troops to Iraq is the covering and establishment of a great assembly base at Basra, and that what happens up-country, except at Habbaniya, is at the present time on an altogether lower priority. Our rights under the Treaty were invoked to cover this disembarkation and to avoid bloodshed, but force would have been used to the utmost limit to secure the disembarkation if necessary. Our position at Basra, therefore, does not rest solely on the Treaty, but also on a new event arising out of the war. No undertakings can be given that troops will be sent to Bagdad or moved through to Palestine, and the right to require such undertakings should not be recognised in respect of a Government which has in itself usurped power by a coup d'état, or in a country where our Treaty rights have so long been frustrated in the spirit. Sir K. Cornwallis should not, however, entangle himself by explanations.[68]

The influx of imperial troops, Paul Knabenshue told Washington, 'relaxed but did not dispel tension', and certainly did nothing to improve Rashid Ali's mood.[69] In a move of calculated threat, he told Cornwallis that the Iraqi garrison at Basra would be increased to a full division, significantly augmenting the size of the force that the British would have to fight at their key port of disembarkation should things turn sour. Rashid Ali disputed Britain's right, under the terms of the treaty, to build up forces in the Basra area without permission, as opposed to landing them and moving them on. But the British interpreted the treaty differently, claiming that Iraq was obliged to give Britain any facility within its power in a war situation. The

Iraqi government stood on the terms of the treaty, believing that Article 5, regarding an emergency situation, did not apply, as Britain seemed to be demanding the right to maintain an unlimited quantity of troops inside Iraq for an unlimited period of time.

But the British would not recognize these restrictions, arguing that Article 4 fully covered things – obliging Iraq in time of war to offer all facilities in the capacity of an ally. It is of note that neither side sought to take their differences to arbitration. Britain was at war, and determined come what may to have a base in Basra for strategic reasons of urgent priority. For their part, Rashid Ali and the Golden Square were determined to prevent it (seeing it as the very epitome of the inequality that the treaty enshrined), and transfixed by the opportunity to expel the British. Knabenshue wrote that in view of the 'many evidences' of the hostile attitude of the Iraqi army, 'it is obvious Gailani hopes to retain Iraq military superiority pending signal and help from Germany'.[70]

Cornwallis informed his American counterpart that Britain would not comply with Rashid Ali's requests, and that the additional troops would arrive as planned. 'Communications will then be taken over by British troops and garrisons established also at Baghdad and Habbaniya.' The reason given by the British for these actions, Knabenshue continued, 'will be the protection of Iraq in accordance with the treaty'. 'In view of illegality of present government and its hostile attitude interfering with British war effort it would seem British would be justified in such action,' he added.[71] Alarmed by the possibility of a German airborne attack on Habbaniya to seize the airbase for the use of the Luftwaffe, the British also decided to airlift troop reinforcements to the airbase.

On 25 April a treaty was concluded between Rashid Ali and the Italian minister by which the Axis undertook to supply financial and military aid to the Iraqi government for war against Britain. It also recognized the union of Iraq and Syria under the Iraqi king, in return for oil concessions for the Axis and access to ports and military bases. The following day and again on 28 April, Rashid Ali enquired of the Germans about the support they had promised, and requested that they send captured British weapons because the Iraqi army was familiar with them.

On the night of 28 April a troop convoy transporting further elements of 20th Indian Brigade arrived at the head of the Gulf accompanied by HMS *Cockchafer*, HMS *Falmouth* and HMAS *Yarra*. Disembarking at Basra in the morning – the day the last Middle East Command troops were evacuated

from Greece – the arrival of the second troop convoy was a big shock to
Rashid Ali and his confidantes. On the same day Cornwallis ordered the
evacuation of 250 British women and children. The situation was tense,
'with the very real possibility of mob action against British civilians'.[72] The
women and children were ferried to RAF Habbaniya in a procession of cars,
buses and RAF lorries, and then removed from Iraq aboard British Overseas
Airways Corporation flying-boats. The nurses at RAF Habbaniya's hospital
remained. 'The total evacuation of British women and children,' Knabenshue
wrote, 'has alarmed Iraqis. It shows the British mean business and it might
have salutary effect.'[73] American women and children were leaving too,
while other civilians sought refuge in the embassy compounds. Around 350
British subjects flocked to the embassy on the banks of the Tigris. Fearing
mob violence in Baghdad, what Ambassador Cornwallis described as 'a
mixed lot of Americans and miscellaneous foreigners and some Iraqi
subjects' took up refuge in the American legation, including at least 160
other British nationals.[74]

The 364 men of the King's Own Royal Regiment that had arrived from
India were airlifted to Habbaniya in order to bolster the airbase's defences.
With British troops arriving in strength, it was time for Rashid Ali and the
Golden Square to make an important decision. They chose war, gambling
that Iraqi forces could hold the British until the Germans arrived. Late on
the afternoon of 29 April Iraqi army units began streaming out of Baghdad,
heading west towards Habbaniya via the bridge over the Euphrates at
Fallujah. The Euphrates bunds were cut and the countryside around the
remote British airbase rendered virtually inaccessible by flooding, making
it particularly difficult to reinforce from the direction of Basra. Ramadi was
also occupied by Iraqi troops, as were the Kirkuk oilfields. The supply of oil
to the British terminal at Haifa was cut, while the flow to Tripoli, closed by
the British when France fell, was reopened for the benefit of the Axis. That
evening, at midnight, 'the last mobile units of the Iraqi army including
tanks, armoured cars, field guns, cavalry and infantry commenced passing
the Legation from their nearby base,' wrote Knabenshue. 'I sent for the
British intelligence officer, my neighbour. He went to the [British] Embassy
and from there notified the British Air Base at Habbaniya. This was the first
notice they received.'[75]

The officers of the Golden Square had probably long believed that one
day they would have to fight the British if they were to achieve their ambitions. They 'chose this particular moment because they were angered and

frightened by the continual build-up of British troops at Basra'.[76] Influenced by recent German victories, encouraged by Axis pledges of support, they thought that they would get immediate assistance. They were also aware of the weak defences of RAF Habbaniya – a sitting duck behind a 'fence designed to keep out wild animals and marauding bedouin'.[77] It was against this particular fence that the Iraqis decided to throw themselves.

CHAPTER 4

Iraq goes to war

'A minor skirmish but extremely uncomfortable at the time' was how F.E. Brown of the Royal Artillery described the Anglo-Iraqi war in a letter to Winston Churchill, nine years after the event.[1] One of over 12,000 people besieged at the Habbaniya airbase 55 miles due west of Baghdad, Brown underplayed the significance of the encounter. For in fact it offered the Iraqis and their German allies a unique opportunity to undermine or even eradicate Britain's position in the country, with potentially grave consequences for the allied war effort.

RAF Habbaniya was one of the two airbases securing Britain's presence in Iraq.[2] Lying behind an 8-mile perimeter fence interspersed with blockhouses and machine-gun posts, it was a military cantonment on the Indian model, an enormous camp backing on to the Euphrates. It was home to over 1,000 RAF personnel and the 1,250 British-officered Kurds, Arabs and Assyrian Christians of the RAF Iraq Levies. The levies' role was to protect the base in conjunction with an RAF regiment operating eighteen vintage Rolls Royce armoured cars. Habbaniya's defences had recently been augmented by the King's Own Royal Regiment contingent airlifted from Shaibah (reinforced by a further 150 troops on 4 May).

The sprawling base was also home to around 9,000 civilian workers and their families. This assortment of nationalities made Habbaniya one of the more extraordinary outposts of empire. Inside its iron fence were hangars, two large repair shops, corrugated iron-roofed military buildings, a water tower, power station, gymnasium, swimming pool, social clubs and tree-lined roads with names such as Cheapside, Kingsway and Piccadilly. Stocks, sweet peas and roses grew around the bungalows and buildings.[3] 'Suites for guests were built around a large cool marble hall,' wrote the photographer Cecil Beaton, who stayed at RAF Habbaniya while on an official visit for the Ministry of Information, with 'huge silent fans propelling in every room'.[4] The headquarters mess, wrote Somerset de Chair, the Household Cavalry Regiment's intelligence officer, was 'a palace panelled with cedar wood'.[5] There were dozens of tennis courts, riding stables, a polo-ground-cum-racecourse, vegetable plots, a large stock farm and a golf course. The base was sited close to Lake Habbaniya, which covered an area of 100 square miles and on which British Overseas Airways Corporation flying-boats from Egypt bound for India and Singapore landed in order to break their journey, and drop off and collect passengers. The airfield itself lay beyond the enclosed perimeter.

Built 'at the cost of many millions of pounds in the desolation of the Iraqi desert', RAF Habbaniya had opened as recently as 1938 and was valued because it was out of the reach of potential enemies.[6] The commanding Air Vice-Marshal had selected the site by going off on mysterious flights into the desert, ostensibly for ornithological purposes. Flying west from Baghdad, he would land at various spots, take out his binoculars and, through an interpreter, question wandering Arabs about the climate and mosquitoes.[7] The problem, given what transpired, was that it was not sited with an Iraqi attack in mind – the Iraqis, after all, were allies. Indicating the friendliness supposed to characterize Anglo-Iraqi relations, recent joint war games had focused on how to capture the airbase. That Habbaniya had not been positioned with defence in mind was further demonstrated by the fact that it was completely overlooked by a 150-foot-high plateau.

Compounding problems associated with its location, in 1941 Habbaniya was bereft of operational RAF units, which had been concentrated in Egypt to support the campaign in the Western Desert. At the time of Rashid Ali al-Gailani's coup, it was home instead to No. 4 Service Flying Training School, comprising pupil pilots, their instructors and outdated aircraft. Altogether, there was a total of ninety-six airframes, including thirty-two Audaxes, eight Gordons, twenty-nine Oxfords, nine Gladiators, five Hart trainers and a solitary Blenheim. Except for the Gladiators, wrote Air Vice-Marshal Smart, Habbaniya's aircraft were either dedicated training machines or obsolete ones, and most of his pilots and aircrew were untrained in operational flying.[8] Of great importance, No. 244 (Bomber) Squadron, equipped with Vickers

Vincent general-purpose biplanes, was based at RAF Shaibah, reinforced during the crisis by a squadron of Wellington bombers sent from Egypt.

Despite its defensive deficiencies, Habbaniya had no choice but to fight when on 30 April the Iraqi army units that had 'streamed out of Baghdad arrived before dawn and took up commanding positions on the heights overlooking the air base'.[9] Comprising over 9,000 troops, the Iraqi force busied itself constructing defences and gun emplacements on the plateau. Smart's reconnaissance flights informed him that the force amounted to an infantry brigade and two mechanized battalions, the twelve 3.7 howitzers of a mechanized artillery brigade, the twelve 18-pounders and four 4.5-howitzers of a field artillery brigade, twelve armoured cars, one mechanized machine-gun company, a mechanized signals company and an anti-aircraft and anti-tank battery.[10]

Though the situation facing the defenders of Habbaniya was unenviable, it helped that the British were confident in their superiority. The 'British Air Force,' Knabenshue told Washington, 'believe they can dispose of the Iraqi Army in short order'. Not only was the Iraqi army held in low regard, so too was the air force. 'I can confirm entirely,' wrote Smart, 'the accuracy of [Major-General Waterhouse's] estimate as regards the Iraqi Air Force from experience at SHAIBA of one of their better units. In the military sense it is valueless.'[11] Though influenced by a prevailing colonial mindset that ascribed lesser capabilities to non-European peoples and organizations, this low opinion of Iraqi forces – expressed also with regard to the Iranian military by commanders such as Major-General William Slim – was well founded for a number of reasons, as events were to prove, despite the apparent mismatch of forces on paper.

The Iraqi commanding officer informed Smart that his troops were there on exercise and that if any British aircraft left the ground they would be attacked. Smart replied that he was also under instruction to exercise, and that if the Iraqi army interfered it would be considered an act of war. Frenetic efforts were made to prepare the base for offence and defence, which included digging trenches in order to provide shelter from artillery fire. Though 'dangerous and disquietening,' wrote Smart, 'the immediate situation was strategically a straightforward one' – he needed to get the Iraqis as far away from his airbase as possible.[12] At first, Smart played for time in the absence of clear direction from his superiors. But during the course of 1 May the need to make a pre-emptive strike against the investing force became obvious. Though troops were being loaded into Basra, it was clear that reinforcements were not going to arrive at Habbaniya anytime soon, though on that day Air Chief Marshal Longmore did order more Wellingtons to Shaibah. Churchill telegrammed his advice to Smart: 'If you have to strike, strike hard. Use all necessary force.'[13] This Smart duly did. An 'Air Striking Force' was improvised, one wing comprising twenty-one Audaxes under Wing Commander 'Larry' Ling, which was to operate from the polo field, the other wing under Squadron Leader Tony Dudgeon, operating from the main runway and comprising twenty-seven Oxfords, nine Gladiators and seven Gordons.

The situation was so critical that it was decided that instead of an ultimatum to the Iraqi government, the RAF would simply start bombing. Smart briefed his officers, explaining that the aim was to achieve surprise and deal the Iraqis the sharpest possible blow. The initial RAF attack, commencing at 0500 on 2 May, lasted for nineteen hours, Habbaniya's gallimaufry of aircraft going in en masse. A cycle developed: bombing, returning to base, debriefing, bombing up, then going out again. A damaged Wellington managed to land but was destroyed by Iraqi shells on the airfield. Overnight, damaged aircraft were patched up. 'As the daylight got stronger,' Dudgeon wrote:

we could see that the air above the plateau was like the front of a wasp's nest on a sunny morning. The ten Wellingtons were there from Basrah making a total of forty-nine aircraft of five different types and speeds, clustering and jockeying over an area not much bigger than a minor golf course. It was a hairy experience. In my Oxford I would peer down into the dusk, trying to distinguish a juicy target like a gun-emplacement – and an Audax would swoop past at some crazy angle. Or a Wellington would sail majestically across my bows, giving me heart failure and leaving my machine bucketing about in its slipstreams. Luckily, no one hit anybody else, but there were some very close shaves indeed.[14]

Pilot Officer Colin Dunford Wood wrote in his diary:

War! I went up at sunrise in the back of Broadhurst's Audax, without a parachute like a fool, and we drop 20lb bombs on the guns in conjunction with Oxfords and Wellingtons from Shaibah. I use the rear gun on an escaping lorry, but it's so damn hard when pulling out of a dive ... Next sortie I go up with Broughton, but we go too low and I feel something tug at my sleeve. Then liquid comes back over me, which to my horror I find to be blood. I can't see out of my goggles so stand up and find Jimmy B. in front is shot through the face and blood pouring out like a perforated petrol tank. I buckle on my parachute, but luckily he is fully conscious and we land on the polo pitch OK. I am a bit shaken and we then get shelled on the polo ground and in the mess, without much effect. Ling, Garner and Broughton get shot, and Chico Walsh with two pupils Skelton and Robinson is shot down in flames in an Oxford.[15]

In response to these intense British sorties, the Iraqi artillery shelled the cantonment, though the muzzle flashes of their guns helped the RAF pick their targets.[16] The Iraqi air force also joined in that afternoon, Audaxes, Bredas, Northrups and Savoias bombing and strafing the airbase at intervals, their sorties met by fire from Lewis guns.[17] Smart recorded that at the end of the first day 'Iraqi morale remained surprisingly high', and there were no signs of a withdrawal despite the heavy RAF attacks. But it was also clear that the attacks had significantly reduced the danger from the Iraqi artillery.

With hostilities under way, the Iraqi government explained the conflict to the people, describing it as a righteous struggle against imperialism and aggression. Broadcasts by the regent and Winston Churchill were jammed. On 2 May, the 'mood in Baghdad was jubilant. From 6:30 AM to 1:00 PM daily, the radio broadcast martial music and news of victories everywhere'.[18] But there were signs of nerves too, as war approached. Blackouts began. Schools closed and business were paralysed when banks were ordered not to pay money; a Jewish student carrying an English book was accused of spying, and a French violin teacher of carrying a wireless set. A woman whose gold button inadvertently appeared through her black garment was detained for signalling to the British.[19]

A radio broadcast emanating from the Ministry of Propaganda was picked up by BBC monitors. Though reception was poor, the gist of the bulletin was clear. There were references to Britain's infringement of Iraqi sovereignty, and tell-tale phrases such as 'shedding blood', 'attacked the Iraqi forces', 'capitalists' and 'British imperialism'. The broadcaster spoke of 'the liberation of our homeland' and 'our love of freedom and determination to defend it'. Other audible sentences noted by the monitor included 'May I stress again, in order to deprive Iraq of its sovereignty and smash its freedom and independence ...' Indicating a particular grievance of the Iraqi government in the run-up to the conflict, the broadcast reported Ambassador Sir

Kinahan Cornwallis's meeting at the Iraqi Ministry of Foreign Affairs, during the course of which he declared Britain's intention to establish a military base at Basra, described as 'a clear contravention of the treaty'.[20]

Casting the British as the aggressors, the broadcast said that the arrival of the Iraqi force at Habbaniya had 'surprised the British military command ... But instead of behaving reasonably, the Britishers, whose nerves have been exhausted ... became excited. They attacked the Iraqi forces at Habbaniyeh and at the same time in Baghdad.' The person transcribing the broadcast noted that at this point the announcer's voice 'rises to a shriek of emotion and becomes inaudible'. 'Mothers, brothers, wives know that you are serving this nation. We are conscious of a just and noble cause.'[21] Another broadcast from Baghdad, this one in Italian, relayed Rashid Ali's message to the Iraqi people: 'Comrades, patriots, heroes, do whatever is necessary to defend the honour of our country and obtain victory.'[22] But it would take more than stirring words to rouse Iraq's people to arms, the majority of whom wanted nothing to do with the fighting.

As British and Iraqi forces traded blows on the ground around Habbaniya and in the skies above, Rashid Ali tried to enlist the Americans for propaganda purposes. Paul Knabenshue wrote that the Iraqi Ministry of Foreign Affairs had officially requested him to tell the State Department that 'a British plane tried to bomb a Mosque in Fallujah at the time tribesmen were making their prayers. The Ministry points out that this horrible action which is not based on any human principles caused public disturbances and consternation and that this action will show the civilized world what British forces are doing now against all rules of war of the civilized world.'[23] The ministry also told Knabenshue that Air Vice-Marshal Smart had sent an ultimatum demanding the withdrawal of the Iraqi army from Habbaniya within four hours, or the British would bomb Baghdad. An Iraqi counter-ultimatum stated that the Iraqi air force would bomb British subjects.[24]

The struggle at Habbaniya continued. Hundreds of Iraqi shells hit the airbase, though achieved little other than causing minor damage and small numbers of casualties. British ground forces patrolled no man's land between the airbase and the Iraqi positions. Troops defending the base identified enemy gun emplacements, and protected the perimeter using machine-gun nests and blockhouses located so as to provide advantageous fields of fire. No. 10 blockhouse, for instance, had a commanding view of the road to Fallujah and was used to harass Iraqi traffic supplying the investing force. There were also sallies by ground forces, such as the attack by No. 8 (Kurdish)

Company Iraq Levies, intended to silence a gun emplacement behind Burma Bund across the Euphrates. The attack failed though was later completed from the air.[25] Ground forces also had to deal with Iraqi attacks on the base: No. 4 (Assyrian) Company Iraq Levies repulsed an assault on the perimeter mounted by armoured cars and light tanks; 'aggressive action during this first day did much to temper Iraqi ardour and no further penetrations by armour were attempted against the perimeter during the siege'.[26]

Robust British attacks on the plateau and on Iraqi forces stationed elsewhere on the first day of operations, 2 May, took the Iraqi military by surprise and shocked Rashid Ali's government. The attack had begun on a Friday as many troops prepared to pray. On hearing the news, the Grand Mufti declared a jihad against the British and the flow of oil to Haifa was 'severed through the sequestration of the Iraq Petroleum Company oil plants'.[27] At the end of the day the Iraqis were still on the plateau, and twenty-two of the sixty-four aircraft that Dudgeon and Ling's Air Striking Force had started the day with had been lost, and ten of the thirty-nine British pilots killed or wounded. Two Vincent bombers had also been shot down near Shaibah.

On the following day, air operations again began at 0500. Douglas DC-2s of 31 Squadron, based at RAF Shaibah, flew to Habbaniya to evacuate the remaining women and children and the wounded, armoured cars racing alongside them as they took off in order to afford extra protection.[28] The transport aircraft arrived with supplies for the defenders, and diversionary attacks were mounted against the Iraqi positions to protect them as they landed and took off. RAF attacks were extended beyond the escarpment, now targeting Iraqi airbases and army lines of communication across the country. They hit the Iraqi air force's Rashid airbase in Baghdad, where Wellingtons of Shaibah-based 37 Squadron dropped 7,100 pounds of explosives. The Baghdad–Fallujah–Ramadi road, along which supplies for the Iraqi force investing Habbaniya passed, was also targeted by RAF aircrews. Four valuable fighter Blenheims arrived on 3 May to supplement Smart's resources. British airpower was further augmented by the presence in the Gulf of the carrier HMS *Hermes*.

On Sunday 4 May the Wellingtons, boosted by the additional aircraft from Egypt, continued the attack on Rashid airbase, dropping 15,700 pounds of bombs, destroying hangars, dispersed aircraft, magazines and ground defences. Low-level machine-gun attacks here and at the Baghdad civil airport were also conducted.[29] Freya Stark, holed up in the British Embassy compound on the banks of the Tigris, witnessed the attack, recording that 'our bombers came over to plaster Rashid camp and machine-gun the airfield'. The attack led to 'wild and ineffectual popping of Iraq firearms ... These attacks proved extremely effective in limiting the offensive capability of the Iraqi Air Force and in severely undermining the fragile morale of Iraqi troops on the ground.'[30] The 4 May attacks on Rashid airbase destroyed or disabled twenty-nine Iraqi aircraft, a devastating loss, and thirteen more were destroyed at Baqubah, north of the city, where a direct hit on the fuel storage facility was also registered. Propaganda leaflets were dropped by RAF aircraft, assuring the population that Britain's quarrel was only with the illegal government of Rashid Ali.[31] Demonstrating a range of air power capabilities, British air attacks were also employed to pin down Iraqi formations, preventing them from moving to support the forces investing Habbaniya, for example by strafing an infantry group moving from Baghdad towards Fallujah. For their part, the Iraqis continued to shell the Habbaniya compound. The defending forces bombed them back, launching night attacks and employing delayed-action bombs dropped during daylight hours.

An 'urgent' broadcast from Baghdad carried an address to the nation by Rashid Ali on 4 May.[32] He expressed his thanks for 'the complete order and discipline they [the Iraqi people] had preserved'. There was cheering war news from the high command:

> Our forces draw the ring around the aerodrome of Habbaniya steadily closer. The garrison is continually being bombarded by our artillery. It is presumed that the enemy will be beaten. Many fires were caused in ammunition and fuel dumps. At the western border of the oil fields our recce troops went into action and are in contact with the high command. Our troops have contacted the enemy and operations are carried out according to plan.[33]

This dry and measured report on the progress of the conflict represents a rare Iraqi commentary on proceedings, though a rather over-optimistic one. The broadcast continued:

> Firstly our bombers dropped bombs on the aerodrome of Habbaniya causing heavy damage. All our aircraft returned safely to their bases. Secondly two enemy aeroplanes of the Wellington type directed a concentrated attack on a military camp this morning. They were intercepted by

our fighters. One was brought down and the other turned back ... The high command announces to the enemy forces surrounded by our forces that good treatment as POW [prisoners of war] is guaranteed to them if they surrender to the high command and put up no resistance ... The western command announces that the Iraqi forces are still besieging the garrison at Habbaniya. The [British] garrison commander received a request to surrender ... [and] avoid senseless resistance.[34]

It was claimed in the broadcast that a hospital was attacked by British aircraft 'although clearly marked by the red crescent'.

On the same day Baghdad news in Arabic issued 'A call to the Iraqi people':

> O believers in God and in his Prophet. Fighting is written for you, to free yourselves and your country, collaborating together as one man supporting your noble government under the leadership of Rashid Ali and with the support of your brave and courageous army ... Our reward will be a great thing in the hereafter, this great thing that we have been promised by God is paradise for all Moslems who struggle for right ... I call you, all Iraqi people, to the battlefield, to the scene of honour, shoulder to shoulder against the tyrant, the British who started aggression against us. We will defeat them with our united effort and with the strength of our great army. Remember that your struggle is for dignity of the country and for freedom.[35]

Despite such stirring injunctions, the military situation was not favourable, the hoped-for popular uprising was yet to materialize and Iraqi leaders were showing precious little initiative. Cecil Beaton shrewdly summarized the situation at this point: 'by continuous [RAF] bombing, the enemy gun posts were quietened by day: and, at night, patrols prevented the use of the cover of darkness to shell the cantonment'. The result was that 'Habbaniya, which itself was cut off from outside help or supply, except by air, was now in fact besieging the Iraqi forces on the plateau'.[36]

Wavell wavers

Whatever the heroics being performed by the defenders of Habbaniya, the strategic picture from a British point of view was distinctly unedifying. They needed to lift the siege as soon as possible and defeat Rashid Ali's attempt to snuff out Britain's presence in the country before the Germans arrived. On the morning of 5 May Anthony Eden summoned the Iraqi chargé d'affaires and 'told him that if matters continued his country would be at war with the whole of the British Empire, and if German help was received Iraq would be turned into a battlefield'.[37] As this was taking place in London, outside Habbaniya a King's Own Royal Regiment patrol was making an unsuccessful attempt to drive out the Iraqi troops defending the village of Sin al-Dhibban, site of the vital ferry point used by the Iraqis to cross the Euphrates to reinforce the plateau. At noon, General Wavell assumed responsibility for operations in northern Iraq at London's insistence, taking over from India Command. That evening, Wavell sent a most secret cipher telegram to General Sir John Dill, Chief of the Imperial General Staff. 'Nice baby you have handed me on my 58th birthday', it said. 'Have always hated babies and Iraqis but will do my best for the little blighter'. Dill replied: 'What a birthday present. Sincerely hope that you will be able to kill the little brute. Many happy returns of birthday but not of baby'.[38]

Iraq was a baby that the taciturn general was reluctant to accept; he remained highly sceptical about the prospects of successful military action, and adamant that he possessed insufficient forces to conduct it. Though Plan Lobster had long envisaged the dispatch of a brigade from Middle East Command to Iraq, in the spring of 1941 Wavell resisted and made his objections very plain to his superiors. But while he was slow to embrace the responsibility, London looked to him to sort out the situation and provide Habbaniya with the relief it desperately needed. Though troops were massing in Basra, flooding and other obstacles made it almost impossible for them to move north in strength and at speed, so relief had to come from Palestine.

On the previous day Wavell had been asked to send troops, a request that he disputed and sought to block: 'You must face facts', he chided the Chiefs of Staff. 'I feel it my duty to warn you in the gravest possible terms that I consider prolongation of fighting in Iraq will seriously endanger the defence of Palestine and Egypt'.[39] The Chiefs of Staff dismissed his protest and ordered him to get a force moving towards Iraq as soon as possible. General Sir Hastings Ismay, Churchill's principal military assistant and the crucial bridge between the prime minister and the Chiefs of Staff, wrote that Wavell's 'protest was vehement'. He argued to the point of insubordination against providing a striking column from Palestine for operations in Iraq, urging instead that Britain pursue its objectives through diplomacy and the acceptance of a

Turkish offer of mediation. 'To this the Chiefs of Staff, with the support of the Prime Minister and Cabinet, replied that no political settlement was possible, and that there was no option but to crush Rashid Ali by military action before the Germans appeared on the scene.'[40] With evident regret, Ismay noted that this was the first time that the chiefs had had to overrule a commander-in-chief on the spot, and it led inexorably to Wavell's eventual dismissal in June 1941. All of this thoroughly depressed Wavell. Peter Coats, his ADC, wrote that he had 'never seen him so low'. Minister Bullard in Tehran, meanwhile, observed that he looked 'the picture of gloom'.[41]

Wavell's reluctance to send forces to Iraq can be explained by two factors: on the one hand, he believed that he had bigger fish to fry, not least Rommel's Afrika Korps and dealing with the aftermath of Britain's evacuation from Greece. The East Africa campaign was still rumbling on as well. He also believed that the region fell naturally within India Command's sphere of responsibility, not his. The fact was that the Iran–Iraq region was of concern to both India Command and Middle East Command. But it was on the outer edge of the responsibilities of both, and so central to neither.

Elie Kedourie offers further insights into Wavell's stance.[42] Wavell, he claims, believed in the 'myth' of a united 'Arab world' that could rise as one if sufficiently provoked. Such provocation could easily be provided by the incendiary Palestine policy of the British government, or by clumsy military manoeuvres like the ones Britain appeared to be mounting in Iraq. Cairo-based experts cautioned Wavell against actions that might light the touch paper of 'Arab public opinion'. This augmented his caution, already firm-set given his focus on the main task in hand, the war in the Western Desert – hence his desire for a political rather than a military solution to the Iraq crisis. Churchill had spotted Wavell's predilection, observing that he was 'strongly pro-Arab like most military officers'.[43]

On 6 May 1941 Dill told Major-General Kennedy, Director of Military Operations at the War Office, that the prime minister wanted to sack Wavell. Churchill was really annoyed and considered him 'to be too weak in his attitude to Iraq'. While the Army top brass loathed siding with a politician against one of their own, the fact was that in this matter they agreed with Churchill. Dill told Wavell that 'Our view is that if the Germans can get Syria and Iraq with a few aircraft, tourists [a name given to German nationals in Iran and Iraq] and local revolts, we must not shrink from running equal small-scale military risks, nor from facing the possible aggravation of political dangers from failure'.[44]

The message from London ended unequivocally: 'We of course take full responsibility for this decision . . . should you find yourself unwilling to give effect to it, arrangements will be made to meet any wish you may express to be relieved of your command.'[45] Wavell's behaviour contrasted starkly with that of Auchinleck, who said that India Command could make the force in Iraq up to five brigades within the month, a 'bold and generous offer' gratefully accepted by the Chiefs of Staff.[46] Auchinleck was very opposed to any negotiation with the Iraqi government and wanted no delay. He fundamentally disagreed with Wavell's contention that the security of Iraq 'was of minor importance compared with security of Egypt and Palestine, and insisted that it was the other way about'.[47] Of course, Wavell's predicament was unenviable, but firefighting across vast regions was the nature of the war as it currently presented itself to the captains of the British Empire. The situation in Iraq required urgent attention; whatever Wavell thought in that first week of May, imperial forces were in trouble, and needed help.

The siege is lifted

On 6 May, two Valentias, each carrying a platoon of the King's Own Royal Regiment, got lost and landed next to a pumping station occupied by the enemy. One of the aircraft managed to regain the air, but the other became stuck in the sand, and was destroyed by Iraqi machine-gun fire; the British troops surrendered. A Valentia escorted by a Blenheim ferried fuel to three Valentias that force-landed after running dry near Hit.[48] But despite such losses, British momentum continued to build and the Iraqis continued to underperform.

On the same day, RAF reconnaissance flights revealed what looked like a large reinforcement of the plateau, and the heaviest Iraqi air raid to date was launched against Habbaniya. It looked like a big push to force the base to surrender was imminent. But then, to everyone's surprise, the Iraqi forces began to leave. While Rashid Ali was desperately appealing for Axis aid, unremitting British attacks and a lack of rations and water had sapped the morale of the Iraqi soldiers. They were now massing about 2 miles from the airbase on the road leading towards Fallujah at Sin al-Dhibban. Smart scrambled all available air assets to attack the forces leaving Habbaniya, and those coming to reinforce them. Pilot Officer Dunford Wood wrote in his diary: 'I get up eventually with "Tiny" Irwin in the back and machine gun the fleeing troops. They stop and shoot me up, but it seems slaughter all the same. Three Iraqi armoured cars come up, my bombs miss but Dan opens them up like a tin opener with a stick right down the road. Tony warns me they "bite" so I don't go too low.'[49]

What followed was indeed slaughter, as advancing Iraqi forces collided with those retreating from Habbaniya. The resultant mass of men and machines were sitting ducks for the RAF pilots, stopped head to head and making no attempt to disperse. 'We made 139 aircraft sorties,' Squadron Leader Dudgeon recalled, 'and when the last aircraft left, its pilot reported that the road was a strip of flames, several hundred yards long. There were ammunition limbers exploding, with cars and lorries burning by the dozen.'[50] The reinforcement column, Smart wrote, had been 'annihilated from the air'. The attack lasted for almost two hours and over 500 prisoners were taken.[51]

A retaliatory raid on Habbaniya destroyed two Oxfords, a Gladiator and an Audax, and killed seven people. But the airbase had been relieved, largely through its own devices. Despite this blow, Iraqi radio broadcasts still sought to rally the people. 'Our fight is an example to the whole Arab world,' declared a broadcast on 6 May. It reported a message of support sent to Rashid Ali from Syria: 'Aleppo stands firmly behind the Iraqi Government. The town is prepared to bring all sacrifices in the interests of the common cause.' The reply sent on behalf of the Iraqi nation thanked the city 'for its assistance and noble attitude towards this holy fight'.[52] But messages of support were no substitute for battlefield success, and the Germans were still nowhere in sight.

On 7 May an armoured car reconnaissance of the plateau overlooking Habbaniya found it deserted. A large quantity of abandoned equipment and supplies was captured, including 79 motor vehicles, 10 Crossley armoured cars, an Italian tank, 7 Czech 3.7-inch howitzers, an 18-pounder field gun, 45 Bren guns, anti-tank and anti-aircraft guns, machine-guns and 340 rifles with 500,000 rounds of ammunition. Many of the captured weapons were of better quality than those being used by imperial troops, and quickly found new owners, Air Vice-Marshal Smart writing that this 'invaluable' booty 'significantly rearmed the garrison'.[53] With the siege lifted, foraging parties were able to leave the airbase and bring in sheep and cattle for food.

In the five days since the beginning of the siege – which seemed like an age to Habbaniya's defenders – the RAF had dropped 5,000 bombs with an overall weight of 50 tons, and expended 116,000 rounds of ammunition. Official figures recorded 647 sorties flown from Habbaniya, though the real figure was much higher. Churchill signalled Habbaniya's defenders: 'Your vigorous and splendid action has largely restored the situation. We are watching the grand fight you are making. All possible aid will be sent. Keep it up!'[54] Air Marshal Sir Arthur Tedder proudly labelled the defence of Habbaniya 'a little classic'.[55] But even though Habbaniya had been relieved, Iraqi forces remained undefeated, and hundreds of British civilians were besieged in Baghdad. The Iraqi army had been dealt a tremendous blow, but remained largely intact. Not so the Iraqi air force: by 8 May, Smart recorded, it had been 'virtually eliminated, approximately twenty-five of their operational aircraft shot down or destroyed on the ground, and 20–30 damaged beyond immediate repair . . . A machine gun attack on 8 May by three Fighter Blenheims against aircraft on the ground at Shahraban was particularly spectacular, all the Iraqi aircraft found there being set on fire.'[56] But all was not lost. On the same day as these devastating attacks, a Luftwaffe bomber squadron based on Rhodes, which had been earmarked for an attack on the Suez Canal, was ordered to Syria, destined for Iraq.[57] German help was on its way.

On 8 May an Audax dropped a message bag into the British Embassy compound in an effort to re-establish communications, though Iraqi ground fire prevented a reply being picked up by cable-and-hook the following evening. 'Yesterday ended with very good news,' Stark wrote on the same day: 'the retreat of the enemy near Habbaniya with loss of 1,000 casualties and 300 prisoners. A series of RAF visits over Baghdad followed, flying quite arrogantly in formation. They must have dropped bombs near, possibly on the railway station, as we shook and rattled.'[58] Later a Gladiator 'came swooping almost to touch the palm trees on the lawn and drop a letter from Habbaniya – all very satisfactory, and all but thirty-two women and children safely evacuated to Basra . . . Last night a huge panache of fire and smoke hung over Baghdad and the steely river: RAF had hit an IPC [Iraq Petroleum Company] oil tanker.'[59]

Radio broadcasts continued their attempts to rally support for Rashid Ali's cause. Also on 8 May, an Arabic broadcast entitled 'Grand Mufti to Islamic World' went as follows:

To all Moslems all over the world I call to work together in a spiritual collaboration. The hour is critical and the chance is here. The British, who are attacking Iraq and the people, or in other words your brother Moslems, were those who fought in the past the Arab nations, no indeed all Moslems all over the world. The British did not give the Moslem world any rest.

You remember the bloodshed of the Arabs in Palestine, and everyone of you in the Islamic World knows the sort of atrocities the British imposed upon the Palestinians ... Their main aim was to destroy an entire Islamic nation in order to build a Jewish country on the bodies of the Moslem. Look at what the British are doing in Iraq now. They are already occupying some parts of the country and want full occupation by violating the freedom and independence of this Moslem country, for the military and Imperialistic objectives. The British atrocities cannot be forgotten or forgiven but God is watching them, and their bad deeds. From that you know that God is helping you if you help each other. Look at what Britain has done to the Arabs in Berka in her recent movements there, or what she has done to the Arabs of Hadramout, Oman, and Transjordan. She is using all these Moslem Arab countries as bases for her Imperialistic objectives. What has she given them? Nothing, indeed tyranny and oppression and has stolen their freedom. In India they have destroyed the Indian Empire and divided people among themselves. What was the result of all these criminal actions? Poverty and weakness for all the Arab countries and for all the Moslems in the world. But there was another result caused by these atrocities. Hatred for Britain in the hearts of all the Arabs, who cannot deny it or hide it any longer. .... God is against the tyrant and the oppressor, and defends those who are struggling against them because God does not like aggressors or tyrants.[60]

Wavell, meanwhile, was still digging his heels in, bridling at London's interventions, and predicting failure. On 8 May he telegrammed to say that though Habbaniya might be saved and Basra secured, the imperial forces deployed were insufficient to take Baghdad against the anticipated level of German and Iraqi opposition.[61] Countermanding him, on 9 May Churchill again decreed that risks should be run. Audacity was called for: in the absence of further reinforcements and with imperial troops in the south stuck in the Basra area, a small force should try and take Baghdad. The following day Wavell wrote of the need to guard against a large-scale Arab uprising. Already, he noted, the loyalty of the Trans-Jordan Frontier Force was 'in grave doubt.' He had learned that some of its units had refused to join the British force that he was reluctantly assembling in Palestine, unwilling to fight fellow Muslims.[62]

But despite all this, Wavell was obliged to yield. On Churchill's insistence that forces be sent from Middle East Command to relieve Habbaniya, Wavell ordered Major-General George Clark, commanding the 1st Cavalry Division, to assemble a brigade group. To be known as Habforce – Habbaniya Force – and built around the 4th Cavalry Brigade, its purpose was the relief of the airbase. General Sir Henry Maitland 'Jumbo' Wilson then arrived to take over command in Palestine following his evacuation from Greece. Clark, now his subordinate, met Wilson in Jerusalem to discuss the situation on 11 May and learned that his secondary objective was the relief of the embassy in Baghdad.[63] Also present in Palestine as decisions were taken about Habbaniya's relief and the wider objectives in Iraq was Air Vice-Marshal John D'Albiac. He had just returned from Britain's abortive Greek venture, during which he had been Air Officer Commanding. Subsequently appointed Air Officer Commanding Palestine and Trans-Jordan, the posting was cut short when Reggie Smart was injured in an accident on the Habbaniya base. D'Albiac was ordered to replace him as Air Officer Commanding Iraq.

Lieutenant-General Quinan arrived at Basra on 8 May to take command of forces building in the Basra region (and eventually all land forces in Iraq). He was to be at the heart of the frenetic military activity that was to occur in Iraq and its environs over the next fifteen months. His initial appointment was as commander of Force Sabine.[64] 'A small, grey-haired, weather-beaten man, he was to inaugurate in Iraq a special tradition of generalship.' With a style of command involving detailed planning and staff work for campaigns, Quinan:

> had an intense dislike for the trappings of office. He refused to have a flag on his car, he much preferred to travel without an ADC, in church he liked to sit next to the sepoys. At a lonely camp an officer would arrive in a trench-coat and ask if anyone could spare him a tent; the residents were startled when their guest came in to supper with crossed swords and crown revealed on his epaulettes. He had a thorough contempt for his own comfort.[65]

The soldiers in Basra and its environs would not be able to move north with any great speed because of flooding and other obstacles, and so it was down to Habforce to reinforce the airbase. On 9 May, 203 Squadron Blenheims, based at H4 pumping station in Trans-Jordan, had attacked the Rutbah fort and were met by ground fire that destroyed one of the aircraft, killing its crew. On 10 May the RAF armoured cars arrived to find the fort deserted. Churchill signalled Wavell that 'every day counts, for Germans may not be long'.[66] Alongside the Household Cavalry, Habforce included units from the Royal Wiltshire Yeomanry and Warwickshire Yeomanry, recalled from Sidi Barrani in Egypt, and the 1st Battalion the Essex Regiment. It also contained No. 2 Armoured Car Company RAF with its Fordson armoured cars under command of Flight Lieutenant Michael Casano, which had been operating in the Western Desert when orders were received to proceed with haste across 1,000 miles of desert to the relief of Habbaniya. It was supported by John Bagot Glubb's 350-strong Desert Mechanized Regiment of the Arab Legion, loaned by the Emir of Trans-Jordan, who 'rushed about the desert in Ford trucks at 60 miles an hour'.[67]

Given the need for speedy action, Clark divided Habforce in two. A flying column, built around Brigadier Joe Kingstone's 4th Cavalry Brigade and known as Kingcol, would lead off. Only recently converted from horses to mechanized vehicles, the brigade possessed some dated equipment, such as Lewis and Hotchkiss guns, but was full of cheer and adventurous spirit and ended up covering 1,200 miles in nine days on its journey to Habbaniya. Comprising 2,000 men in 500 vehicles, Kingcol was ordered to hasten to H4 and link up with Glubb Pasha's force and then proceed to capture Rutbah. The armoured cars led the way, and then on 11 May the bulk of Kingcol left Beit Lid, moving across the clay-covered plains of Esdaelon into the Jordan valley and over the Jordan river, a column of men and machines stretching for 7 miles.[68] The 1st Household Cavalry Regiment formed Kingcol's spearhead.[69] Camping at night, Kingcol laagered and dug slit trenches, forming a huge defensive square with the ambulances and field hospitals at its centre, the field artillery facing outwards on the perimeter. Kingcol arrived at H4 on 12 May, bivouacking in the desert away from the station in case of air attack, and two days later Rutbah was reached. Leaving the fort on 15 May they headed for Kilo 25, a point on the Baghdad road 14 miles west of Ramadi, where a brigade of Iraqi troops waited.[70]

Kingcol was to turn south-east at this point to avoid the Iraqi force as it closed on its objective, Habbaniya. Making this move away from the main track, however, the column's inexperienced drivers hit soft sand, which meant digging them out in the blazing heat and hoping that German aircraft did not find the immobilized column. With water running perilously low, a reconnaissance by the Arab Legion found an alternative route. Looking back from the vanguard, Somerset de Chair beheld the entire brigade, 'stretched back in an apparently endless line over the desert for twenty or thirty miles'. While looking back, 'I saw, with surprised eyes, two black tulips of smoke blossom far down the line, and, while the bomb burst still hovered in the air, I saw the bright white-hot flash of anti-aircraft fire stream upwards across them'.[71] Kingcol had been discovered by the Luftwaffe, but the German attack was not pressed home.

The column's advanced formations reached the outposts of Habbaniya on 18 May. 'At the edge of the plateau,' wrote de Chair in *The Golden Carpet*, his paean to Habforce, 'I came abruptly on the cantonment. From the foot of the red sandstone spurs, a level mud aerodrome stretched to the settlement itself, where hangars gave way to a maze of leafy avenues and the red roofs of bungalows'.[72] De Chair made his way to the Air Force Headquarters building. On the roof, tin-helmeted watchers searched the sky for enemy aircraft. The door was guarded by an Assyrian levy, a man of truly martial appearance, who wore a pale blue uniform shirt open at the neck and a dark brown felt hat turned up at the side, Australian fashion. He also wore khaki shorts and puttees. His boots were actually polished and the sling of his rifle whitened to a wonder. He was an apparition – a testimony to the stability of the British Empire.[73]

Although the siege had been lifted, Kingcol's march was a feat of historic significance. Major-General Clark arrived at Habbaniya by air, in advance of his troops, together with D'Albiac. With the base relieved and reinforced, and Basra also secured, the British had cause to be pleased with how events had panned out thus far. RAF sorties continued to take the fight to Iraqi forces across the country. Apart from reconnaissance flights and standing patrols, aircraft from Habbaniya and Shaibah continued to attack Iraqi aerodromes and military establishments, as well as strategic strongholds such as Rutbah. Rashid airbase had again been visited by the RAF; 'direct hits were obtained on hangars, barracks, and other buildings, and on three occasions the petrol dump at the aerodrome was attacked'.[74] The RAF also attacked aerodromes in Baqubah, Mosul and Shahraban (modern Miqdadiyah), where ten aircraft were destroyed on the ground, and barracks were hit at Washshash, Nasiriya and Qaraghan. The problem was that German forces had now taken to the field, and the roads to Baghdad had been rendered almost impassable by flooding and the destruction of bridges. But a way would have to be found, because from Habbaniya, imperial forces needed to close on the capital.

CHAPTER 5

Fallujah and the advance on Baghdad

Two weeks into the campaign and the British were secure in Basra and had lifted the siege of Habbaniya. They had also degraded the Iraqi air force, which had been reduced, the War Cabinet were told, to about fifty aircraft, of which only six were first-line operational types.[1] But though the Iraqi army had suffered a demoralizing reverse, it was still largely intact, with 20,000 troops in and around Baghdad and 15,000 in the north. Rashid Ali's government still ruled unmolested in Baghdad and the Indian Army troops decanted into Basra were bogged down and making exceedingly slow progress in their endeavours to move north to threaten the capital. Most worryingly, German forces and ammunition trains had started to arrive. The British government believed that the Germans might send up to sixty fighters and bombers. About thirty Luftwaffe aircraft were reported to have landed in Aleppo and Damascus en route to Iraq. By this stage, British objectives had crystallized around the overthrow of Rashid Ali, the removal of the Golden Square and the return of Prince Abdulillah as regent.

The Chiefs of Staff remained distinctly worried, despite the success at Habbaniya. Dill confided to Auchinleck on 21 May: 'If we cannot quickly scotch the trouble that has started with Rashid Ali it is difficult to see where it will all end.'[2] There were wider implications, too, the longer the situation in Iraq remained unresolved. As Eden wrote to Churchill on 19 May, 'these developments cause me most concern on account of their influence on Turkey's policy [as to whether to remain neutral or actively assist Germany]. The Turks are concentrating troops on the Iraqi and Syrian frontiers and are asking us in return for our plans for dealing with the situation in these recalcitrant countries'.[3]

A message from Churchill to Roosevelt on 14 May reflected the finely balanced situation, as well as allied ambitions. 'In Iraq,' the British prime minister told the American president, 'we are trying to regain control and anyhow we are making a large strong bridgehead at Basra where later on in the war American machines may be assembled and supplies unloaded.' But, Churchill cautioned, 'there is no doubt' that Admiral Darlan, leader of Vichy Syria, 'will sell the pass if he can, and German aircraft are already passing into Iraq.'[4] The unfolding situation was difficult to read, and the British needed a quick resolution, not least so that Iraq could play its part in the wider war effort. It was infuriating to be fighting the locals – who were supposed to be allies – when there was a world war to be won. For both sides, it was a race against time: for the British, to get more troops into Iraq and onto the battlefield, and for the Iraqis, to get the Germans in and crush British resistance before it was fully mobilized.

Fevered Iraqi appeals to Berlin had been made from the start of hostilities. On 4 May a coded radio message had been picked up by the British. 'This is Baghdad,' the announcer repeated three times. 'This is a message to the Iraki legation in Ankara [repeated]. It is the Iraki Foreign Office.' The message instructed Iraq's Ankara legation to keep the pressure on German officials to send military aid forthwith.[5] War Minister Naji Shawkat also travelled to Ankara 'to impress upon the German authorities Iraq's urgent need for military assistance.'[6] But the Iraqi government was simultaneously exploring options for a return to peace. On 13 May the American ambassador in Ankara, John Van Antwerp MacMurray, reported that Shawkat had 'sought to obtain [the Turkish] Government's assistance in formulating acceptable basis of understanding with the British'. In response, Turkish officials made plain their conviction that Iraq had violated the Anglo-Iraqi Treaty and taken a 'course whose successful outcome could only place it and [the] Moslem world at [the] mercy of [a] power far less indulgent and more oppressive.'[7] Rashid Ali also sent his Foreign Minister to Saudi Arabia, where he was given short shrift by King Ibn Saud. The British also appealed for the Saudi king's aid, on 2 May telegramming Jeddah to ask him to make a public statement 'deploring the situation, to which Rashid Ali's disastrous policy has brought Iraq, and expressing the hope that Iraqis would disown him'.[8]

Intelligence decrypts kept London informed about the build-up of Fliegerkorps XI in the Balkans, for a time entertaining the idea that the threat to Crete might be a cover for an operation in Iraq. On 9 May, Ultra had revealed that an alternative had been chosen. From Luftwaffe cyphers it was learned that an airfield near Athens had been set aside for special operations and that bombers and fighters, stripped of their Luftwaffe markings, were being ferried through Syria to Iraq. The War Cabinet's weekly resumé reported that:

> French authorities are known to have sent two train loads of ammunition eastwards but deny this destined for Iraq on German demands ... Enemy agents are believed to be entering Iraq from Turkey and Iran, presumably assisted by Fifth Column already organized there to prepare for reception German airborne troops ... By advancing through Turkey into Syria and at the same time renewing their offensive in North Africa they could develop once again the pincer movement which they have used so consistently in all their recent campaigns.[9]

It was on this day, 9 May, that the Foreign Office in Berlin announced Germany's military aid package to Iraq. Major Axel von Blomberg was on his way to conduct a reconnaissance of Iraqi airfields for Luftwaffe use, the first twenty aircraft were due to arrive soon and supplies were moving through Syria. Though in the end it did not transpire, the original plan was also to deploy a reinforced battalion containing at its core elements of the Brandenberg Regiment, a specialist unit controlled by the Abwehr and used on intelligence and sabotage operations. General Hellmuth Felmy was in overall command. He had retired as an air force general in January 1940, but had been recalled in May 1941 and appointed head of Sonderstab Felmy, the German military mission to Iraq.[10] It would perform the role of a 'central agency for all Arab questions applying to the Wehrmacht'.[11] Luftwaffe colonel Werner Junck was the officer tasked with taking Fliegerführer Irak to Mosul, from where its aircraft would operate bearing Iraqi air force markings. The force initially comprised a squadron of twelve Messerschmitt Bf 110s, a squadron of twelve Heinkel He 111s and thirteen Junker transport aircraft. A squadron of Italian Fiat CR.42s also arrived from Rhodes. German forces made their presence felt as soon as they arrived in theatre. On 12 May a Heinkel bombed men of the 1st Battalion the Essex Regiment, part of Habforce, as they began their journey towards Habbaniya, and the following day a Blenheim was attacked by a Messerschmitt over Mosul. On 14 May six Messerschmitts were seen at Erbil and three Heinkels were also reported. By this time, the bulk of Junck's force had arrived in theatre. The deployment of German forces was intended to provide 'what the Germans tellingly described as "spine straightening" for the Iraqi army, much of which had become terrified of bombing by British aircraft'.[12]

Crucial to the outcome of the campaign would be how well German forces could be integrated with their Iraqi allies, and the extent to which these unlikely bedfellows could agree upon and execute an effective joint plan of action. Major von Blomberg was charged with the task of supervising this integration, and travelled to Baghdad on 15 May to arrange a council of war with the Iraqi leadership. Unfortunately for both him and the nascent German–Iraqi alliance, an Iraqi soldier 'guarding a bridge in Baghdad, not recognizing the shape and silhouette of the He 111, and believing it to be British, placed a few well-aimed rounds into the fuselage as it cruised low overhead'.[13] Von Blomberg was discovered to be dead on arrival, a bullet through his neck. Following this inauspicious start, Junck himself flew to Baghdad the following day to confer with Rashid Ali, Chief of the General Staff Major-General Amin Zaki, Colonel Nur ed-Din Mahmud and Colonel Mahmud Salman (of the Golden Square).[14] It was agreed that the German priority should be to prevent Habforce arriving at Habbaniya, followed by the capture of the RAF base. Only a few days later, however, Habforce arrived at its destination unmolested, the Germans having arrived too late.

While in Baghdad, Junck conferred with Fritz Grobba, reinstalled as Berlin's representative after a 'triumphal return'. His party had flown in from Rhodes via Aleppo and Mosul in Heinkels accompanied by Messerschmitt fighters. His mission was to prepare for a new German–Iraqi alliance after the British had been ejected. As part of this initiative, the Germans were quick to get a team to Baghdad to examine the Iraqi oil industry with a view to its transfer to Nazi use. The German Petroleum Mission, a group of 'reputable scientists', came well prepared with equipment and supplies, and were led by a very able petroleum technologist, surmised by the British to be one Colonel Geissman: he informed staff at the Baghdad Chemical Laboratory 'that he had been in charge of the immediate utilization of seized petrol supplies in most of the major German campaigns' to date. Geissman's immediate object was the production of the maximum quantity of aviation spirit of at least 87 octane rating. The German scientists 'succeeded in blending all spirits in Baghdad derived from Abadan up to about 92 octane rating'.[15]

The Germans were also sending weapons. An agreement with the Vichy authorities allowed the Syrian government in Damascus to recover a quarter of the weaponry impounded under the terms of the French armistice in return for turning over the remainder to the Iraqis.[16] The agreement had also permitted Axis forces to use Syrian airfields and facilities, and provided for the establishment of a Luftwaffe base at Aleppo. The first trainload of ex-Syrian weapons had arrived in Mosul on 13 May via Turkey, and included 15,500 rifles, 200 machine-guns and four 75-millimetre field guns, all with ammunition and shells.[17]

Junck attacked Habbaniya on 16 and 17 May using six Messerschmitts and three Heinkels operating from Mosul. The problem for the Germans was that the British had forces up and running inside Iraq and were imbued with an offensive spirit, determined not to allow the Germans the chance to get a grip on the situation. Air Vice-Marshal D'Albiac, now directing British air operations, was quick to take the attack to the Germans, sending aircraft against their Mosul stronghold. Attempts were also made to disorganize the German movement of supplies by bombing Mosul railway station and the railway lines and sidings surrounding it. On 17 May British reinforcements arrived in the shape of four Gladiators from 94 Squadron and six Blenheims from 84 Squadron.

> Although the nine remaining Wellingtons in Basra had been withdrawn to Egypt on 12 May to assist in operations against Rommel in the Western Desert, two new long-range cannon-firing Hurricanes had also arrived from Aboukir in Egypt. Together with the Blenheims, they made a daring, long-range sortie to hit back at the Luftwaffe at Mosul on 17 May, destroying two and damaging four aircraft for the loss of a Hurricane. On the same day, two Gladiators from Habbaniya, loitering around Rashid Airfield at Baghdad, encountered two Bf.110Cs attempting to take off, and destroyed them both.[18]

All in all, this represented a disturbing rate of attrition for the newly arrived Germans.

Nevertheless, the Foreign Office in London urged a quick solution. Eden wrote to Churchill, again raising the fear that if Germany was successful in Iraq and Syria, Turkey would 'be effectively surrounded and it would indeed be difficult then to count upon her enduring loyalty'. In connection with this, the Foreign Secretary noted that 'the mobile brigade [Habforce] had evidently had difficulties in its approach to Habbaniya'. He had not, he continued, 'appreciated when the Defence Committee recommended this move that its development would take so long. The delay has enabled German arrivals to hearten the Iraqis.'[19] Meanwhile, in Baghdad and several Iraqi outposts incarcerated American and British subjects also wondered at the delay, none more so than those crammed into the diplomatic compounds.

The embassy siege

In outlying districts British and other alien nationals had been rounded up by the Iraqi army and police. In Kirkuk, rumours flew as hostilities began, and soon, according to British political adviser Wallace Lyon, 'the [Iraq] Petroleum Company got orders to evacuate all women and children; after that, communications were cut'. He himself was taken away: 'Police arrived and ordered Brady and me to go to IPC [Iraq Petroleum Company] Club. There all men rounded up (bar not dry so okay; payment by IOU).'[20] Here he and his fellows were incarcerated, shortly to be joined by captured RAF aircrew. Meanwhile hundreds of British civilians were sheltering in the American and British diplomatic compounds in Baghdad, cut off from news of the war's progress. Paul Knabenshue knew nothing other than that he had 'seen British bombers operating over Baghdad and Rashid camp near the Legation'.[21] This was the same across the country and was to be a feature of the campaign; the Iraqis had effectively severed communications, and so the various British parties on the ground – the Baghdad Embassy, the imperial forces concentrated in and around Basra, the thousands of service personnel and civilians at RAF Habbaniya, and Habforce as it moved east from Palestine – had no clear picture of what was going on.

The British Embassy stood on the west bank of the Tigris, its gardens set about with buddleia, hibiscus and pomegranate. 'Passing through the gates in the high wall,' wrote John Masters, 'I entered Arnold's Rugby, with rooks cawing in immemorial elms and chestnut trees spreading their gaunt branches across gravelled paths; and there was a big grey English country house, and the smell of tea and crumpets in the Counsellor's study.'[22] Freya Stark's memoir offers a vivid account of the month-long incarceration of the 'small Lucknow of imprisoned British'; 350 men, women and children, as well as the ambassador and his staff, crammed into the embassy compound living in dormitory-style makeshift accommodation.[23] Overflowing with European refugees, the embassy's ballroom was 'like pictures of the first emigrant ships'. Each defending his or her own privacy, she wrote, we 'vainly try to make small barricades of our boxes and belongings'.[24] Anticipating

'Ash Wednesday', the famous occasion on which secret documents were burnt by the British Embassy and Middle East Command headquarters as Rommel closed on Cairo, official papers were destroyed.[25]

Defences were improvised around the perimeter, including sandbags in case the compound was shelled or bombed. There were loopholes in the sandbag wall at the front entrance, and barbed wire connected the cypress trees to form an inner defensive ring. To create more obstacles, cars were parked on the lawn. Improvised bombs were stockpiled at various locations throughout the compound. Known as the 'general's bombs', the arsenal included petrol tins of sand and beer cans filled with paraffin with cotton-wool fuses. Iraqi policemen ensured no one left the compound, and a drum-beating, war-chanting 'mob' sometimes gathered outside. Its efforts appear to have been rather desultory, however, the result of official encouragement and the passion of a small group of enthusiastic nationalists, rather than a reflection of a seething anti-British population. Though most of the British people affected indifference and good cheer, it was a worrying time. Stark described the 'pathetic look of dog-like trust of Indians; gloomy look of Iraqis; imperturbable, hot, but not uncheerful looks of the British'.[26] Attempts were made to fashion a receiving set, and activities were planned to sustain morale, such as a concert, during which the audience was 'not allowed to applaud, fearing that the sound of it across the river might be thought of as rejoicing over the air raid'.[27]

The inmates were cheered by RAF activity overhead. A large V was marked out on the lawn in white sheets 'to tell the air that we are lost to news', and Union Jacks were spread out on the roof to prevent British aircraft attacking their own embassy. With increasing regularity the throttle of 'British bombers, black in the blue sky', was heard.[28] On one occasion Stark observed the 'very beautiful sight' of a Wellington bomber 'slowly sailing along at about 1,000 feet, up the river from south to north, very dark against the green sky and the sleeping houses'. An aspect of the British campaign that Stark found less impressive was the propaganda material dropped by the RAF, a 'dead sort of animation of Arabic leaflets'. Ambassador Cornwallis agreed that their tone was 'insulting'.[29] They had a threatening tenor that Britain's precarious position hardly justified. Stark wrote scathingly of the 'monstrous leaflet drop by the British Government to say they will bomb Government buildings in Iraq, so condemn all here to destruction – and of course it can't be carried out. Why spread *empty* threats? HE [His Excellency] telegraphs urgently to stop *violent* leaflets written by ourselves.'[30]

To replenish the embassy larder, the Iraqi guards would escort a lorry to the shops. During and after RAF raids this was impossible as the shops were shut, their owners 'terrified by our bombing'.[31] As stocks dwindled, rationing was introduced. Portions were 'quite sufficient though one could easily eat every meal twice over'.[32] A typical day's rations might comprise, for breakfast, 'cocoa, one sardine on bread, one bread-slice and jam. Lunch: rice, corned beef, half tomato, two small bread *bibi*; two prunes and half slice pineapple. Evening: fish, curry and stewed fruit: very little of each.'[33]

A mantle of depression settled on the embassy as the realization set in that the siege might last a long time. We 'must admit that in the map of the whole Middle East we are not so very important, but console ourselves by reflecting that our neighbourhood to Oil will prevent us from being forgotten'.[34] Furthermore, it was not just the RAF that was active in the skies above Baghdad; on 15 May, German aircraft were spotted for the first time. The Iraqi police outside the embassy became less amiable and 'call the inside Iraqis *Ingliz* and promise massacre', inspired by the Grand Mufti's speeches.[35] One of the policemen guarding the compound told Stark that if she became a Muslim he would keep her himself: 'I am sorry that their minds dwell on loot and rapine – evidently the result of the Mufti's preaching of a holy war last night'. She worried about the embassy's Iraqi and other non-British servants and attendants, for a death sentence had been placed upon them. There were also threats directed specifically at the women, a policeman telling Stark that he could not imagine what use 'the harim' about to be murdered had for so many items of cosmetics. 'I mean to be killed, if it comes to that, with my face in proper order.'[36] Things were little better at the American legation nearby, to the anger of Paul Knabenshue. His mission, he wrote, had to deal with 'a hostile gangster fifth column illegal government under the direction of Grobba, the former German Minister to Iraq'. The Iraqi police guard deployed around the American compound 'for our protection' had, in fact, 'made us prisoners'.[37]

Breakout from Habbaniya and the capture of Fallujah

The British needed to get to Baghdad and oust Rashid Ali al-Gailani, the Golden Square and the Grand Mufti. They planned to move forces towards the capital from Basra in the south and from Habbaniya in the west. But the former were delayed leaving Basra and made slow progress because of the deliberate flooding of the Euphrates and the fact that the Iraqi army controlled the railway line. Colonel Ouvry Roberts, Chief of Staff of the 10th Indian

Division, had been given command of Habbaniya's land forces earlier in the campaign. Including the RAF Levies, these amounted to 2,200 men supported by the RAF's armoured cars.[38] These forces were supplemented by the arrival of the men of Kingcol. Roberts grouped together the Gurkha infantry reinforcements from Basra and from Kingcol to form Habbaniya Brigade, and put together a plan to attack Fallujah as the first stage of a move on Baghdad. He decided to bypass Ramadi as it was strongly garrisoned and 'largely cut off by self-imposed flooding and could be isolated in favour of securing the strategically important crossing over the Euphrates at Falluja'.[39] Upon leaving Habbaniya, Iraqi forces had retired east to Fallujah and westwards to Ramadi, 'carrying out demolitions and inundations covering these two towns'.[40] Urged on by Churchill, the commanders on the ground decided that a quick bid for Baghdad was essential, especially as Glubb Pasha had made it clear to General Clark that, with no preliminary work in place, it would take weeks to achieve Rashid Ali's overthrow by political means.

In order to move on the capital, imperial forces first needed to overcome the natural obstacles in the vicinity of Habbaniya. A section of No. 10 Field Company Madras Sappers and Miners was flown in to make a crossing at Sin al-Dhibban on the banks of the Euphrates. Here, the river was 750 feet wide with a strong current. Bridging was not possible at short order, so a ferry was made with 1,500 feet of wire rope. The first experimental trip across was made on 18 May, just as Kingcol was processing into the base after its pell-mell rush across the desert, and by 0930 the following day all of Roberts' troops were across and heading east towards Fallujah.

Fallujah was strategically important because the main Baghdad–Habbaniya road, 4 miles west of Fallujah, had been flooded over a stretch of 2 miles, presenting an impassable obstacle. The British needed, therefore, to approach Baghdad by way of Fallujah's bridge over the Euphrates, a steel-girder structure of five spans' width, 177 feet in length.[41] The British troops assaulting it were divided into five small columns of about 100 each with supporting weapons, one being a section of RAF armoured cars and another including captured artillery. One was to move up along Hammond's Bund, wading through the waters of the breach, three to cross the Sin al-Dhibban ferry with guns and armoured cars, the fifth to be landed by four Bombays and two Valentias at dawn in a position astride the road, to cover the main Fallujah–Baghdad artery with fire. This would seal all roads from Fallujah bar the track leading south-east to the Abu Ghuraib regulator, and this track was to be covered by a Kingcol troop of 25-pounders.[42]

Once the columns were in position around Fallujah, air attacks commenced at 0500 on 19 May. During the day an RAF aircraft cut all telephone communications with the town, the crew landing, chopping down poles with hatchets and using wire clippers to cut the lines. Pamphlets calling for surrender were then dropped after an hour's bombing, though they failed to induce the Iraqis to give up. Thus it was decided to try to capture the bridge using the column facing it from the west. The town was subjected to dive-bomb attacks, 134 sorties dropping 10 tons of bombs. The position was secured after it was bombed, machine-gunned and shelled by 25-pounders and the town was captured, together with 300 prisoners of war.[43]

The British propaganda machine set to work immediately: 'The rebel Iraq Army fled in disorder from Fallujah yesterday when they were attacked from three sides by British and loyal Arab troops,' the British-controlled *Basrah Times* declared. 'There were no British casualties. The inhabitants of Fallujah welcomed the troops and the restoration of law and order.'[44] 'Things were beginning to look a lot more promising,' wrote Freya Stark: at four o'clock on 20 May, news was received in the embassy compound that 'Fallujah is taken, bridge, town and all. Thank God.'[45]

But the Iraqis were not done yet. As the British cleared over 1,500 civilians from key parts of the town, on 22 May they launched a counterattack with the 6th Iraqi Brigade supported by Fiat tanks. Their main purpose was to blow the bridge to prevent the British advancing on the capital. Imperial forces in the town had been reduced since its capture and some intense combat followed, including house-to-house fighting, in which the King's Own Royal Regiment suffered fifty casualties. A lorry containing gun cotton intended for the destruction of the bridge was hit and 'blown to minute fragments'.[46] The RAF Iraq Levies were to the fore in this engagement, with the role of the Assyrian soldiers particularly noted by their commander. D'Albiac told the British ambassador that the 'determination of the Assyrians at FALLUJAH when a weak company defied an 'Iraqi Brigade, supported by tanks, and one platoon counter-attacked and cleared the town when full of 'Iraqi soldiers was one of the most important factors in breaking the morale of the 'Iraqi army which certainly was broken at Fallujah'.[47] The fighting had been hard. 'In daylight,' wrote de Chair, 'the damage to the town, after consistent shelling by both sides, was an impressive sight and recalled pictures from youthful memory of the battered towns of Flanders in the Great War.'[48]

Victory at Fallujah was a campaign turning point. Demonstrating the disconnect between German grand strategy and operations on the ground, it was not until the fourth week of the conflict that Hitler articulated his ambitions for Iraq. Directive 30, issued on 23 May, stated that:

> The Arab Freedom Movement is, in the Middle East, our natural ally against England. In this context, the uprising in Iraq is of special importance. This strengthens the forces which are hostile to England in the Middle East, interrupts the British lines of communication, and ties down both English troops and English shipping space at the expense of other theatres of war. For these reasons I have decided to push the development of operations in the Middle East through the medium of going to the support of Iraq. Whether and in what way it may later be possible to wreck finally the English position between the Mediterranean and Persian Gulf, in conjunction with an offensive against the Suez Canal, is still in the lap of the gods.[49]

The directive promised to help support the Iraqis with an air contingent, a military mission and arms deliveries. In addition, a German-led Arab Brigade would be formed using volunteers from Iraq, Syria, Palestine and Saudi Arabia. This was an extension of Sonderstab F (Special Staff F – 'F' standing for its commander, Hellmuth Felmy), a German–Arab unit for deployment in Iraq and elsewhere in the Arab world in conjunction with invading German armies, with a prospective strength of 6,000.

But ideas and plans for the future were one thing. What the Iraqis needed was immediate military assistance. The problem for the Germans was that they were too confident of eventual success in the war to invest properly in this operation. And, like the British, they were also hampered by distance, terrain and the demands upon resources. The Luftwaffe had strafed Fallujah on 23 May, but to little effect, and the Iraqis were mounting little more than nuisance raids and employing delaying tactics. On 21 and 22 May, for instance, they made an attempt, 'frustrated by our patrols, to breach the bunds protecting Ashar [the business district of Basra] and Shuaiba aerodrome'. An operation on 25 May by a British battalion with Royal Navy and RAF support was successfully mounted against enemy troops 6 miles up the Tigris from Basra as efforts continued to push Iraqi forces back from the port.[50] All of this ground activity was accompanied by ceaseless RAF sorties, recorded in the daily operational summaries. On 25 May Habbaniya-based aircraft flew 82 sorties, dropping 8 tons of bombs in the Ramadi area and bombing Mosul aerodrome. On the same day, 94 Squadron mounted standing patrols over Habbaniya and fighter escorts over Ramadi, and machine-gunned Iraqi vehicles discovered on the Baghdad road. Four enemy aircraft were machine-gunned at Mosul, and two of the five seen at Baqubah set on fire in a low attack. Habbaniya itself, meanwhile was bombed on that day by two Heinkel He 111s and three Messerschmitt Bf 110s. A successful attack on the Iraqi army and air force reserve petrol dump at Cassels Post destroyed a million gallons of fuel.

To Baghdad

During the Habbaniya-to-Fallujah phase the RAF had kept up its attacks on Baghdad. On 20 May Freya Stark watched a heavy attack, counting twenty-six RAF aircraft: 'Over Rashid [airbase] the bombers sail and dip and the dull noise follows; they circle in far wide curves in the early sky. One fighter flies the whole length of New Street almost touching the minarets, dropping leaflets, and the first burst of ground fire comes only from the line of defence in north Baghdad.'[51]

With the 10th Indian Division, now commanded by Major-General William Slim, only ordered to advance north from the Basra area on 25 May, it was decided to press ahead with Brigadier Kingstone's 1,450 men (including around 250 men of the Arab Legion) who had come from Habbaniya via Fallujah. The most obvious and therefore best-defended route to the capital was from the west along the Fallujah road. Another option was an approach from the south, through Karbala, or to come from the north along the Mosul road. The British banked on the Iraqis thinking they were in much greater number than they actually were, and wanted to keep them guessing as to the direction from which the main attack would develop.

The advance of Kingcol on Baghdad commenced on 27 May. Brigadier Kingstone was now firmly in charge. He struck across the Fallujah plain to Khan Nuqta, while a column of the Household Cavalry went to the main road from Mosul north of the city, around 700 men per force. The Arab Legion cut the Mosul–Baghdad railway and RAF armoured cars chased the enemy from Taji station, activities that, according to Glubb, provided Rashid Ali with a real shock as the capital was cut off from the north.[52] On the evening of 27 May the northern force camped 6 miles from Baghdad, though met stiff resistance the following day. In the south, on the same day,

Slim's two brigades moved north along the Euphrates and Tigris and captured Ur, 80 miles east of Basra. Severely hampering progress from the south, however, the Iraqis had not only created floods but had removed hundreds of railway sleepers. For its part, Kingcol's advance to Baghdad was greatly hindered by the destruction of the road bridges over the canals carried out by the retreating Iraqis, and the extensive flooding caused by the opening of the Abu Ghuraib regulator. It is worth reflecting on the issue of flooding, because it is easy to overlook just how significant an obstacle it was to military operations. There was a real risk, for example, of the rear of Kingcol being marooned as the waters rose. Fortunately, some water was allowed to escape when locals, whose crops were threatened, opened another bund. Travelling with Wavell for a meeting with Auchinleck at Basra at this time, Peter Coats, Wavell's ADC, described how they flew along the southern oil pipeline so as to avoid German aircraft in the north, 'which they say are numerous and aggressive'.[53] 'Finally we reached the Euphrates (or Tigris – they look exactly alike). Both were flooded, making the already hideous country of Iraq one vast and inattractive duck-pond. What a terrain for warfare!'[54] When Lieutenant-General Quinan stated that his priority was securing the Basra base and that a move on Baghdad might take up to three months because of the flooding, Wavell felt fully justified in his gloomy assessment of the situation in Iraq.

Nevertheless, British forces were approaching Baghdad from the west, though hardly in strength. Kingstone seized the fort at Khan Nuqta first thing on 28 May and arrived at the demolished bridge over the Abu Ghuraib canal on Baghdad's outskirts. The British had now left the desert behind, and entered a region irrigated by dykes and canals, with thick scrub. On the same day, Fritz Grobba sent a desperate message to Berlin reporting the arrival of British forces at the gates of Baghdad with 100 tanks, a false rumour put about by Kingcol's enterprising intelligence officer, Somerset de Chair. By the evening of 28 May the northern column had reached Taji and was advancing on the Khadhimain railway station. Here it was held up, though it was to prove valuable in threatening Baghdad from a different direction and further demoralizing the enemy.

On 29 May Kingstone's troops were engaging Iraqi positions in front of Baghdad.[55] Fortunately, Iraqi opposition was only slight and by nightfall on 30 May the column had reached a point only 3 miles from the iron bridge over the Washash Channel on the outskirts of Baghdad West. It had been assisted by constant air reconnaissance and occasional close support bombing, and on 30 May very heavy bombing attacks with screaming bombs were launched on the Washash and Rashid camps, and on Iraqi troop positions in the vicinity of the Kadhimain railway station.

Air power remained a decisive factor. The RAF's close air support had been vital in the campaign so far, and had had a devastating effect on morale as Iraqi resistance weakened. On 29 May there was some air combat and enemy transports north-west of Ramadi were machine-gunned, along with boats observed on Lake Habbaniya. On the following day RAF Habbaniya flew forty-two sorties, bombing troop concentrations and transports around Kadhimain in support of forward British formations on Baghdad's outskirts. There was a mass leaflet drop over the capital, and a large fire was started at the motor transport depot at Rashid airbase. On 30 May Habbaniya's aircrew flew twenty-nine sorties concentrating on a heavy bombing attack on Rashid and Washash, attacks made with screaming bombs 'which proved most effective', with aircraft of 94 Squadron escorting the bombers. 84 Squadron, meanwhile, performed reconnaissance flights over Ramadi, Hit, Mahmudiya, Musayyib and Karbala, and conducted a photo reconnaissance of Mosul and the K2 pumping station.[56]

As British forces approached the capital, the rebel Iraqi regime disintegrated. With the city seemingly surrounded, Rashid Ali, the Grand Mufti, Grobba and the officers of the Golden Square scattered. It was left to the Mayor of Baghdad to sue for peace, and wireless sets were returned to the embassy. 'After this,' wrote Freya Stark, 'in a sort of golden mist of sunset our bombers and fighters came sailing: they came in troops and societies, their outline sharp in the luminous sky: they separated and circled and dived, going vertically down at dreadful speed, like swordfish of the air.'[57] A message was received at RAF Habbaniya from the British Embassy, just reconnected, requesting that an Iraqi flag of truce accompanied by an embassy representative should be received as soon as possible at the iron bridge. 'As soon as we got this message,' wrote Smart, 'both the GOC [General Clark] and I decided to go ourselves to the Iron Bridge to meet the Iraqi Envoys', the commanding officers keen to be in at the kill.[58] A signal was sent to the ambassador fixing a time of 0400 on 31 May for the car with the flag of truce to be at the rendezvous. It was in this vehicle that de Chair entered the capital and pulled up at the embassy. Cornwallis, stirred from sleep, greeted him in his dressing gown and cummerbund, but he was soon kitted out in a white drill suit topped with solar topee and they were speeding back to the iron bridge.[59]

The Mayor of Baghdad led the Iraqi delegation, accompanied by Cornwallis. In the cold light of dawn, the terms of the armistice were agreed. The Iraqi army was permitted to retain its weapons though was to return forthwith to its normal peacetime stations, and Ramadi was to be evacuated. All POWs and civilian internees were to be released, and all German and Italian personnel and equipment were to be detained by the Iraqi government. Fighting ceased at 0430, and the armistice was signed. Prince Regent Abdulillah and his entourage had already returned to Iraq in a procession of vehicles purchased in Palestine with the intention of drumming up support for his return to Baghdad, and were waiting in the wings at RAF Habbaniya, where the party was billeted in the Imperial Airways building that had been smashed up by the Iraqi army. Now, Abdulillah returned to Baghdad and resumed the regency. The Iraqi army was allowed to retire, 'many of them deceived by their leader and not in fact disloyal'.[60] This was a wise move, and made ensuing relations better than they might otherwise have been.

Knabesnhue reported on events to Washington. At 1430 on 30 May the Mayor of Baghdad 'telephoned to inform me Rashid Ali and Axis group had left Iraq and that he headed a temporary Government to bring [the] conflict to an end'. He invited foreign diplomatic chiefs to his office. 'I went first accompanied by Commandant Police to see the British Ambassador and thence with his Counsellor to the Mayor's office'.[61] At the British Embassy, the armistice led to an 'absolute orgy of activity all over the Chancery with typists flying in and out'.[62] The embassy resembled 'a railway station: officers from Habbaniya, colonels from Basra, Cawthorn from Cairo, Iraqis, people here leaving, cars scrunching, cawasses returning'.[63] Members of the embassy community were told to wear their solar topees, presumably in an attempt to bolster British prestige rather than as a precaution against sunstroke.

Captain Sowerby of the 2nd Battalion the Essex Regiment, part of Habforce, had what he termed an 'exciting night' on the day the armistice was signed. In a letter to a friend he boasted that he 'had had the satisfaction of being blooded in this war, though against the Iraqi rebels and not the Hun'.[64] Arriving in Iraq his battalion had marched 50 miles in three days in full service marching order. 'Then we had a few weeks of civilization and when the Iraqi show burst forth we were the first Company away and left barracks within an hour of receiving notice and were front line troops until after Rutbah and again later on … We had several scraps with very few casualties'. On the eve of the armistice, Sowerby:

had to get a message to the Hq outside Baghdad, with the instructions for the reception of the envoys. I had two hours to do 25 miles of desert and 8 miles of flooded tarmac and then find the Hq which I was given to understand would probably be near the road and somewhere near Baghdad! Just as I got into the floods an outpost sentry told me that the road had been under heavy shell and MG fire all day, to cheer me up I suppose! I nearly overshot our front line but luckily spotted an Ambulance in time.

Finally locating the headquarters, Sowerby 'panted in to the Brigadier', Joe Kingstone, only to discover that his message had already been received as wireless communications had been re-established. 'I managed to scrounge some tea though!' he wrote.

Sowerby's cheery tone reflected the fact that imperial ground forces had had a relatively easy campaign and suffered minimal losses. 'For us it was but another campaign along the eastern marches of our Empire', wrote de Chair; 'for them it was a war against the whole distracted might of Britain.'[65] British land and air forces had carried the day through resolute action, speed and deception. The armistice was finally forced by the small British contingent of approximately 1,400 men that had come from Habbaniya to Baghdad, with very little artillery or armour. As Freya Stark wrote, 'we have done this with only two battalions': the battle had been won by a 'colossal bluff'.[66]

Accounting for Iraq's defeat

Though Baghdad had been taken by legerdemain, the British had fought an excellent campaign and many factors accounted for the final result. The campaign's most striking feature was the remarkable stand of the RAF's No. 4 Flying Training School at Habbaniya. Using obsolete aircraft, a handful of experienced pilots and their inexperienced pupils lifted a siege by about 9,000 Iraqi troops, crippled German aircraft sent to the country and destroyed most Iraqi air assets before taking the fight to Baghdad via Fallujah. By holding out and then going over to the offensive, RAF Habbaniya bought crucial time for imperial relief forces from Palestine and India to concentrate and then deploy. In achieving this, Habbaniya was ably assisted by the air assets based at RAF Shaibah: the RAF had flown 1,600 sorties. Special forces had also played a role, with agents from the British Secret Intelligence Service (SIS) and Special Operations Executive (SOE), and even Palestinian Jews recruited by SOE from the Irgun, undertaking sabotage missions: fuel dumps were targeted and sixteen newly arrived, American-built Northrop aircraft belonging to the Iraqi air force were destroyed on the ground. The Arab Legion played an unobtrusive but important role:

> Glubb's desert patrol was a talisman among the bedouin [sic], who would otherwise have molested our straggling supply column, thin-drawn out across the blinding desert, and have raided our solitary outposts along the route. In the event, we had no trouble from the tribes, who remained amicable with so many cousins under our flag, while the town dwellers of Iraq were loathing us with deadly passion.[67]

To stand any chance of winning, the Iraqis needed to have eliminated the British at Habbaniya. As it was, though the airbase's Assyrian and British churches were damaged along with messes and billets, the all-important water tower and power generator escaped unscathed and RAF aircraft never ceased using its runways for offensive purposes.[68] Perhaps more importantly, if the Iraqis could have removed the British from Basra and blocked the Shatt al-Arab, they could have prevented British reinforcement by sea. Mahmood al-Durrah, a member of Rashid Ali's government, ascribed defeat to a range of interconnected factors. The four members of the Golden Square, each in command of a major army unit or air force group, had pursued their own political ambitions and tribal interests.[69] 'As there was no overall command and control of Iraqi forces,' he wrote, 'their military fate was sealed.' There was then the fact that no clear objectives had been provided to army group commanders except to be prepared to defend their regions. In contrast 'the British had clear objectives that included securing Basra first and secondarily the airfield at Habbaniya.'[70] There were other reasons for defeat, stemming in part from ministerial indecision at the beginning of May, which enabled the British to break out of Habbaniya before the Germans arrived. The Germans had warned Ali that they could not act to full effect before they had wound up their occupation of Crete and built up their air force and associated supply lines to Iraq. This indecision was caused by a split in the Iraqi ruling clique and also within the army. Essentially, the Iraqis went to war a month too early, and thus had to do without the German assistance that they were depending upon. Al-Durrah also highlighted the quality of British intelligence about the Iraqi forces, particularly as British officers had been employed in the army and air force as advisers and instructors until only weeks before fighting broke out.

A mordant critic of the Anglo-Iraqi Treaty, Rashid Ali was later to write that he saw German battlefield success as a golden opportunity. 'Believe me, I was ready for an alliance with the devil to get hold of the weapons I needed for the army to fight British troops.'[71] But he blamed failure on the lack of Axis support, and 'bitterly concluded that as a puppet in Germany's game he was not even of sufficient importance to receive her whole-hearted support'.[72]

General Ismay offered a succinct appraisal from the British point of view a fortnight after the armistice. 'I think we were lucky to get away with Iraq so lightly – assuming that we have got away with it. India played up splendidly in getting troops to Basra in record time, and forcing Rashid to fire the mine before his Axis friends were ready.'[73] Vice-Chief of the Imperial General Staff, Lieutenant-General Sir Henry Pownall, reached a similar conclusion:

> There are, however, plenty of indications that the German timetable has gone wrong and is at least a month in arrear. Crete added to those delays. The most important result so far is the obvious fact that their plans for Iraq have miscarried. Gailani went off at half cock, and too soon. Crete prevented the Germans from giving him any effectual aid and we are now back in Baghdad, Rashid and his confederates having fled to Persia.[74]

The Germans proved to be possibly the harshest critics of their own performance. General Franz Halder, head of the supreme high command of the German army, described the Iraq venture as a lesson in how things should not be done. 'German efforts to exploit the Arab nationalist movements against Britain lacked a solid foundation. Occupied by other problems more akin to his nature, Hitler had expended too little interest on the political and psychological currents prevalent in the Arab world.'[75] The German high command, he wrote, had been taken by surprise by Rashid Ali's coup.

> In the diplomatic, propaganda, and military fields, Germany had neglected to prepare the ground for a serious threat to Britain in the area . . . Germany's belated and feeble efforts were doomed to failure from the outset against a Britain served by an excellently functioning intelligence service, valuable bases, and immediately available military forces . . . Secret doubts as to the possibility of success for German military improvisations in the Arab regions probably contributed toward the remarkable degree of inactivity displayed by the top levels of German

command ... [N]o uniformly thought out plan was developed for the exploitation of the Arab nationalist movements.[76]

The Luftwaffe, leading Germany's military support for Rashid Ali, was woefully late. Luftwaffe general Hellmuth Felmy had reached Aleppo on 1 June. By that time reports of British units fast approaching Mosul – false, as it turned out – meant that German aircraft were leaving for Syria. They then left Syria for Greece, as reports suggested that the British would invade Syria if the Germans remained. The temporary loan of French airbases in Syria had already given the British an excellent excuse to invade. 'The chief reason for the failure of the Germans to provide the Iraqis with adequate assistance in their struggle against the British was the lack of political fore-sight shown by the German Government.' But it would have been helpful if the Iraqis had made an arrangement before starting the revolt, wrote Felmy, with measured understatement.

There were more general reasons too for the failure of the original coup: the brief war turned out not only to be a lesson in the ineffectualness of the Iraqi army and air force, but testament to the Iraqi government's isolation. There was little popular support for the movement to evict the British. 'The government received no support from the Shia majority, who had been alienated by the brutal suppression of the rising in the Euphrates region in 1935–36. Nor was it supported by the Kurds, who were bitter at their failure to achieve autonomy or even a fair allocation of official posts in their region.'[77] The great majority of Iraqis were not 'particularly involved in the plight of the government':

> Despite calls for *jihad* by a number of clerics and despite the best endeav-
> ours of the government media, those sections of the Iraqi population
> which might have made a difference to the military outcome – the Shi'i
> tribes of the south and the Kurdish population of the north – failed to
> respond to the government's rallying cry. On the contrary, in many cases
> Kurdish and Shi'i tribal leaders assisted the British forces.[78]

Shiite tribes in the south did not support Rashid Ali, and remained resentful of the suppression of the Euphrates rising of 1935–36; troops stationed in the north did not move; desertions increased as the campaign progressed; and the sentiments of villagers and townspeople became increasingly luke-warm, if they had ever been warm at all.[79]

Rashid Ali's movement was 'not in favour of fundamental changes in the economy, society, or political structure of Iraq'.[80] All leaders were part of a small Sunni ruling clique, and were nationalists, not social reformers. The coup, according to Daniel Silverfarb, was a dispute within the governing class. Rashid Ali's administration did not differ from previous ones, containing the same people. This 'reduced its ability to mobilize large-scale popular support for the war effort ... Their history of rapacity and indifference to the problems of the poor made them ill suited for the role of leaders of a truly national resistance.'[81] Rashid Ali had also done nothing to win over the allegiance of most Shiites or to develop a strong Iraqi national identity able to take precedence over local, tribal or religious loyalties.

During the course of the conflict 'important Shiite tribal leaders in southern Iraq offered their services to the British'.[82] The Kurds were also alienated from the government. Their leader Sheikh Mahmud, who since the early 1920s had been calling himself 'King of Kurdistan' and agitating for independence as envisaged by the Treaty of Sèvres (for which he had been bombed by the RAF), capitalized on the upheaval by repudiating government authority and offering friendship with Britain. Rashid Ali had been prime minister at time of the Assyrian massacres in 1933, so he was not popular with that community. Also, while most Iraqis may not have welcomed the British, they were hardly going to risk their lives for the sake of Rashid Ali's government.

To poor leadership and poor-quality forces must be added effective leadership on the British side, along with fighting quality and spirit. In many ways, the campaign was meat-and-drink to the forces of the British Empire, blending improvisation with an understanding of the precepts of imperial defence, a system that, at the end of the day, functioned as it was supposed to. Forces, in sufficient strength to do what was necessary, were either already present or subsequently deployed in time. Nevertheless, in spite of Iraqi deficiencies and British skill, things might have been very different had not Hitler missed the bus. The pessimistic appreciations in London before the campaign were well founded. General Ismay wrote that 'it was clear that Habbaniya must succumb to any serious attack unless it was immediately reinforced'.[83] 'It is difficult to know why', therefore:

> the Germans let such a golden opportunity slip through their hands. If they had sent a military mission to Baghdad directly Rashid Ali usurped power, they could have vitalised the Iraqi Army and arranged for their

reinforcement by German aircraft and possibly air borne troops. Habbaniya could have been overwhelmed without much difficulty and the troops at Basrah compelled to evacuate the country ... We were in fact saved from a disaster of some magnitude by the ineptitude of the German High Command. One can only suppose that their minds were full of the impending attack on Russia.[84]

Hitler had had a viable option to use General Kurt Student's air corps against Iraq, working through the Dodecanese, instead of against Crete. What was sent to Iraq was far too little and far too late. Even what arrived was quickly shot up by the British; by the end of May, Junck had lost fourteen Messerschmitts and five Heinkels, 'an overall loss of 95 per cent of his original fighter and bomber strength'.[85] At the end of hostilities, Smart reported that British forces found twenty-one damaged and unserviceable German and Italian aircraft at Mosul, Kirkuk, Rashid and elsewhere that had either been shot down or force-landed.

German Middle East experts and military personnel involved on the ground lamented Germany's failures. In his memoirs Fritz Grobba wrote that 'the rejection of every unilateral German initiative in the Arab region was due to the fact that Hitler's enemies at the Foreign Office worked against any expanding of the war to the Middle East. In part, they did not recognize the opportunity there and in part obstructed it.'[86] The Italian position was also a spanner in the works. The terms of the Rome–Berlin Axis obliged officials in Berlin to refrain from taking any lead in Arab affairs. Furthermore, Germany wanted to avoid liberation movements in the Levant and destabilizing relations with Vichy France. According to Fritz Grobba:

> The Iraq conflict offered Germany a unique opportunity to gain a foothold behind the British frontline in the Middle East from which to launch a very effective pincer operation against Egypt and the Caucasus. Successful German operations on Iraq and Egypt would have opened the way to India and, by posing a serious threat to India, would have created favourable conditions for an agreement with England. Churchill writes about the Iraq conflict: 'Hitler certainly rejected a brilliant opportunity to gain a great prize in the Middle East with a minimum of investment.'

This opportunity was not recognized in time by influential policymakers at the Foreign Office and the Army High Command, and was, in part due to their opposition to Hitler, consciously not seized upon. The lack of understanding of the Middle East on the part of high-level German authorities, together with the potential opportunities arising from exploiting indigenous movements, had already come to the fore in the First World War.[87]

There is no doubt that the German response was muted because Iraq was not the focus of attention. Preparation for the imminent invasion of the Soviet Union was everything, and locally, paratroops, transport aircraft and large numbers of fighter aircraft and bombers were tied up in Crete. Turkey blocked the overland route, and many influential Germans were reluctant to get sucked into a campaign where Britain had good forces in the field and where German forces would have to operate so far from their own bases in Greece and the Dodecanese. They were keen, however, to maintain prestige and tie down British troops. The Iraqis had 46,000 troops and 12,000 police, mostly armed, at the start of the campaign, and they sued for an armistice when they still had 20,000 troops available for the defence of Baghdad and 15,000 in the vicinity of Mosul. More Germans were on the way, and in Athens large quantities of arms were being prepared for shipment. In his forensic study of Anglo-Iraqi relations, Daniel Silverfarb hits the nail on the head as to why Iraq lost: first, he writes, to 'a considerable extent Britain's rapid and complete victory in the campaign was due to Germany's failure to act quicker and in greater strength.'[88] Second, and perhaps most tellingly, Rashid Ali should not have hesitated, and should have wiped out Habbaniya – he failed 'to cross the threshold from a diplomatic challenge and a military maneuver into open warfare.'[89]

'In the end the Axis was too distant and uninterested actually to provide the wedge the officers sought, and British naval and air power too close and easily deployed, so that it could secure the former colony for British war aims.'[90] Historian Simon Davis claims that diplomatic frictions between the Abwehr and the SD, along with the Crete campaign, delayed Hitler's orders for three weeks; Vichy cooperation, vital for access via Lebanon and Syria, was confirmed too late to prevent Iraq's surrender, despite German agents securing arms and airfields and a Luftwaffe base at Mosul. Correspondence between General Ismay and the biographer John Connell offers a different angle. Connell wrote that Wavell criticized himself 'very strongly for what he thinks were his mistakes over the Iraq episode ... [and] gives generous credit to Winston and the C. O. S. for their attitude.'[91] In his reply, Ismay said that he had 'only recently heard' why the Luftwaffe failed to intervene:

A train load of high octane fuel which the Germans dispatched for the use of their aircraft in Iraq, not only arrived at Mosul from Germany three weeks late owing to obstruction planned by the Turks, but when it got there it was found that the tank cars were full of water. They had been drained of petrol and refilled with water by our friends of the Turkish Air Force, while the train was standing in a siding alongside the Adana Airfield.[92]

Wavell might justly be permitted the final word. The relief of Habbaniya and advance on Baghdad, he wrote, 'was a remarkable bit of work by George Clark and Kingstone. I must say I very much doubted whether the bluff, for it was almost entirely bluff, would succeed.'[93]

The *Farhud*

The collapse of government authority at the end of the Anglo-Iraqi war led to a brief period of violence, in which Baghdad endured a wave of looting and disorder. Most notably, the Jewish community was targeted on 1–2 June. This was the *farhud*, a term used from the very start, meaning a breakdown of law and order imperilling life and property. When Rashid Ali fled the capital, Yunis al-Sabawi, the cabinet minister and leader of several small Nazi groups, declared himself governor of central and southern Iraq. He told the president of the Jewish community, Sason Khduri, that all Jews should stay indoors for three days. The Committee of Internal Security formed by Baghdad's mayor then deported Yunis and declared all youth movements dissolved and ordered all weapons to be handed in.

When the regent returned, many Jews were pleased, some going to the airport to welcome him. They also hoped to celebrate Shavuot, the Feast of Weeks, to be held that year on 1–2 June.[94] The violence appears to have started when a busload of Baghdadi Jews, returning from the airport, were attacked and murdered. Police, civilians, troops and slum-dwellers from Karkh on the other side of the Tigris soon joined the carnage. Jews were killed along with non-Jewish civilians as the authorities attempted to restore order. Tragically, the British units that had forced the surrender of Baghdad were not asked to intervene, and did not do so of their own volition. The regent did not order the Iraqi army to quell the unrest given its highly volatile state in the aftermath of its defeat, and the fact that it was suffused with pro-German, anti-British and anti-regent sentiment. He did, however, order Kurdish troops of the Northern Division to come to the capital. The anti-Jewish and Nazi-style clubs and societies that had formed before the war were the key instigators of the violence, and soldiers, policemen and young men imbued with a hatred of Jews were responsible for the murders. Things were made worse in Baghdad, because Jews there lived in a segregated quarter, unlike in other towns and cities, and so were more easily targeted. Freya Stark heard reports of between a dozen and 500 deaths, and Abdullah Ezra said that he was 'wading in blood' up Ghazi Street.[95] This orgy of violence, in which Jewish homes and businesses were ransacked and looted, led to the deaths of around 200 people and injury to over 1,000.[96]

There were other examples of anti-Semitic persecution, and things had generally been difficult for Jews across the country during the coup period, when there had been anti-British and anti-Jewish demonstrations. British political advisers recorded the popularity of Berlin radio broadcasts in private houses in Zubair near Basra. Their 'anti-Jewish attitude is regarded favourably by the Zubairis who are the trade rivals of the Jews in Basra'. In Basra, a date trader sheltered 200 Jewish Iraqis in his house during the looting.[97] The fact that the British were occupying Basra reduced the number of casualties too, though apparently some Gurkha soldiers also took part in the looting.[98] In Fallujah, RAF Assyrian Levies looted homes indiscriminately. A key role in suppressing the looting in Basra was played by a Muslim trader who set guards. In May the Iraqi troops at Ezra's Tomb in Al-Uzair 'claimed that the Jews there were British spies and sent them all at short notice with only hand luggage to Amara'. When the people returned in June after the conclusion of hostilities, all their property had been looted.[99]

Though these terrible events represented the worst of the post-conflict violence, there was a lot of strife still to come, as Iraq settled down to what amounted to a British occupation under a restored government, with the difficulties and recriminations that such a situation was bound to breed.

CHAPTER 6

Mopping up and de-Nazification

Victory in Iraq secured what Auchinleck dubbed an 'absolutely vital outpost' of imperial defence.[1] Now Britain needed to mop up, get forces into position in key strategic locations and prepare to defend Iraq from German or Soviet attack – or to lay waste to its vital infrastructure in a scorched-earth withdrawal should an enemy appear in irresistible force. Lieutenant-General Quinan was instructed by GHQ India to accomplish three tasks. First, he was to 'develop and organize the port of Basra ... to enable it to maintain such forces as may be required to operate in the Middle East, including Egypt, Turkey, [and] Iraq.'[2] Second, to secure control of all means of communication and develop them. Third, to take measures to protect the Basra base and RAF installations at Habbaniya and Shaibah, the Kirkuk oilfields, the pipeline to Haifa and the lives of British subjects in Baghdad and elsewhere. Beyond Iraq, Quinan was also to make plans for the defence of the Anglo-Iranian Oil Company installations in south-west Iran. For its part, America kept an eye on developments here. For its own strategic purposes, it had to contemplate the prospect of significant British reverses, and assess areas in which it could aid Britain without compromising its non-belligerent status. Iraq was one of them. W. Averell Harriman, Roosevelt's special envoy to Europe and a key Lend-Lease coordinator, visited Baghdad and Basra on 6 July 1941 to see how America could help build up the presence at the head of the Gulf if Britain were forced to leave the Suez Canal Zone, as the Anglo-Americans came to envisage the development here of an enormous supply base capable of handling weapons and military supplies for distribution to formations fighting in the Middle East and beyond.[3]

In the broader context of the war, Britain's position remained extremely vulnerable – especially when Hitler took the decision to invade the Soviet Union, launching Operation Barbarossa on 22 June 1941, less than three weeks after the surrender of Baghdad. The Germans retained a very active interest in the region, and an expectation that it would soon be theirs, despite the disappointing result of the Anglo-Iraqi war. Hitler's Directive 32, 'Preparations for the time after Barbarossa', promulgated on 30 June, envisaged continued pressure on Britain's position in the Middle East from Egypt, from Bulgaria through Turkey and from Transcaucasia through Iran.[4] In the following month, Field Marshal von Brauchitsch, Commander-in-Chief of the German army, sent OKW a detailed plan for these operations.[5] Iraq remained in Germany's crosshairs.

Reflecting the danger of invasion, the British immediately began enacting plans for a scorched-earth retreat once they had taken over Iraq. Extensive plans were drawn up to destroy oil wells and vital infrastructure to stop them falling into German hands should the worst happen.[6] The scheme was considered urgent and began as early as May 1941, with 200 army engineers being diverted from other important projects in order to supervise the work. By August the British had junked – rendered inoperable – forty-five of the fifty-five wells at Kirkuk. So too at Ayn Zalah, Qayyarah (except for the one producing bitumen for the construction of British airfields) and Naft Khana. The wells were not fired, as the British hoped to reconquer the area and did not want to attract Iraqi attention. All of this represented work both of a specialist and dangerous nature. Sapper Jim Hancock was part of the Royal Engineers team responsible for oil denial, an operation that he insisted was called, formally or informally, Operation Chinese Junk. During this mission a well exploded, killing three of his colleagues:

Jim survived but was unable to see and crawled around the scene for a few days finding various body parts of his comrades who had all died. He also lost all his teeth in the explosion and his back was badly injured. After some time alone in the desert, he was picked up by a unit of the 4th Indian Division. He was covered in oil and sunburnt and his rescuers did not, at first, think he was a European.[7]

Both of Hancock's eyes were removed in a field hospital.

Drilling equipment and other essential machinery was removed from the country or destroyed. The British also made plans for the destruction of railway lines and the evacuation of rolling stock along with roads, bridges, communications infrastructure and water sources. Should the invader come, they would resort to flooding in order to hamper his advance, inundating some parts of the country while drying up other parts. All of this was done without Iraqi knowledge or permission.[8]

Barbarossa brought German forces a dramatic step closer to the Iran–Iraq region. While the British made extensive preparations for defence against external foes, internal sources of insecurity remained. To insure against further combustion inside Iraq, the British, in league with the restored Iraqi government, began a purge of pro-Nazi elements in the political elite and the military. They downsized the army, having contemplated disbanding it altogether, while significantly expanding the size of the RAF Iraq Levies.[9] But as well as danger, British victory in the Anglo-Iraqi war brought new opportunity. With imperial forces now present in strength inside Iraq, the British contemplated moving against equally suspect regimes in neighbouring Iran and Syria.

Casualties and compensation

In the aftermath of the Anglo-Iraqi war, with the dead buried, it did not take long before claims for compensation began to arrive at the British Embassy in Baghdad. Casualty figures are difficult to gauge with accuracy, even more so for the wounded than for the dead, and for civilians, usually killed or injured as a result of bombing or artillery fire. On the British side they numbered in the tens, not the hundreds; on that of the Iraqis, between 500 and 1,000 were killed – though some put the figure well in excess of 2,000 – and many more were wounded.

A gruesome post-conflict task was the exhumation of Iraqi dead, a process undertaken with great care because the bodies were decomposing.[10] Grieving relatives wanted their sons' and husbands' bodies returned so that traditional customs and burial rites could be observed. There were scores of graves on the plateau overlooking RAF Habbaniya and at least eighty in the vicinity of the village of Sin al-Dhibban. In the aftermath of battle, British burial return officers had listed the names of the dead soldiers, their religion and date of burial, and drew sketch maps of the locations of the graves. Each burial site was marked with an upturned bottle containing the dead man's personal effects and papers concerning religious and other particulars.

The archives offer fragmentary evidence regarding the range of civilian casualties. For instance, an Iraqi national employed by the British Embassy had been accused of being a spy. Because of this his shop was looted by followers of Rashid Ali, and on 2 May, while washing the embassy's motor launch, he had been accosted and beaten up.[11] More serious was the case of Guairry ibn Sarhan, who lived in the railway quarters of Baghdad West, near the Rashid airbase. He wrote to the British Embassy stating that on 7 May an RAF bomb had killed his mother, wife and four small children on the spot. Death certificates from the Iraqi Royal Hospital were attached, and he sought compensation for the loss of his family. Despite the tragedy, a note on the letter said that paying compensation would create a 'dangerous precedent'. 'We can do nothing officially of course,' wrote the official, but 'Do you think that from the propaganda point of view Colonel Astor might be asked to look into it and hand out a dinar or two if he thinks it a deserving case?'[12]

Businesses that suffered as a result of the conflict also made claims. The construction firm Balfour Beatty requested recompense for damage caused when its Ramadi offices were looted. No item was too small to be omitted; soup ladles, bed-sheets, napkins, typewriters, wicker chairs, shaving mirrors, dessert forks, lavatory brushes and a solitary cheese dish with cover all appeared on the itemized claim. There were also claims from the British Overseas Airways Corporation, whose headquarters building on the shore of Lake Habbaniya had been vandalized by the Iraqi army; 'a more devastated place it would have been difficult to imagine,' wrote Somerset de Chair when his unit camped there in the aftermath.[13] The British Oil Development Company, the Rafidain Oil Company and contractors working for the Iraqi government's Irrigation Department all put in claims too.[14] Claims from American nationals were also submitted to the British authorities.[15]

Local businesses joined the queue of those seeking financial compensation. A general contractor from Mustansir Street near the Tigris in central Baghdad had a contract to supply fresh mutton and beef to RAF Habbaniya. He was in the process of making a delivery when the fighting supervened.[16] On 29 April three shepherds, acting on the instructions of the airbase's imaginatively titled Officer-in-Charge Butchery, drove 582 sheep towards Fallujah, crossing the bridge over the Euphrates on 1 May. The men, Khasan al-Aziz, Amanah Ibu Ibrahim and Abood ibn Dhebab, soon reached al-Hamra. But here they were intercepted and detained, along with their flock, by the Iraqi army. Subsequently beaten, they fled for their lives. John Chaplin's brusque embassy note decreed that compensation could not be funded.[17] Other claimants met with similar responses. A Palestinian firm submitted a claim for a quantity of olive oil that had been in transit through Iraq to Australia when it was destroyed by military action at Ramadi. The British authorities denied responsibility, arguing that the conflict had been caused by Iraqi aggression.[18]

The British did, however, make payments to the dependents of RAF employees killed during the conflict. These included eighteen Assyrian, Iranian, Iraqi and Indian men who lost their lives as a result of the Iraqi shelling and bombing of Habbaniya. They had variously been employed as clerks, storekeepers, labourers and carpenters.[19] The Claims Committee also received appeals from civilians whose houses had been destroyed by RAF bombs in Fallujah and then allegedly looted by Assyrian troops of the RAF Iraq Levies.[20] In February 1942 the Iraqi government sought financial aid from Britain because of the 'unusual expenditure' caused by the events of the previous year and war-related inflation. It had spent 120,000 Iraqi dinars on compensation for British subjects, 150,000 on payments to people who had suffered because of excessive flooding – much of it caused by the Iraqi army – 150,000 on bonuses to state employees in light of the high cost of living, 300,000 for the Ministry of Defence covering the costs of the war and 120,000 for the police.[21]

Showing the flag, mopping up and invading Syria

From the British government's perspective, the political position in Iraq 'cleared up with the flight of Rashid Ali and his Government'. On 3 June 1941 the Foreign Office sent a telegram to the Soviet government, repeated to Ankara, Tehran and Cairo, heralding Britain's victory. The action taken in Iraq, it stated, was 'only one example of our determination to maintain our position throughout the Middle East', including in Iran and Afghanistan. The Germans were 'scheming' in those places and attempting to set British interests against those of the Soviet Union; Britain was determined to show resolution.[22] The brisk campaign served as a warning to the Axis, to Moscow and to local leaders throughout the world who thought to prosper while Britain's attention was concentrated elsewhere.

Nevertheless, to those on the ground in Iraq things did not feel quite so secure. Somerset de Chair, in Baghdad in the immediate aftermath of the armistice, felt that at any moment the Iraqi army might resume hostilities, especially if they realized how small the force that had defeated them was. De Chair noted the anger and resentment directed towards him and, with thousands of Iraqi soldiers still around, feared a mousetrap. Out on a limb, de Chair spent days in Baghdad after the armistice as Brigadier Kingstone's personal liaison officer to the embassy. He was given three codes to be used in the event of trouble: 'Brigadier come', which would summon Kingstone from the British encampment outside the city; 'Casano come', which would bring Squadron Leader Casano and his armoured cars racing into the capital; and 'All come', 'which meant the whole shooting match'.[23]

Concerns regarding a reignition of hostilities were heightened because of the still very strong belief that the Germans were going to win the war, and that therefore the armistice was not an end to hostilities, merely a pause. Glubb Pasha, leader of the Arab Legion, insisted that the vast majority of people believed at the time of the Anglo-Iraqi war that Germany would win the world war; even his soldiers, though fighting valiantly for the British cause, believed this.[24] Given this, priority was given to 'show of force' activities deliberately mounted to impress upon the people that the British were there in numbers. Their objective was to offer reassurance, support the reinstalled regent and his government and deter those who were disposed to resent Britain's presence or conduct acts of 'brigandage' against its bases, lines of communication and oil pipelines.

De Chair breathed a sigh of relief when British forces eventually entered Baghdad in force. Led by Casano's armoured cars they crossed the iron bridge over the Washwash channel and encamped next to the Anglican church of St George's. The armoured cars were followed by the Blues and Royals, two companies of the Essex Regiment, a lengthy stream of heavy Royal Armoured Service Corps vehicles, the Bren gun carriers and, finally, 'the murderous snouts of the 25-pounders' and the ammunition limbers. It took over two hours for Kingcol to file in, watched by Iraqis with a 'dawning look of wonder' at this 'evidence of British striking power'.[25]

Troops fanned out across the country. Rupert Hardy took 'Harcol' 'racing across Iraq to show the Union Jack in the oilfields of Kirkuk', and the RAF undertook demonstration flights.[26] RAF aircraft flying between Habbaniya and Iran were explicitly ordered to pay special attention 'to formation flying over BAGHDAD and other towns' in an effort to impress the population with British air power. On land, the 20th Indian Infantry Brigade's journey up the Tigris was reported to have had 'a salutary effect on the population'.[27] In post-invasion Iraq, British imperial troops travelled in convoy on Iraq's roads and railways, through towns and across the desert. Large concentrations came to form around towns such as Kirkuk and Mosul, Basra was effectively under occupation and, more discreetly, Baghdad was garrisoned.

British troops had not been present in Iraq like this since the early 1920s, and it reminded people of the previous occupation.

The 20th Indian Infantry Brigade's progress north illustrates the manner in which British forces spread across the country. Formed from part of Slim's 10th Indian Division, now concentrated around Basra, the brigade had left Ur on 10 June to release Habforce for other duties by taking over its positions in Baghdad, Mosul, Kirkuk, Haditha and Rutbah. Elements of the 21st Indian Infantry Brigade, together with two troops from the 13th Lancers, one troop of the 15th Field Regiment and ancillary units, formed what was known as the Tigris column. Over 1,400-strong and travelling in 210 vehicles, the column proceeded by river as far as Kut al-Amara aboard steamers and barges, departing from Maqil on 11 June and reaching Kut on 17 June under naval escort. The British were firmly in control of Iraq's major towns, ports and lines of communication. On 18 June Slim was appointed to command the whole of northern Iraq.[28] His orders were to keep mobile troops round and about and prepare landing grounds in the Mosul province, and to make administrative arrangements for the maintenance of four RAF squadrons. Within two days his forces were spread across the Iraqi plain inside the Baghdad–Haditha–Mosul triangle.

Victory over Rashid Ali's government and the Iraqi military meant that the country could now be used by the British for their own strategic purposes in an unfettered manner and with the cooperation of the government. To the victor the spoils, and Iraq, now a British encampment, was used as a launch-pad for further military operations across the region. As well as conducting mopping-up operations in the weeks immediately following the end of hostilities and 'showing the flag', imperial troops began digging in to defend the region in anticipation of invasion.

When hostilities ended it was deemed essential to infuse British power into the north and prepare to meet a German or Soviet invasion. There was also a multitude of military tasks to be performed in the aftermath of the armistice. Even when ceasefires have been agreed, there is no guarantee that they are going to be observed by all military units: sometimes it takes time for news of the ceasefire to reach all commanders, and sometimes pockets of the erstwhile enemy are unprepared to accept the ceasefire and keen to continue hostilities. On 2 June, RAF units flew reconnaissance flights to check that Iraqi troops were retiring in accordance with the armistice. On the following day, six Blenheims of 84 Squadron escorted the DC-2s and Valentias of 31 Squadron as they conveyed a Gurkha battalion from Habbaniya to Mosul. This was John

Masters' unit, and its orders were to take over the city or capture it, 'according to circumstances.'[29] Units of the Household Cavalry and the King's Own Royal Regiment were airlifted from Habbaniya on 4 June. As well as securing the oil wells, this force was soon operating in Syria and attempting to capture Fritz Grobba, while another column – Mercol – headed for Haditha to engage irregular forces led by Fawzi al-Qawuqji, a prominent Iraqi officer who had resigned his commission to lead armed resistance during the Arab Revolt in Palestine between 1936 and 1939. Subsequently returning to Iraq and teaming up with the Grand Mufti and other nationalists, and in touch with the Germans through Fritz Grobba, he had led around 500 irregular troops during the Anglo-Iraqi war. Gocol and Harcol (as we have seen) were the names of other British flying columns tasked with securing Kirkuk, pursuing Grobba and fighting al-Qawuqji. On 8 June a small column proceeded to Tel Kotchek on the Syrian border. Finding no signs of German activity, they returned to Mosul. On 9 June, passing through Haditha, a flying column made contact with insurgent elements at Abu Kamal over the border in Syria.

With regimental headquarters located at Habbaniya, the Household Cavalry's 'B' Squadron went to Mosul, 'A' Squadron to K3 pumping station near Haditha on the Mosul–Haifa pipeline and 'C' Squadron to Kirkuk.[30] 'B' Squadron mounted patrols to both the Turkish and Iranian borders in the hope of capturing Rashid Ali and raided 60 miles into Syria to capture fleeing Germans. 'A' Squadron took part in the operations against al-Qawuqji, which succeeded in driving him and his 500 men out of Iraq into Syria. The regiment was then used to give the impression that an attack on Syria would develop from the Euphrates valley, as Britain planned its next invasion in the region.

This began on 8 June, as British forces invaded Lebanon and Syria from Iraq and Palestine. Auchinleck told Quinan that Syria took priority over securing southern Iran. Quinan's Iraq-based forces combined with largely Australian forces in Palestine to advance towards Beirut and Damascus (from Palestine) and Palmyra and Tripoli (from Iraq). Having been only a bit-part player in the Iraq campaign, Slim was now to share the centre stage. 'My division was suddenly transferred from the Iraq to Syria Command, and I was told to advance as speedily as possible up the Euphrates into Syria. The objective was the town of Deir-ez-zor, capital of eastern Syria.'[31]

For this invasion, Iraq's desert convoy route again came to the fore. Familiar challenges of distance, transport and supply faced Slim and his senior commanders as they launched into Syria from Iraqi bases: 'At Habbaniya, I was 300 miles from the objective, 500 from Aleppo.'[32] Fortunately, Slim had poached

Lieutenant-Colonel Alf Snelling from the line of communication forces and put him in charge of the division's logistics. Snelling was a master at 'pulling rabbits out of hats', as Slim described him.[33] Under Snelling's direction, the division employed Iraqi boats on the Euphrates, hired all available civilian lorries from Baghdad, and even dragooned village donkeys into service. Slim chose Haditha, 'a crumbling mud village on the river bank about half midway between Habbaniya and the French frontier, as my next base, and Snelling began, using every form of regular and irregular transport he could scrape up, to stock it with fifteen days' supplies for two brigade groups', and enough fuel for two lorry-borne brigade groups, an armoured regiment and an RAF squadron.[34] He moved his division's tactical headquarters to T1, the first pumping station on the now idle pipeline from the Iraqi oilfields to Tripoli. Slim's line of communication stretched from the Syrian border back to Baghdad.

From Habbaniya and their new base at Mosul the RAF mounted numerous long-ranging aerial reconnaissance and bombing missions across Iraq and into Syria and Lebanon in support of ground troops under Slim and the commanders invading from Palestine, backing, for example, imperial and Free French troops advancing on Damascus. There were many attacks on Aleppo and a detachment of Habbaniya's aircraft also opened a temporary base at Amman. Iraq-based RAF armoured cars also struck deep into Syria in support of the Household Cavalry, while Blenheim bombers from 4 Squadron based at RAF Habbaniya flew reconnaissance missions over Abu Kamal in southern Syria and observed Habforce in contact with enemy formations inside the Vichy-held territory.[35] Though Damascus fell to imperial and Free French forces on 21 June 1941, Vichy still held four-fifths of the country, including the major ports. The third and decisive thrust was made by the Indian troops stationed in Iraq. Slim's objective was the capture of Aleppo, thereby threatening the rear of Vichy forces in Beirut.

Troop numbers inside Iraq rose steadily as the British government prioritized the defence of the region against possible German invasion. The 25th Indian Infantry Brigade arrived, completing Slim's 10th Indian Division. In June the 17th Indian Infantry Brigade under Brigadier Douglas Gracey reached Basra and the 24th Indian Infantry Brigade under Brigadier R.E. Le Fleming also arrived, thus completing the 8th Indian Division. In September the 6th Indian Division, created at Secunderabad earlier in the year, landed, destined to spend its entire existence in Iran and Iraq, until disbanded at Basra in 1944.

The continued German threat to the region meant that extensive defences had to be developed and lines of communication improved and secured. Thousands of Iranian and Iraqi civilians were employed digging tank traps, roads, airfields and other military positions and defensive lines. Anti-aircraft defences in the key Basra–Abadan region were beefed up in case German bombers came within range, as well as in the Mosul area. Among them, Brigadier John Crumb's brigade was instructed to divert from its course to Singapore and disembark at Basra:

[The] abortive Nazi inspired revolt led by RASCHID ALI had been put down by the time the Brigade arrived in IRAQ, but the conditions were far from settled. HQ IRAQ FORCE was situated at BAGHDAD and Bde HQ was set up there . . . No previous AA [anti-aircraft] troops had been in the theatre and it was vital that immediate protection be afforded to the Oil refinery at ABDAN [sic], the largest in the Empire and containing the only cracking plant, then under direct British control. Accordingly the first deployment was in defence of ABDAN and BASRA by 87 HAA [Heavy Anti-Aircraft] Regt and of the oilfields at MOSUL and KIRKUK by 12 LAA [Light Anti-Aircraft] Regt.[36]

To augment Iraq's defences, additional RAF squadrons were also deployed, such as 237 (Rhodesia) Squadron, which arrived in February 1942 and remained until after the Battle of Stalingrad.

De-Nazifying Iraq

Despite these deployments, Britain's position in Iraq remained vulnerable as long as German forces remained successful in the field – both because of the actual threat from those forces, and because of the manner in which their success kept alive the prospect of internal unrest and uprisings. Paul Knabenshue, the American consul-general, wrote: 'It is my considered opinion that most of the Iraqi Army and Iraqi people are anti-British and that if the Germans make an appreciable thrust in this direction the Iraqi Army will rise against the British unless the British maintain here a force adequate to stop a German thrust and at the same time keep the Iraqis under control.'[37] The British felt the same; the weekly report compiled for the War Cabinet two weeks after the armistice in Iraq stated that:

Rashid Ali's propaganda has left a deep impression in certain quarters. His agents still control a large section of the armed forces, and are sedulously spreading the belief that the Germans will again be in Iraq within the next few weeks. The army has by no means lost cohesion and discipline. Its present temper is sullen, and until the unreliable officers are replaced by trustworthy men its future attitude remains uncertain.[38]

A letter from Rear-Admiral Cosmo Graham, Senior Naval Officer Persian Gulf, reflected deep concerns about the security of British interests in the aftermath of the Anglo-Iraqi war, and emphasized that there was no room for complacency. What concerned him was the unreliability of the Iraqi governing and military elite, based on 'the personal and vicarious experience I gained during the period of hostilities against the IRAQIS and days immediately preceding this period'. In this connection he referred to a 7 June 1941 paper issued by the Combined Intelligence Centre Iraq (CICI, the British intelligence and secret service propaganda agency headquartered in Baghdad, created by a £1 million grant to Middle East Command). The paper stated that during the conflict it had been widely proclaimed that Britain was 'not fighting the IRAQI nation, but only RASHID ALI and his small group of Generals'.[39] But in Graham's reckoning, the rot spread a lot wider than that, and defeat had not brought an end to the danger:

> Ali's Cabinet contained 3 ex. Prime ministers. In parliament, where there were a few absentees, no deputy or senator opposed the dismissal of the Regent or his replacement by RASHID ALI'S nominees. The whole Army and Police Force cooperated actively in the rebellion and were supported by the entire civil administration. The Youth Movement or 'FETUWA' were most active against us ... The Iraq Army has not been sufficiently cowed by defeat to be an entirely negligible quantity ... With German support and equipment they might start trouble again ... I do not, now, trust any IRAQI at all since they have demonstrated that they are adherents only to the potential victors.[40]

Graham's suspicions extended all the way from lofty Iraqi politicians down to individual workers. He expressed mistrust of the pilots at Abadan responsible for guiding ships in to moor, and the potential for them to deliberately ground ships in the channel below the port. He was worried by the prospect of the Iraqis mining the Shatt al-Arab and the potential effect on Britain's ability to use the vital waters around Abadan and Basra. He was also concerned about the security of communication systems, recounting the case of an Iraqi signaller who had confessed to giving copies of messages to Iraqi authorities outside the port and the fact that the whole Iraqi staff of the transmitting station had been found asleep on duty at 0200 two days previously. There was the risk that such employees might corrupt messages in transmission or cause delays. 'If we must keep them do not let us make a second mistake in trusting them.' To increase security in the light of recent events, British naval guards were now deployed aboard the Examination Service vessel in Basra harbour, the port wireless transmission station, dredgers and at al-Faw and Harmaw. Graham emphasized the fact that the British military and naval authorities agreed that the Shatt al-Arab defence scheme should be a British, not an Iraqi, responsibility. He also feared, not without cause, that the Axis merchant vessels present in Iranian harbours could be scuttled in order to effectively block the Shatt al-Arab.

Pro-Axis and anti-British propaganda and political activity was still a potent force, and in the months following the British invasions of Iraq and Syria the British had to deal with disgruntled politicians, angry and bewildered people, and the fact that, despite their recent triumphs, many still believed that they would eventually lose the war. Freya Stark, the British propaganda specialist, wrote that post-invasion Iraq 'was seething with disguised Nazis and swastikas were appearing everywhere – even on the back of my car':[41]

> The country was soaked in German doctrines; the Berlin radio blared from every coffee-house; the army was surly over its defeat and none too pleased to discover that it had been effected with less than two British battalions; and the worst of the Middle East war was beginning. The German advance in the Soviet Union, the entry of Japan, the fall of Singapore, Sebastopol, and Tobruk lay ahead. The enemy plan of July that year foresaw a Panzer corps through Persia in the winter. Ten divisions would traverse Anatolia to Iraq . . . With the appearance of Rommel and our withdrawal on Tobruk, the desert was then swinging against us, and in Iraq itself the situation – according to my diary – 'was frothing like milk about to boil'.[42]

The Grand Mufti and Rashid Ali al-Gailani continued their activities from Tehran and later Berlin, fomenting anti-allied and pro-Arab sentiment and working hand in hand with the Germans. Both men maintained regular contact with German political and military officials, and met with

Hitler and other very senior Nazi officials on numerous occasions. German agents continued to deploy to Iran to coordinate fifth-column activity, and an Iraqi government in exile was formed in Berlin.[43] German interest in the region, despite setbacks, remained strong, and this is why they kept close tabs on the Grand Mufti and Rashid Ali, expecting that victories won by German arms in Africa and the Soviet Union would in the fullness of time see the region drop like a ripe plum into Berlin's lap.

Though the regent and his political allies, backed by the British, were now able to assert themselves without the risk of army intervention, the upheavals of April and May had had little noticeable effect on the highly personalized nature of politics and the hierarchies of power. Though Jamil al-Midfai had succeeded Rashid Ali, Nuri as-Said dominated Iraqi politics, returning as prime minister himself in October 1941 and remaining in office until June 1944. He had a vision of a Hashemite-led federation of Arab states and 'presided over a government intent on retribution'.[44] Some Rashid Ali supporters were captured in Iran and interned in Southern Rhodesia. Courts-martial sentenced to death three of the four Golden Square officers in absentia, and they were eventually all run to ground and executed: in May 1942 Fahmi Sa'id, Mahmud Salman and Yunis al-Sabawi were hanged. Kamil Shabib met the same fate two years later. As for Salah al-Din al-Sabbagh, he escaped to Iran and then to Turkey, where he was interned. When he was eventually handed over to the Iraqi authorities, he was hanged at the gates of the Ministry of Defence.[45] Rashid Ali, also condemned to death, evaded the sentence through safe haven in Egypt, Germany, Iran and Saudi Arabia.

As British occupation settled across Iraq in the months following the restoration of Prince Abdulillah, efforts were made to purge the country of pro-Rashid Ali and pro-German officials, officers, teachers and community leaders. The British once again took over the Education Department and ensured that the pro-German and nationalistic school curriculum formally adopted in 1939 was thrown out. British power in Iraq was manifest as imperial troops flooded in, but there were also more subtle approaches. These included the secondment of British officials to Iraqi government departments, and the creation of a new political service controlled by the British Embassy and designed to serve British political and military ends.

Britain aided, indeed to a large extent directed, the Iraqi government in a wide-ranging process of de-Nazification. Hundreds of alleged Nazi sympathizers and supporters of Rashid Ali were sent to a special detention camp on the al-Faw peninsular near the Shatt al-Arab, described by a British political adviser as an 'isolation hospital' for those suffering from the 'infectious disease' of Nazism.[46] British nationals played their part too, the director-general of the Date Association promising that he 'would use his position to make it as difficult as possible for our late enemies to profit in the date trade with Britain'.[47] The British, afraid that the Iraqi army might yet stab them in the back, considered disbanding it. Instead, they decided to cut its size in order to structurally weaken it, a process put into action by starving it of equipment and uniforms, and even limiting daily rations to 1,000 calories less than what was considered necessary for 'Eastern' troops.[48]

This was a pivotal moment in Iraq's history. Up to the time of King Ghazi's death, the monarchy had been gaining in popularity, largely because of its nationalist and pan-Arabist timbre. But from the end of the Anglo-Iraqi war, the monarchy became increasingly identified with the British, having been restored by British bayonets. 'Clearly it was urgent for the Iraqi regime to seek local support. Instead, Abdulillah and Nuri al-Said relied on martial law and remained defiantly pro-British', with deleterious long-term consequences.[49] The power of the monarchy vis-à-vis the government increased; not only did the king appoint the prime minister, but he soon gained the power to dismiss him too. He could appoint members to the upper house of parliament, and the prime minister collaborated with him in choosing lists for election to the lower chamber. The power of Britain vis-à-vis the regime greatly expanded, too. In June 1941, Prime Minister al-Midfai agreed that Britain could station troops anywhere it liked, and gave all possible assistance when they turned their attention to the invasion of Iran. Nuri, when he returned as prime minister in October, went further, pledging all assistance and the use of the Iraqi army in whatever way the British thought best.

As a result of the occupation, the British Embassy, in the words of C.J. Edmonds, a British adviser to the Ministry of the Interior, 'pushed its tentacles into the internal administrative machine even more deeply than the High Commission in its later days'.[50] A British general continued to act as inspector-general of the Iraqi army, and British officers were embedded in the police force, where they had 'been given wider powers than for many years'.[51] British officials were given 'considerable administrative authority in the Ministry of Interior, which controlled the police'.[52] A Briton headed the Criminal Investigation Department, another the Port of Basra authority. Britons also led in the fields of river, road and rail transportation, foreign currency, imports, local produce, irrigation and the veterinary service, and had advisers in the Ministry of the Interior and the Department of Education.

Some of Britain's Iraqi friends and supporters were keen to declare their position in a post-invasion climate where 'loyalty' or 'disloyalty' was of heightened importance. Rashid Subhi, for instance, an official in the Ministry of the Interior, wrote to Ambassador Cornwallis thus:

> I pray God to grant you prosperity and to grant victory to your noble nation and success in its struggle in order to overcome the evil power of the Nazist pagans, the criminal refuse of humanity, the blood-stained Italians who have covered themselves with shame by their dastardly acts of aggression against peaceful peoples, and also the refuse of humanity, apes of the Far East. It is through the destruction of those depraved and degraded elements that humanity wold be able to enjoy peaceful and prosperous life.[53]

Some Iraqis, along with members of the British community, donated money to war funds. In October 1941, the Baghdad and Northern Iraq War Contributions Fund raised £7,500 and a 'War Charities Fête' £12,000. Another £6,400 had been raised by the Imperial Forces Welfare Committee, 'Ladies' Working Parties' and the Spitfire Fund.[54]

The British controlled the postal and telegraph network, including the General Post Office. Through the Directorate Chemical Laboratory Baghdad, the British had conducted 'technical censorship' for years, and general censorship under the Director-General Propaganda had commenced on the outbreak of war. Now, in post-coup Iraq, 'full postal censorship' began, and the laboratory increased its activities. Baghdad Postal Censorship was located in a building next to the main Post Office headquarters, and a new Iraq Postal and Telegraph Censorship Office was established. A censorship office in Basra examined mail to and from Iran, and a censorship office was also opened in Mosul.

Most of the censorship work was conducted 'outside office hours to try and maintain secrecy'.[55] It was painstaking work, 'Iranian derived mail' being particularly 'difficult to manipulate due to the general use of poor paper and the habit of plastering the back of the envelopes with stamps'. The record to date was held by an envelope from which '26 stamps had to be removed before the main manipulation was possible. The replacement with interlocking post marks was most difficult.'[56] With the approval of the Iraqi authorities the British also conducted mail spot checks. For example, checkpoints were set up to look for mail carried illegally in frontier areas around Mosul. On one occasion, 33 lorries and buses were examined, 101 people searched and 31 sealed envelopes discovered and examined. All letters were found to deal with family or business matters, and it was noted that the exercise had 'told more about smuggling than censorship'.

The creation of a network of political advisers, working directly under the British Embassy's Oriental Secretary, Vyvyan Holt, was a major post-coup initiative aimed at enhancing British knowledge and power. The country was divided into three areas and political advisers were positioned within them. The Northern Area, including the provinces of Mosul, Erbil, Kirkuk, Sulaymaniyah and Diyala, was headquartered at Kirkuk; the Central Area, comprising the districts of Dulaim, Baghdad, Hillah, Karbala, Diwaniyah, Kut and Amarah, was headquartered at Baghdad; and the Southern Area, comprising the districts of Basra and Nasiriyah, was headquartered at Basra. Most of the men recruited were former employees of the Iraq Petroleum Company or government, and had served in the military.[57] They were attached to the Combined Intelligence Centre Iraq.

The political advisers' military duties were several: to keep in close touch with British commanders on the ground and provide political intelligence; to facilitate the cooperation of Iraqi civil authorities on behalf of the British military; to ease good relations between the population and British forces; and to accompany military columns where necessary. Their political duties were both less easy to define and more difficult to pursue. They were to fight Nazi influence, prevent the possibility of another rising and to make preparations to meet a German advance. Ambassador Cornwallis admitted that it was 'difficult to know how' they would achieve these objectives: 'A month ago this country was completely in the hands of fifth columnists and although the arch-villains have fled, the machine remains with plenty of smaller villains to work it. Thanks to their intensive propaganda over a period of years, the Germans have created a hatred of us amongst certain classes.'[58]

Wallace Lyon, an old Iraq hand, was one of the newly appointed political advisers, re-commissioned into the Indian Army in order to undertake the role. While commanding British forces in the Nasiriyah area in the aftermath of the Anglo-Iraqi war, Slim had required 'a suitably qualified Political Officer to help him with all his dealings with the Iraq Army and local inhabitants'.[59] This role was one aspect of Lyon's appointment, the other being political affairs in an area which stretched from Diyala province in the south to the Turkish frontier, and from the Syrian frontier to the Iranian – 'In short, the top half of Iraq which a British Corps and the Polish Army were subsequently to occupy.'[60] His duties were to maintain a close liaison with Slim and his subordinate commanders, to report any 'subversive activities to the British Ambassador and the General Officer Commanding-in-Chief [Quinan]', to provide all commanders with information on local communications and resources, and 'advising and assisting them in all matters involving the natives of the country'.[61] He was responsible for settling all claims for compensation lodged against British imperial forces, leaving them free to devote their attention to training, defensive preparations and military operations. He was also to advise and assist the five Iraqi provincial governors in his area as they sought to restore stable government, public morale, friendship and support for the allies and confidence in ultimate victory. 'Small job then!', as Lyon remarked in his diary.

As weeks stretched into months following the conclusion of the Anglo-Iraqi war, British political advisers and their Iraqi friends worried about the slowness of the anti-German and anti-Rashid Ali purge. The British Political Adviser Northern Area wrote that 'the Matasarrif [local provincial governor] continues to work energetically in suppression of Nazi supporters'. The problem, however, 'is that government doesn't seem inclined to deal firmly with Iraqi Nazis ... The Iraqi army are still untouched and the Iraqi Air Force Officers are probably the most Nazi of the lot and openly spurn any allied propaganda.' The civil authorities 'have made such little progress in following up and weeding out sources of Nazi culture that our well wishers despair of any success under the present regime'.[62]

The British put pressure on the Iraqi government to take action. Nazi supporters, the British claimed, remained in abundance, particularly in the military and the schools. A political adviser estimated 'that 50 per cent of teachers and officers were still anti-British'. Younger officers 'find it tough to adjust views: There are the two most powerful incentives of revenge and shame and professional admiration for the success of the German Army'.[63] The adviser had toured Samarra and Tekrit in September 1941, reporting that the first location 'appears to have cleared up somewhat but I am credibly informed that many of the holy men there are still convinced that Germany will win'.[64] Individuals such as Suleiman ibn Daoud of Mosul were arrested, in his case for allegedly being in possession of hand-written anti-British and pro-Nazi pamphlets. He had been introduced to a German secret service officer in Mosul, who had given him money.

Perhaps unsurprisingly, the presence of imperial troops in Iraqi towns and cities usually had a salutary effect on the situation from a British point of view, as did military success in the wider region:

The entry of British Troops into Iraq has been a definite shock to those people – and there are many in Mosul – who have been saying that the Nazis would be back in two or three weeks. People are now asking from where can the Nazis come? The answer is Turkey, but opinion is that the moral of the British occupation of Syria, Iraq, and Iran will not be lost on Turkey who will therefore be much too afraid of the British to allow her territory to be used as a centre for Nazi propagandists. The show of British strength has impressed and people are beginning to realise that Britain means business and further that Britain has the means and the will to beat the Nazis.[65]

Nevertheless, the adviser noted, 'Nazi propaganda among civilians in the Kirkuk Bazaar seems not to have subsided to a great extent ... when the British Air Force passed over in strength on September 9th there was clapping in the tea shops by those who thought they were German. It subsided when the true identity of the machines was established.'[66] The mutasarrif had started a new paper called *Kirkuk*, the first issue of which contained a fatwa by the imams 'cancelling out the [anti-British] fetwa they gave during the rebellion'.

[It is] obvious to everyone that the government does not intend to deal firmly with the Rashid Ali party. Though there is less open propaganda in the towns it is for the most part due to the presence of British Troops and to the success of the operations in Iran. The chief offenders have gone unpunished and their jackals are still lurking under cover. This is especially the case in the Iraqi Army. The people who have been associated with the British are still looking over their shoulders and frankly admit they do not understand why the British do not exercise more control over the Iraq Government. They know, as do office holders that but for British arms the government would be quizling [sic] only. Yet the conscription and the petty oppression associated with it continues as if there had been no rebellion and no British occupation.[67]

As an example he cited the case of Amin Khaki, a lieutenant-colonel in the Iraq army in Kirkuk, and a known Nazi sympathizer. Khaki:

refused to take any action against officers residing in town found to be listening to German broadcasts despite repeated requests [from the provincial governor]. Has repeatedly refused to allow Police to search Officers houses suspected of containing stolen property. Mustarrif suggested to him that he should be as co-operative as possible with the British in accordance with CGS [Chief of General Staff]'s instructions but he replied that he would have nothing to do with them.[68]

The report also singled out one Ibrahim Saleh Shukr, described as Rashid Ali's 'No. 1 man in Diyala during May', who had 'made life as unpleasant as possible for Britishers in Khaniqin Oil Company'.[69]

The Political Adviser Central Area reported that Iraqi officials were being transferred in order 'to break up Nazi cells', but that these:

> alleviations are not sufficient to eradicate the Nazi disease, however. Only major operations, inflicting the most severe sentences on the principals responsible for the May disturbances and on those responsible for the Baghdad pogrom of 1st/2nd June; sentencing those officials prominent in their support of Rashid Ali in May or in propagating their Nazi persuasions since May to at least suspension from service for the duration; cleaning the Augean stables of the Iraq Army and of the schools; and insisting on just retribution for [crimes against British military personnel]; can be expected to cut out the roots of Nazi influence here.[70]

In Baghdad the more notorious pro-Nazis were being removed from office, though evidence of Nazi sympathies was not difficult to find. The arrival of an American aircraft, for instance, 'led some to believe the Germans are coming', and there was 'some rejoicing in Nazi circles at the fall of Kiev and I heard several reports that some coffee shops were giving free drinks to celebrate'.[71] Despite the outcome of the Anglo-Iraqi war, the simple fact was that many people still expected ultimate German victory to transform the situation. The tide would turn again; fleeing rebels passing through the region on their way to Iran said that the April coup 'had failed because of too hurried planning but that they would without doubt return in four months with a well prepared scheme for taking over control'.[72] The Political Adviser Central Area wrote that the 'force of Nazi propaganda in Baghdad varies day by day in direct relation to the success or failure of the Nazi armies in the Russian battlefield as reported in the Radio announcements'.[73]

In September 1941 the Political Adviser Central Area reported the 'extensive movement of troops through Baghdad this week'. Nazi sympathizers were still at large; sixty deserters from the Iraqi army had been rounded up in Najaf, and the town had 'undergone a considerable change of heart in its attitude towards us'. Nazi propaganda had been 'still further diminished though not yet eliminated among the schoolboys'. On 2 September the political adviser called on Amin Khalis, mutasarrif of Hillah, who had his own methods of dealing with pro-Germans. He 'seems to think he has curbed the pro-Nazi activities of several Hillah-ites by inviting them to his residence after dark and handing out some well-chosen admonition cum a few well directed blows!'[74]

Iraqis deemed loyal by the British continued to express their dismay regarding the slowness with which anti-British and pro-Rashid Ali individuals were being rooted out. They believed that Britain was running the country now, and so did not understand why the British permitted so many pro-German and pro-Rashid Ali men to remain in important positions.[75] The Political Adviser Central Area complained that there had been no progress in punishing the principal offenders responsible for the May rebellion; it was 'difficult to understand why no action has yet been taken to deal with Rashid Ali, to bring him to trial ex parte, to pass sentence, and to confiscate his property ... Similarly no decisive action has yet been taken either against the golden square or against the black pillars of Rashid Ali's edifice, Abdul Wahid, Sayed Alwan al-Yasiri and Sayed Gata al-Awwadi.'[76]

Given this state of affairs, it was not surprising that 'rumours of Rashid Ali's impending return to power at the head of a conquering army of Germans should be of constant recurrence and should gain considerable credence'. The 'lack of decisive action has persuaded the tribes in most districts that they need fear no punishment for their misdeeds and the reaction has been a widespread outbreak of petty tribal quarrels'. 'Assiduous propaganda' produced by supporters of Rashid Ali claimed that the present situation 'is only interim and that the Germans will soon bring him back'. Activity had included pro-Nazi pamphleteering in Baqubah and Baghdad, with Iraqi army officers and government officials known to be behind most 'subversive work'. On a brighter note, the adviser reported, the 'stout resistance of the Russians and our advances into Syria reacted very greatly in our favour'.[77]

Ambassador Cornwallis offered an explanation as to the relative slowness of de-Nazification in a letter to Wallace Lyon. Lyon had written to him expressing frustration. In his avuncular but authoritative reply, Cornwallis agreed that many pro-Nazis still remained in place and believed that they were sheltered because of old friendships with those currently in power.

In the meantime I plug away steadily at a selected and gradually decreasing list and lose no opportunity of saying just what I think about them. But I want to make it quite clear that I think it would be extremely stupid if I were to force a Cabinet crisis over any or all of these men. Our essential tasks are, firstly, to prepare our defences with the ready coop-eration of the Iraqi Government and, secondly, to bring about an improvement in the feelings of the people as a whole towards us.[78]

This would not be achieved, the ambassador said, if Britain started throwing its weight around. Tellingly, Cornwallis told Lyon that if there was a sudden emergency – such as a German breakthrough – the remaining pro-Nazi elements could be dealt with very swiftly, a glimpse of Britain's own assess-ment of its dominant power in Iraqi affairs.

Slowly the tide turned. The Political Adviser Northern Area reported in November 1941 that hostile propaganda was diminishing, hastened by the purge and the steady stream of people being sent to al-Faw. 'The effects of the purge have been so great that it is becoming difficult to provide the victims. I have no doubt, however, that they will be found.'[79] The following month he reported that:

Now practically no enemy overt propaganda reported, occasionally one hears of pro axis remarks in Tea Shops but the more important axis sympathisers have apparently decided to lie low or change their tune. A typical example of this is Yusif Zainal Director of Education Mosul who since his visit to Baghdad has warned his teachers that anyone expressing Nazi views would be immediately removed. This sounds rather like Satan rebuking sin but at any rate it indicates a growing respect for the Cabinet since it has started its purge. The recent axing of Judges has also proved popular and the time should now be ripe for making a thorough clear up in the Iraq Army.[80]

Enemy propaganda had been 'practically silenced though no reason to believe that the agents have been put out of action'. Here, as in other parts of Iraq (and Iran for that matter), there were complaints that there was insufficient allied propaganda, though the adviser noted that the six free cinema shows for chil-dren in Mosul had been well received.[81] This contrasted with an incident in the same month, in which 'two little boys "Heil"ed Hitler and cheered the German soldiers before scuttling out' of the ornate façade of the popular al-Zawra Cinema in Baghdad. Many such incidents were recorded: two people in Nasiriyah were fined for tuning into Berlin, people in Baghdad were caught drafting pro-Nazi and pro-Rashid Ali pamphlets and the Führer's portrait was clapped and cheered during showings of the film *Freedom*. 'Down with the regent! Hurrah for Rashid Ali' was chalked on a Baghdad road.[82] It was reported that the extensive distribution of British propaganda pamphlets and literature in the Euphrates area was having a good effect, though there was 'more Nazi propaganda than there should be in Samarra and Tekrit'.

The Political Adviser Central Area drew Ambassador Cornwallis's attention to Abdur Rezak Hilm, who was 'acknowledged on all sides to have done excellent work for our cause in cleansing Basrah of Nazi influence'. The 'cumulative effects of literature propaganda and the removal of undesirables to Fao [al-Faw],' he continued, 'has had a great effect throughout the country particularly regarding loose talk of rapid German advances into this country which has almost ceased except in the circles of Junior Iraq Army Officers'.[83] He also reported that the 'ban on programmes other than Baghdad Radio is still in force and continues to be resented in Basrah, Nasiriyah and Diwaniya' (reception of Baghdad Radio was very poor in the latter two locations). The Political Adviser Northern Area wrote that in Kirkuk, Baghdad Radio was 'weak and commands little attention'. The favoured and most influential broadcasts were those from Ankara, which were considered to be 'pro Nazi and damaging'.[84]

Pro-British propaganda was disseminated in the months following the Anglo-Iraqi war. Initiatives included articles in local newspapers and the distribution of souvenir-like trinkets, such as pro-British badges. The Political Adviser Northern Area wrote that 'many people are to be seen wearing "V" cuff links or a "V" sign badge in their buttonholes'.[85] It was reported from Erbil that allied propaganda leaflets 'go down well in the town and the British troops passing through the town have made no complaints'.[86] The British Embassy maintained public relations sections in Baghdad, Basra and the northern cities. The Basra section reported in late 1941 that it was sending propaganda material to hundreds of addresses in Amarah, Basra and Muntafiq, and propaganda was also being distributed in out-of-the-way areas by touring military officers.[87] There was apparently a 'keen demand for maps of war areas in English and Arabic'. The British also published a special newspaper for dhows calling at al-Faw, emphasizing British sea power, and the *Basrah Times*.[88] Specific publications included *Jerida el Muhit al Hindi*, *The New European Order* and *Akhbar al Harb*. Five thousand copies of an

Arabic version of 'The truth about Iran and Russia's struggle and reserves', a Government of India publication, were printed.[89] In December 1941 a public relations branch was opened in Mosul. Its employees used printing presses and local newspapers for their work. The British kept a close eye on rival propaganda and trends in public opinion. For example, in late 1941 it was reported that in the Middle Euphrates region the rise in the cost of living was being viewed as 'policy of the British to avenge the events of May'.[90] A publication called 'Brothers of Virtue', criticizing Rashid Ali and the leaders of the April rebellion, also came to light.[91] Another development, which was to become of greater concern in the post-war years, was the spread of communism in Iraq. There was a 'small but growing' party in Baghdad and a communist magazine called *Sparks*. The growing popularity of the Soviets was noted by British political advisers, one reporting a cartoon that depicted Hitler being beheaded by a sickle and beaten by a hammer in a communist paper called *Al Majjalla Iraqi*.[92]

A year after Rashid Ali's coup, the situation was such that one British Embassy official was moved to write:

> As regards Iraq, I think I need only add this. I have been here now nearly a year and have seen one of the most extraordinary political and psychological transformations that I am ever likely to witness. A year ago Iraq was bitterly hostile and disorientated. If you showed a Swastika in a propaganda film it was applauded. If you put up a poster with a Union Jack in it it would probably be pulled down. It was the ideal atmosphere, in fact, for an experiment of propaganda and conversion. The Ambassador, who knows the country I think better than any living man except Nuri, laid solid plans for a comprehensive campaign which was to include every known method of influencing people, e.g. political reform, economic help, military infiltration and what is best described in Burke's phrase as 'the soft collar of social esteem'. The results, as I say, have been remarkable, though to those who believe in the efficacy of ideas, not unforeseen. Now the country is predominantly friendly.[93]

So much for Iraq, firmly under the British mantle following an unpleasant war, though bracing itself for a possible German advance. It was to Iran that attention was soon to shift, and where it was to linger for the remainder of the war.

CHAPTER 7

Barbarossa and Iran

With Iraq and Syria settling under British occupation, the circumstances of war now cast a spotlight on Iran. The German invasion of the Soviet Union on 22 June 1941 changed things dramatically, as 3 million German troops attacked across a 1,000-mile front. The southern army group had the Caucasus and the region's oil resources as one of its key objectives. Having spent years contemplating war against each other, Britain and the Soviet Union were thrown together as allies by Operation Barbarossa. Both now looked at Iran anew and considered invading it, to secure its oil, to seize an historic opportunity to 'round out' their respective spheres of influence and to use it as a bridge for military supplies flowing from the one to the other. Also, on the part of the British, to defend the country lest the Germans defeat the Soviets – a source of awkwardness between the new-found allies, because the Soviets understood only too well that the British planned to move into the Caucasus to resist the Germans if the Red Army crumbled. The advent of Lend-Lease emboldened Britain and plumped up its regional ambitions. It also brought America into the equation in a more forceful manner than ever before. Extending Lend-Lease to Moscow, American authorities agreed with the British that the ports, roads and railways of Iran offered the best route for sending war material to Stalin. While prepared to accept such help, though never gratefully, this new situation was a cause of resentment for Moscow: it had made perfectly clear that it did not welcome America anywhere in the country.

Until Barbarossa, the British had not been unduly worried by the presence in Iran of German nationals – 'tourists', as was the persistent euphemism employed in diplomatic and military circles at the time. But the sudden alliance of Britain and the Soviet Union made both countries keen to secure their respective positions there. Britain evinced a strong desire to do something in unison with the Soviets, especially as Stalin's most ardent wish – for the opening of a 'second front' in western Europe to relieve pressure on the new Eastern Front – was something that the British, in mid-1941, were utterly unprepared to countenance. Therefore, 'doing something' in Iran became a distinct possibility.

The American War Department had been sceptical about the Soviet Union's capacity to resist the German onslaught, and was therefore reluctant to extend supplies to it and redirect Lend-Lease, with all of the work that that would entail. 'With little knowledge of the Soviet Union's real capabilities of resistance, the General Staff felt the best method of aiding the USSR would be to continue aid to Britain.'[1] But evincing an optimism shared by few at the time, Harry Hopkins, Roosevelt's personal emissary, returned from his visit to Moscow in late July with a firm conviction regarding the Soviet Union's ability to resist. The man who six months earlier had been sent as Roosevelt's personal emissary to Churchill in order to check Britain's fighting mettle was now taking Moscow's pulse and establishing presidential contact with Stalin.[2] He recommended that Lend-Lease be extended to the Soviets.

The German invasion of the Soviet Union ratcheted up the pressure on the shah. Britain and the Soviet Union were still there, breathing down his neck, but now his German big brother appeared to be a giant step closer. It was no wonder that the shah felt more than ever like a sheep among wolves. 'The Iranian government,' wrote British diplomat Sir Alexander Cadogan the day after the German invasion began, 'will surely wait and see which way the cat jumps.'[3] The British believed that Germany would soon take Baku and Ukraine and enter Iran, and began discussing what they could do. For the British, Barbarossa brought new danger to an area of primary strategic importance – but it also meant new opportunity to cement their position in the Middle East. Having cleaned up in Iraq and Syria, there was now a tantalizing chance to take control of their vital interests in Iran. Those interests were threatened by the presence of German nationals, though this was not an insurmountable problem, even though it did become a pretext for action. Of greater concern was the threat should the Soviets fold and Britain need to defend the oilfields from German troops and aircraft. Aside from guarding the all-important oil, defending Iran was also part of the defence of India and would encourage Turkey to cleave to its neutral line. What made military action against Iran even more likely was London's desire not to rebuff the Soviets in their first approach, as an ally, for tangible cooperation.[4]

From Moscow's point of view, there were several compelling reasons for invading Iran, both historic and immediate. In a cypher to Britain's representatives in Baghdad and Tehran, Foreign Secretary Anthony Eden explained Soviet attitudes towards the British, and their activity in Iran, in the following terms: 'The Soviet Government has always regarded proximity of the BAKU oilfields to the Persian frontier as almost, if not quite as dangerous as proximity of Leningrad to the old Finnish and Baltic frontier; and as with these latter frontiers their only chance of making a change is to take action while the war is still on.'[5] Basically, the Soviets wanted parts of northern Iran under their own control, as colonial or semi-colonial zones to be employed as buffers and to be tapped for their resources. Moreover, the Foreign Secretary continued, it was not only a question of long-term policy:

> our undisguised interest in CAUCASIA though in fact based on perfectly sound considerations of joint resistance to the Axis, has never ceased to excite Soviet suspicions. They believe, – not without some reason – that the result of another German drive and consequent weakening of their own position in the CAUCASUS might be a situation in which we should consider British intervention essential, while they did not . . .[6]

This, then, was one cause of tension between London and Moscow with regard to this region – Russia was not only suspicious of British intentions regarding Iran, it *knew* that at a certain point, if the Germans continued to advance, the British would deploy troops to Soviet soil in order to protect its vital interests in the Iran–Iraq region.

Shortly after the launch of Operation Barbarossa, Winston Churchill addressed the House of Commons:

> If anyone had predicted two months ago, when Iraq was in revolt and our people were hanging on by their eyelids at Habbaniya and our Ambassador was imprisoned in his Embassy in Baghdad, and when all Syria and Iraq began to be overrun by German tourists, and were in the

hands of forces controlled indirectly but none the less powerfully by German authority – if anyone had predicted that we should already, by the middle of July, have cleaned up the whole of the Levant and have re-established our authority there for the time being, such a prophet would have been considered most imprudent.[7]

Churchill, bullish and ebullient as ever and keen to boost morale, was right to put a positive spin on Britain's achievements in Iraq and Syria. But he was well aware, if more circumspect in his public pronouncements, that the German invasion of the Soviet Union meant that the threat to Britain's position in the region not only remained alive, but was reinvigorated. It would come down to the Soviet Union's capacity to resist, and there remained a big question mark over the capacity of the British to repel Axis forces attempting to eject them from North Africa. As Eden told Churchill only a week after his Commons speech, 'should Russia be defeated, we shall have to be ready to occupy the Iranian oil fields; for in such an eventuality German pressure on the Iranians to turn us out would be irresistible'.[8]

For their part, the Germans told splendid fibs regarding the invasion of the Soviet Union, designed to court favour in countries such as Iran and Iraq where, very soon, they expected to arrive in person. On 22 June 1941, the day Hitler sent his armies crashing across the Soviet border, Berlin radio told Iranian listeners that 'the Soviets have directed foreign policy entirely against Germany and are ready to attack Germany'. The Soviet government 'has betrayed its pledges to the German government':

> With unparalleled enmity the Bolsheviks of Russia have prepared them-
> selves against National-Socialist Germany. The Moscow Bolsheviks are
> on the point of stabbing National-Socialist Germany in the back at a
> time when Germany is engaged in a war for her existence. Germany
> cannot leave this active menace to her Eastern frontier unanswered ...
> The German nation knows that in this war it has not resorted to arms
> only to defend its existence but also to save the whole civilised world
> from the dangerous Bolshevik intrigues and threats, and to open the
> way to the prosperity of the whole world.[9]

Sir Claude Auchinleck and Sir Archibald Wavell, the generals controlling the vast Middle East–South Asia region, as well as the British Chiefs of Staff and the American War Department, believed that Soviet resistance to Germany's ferocious invasion would crumble within six weeks. Yet despite these gloomy assessments, and despite historic differences between them, the Anglo-Soviet marriage of convenience was a potent one. The immediate problem was how to support Moscow and stave off its widely predicted capitulation. Almost straight away, Churchill and Roosevelt saw that the Iran–Iraq region could become a major conduit for military hardware hastening to help the Soviets fight the Germans. This was an especially attractive prospect because the alternative route – through the North Sea to Arkhangelsk and Murmansk, braved by the Arctic convoys – was exceedingly dangerous, and would soon be shut. Stalin proposed a supply route through Iran as early as 29 June, the origin of an Anglo-Indian intiative – the East Persian Auxiliary Transport Route – that was to see supplies delivered from Nok Kundi in India (now Pakistan) to Mashhad in Iran.

The situation in Iran and the growing German threat to the region from the Western Desert and the Caucasus coloured British military thinking through the summer months. Viewing proceedings from his eyrie in the War Office, Major-General John Kennedy wrote that the 'situation in Iran is not too happy':

> A large number of German agents are established in the country. We are now in communication with both India and the Middle East as to action which might be taken in the diplomatic, and possibly the military, sphere to secure their expulsion and establish ourselves in a controlling position. If the Germans were to appear in force in Iran by way of Russia, our whole position in Iraq would be threatened and our communications in the Persian Gulf might be cut.[10]

From the British point of view, it was certainly better to be safe than sorry, to act decisively rather than to dally and lose a valuable opportunity, or worse, see the enemy steal a march. Though estimates of their numbers varied, Iran was 'infested with German undercover agents'.[11] On 23 June 1941 Under Secretary of State Sumner Welles telegrammed Louis Dreyfus, America's minister plenipotentiary in Tehran, saying that the State Department had 'received information from a reliable source that the Germans have established a skeletal General Staff in the German Legation in Tehran with branches located in German business firms throughout Iran'. Dreyfus was asked 'to ascertain the authenticity of this report'. In reply, he said that he was unsure as to the exact facts, but that it was often claimed that the fifth column in Iran was large and that it was capable of putting 500 well-armed men on the streets of Tehran within a few hours.[12] While the Iranian authorities were aware of fifth-column activities, 'their police action has been too desultory and weak to prevent the building up of an efficient organization which is ready to strike at the proper moment. It is considered not unlikely that this moment will arise when German forces penetrate into the Caucasus.' Sir Stafford Cripps, British ambassador to Moscow, told Eden: 'I consider that Stalin is right regarding the Fifth Column menace in Iran as an urgent problem which calls for immediate vigorous action before the German advance towards the Caucasus renders effective pressure impossible.'[13]

Cripps and Stalin discussed the situation on 8 July, and the Soviet leader appeared profoundly concerned about the number of Germans inside the country. Soviet estimates put the figure at between 5,000 and 10,000 Germans. British estimates invariably came in lower, though always mentioned them as a menace. In May 1940 British Minister to Tehran Reader Bullard put the figure at 1,700 to 2,000.[14] On 29 July 1941 the Commander-in-Chief India estimated the number of Germans in Iran at between 2,000 and 3,000, 'many of them active fifth-columnists.'[15] Orders issued to the RAF in Iraq in the event of hostilities in Iran stated that there were 'at present considerable numbers of Germans (approx. 2,500) in Iran, highly organized as a fifth column': 'There is no doubt that at any moment decided upon by the GERMAN government, this Fifth Column will be used to damage by sabotage BRITISH and RUSSIAN interests in and near IRAN, and may be used to stage a coup d'etat with the object of bringing IRAN into the war actively on GERMANY'S side.'[16]

Germans occupied key positions – on the state railway, in the postal service, in car firms and road transport services and in war industries such as the Škoda small-arms factory near Tehran. Two technicians at the Tehran radio station were known to be key members of the German secret service, while others included a doctor at Kermanshah, the director of the Technical College at Kerman, and a lecturer at the Karaj Agricultural Institute. Over 100 Germans had illegally entered Iran as Rashid Ali's coup collapsed in Iraq, German ideological penetration was well developed, and anti-British and anti-Soviet propaganda widespread.

Nevertheless, Reza Shah was not indiscriminate in his attitudes towards and dealings with the Germans. Germany's apparent complicity in the coup against the monarchy in Iraq had displeased and disquieted him; he refused

Berlin's request for a German military mission in Tehran; and he circumscribed contact between Iranian officers and Germans. But on the other hand,
the shah's government tolerated activities and hosted pro-Axis individuals in
a manner bound to raise hackles in London and Moscow. Following the overthrow of the Iraqi government in May 1941, Rashid Ali, the Grand Mufti and
their discomfited associates had found sanctuary in Tehran, from where their
anti-British activities continued. Furthermore, German agents exhorted the
shah to remain on friendly terms with Germany, particularly when it came to
allied requests to eject German nationals inside his country. The shah's
prevarication was understandable: he wanted to convince Britain and the
Soviet Union that he was not a Nazi stooge and believed, correctly, that
acceding to their demands would only lead to further demands. But he also
knew that the Soviets might fold at any moment, and had the Germans on his
back too. Erwin Ettel, the SS officer serving as German minister in Tehran,
kept pressuring him not to relent on Iran's neutral stance, even conveying a
personal message from Hitler. Germany, the Führer said, was doing well on
the Eastern Front, so the shah would not have long to wait for his 'friends' to
arrive. The message said that 'the Reich Government trust that until this brief
period of danger [the German-Soviet conflict] will have passed away the Shah
will resist with all means at his disposal any such attempt on the part of the
British, which would carry the devastation of war also into Iranian territory'.[17]
Reza was also suspicious of rumoured German plots to replace him with a
pro-German government, the Germans apparently calculating that a pro-
German coup would be a good distraction for the Soviets.[18] It was a terrible
predicament, captured in Freya Stark's description of Iran as 'a rabbit hypno-
tized by a snake', or a 'frog in front of the German python'.[19]

In the light of this, and not really knowing what else to do, Reza Shah
withstood British and Soviet pressure to expel the Germans. The Iranian
position was that they would expel them if presented with clear evidence of
subversive activities, but they would not do so en masse. Surrounded by
sycophants and tight-lipped counsellors, the shah was unaware of just how
precarious his position was. The American diplomatic chief was sure that
he had failed to grasp the situation. 'I gained the distinct impression in a
long conversation yesterday with the Foreign Minister,' Dreyfus told
Washington on 19 August, 'that the Iranians are temporizing and parrying
without realizing the seriousness of their situation. Unless they abandon
their search for a magic formula and face the immediate realities of the situation they will perhaps within the next few days find it is too late'.[20]

British deliberations and preparations

In stark contrast to his reluctance to supply forces for the invasion of Iraq in the spring, in the summer of 1941 Sir Archibald Wavell was all action with regard to Iran, berating London for not getting a move on and intervening decisively. The reason was that he was now Commander-in-Chief India, having swapped places with Auchinleck in June. Things looked different from Delhi than they did from Cairo; in April, Iraq had seemed like a peripheral irritant to a commander-in-chief focusing on the Western Desert and southern Europe. But in July, Iran loomed large as an urgent problem to a commander in the Indian capital, desperate to shore up India's defences and with the weight of the Government of India's historic steward-ship of the Gulf region on his shoulders.[21]

On taking up the reins in India, Wavell had identified Burma and Iran as his most immediate concerns, and determined to stop Nazi infiltration of the latter. On 17 July he sent a pugnacious telegram to the Chief of the Imperial General Staff, General Sir Alan Brooke, arguing that the:

> complaisant attitude it is proposed to adopt over Iran appears to me incomprehensible. It is essential to the defence of India that the Germans should be cleared out of Iran now. Failure to do so will lead to a repeti-tion of events which in Iraq were only just countered in time. It is essen-tial we should join hands with the Russians through Iran, and if the present Government is not willing to facilitate this it must be made to give way to one which will.[22]

Wavell need not have worried, because the Iranian situation was commanding the full attention of the government back home. As Wavell penned his letter to Brooke, the War Cabinet was being apprised of the diplo-matic pressure being brought to bear on the Iranians 'to expel the German community now in their country'. Soviet pressure was also being applied, and Foreign Secretary Anthony Eden reported that Ivan Maisky, Soviet ambas-sador to Britain and the man charged with normalizing relations with the Western powers following Barbarossa, had indicated that his government was anxious to clear up the position in Iran.[23] Moscow agitated for the expul-sion of the shah and seizure of Iran's road and rail network and informed the British that they were 'willing to take part in joint military plans'.[24]

Throughout July, Major-General Kennedy and his staff in the Military Operations Department at the War Office worked on a British 'plan to get the Germans out of Persia'. The idea 'was to try diplomatic pressure and then if necessary deliver an ultimatum, backed by a threat to bomb Tehran and occupy the oilfields'.[25] In the first week of August Kennedy attended two meetings chaired by Attlee in the absence of the prime minister, who was at the Atlantic Charter meeting with Roosevelt. The need to get the German 'technicians' out of Iran was stressed, as was the need to take control of the country lest the Soviet front break up and German armies move on the Caspian and the Caucasus. 'If this happened, Persia would then become the essential bastion of our right flank in the Middle East, and an outpost for the defence of India; moreover, it was necessary to be sure of Persia if we were to continue to draw the vital supplies of oil from the Gulf.'[26]

On 18 July the Chiefs of Staff concluded that the Iranian military was in no position to resist an invasion. Of nine divisions, only two 'could be considered moderately efficient'.[27] The air and naval forces were considered negligible. Joint Anglo-Soviet notes to the Iranian government were presented on 19 July requiring the removal of the Germans, though they explained that the allies advocated the maintenance of Iran's independence and that it was in the interests of Iran to get rid of the Germans too. Tehran refused, but promised to watch them closely; the Germans threatened to break off diplomatic relations. While making military preparations, the British hoped that a display of force would be enough to serve their purpose. The Foreign Office opposed the military option, concerned about Britain's capacity to limit Soviet designs in the country if invasion occurred, and concerned lest the Germans use it as an excuse to press for similar rights in Turkey. They were also concerned lest military forces across the region become too thinly spread, especially as it was possible that the Iraqi army could cause further trouble.

In particular, the Foreign Office worried about the impact on world opinion of invading a neutral country.[28] Even in the desperate circumstances of a world war, violating a neutral state had significant moral and political costs attached, and was the kind of action that the British had gone to war to prevent. Iran's neutral status was given due regard by senior British politicians, and the pros and cons of using force were vigorously debated. The British were not just battling against fascism and Nazism, but were fighting to preserve a rules-based international system that protected the rights of weak nations against the strong. They were fighting, in essence, to re-establish international law, and in doing so, claimed that they represented a higher moral order.[29]

Senior soldiers shared these concerns. Writing of the plans swirling around Whitehall for operations in places as diverse as the Azores, Iran and Siam, Lieutenant-General Sir Henry Pownall, Vice-Chief of the Imperial General Staff, wrote: 'I do *not* like these new commitments, started by small forces and growing, as they always do, into larger ones. The game may be worth the candle, but there's no estimate of the eventual number of candles required to get the game.'[30] There were doves as well as hawks, Eden in the former camp, the Viceroy of India, Lord Linlithgow, the latter. Churchill was positioned somewhere in between, though leaned, as ever, towards decisive action. But in the end, Churchill and the Chiefs of Staff were strongly influenced by the situation on the Eastern Front, where a collapse was expected. The British were also concerned to ensure that America supported and understood British actions, even if that support was *sotto voce*. The War Cabinet sanctioned the use of force if necessary, and Wavell was told to make his dispositions for an invasion.

Diplomatic correspondence and meetings smoothed the way for joint military action. Maisky, the Soviet ambassador, was invited to Chequers, the country residence of the British prime minister, on 20 July. Arriving at the Buckinghamshire mansion, he was taken to a room where Clementine Churchill was pouring tea for her husband and assembled family and guests. 'Everyone was talking, laughing, exchanging remarks,' Maisky wrote. 'The air was filled with chatter. Churchill, dressed in strange blue-grey overalls and a belt (a cross between a bricklayer's work clothes and an outfit suitable for a bomb shelter), was sitting in the other corner playing *Halma* with some pretty young girl.'[31]

The Soviet diplomat was being plied with tea and biscuits by Pamela, Churchill's daughter-in-law, when the prime minister rose, 'nodded to the guests and led me downstairs to a dreary drawing-room'. Here Maisky presented him with a personal message from Stalin. Responding to it, Churchill warmed to the idea of operations in Norway, poured cold water on the prospects of a second front in France anytime soon and enthused about the RAF's bombing campaign over Germany.

Then Churchill suddenly shifted to Iran, repeating everything that I had heard from Eden this morning, but in a sharper and more resolute form . . . 'The Shah must not be allowed to pursue *monkey tricks*,' the prime minister uttered heatedly. 'Persia must be with us! The Shah must choose one way or the other'... Churchill added that if the Shah persisted, a military occupation of Persia by Anglo-Soviet forces would be necessary. He hinted, moreover, that the Persian operation, along with Norway, could also be a sort of 'second front' [though there was little chance that Stalin would buy *that* as an alternative to an invasion of France].[32]

Two days later Lieutenant-General Quinan, commanding British forces in Iraq, received orders from Wavell to make ready to occupy the oilfields at Abadan and Naft Shah and the ports of Bandar-e Shahpur and Bushire. He was told that the government had approved a proposal to apply diplomatic pressure, backed by a display of force. Another note was to be presented to the Iranian government on 12 August, and Quinan was to have his troops concentrated by that date. Consequently, British forces were rushed into position on the Iran–Iraq border. Local inhabitants were enlisted to help, particularly the Kurds. Ambassador Cornwallis wrote that 'probably the best method of raising Kurdish saboteurs for work on Iraqi frontier passes would be to choose suitable local chieftains and arrange with them to produce a given number of men in a specified place at a given signal'. He told Sir Reader Bullard, his counterpart in Tehran, that 'reconnaissance detachments of British forces in Iraq were visiting Penjwin, Halabja, Rowandaz, Rayat and other points near the frontier'.[33]

On 31 July 1941 the War Cabinet discussed the Iranian situation again. Eden hoped that British forces in Iraq 'would be sufficient to enable us to bring pressure to bear on the Iranian Government to eject the German community without leaving us too weak in Iraq', where the situation remained tense following the recent war. A timetable for invasion was now in place, should it be necessary, as Quinan would have his forces ready by 12 August. Another division would be available by the end of August if required, and RAF squadrons were primed to support the ground forces.[34] Translating these orders down to units on the ground, on the same day, in Aleppo, the Household Cavalry regiment that had been at the core of Habforce was given the order to move to the Iran–Iraq border. Having taken part in the invasions of both Iraq and Syria, the regiment was presently garrisoning the conquered Syrian capital. Now it began another dash along the Iraqi trans-desert line of communication, the formation's transport supplemented by vehicles taken from vanquished Iraqi forces and 'enormous six-ton Peugeots' liberated from the Vichy French.

Barrelling in from Syria in a cloud of sand, the Household Cavalry bivouacked the first night on the edge of the Euphrates near Raqqa, and the next day moved through a sandstorm to Deir ez-Zor. The following day, it drove 'at a furious pace' to T2, then turned east down the pipeline, spending the night at T1. Then on to Habbaniya, camping on the lakeside, reaching Baghdad the following day. 'We moved through that horrible city, which has a main street eight miles long which smells of bad fish.' After that it was 20 miles on tarmac, then desert to Qizil Ribat en route to Kirkuk and the oilfields, where the regiment occupied slit trenches dug by recently departed Indian troops. Here it temporarily halted, having travelled 850 miles in six days.[35] The unit now awaited further orders while its men found ways to kill time. They bathed, took rifle practice on an Iraqi army range, sent patrols to the Rawandiz gorge and Sulaymaniyah, and 'killed hundreds of fish with a Mills bomb in a river', while on 12 August – the 'Glorious Twelfth', traditional opening of the red grouse shooting season in Britain – the officers shot sandgrouse.[36] As one soldier of the unit wrote, nevertheless 'We all had a fairly shrewd idea as to what was on. We had chased Germans out of two countries and we knew that their activities in Persia were causing consterna- tion.'[37] But the Iranians and Axis powers were not to know what was to come next, and measures were taken to deceive them as to British intentions in this theatre. The story was spread that an Indian division was being sent from Basra to Palestine along the desert convoy route in an attempt to explain the supply dumps that were being built up in anticipation of the invasion of Iran.[38]

The Household Cavalry now came under Slim's command. Having played a part in the invasions of Iraq and Syria, Slim had been hoping for a rest come August 1941. Leaving his troops in Iraq, he boarded a flight for a conference in Palestine, 'looking forward to the luxury of the King David Hotel'.[39] But half an hour into the flight the pilot handed him an urgent signal from Quinan, ordering an immediate return to Baghdad. This gave Slim pause for thought, as the two were not on the best of terms. Quinan had recently travelled aboard an aircraft carrying a jazz band's instruments from Jerusalem back to Iraq, at Slim's request. Given Quinan's orders regarding absolute economy in transport, the episode had earned Slim a 'stinging rebuke'.[40] Things were made worse when Quinan caught Slim using French lorries captured during the Syrian campaign to import thou- sands of bottles of Australian beer from Haifa – none of which he was prepared to part with for the benefit of Quinan's army headquarters staff in

Baghdad. 'I was therefore considerably relieved,' Slim recounted, 'to be told that I was forthwith to take command of a small force now collecting at Khanaquin and with it in three days' time invade Persia. It seemed a fairly tall order. Persia was a big country with a large if not reputedly very efficient army.'[41]

The War Cabinet now formed a special 'Persia Committee' to steer political and military policy and resolve the situation as quickly as possible. It met on 4 August in the Lord President's Room in Great George Street, chaired by Sir John Anderson, Lord President of the Council. If Quinan's invasion force met no substantial opposition, it should be in possession of the oilfields within two days of the order to move. The Persia Committee recommended that the Iranian government be approached on a 'firm but friendly basis', and that British troops employ minimum force if the invasion went ahead. From a political point of view it was also important to discourage the Soviet Union from 'gratifying any ambitions they might have of occupying Northern Persia. It should be explained to them that our intentions were limited to ensuring that the Persian Government exercised their neutral rights without detriment to our interests.'[42]

The Persia Committee drafted a note for the Foreign Secretary to send to the Iranian government, amounting to a list of demands to be met if military action were to be avoided: 'His Majesty's Government regarded the continued presence of German technical advisers and others in Persia as a danger to their rights and interests; they would accordingly wish to see the whole community removed.' It was acknowledged that this could not be done 'all at once', but the British insisted upon the expulsion of Germans whose presence was unexplained, or who worked in potentially dangerous occupations, such as the Posts and Telegraph Department. They also demanded 'vigorous steps' for monitoring and restricting the movements of those whose presence might be essential for German industry. No further German nationals were to be admitted, and the British government was to be given a list of those Germans that the Iranian government wished to retain, a list not to exceed one-fifth of the total number currently in the country. The Iranian government was also required to give assurances that it would curb the anti-British activities of politically malcontent Iraqi exiles, and was told that the British attached 'very great importance' to the granting of transit facilities through Iran for the supply of material to the Soviet Union. By way of mollification, Lord Hankey thought it might be possible to get British replacements for some of the German experts that the shah was required to expel, and the Persia Committee suggested that it might be politic to offer him an inducement, possibly in the form of doubled oil royalties. But if carrots did not work, then sticks would be used, to wit invasion, the seizure of key strategic assets and, if necessary, the bombing of Tehran.[43]

To help prepare the ground, military, diplomatic, economic and propaganda activities were aligned, and measures to withhold Anglo-Iranian Oil Company royalties from the Iranian government drawn up.[44] Throughout August the Foreign Office and the Government of India worked together to disseminate anti-shah propaganda claiming, for instance, that he treated his ministers in a 'medieval manner'.[45] Broadcasts from Britain and Delhi suggested that constitutional government should return to Iran and denounced the shah's autocratic ways. A secret memorandum of 7 August entitled 'Propaganda in Persia', prepared by Minister Bullard, argued that to 'forestall the Germans we might, simultaneously with the ultimatum, release articles and wireless talks about Iran, referring not only to the good points, but also to the great defects of the present regime'.[46] Anticipating the climate that would follow an invasion, Bullard continued in this vein:

> Tribute could be paid to the Shah as a soldier in early days but it could be hinted that greediness and tyranny have made him a different man ... forcible acquisition of land, forced labour, general poverty and corruption, acute shortage of water, Shah's own wealth and ownership of factories ... his monopoly of all prices ... his involvement with opium trade ... his bad treatment of soldiers ... weakness of the political structure ... Constitution only in name, a powerless parliament, dictated elections ... could be highlighted. Also it could be stressed that England has a democratic Government whereas the Shah, like Hitler, thinks the people are like sheep and are only fit to carry orders blindly.[47]

Britain sought both to garner American support for their actions in Iran, and to seal off the shah's regime from potential American support. To the shah's chagrin, Britain moved to block purchases of American arms. The Iranian government had approached American firms earlier in the year because Britain was unable – or unwilling – to meet its requirements. Key individuals such as Bullard and Wavell did not think Britain should supply Iran with war material in case the Germans got hold of it. American attitudes towards the shah had hardened. Despite concerns about souring relations with the Iranian government, and reservations about the motives of British and particularly Soviet policy, there was clear common ground. Supporting Britain's war effort was a cardinal tenet of American foreign policy, and because America was convinced of the seriousness of the German threat to Iran. Minister Dreyfus in Tehran told the State Department that the 'stormtroopers Gamotta [Gamotha] and Mayer who are ostensibly employed by Shenkers Transport Company, head an efficient Nazi party organization with branches throughout the country and with members strategically placed and instructed as to their part when the day of action arrives'.[48] An archaeologist called Eilers was the main person responsible for German propaganda, Dreyfus reported, and Germans were 'strategically placed' in the railway, radio and other public services, 'scattered throughout the country as agents of commercial organizations such as Shenkers and Ferrostahl'.[49] The Nazi club in Tehran, known as the Brown House, was the centre of their activity. Until outlawed by the Iranian authorities, club activities included enthusiastic military drill and target practice:

> The organization is said to be trained and disciplined with each man trained as to his duties either for sabotage or as an adjunct to invading German forces. An experienced American radio expert who is installing radio equipment for the Government is convinced that the Germans at the governmental radio station have set up special equipment which they are using to direct jamming operations originating in Berlin and directed against Allied broadcasts to this entire area.[50]

The British were keen to keep the Americans abreast of developments. On 8 August Eden showed John Winant, the American ambassador in London, the draft memorandum to the Iranian government. By this time British propaganda in Iran had reached 'an intense pitch' and, offering a further indication of where American sympathies lay, the American press was helping the British cause. For example, American newspapers printed a report from Delhi that a trainload of Germans had arrived in Iran, a report from Cairo about a rebellion in the Iranian army and reports of tribal uprisings in the Iranian countryside.

On the same day Lieutenant-General Pownall wrote that 'a very strong message' was being given to Iran:

> she *must* get rid of her 5–8,000 German 'technicians'. We really want not only that but physical control over the Anglo-Persian Oil Company

oilfields and the refinery at Abadan. That means employing a division and a cavalry brigade who are now being concentrated near Basra, partly as a threat and partly for use. The position is complicated by that fact that the Russians want to be in on the party. If we go in from the south they want to come from the north. India doesn't like that idea a bit – no more will Turkey.[51]

The Iranian government rejected the joint Anglo-Soviet note of 16 August, a document that demanded the expulsion of Axis nationals and the closure of their legations and consulates. By the time that the note was presented to the shah, the issue of expelling the Germans – over which the Iranian regime had temporized – had become little more than a *casus belli*. Both the British and Soviet governments had convinced themselves of the strategic wisdom of occupying Iran for the duration of the war. In the week following the presentation of the 16 August notes by the British and Soviet representatives, German forces made good progress on the Eastern Front and were seriously threatening Kiev and Odessa. Germans in Tehran boasted that they would soon be across the Dnieper. They would quickly arrive at Batum to cut off Soviet communications if they invaded Iran. If only the shah could stand firm for a few more weeks, German forces would be in Tehran to help him.[52]

Dreyfus told Washington that while he had no doubt about the existence of a Nazi fifth column and of its disruptive potential, he was convinced that 'the Brits' were using it as a pretext for eventual occupation 'and are deliberately exaggerating its potency'. 'I have come to the conclusion,' he wrote, 'that the British and Russians will occupy Iran because of overwhelming military necessity no matter what reply the Iranians make to their demands. I must add emphatically to avoid misunderstanding that I am in full agreement with the British action and believe it to be vitally necessary for the furtherance of our common cause.'[53] This was a significant judgement, because Dreyfus was generally highly critical of British motives and actions; Milani writes that he was a 'preacher turned diplomat who despised some of the bare-knuckle tactics of his British counterpart'.[54] Nevertheless, writing on 22 August Dreyfus emphasized that Iranians remembered 'with sorrow the great misfortunes of the last war, the unbelievable number of the population which died as a result of famine and epidemics caused by foreign interference'. The official Iranian line was that it would agree to expel the Germans but 'deeply resented' the peremptory nature of the demands, and did not like 'being pushed around by the British'.[55]

As British and Soviet diplomatic pressure mounted, reinforced by the troops massing on the borders, Iran held its breath. There were food shortages in Tehran as people stockpiled supplies; riots were only narrowly avoided in food and kerosene queues. As a precautionary measure, British citizens were evacuated; about 800 Germans took refuge in the German legation, and 350 British and other allied civilians crammed into the American and British diplomatic compounds. The German agent Berthold Schulze-Holthus wrote that although citizens of other nations were leaving, Germans had to remain. 'Acting on the highest orders, Ettel announced that any German who abandoned Persia would be looked upon as a traitor to his country.'[56] The prospect of Soviet invasion and bombing terrified people. Dreyfus predicted that if an invasion took place, rioting and civil disturbances would occur until 'the invaders get a firm hold . . . in view of the bitter feeling among the masses against the British and the Shah'.[57]

British preparations proceeded apace. Churchill and Dill returned from the Atlantic Charter meeting on 19 August. 'Roosevelt agreed to our proposed action towards Persia (which will come to a head very soon indeed),' wrote Pownall. 'Winston himself is strongly in favour of military action', specifically because of his interest in Iran as a supply line to the Soviet Union, and because of his fears 'that Turkey might welsh at any moment'.[58] Working late at the War Office on the following day, Major-General Kennedy received a visit from the Russian military attaché. 'I took him to Dill's room, where I gave him an outline of our plan for the operations in Persia. We asked him what the Russian plan was, but he did not know it, and he promised to ask Moscow.'[59] But generals Dill and Kennedy 'expected no answer', based on Moscow's extreme reluctance – indeed, its blunt refusal – to share even basic information with its allies. Nevertheless, four days later, on 24 August, the attaché visited again, to say that Ambassador Maisky 'had heard from Moscow that a Russian force would cross the Persian border at dawn next day'. He added that 'Moscow thought we had underestimated the Persians, who were about twice as strong as we had calculated'.[60] The British Embassy in Baghdad reported that a Soviet military mission was due to arrive in Mosul on 23 August. The embassy was 'informed by wireless that Russian forces cross into Iran at dawn on 25 August, their immediate objective being the line from Tabriz to Ardebil'. The Soviet force would comprise three infantry divisions, two cavalry divisions and two tank brigades. The most secret message was delivered by hand to Major-General Charles Harvey and Major-General Slim, commanding the two British land forces poised near the Iranian border.[61]

The British intensified their efforts to ensure that the Americans were onside in the hours immediately preceding the invasion. On 23 August Ambassador Winant contacted the American Secretary of State, telling him that he had spoken to Eden that morning, and that the British Foreign Secretary 'wanted you to know how seriously they view the German agents in Iran. The British are certain that their negotiations with the Iran government are being directed by the Germans.' Despite their reservations, the Americans continued to back the British.

Churchill kept an eagle eye on the situation. In particular, he was keen to keep the pressure on Wavell, reminding him of the seriousness with which the War Cabinet viewed a successful outcome in this latest Middle Eastern venture. On 24 August, the day before imperial forces crossed the start line, the prime minister dispatched one of his 'action this day' communiqués. Addressing the Secretary of State for War and the Chief of the Imperial General Staff, and pursuing his animus towards Wavell, he wrote: 'Remember, please, that General Wavell is the Officer responsible for the Persian campaign. It seems astonishing that he should leave for England the very moment when all hangs in the balance. I suppose he realizes that I am holding him responsible for this campaign.'[62] Both anxious and excited about the impending operation and the range of possible outcomes, on the same day Churchill wrote to the Chiefs of Staff, stressing the need to send more forces to the theatre and fretting over the detail. If it were true, for example, that Slim's 10th Indian Division did not have a European battalion per brigade (a standard Indian Army practice), then three should be sent forthwith, he declared. This was in response to a telegram expressing concern that there might not be sufficient forces to launch Operation Countenance, the name given to the British invasion. It was typical Churchill. 'Where is the last brigade of the 50th Division?' he asked. Surely its current place of residence, Cyprus, was in no immediate danger, so why were forces being retained there? And so on.[63]

On 25 August, the day British and Soviet forces went in, Under Secretary of State Sumner Welles met the Iranian minister in Washington, and told him that he felt sure that British policy would be 'one of eventual restoration of the liberties of the Iranian people, no matter what temporary measures might be undertaken, whereas if Germany acquired any form of domination over Iran, that domination would never be relinquished were Germany to find herself in a position of world domination'.[64] Assistant Secretary of State Wallace Smith Murray had a conversation with the Iranian minister in Washington, during the course of which he shocked him by venturing the opinion that working with the British for the defence of the region was a good thing, and that 'we [the United States] regard the British cause as our cause'.[65] Cordell Hull stated things even more explicitly: 'My country has no notion of sitting still and listening to the siren voice of Hitler discussing the merits of neutrality while he conquers all other areas and gets around to the point of attacking us just as he has some fifteen countries in Europe.'[66] Thus isolated, Iran was now at the mercy of the British and Soviet militaries, and was about to be dragged into the shooting war.

CHAPTER 8

Anglo-Soviet invasion

Regardless of the strategic logic of invading Iran, breaching an independent country's sovereignty and neutrality bothered the British government. It was supposed to be the Germans, not the British, who did such things. Jock Colville, Churchill's assistant private secretary, reflected this unease, confiding to his diary on 25 August that 'today our long-planned invasion of Persia began. I am afraid it is an aggressive and not really warranted act, which is difficult to justify except on the, in this case dubious, principle of *Salus populi suprema lex*' ('the welfare of the people should be the supreme law').[1] John Masters put it more bluntly: 'We had started the great war for democracy by invading three neutral countries against the wishes of their inhabitants or, at least, their governments.'[2] Britain could feel 'rather ashamed', wrote the diplomat Oliver Harvey, of its 'first act of "naked aggression"'.[3] But setting aside such democratic squeamishness, there was a war on, and the initiative had to be seized. Adrian O'Sullivan, the foremost expert on German penetration in Iran during the war, summarizes matters in this way:

> Any suggestion that the Anglo-Soviet invasion was an avoidable, egregious violation of a neutral state fails to take into account the fact that the Germans were poised to complete this fourth stage of their plan ... The German presence in Persia, astride the lines of communication between the British Middle East and India, and immediately to the rear of the Red Army in Transcaucasia, was politically provocative and strategically unacceptable: invasion was inevitable.[4]

The Soviets had been building up their forces on Iran's borderlands since early in the war. On 25 August they invaded mainly from Transcaucasia, with the 44th, 47th and 53rd armies under General Dmitry Timofeyevich Kozlov, commander of the Transcaucasian Military District. Entering Iran along both the eastern and western shores of the Caspian, the invasion force comprised around 40,000 men and 1,000 tanks, mostly of the T-26 variety. The 47th Army struck from the Soviet Socialist Republic of Azerbaijan into the Iranian province of Azerbaijan on the morning of 25 August, led by Major-General Vasily Novikov. The force comprised two powerful mechanized columns, one moving down to the shore of the Caspian through Bandar-e Pahlavi, the other crossing the frontier 200 miles farther west, moving on Tabriz.[5] Spearheaded by an overwhelming force of tanks, the Soviet intent was to swing towards Qazvin, the traditional invasion route used by Tsarist armies in the past. Novikov's second objective was to capture Rezaiyeh (today's Urmia) and then drive into Kurdistan. Novikov also thrust towards Maku, which had been bombed, to cut off Iran from the Turkish frontier. The Soviet objective was the occupation of the Iranian provinces of Azerbaijan, Gilan and Mazanderan.

Iranian forces failed to counterattack or to blow bridges and other transport infrastructure, and in the air, while the Soviets had over 400 aircraft to call upon, they were opposed by the fourteen outdated Audax and Hind biplanes of the Second Iranian Air Regiment at Tabriz. Clarmont Skrine, consul in Mashhad, wrote that as Soviet bombers flew overhead the 'streets filled with military transport and commandeered civilian lorries' as the bulk of the garrison left towards where it was thought that the Soviets might appear. 'Behind them they left chaos, thousands of people pouring into the country as they escaped the beleaguered city, crammed along with their belongings into cars and carriages and on barrows and mules.'[6]

Further to the south, British forces, using Iraq as their springboard, attacked from the Basra bridgehead towards the oil-rich province of Khuzestan, and from Khanaqin towards the northern oilfields and the cities of Kermanshah, Hamadan, Tehran and Qazvin, where they would meet up with the Soviets. The British invasion featured synchronized activity by air, land and sea forces. Units involved included regiments from the British and Indian armies amounting to around 20,000 soldiers, RAF squadrons and warships from the Royal Australian Navy, the Royal Indian Navy and the Royal Navy. Strategically, Britain's intention was to take over the oilfields, see off German filibusterers and get into a position from which it would be able to defend the oilfields should the Germans invade. An additional strategic objective, for both invading powers, was Iran's transport infrastructure, which was to be seized and used to channel supplies from America and Britain to the Soviet army and air force. As the military orders succinctly put it, the British intent was 'the capture and the occupation of the oilfields in the North West (NAFT-I-SHAH district), the oilfields in KHUZISTAN with the refinery at ABADAN, and to gain control of the Trans-IRANIAN Railway from BANDAR SHAHPUR in the South to the railhead on the CASPIAN SEA at BANDAR SHAH'.[7]

Quinan's land forces were divided into two groups. Southern Force under Major-General Harvey was built around the 8th Indian Division's 18th and 24th Infantry brigades, supplemented by the 25th Infantry Brigade borrowed from the 10th Indian Division, which had been transferred from Kirkuk to Basra for the purpose. Northern Force, commanded by Major-General Slim, comprised the rest of the 10th Indian Division – the 21st Indian Infantry Brigade and 2nd Indian Armoured Brigade – and a field artillery regiment. In addition, Slim had the British 9th Armoured Brigade – the new designation of the Household Cavalry brigade – and the other units that had been part of Habforce during the Iraq campaign. It was, in Slim's words, 'rather a composite force', the 2nd Indian Armoured Brigade, for example, having 'no armour but dismounted cavalry in 30 cwt [hundredweight] trucks'.[8]

Supporting Slim's troops was the RAF's Northern Group, operated from RAF Habbaniya under Air Vice-Marshal D'Albiac's direct command. It comprised the bombers of 11 Squadron, 14 Squadron and 45 Squadron.[9] With twelve aircraft apiece, the three squadrons would 'operate against objectives in the TEHERAN Area and elsewhere in Iran as required, and may be called upon to operate in direct support of the military force attacking Naft-I-Shah'.[10] Group Captain Donald Thomson commanded the RAF's Southern Group or 'Basra Wing' which operated from RAF Shaibah in support of Harvey's force. He stated that his intent was: 'To destroy the IRANIAN Air Force in the Khuzistan Area ... To protect the Army and Navy forces from air attack ... Strategic bombing of military objectives in close support of ground forces and destruction of Iranian aerodromes and air forces on the ground.'[11] Thomson had at his disposal the Hurricane and Gladiator fighters of 261 Squadron, dedicated to the protection of land and naval forces, 84 Squadron's Blenheim bombers, 31 Squadron's battlefield transport Valentias dedicated to the transport of troops, equipment and supplies and 244 Squadron's Vickers Vincents, which performed light bomber and army cooperation roles such as tactical reconnaissance.[12]

The RAF would also be employed to drop propaganda leaflets aimed at the civilian population, stating that the war was against the 'corrupt' shah and his regime, not the people, though warning them that 'if any oppose or help the Germans they will be destroyed'. Hundreds of thousands of pamphlets were ready for dispersal from the skies above Tehran, Kashan, Isfahan and Shiraz. A secret communication to squadron commanding officers, dated 25 August, gave all necessary map references for targets in central and southern Iran. The RAF's No. 2 Photographic Reconnaissance Unit, comprising long-range Hurricanes and a Lockheed Electra, had arrived at Habbaniya to photograph potential targets and Iranian naval vessels in order to assist naval operations in the Gulf.

The Royal Navy's Commander-in-Chief East Indies, Vice-Admiral Geoffrey Arbuthnot, was told about the forthcoming invasion on 20 August. He instructed his subordinate officer, Commodore Cosmo Graham, Senior Naval Officer Persian Gulf, to prepare. Graham's Persian Gulf Division was an eclectic little fleet. There was the armed merchant cruiser HMAS *Kanimbla*, particularly valued because it was big enough to transport large numbers of troops, the corvette HMS *Snapdragon*, the river gunboat HMS *Cockchafer* and the sloops HMS *Shoreham*, HMAS *Yarra* and HMS *Falmouth*. There were also a couple of tugs, the armed dhow *Naif* (manned by Australians) and the Royal Indian Navy's *Lawrence* and *Lilavati*. These ships were to capture or sink Iranian sloops and gunboats in the Karun river and at their naval base at Khorramshahr, attack shore batteries, seize Axis merchant vessels in neutral Iranian ports, and, with army assistance, capture the Iranian naval station and barracks.[13]

The Iranian forces opposing generals Kozlov and Quinan consisted of about 130,000 men, with 200 outmoded aircraft and naval forces amounting to 7 sloops and gunboats. Since coming to power Reza Shah had taken 'special pride in re-establishing Iran's military might after more than a century of Iranian humiliation as a victim of Russian and British imperialism'.[14] The army was prominent in Iranian affairs and had been instrumental in the centralization project that had seen Tehran's power extend into the regions. The shah strove to ensure the loyalty of the military, particularly the officer corps. In Tehran he built an impressive array of military establishments, including an arsenal, machine-gun factory, aircraft repair shop, military hospital, officers' club, army bank and the military college in Tehran, modelled on the elite French academy of Saint-Cyr. But suppressing nomadic communities in pursuit of the shah's policy of sedentarization and centralization was one thing. Now, for the first time, the Iranian military was to be pitted against the forces of the great powers, a different prospect altogether.

Unlike in Iraq, there were no German forces fielded in support of the Iranians, though German agents were active across the country, garnering intelligence regarding Soviet forces in Transcaucasia and developing a fifth-column movement intended to prepare the ground for the arrival of the Wehrmacht. Berthold Schulze-Holthus was a member of Abwehr I deployed to Iran to gather intelligence on airfields, factories, railway junctions and the location and strength of Iranian and Soviet garrisons.[15] Working initially under the cover of his role as Vice-Consul Tabriz and the Deutsche Haus, Tabriz's social centre for Germans, he was particularly interested in the Baku area. Azerbaijan was an ideal region in terms of location and the fact that the national aspirations of the Azeris were split either side of Soviet–Iranian border, making it good ground for conspiracy and espionage. There was an underground movement here sympathetic to Germany, and another in Armenia. Ahead of Barbarossa he was reporting to Abwehr chief Admiral Wilhelm Canaris, and thereafter gathered information from Soviet Azerbaijan, mainly from the oilfields. He provided information about airfields, underground installations, emergency landing grounds, bunkers, garrison buildings, new industrial factories, pumping stations, refineries, power stations and waterworks.

Surviving transcripts of radio broadcasts from Tehran reveal the turmoil inside the country as enemy forces massed on the border and the government attempted to conjure a spirit of popular resistance. There was widespread coverage of the shah's speech to graduates passing out from the officer training college on 20 August:

> There is no need for me to attract your attention any more than I have done to your public duties and the grave situation of today. It is sufficient to say that all soldiers and officers of the army must pay great attention and have due interest in the circumstances now prevailing and should in no way refrain, when the time comes, from any sacrifice ... Not only from time immemorial has it been the characteristic of the brave soldiers of Iran to sacrifice their lives for their country and even today all the soldiers and officers of the powerful imperial army are endowed with this quality, but also every one of the inhabitants of this ancient country is filled with the same spirit, and it is through this spirit of sacrifice and observance of the duty of giving their life for their

country that the Iranian nation has been able to resist throughout the length of its long history in the face of the most formidable and terrifying events of the world's history, and continue for some 27 centuries to live a life full of honour and glory. As the course of events is today become increasingly grave, the Iranian nation must also increase its attentiveness and endeavour not to let any blow be struck at its dignity and honour, and should prepare itself for immediate action.[16]

Presenting certificates to the cadets, the shah declared: 'Unfortunately this year you cannot take your month vacation upon graduation . . . You must go immediately to the regiment to which you are assigned . . . For your information, sons, our country is on the edge of very dangerous times.'[17] Lieutenant Mohammed Ali Sobhani was one of a group of officers who boarded a bus in Tehran bound for Tabriz in Azerbaijan to join the 3rd Division. During the journey the soldiers learned of the Soviet invasion while at a checkpoint. 'I remember as soon as we heard we were all very happy because now we would be fighting our real enemy – the Russians.'[18]

The troops go in in the south

At first light on 25 August 1941 the sloop HMS *Shoreham* opened up with her main armament on the Iranian sloop *Palang* at Abadan pier, signalling the start of the offensive. The Iranian vessel exploded in a fireball and quickly sank, and *Shoreham* also shelled the *Babr*. Several synchronized troop landings were made in the southern sector, while Slim's forces crossed the border from their Khanaqin assembly point and Soviet forces rolled across Iran's northern borders. Harvey's objectives in the southern sector of British operations were to capture the Khuzestan oilfields and to dislodge Iranian forces deployed near the Gulf. Simultaneous operations were launched on three axes. The 24th Indian Infantry Brigade spread out along the Gulf coast in a gallimaufry of vessels to capture the ports and towns of Abadan and Bandar Shahpur; the 18th Indian Infantry Brigade attacked the river town of Khorramshahr; and the 25th Indian Infantry Brigade made for the fort at Qaisr Shaikh.[19]

The invasion of Iran, according to a British intelligence report, 'took the German colony there completely by surprise.'[20] Schulze-Holthus and his wife were 'awoken brutally out of our sleep at five o'clock by the sound of heavy anti-aircraft fire. In the meantime came the hollow thud of the first bombs.'[21] German nationals had assembled and left the capital in a convoy. At the German Embassy, Ettel, in company with the SD chiefs in Iran, Roman Gamotha and Franz Mayr, was burning documents, and looting had commenced on the streets outside. As he moved to Isfahan and onwards, Schulze-Holthus continued to take note of landmarks and features that might be useful to Luftwaffe pilots in the future.

Learning of the coordinated attacks, the shah summoned the British and Soviet ambassadors. 'I need to know why your forces have invaded my country,' he said. 'You haven't declared war on us.'[22] He said that he could have the Germans out within the week. But military operations were now irreversible and, back in London, the War Cabinet decided on this day that more forces needed to be sent to ensure that the Iranian road and railway system were adequately secured after the cessation of hostilities. Ceasefire terms and zones of occupation were already being discussed, and Eden had proposed a line of separation between the two zones to Maisky. Revealing their core interest, before doing so the War Cabinet had consulted the Petroleum Department to ensure that Britain got the areas it wanted. The consultation led to alterations, ensuring for example that the British zone included the new oilfield at Gachsaran.[23] Furthermore, with operations now proceeding, Britain's ideas of what it wanted from Iran were growing. No longer, for example, was the Iranian facilitation of the dispatch of supplies to the Soviet Union considered sufficient. Now, 'the right to control and develop Iranian communications' was to be demanded.[24]

Securing the oil wells and refineries intact, along with the people that operated them, was the priority, and that meant Abadan. Abadan was an impressive sight: 'Like the skyscrapers of New York,' wrote Alan Moorehead, 'the towers of the Abadan refinery rise out of the delta. All around lay the cottages and gardens of the officials and the workers.'[25] To capture Abadan and its refinery, two battalions of the 24th Indian Infantry Brigade – the Rajputana Rifles and 1st Kumaon Rifles – were transported under cover of darkness down the Shatt al-Arab from Basra in naval vessels, motor launches and barges from Basra's RAF wharf. At dawn, they were in position and ready to storm the jetties and creeks on the waterfront, achieving complete surprise. The enemy was driven off the waterfront and through the residential areas. There was 'stiff fighting' when they moved against the town and several incidents of Anglo-Iranian Oil Company (AIOC) workers in overalls being mistaken for enemy troops and killed. When Abadan had been secured, a cordon was formed around the refinery.

HMAS *Kanimbla* landed two companies of the Baluch Regiment at Bandar-e Shahpur to seize harbour works and oil facilities, and it did not take long before it was 'completely in [British] hands' and an Iranian warship sunk. The British hoped to seize intact a number of Axis merchant vessels sheltering in the port – three Italian and eight German ships, the latter including *Wiessenfels, Hohenfels, Marienfels, Sturmfels* and *Wildenfels,* all of the Hansa Line. Given the global shipping shortage and the predations of the enemy, the opportunity to capture additional hulls was welcomed; more importantly, the British wanted to prevent the Germans from scuttling them and blocking the Shatt al-Arab – orders for which were issued by the German navy's high command.[26] Unfortunately, 'considerable damage' was 'sustained by Axis vessels through sabotage before our forces could prevent this action', though salvage operations were soon under way.[27]

Two battalions of Gurkhas and one of the Mahratta Light Infantry, together with a squadron of the Guides Cavalry and a field artillery battery, crossed from Basra and moved on Khorramshahr in order to subdue the naval base. HMS *Falmouth* transported two platoons and the company headquarters of the 3/10th Baluch Regiment. Mahratta and Sikh battalions and units of the 13th Lancers advanced on a northerly route to round up Iranian troops in the Qasr-e Sheikh region. The oilfield at Haftkel, 40 miles east of Ahwaz, was secured by an airborne landing. A company of the 3/10th Baluch Regiment was conveyed in 31 Squadron Valentias, the workhorse cargo aircraft used throughout the Middle East. Their job was to protect and escort British women and children evacuated from Masjed-e Soleyman to Haftkel. 'Arrangements had been made with the staff of the AIOC to indicate whether it would be safe for the BT [bomber transport] aircraft to land by displaying large white XX on the landing ground and this was done. The BT aircraft were escorted from Shaibah on outward and return by 2 LR [long range] Hurricanes.' Two of the Valentias overshot the landing ground and had to be written off, though there were no casualties and all useful parts were salvaged. The remaining four Valentias and the Hurricanes returned safely to Shaibah in Iraq.[28]

Supporting the troops in the southern sector, Group Captain Thomson's Basrah Wing maintained Hurricane standing fighter patrols over Abadan, Bandar-e Shahpur and Khorramshahr. Hurricanes were sent to attack enemy airbases and landing grounds. Three Gladiators were retained at Shaibah for the defence of the Basra dock area, the airport and the aerodrome itself. A flight of three Blenheims was sent to destroy the enemy airbase at Ahwaz and any aircraft found there, while another flight was dispatched to attack the naval barracks at Khorramshahr and the military barracks at Abadan. Blenheims also gunned Iranian positions at Khosrowabad. All available Vincents stood by for reconnaissance over the Ahwaz column of troops and over Abadan and Khorramshahr.

The Iranians put up virtually no resistance in the air, allowing the RAF a free hand. They hit key facilities such as the Ahwaz airbase hard:

> The first flight of our aircraft surprised three Hawker type enemy aircraft running up on the ground at AHWAZ aerodrome and success-fully strafed them. A flight of Blenheim bombers then attacked the hangars. They reported further aircraft seen dispersed on the aerodrome and the fighters were again despatched to deal with them, followed by a second bombing raid in which one of the two hangars was hit and set on fire. The ground strafing by the fighter aircraft had also been successful and it was thought that a considerable number of the enemy aircraft had been rendered unserviceable.[29]

Reports were positive throughout the southern sector. Tactical recon-naissance had been carried out by Vincents of 244 Squadron and 'proved of value to the various brigades carrying out the operations ... Opposition from the forces at KHURRAMSHAHR on the West bank of the Karun has been overcome. The Wireless Station and the Customs Post at PUL-I-NAU were in our hands and although Khurramshahr had not been occupied, our Armoured Cars had entered the town and returned to report all quiet.'[30] On the east bank of the Karun, one Iranian sloop had been sunk alongside its jetty, the two gunboats and the rest of the naval craft had been captured and barracks and other military installations were occupied. The 25th Infantry Brigade encountered and overcame resistance at Qasr-e Sheikh and bivou-acked for the night, ready to resume the advance towards Ahwaz the following day.

Responding to the attacks, the shah ordered Major-General Azizollah Zarghami, Army Chief of Staff, to deploy the Central Garrison to defend the capital, but offered no instructions for the divisions bearing the brunt of the invaders' attacks elsewhere. The provinces of Azerbaijan and Kermanshah were reinforced, and Khuzestan was to be defended at all costs. Large concentrations of Iranian troops were located across the country, but not where they were most needed.[31] A significant problem for the Iranians was that they had no experience of coordinating the operations of ground and air forces. This was not the only problem; army formations outside of the capital suffered from poor mobility, there were major equipment deficiencies and there was no effective coordination of defence across the vast country.[32]

The British attack in northern Iran focused on occupying the Naft-e Shah oilfields on the frontier near Khanaqin, and securing the road through the mountains to Kermanshah and on towards Tehran. The only way to do this was to take the Pai Tak Pass. On the approach to this bottleneck point of access, a V-shaped gorge led into a narrow valley with a swift-running stream. 'After ascending this for nearly ten miles', wrote Captain Summers of the Household Cavalry, 'the valley abruptly ended in an apparently impassable cliff of 2,000 feet of sheer perpendicular rock, and we were face to face with the famous pilgrim pass, the Tek-i-Gehri, which gives access to Persia proper and is the only pass negotiable by wheeled vehicles for some hundreds of miles on either side.'[33] At the foot was the small village of Pai Tak. The narrow track running up the cliff face in a horseshoe fashion, as it made the circuit of the recess of cliff forming the actual 'end' of the valley, was 'an insignificant ledge in the sheer wall of the rock'. Before ascending, the checkpoint at the summit had to be telephoned to ensure there was nothing coming down the track.

Slim arrived at the rallying point at Khanaqin less than twenty-four hours before the attack went in. This was hasty planning by any standards. Fortunately, Slim's subordinates had the situation under control. He was able to adopt a plan designed by Brigadier John Aizlewood, commanding the 9th Armoured Brigade, for 'the forcing of the formidable Pa-i-Tak Pass, which within thirty miles of our crossing the frontier would bar our way'.[34] The plan was to send one force to secure the oilfield at Naft Shah, 25 miles south-south-east of Khanaqin, and to send another, fast, column south, to outflank the Pai Tak Pass position and threaten its rear. Meanwhile, a third force, at the allotted moment, would assault the pass frontally.

'Before dawn on 25 August', wrote Slim:

led by the Hussars in their always gallant but decrepit and slightly ridiculous old Mark VII tanks, whose only armament was a single Vickers machine-gun apiece and whose armour almost anything could pierce, we crossed the frontier. By that time I was becoming accustomed to invasions; this was the fifth frontier I had crossed in the past year. All the same, there was a thrill about it. But very little happened. A few harmless shots from vanishing frontier guards greeted us as we encircled the village of Qasr-i-Shirin, about ten miles inside Persia, but we met no real opposition. As it grew lighter, Aizlewood and I pushed on with the advance-guard, and by mid-morning we were almost at the entrance to the Pa-i-Tak Pass. Here we stopped and, covered by a screen of light tanks, stood on the roof of my station-wagon to study this historic gate through which, over the centuries, so many armies had passed or tried to pass ... Viewed from below it was a most formidable and threatening obstacle. The interminable flat plains of the Tigris and Euphrates which stretched behind us for hundreds of miles here came to an abrupt end at the great boundary wall of a mighty escarpment stretching from north to south across our path. The road to Kermanshah which we must follow rose sharply into the mouth of the pass and, climbing in curves and loops, vanished among cliffs and gorges to emerge, three thousand feet higher, on to the plateau of Gilan. It looked as if a handful of men could hold against an army many times the size of mine.[35]

Confirming Slim's assessment, Summers reckoned that a 'stubborn enemy could have prevented any forward movement through the pass down the main road to Kermanshah'. But though British intelligence suggested that a dug in force of between 5,000 and 10,000 Iranian soldiers guarded it, the narrow entrance seemed 'still and deserted'. Slim could not resist driving cautiously up the pass himself, intrigued to see if the enemy was there at all. They drove on until gunfire was heard from behind. 'By God, they're shooting at us!' exclaimed the brigadier in an aggrieved voice, and they beat a hasty retreat from what turned out to be Iranian anti-tank gunfire.[36] Below, John Masters and his Gurkhas were waiting in battle formation ready to go up the pass, having been told that enemy guns were ranged on all possible access points. Suddenly a khaki saloon appeared, flying the divisional flag from the radiator cap. 'How the hell did he get past us?' asked the battalion commander when Slim emerged from the vehicle. 'Morning Willy. There's nothing til you get round the fourth hairpin,' the general said. 'They've got an anti-tank gun there.'[37] There was a large shell hole through the back of the car body: Slim, who would later gain fame in Burma, had come close to an early exit from the stage.

Having seen things for himself, Slim ordered the attacks to go ahead:

The idea of a frontal attack up the rugged and in places almost vertical escarpment was not attractive, but the brigadier when studying his map before my arrival had spotted a route by which any position at the Pa-i-Tak itself could be by-passed. This was a track which crossed the escarpment some twenty miles further south and went via the village of Gilan to Shahabad on the main Kermanshah road, about thirty miles south-east of the main pass. It was a long – about ninety miles – and rough track but it was said to be passable by wheels.[38]

As British and Soviet forces penetrated Iranian territory on 25 August, Tehran radio reviewed the current 'unfortunate situation'. It restated the country's neutrality, recounted Britain and the Soviet Union's unreasonable demands for the expulsion of German nationals and the takeover of Iran's transport infrastructure, and lamented their deplorable preference for war over diplomacy.[39] Under the headline 'Bombing of open cities', the newspaper *Iran* published an article claiming that casualties had been suffered as the allies attacked civilians 'against the principles of warfare'. This 'act of aggression will create astonishment among the civilised world, to whom we protest and declare that the Iranian government which is supported by the people had no intention of going to war, and only wished to maintain peace and security'.[40]

The shah made frantic last-minute efforts to forestall the allies as hostilities got under way. He summoned the British minister Sir Reader Bullard and his Soviet counterpart, Andrey Smirnov, and offered to expel all German subjects in return for a cessation of hostilities. But it was too late for any of that, and the unexpected tepidity of the Iranian army's resistance created its own momentum. Reza Shah sent urgent telegrams, written in French, to President Roosevelt, one neutral head of state appealing to another. Addressing the American leader as 'Your Excellency', he reported that British and Soviet forces had entered Iran brusquely and without notice. They had occupied certain locations and bombarded open cities. The pretext regarding German nationals was insufficient to warrant such extreme action, he argued. Anglo-Soviet acts of aggression had no basis in reason, and in asking for American intervention he referred to President Roosevelt's own declarations regarding the need to defend the principles of justice and the rights of people to freedom and neutrality.[41]

The atmosphere was gloomy as the royal family wondered what to do, staring into an abyss that might spell the end of all that Reza Shah had built since ascending the throne:

> On the day of the invasion the Imperial Family gathered for lunch. The mood at the table was 'so tense and so grim that none of us dared speak', recalled Princess Ashraf. 'What I knew was inevitable has happened', her father told them. 'The Allies have invaded. I think this will be the end for me – the English will see to it.' In a moment of great drama, the Crown Prince handed his sister a gun. 'Ashraf, keep this gun with you, and if troops enter Tehran and try to take us, fire a few shots and then take your own life', he told his sister. 'I'll do the same.' The next day, bombers reached the outskirts of Tehran and dropped explosives. The queen and the princess sheltered in the palace basement and as soon as the all-clear was sounded packed and fled south to Isfahan.[42]

There was an element of bathos, as a dynasty and the state it had founded teetered on the brink of destruction at the hands of a relatively small number of alien soldiers fighting a routine campaign on the distant fringes of their countries' empires.

In the south on the second day of the invasion, 26 August, the 24th Infantry Brigade continued mopping up operations and secured the whole of Abadan island. The 18th Indian Brigade was tasked with the capture of Khorramshahr and the area up to the Iran–Iraq border. This involved advancing under cover of darkness in motor transport and making a wide detour to attack the town from the north. The 18th and 25th brigades consolidated their positions and made some small advances up the banks of the Karun river. They crossed the river and secured the AIOC pumping station at Darkhoveyn. The RAF maintained standing fighter patrols over Ahwaz and Abadan, while Vincents conducted tactical reconnaissance flights above the soldiers of the 25th Brigade as they advanced towards Ahwaz. During the morning two Iranian aircraft, believed to be Audaxes, took off from the local airbase. Squadron Leader Mason, on patrol in a Hurricane, shot one down, the Iranian pilot force-landing 5 miles south-east of Ahwaz. Tellingly, 'this was the only occasion in the South in which IRANIAN aircraft took to the air'.[43]

On 27 August, Abadan, Khorramshahr and Qasr-e Sheikh having been successfully 'cleaned up', General Harvey developed his plans for the capture of Ahwaz. The 18th Indian Infantry Brigade continued its advance up the east bank of the Karun through the Kut-e Abdollah pumping station, whilst the 20th Indian Infantry Brigade advanced up the west bank to capture the barracks, aerodrome and bridgeheads over the river.[44] 84 Squadron Blenheims bombed Iranian troop concentrations and barracks at intervals of twenty minutes, commencing at 0530. The aircraft returned to Shaibah, bombed up, refuelled and remained on call. 261 Squadron provided continuous fighter cover over Ahwaz from 0600, while 244 Squadron Vincents continued to provide tactical and reconnaissance flights over the infantry columns either side of the river.

Journalists followed in the wake of Harvey's force. 'Can you fly to Persia at once?' the editor of the *Daily Express*, Arthur Christiansen, had asked Alan Moorehead.[45] Hurriedly, the Australian journalist obtained a visa from the Iranian Embassy in Cairo, and with a gaggle of fellow newsmen headed east, reaching Basra via Lydda and Habbaniya, where 'bullet holes made by Nazi fighters were still letting in shafts of sunlight' in the mess.[46] The Shatt al-Arab had been bridged, 'about thirty Arab dhows lashed side by side, their midships covered with planking. Across this the rear remnants of the Indian Army were hastening into battle. We began a weird drive in their wake ... hundreds of army vehicles bouncing pell-mell towards the east.'[47] He met Harvey at a riverside headquarters. 'It was like no war I had ever seen before. We sat around in easy-chairs drinking whisky and soda and it was all explained to us on maps like some parlour game', the scene reminiscent of accounts of nineteenth-century campaigns like the advance before the Battle of Omdurman.[48] 'Months of planning had preceded this invasion. Months were going to elapse while Persia was conditioned to her new role in the war. But the actual fighting, the actual event which changed the country's history, was really a very small thing.'[49]

Moorehead moved around in search of news, loitering at the English Club at Kermanshah before witnessing the dual-pronged advance on Ahwaz: 'Next morning at 5am the majority of the British Army went coursing up both banks of the river in pursuit of the Persian Army at Ahwaz. It was an incredible drive. Thousands of vehicles were moving northwards at high speed across the dusty plain.'[50] At 0730 GMT, a white flag of truce was displayed over Ahwaz and firing ceased. General Harvey met the Iranian commander at 1300 and agreed the following terms: Iranian troops would be confined to barracks on the west bank for twenty-four hours; all British prisoners would be released immediately; British forces would camp on the east bank of the Karun, north of the town. The general attitude among the people was reported to be friendly.

The British attack in the north

On 26 August, at Slim's request, the RAF located enemy defences on the Pai Tak Pass and along the escarpment. Later in the afternoon, a dozen 45 Squadron aircraft bombed enemy positions, 'all bombs falling on the target area', the pass having been cleared of British troops in order to give the RAF a clear field of fire.[51] Throughout the day the infantry carried out reconnaissance and preparations for the attack. The southern flanking force had begun 'its arduous and hazardous march, the first stages of which were to be completed before daylight'.[52] 'Our Brigade,' wrote Captain Summers, 'being highly mobile, was to be used to outflank this position in the Pai Taq Pass. We were to move by the new military road through Gilan to Shahabad, thereby cutting off the line of withdrawal of the division holding the Pai Tak ... Enemy air activity was expected and would have been very telling in the narrow gorges.'[53] Arriving at Gilan, the 9th Armoured Brigade's Warwickshire Yeomanry 'bumped' the Iranian forces and drove them out of their positions, and pushed on. The nearest the Brigade's Household Cavalry regiment came to enemy gunfire was when a non-commissioned officer pulled a piece of string on a captured anti-tank gun, causing a shell to whistle over the column. The regiment pushed on through Gilan into the country beyond, 'high mountains covered with small oak trees with beautiful, fast-running streams', and headed for Shahabad.[54]

With the southern force making good progress, the frontal infantry assault on the pass went in before dawn on 27 August. Slim wrote:

> two Gurkha battalions, one each side of the Pa-i-Tak Pass, began in real mountain warfare style to scramble up the escarpment. Hardly had they got going when I was almost relieved to receive a signal from the flank column that it had taken Shahabad. The news of this had proved too much for the Persians, already shaken by the bombing, and they had pulled out hurriedly across country north of the road while it was still dark ... When I drove up to the top of the pass early that morning I found a very cheerful brigadier, with his headquarters established beside the road, issuing orders to his first battalion to arrive to press on hard along the road for Shahabad.[55]

So, Slim's 'northern' column, formed of the 21st Infantry Brigade, found no opposition on the pass, over which a 45 Squadron Blenheim made a recon-naissance flight. By the afternoon, the troops had advanced to Kerend-e Gharb. The heights had been taken and the road into Iran secured. It was now a question of pursuing the retreating Iranian army and pushing towards the capital and the anticipated meeting with the Soviet forces coming from the north. Slim issued orders for two of his brigades to push hard for Kermanshah. Following on himself, he reached a point about 15 miles east of Shahabad when 'the discovery of a strong Iranian force [at Zibri] made it imperative to close up our strung-out units. This we did behind a ridge astride the road and there, covered by outposts, we passed a quiet night.' The next morning, shelling began from distant hills forming the eastern horizon. Concealed here was a battery of artillery, 'and I cursed their modern 155-mm guns which so easily and so far outranged our old 18-pounders'. It was well known that 'the Persians were well equipped with modern Czech-Slovak weapons,' Slim wrote.[56] The Iranian shells were getting 'uncomfortably close', and the tactical problem 'was immediate and formidable. Facing us, in position along a line of hills astride the road about four miles away, was a Persian army corps of two divisions and a cavalry brigade', and British patrols had reported armoured vehicles too.[57]

The situation was an interesting one. 'We had no very high opinion of the enemy's military qualities,' wrote Slim, 'but a couple of brigades was not quite the force with which I would have chosen to attack a full strength corps, even a Persian one. But it was no use waiting. I issued orders for a general advance to begin at ten o'clock, with a view to an attack, if possible, that afternoon.'[58] But then a black saloon car drove towards the British lines, exhibiting a white flag. The vehicle was met by two light tanks, and from it emerged a dapper Iranian officer, wearing high-heeled field boots and an immaculate uniform. He told Slim that the shah had ordered his commanders in the field to organize a ceasefire. Slim dictated his own ceasefire terms: all hostile action was to cease on both sides; Iranian forces were to withdraw from their present position 'at a time I would state and assemble in areas I would designate'; there was to be 'unrestricted passage to Kermanshah for my force and facilities for its maintenance there'; and 'the delivery to our forces of all British subjects in Persian hands unharmed and well treated'. Kermanshah was to be surrendered and handed over at 0600 on 31 August. Slim's superior, Quinan, approved these terms as well as his intention to advance into Kermanshah. The RAF dropped its pamphlets and conducted photo reconnaissance missions. Though the Warwickshires had sustained casualties in an ambush as they pressed forward, on the whole, the 'enemy had melted into thin air'.[59]

As Slim approached Kermanshah in strength, Mr Robertson, the British manager of the oil refinery, drove out to meet him. He confirmed that all British citizens were safe, and that the locals were delighted the fighting was over but 'terrified of the Russians, rumours of whose advance from the north had reached them'.[60] Slim drove to Robertson's bungalow in the city, which had been placed at his disposal. He demanded an immediate interview with the Iranian commander and went off with Robertson to find him. They also located and arrested a German 'medical man' who was a 'notorious Axis agent' wanted by British intelligence. In the morning 'we marched into Kermanshah in style and formally occupied it'.[61] Alan Moorehead had left the southern sector to observe proceedings in the north for the *Daily Express*, travelling from Basra to Baghdad and then across the border. In Kermanshah he 'passed many demobilized Persian soldiers on the road. They tramped along stolidly, sometimes raising enough energy to throw a curse or a stone, but mostly they were just bored and anxious to get home.'[62]

Throughout the operation, the British were concerned lest the Soviets exceed the agreed territorial limits of their zone. The British needed to occupy as much of their designated zone as possible in order to prevent the Soviets from exceeding theirs. As hostilities drew to a close, Slim was perturbed by the reports of Soviet columns advancing on Kermanshah. 'Hamadan and Sinneh were in our zone', so Indian troops were hurried north to meet them and establish roadblocks. They were ordered to be as friendly as possible, though to assure the Soviets that their forces were not needed in these cities. Slim reached Hamadan 'in time to see the admirable way in which Aizlewood disposed of his force to occupy the city'. Here again the British forces were 'welcomed with evident relief' because they were not Soviets. Whether the Soviets 'ever seriously intended to occupy Hamadan', wrote Slim, 'especially after they learned we were there, I was never able to discover. But I had a feeling that they would very much like to have done so.'[63]

Having expected stiff opposition, it had turned out to be an easy campaign, concluded within four days.[64] But that should not be permitted to belie its importance, because it secured Iran for the allies at a time when it was threatened by Germany's continued military presence in North Africa and the Soviet Union. The 'Battle of Persia' was over, wrote Captain Summers as the Household Cavalry moved into Kermanshah and bivouacked by the oil refinery. Crowds watched the 8-mile-long procession of British military vehicles: 'some persons waved and appeared pleased to see them, and some looked gloomy and unfriendly'.[65] Then, for Summers and the Household Cavalry, it was on to Sanandaj. British and Soviet forces met here and at Qazvin on 30 and 31 August respectively. Newsreels captured the moment, Churchill and the British keen for the world to see the new allies joining hands for the first time.

Iranian radio broadcast a declaration of martial law and Prime Minister Ali Mansur ordered people to refrain from all resistance.[66] On 30 August a mutiny occurred at the headquarters of the Iranian air force in protest at the ceasefire, and there were threats to bomb Tehran. As had been the case with the Iraqi army three months before, many units of the Iranian army disintegrated and disbanded, men taking their weapons home with them. There were incidents of ill-discipline, such as the Iranian 11th Division's use of anti-aircraft guns to fire on Soviet aircraft dropping leaflets, which provoked a bombing raid on a barracks complex in which over 100 soldiers were killed. Attempts were made to reassure the public. 'Many untrue and forged pieces of news are current,' said the prime minister on Radio Tehran, 'and it is even said that people are leaving the capital. There is no danger for Tehran. There is a plentiful supply of bread and wheat but of course if each person buys ten pounds of bread instead of one pound, the government will be faced with some difficulties.'[67] For many ordinary Iranians, the extent to which the war affected food supplies became its most important ramification. There were acts of sabotage, such as on the western frontier where troops of the 9th Armoured Brigade and 21st Indian Infantry Brigade were deployed to protect the lines of communication between Khanaqin and Kermanshah against sporadic raids.

Fighting had been heaviest in the British sectors around Abadan and on the western border with Iraq. But victory had been cheaply bought. The Iranians lost six warships sunk or badly damaged, six aircraft and around 800 service personnel. About 200 civilians were killed when the Soviets bombed Gilan, and the British and Soviets lost about 80 killed between them. The Iranian army offered little resistance as Soviet troops and tanks entered Tabriz, their progress aided by pre-positioned spies and informers. Indeed, it offered little resistance anywhere at all, at least, none that had any chance of successfully repelling the invaders. Having been built up, in terms of size and self-importance, to defeat internal foes, the shah's beloved army was 'ill prepared for any mission larger than the suppression of Iran's tribes', and particularly unprepared to ward of an invasion from two great powers.[68] Though they had started building fortifications designed to resist invasion in 1940, work was incomplete. Command and control was rudimentary, 'mainly because even some of the least significant decisions had to be personally approved by the shah'.[69] Poor preparations, the suddenness of the invasion and unrestrained Soviet bombing of cities in the provinces of Azerbaijan and Gilan 'caused utter confusion, fear and even desertion among Iranian officers'.[70] Troops defending Azerbaijan under General Mohammad Shahbakhti did, however, fight credibly, and the British also had to spend four hours fighting for the Abadan refinery.

The shah was isolated and now beaten, all that he had built since the mid-1920s crumbling around him. The telegram he had fired off to Roosevelt as troops crossed the border was answered a week later, by which time it was all over. The president offered no succour. He formally thanked Reza Shah for his 'communication regarding the recent entry of British and Russian forces into Iran', responding as if the shah had asked him for a charitable donation rather than intervention to protect a principle of international law. The president assured the shah that the matter was receiving his most serious consideration, not least because of the principles involved.

> At the same time I hope Your Majesty will concur with me in believing that we must view the situation in its full perspective of present world events and developments. Viewing the question in its entirety involves not only vital questions to which Your Imperial Majesty refers, but other basic considerations arising from Hitler's ambition of world conquest. It is certain that movements of conquest by Germany will continue and will extend beyond Europe to Asia, Africa, and even to the Americas, unless they are stopped by military force. It is equally certain that those countries which desire to maintain their independence must engage in a great common effort if they are not to be engulfed.[71]

Clearly, and to the shah's disappointment, America was not about to rush to Iran's defence. Small comfort though he surely knew it would be, Roosevelt did emphasize America's continued interest in the situation, and assured the shah that 'My Government has noted the statements to the Iranian Government by the British and Soviet Governments that they have no designs on the independence or territorial integrity of Iran'.[72] It was a polite but very firm rejection letter.

A leaf from Hitler's notebook

Jock Colville, now serving as Churchill's assistant private secretary, recorded the mood during the invasion. He wrote with cautious optimism on 25 August that 'the Persian adventure has started successfully, though we do not seem to have a very large force employed'. By the end of the week, dining at Chequers, he was writing of the 'jubilation over our success in Persia, which had been very well received all over the world. The PM said that last Sunday morning [the day before the invasion] he had had qualms. We had been doing something for which we had justification but no right. The man in the street, on the other hand, seemed elated that we had at last taken a leaf from Hitler's notebook'.[73] Churchill told his son Randolph that he thought the invasion of Iran was 'questionable', 'like taking a leaf out of the German book'.[74] Anthony Eden, meanwhile, described the operation as Britain's 'first act of "naked aggression"', and told the Soviet ambassador that he was 'ashamed of himself'.[75] Major-General Kennedy at the War Office wrote that 'there was a general feeling that this short war had been unnecessary, and that our diplomatic action had been bungled'.[76]

But these men had no need to be ashamed; in much chirpier vein, the guidebook written for the American GIs who would subsequently serve in Iran referred to it as 'one time we got there first'.[77] Furthermore, such equivocal assessments reflect the democratic nature of British decision-making, and the fact that the summer of 1941 was a touch-and-go moment in the war. No one knew if the Soviet Union could hold and it was clear that the danger to vital strategic interests in Iran and the wider region were gravely threatened at that moment. The invasion also reflected something that is clearer with hindsight – that the British, in the final analysis, had decided by August 1941 that the occupation of Iran was what was required, not the shah's compliance. This was one of the reasons why there was never an actual ultimatum; if there had have been, then the shah probably would have acceded to allied requests, especially if they were delivered down the barrel of a gun.

The invasion of Iran was the final act by which the great arc between the Mediterranean and the western frontier of India was freed of Axis interference, following the actions in Iraq and Syria earlier in the year. The invasion was conducted in order to forestall an enemy attack in a region of prime geostrategic concern, to safeguard what was an important allied supply route and to stamp out disruptive enemy intrigue. John Masters' Gurkha battalion was typical of the imperial forces deployed to the Iran–Iraq–Syria region in 1941. The battalion's movements that summer, he wrote, 'took us through the Middle East like the writhings of a demented snake'. They began by pushing the Iraqis back from Basra until they could present no threat to the port and the large British military base that was being built up around it. After this they flew to the centre of Iraq to take part in the relief of the RAF base at Habbaniya. Writing of the three brisk campaigns that saw the British secure their interests in the vast region stretching from Syria's Mediterranean coast to Iran's borders with British India, Masters envisioned them in the following manner:

> The Habbaniya–Baghdad area then became, as it were, our launching pad. From it we made three boomerang-like sallies. First, in June, we went to Mosul, in the extreme north of Iraq, held that until conditions quietened – and returned to Habbaniya. Sally Two, in July and August, saw us hurtling northwest into Syria, almost as far as Aleppo and the Mediterranean – then back to Habbaniya. Sally Three, in August, September, and October, launched us northeast into Iran – then back to Baghdad.[78]

The historian Adam Tooze offers a penetrating analysis of the strategic situation, contending that Italy's entry into the war had enabled Britain to direct its imperial armies against the Axis's soft underbelly. 'By the end of January 1941 they had defeated the Italians in North Africa and were poised to seize the entire southern coast of the Mediterranean':

> A month later they completed the destruction of the Italian Empire in East Africa ... In April 1941 decisive German intervention tilted the balance back towards the Axis with Erwin Rommel taking charge of a combined German and Italian force based on Tripoli. In addition, the Wehrmacht drove the British out of Greece and took Crete with dramatic parachute landings. But in strategic terms these Axis triumphs were less significant than Britain's success between April and July 1941 in putting down the German-sponsored insurgency in Iraq and seizing Syria from Vichy forces [and occupying Iran in conjunction with the Soviets in August]. In military terms these encounters may have been relatively minor. But they ensured that the African possessions of Italy, France and Belgium would not be combined into a single Axis empire and consolidated Britain's grip on the Suez Canal zone. With Britain entrenched on

both sides of the Indian Ocean, a blocking position was established between Germany's European empire and Japan in the East. This in turn enabled President Roosevelt to declare the approaches to the Suez Canal no longer a war zone, removing the legal obstacles that prevented American shipping from making direct deliveries to the forces of the British Empire in Egypt.[79]

So, the allied position had been reinforced. Flying to Tehran shortly after the Anglo-Soviet invasion, the journalist and writer Eve Curie wrote that 'a continuous front had been built from Libya to India for defense or offense'. Flying from Cairo across Palestine, Syria and Iraq, 'I had seen, from the plane, the British military tents that looked like countless pale mushrooms. As soon as I had stopped seeing them, I knew that I was approaching the Russian camps of northern Iran. I was thus following, link by link, the chain of troops and of war machines that the allies were slowly spreading around the Nazis.'[80]

Nevertheless, at that moment the prospect of significant German victories on the Eastern Front and in North Africa meant that the situation remained critical. For the people of Iran and Iraq, meanwhile, the manifestations of world war were about to become a lot more evident.

CHAPTER 9

Abdication and occupation

Apprised of the shah's capitulation, Churchill focused immediately on the prizes brought by victory – in particular, the ability to use Iran to supply the Soviet Union. He badgered commanders on the ground via the Chiefs of Staff. An 'action this day' communiqué asked, 'In view of Persian plan to effect demolition of the railway from the Persian Gulf to the Caspian, what arrangements are made to follow up our advance with a strong force of engineers and rail repair parties? What arrangements have been made to construct blockhouses and to guard bridges and deviations? All this ought to have been thought out and prepared for. How does it stand?'[1] Churchill had behaved in this manner throughout the short campaign. When, on 27 August, it appeared that the invasion was going well, he urged the local commander on towards the next objective: 'Now it seems that Persian opposition not very serious', what are the 'plans for joining hands with Russia', and 'are the railways – crucial to turning Iran into a conduit of Anglo-American supplies for Russia – in working order?'[2] 'We do not simply want to squat on the oilfields', he wrote, betraying both his customary impatience and his impeccable phrasing, 'but to get through communication with Russia.' 'We will employ large forces to keep the supply route to Stalin open', he enthused.

His strategic antennae aquiver, Churchill wanted to focus on the region's affairs only inasmuch as they pertained to the allied war effort, and had a very clear sense of what he was *not* interested in. As he told Stalin, he did not want to tie down precious resources dealing with internal security or local squabbles, but, rather, to get on with the job of using Iran as a supply route as rapidly as possible: 'Our object should be to make the Persians keep each other quiet while we get on with the war.'[3] The prime minister told Stalin on 31 August that the 'news that the Persians have now decided to cease resistance is most welcome. Even more than safeguarding the oilfields, our object in entering Persia has been to get another through route to you which cannot be cut.'[4]

In getting the supply route up and running, there was to be no pussy-footing around. As Churchill told Sir Alexander Cadogan of the Foreign Office on 2 September 1941, the Iranian government 'should be told we hold them responsible for the capture and surrender to us of the Grand Mufti and any other objectionable person you may wish to mention'. Churchill wanted the Mufti 'dead or alive'.[5] On the following day, he made the point forcefully to Britain's minister in Tehran: 'Don't be lenient with Germans to appease the Persian Government.' The overriding strategic objective was to make Iran the 'best possible through-route from the Persian Gulf to the Caspian ... developed at the utmost speed and at all costs in order to supply Russia'.[6] Churchill said that while he did not want to sanction the occupation of Tehran, with Anglo-Soviet troops stopped short of the capital, the 'Persian Government will have to give us loyal and faithful help and show all proper alacrity, if they wish to avoid it'. With the German threat still very much alive given the Wehrmacht's lunge for the Caucasus, the prime minister antici-pated a significant British military build-up: 'Large forces will be operating in and from Persia in 1942 and certainly a powerful Air Force will be installed.'[7]

The shah's procrastination

Ideally, the British wanted existing state structures to continue to function, for if they failed, it would be they who had to step in and fill the breach. As an occupier, Britain shared responsibility for internal security in Iraq and much of Iran. This required the deployment of scarce military resources, the provision of which hampered Britain's capacity to get on with the job of preparing to defend both countries and develop the supply line, a task that had become paramount in the minds of both Churchill and Roosevelt. In their zone, meanwhile, the Soviets took over where they wanted to, refused to allow the forces of the Iranian state to effectively deal with unrest and armed and supported communities and movements that furthered Soviet political ends. For their part, the Iranians pursued their own interests using the scant resources that the situation dealt them. They attempted to play the occupying powers off against each other, and strove to inveigle the

Americans into becoming involved in Iranian politics in an effort to use them to curb the influence of Britain and the Soviet Union.

As German successes accelerated on the Eastern Front, people 'gathered in Tehran's Sepah Square to cheer loudly each time the media announced the fall of a Soviet city'.[8] The Germans remained popular and, as in post-invasion Iraq, plenty of people still thought ultimate German victory was likely. Astonishingly for the British, despite the invasion of Iran, the Tehran government still seemed to be equivocating, dragging its heels over the expulsion of German nationals. 'The prestige of the Allies wears very thin,' wrote the British consul Clarmont Skrine from Mashhad. When rumours of a Soviet deal with Hitler circulated, 'swastikas appeared in unexpected places'.[9] In the days following the Anglo-Soviet invasion, exasperated British nationals on the ground had cause to wonder what, exactly, had actually been achieved by military action. As in Iraq, although a 'feat of arms' had taken place (to borrow Churchill's antique phrase), enemy influence endured, and in the wider context of the war the threat to the region remained high. A week after the invasion, the *Times* diplomatic correspondent reported that Germans were still 'dashing about in high-powered cars, hanging out the swastika, cutting a figure in Persian homes, insulting British passers-by, and spreading anti-Ally rumours'.[10] Reports of this nature led to searching questions in London, and on 9 September Churchill described the recent intervention in the House of Commons and promised that all necessary action would be taken to ensure the final expulsion of Axis personnel and influence. Anthony Eden had written to Churchill the previous day, referring to the press criticism which claimed that the British were 'havering and dilatory in Persia' now they were there, and asking him to give reassurances in the Commons debate.[11]

The shah's failure to expedite the expulsion of German nationals even after the ceasefire exasperated the allies and would have grave consequences for him and his people. Churchill was understandably irritated, and on 2 September had pressed the Foreign Office to get all Germans and Italians into British or Soviet custody and all diplomatic and consular officials ejected from the country, some of them to be held back as bargaining chips for the release from Nazi custody of Sir Lancelot Oliphant, British ambassador to Belgium.[12] On 6 September the prime minister was on the warpath again, telling Eden in an 'action this day' minute:

> Your Minister at Tehran does not seem to be at all at the level of events. We mean to get the Germans in our hands, if we have to come to Tehran and invite the Russians there too . . . I feel this business requires

your personal grip. It is a matter between you and your Officer [Bullard]. Undoubtedly we must acquire complete military control of Persia during the war. Please let me know what action you propose to take.[13]

The subsequent decision to occupy Tehran was not taken lightly – at least not by the British government. Nevertheless, as it looked as if the Iranian government was unwilling or unable to act the part of a defeated foe and comply with the terms of the ceasefire, and as allied ambitions for Iran grew exponentially, it became more and more likely that it would be taken over. As early as 3 and 4 September, in War Cabinet meetings, Churchill defended the Chiefs of Staff's desire for military occupation. The British argued that by failing to meet the demands made of them the Iranians had brought the occupation of the capital upon themselves, but more importantly, that they needed to prepare to defend the country against German attack. Churchill told Bullard to 'dismiss from your mind any idea of a generous policy towards the Germans to please the Persians or anyone else'.[14] On 13 September the War Office informed Wavell of the War Cabinet's decision. Intelligence suggested that serious disorder could break out at any moment, spearheaded by a revolt against the shah.

The army and the monarchy were in disarray following their defeat, and Tehran's power over the regions waned precipitately. The prime minister resigned, and on 10 September Radio Tehran broadcast a statement from his successor, Mohammad Ali Foroughi. He 'expressed his utmost regret and deplored the raging of the world war and the sufferings of humanity and the spreading of this war to Iranian territory'.[15] People were bewildered and took precautions, such as stockpiling food, and this and other reactions to the invasion led to serious problems. Hoarding became widespread and it was increasingly difficult to obtain sugar, meat and bread. A broadcast claimed that 'while this no doubt temporary hardship was to some extent the result of the unexpected recent happenings, the main cause was hoarding and profiteering', and it was alleged that 'officials handling foodstuffs use discrimination in favour of friends'.[16] The situation bred recriminations and long-standing political and social divisions came to the surface.

The state newspaper *Ettela'at* carried an article headlined 'The people's bewilderment':

The government of Iran has ever since the beginning of the present conflict made great efforts in preserving the neutrality and in preserving its friendly relations with the neighbouring countries. But as our PM stated in his effective speech in Parliament, Fate would have it that we should also be dragged into the fire of this world-burning war and that a peace-loving and disinterested nation should be involved in troubles and hardships. Of course, our readers are right in being sorrowful as a result of these events for we are now faced with great difficulties quite outside our expectations and which we did not deserve, but our government had no other choice and there did not seem any way out of the crisis but that which the government has taken. We must point out that the expectations of the Iranian nation from the two governments of the USSR and Great Britain in view of friendship and good neighbourliness, was much more, and we are disappointed.[17]

But few people were prepared to let the government off so lightly. While Iranians welcomed the ceasefire, many felt a sense of shame given the rapid and humiliating capitulation of the army. Anger was directed not only at the invaders, but at the regime, which after years of demanding taxes and other sacrifices in order to build up the armed forces, had spectacularly failed to defend the country. Everything that Reza Shah had built since coming to power had been dashed to pieces in a few short days. His protestations had fallen on deaf ears; though British and Soviet actions were compared to Germany's invasion of Poland, no one seemed to care. The shah fulminated, summoning generals and ministers and hurling abuse at them, some of it physical. Minister of War General Ahmad Nakhjavan was assaulted, his insignia of rank ripped from his uniform.[18] The shah ordered generals stripped of their rank and arrested, and courts-martial were scheduled. The regime's disgrace was clear for all to see. 'Fear of revolution was palpable in Tehran as British and Soviet propaganda against the shah fed popular resentment against Reza and led to major misjudgements by the military leadership.'[19] Conscripts were released and sent home and regular soldiers deserted, many taking their equipment and weapons with them. An *Ettela'at* article on 10 September expressed regret at the invasion and said that the German, Italian and Hungarian legations would remain. This seriously damaged Reza Shah's standing with the allies.[20]

Anthony Eden reported to the War Cabinet that in the weeks following the invasion German nationals in Tehran had been putting all sorts of obstacles in the way of their internment. Reza Shah continued his pre-conflict procrastination, havering over a settlement with the allies. On 16 September the British War Cabinet was told that 'matters had been going so slowly that it had been decided that we must send troops into Tehran. After consulting the Prime Minister, he had proposed to the Soviet Government that our forces and the Russian forces should make a joint advance on Tehran forthwith.[21] This had not been part of the original plan; to avoid undue unrest and to allow the shah and his army to retain some dignity and authority following their defeat, British and Soviet troops had deliberately stopped short of the capital city (as had been the case in Iraq). This, Eden claimed, was the best way to secure Britain's objectives in Iran, namely the control of the railway and the avoidance of anarchy, not to mention the securing of Iranian oil. The intention had been to work with the 'present Persian Government', but the British were ready to tighten the thumbscrews if necessary. As regards the shah, 'if he remained in Tehran after we occupied the Persian capital, he would be under our control'.[22] Lieutenant-General Quinan was given orders to the effect that if he tried to set up an independent government away from Tehran, for instance at Isfahan, he 'should be seized and held'. As in Iraq, in the days and weeks immediately following the ceasefire, nobody knew quite how things would pan out. The shah was deeply worried about the allied occupation of Tehran, and contemplated abdicating and moving to Isfahan. Among the general populace, the prospect of the capital's occupation caused

> paralysing panic. Sporadic bombing of the city, the speedy disintegration of the army which flooded its streets with 50,000 shabbily dressed and hungry conscripts, an acute shortage of petrol and insufficient supplies of grain all aggravated the looming sense of catastrophe. The royal family, along with many other prominent families, had already left for Isfahan and it was becoming increasingly difficult to persuade Reza Shah and the Crown Prince, Muhammad Reza, to stay.[23]

With news of Soviet troops approaching the capital, numerous bonfires were lit, as soldiers burned their uniforms, terrified by the rumour that the Soviets would go from door to door to find and then execute military personnel.[24]

The Iranian government's refusal or inability to carry out the surrender terms meant that further action was required to 'enforce compliance'.[25] Preparing to occupy Tehran, imperial troops were also used for 'show of force' demonstrations across the British zone. As Slim wrote, 'I had to tour my extensive area and visit the chief towns to impress on them the reality and effectiveness of our occupation.'[26] In these circumstances Slim decided that Kermanshah was too far away for his headquarters, so he moved with the bulk of his force to Arak. It was not only closer to Tehran, it was also on the railway which would soon be used for supplying the Soviet Union. Slim wrote that Qom, 'eighty miles nearer to Tehran, would have suited better. Unfortunately, with the domes of its Golden Mosque flashing in the sun, it was a very holy city, and the stronghold of Shia orthodoxy. Its ecclesiastics and citizens remained smoulderingly hostile to us Infidels and this was no time to inflame their fanaticism by our presence.'[27] Despite Slim's restraint, it would not be long before Qom was the site of a significant British military presence.

Tasked with occupying the capital, Slim visited Tehran in civilian dress to confer with Bullard. Captain Summers waited with Slim's troops to see what would happen. It was 'a week of indecision . . . No one knew if we were to go forward to Tehran, to Russia or back to Palestine.' The army, as always, found work for idle hands: 'PT [physical training] was started, we fired our mortars, we ate and we slept. A new system for laying out kits and the contents of our trucks was started.'[28] But then Summers' Household Cavalry regiment joined the troops detailed for Tehran. Via Hamadan and Qom, they halted 20 miles short of the capital and were joined by Soviet liaison officers. There was a chance that the entrance of British and Soviet troops would be opposed, and among other measures, 'a scheme for the surrounding of the German Legation had been prepared'.[29]

Abdication and the occupation of Tehran

Anglo-Soviet forces were poised to occupy Tehran when on 16 September, three weeks after the invasion, Reza Shah gave up his throne. His hand-written instrument of abdication was read out by the prime minister during an extraordinary session of the parliament. He gave a detailed explanation of the shah's decision to leave, 'on account of failing health, in favour of the Crown Prince'.[30] According to Bullard, what finally persuaded him to abdicate was the movement of Soviet troops from Qazvin towards Tehran. On this momentous day in Iran's history, Radio Tehran assured the people that the comings and goings of allied troops would 'not interfere with the affairs of the country', though this would have been very hard for people to believe, and a bitter pill for them to swallow.[31] The Iranian broadcaster was anxious to explain the state of affairs to the city's population:

As the people of the capital know the Soviet and the British forces have come to Iran only for the purpose of protecting their military and strategic interests and as the official notes have made it clear their action is in no wise directed against the country. People are expected to act courteously and kindly towards them ... The people of the capital must conduct themselves according to the moral principles of the Iranian people. Should any member of the Soviet and British forces perhaps do something to the people the people must not retaliate but must immediately inform the police.[32]

Not only would people across the country have to suffer the presence of the foreign troops who had defeated their leaders and their army, they would have to stomach the takeover of the national transport infrastructure too. Unlike Iraq, where the British intervention had effectively led to a restoration following the coup, this amounted to regime change, with serious ramifications for law, order and political stability.

The Soviets dropped a parachute battalion east of the city and their mechanized forces advanced from the north and the west. 'The British advanced from the south ... and all the exits from the capital were blocked. Russian bombers flew overhead and very impressive they looked.'[33] The day after the shah's abdication, British and Soviet forces entered Tehran, marching down opposite sides of the street. It was not, Slim wrote, 'a particularly triumphant or spectacular affair. We just marched quietly to the areas allotted to us, through undemonstrative crowds of depressed-looking citizens, in shabby, down-at-heel European clothes.' Tehran, he wrote, 'was very much like an ant-hill that had just been kicked over'.[34] The army was embarrassed and embittered. In a letter to army headquarters, the British political adviser in Kermanshah provided intriguing intelligence about the attitudes of Iranian troops. Regarding the sentiments of Iranian officers in the Kermanshah and Hamadan regions, the consul reported:

General attitude summed up as We hate all foreign troops – be it English, Russian or even German. We like them as individuals apart from the Russians whom we all loathe. Will fight for the British against Russians anytime but against Germans can't yet say. They doubted that the British would help them get the Russians out of Azerbaijan. The British were disliked because they were occupiers: 'we have the same feelings on this point as an Englishman would have if the Germans had occupied parts of ENGLAND' . . . Why do you like the Germans, the Iranian soldiers were asked: 'Because we have nothing to dislike them for', was the answer. Germany was powerful through deed and propaganda.[35]

Captain Summers of the Household Cavalry and his men were stationed on the outskirts of the city, 'where the English residents came to see us, and it gave a thrill to be welcomed in such a whole-hearted manner'. Then, he wrote:

> began the orgy of our stay in Tehran. The British community could not have been more helpful or more thorough in their entertaining. Beer was 6d. per bottle, caviare [sic] 5s. per pound. Leave was allowed nightly in the town. The cabarets were packed. Tehran was civilization and we revelled in it. American bands, one English cabaret girl and the usual crowd of Greek, Rumanian, Bulgarian, Hungarian, Egyptian and Persian girls who regularly make the tour Alex–Cairo–Athens–Beirut–Baghdad–Tehran formed the cabarets . . . We had a joint parade with the Russians, who later entertained us with their band and dancers.[36]

The arrival of allied troops in Tehran expedited the expulsion of Axis personnel; finally, the 'Italian and German legations disgorged their inhabitants'.[37] German, Hungarian and Bulgarian diplomats left by special motorcars, buses and lorries via Tabriz for Turkey.[38] It was announced that 'Germans without a permit from the Soviets or British are to report to the local police by 24 September. Those who do not will be arrested and punished.' A month after troops entered the capital, the bulk withdrew, the occasion marked by a big parade at the Maidan-e Jalaliyyeh, a racecourse outside Tehran that was also used for military purposes.[39] Summers' unit was ordered to return to Palestine, sorry to leave 'that modern city that the late Shah built which is so strikingly rich in comparison with the poverty of the country'.[40] But the British had decided that some garrison forces would remain indefinitely. This was against the advice of Bullard, the British minister and the Foreign Office's Eastern Department.[41]

Though Iran could not be as thoroughly gripped by the British, in the aftermath of invasion, as Iraq, they did make inroads into the state for their own purposes in addition to the deployment of troops. Defence Security Office (DSO) Tehran conducted postal and press censorship and visa control, and had a network of area liaison officers. The Tripartite Treaty of January

1942 formed a joint Anglo-Soviet censorship administration, taken much more seriously by the British. Censorship was used 'as a substitute for general security controls [and] as a counterespionage weapon.'[42] Using this, the British established the identity of the principal couriers between the pro-Axis fifth column and the German intelligence services in Turkey. There was a great deal of painstaking work opening and examining mail leaving Iran. This required a significant multilingual staff working for DSO Persia.

Though the extraordinary conditions of global war had provided the catalyst, the causes of the shah's abdication had deeper roots. He would not have had to abdicate 'if the public had been sympathetic to, rather than angry with him, given the fact that, after the cease-fire following the allied invasion was declared, he was fully prepared to cooperate with the British and the Soviets.'[43] His failure to stay in power, ironically, was a result of his success in establishing himself as an absolute – and arbitrary – ruler, for in achieving this, he managed to alienate all social classes and groups, including powerful landlords, merchants and the religious elite, traditionalists as well as modernists.[44] Reza Shah's 'contemptuous and insensitive style of personal rule and his suspicion-ridden mind and crude political disposition effectively eliminated all those capable politicians he considered insufficiently servile.'[45] The shah's 'astonishing lack of nerve in the face of the allied invasion ... can only be explained in terms of his complete lack of any popular power base'; his one-time Justice Minister, Muhsin Sadr, said that in his view 'Reza Shah was forced out of the country neither by the threats of the Russians nor by the tricks of the British; it was his unbounded arrogance and the unbridgeable rift between him and the nation which resulted in his exile.'[46]

A consequence of his isolation was that there had been no one close to him able to offer informed advice. When the allies began to warn Iran about its tolerance of German war activities:

there was no one who could either gauge the situation correctly or who had the courage to explain it to the shah. He responded to the warnings with simple denials and dismissals, and by the time the Allies were poised to cross the Iranian border, it was too late to stop them. Even then, things could have been different if the shah had had a genuine domestic power base ... In other words, even if Iran's occupation during the Second World War had been inevitable, the shah would not have had

to abdicate in disgrace had he had real internal backing. The shah
himself became the last victim of his own absolute and arbitrary rule;
for where there are no rights there are no obligations either.[47]

When the British resolved to push for the shah's abdication, they enlisted
the support of the BBC Persian Service. It broadcast items 'that revealed
Reza Shah's autocratic style of leadership'.[48] He had always viewed the BBC
with strong suspicion, rightly as it transpired. The British broadcasts 'seriously damaged his standing' and pleased domestic opponents of his rule.[49]

The parliament was encouraged by BBC reports of royal malpractice to
ask for reforms. On 16 September a deputation asked the shah to resign,
and there was also news that the Russians were at Qazvin and had drawn up
an abdication instrument.

> Soon after his abdication, some politicians began denouncing the shah's
> massing of wealth, dispossessions, and murder of civilians. In his book
> *War of Words* Asa Briggs acknowledged the significance of BBC broad-
> casts in bringing about the shah's abdication, quoting Richard Dimbleby's
> dispatch from the area: 'I doubt if the power of broadcasting has ever
> been shown in such a way as by the success of these [Persian language]
> broadcasts.'[50]

Boarding the steamer *Bandra* at Bandar-e Abbas on 27 September 1941,
Reza Shah left his land behind. On his journey into exile, he complained of
not having been told frankly what the British had wanted. His complaint,
uttered in conversation with the consul Clarmont Skrine, who accompanied
him on the voyage, chimed with the British minister Bullard's frequent
lament that the shah's advisers had kept the two men apart in the lead-up to
the invasion. 'I never could get near the man,' he said.[51] A British legation file
noted that Reza Shah 'absolutely refused to have anything to do with the
British representative directly. I do not believe that in the last ten years of
Reza's rule he saw the British representative once on matters of business.'[52]
The Arabist Gerald de Gaury remarked that the shah had 'adopted much the
same attitude towards foreign representatives as the Ottoman Sultans had
taken in their day ... His family was forbidden by him to receive foreigners.'[53]
The ex-shah's destination of choice was Argentina, but the British had other
ideas. None of the passengers aboard the *Bandra* were allowed ashore when
the ship reached Bombay, as secrecy was considered paramount. Switching

ships, the shah, his family and servants headed for the British colony of Mauritius, deep in the Indian Ocean, aboard the *Burma*.[54] He left behind the crown prince, his son Mohammad Reza Pahlavi, to pick up the pieces.

Britain and the new shah

The early years of Shah Mohammad Reza Pahlavi's reign were to be dominated by the consequences of invasion and occupation, and Iran's unwanted involvement in the war. The invasion ended a chapter in Iranian history characterised by absolute monarchy ruling through court patronage and control of the military and the bureaucracy. The reforms undertaken by Reza Shah following his seizure of power in 1925, and the accompanying extension of Tehran's grip across the country, had stimulated anger and opposition – among tribal groups pacified by his new army, for instance, and among religious leaders and the intelligentsia. Now, with Reza Shah gone and the army defeated, pent-up opposition burst forth. On its own, the Iranian government and state apparatus was ill-equipped to cope with the resulting disorder, as regime change threatened state collapse. Though retaining control of the armed forces, in large measure the new shah lost control of the bureaucracy and the patronage system. The centre of gravity in the country shifted back to the local notables who had ruled the country before Reza Shah's reign. These notables dominated the regions, the cabinet and the Iranian parliament.

The British became key brokers in Iranian politics and arbiters of security, propping up the Iranian state because the alternative was a general chaos that would have grossly impeded Britain's strategic ends. There was also a clear if unofficial bargain in play. As Sir Reader Bullard phrased it, 'the Persians expect that we should at least save them from the Shah's tyranny as a compensation for invading their country.'[55]

The British concluded that the best post-invasion settlement was one that would preserve the monarchy and the state apparatus. This was because they did not have any particular interest in getting involved in the business of creating a new state; from the British perspective, there was a war on. Churchill set the tone, making it clear that he was only interested in Iran in so far as it served British strategy in supporting the Soviets and defeating Germany. The 'deal' that emerged between the invaders and the new shah, therefore, meant that while the allies took over Iran's transport infrastructure, other things would be left in place and the shah would be granted the wherewithal to rule effectively, with the central government left unhindered to administer the country – if, indeed, it was capable of doing so. Importantly, the allies also pledged to sustain Iran by meeting food and other essential commodity requirements that could not be realized internally, largely as recompense for the takeover of the ports and the rail and road network. It was agreed that the armed forces could remain under the shah's direct control and at a minimum strength of 80,000, with the gendarmerie at 24,000. Furthermore, it was agreed that British and Soviet forces would evacuate the country once the war ended. On his side of the bargain, the shah agreed to cooperate fully with the allies, though this was to prove difficult to accomplish.

Reza Shah had planned a gradual transfer of power to his son whom he had tutored in the role and responsibilities of kingship. But in the event, the transfer of power was sudden, and took place in a moment of crisis. The allies considered 'turning out the Pahlavis and replacing them with the more pliable Qajars. Fearful of nationalist opinion, they abandoned the scheme.'[56] Crown Prince Mohammad Reza Pahlavi, still only twenty-one, was a:

> young, timid as well as intimidated man, suffering from a basic sense of insecurity which was further exacerbated by his own superficiality as well as lack of knowledge and experience. He disliked older men of knowledge and wisdom because he felt dwarfed by them. He enjoyed the company of women and of sycophants but did not trust them. He was acutely worried about a foreign (mainly British) plot to dislodge him, and he therefore took extreme care not to displease them. He had an idealistic view of the United States, not just as a potential patron and benefactor, but also as the best and most advanced society on earth.[57]

Radio Tehran offered a running commentary on his swearing-in ceremony, which took place in parliament on 18 September. Huge crowds gathered on both sides of Pahlavi Street and Shah Street as Reza Pahlavi processed from the Royal Palace. Dressed in civilian, not regal, attire, he swore an oath of office before the parliament. This in itself was a public statement of the monarchy's diminished post-invasion status, and the concomitant elevation of parliament. 'With God Almighty, the Omnipotent, as my witness, I swear by the Holy Koran and by whatever else is holy in His eyes, that I will devote all my endeavours to preserving the independence of Iran and to safeguarding the frontiers of the country and the rights of the nation.'[58] The shah promised to be a 'completely constitutional king [who] would do his best to amend the wrongs done to the people' during his father's reign: 'Now that the internal conditions of the country necessitate that I should undertake the onerous duties of kingship and carry the burden of the affairs of the country according to the law of the constitution, I find it necessary to point out that perfect and continuous cooperation between the government and the parliament is essential.'[59] The prime minister enunciated parliament's expectations of the shah, striking a new tone in Iranian politics as parliament used the extraordinary circumstance of war to trump the monarchy: 'the ex-king had been an absolute ruler of the country, and people who wanted to raise matters concerning the country's management did not dare to ask questions. They wanted the rights of individuals and privileges of the members of the Government clearly defined, and public finance expenditure inspected by the representatives of the people.'[60]

The young shah felt keenly the humiliation of his country and his throne. There were everyday reminders, such as having to present his identity papers to Soviet troops when entering and leaving Tehran. Shah Reza Pahlavi sought help from senior politicians in order to prevent the demise of his dynasty. The private session of parliament on 18 September discussed the momentous developments of the preceding month, and agreed that fundamental reform was necessary. The deputies discussed the fate of the crown jewels, the rendering of justice, the need to return property to individuals dispossessed by the former regime, the need to assure tranquillity and peace, to cancel severe laws, to lower budgetary expenditure, to reduce tax and to declare an amnesty for political prisoners. All of this meant loosening the iron grip on Iranian society that Reza Shah had striven to achieve. Press restrictions were relaxed, political parties were permitted to form and campaign and new parliamentary elections were announced. Contentious legislation was repealed, such as the 1935 Forced Unveiling Act, which had decreed all women 'should immediately go bareheaded or face verbal and physical violence followed by arrest and punishment', and which had meant 'Many urban women over the age of forty stayed indoors until 1941, when, upon Reza Shah's abdication, the order was lifted.'[61] Muhammad Mossadegh had been one of the few men who had opposed this law, and the new political climate enabled him to rise to political prominence.

For a 'brief period after the abdication a wave of optimism swept over the country,' wrote Ann Lambton, an important official at the Tehran legation and a Persian scholar of note. 'It was generally assumed that with the disappearance of RIZA Shah constitutional democracy would automatically replace the hated dictatorship.'[62] But there was a failure to realize that democracy requires a degree of political maturity that Iran did not possess, even though political parties, banned by the shah, now 'sprang up like mushrooms'. Iran 'faces the future without confidence in her own ability or any assurance as to the stability of her independence. To expect her in such circumstances to put her internal affairs in order, while her political independence and future existence are uncertain would seem to be demanding the impossible.'[63] While the new situation 'led both to a restoration of basic rights and freedoms to the people at large', it also saw the 'emergence of the higher social classes as powerful socio-political entities. Landed property began to become secure once again ... The landlords became powerful in the provinces where they had rural estates, and they could send deputies to the Majlis to share in the global power. The merchants could now replace the state in its monopolies of domestic as well as international trade, and use their wealth to acquire political power.'[64] Few politicians pursued the interests of 'the people' over the interests of themselves and *their* people. The political scene became a battleground on which parliament, the monarchy and regional notables struggled for advantage, often intriguing against each other. This was invariably to the detriment of the lives of ordinary people, manifest most conspicuously in hunger and poverty.

In a broadcast on 7 October, Prime Minister Mohammad-Ali Foroughi praised God that 'under the aegis of their young sovereign, [the people had] become free again', and 'expressed the hope that they had learnt from the difficulties of the past 35 years the value and meaning of freedom, which must have limits set to it in order to be effective and to prevent the strong making slaves of the weak'.[65] On opening parliament in November, 'His majesty began his speech by expressing his regret that Iran was affected by this world war, despite the Government's efforts to keep the country at peace and isolate it from this world tragedy'.[66]

Understandably, given the manner of his coming to power, the shah worried over whether the British and Soviets liked him and supported him, or whether he might go the way of his father. Having expressed his concerns in a meeting, Bullard tried to reassure him, but shortly after 'heard that a battalion of 600 Iranian soldiers was now stationed at Saadabad [palace complex in northern Tehran], the Shah not being quite oversure of his position'. He wanted to reform government departments and resist the pull towards a more dictatorial style of rule. There was a lot of opposition to the shah, it was noted, especially from among those who feared he would try to re-establish his father's dictatorship.[67]

The British, naturally, were keen to get the measure of the new shah. J.D. Greenway of the British legation wrote to Anthony Eden reporting that the shah bore 'little resemblance to his father in character but he shares with him a deep interest in the Persian army'.[68] Nevertheless, he suffered from illusions as to the Iranian army's value and the role it could play in the war, and 'talked quite seriously about helping us with an army of 300/400,000'. Greenway wrote that the manner of the Anglo-Soviet invasion continued to rankle:

> It is well to remember that however great the material gain we may obtain from the Allied occupation, the manner in which it was effected is not to be easily distinguished by Persians from the 'treachery' of the attacks without warning effected by the Germans and the Japanese; and that consequently one of the moral arguments on which we build our case against the Axis and its associates carries little or no weight in this country.[69]

Reza Pahlavi promised the British minister that he would try to convince his government and people that throwing in their lot with Britain was for the best. In order to restore morale, he needed to convince the Iranian army that it had a part to play in the country's defence, especially if the Germans arrived. It needed to be 'inspired with a determination to defend Persia against the Axis'. The young shah upbraided Bullard for the manner in which the invasion had taken place; presenting the Iranian government with an ultimatum at four o'clock in the morning, the shah said, and at the same time launching an unannounced attack, 'was not what they had expected from us ... He is obviously greatly feeling the humiliation of his army, with which he associates himself closely'.[70]

The shah expressed his wish that the allies would support his regime by refraining from encouraging separatism. He hoped that, with the signing of the treaty between Iran and the allies, Britain and the Soviet Union 'would do something to ensure that the Kurds were convinced that we were entirely out of sympathy with their attempt to throw off the Persian yoke'. The shah intimated that he wanted to have regular private meetings with Bullard, but without Iranian politicians knowing.[71] Reza Pahlavi's understanding of the post-invasion deal between Iran and the occupiers was articulated by Bullard in a telegram to the Foreign Office:

The Shah summoned me for [a] meeting. Gist of conversation was that Shah since his accession had thrown in his lot with the Allies. He had given instructions to his Government to cooperate as closely as possible with us. He hoped that we, on our part, would not interfere in the internal politics of the country, and that, if we were dissatisfied with the Government or any of its actions, I would come to him personally, so that we could settle the matter together. He would not put in any new Government unless he was sure that we had no objection … He trusted that we would refrain from giving the impression that we could change the Government ourselves at will by our own means, otherwise authority would break down.[72]

A minute on the file captured the British point of view and reflected Britain's extraordinary influence upon Iranian affairs:

I am entirely in favour of our having more relations with the Shah. He is an organ of Government and in an oriental country has a much more important position than in a western democratic country. He is the key to the feeling in the army (or should be) and the bureaucracy in any oriental country has a certain tendency to take its views from the Court. Personally I think we should get the whole lot into our orbit without delay … We want the whole lot to be unostentatiously, perhaps unconsciously, and quietly in our orbit and spreading our point of view throughout the country … [We n]eed to take urgent steps to get the Majlis on side too – this Legation should take active daily measures to see that we have the Majlis where we have to have them – preferably in our pocket. In no other way can we fulfil our responsibility to the British Empire to see that we get all our vital desiderata from Persia for the conduct of the war without immobilising troops.[73]

In a succinct expression of Britain's new role in Iran, R.M.A. Hankey of the Foreign Office's Eastern Department, son of Sir Maurice Hankey, minuted: 'We are no longer observers here but an essential and dynamic factor in running this country.'[74]

Internal security and post-abdication political change

The allied invasion and the shah's abdication heralded a period of political chaos in Iran. The chaos was at work 'not only in the provinces but also at the centre, and in the very centre of politics, among the political parties, the press, the notables, the Majlis, the very frequently changing cabinets (it would be misleading to call them governments) and the royal court'.[75] In the 'sudden changeover from pure despotism ... to an alleged constitutional and democratic regime, there was a general scramble for the fruits, though not for the responsibilities, of privilege and office'.[76] The abject power vacuum that this situation might have caused was partially mitigated by the presence of powerful external actors. The Anglo-Soviet occupiers, with their considerable political, economic and military resources, found that they had to help preserve law and order, because it was in their own interests to do so.

The Americans also became increasingly involved, seeing in Iran a nation-building project as specialist missions to reform key elements of the state were requested by the Iranian government, and duly dispatched. But the occupying powers were ill-prepared to assume the role of arbiters of security and governance. Ann Lambton, observing affairs from Tehran, wrote that the allies 'perhaps did not clearly realise or make sufficient allowance for the very real difficulties which the invasion and virtual occu-pation of Persia by the British forces in the south and the Russia in the north, and its division into two virtually separate zones, would involve'.[77] The removal of the shah's authoritarian rule led to anarchy and the re-emergence of problems not solved but driven underground during his reign.

Lambton explained the privileged position that the army had occupied under Reza Shah's rule, a position dramatically altered by the Anglo-Soviet invasion:

> The Army administration had proved itself unequal to the task of modern war at the time of the invasion and many units had virtually disintegrated. These events had been a great blow to the national vanity in general and left much resentment behind among the military classes. In the interests of internal security the reformation of an efficient army seemed desirable. But, as in the case of the administration, the only tools at hand were the army as it existed. This was both hated by the public for the abuses it had committed during the Riza Shah regime and discred-ited in their eyes for its performance at the time of the invasion. Furthermore it was divided into factions and its confidence in its ability severely shaken.[78]

The army was left embarrassed and embittered. In a letter to Tenth Army's headquarters, the British political adviser in Kermanshah provided intriguing intelligence about the attitudes of Iranian troops, as well as Britain's own Indian forces. Indian troops stationed in Iran had been telling their Iranian confreres that they 'would like to be rid of us'.

The ineffectualness of the Iranian army meant that British forces were expected to contribute to the maintenance of law and order and general security. Beyond this lay more strategic tasks. Imperial troops were now present in force, and would remain at least until the German threat receded. In the post-invasion months, the entire Iran–Iraq region needed to be made to work for British and allied strategic ends, which in addition to defensive and offensive military preparations and operations included the takeover of transport infrastructure in order to deliver Anglo-American military aid to the Soviet Union in ever-increasing quantities. There was even the chance that British forces might be sent to support the Red Army, or to replace Red Army units stationed in the Soviet zone of Iran in the north.

Following invasion and abdication, the Iranian state entered a rudderless period. With the breakdown of the shah's centralized state, tribal communities reclaimed land that had been confiscated by Reza Shah: 'almost all settled nomads returned to nomadic life'.[79] 'The benefit of the Shah's greatest achievement, subduing the tribes,' wrote Louis Dreyfus, 'may be lost'.[80] The weakness of the Iranian state post-invasion led the Kurds to assert their demands for independence, and the Anglo-Soviet allies allowed a vacuum to develop in Kurdish regions between the fringes of their two areas of occupation.[81] British officials urged the Tehran government to settle claims against the state made by those dispossessed under the former shah; the government established a commission to look at the land claims of individuals and groups, but it proved 'pretty much useless in the working of its local commissions'.[82]

There were almost continuous incidents of disorder up and down the country. 'Some of these were large and historic', such as the major revolts that were to occur in the provinces of Azerbaijan and Kurdistan when the war ended. 'Some were less spectacular but made up for it in frequency, becoming a matter of monthly and weekly, if not daily, occurrence.'[83] While these tensions and revolts were of great significance for the integrity of the Iranian state, for the allies they were also of importance because they threatened to disrupt their ability to use Iran for strategic war purposes. Some of the most serious threats to the all-important railway were to be found in the hill region of Dorud, where British garrison forces were maintained, and on the stretch of the Bushire–Isfahan road which passed through Qashqai territory. Here, imperial troops conducted military reconnaissance and assisted the local military governor. In key areas, tribal communities were anti-British and there was a fear of uprisings and sustained sabotage attacks.

Threats to the lines of communication included thievery and raids from gangs or 'tribal' groups, as well as German or German-sponsored saboteurs. The British were more interested than the Soviets in improving the capacity of the Iranian state to cope with its immediate and long-term problems, tackling, for example, the lethargy and corruption of state officials.[84] Bullard explained the British position regarding Iranian internal security and the challenges it presented:

> We accept responsibility for, and in actual fact the Russians hold us responsible for, security of routes from the Indian border and from the ports of the Gulf to the places in North Persia where the Russians take over. To ensure the security of routes one must take a broad view of the security question. The Russians are far less concerned with the security situation than we are. They maintain many more troops in Persia and concern themselves with a far smaller area. They are practically independent of Persian cooperation. We are not. We are far more intimately concerned with the economic situation than the Russians.[85]

In their zone, the Soviets supported separatist ambitions and permitted Azeris and Kurds to ignore Iranian laws on dress and language, to take over provincial administrations and to create armed militias. The British came into possession of a document entitled the 'Programme and Desires of the Azerbaijan Workers' Committee', written in the Azeri Turkic language.[86] It was, according to Bullard, clearly of Soviet origin, asking among other things for the protection of vernacular theatre, for brothel workers to be absorbed into productive factory work and for equality of women with men in social and political affairs – 'all matters remote from the views of the oriental and the Moslem'. Bullard told Eden that he 'mentioned this programme to my Soviet colleague as the kind of thing that did us great harm in adding to the suspicions of the Turkish Government that the Soviet Union had designs on Azerbaijan'. But ambassador Smirnov denied that there was any Soviet influence at work here.

Ann Lambton described local administration in the Soviet zone as 'virtually paralyzed' because of the Soviet policy of disarming Iranian security forces, 'preventing their freedom of movement and the freedom of movement of government officials, and by preventing the movement of foodstuffs to other parts of Persia.'[87] Refugees were arriving in Tabriz from Rezaiyeh. The Azerbaijan Workers' Committee was 'reported to be living on loot and robbery while police do not venture out. Some members said to be forcing villages to sign in favour of independent government of Soviet type.'[88] On the streets of Tabriz, red flags were hoisted and calls made for an independent Bolshevik Republic of Azerbaijan. This could only happen because the Soviet government refused to allow the Iranian government to maintain adequate military and police forces in the province. The virtual disappearance of Iranian government authority in the Soviet zone, especially in Azerbaijan province, had commenced when officials and military officers ignominiously abandon the region as Soviet forces crossed the border. The Soviets subsequently armed what the British consul called 'Armenian riff-raff' to keep order, and confiscated goods and property, causing many to flee to Isfahan and Tehran.[89] 'It is difficult,' writes the Iranian historian Fakhreddin Azimi, 'to defend the Soviet policy of first disarming the gendarmerie and police and then refusing to assist in the maintenance of order on the grounds that this would be interference in the internal affairs of Persia.'[90]

In the south, the British military was helping the Iranian government 'fulfil its internal security responsibilities'. But in so doing, 'we are being inexorably drawn into the net of another frightful and insoluble question: the age-long squabble between the Persians and the Arabs'.[91] Before Reza Shah extended Tehran's writ across the country, the western portion of Khuzestan had been an autonomous region known as 'Arabistan', and tensions between Arabs and Persians revived in the aftermath of the invasion. In a typical example of the petitions submitted to British civilian and military authorities in the aftermath of invasion, the chief of the Dris tribes craved British support for Arab communities struggling against the Iranian government:

> We have the honour to forward to your Excellency our high esteem and devotion. The Arabic district of Arabistan has suffered at the hands of Persian Officials the severest tyranny and all sorts of torment and humiliation ... Our hearts overflowed with delight and our faces were lighted with joy on the arrival of your victorious armies to the district of Arabistan because of our belief that you will uproot tyranny and restore

to us the liberty for the sake of which you are fighting and thus set us free from the fetters of dictatorship of which we have been suffering for the last sixteen years.[92]

But British officials in both Iran and Iraq were exhorted to keep out of local and national territorial disputes. Vyvyan Holt, writing from the Baghdad Embassy, told Major V.H.W. Dowson, British consul at Basrah, not to encourage talk of Arabistan. British policy was to 'respect borders so no sympathy with movement to include Arabs of Arabistan in Iraq'.[93]

The nature of British involvement in local affairs is reflected in the reports filed by the officers of the consular service. Like those of the political advisers in Iraq, they were strikingly reminiscent of the reports of district officers in the colonial empire. They furnished copious intelligence on political activities, and offered opinion and analysis. Routinely written with paternalistic authority and insight into local customs and personalities, they airily described what Iranians were 'like' and what they could and could not be expected to do. They proffered pen pictures of 'tribal notables', the genealogies of individuals and their disputes, the pedigree of parliamentary candidates and the provenance of newly formed political parties.

The official British position with regard to involvement in Iran's local affairs was clear – it was to be avoided as much as possible. But that was easier said than done. The fact was that, like it or not, the post-invasion political and strategic situation meant that the British were inexorably drawn in. For the sake of national unity, Britain undertook to preserve the shah's state and to discourage regional challenges to its integrity; directly contrary to this, regional leaders sought to enlist British help against the state in order to further their own ends and seize upon the opportunity presented by a stricken Iranian national government. They supplicated British officials for assistance in getting properties confiscated by the old shah returned to them, or for help in achieving goals of national self-determination and regional autonomy. This was always going to be a 'damned if they did, damned if they didn't' situation for the British, and they knew that the very fact of their presence could be used to justify government inaction: the assumption that the British would act to maintain security 'may account for complete apathy of the Persian authorities', as one official put it.[94] The British did not want to forward regional agendas – Kurdish autonomy, for example – but neither did they want to do the Iranian government's job for it nor actively to incur the disfavour of influential individuals and communities. Although the British were pledged not to act in any way detrimental to the state's integrity, the mere fact of their presence and its puissance gave great prominence to their long-standing involvement in the country. This, coupled with their military activities, meant that they were much more than bystanders.

An example of the manner in which the British became embroiled in local affairs is provided by the reaction to a spate of robberies in Fars province. Sending British troops was ruled out, and there were no additional forces being sent by the Iranian government. But the region's Anglo-Iranian Oil Company station needed protection. The AIOC had a trans-shipment base and landing ground at Ganawah and an oil installation, so unrest in the region dismayed the British. To provide a modicum of security, it was proposed to arm a local tribe, the Hayat Dawudi, with rifles. The British consul made it clear to the commander of Iranian forces in the region that 'the responsibility for protecting the Company's installation is his'.[95] Lorries, some of them British, were being held up and looted, and on 20 December 1941 the governor of Bushire reported that around 400 insurgents had captured Mazasuri, 10 miles from Ganawah, and looked like attacking Ganawah itself. He had sent 30 road guards and was sending 30 more, and requested that the governor of Shiraz dispatch 1,000 regular troops to Ganawah. The governor of Bushire visited the British consul and requested the aid of British troops, as his guards had proved ineffectual and even made the situation worse because of their unpopularity. He also suggested 'that a small air reconnaissance would cause them to scatter'. But if no action were taken, the city of Bushire itself would be endangered. 'Discontent in the area is partly due to the fact that people are starving and nearly naked,' the consul observed.[96]

And so things went on, unsatisfactorily. Nine months later the British consul toured the area and reported that the question of the AIOC's position had returned 'in aggravated form'. The local Iranian military commander had machine-gunned caravans of the Boir Ahmadi tribe, and in the aftermath the AIOC guards had taken the opportunity to loot their flocks. Relatively minor stuff, one might think, but the region had gained new strategic importance: until recently, the consul explained, 'Gach Saran was important but not vital to oil production and the war effort. This has now changed. As a result of the production of butane – apparently an ingredient which enables high octane aviation petrol to be produced in Abadan, Gach Saran has become vitally important and production is also being opened up at Pazanun.'[97] Therefore, measures for the protection of the roads were urgently required, and British soldiers became involved.

Minority groups in Iran and its environs were being stirred up by the ideological struggles of a world war and their actual or potential local permutations. A Foreign Office paper entitled 'The Problem of the Near East minorities: Pro Axis or Pro Ally?' considered the probable effects of German victory over the Soviet Union. If this eventuality were to occur, the document anticipated thousands of Caucasian soldiers returning home with arms in hand, and Turkey joining the Axis. It also contemplated the likely attitude of Kurds and other ethnic communities in the region.[98] Many people were being wooed by Axis propaganda, including daily broadcasts in the Armenian, Tartar and Georgian languages. Their theme was that Germany had given the Baltic states their independence and that now 'we will do the same for you.'[99] On the other hand, and rather less attractively, Britain's policy was to encourage the Iranian government to establish proper control and redress all legitimate grievances – not to champion local separatist movements.

Troubles in Kurdistan

The Kurds wanted far more than that and, in the north, they got it, as the Soviets encouraged their separatist desires in order to further their own ambition to create client states. Unrest in this region provides an example of the destabilization brought by war, and it began as soon as the British and the Soviets invaded and in the wake of Tehran's disintegrating authority. Armed rebellion and raiding broke out as the Kurds drove Iranian army detachments into the major towns. Major-General Slim's forces had to quell the worst of the Kurdish attacks, delivering the final blow to the military's ruined honour.

After the ceasefire in Iran, as Slim led his division to secure Hamadan and meet up with the Soviets, there had been an upsurge in civilian unrest; 'the Kurds were rising,' he wrote, and though the 'last thing we wanted was to tie down our forces in Iran', it was to prove impossible to stand aloof. Setting the tone for what was to happen in many parts of the country, the defeat and subsequent disarray of the Iranian state and its army caused disorder. 'That night,' Slim wrote:

before my orders for the withdrawal of Persian troops could be carried out, local tribesmen saw their opportunity in the demoralization of the garrison and raided the magazine. In the confusion they made away with a large number of modern rifles and considerable stores of ammunition, thus making all the problems of internal security much more difficult for the unfortunate Persians and for us.[100]

Iranian soldiers attempted to restore order, but were ill-prepared to do so. 'Unfortunately the troops were not in good shape; morale was low even for Persia, there had been many desertions, pay was in arrears and the soldiers had lost what confidence they may have had in their leaders ... Villages had been sacked, the countryside laid waste, and now larger towns were being threatened.' Slim's orders were to assist the Iranian forces but not to fight the Kurds. He sent small columns of troops into the area under junior officers, who had some success in quelling unrest. But general insecurity was going to be a problem: 'armed deserters roamed the countryside, and frequently joined forces with more established bandits or formed robber gangs of their own.'[101]

Captain Summers was part of Slim's force. In his words, after the invasion, 'chaos reigned in the country':

The conscripted soldiers deserted with their arms or were disarmed by the Russians. Thousands of soldiers straggled along the roads returning to their homes and villages. The majority had no boots and no food. Their clothes were in tatters. Somewhat naturally these soldiers formed into bands. They were robbing villages and fighting the police. The police were the pick of the old soldiers, were loyal to their country and most helpful to us. Considerable fighting was also going on on the frontier between the Kurds and the Persian soldiers.[102]

The widespread distribution of firearms was a problem in Kurdish – and other – regions of both Iran and Iraq. In conversations with the shah and government ministers, the American soldier, statesman and diplomat Patrick Hurley learned that at least 50,000 rifles had fallen into the hands of 'tribesmen'. The British consul in Shiraz, meanwhile, reported that after the Anglo-Soviet invasion, the southern tribes rejoiced in their new freedom, dug up and cleaned buried weapons, bought new rifles from traffickers, seized weapons from Iranian army outposts, or simply added the rifles kept by tribal conscripts to their stockpiles when they left the army. The Kurds meanwhile were in possession of large quantities of rifles thrown away by fugitives from the Iranian army, and also some procured in the aftermath of the Anglo-Iraqi war. The Anglo-Soviet invasion caused intense activity on the border and the 'sudden invasion of Persian Kurdistan by Iraqi Kurds said to be under orders of Sheikh Mahmoud . . . Invading bands reported to number about 1,000 have surrounded several Iranian frontier posts', penetrating about 50 miles into Iran. The Iranian posts had been called upon to surrender in the name of the sheikh. 'As Iranian military authorities in their present difficulties are almost powerless to resist these attacks', wrote the consul, 'British military authorities are taking measures to repel these invaders by reinforcing the British garrison at Sanandaj.' The consul hoped that 'British troops in north east Iraq will be ordered to collaborate in crushing this movement which appears to have been launched to encourage Iranian Kurds to support Sheikh Mahmoud's efforts to take advantage of present chaos in western Iran in order to create an autonomous Kurdistan.'[103] Captain Summers heard rumours that a local leader named 'Sheikh Mahmud' was leading 1,000 marauding men, and that it was claimed that he 'cannot die in battle or be harmed by any bullet'.[104]

Ambassador Cornwallis in Baghdad assured London that he was doing his 'utmost to persuade the Iranian Government to redress grievances of Kurdish population' in an effort to win their support.[105] The Iraqi Kurds, seeing what was happening in Iran, where regional groups were rising up against state forces, 'followed suit by taking every Persian army and police post along the whole length of the frontier. For them it was a real bonanza; crates of Czech rifles and ammunitions, some of them still packed in grease, were the prizes of war.'[106]

Wallace Lyon, political adviser in northern Iraq, reported that instability on the border was a constant source of concern. The seizure of weapons from Iraqi and Iranian military and police forces, and the use of coveted Brno rifles as currency, meant that hijackings, sheep stealing and cross-border raids increased. The Political Adviser Southern Area received a Combined Intelligence Centre Iraq report stating that 'the tribes in N. Iraq were now more heavily armed than ever before. Majid al-Khalifa had a brace of machine-guns, and Iraqi army Bren guns were available at good prices, most of them guns looted after the battle of Taji' (an encounter between British and Iraqi forces as the British advanced on Baghdad in late May 1941).[107]

The invasion of Iran had 'led Kurds on Iranian side to clean up all the Frontier posts. It is said that British troops disarmed the Baneh Garrison and the Russians came as far south as Khaneh and Serdesht where they likewise disarmed the Persian Army. As a result of this all the Iranian police posts have been shot up and looted, and there is a state of lawlessness just across the border.'[108] It was a free-for-all on the border: 'The lawlessness that followed the disarmament of the Persian Army and the looting of the Amnia [Iranian road police] posts has so far not spread into Iraq though there is good reason to believe that some of the Iraqi tribes got their share of the loot . . . Now there is no customs post or Amnia on the frontier, wheat, sugar etc are being smuggled into Iraq where the prices are much higher.'[109] Slim sent Colonel Ouvry Roberts to discuss the matter with the local Iranian commander in view of the possible threat to the British garrison in Sanandaj and the lines of communication. A memorandum on 'Unrest in Kurdistan' reported that additional mechanized forces were being dispatched, and that during 'the past fortnight British patrols have scoured large areas in search of Iraqi invaders and hidden rifles.'[110]

In October 1941 an emissary of the Kurdish leader Hama Rashid Khan, now in control at Baneh, visited the British Embassy in Tehran. He had been sent to ask the British to establish a protectorate over 'Persian Kurdistan' and to 'save them [the Kurds] from Persian tyranny'.[111] The situation was extremely difficult:

> for whereas most Persian officials are incorrigibly corrupt and uncon-scientious, the Kurdish ideal is plenty of smuggling and looting, no government control and no taxation, so that the minimum programme which any government must impose, viz. establishment of customs police, disarmament of persons not authorised to carry arms and levying of minimum of taxation must appear tyranny to the Kurds.[112]

The Iranian army deployed tanks and armoured cars against Kurdish forces. In operations to reoccupy Baneh, the Iranians had to seek Soviet permission to send a cavalry regiment to Mahabad.[113] As a further indica-tion both of the constraints imposed by the occupation and of where ulti-mate power resided, the Iranian government asked the British if they had any objection to its plans to occupy Baneh in order to suppress Hama Rashid and the movement for Kurdish autonomy, and to install regular Iranian officials and gendarmerie. The British Embassy in Baghdad thought that 'The problem, in its essence, is how to keep the Kurds well enough disposed towards the British to prevent their being captured by Axis blan-dishments, without encouraging them to think that we are supporting them against the several governments whose subjects they are. This political tight rope walking can only be performed if policy is carefully balanced every-where by one authority.'[114]

The British were not the only ones concerned about unrest in the Kurdish regions of Iran and Iraq. The Turkish government was disturbed by Kurdish independence declarations in western Iran, and 'vitally interested in main-taining status quo of Persian AZERBAIJAN'.[115] Kurdish chiefs had travelled to Baku to discuss plans for an independent Kurdish state. They had received rifles, clothes and wireless sets from the Soviets. On returning to Rezaiyeh they were welcomed by hundreds bearing flags and portraits of Stalin and Molotov and shouting 'Long live Bolshevism'. An oath of independence was administered to members of the committee, already alleged to comprise 10,000 members.[116] In May 1942 the American legation chief reported on disturbances and a 'deteriorating situation' in Rezaiyeh, 'where Kurds are attacking 800 gendarmes outside [the] city'. The Soviets refused to allow Iranian reinforcements to proceed there. In the British zone in central Kurdistan, he wrote, there had 'been large scale clashes between troops and Kurds under leadership of Hamarashid [Hama Rashid] and many casualties … Thousands of peasants and peaceful inhabitants, whose property has been pillaged, have had to abandon their fields and homes and take refuge in the city [Rezaiyeh] where famine already reigns.'[117]

Ultimately, opposition to the Iranian and Iraqi governments in Kurdish territory was to lack the 'combination and leadership' required for a successful secessionist drive. Men like Hama Rashid, it transpired, were brigands as much as they were political leaders, and could treat their own people worse than they were treated by the governments they purported to despise.[118]

Quinan's tasks

Lieutenant-General Quinan received a new directive following the invasion of Iran. In addition to preparing to defend Iran and Iraq against German invasion, he was now ordered to develop the road, rail and river communi-cations necessary to ensure the delivery of the maximum possible aid to the Soviet Union. Now commanding what amounted to a corps (three divi-sions) and with more troops arriving in theatre, in late 1941 Quinan's force was formally designated the Tenth Army, its symbol a golden *lamassu*, an Assyrian deity with a bull's body, eagle's wings and the head of a man.

There was an immense amount of infrastructural work to be under-taken, for example the installation of water pipelines. No. 1 Engineers Base

Workshop Company eventually numbered 1,350 men – Sikh, Punjabi, Madrassi and Iraqi – while the Royal Electrical and Mechanical Engineers Base Workshops in the Maqil area came to employ 3,300 men. Indian Posts and Telegraph Department units took six weeks to build a reliable speech and telegraph line from Basra to Baghdad, following the line of the Euphrates. The Vehicle Assembly Unit near Shaibah, assembled 16,000 lorries for the long overland journey to the Soviet zone. Bulk oil vehicles were shipped to Iran, so that by the autumn of 1941 there were 110 tank cars on the railway (a figure that had risen to 400 by the spring of 1943). The number of tanker lorries rose over the same period from 260 to 500. The next task was to develop communications between the Persian Gulf and the Caspian. This was a formidable additional burden on top of the administrative development to which India was already committed, undertaken in order to maintain forces in Iran and Iraq to meet a German invasion from the north.[119]

With Quinan's troops providing security and developing the transport infrastructure, a large civilian organization also became involved in the mission to send military hardware to the Soviet Union. In August 1941 the British government ordered the United Kingdom Commercial Corporation (UKCC) to spearhead this task. Based at Plantation House on Fenchurch Street in the City of London, it had been created in April 1940 for the purposes of economic warfare with the object of denying sources of supply to the enemy and procuring goods for Britain from neutral countries. In Iran it was responsible for road transport and the importation of all British goods, as well as exports, and became the 'consignees of all "Aid to Russia" stores'.[120] The UKCC was asked to organize local transport on the Tenth Army's behalf, which it did from bases in Baghdad, Basra and Mosul. By October 1941 UKCC lorries were operating over 3.5 million ton-kilometres a month. Soon, employing over 5,000 lorries, that figure had risen to 25 million a month.

Quinan's other main task remained the preparation of Iran and Iraq to face invasion, very much now focused on Germany since the Soviets were allies. The seriousness with which this threat was viewed in London can be gauged by the urgent priority that was given to the construction of defences. 'The utmost speed must be exercised in planning and execution of defensive works', Quinan's headquarters signalled divisional commanders. 'Speed is truly vital. Every hour matters. Preparation of defences in the forward areas must be pressed on at maximum speed.'[121] It was an all-hands-to-the-pump moment, commanders being told to cut guard duties, training and patrols in order to expedite the construction and preparation of defences. In one of those ironies of war, while some military resources were being employed to destroy infrastructure lest the enemy get hold of it, or to plan to do so, other resources were being pumped into extending and building new infrastructure to enhance defensive capabilities. Thus 2,000 soldiers were allocated to work on the railway network, which was augmented by 9,000 new locomotives and wagons and the construction of 600 miles of new track. Quinan forwarded other initiatives to increase the load-bearing capacity of the region's transport infrastructure. His command gave priority to port development, ensuring that material could be off-loaded from allied merchant vessels and then stored, or – in the case of the many crated vehicles that arrived in kit form – assembled nearby. Onward distribution and the development of the rail, river and road transport networks upon which it depended was a separate though entirely comple-mentary activity.

All of this took place against the backdrop of possible German invasion. In January 1942 Churchill told Roosevelt that at least fifteen allied divisions were needed to defend the oilfields of the Persian Gulf region. In the same month the Commander-in-Chief Middle East outlined his thinking on Quinan's Iran–Iraq command in a telegram to the War Office. He explained that the minimum security requirements entailed keeping the enemy away from Egypt and the Persian Gulf bases and supporting the Turks. Should the Germans break through the Caucasus, the plan was to fight forward on the general line stretching from Qazvin to Hamadan, Mosul and the fron-tier with Syria and Turkey. But the forces for such a defence would not be available if the German attack commenced on 1 April (for planning assump-tions, the likely start of a spring offensive). Given this, if attacked the 'only course will be to fall back on defences in rear in Persia, Central Iraq, and South Syria and to fight a defensive battle'.[122]

Unfortunately, planning the region's defence was hampered by the Soviet attitude. They would not allow the British 'to reconnoitre one inch of the ground over which they would have to fight if they were to keep the German air bases at a sufficient distance from the port of Basra and the vital oilfields of the Persian Gulf'.[123] There was no word of their plans, either, to hold the passes in the Caucasus. To attempt to fill in the gaps, Quinan needed an experienced, highly mobile reconnaissance unit to watch the approaches on his front. The 11th Hussars were duly sent. The unit drove out of Cairo on 27 April 1942 across the Sinai into Palestine and then along the Iraq desert convoy route, reaching Mosul on 6 May. Here it came under the command of Brigadier Gerald Carr-White's 252nd Indian Armoured Brigade as part of the Tenth Army, having travelled 1,000 miles in 7 days. The brigade was soon ordered to Kermanshah, where it trained in the mountains and sent forward patrols to reconnoitre the approaches to British-occupied Iran. The men of the 11th Hussars, like so many others, longed to get to the Western Desert. So, too, Captain John Masters. Having taken part in the invasion, he wrote, 'the supply of opponents was now running out. Surely our next move must be the big one – to the Western Desert, to fight Rommel'.[124] Nevertheless, Masters next found himself on leave in Tehran, before being sent north, with three trucks, half a platoon of Gurkhas and an Iranian interpreter, to reconnoitre routes that the Germans might use in invading the country, reporting on their feasibility and making recommendations for their defence.

Differences with the Soviets

Conversing with Anthony Eden in August 1941, Ambassador Maisky described the mood of the Soviet people. He spoke of the huge losses already suffered in the two months since the German invasion. 'And what has England been doing all this time?' the people asked. The idea of a second front had been knocked back, at least for the time being. 'Something is happening, sure,' Maisky told Eden. 'Thanks. But ... it's not enough to pinch the rabid beast's tail; it must be hit round the head with a club!'[125] British bombers had not made the Germans withdraw a single squadron from the east, Maisky said. Eden would like a second front himself, the ambassador recorded, and was 'a little embarrassed' as he took the point about the Soviet Union's sense of disappointment and bewilderment. Eden repeated the usual British responses, talking optimistically of the bomber offensive over Germany, planned operations in Libya, the good prospects in the Middle East and Anglo-Soviet cooperation in Iran. But Maisky, in turn, gave the standard Soviet response. 'I replied: "Iran and Libya are secondary tasks. The main one: how to beat Germany?"'

As well as the challenges posed by Iran's fissiparous internal politics, the politics of the Anglo-Soviet alliance required careful handling. The two powers – soon joined on the ground by American forces who began entering Iran in strength in December 1942 – had to rub along together in order to make the

Iranian supply route function, both acutely aware of the fact that the Germans were advancing. Sir Oliver Lyttelton, Britain's Resident Minister in the Middle East, told Clarmont Skrine that the British government did not like having the Soviets in Iran and would gladly relieve them of the defence of the northern provinces 'so that they can defend the Caucasus but the Russians won't hear of it'.[126] In October 1941, as the Germans reinforced their positions in the Murmansk area, Anthony Eden and Sir Stafford Cripps, British ambassador to Moscow, discussed the practicalities involved in sending troops to fight along-side the Soviets.[127] Britain's willingness to help the Soviets defend the Caucasus was viewed by the Soviet ambassador 'as the main indicator of our attitude'. 'We thought a useful first step would be for us to relieve the bulk of Soviet forces in Persia, freeing them for the Caucasus.'[128] But the Soviets were never comfortable with the idea of British forces replacing their own troops in 'their' zone, consisting of the long-coveted northern provinces, or setting foot on Soviet territory to help defend it against the Germans. While encouraging, even demanding, that such plans be made, the Soviet official mind could not shake off its suspicions and fears regarding British imperialism.

Nevertheless, in their desperation the Soviets clamoured for large British forces to be dispatched to their aid, while also maintaining their demand for a 'second front' in the west. In doing so, Moscow expected far more from the British than they could possibly deliver. Writing to Eden on 23 October, Cripps said that there was 'no way we can send 25 to 30 divisions anywhere, Russia or elsewhere'. But he hoped that Britain could act in a more modest manner: 'Surely it is possible to send either to Murmansk or through Iran at least one or two fully armed divisions to fight on the Russian front.'[129] In replying Eden agreed that the chance of Britain sending twenty-five to thirty divisions was pie in the sky – a 'physical absurdity', as he put it. At the start of the war, the Foreign Secretary recounted, Britain had only managed to send ten divisions the short distance across the English Channel, at a time when shipping was plentiful and U-boats scarce. In the last year London had managed 'with the greatest difficulty' to get a solitary division (the 50th) to the Middle East, and Britain was at the time of writing sending another division overseas 'only by extraordinary measures' (the ill-fated 18th Division, originally embarked for the Middle East but diverted to India and thence Singapore, where it arrived just in time to be captured by the Japanese). All Britain's shipping, Eden explained to Cripps, was fully committed, and the 'margin by which we live and make munitions of war has only narrowly been maintained'.[130]

But where Britain could help the Soviets physically and materially, it would – and Iran was a place where it could do so. The position on the 'southern flank' was that the Soviets had five divisions in Iran 'which we are willing to relieve'. Lest they be reluctant to agree to this offer of British help, for fear of their old rival stealing a march in their absence, Eden suggested that they might leave a token force to 'maintain their position' in northern Iran. He also said that Britain could send the same in the opposite direction. To put two British divisions (hardly a 'token force') into the Caucasus, he thought, would take at least three months and they 'would then only be a drop in the bucket'.

Cripps replied to Eden on the same day, 25 October 1941. He reported that the feeling in Soviet government circles and among the population as a whole about the lack of armed help from Britain 'is very strong indeed'. Diplomatic relations were worsening, and 'probably nothing less than the dispatch of a force not less than a corps' and RAF resources 'is our only hope of checking a dangerous deterioration, not only in the will of the Russians to resist, but also in our relations with the Soviet Government ... There is an obsession that we are sitting back and watching them.'[131] The Soviets, Cripps wrote, were 'obsessed we are prepared to fight to the last drop of Russian blood as Germans suggest in their propaganda ... An attack on Libya would no doubt be interpreted as our taking our chance of conquering Africa while they are holding the Germans for us here.'

This was too much for Eden, who was in no mood to be lectured by the Soviet Union and robustly defended Britain's position. While he sympathized with Cripps' awkward position and Russia's 'agony', he believed that the Soviets 'certainly have no right to reproach us. They brought their own fate upon themselves when, by their Pact with Ribbentrop, they let Hitler loose on Poland and so started the war.'[132] The Soviet Union gave Britain no support for a year and would have been 'utterly indifferent' if we had been defeated. 'That a Government with this record should accuse us of trying to make conquests in Africa or gain advantages in Persia at their expense or being willing to fight to the last Russian soldier, leaves me quite cool.' Eden reiterated that Britain could replace the five Russian divisions in Iran 'with Indian troops fitted to maintain internal order, but not equipped to fight Germans', and Britain was building up divisions in Iran 'which might be joined up with Russian forces in the Caucasus'. Eden also sent Cripps a copy of Churchill's letter to Stalin of 4 November, and said that he would be happy to send Wavell to meet the ambassador. Take it or leave it, was the *sotto voce* message.[133]

American involvement

For their part, American diplomats were quick to recognize the 'entirely new state of affairs' ushered in by the invasion and subsequent occupation of Iran. 'With the disappearance of the authoritarian regime ... which was highly nationalistic and had a strong element of xenophobia, a more liberal attitude towards foreign institutions is to be anticipated.'[134] In order to take advantage of this change and to encourage the growth of free institutions, the Americans wanted to reintroduce sponsored schools, and it was soon clear that this was a welcome opportunity for the Iranian government to reignite the policy of 'positive equilibrium', attempting to draw in the American government to act as a counterweight to the British and the Soviets. Even at this early date, one of the key reasons for proposing involvement was to counter what the diplomat termed 'Sovietization', an early sign of the tensions that led towards the Cold War. The American schools initiative was immediately challenged by a Soviet demand for equal rights. From as early as September 1941, American and British diplomats were expressing anxiety about Soviet-inspired separatism, which was manifest from the start of the occupation, as well-directed Soviet propaganda sought to drive a wedge between people in the Soviet zone and the government in Tehran, through the spread of communism and the encouragement of separatism.[135]

Churchill and Roosevelt had agreed, in the summer of 1941, that Iran and Iraq formed a key region in which America could relieve the pressure on British resources, especially as Britain was preparing to operate and sustain a fighting army as well as endeavouring to channel military supplies to the Soviet Union. Heeding Harry Hopkins' advice, Roosevelt decided that the utmost aid possible should be given, and on 15 September 1941 a conference was held in London. Resisting Britain's desire to control all aid to the Soviet Union, a new supply programme second only to that supplying Britain came into being. America started sending experts and supporting British efforts to develop the supply route, and also to help Britain equip and move its forces as they prepared to fight the Germans should they break through in the Caucasus. Because of these decisions, it was decided to deploy specialist American servicemen to Iran.

By late September the Germans had captured nearly one-third of the Soviet Union's industry and much of its best agricultural land, taking nearly a million prisoners. In that month Roosevelt's special envoy W. Averell Harriman and British Minister of Supply Lord Beaverbrook flew to Moscow to discuss Lend-Lease supplies, and between them pledged 1.5 million tons of war material to be delivered by the end of June 1942.[136] The so-called Moscow Protocol was signed on 1 October, inspiring one of Stalin's aides to exclaim 'Now we shall win the war!'[137] While Quinan prepared to supply ten divisions for three months of fighting, the UKCC delivered British aid to the Soviets, including Australian wool, Canadian aluminium and cobalt, Indian jute and shellac, Ceylonese rubber and tea, West African oilseeds, tents from Palestine, industrial diamonds from South Africa and machine tools from Britain.

The requirement to build up American forces in this region came all of a sudden, leading to feverish military planning in late 1941 and a steep learning curve for American officials. War Department intelligence officers had to turn to the consultant in Islamic archaeology at the Library of Congress for information on highways and transportation routes to Iran.[138] The US Military Iranian Mission was formed to help the British deliver Lend-Lease to the Soviets, and the Iranian District of the North Atlantic Division was created to provide construction support from the Corps of Engineers. It was led by Colonel Raymond A. Wheeler, a career engineer specializing in road and railway construction who had been governor of the Panama Canal Zone.[139]

Wheeler's mission was to help the British 'by building up supply facilities for their forces in the Persian Gulf and by assisting their efforts to support the Soviet Union.'[140] From 30 November, the new Iranian Mission was headquartered in Baghdad. Wheeler felt that the Persian Gulf would eventually offer the best avenue for supplying the Soviet Union: the Antarctic route's utility was limited and Vladivostok could only take civilian supplies because of Soviet–Japanese complications, leaving the Middle East as the only alternative route for shipping war materials. At either Umm Qasr or Baghdad, Wheeler proposed to develop ordnance repair facilities to support the British Tenth Army. In Iran the Americans agreed to undertake the construction and repair of roads, railways and ports, and to operate truck and aircraft assembly plants to serve both allies.

On a mission in the Soviet zone of Iran, John Masters' driver pulled over for a speeding car, 'a flag whipping furiously from its radiator cap ... the Stars and Stripes. The American Ambassador, I thought. Very odd; and what was he in such a hurry about? It was December 8 1941.'[141] With America's entry into the war as a full belligerent, earlier plans to deploy forces to Iran were galvanized. Moves towards establishing dedicated

American facilities in Iran and Iraq took a significant step forward when, on 30 December, Secretary of War Henry Stimson reported an agreement with the Commander-in-Chief India and the Air Officer Commanding Iraq for the use of facilities at Abadan and Basra. These would enable 200 American aircraft to be delivered per month, assembled, and then flown to Soviet territory.

By early 1942 the first direct consignments of American Lend-Lease began arriving from Boston and Philadelphia: wheat, flour, meat, eggs, milk, lard and butter for the Soviet people; rubber boots, shoes, clothes and blankets for the Red Army; and arms, ammunition, barbed wire, communications equipment, trucks, jeeps, scout cars, tanks, bombers, fighters, petrol, high-grade steel, copper, dynamos, tools, a hospital train and even toothpaste.[142] A treaty of alliance between the allies and Iran was signed in Tehran in January 1942. It committed the allies to leave Iran six months after the end of the war, and afforded them the right to develop all means of communication across the country in the meantime. The hotels, bars, cinemas and offices of Tehran filled with allied military personnel and civilian experts – 'oil experts, plane experts, automobile experts, road and railroad experts, most of them toiling on the problem of supplies for the Soviet Union' – while senior military officials 'seemed to be playing with their large maps and sharp pencils, at some fascinating game, full of invisible traps'.[143] Allied forces were growing in strength in Iran and Iraq, and their activities, and the wider ramifications of world war, were becoming a significant factor in the lives of ordinary Iranians and Iraqis.

CHAPTER 10

The consequences of occupation

The arrival of allied troops following the occupation of both Iran and Iraq had a deep impact on the people of both countries. In Tehran, an 'astonishing variety of uniforms mingled with the crowds, Persian, Indian, Polish, and British,' wrote Hermione, Countess of Ranfurly, while convoys of troops and military supplies became commonplace on roads and railways.[1] Erstwhile enemies, including British and Iraqi soldiers, needed to adjust to new realities. Efforts were made to get along, and at least give the outward display of friendship and cooperation. Another key theme in the post-occupation environment was the need to accommodate large numbers of foreign soldiers – to find space for their encampments, and to adjust to the economic changes that the sudden arrival of large numbers of relatively wealthy individuals in need of a range of services inevitably caused. The stationing of allied troops in Iran and Iraq, and the significant work on defences and infrastructure that they undertook, brought job opportunities for thousands of people.

British political advisers noted that reports of British military successes had a good effect: 'Reactions to the march into Persia and to the successful conclusion of hostilities have been excellent. Iraqis feel that it has removed the menace of war at least a step further from their doorstep and cleared up the source of a considerable proportion of the subversive propaganda in this country . . . No doubt whatsoever that this successful use of power politics has made a very deep impression.'[2] Similarly, during the Eighth Army's 'Crusader' offensive in the Western Desert in November, which relieved the siege of Tobruk, the Political Adviser Central Area reported that the

Initial success of the Libyan offensive has overshadowed all other polit-ical effects. With a people as volatile as the Arab the effect is much exag-gerated – indeed to talk to some of them one would think that not only are the Axis driven out of Africa but the war is as good as over. The more sober minded have watched the Russian campaign with renewed misgiv-ings but there can be no doubt that Libya has riveted most of their atten-tion. The effect of this blow, coming on top of the cumulative effects of the capture of most of Rashid Ali's supporters in Persia, and on top of the transportation of the many Nazi supporters to Fao [al-Faw] and the obvious pro-British politics of the present Government, has certainly been very great.[3]

But things could swing both ways, and news of German victories, of which there continued to be many, caused great excitement and kept the flame of anti-British and anti-Soviet sentiment burning brightly across the region.

Attempting to forge cordial relations was an important facet of the work of the political advisers in Iraq and the consular network in Iran. Key relation-ships were those between the British armed forces and local political figures, tribal leaders, landowners and businessmen. Another was between the Iraqi army and British imperial forces. Not only had they recently shed each others' blood, but Iraqi officers were known for their anti-British and pro-German persuasions. Special efforts were made to encourage good relations and mutual respect. In this regard the five mutasarrifs of Iraq's northern provinces were 'most helpful and co-operative in matters connected with the British Forces.'[4] The political adviser recorded the Iraqi army's 'increasing disposition towards British community and troops', and a number of joint events including polo matches and parties.[5] Ambassador Cornwallis had cause to write to Minister for Foreign Affairs Ali Jawdat al-Aiyubi, conveying Lieutenant-General Quinan's gratitude for Iraqi help. Examples of cooperation included arrange-ments with landowners for leasing property to the military and the continuous watering of the King Ali and Mansar roads by Iraqi authorities in order to keep dust down for the benefit of imperial forces using them.[6]

Though the arrival of large British imperial formations in northern Iraq, massing around Kirkuk and Mosul, had brought problems, these had been met with 'friendly cooperation'. The region provides an excellent case study of the impact of the occupation and the attempts to mitigate its more nega-tive effects. The officer commanding Iraqi troops in the Mosul area had invited British officers to join the Iraqi Military Club, and the mayor of

Mosul invited British officers to judge the flower show during Eid al-Fitr, a festival marking the end of Ramadan.[7] A 'Mosul British Community Council' was created and British military personnel held a number of joint events with their Iraqi peers. Major-General Harvey, commander of the 8th Indian Infantry Division, made a courtesy call on the mutasarrif in October 1941, and large crowds assembled to see him inspect a police guard of honour.[8] British forces in Mosul were offered the use of the civil hospital, and the mayor, 'who is president of the Red Crescent Society handed over the big Red Crescent Hall and gardens to the British Troops as a recreation centre'. A formal ceremony followed by a tea party marked the occasion. It was attended by the mutasarrif, Major-General Harvey, members of the municipal council, senior officers of the Iraq army, senior civil officials, local notables and large numbers of British officers and men.[9] In December 1941 a party was given for the mutasarrif at the Officials' Club in Amarah, attended by Iraqi officials, notables, tribal sheikhs and officers of the Iraqi army's 7th Brigade. A poem against Rashid Ali al-Gailani was read out, the first time he had been publicly condemned in the town. In his speech, the mutasarrif said that there were three reasons why Iraqis 'should be friendly to the British'. One was the Anglo-Iraqi Treaty and the 'need to keep one's word'. Another was the pursuit of Iraq's own interests, the mutasarrif drawing attention to the manner in which Hitler treated the countries he occupied, including shooting civilians. This was not something that the British would do. Finally, the mutasarrif claimed, the British were a just and merciful people.[10]

Considerable effort was made to promote British popularity, the charm offensive including propaganda articles in local papers and the distribution in places such as Kirkuk of 'V' (for 'Victory') cufflinks or buttonhole badges.[11] In Mashhad in Iran, there were tennis parties and gramophone dances, and Clarmont Skrine inaugurated the Meshed Victory Cup Tournament for which high schools and club teams in Khorasan competed. The Tehran legation's Public Relations Bureau (later, the British Embassy Information Department) sent its consuls 'large quantities of books, posters, leaflets, and photographs and other propaganda material for our "British Reading Room", and lent us famous British war films, such as *Target for Tonight*, and Hollywood films such as *Fantasia* and *The Great Dictator*, which packed Meshed's biggest cinema'.[12] The British legation in Tehran also sent travelling cinemas around the country giving 16-mm shows at every town and large village on the main roads.[13] In an attempt to counter

A firing party of British infantrymen provides cover for Royal Engineers building a temporary bridge near Ramadi, 1 June 1941. The sun was a constant menace and British troops were ordered to wear their sun helmets and observe strict water discipline.

2 Blenheim Mark Is of 84 Squadron based at RAF Shaibah, Iraq, flying in formations of three over the Iraqi desert. RAF aircraft played a vital role in the Iraq, Iran and Syria campaigns of 1941. Aircraft from RAF Shaibah attacked Iraqi forces investing RAF Habbaniya and bombed targets in Baghdad and across the country.

3 The fort at Rutbah, Iraq, under attack from Bristol Blenheim Mark IVs of 84 Squadron, based at H4 landing ground in Trans-Jordan, on 9 May 1941. The bombing was observed by Arab Legion units to the south. Ground fire from the defenders brought down one of the aircraft, killing its crew. The fort, defended by Iraqi desert police and irregular troops, was attacked by Arab Legion and RAF armoured car ground units and, once captured, was used as a staging post by Kingcol.

4 A crew of No. 2 Armoured Car Company service a .303 Browning machine gun beside their GMC Mark I Otter light reconnaissance car at RAF Habbaniya after practice manoeuvres in the desert. This company was transferred from the Western Desert to take part in the Iraq campaign, joining No. 1 Company which was based at Habbaniya. The RAF armoured cars were responsible for defending RAF bases and patrolling the trans-desert line of communication and its forts and outposts.

5 British troops look out across the Tigris from the roof of the British Embassy in Baghdad, 11 June 1941. For the first time in many years, soldiers of the British and Indian armies were seen throughout the country.

6 The commanding officer of 84 Squadron briefs his aircrew before a training sortie at Shaibah, Iraq.

7 Recruits for the RAF Iraq Levies at drill, still wearing their civilian clothes. Men from some of Iraq's minority communities, such as Assyrians, Kurds and Yazidis, were the mainstay of the levies, which expanded from around 1,200 at the time of the Anglo-Iraqi war to more than 10,000 over the course of the following year.

8 A wooden painted plaque of the British 10th Army insignia: a golden *lamassu*, an Assyrian protective deity with a bull's body, eagle's wings and the head of a man.

TENTH ARMY

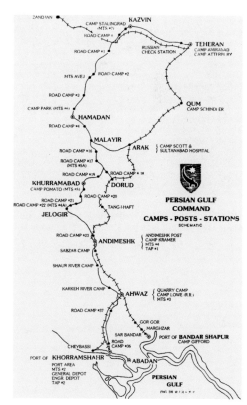

Persian Gulf Command: a map showing the extent of America's base infrastructure spread along the Iranian lines of communication.

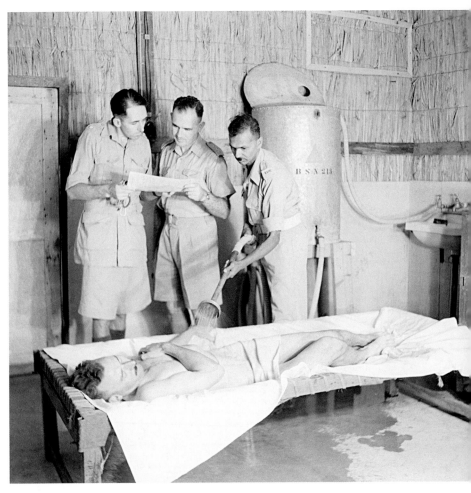

10 One of a series of photographs demonstrating the treatment given to sufferers of heatstroke in Iraq. This patient is being sprayed with cool water, 20 September 1943.

11 Indian troops guarding the Abadan oil refinery in the immediate aftermath of the Anglo-Soviet invasion. Abadan island, its extensive refining facilities, and the oilfields of south-west Iran were the major cause of Britain's joint invasion of the country in August 1941.

12 Soviet tankmen of the 6th Armoured Division drive through the streets of Tabriz on their T-26 battle tank.

13 Winston Churchill is given 'three cheers' by officers and men of Persia and Iraq Command on the occasion of his sixty-ninth birthday, Tehran, November 1943. The prime minister was in the city to meet Roosevelt and Stalin for one of the seminal grand strategic conferences at which they decided the future course of the war.

14 Sherman tank crews of the Scinde Horse Regiment, part of the 31st Indian Armoured Division in Iraq, March 1944. In the foreground, a party of Sikhs is being given instruction on stripping and cleaning a Browning gun by a viceroy's commissioned officer. The division's armour did not see action during the war, and was indicative of the need to sustain reserves and guard vital strategic regions which might see combat depending on outcomes in other theatres.

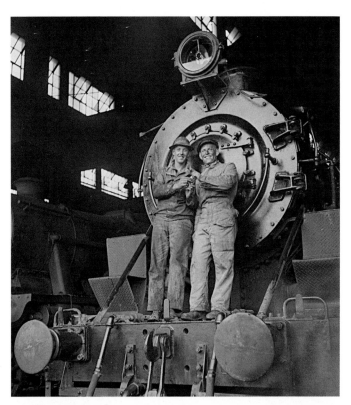

15 An American and a British engineer standing on an American locomotive in Iran, 1943. Between them, the two allies greatly increased the amount of rolling stock using the Iranian railway, which was responsible for carrying the lion's share of military aid that was sent to the Soviet zone in the north.

16 An assembly plant for American aircraft destined for the Soviet Union, Iran, 1943. Over 4,000 aircraft were assembled in allied factories in the region for onward flight to the Soviet Union, and nearly 1,000 were flown in direct.

7 Crated fighter aircraft waiting to be assembled at an assembly plant in Iran, 1943. The allies developed extensive infrastructure for the construction and movement of all manner of supplies. The largest crates contained the wings of aircraft complete with landing gear.

8 Soviet officers in black leather coats surrounded by a group of American soldiers at a dumping spot for supplies which the Americans brought through the Persian corridor. This was one of the first all-American convoys to make the trip bringing aid to the Soviet Union, 1943.

19 British, American and Soviet servicemen at a delivery point for allied aircraft, Iran, March 194.
Iran was the only place where service personnel of America, Britain and the Soviet Union operatec
side by side.

20 Captain C.B. Cutler of
Chicago, Illinois, dust-covere
and wearing sand goggles.
The leader of a convoy, he
rode a jeep at the end of the
line, checking disabled truck.
as he passed, 1943.

21 Renata Bogdańska (Irena Jarosiewicz) as a flower girl and Feliks Fabian as Charlie Chaplin, both of the 'Polish Parade' (Polska Parada) band, performing for the troops at Tehran, 7 November 1942. Bogdańska later married General Władysław Anders, commander of the Polish divisions formed in Iran and Iraq after the release of Polish people from Soviet labour camps.

2 Mrs Louis Dreyfus, wife of the United States Minister in Iran, visiting a poor section of Tehran, 1943. The American Red Cross and other charities worked to alleviate poverty and provide for the tens of thousands of Polish refugees who entered Iran from the Soviet Union in 1942.

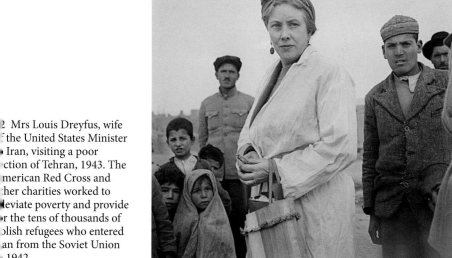

23 Iranian women watch an allied supply convoy halted somewhere in Iran as it makes its way from the British zone to the Soviet zone. The photograph captures both the distance between and the proximity of the allied forces in Iran and the local population.

24 A Polish boy carrying loaves of bread made from Red Cross flour at an evacuation camp, Tehran, 1943.

Soviet influence and raise British prestige in the eyes of the locals, the British community in Mashhad set about things in a typically British way. They formed an amateur dramatics society and held fêtes (one was held in the summer in Mashhad's municipal gardens in aid of Red Army charities),[14] while the Government of India funded a 'Victory Reading Room' on Pahlavi Avenue, where people could peruse British literature and even learn English under the tuition of Muslim graduates from India. At one fête, the British pavilion – a medieval castle constructed by the UKCC and members of the Indian community from jute sacking and timber – featured a pub inside its walls. The Castle Inn was run by an Essex UKCC employee who was a landlord back home. A 'mysterious Indian princess' told fortunes and there was horse racing and 'Aunt Sallies', a pub game that here involved sticks thrown at effigies of Hitler and Goebbels.

In an effort to lessen friction with the civilian population, allied servicemen deployed to Iran and Iraq were given briefings on local customs and culture and how to comport themselves. Small numbers of Americans served in or visited Iraq throughout the war, sufficient for the US Army to publish *A Short Guide to Iraq*.[15] The much larger US Army deployment to Iran warranted the production of a special army *Pocket Guide to Iran*.[16] In Iran, American soldiers were concentrated in eight principal installations, at Ahwaz, Andimeshk, Camp Amirabad and Atterbury near Tehran, Hamadan, Qazvin, Khorramshahr and Khorramabad. On their initial deployment, many Iranians viewed American troops as dynamic, cheerful and friendly, not aloof like the British or fearsome like the Soviets. American soldiers were told that 'American success or failure in Iraq may well depend on whether the Iraqis (as the people are called) like American soldiers or not. It may not be quite that simple. But then again it could.'[17] The guide told troops in both Iran and Iraq not to expect what they had seen in the movies, the Middle East of the *Arabian Nights*. The pleasure evinced by some Americans when they learned they were going to Iran was based on 'memories of a Technicolor Persia from the movies' (leaving some soldiers feeling seriously betrayed by Hollywood when they encountered the reality).[18]

Germany's efforts to influence the country were also explained, as well as the 'pro-Nazi' predilections of some Iranians. There had been Axis agents in the country 'before we came,' the *Pocket Guide to Iran* asserted. Nazi propaganda claimed that Hitler was a Muslim; and the Nazi film *Victory in the West* had played to capacity crowds in Tehran.[19] This, along with the country's strategic significance, had justified the Anglo-Soviet invasion.

The importance of protecting America's good name was emphasized. After explaining why allied forces were in Iran, and the value of their work there in the context of the global war effort, the *Pocket Guide* emphasized the role of American troops as ambassadors:

> Your country has a reputation throughout the world for decency and unselfishness in its dealings with other nations. That reputation is a major asset for us in this global war. By your actions you can uphold or destroy it ... You'll need to respect the ways of thinking and doing things of the Iranis and of the British and Russian soldiers, no matter how different they may be from your own ... If you adopt the attitude that we Americans don't know all the answers and that the world doesn't revolve around Kankanee, Ill., you won't be very far off target in your dealings with other peoples ... And remember always that you aren't going to Iran to change or reform Iranis or to tell them how much better we do things at home.[20]

The Iraqi guidebook likewise emphasized that the troops were not going to Iraq to change the way people lived: 'Just the opposite. We are fighting this war to preserve the principle of "live and let live".'[21]

Troops in Iran were warned to avoid two 'principal danger points' in their relations with Iranian people – politics and religion. 'Stay out of arguments or discussions of either.' The *Pocket Guide* offered a crash course in Iranian society and culture, describing forms of agriculture, the Islamic faith, the role of mullahs, carpet-manufacturing, the technique of bargaining, sanitary conditions, currency, the calendar, weights and measures and history and geography. It supplied useful phrases and specific advice: 'Eat only with your right hand, even if you are a southpaw.'[22] Soldiers in Iraq were urged to '*Keep away from mosques*' because Muslims 'do not like to have any "unbelievers" come anywhere near' them, and to avoid political or religious discussions.[23] Women were to be 'avoided', and men walking hand in hand were not 'queer'.

The *Pocket Guide* contended that the 'position of women in Iran is far more advanced than in many Moslem countries'. Nevertheless, 'you cannot pick up or date an Irani girl. You must wait for a formal introduction.' Even better, 'keep your distance. Don't make passes. Don't even stare at the women.'[24] The authors recognized that in an ideal world, American troops would have nothing to do with Iranian women, but that in the real world, this was never going to happen. Lieutenant Colonel Ernest Norberg, commander of Camp

Park, Hamadan, claimed that venereal disease was 'quite prevalent' in Tehran, and 'the control system we tried to install was squelched by the higher authorities. We had planned on a brothel operated by the civil authorities which would be closely, but unofficially, watched by Army men. This system had worked well in certain sections of Africa, we had learned. We were, however, strictly forbidden to engage in such activity in Iran.'[25]

As in any part of the world where troops were stationed in or near urban areas, red-light districts were a cause of concern for the authorities. Following the establishment of a British camp at Diwaniyah railway station in Iraq, 'some fear clashes with local rapscallions when visiting houses of ill repute'.[26] The Baghdad mutasarrif 'brought to notice complaints from houses of ill repute in the Betaween [Battawin] quarter of trespass or assault by our troops. Another more important aspect is that some complaints have been received of troops knocking up houses of good repute.' The mutasarrif suggested that designated houses for the purpose might be placed under proper control, but 'apparently this doesn't meet with the approval of the military authorities', which did not officially approve of, never mind manage, brothels.[27]

Despite the admonishments of commanding officers and guidebooks, expressions of discontent towards allied troops were common, as were incidents of crime committed against them or perpetrated by them. As is normal in situations where foreign forces arrive amid a local population in significant numbers, reactions and interactions were mixed. From friendliness through tolerance to active hostility, there was a full gamut of reactions, often depending on the specific experience of a person or community. Allied troops encountered violence and resentment; a detachment of Indian troops at a staging camp at Khan Jadwal in Iraq were fired upon by unidentified assailants, as were troops stationed at Deltawa Camp in the north.[28] During the Anglo-Iraqi war the British war cemetery in Baghdad North, commemorating nearly 7,000 First World War dead, had been desecrated, and it remained a focal point for unsavoury incidents thereafter.[29] A German document spoke approvingly of 'continual assassinations of British officers' and 'attacks against English military transports'.[30] On the other side of the ledger, the presence of British forces around Khorramshahr in Iran actively reassured sections of the population frightened by 'rumours of Arab "gatherings"'. Each night a platoon of the Hyderabad State Forces and a naval force, supplemented by a company from the 10th Indian Division's Kumaon Rifles (responsible for security in the Abadan–Khorramshahr region), took up positions across the city in order to reassure the population and keep the peace.[31]

Some other people had good reason to be angered and inconvenienced by occupation; even if Iranians had little love for the governments under which they lived, foreign troops were seen as invaders. As well as the sheer inconvenience caused by large numbers of troops, some had religious or cultural reasons for objecting to their presence. Few welcomed the appearance in their midst of armed foreigners immune from local law, or indignities such as being body-searched by children, under the watchful eye of armed soldiers, as employees left American bases. Photographs document such occurrences, as well as armed American and British troops searching vessels on the Shatt al-Arab, and guarding lorries and trains, guns at the ready.[32] Britain's Defence Security Office and eight field security sections of the British Army's intelligence corps, each of platoon-to-company size, became the backbone of law and order in the British zone of Iran.[33] In postoccupation Iran, the British also took control of postal and press censorship, travel and visa permissions and instituted a system of positive vetting.[34] There were sometimes very practical reasons for resenting the presence of the allies; the entire town of Ahwaz had to be blacked out when the enormous imported cranes were in use at nearby docks, offloading locomotives, tanks or other large objects.[35] The arithmetic involved in supplying war while also supplying basic existence could have less obvious but equally direct repercussions. While the building of fixed installations for the Iranian supply line to the Soviet Union alone cost in the region of $100 million, tens of thousands of jobs were created.[36] But this could bring its own problems; in August 1943 the British consul at Khorramshahr reported that the demand made by American-employed labour on the town's milling capacity had created a serious shortage of flour.[37]

Friction was also caused when allied troops attempted to recover property stolen from bases and lines of communication or during ambushes. This often resulted in 'search-and-seizure' operations during the course of which military policemen raided people's homes. On one occasion the RAF, 'despairing of recovering any of the arms stolen by Dulaim [a large community in Anbar province] from the camps at Habbaniya through the Dulaim police, raided various encampments themselves and recovered stolen arms and equipment'.[38] On the Shatt al-Arab, British and American patrol boats would routinely stop and search dhows.[39] Intrusions – sometimes for good reason – could occur in surprising ways. The edges of the Diyala river in Iraq, and neighbouring swamps, were notorious breeding grounds for mosquitoes. This meant Khanaqin and its environs were riddled with malaria, not a situation that could be allowed to go unchallenged when it became home to thousands of imperial and allied troops. British medical authorities decided to clean it up. Stagnant pools were drained and sprayed with oil and 'sanitary squads combed every house, flitting everything and everybody with pyrethrum solution'.

> Such an intrusion into Moslem harems had never before been heard of, still less attempted, and was certainly beyond the capacity of any civilian authority to enforce; but with the whole-hearted cooperation of Ramzi Beg, the Kurdish district governor, the operation was explained to the religious leaders and the local town councillors; local police accompanied each squad and the programme was carried out with little fuss and no complaints. As a result of this operation the incidence of malaria in the town in the following year was reduced by about 75 per cent and if ever the British Army did a fine job this was it. It was one of the few occasions when overawing the civil population with the presence of force proved to be justified.[40]

While foreign soldiers brought opportunities for gain, they also competed for scarce resources and contributed towards spiralling inflation. They hunted wild animals, for food and for fun, often in areas where game was scarce; accounts written by British officers often mention a day's shooting, usually for grouse and partridge, and American documents record 'organized hunting trips, the bag usually consisting of gazelle and wild boar'.[41] Somerset de Chair records his harrowing pursuit of a gazelle, finally killed by hand after many botched attempts with a rifle, and delivered to an army cooking pot.[42] American troops were provided with very little imported fresh meat, and would therefore shoot what game or fowl they could to supplement the Spam and Vienna sausage shipped in from home. Foreign troops could bring unwelcome animals of their own; Ezra Scott, a warrant officer in the US Army's 3410 Ordnance Medium Automotive Maintenance Company, remembers a bear cub that a neighbouring British unit persuaded them to adopt. As it grew it became a rather volatile unit mascot, so much so that one day 'we loaded him into a weapons carrier and took him back to the British railhead and turned him loose'.[43] Foreign troops caused pollution, for example by pumping sewerage into rivers. They left rubbish behind them, not all of it unwelcome; crates used to pack military equipment offloaded at Iranian and Iraqi ports found their way into the local construction industry and formed homes for many people, and in the Iraqi desert, British units striking camp would assiduously bury their waste in the knowledge that, as soon as they departed, local Bedouin would dig it up and sift through it.[44]

Despite unusual sources of friction – such as resentment in Baghdad caused by 'the manner in which the [Indian Army] Sikhs attract the ladies' – trouble usually came in the form of stone-throwing and spitting, assault, road traffic accidents, drunkenness and theft.[45] Passing through Baghdad with his unit, Lieutenant Basu was struck 'by how averse the Iraqis were to the presence of British and Indian troops there. Street urchins jeered at us and people were spitting on the ground at the sight of us.'[46] The Political Adviser Northern Area reported in September 1941 that 'there was considerable stone throwing by children at British Army trucks' in Kirkuk and Mosul. In one incident an attempt had been made to force a British car off the road, and some children were reported to be darting into the road to impede lorries. To get to grips with the situation, the number of local policemen on duty in the town had been almost doubled. 'This had an immediate effect and the police have been bringing between 50–100 boys to the police station daily for stone throwing at cars.' The young rascals 'would be kept in custody for several hours before being warned and released'.[47] In the same month the Political Adviser Central Area reported that 'incidents involving troops in Baghdad such as stone throwing or pelting with garbage appear to have come to an end at least for the moment and I understand that there have even been cases of children cheering our troops on the move through the town'.[48]

But displays of hostility took time to die down, and never died out. In November 1941 the same British official reported the looting of a British Army ration car, and 'complaints of children gathering round lorries and throwing stones at them'. As a counter to this, Iraqi authorities asked that 'Indians with lorries should not encourage the boys to crowd round the lorries by giving them dates, sugar etc'.[49] In Iran, Captain Rimmer, a British survey officer, was stoned inside his lorry by 300 women and children at Saveh.[50] In the Mosul area, though the arrival of the 17th Indian Infantry Brigade 'had an excellent effect on [the] population', Hugh McNearnie, deputizing for Wallace Lyon, soon had incidents to deal with.[51] Less than a fortnight after the brigade's arrival, its commanding officer lodged a complaint about increasing 'anti-British feeling'. Children had been throwing stones at army lorries and darting into the road to block their passage, and Iraqi drivers had attempted to interfere with military traffic.[52]

To top it off, as McNearnie went to visit the mutasarrif to complain, a little girl spat at his car. Men, women and children were often reported spitting at allied vehicles.

The military brought thousands of extra vehicles onto roads and tracks and into town centres, and took over almost all state- and privately owned lorries in Iran in order to supply themselves and run military aid to the Soviet Union. Civilians reacted angrily to soldiers taking over the roads and performing road traffic control duties; Indian soldiers were barracked for refusing to allow traffic to cross a bridge, and in Baghdad 'perturbation was caused by the military holding up the last batch of pilgrims on their way to Mecca at Khirr Bridge. The piquet was enforcing orders to prevent the use of the roads during rain.'[53] Much of the hostility directed towards army and UKCC vehicles and convoys was caused by the danger they posed. The British consul in Isfahan wrote that 'the behaviour of the drivers of these [UKCC] lorries has not contributed to British popularity here. Many of them drive fast through the town, park in rows wherever they fancy and refuse to obey the directions of the police.'[54] Road traffic accidents, which were frequent, caused dismay. Compensation was paid to the family of a boy killed by a 10th Division truck, a common resolution in the case of fatalities; an officer driving to Baghdad killed a woman at Baqubah; and a labourer died when a military lorry overturned at night near Tauq.[55] During night driving practices around Habbaniya, recalled John Masters, two 15-hundredweight trucks drove over a 30-foot cliff, the one landing on top of the other 'in an early example of vertical parking. The trucks were undamaged, as of course were the Gurkhas in them.'[56]

In Iran, there was a 'growing volume of complaints from the [Iranian] Foreign Office about the conduct of the American troops and the frequency of automobile accidents.'[57] Persian Gulf Command investigated these, though American drivers were rarely blamed even though it was acknowledged that they often drove fast; indeed, a dubious attempt was made to attach the blame to the victims of accidents: 'It is impossible however, to expect the oriental Iranian pedestrian to behave when alarmed by an approaching automobile in the same manner as a similar person would in the United States. The reflexes of the Iranians, to whom the automobile is still a comparatively recent innovation, are relatively slow, and by the time the pedestrian endeavors to get out of danger it is apt to be too late.'[58] In response to mounting complaints, American military authorities took what measures they could, such as instigating traffic patrols and fixed speed limits.

Theft, petty sabotage and ambushes

Interactions between occupying forces and local communities sometimes involved violence. Armed troops patrolled city streets and rural roads, while some people saw allied convoys or allied bases as inviting targets for theft or sabotage. On arrival in Iran securing the oil installations of Khuzestan had been a British priority, and the AIOC often appealed for help from the British forces now stationed in the country, and lobbied for the employment of British battalions for internal security displays and operations targeting certain trouble-spots. The robust response that tended to result if locals tangled with soldiers had its own salutary effect. In a typical incident that occurred on the Behbahan road, 'an attack on a British Army lorry resulted in a number of the robbers being immediately shot dead by the escort', and this was 'reported to have created an excellent impression'.[59] It was decided that the dispatch of 'small British columns from time to time on a tour would have a good effect'.[60]

Ambush attacks on UKCC lorries and British military cars were common.[61] Crime was a constant concern for the British and was particularly problematic when it threatened military installations and lines of communication. Lieutenant-Colonel Gerald Pybus, assistant military attaché in Tehran, was tasked with investigating incidents on the Bushire–Shiraz–Isfahan road, where there had been a heavy increase in traffic, consisting mainly of American convoys carrying aid to the Soviet Union. Along with a representative from Persia and Iraq Force (PAIFORCE) headquarters in Baghdad, Pybus investigated the nature of robberies on the road and what the British and Iranian militaries could do to prevent them.[62]

Theft and robbery were major problems, usually born of the proximity between desirable resources and hard-up people. As General Sir Henry Maitland Wilson put it, 'the propensity of the tribes to attack anything likely to yield food and clothing' was 'intensified by Axis propaganda and by economic distress'.[63] The first imperial troops to reach the Kirkuk region as the Anglo-Iraqi war concluded were a battalion of Gurkhas. As soon as they arrived, they began to experience 'the usual attentions of pilferers' as political adviser Wallace Lyon phrased it. 'So the Colonel decided to give them a sharp lesson, and every night a soldier armed only with his kookri crouched in every truck. As soon as a hand appeared in the gloom down came the kookri and in the morning the soldier paraded at the battalion office and claimed his reward – a rupee for each finger. They were all volunteers, for it was just the sort of sport that appealed to Gurkha and the pilfering ceased.'[64]

In April 1943 Churchill and Eden were drawn into correspondence with the British minister in Tehran regarding an Indian soldier who had shot five Iranians stealing telephone wire. He was clearly a murderous individual, having already shot one civilian, and he was to shoot yet another four days after this latest incident.[65]

American forces resorted to similarly violent deterrents. 'Amid the general poverty of Iran, large and well-supplied encampments housed American troops, where muffled booming [was] heard that marked, day after day, the detonation of antipersonnel mines set off by native prowlers attempting the barriers enclosing the foreigners' stores of goods and food.'[66] There were often clashes when Iranians entered American base territory or attempted to steal. A sentry at Camp Atterbury, for example, shot and killed an Iranian whom he was endeavouring to dissuade from defecating in or near the camp's water supply.

The British Embassy's May 1944 complaint to the Iranian Foreign Ministry about increasing 'hooliganism and lawlessness' in Abadan and Khorramshahr was typical. To the complaint the embassy staff attached a list of eighty-eight alleged miscreants.[67] The British officials maintained a ledger of reported criminal incidents, all of which were assiduously taken up with the Iranian authorities. During the first nine months of 1942, incidents included the burglary of the house of three British-Indian subjects; the murder of the British-Indian subject Channan Din, an employee of the Anglo-Iranian Oil Company; the apprehension by British soldiers of one Reza Hassan as he was stealing telephone cable and poles; the theft of American materials from the new jetty at Khorramshahr; the arrest of four Iranians for knifing the tyres of an American truck in the bazaar at Khorramshahr; and numerous complaints from the British naval authorities regarding thefts from the naval base.

The AIOC asked the British legation if something could be 'done to make local courts pass heavier sentences for acts which amount to sabotage, such as stealing telephone wire and removing the supports of the pipe line.'[68] In Iraq, the Political Adviser Northern Area wrote that the 'vast area of the Kirkuk [army] camp under the new dispersal system leaves it very vulnerable to pilferers . . . A party of twenty-one including the Mukhtar of Bajwan and many donkeys were caught red handed with mats and poles from the Garrison Engineers Dump.'[69] In Baghdad a shepherd boy was convicted and lashed for tampering with telegraph lines.[70] In Hillah, thefts of copper wire from the new military telephone line were reported.[71] On 15 December 1941, at Mahawil, schoolboys damaged the military water station, while three days later, near al-Hashimiyah, the military telephone line was cut and 'it was reported from Khan Jedwal staging post that an armed repair party was met by armed Arabs who prevented them from carrying out repairs'.[72] On the same day Sergeant Armstrong 'who is employed on the road work, and who was on the road with 4 cars, was held up some 3 miles north of Hamza in Diwaniyah Lewa and one car looted'.

This was a significant problem, more than a minor inconvenience, because it degraded operational effectiveness. In a document entitled 'Security of war material', British Force Headquarters Baghdad, Quinan's HQ, complained to the British minister that signal wire leading from 34th Anti-Aircraft Regiment Royal Artillery to their troop headquarters at the Kirkuk railhead had been cut ten times in a fortnight. This despite the fact that the wire in question was buried a foot deep. Each time it was cut, it was in the same location, near the Iraqi army barracks.[73] The wire was cut at Diwaniyah, and when a military telephone line was cut and the wire removed, the local mutasarrif was told by the British that the 'time for infliction of a fine on the area involved has come unless the miscreants are caught and severely punished'.[74] There were numerous incidents on the Iraq–Syria border. The oil pipeline was repeatedly tapped near T2, 'and a number of encounters with our garrison troops took place. Some casualties were inflicted and a large number of donkeys of raiding parties was confiscated and sold'.[75] While sometimes wire was cut in acts of sabotage, it was just as likely to go missing through theft; copper wire was a very popular material for the manufacture of jewellery. Persian Gulf Command, the American military establishment created in Iran, estimated that it had to replace at least 250 miles of telephone line during its three-year operation in Iran.[76]

Some areas, particularly in Iran, were known for their lawlessness, exacerbated by the breakdown of the shah's state, making it dangerous for military personnel to move unless under guard. 'This area is seething with intrigues of all kinds,' wrote the British consul in Khuzestan. 'There is nothing we can do.'[77] During an attack on a convoy of eight AIOC vehicles, the assailants discussed whether to kill all the Britons in cold blood, though only killed one. The consul had been in touch with military headquarters in Baghdad asking for a beefed-up troop presence, and elements of the 12th Indian Division, stationed in the district, had already been helping the Iranian authorities disarm people. It was suggested that pressure should be brought to bear on the Iranian government to station more troops in the region. But while agreeing as to the desirability of 'asking Persians to accept [a] greater share of responsibility for maintenance of security', the consul emphasized that the 'establishment of a Persian Military Camp here is bound to lead to the recrudescence of petty repression of Arabs', which would worsen the situation.[78]

American authorities were also concerned about insecurity on the roads and railways, as US troops entered Iran in large numbers and worked on the transport network the length and breadth of the country. The 'security situation in Iran north of Andimeshk was uncertain ... The nomads of the plateau and mountains were less friendly than the people of the south.' Because of this, the War Department militarized all overseas construction contracts.[79] American capacity-building missions sent to Iran sought to buttress state institutions, and the problems of internal security were a factor in the decision to create them. In January 1942, for example, American specialists were requested to take charge of the police force. Adolf Berle, the chief of the Division of Near East Affairs, told Assistant Secretary of State Wallace Smith Murray that this would 'help internal security and contribute to the running of the supply route'.[80] Well-armed tribal factions had 'resumed their lawless predations', said the American diplomatic chief in Tehran. They had been 'the scourge of Iran before the ex-shah Reza brought them under control'. Now, in the post-invasion period, 'these rearmed tribes are becoming a serious menace to the internal peace and security of the country'. American officials in Iran were in little doubt as to the root cause of this disorder. 'Politically the present confused and unsatisfactory situation derives from the violent change from dictatorial to democratic government for which the country was ill-prepared and from popular reaction to virtual occupation of country by two powers regarded as hostile.'[81]

A fascinating strand of activity that would certainly have been deemed illegal by the Iraqi and British authorities involved attempts to tamper with the loyalty of imperial forces. In December 1941 the British Embassy in Baghdad reported 'stories of Rashid Ali's adherents and other ill-disposed persons efforts to tamper with the loyalty of the Indian Muslim troops'. This was worrying, because there were thousands of Muslim Indian troops in Iran and Iraq at the time – 2,000 at Habbaniya alone.[82] Two of the alleged miscreants were 'Indians who have become naturalized Iraqis'. Their propaganda asserted that the British 'intend to use the Indian troops as cannon fodder against the Germans', and that 'the Germans are true friends of Islam'.[83] Measures to prevent the dissemination of such material included sending security personnel to accompany Indian troops visiting the Gailani

Mosque, outside of which such activity had been reported. A man named Khan Sahib Rafique, employed in the office of the controller of enemy property, was deported for serious anti-British activities. He had translated into Urdu 'lies such as RAF bombing of Mosque of Abdul Qadir Gailani,' reported Grice, a British official working in the Iraqi Ministry of the Interior, which were broadcast by his son. Rafique had also prepared a book in Indian languages 'containing all the Fatwas and which was intended to be printed in tens of thousands for distribution in India.'[84]

Crimes committed by allied forces

Criminal activity cut both ways, and documented in the archives are complaints from local authorities to the British representatives in Baghdad and Tehran. In Iraq there were 'complaints from the mutasarrif of vandalism at Hit and Anah by our troops.'[85] Also in Iraq, four British imperial soldiers were accused of rape in December 1941. Three were court-martialled. One turned king's evidence, and the other two were convicted and sentenced to two and a half years' imprisonment each.[86] In the same month the Iraqi Ministry of Foreign Affairs wrote to the British legation regarding the alleged murder by British troops of Shahab ibn Ahmad al-Khalaf from Albu Mahal. While watering his camels, al-Khalaf had been frightened by the approach of military vehicles carrying troops. He feared that they would try to confiscate a pair of German rifles in his possession, and so ran away towards the desert, and was shot while doing so.[87] Formal complaints were made regarding assaults on Bedouin women by Indian soldiers and clashes between Gurkhas and shepherds of the Nidda tribe near Naft Khol.[88] A representation from the Ministry of Foreign Affairs alleged that five nomad dwellings were set upon by Sikh soldiers near Abila, as the nomads were seeking a watering place for their livestock.[89] In Basra, meanwhile, British soldiers entered the premises of Messrs Spinney and Company, a British business, and stole cigarettes and alcohol.[90] Incidents of looting by forces under British command were recorded in Basra and Fallujah during the Anglo-Iraqi war. In Tehran, British soldiers broke into the German legation 'and smashed several portraits and removed a bust of Hitler and a flag,' wrote Bullard. This was to be regretted, he continued, as Soviet troops are not allowed to enter the town 'and appear to the public to be under better discipline.'[91]

As time passed, America's image became tarnished, as everyday frictions between soldiers and civilians took their toll. The American legation in Tehran constantly complained to the military authorities about the damage being done to the country's reputation by poorly behaved GIs. Fearing that this not only damaged America's reputation but also contributed to a growing Iranian tendency to classify America alongside the other allied powers – as occupiers, not friends – the matter was raised with the State Department and the War Department.[92] American troops were an 'ever present source of friction,' complained the legation chief. This despite the efforts of American military authorities to keep soldiers out of Tehran by building barracks on its outskirts. The problem was compounded by the fact that the very presence of American troops in Iran was a source of contention. The Iranian parliament asserted that American forces were 'here without consent or permission', amounting to a breach of sovereignty. This was because they had been brought in under the auspices of the British, rather than as a result of an agreement between the American and Iranian governments. In the opinion of the Iranian prime minister, the American military presence violated international law.[93]

Because of this, incidents of troop misbehaviour were of great significance. The conduct of American troops in Tehran, the legation chief observed, 'leaves something to be desired. Iranians are apt to notice and remark on drunkenness and disorder on the part of foreign troops'. The legation kept a ledger of all reported cases. 'The incidents of drunkenness are particularly offensive to a Mohammedan people,' wrote Dreyfus, America's senior diplomat in Iran, as was general rowdiness. Why are Persian Gulf Command troops so badly behaved? the diplomat asked.[94] It was partly, he mused, down to a lack of military discipline. 'They were not an army at all,' he suggested 'but civilians in uniform, doing dull jobs away from the front line and keen to get back to America' – 'raw and untrained technical forces'. Dreyfus wrote to General Connolly, commanding all American forces in Iran, about the poor behaviour of American troops. 'I regret to state that I hear reports from all sides of drunkenness, disorderly conduct and molestation of women by American officers and men ... It is reported, and widely believed, that the recent ban on dancing was put into effect because of the poor conduct of American officers and men in the cafes and cabarets of Tehran.' The Iranian press 'was beginning to call attention to the behaviour of our forces ... Respectable women avoid streets at night for fear of molestation.' Dreyfus also pointed out how, in contrast, Iranians were impressed by the superior conduct of Soviet as opposed to American, British and Polish troops. 'There is circulating an apparently authentic story of a Russian officer who was first broken in rank and later in the day executed for drunken conduct in the Palace Hotel.' On another occasion the American diplomat wrote that 'while Russians cannot be said to be liked by Iranians there is no doubt that their restraint and good conduct are turning many Iranians increasingly in their favour'.[95] Writing from Tehran, Belgian diplomat Harold Eeman put an interesting spin on this matter:

> The British troops were left in no doubt of their unpopularity. They were openly derided and abused, it being known that they were under orders to refrain from retaliation. In the face of much provocation they showed remarkable self-control. The Russians, who were equally unpopular, were seldom seen in Tehran. Once a Red Army lorry full of soldiers, driving across the capital, had been subject to the treatment which could with impunity be inflicted on the long-suffering British. One of the Russians had whipped out his revolver and shot a mocking Iranian dead. No more was needed. Henceforth the Russians were feared and no one dared taunt or mock them.[96]

Murders and unexplained deaths

Some deaths remained unexplained, such as that of a Gurkha soldier found hanging from a pole near the railway line a mile north of Ur junction in Iraq. He had possibly been strangled, though it might have been suicide as the man had recently lost his rifle and left a train to walk the railway line trying to find it.[97] The Political Adviser Central Area reported the unsolved murder and mutilation of British soldiers at Abu Gir in Iraq's southern desert.[98] In September 1941 Headquarters Northern Line of Communication District reported the ambush of a British Royal Army Service Corps Motor Transport Company convoy on the Ramadi road. After the soldiers inside the vehicles had surrendered and been disarmed, Driver Pearce was shot in the head from a distance of a yard, his body later mutilated. Driver Gregson was shot in the face at point-blank range. When he tried to escape, he was shot twice in the chest, though miraculously survived the assault.[99] In Iran, Master Sergeant Mario Pomato of 334th Engineering Regiment, US Army, was murdered by mountain bandits in the cab of his truck while driving north from Tehran on 23 August 1943.

In December 1941 the Political Adviser Central Area in Iraq asked the ambassador if he could obtain witnesses from the crew of an RAF Wellington that had been forced to land near Ctesiphon on 4 May during the Anglo-Iraqi war. They were needed in connection with the subsequent murder of Sergeant Campbell and the injuries sustained by the rest of the crew. The 37 Squadron aircraft had come down on the right bank of the Tigris near Selman Pak. Local 'tribesmen' had taken the crew to their village, where they were attacked with clubs and sticks, Campbell later dying in hospital in Baghdad.[100]

Serving with the RAF's 37 Squadron on detachment to Shaibah, Pilot Officer Charles Rash was on a sortie during the Anglo-Iraqi war. His mission was to bomb Rashid airbase near Baghdad, drop propaganda pamphlets on the city and reconnoitre Baghdad airport. After successfully completing the mission, the crew set course for the return journey to Shaibah. While passing over the airport buildings the aircraft was hit by 20-millimetre cannon fire. After flying on for another 10 miles, 'the starboard engine began to run rough', and they were forced to land. On leaving the aircraft, the crew removed the 'K' guns, ammunition, Very pistol and cartridges. Then, as Rash recalled in his sworn statement:

[We] noticed some tribesmen standing by and approached with intention of asking if we could use one of their boats. Did not understand and made us go to their village where I offered an Egyptian pound note for use of a boat. Took note but refused boat. I then produced the 'ransom card', of which they took no notice. They then suddenly attacked us, using clubs, sticks, etc. and relieved us of our valuables and disarmed us. All injured to various degrees. Eventually [Iraqi] soldiers arrived and took us to their barracks across the river, then to Baghdad.[101]

Having reviewed this material, Foreign Secretary Anthony Eden telegrammed Ambassador Cornwallis: 'Any other cases? I attach great importance to every case being followed up and to prompt and drastic punishment being administered.'[102]

The sworn statement of pupil pilot Ralph Ritz of No. 4 Flying Training School Habbaniya documented a similar incident during the Anglo-Iraqi war. Ritz was detailed as an air gunner on an Audax piloted by Airman L.A. Blackhall. Their mission was a reconnaissance flight over the Karbala area, during the course of which they noticed the aircraft's tail becoming 'wet', and diagnosed engine failure. Landing about 10 miles north of Karbala, the airmen removed the aircraft's rear gun, magazines and maps, and started walking towards an Arab man, who was soon joined by about twenty more. The RAF men attempted to bribe the first man to take them back to Habbaniya. The man said that others would think it unfriendly to walk about with a machine-gun, so the airmen gave it to him and he put it in his tent. The airmen consulted and agreed that their chances of escape were best if they did not use violence. They then sat inside the tent with about ten Iraqi men who seemed quite friendly. The ransom cards that they carried with them had no effect, and for about an hour the flyers sat there attempting to bribe the Iraqis. A commotion outside heralded the arrival of six or seven Iraqi policemen on horseback. Their leader dismounted and aimed a rifle at Blackhall, cocked it and fired without warning. He then fired at Ritz, hitting him on the hand, then took another shot at Blackhall. The fourth shot hit Ritz in the back as he endeavoured to roll away. He was taken prisoner, returned to the site of the crashed aircraft and then taken to Karbala.[103] Further intelligence regarding Blackhall's murder emerged later. Muzahim Furman was an Iraqi non-commissioned officer in charge of the post at Utaishi to which the airmen were first taken. He allegedly announced his intention of killing the airmen despite the protests of the Iraqi man who had first found them. He then shot Blackhall dead, wounded Ritz and took their property.[104] The Iraqi Ministry of Foreign Affairs informed the embassy that the assailant had been sentenced to death.[105]

Another murder victim was Captain J.F.D. Jeffreys, a political officer serving with the Indian army at Basra. On 4 June 1941 he was canoeing between Ur and Nasiriyah, intending to get the officer commanding British forces in Ur to close the break in the bund as the canal water was flooding roads and delaying traffic. Someone tried to dissuade him from visiting the souk in Nasiriyah to buy goods because of 'inflammation of the minds against the English after the last incidents[,] especially as this visit was preceded by the British aeroplanes having dropped bombs on Nasiriyah Town[,] killing and wounding some people'. But Jeffreys insisted, saying he knew the area very well. Many people, it would appear, were involved in the sustained attack that subsequently killed him and his Iraqi police guard. The post-mortem revealed bruises, stab wounds to the left temple and left forearm, a fracture of the thigh and a gunshot wound to the dome of skull, with an exit wound in front of the right ear. In the absence of any arrests, the British Embassy recommended a collective fine on the quarter of the town in which the incident had taken place.[106]

Cash and employment

Large concentrations of foreign troops brought with them cash, employment and inflation. A few hundred or a few thousand soldiers stationed near a town meant a sudden demand for consumables, land, property, labour and a range of goods and services. Persian Gulf Command depended heavily on local labour, employing approximately 50,000 Iranians as well as smaller numbers of Iraqis and Poles. The British employed at least twice that number in Iran, and military employment in Iraq peaked in 1943 at 70,000 labourers and servants, with a further 10,000 men serving in the rapidly expanding RAF Levies.[107] Basra was flooded with imperial troops leading to all manner of construction programmes and an almost insatiable demand for buildings and land. The Basra–Amarah road was to be given an all-weather surface, and the embankment on the railway line to Baghdad dug up so that the track could be doubled. Labour was sourced from contractors and tribal sheikhs. House rents in Basra became prohibitive because of military demand, and prices paid by British forces were 'out of proportion to the cost of building the house'.[108] There were other inevitable ramifications, as British forces and the UKCC monopolized transport infrastructure. Complaints 'from Kerbela and the Euphrates regarding the lack of transport for their dates are increasing and it is widely stated that the small allotment of railway trucks for civil purposes is giving rise to much corruption among the station masters'.[109] It was reported that 'the Kerbela landowners are somewhat perturbed with regard to the marketing of their dates. It appears that the Railway authorities recently forbade the carriage of dates to Basrah as the Port warehouses were full up with Army supplies'.[110] Renting land and buildings for military purposes was an important element of interaction with local people. At Hillah, 'with a brigade settled at the Hindiyah Barrage, the question of compensation for land taken up has arisen'. As a base, the unit had leased the customs and passport building at Mundhariyah.[111]

The Kirkuk and Mosul region was designated an area of possible offensive and defensive operations against German forces. As a result, over 20,000 imperial and Polish troops concentrated in the area, from RAF observation posts on the frontier with Iran to heavy garrison forces around the towns. Extensive military construction and fortification work was undertaken. The officer commanding 'Sub Area 5 Line of Communication' reported 'signs of resentment on the part of the [Iraqi army's] Kirkuk garrison at their gradual encirclement by the British Forces there'.[112] Wallace Lyon, the Political Adviser Northern Area, wrote that 'large military tenders have set Mosul agog and the sudden demand for billets has started a house boom'. The size of the garrison was 'causing a boom in all commodities'.[113] It was reported from the border town of Khanaqin that the 'atmosphere is quite bright under the influence of fairly large sums of money being spent by the Troops on local commodities.[114] A month later he wrote that the town had 'been unable to supply the needs of the troops stationed there and passing through, consequently although the tone of the town is much the same people are too busy making money to have time to sit around and indulge in open display of their real feelings.[115]

Lyon wrote that 'large engineering contracts have done much to relieve unemployment in the larger towns';[116] also, that 'the extensive military works programme undertaken in this region employed people in winter months.[117] He continued:

> the increase in British Forces in the Northern Area has stimulated business and the large engineering contracts have attracted labour from the most remote villages in Kurdistan. By now there must be anything up to 20,000 labourers engaged in road and excavation works and this has done much to relieve unemployment. Compensation and rent for lands occupied around Kirkuk are now working smoothly. The Arbil [Erbil] garrison has now got the camp site marked and there should be little difficulty in the matter of rent and compensation. The Mosul area still remains the biggest problem.[118]

Here and in Kirkuk there were practice blackouts and air raid precaution drills in case the town was bombed.[119] Major Kinoch reported from the Khanaqin area that line of communication troops were making shades for street lights as a blackout measure, and digging trenches.

In Mosul, 'when the British troops entered the town and began to employ many labourers', problems began:

> prices started to rise very sharply till it reached a fictitious standard of which nobody could dream. It was true that labourers were well paid by the British but there were still thousands of labourers and shopkeepers who were not paid by the British and could not keep up with the rising standard of living. Even the wages paid by the British Troops were not enough to let the workers keep up with that rising standard. As a result of that situation poverty spread in the town on a very large scale.[120]

The troops had been a 'great source of prosperity to the town', but associated price rises and profiteering were a problem and benefits were certainly not shared equally. Cinemas and public places were packed with troops at night, leading to inevitable 'issues with drunken soldiers'. Most shops stayed open at night to take advantage of the situation. The Northern Area report for 10 November 1941 recommended 'speeding up land rental and compensation which has now reached a scale demanding special measures because of the presence of troops'.[121]

The presence of allied forces created tens of thousands of jobs. The arrival of two divisions of imperial soldiers in northern Iraq as 'hasty preparations' for the region's defence were undertaken created an insatiable demand. The military authorities were 'determined to prevent contractors profiting at the expense of exploited poor people as had happened in the previous war'. Lyon wrote:

> The proposed field fortifications would provide employment where it was most needed, and there was no propaganda better than a full belly. Moreover, if suitably handled, these same people might afterwards prove most useful in providing shelter for the Special Officers leading guerrilla forces in the event of a withdrawal. The plan was approved by the C-in-C [Commander-in-Chief] and I then gathered the Kurdish tribal chiefs from all over the countryside and explained it to them. They all knew me well and were quite willing to have a go. Colonel Grand, whom I had known many years before as a Sapper subaltern seconded to the Levies, was now responsible for constructing the field defences, which consisted for the most part of earthworks, trenches, tank traps, strong points, etc.... The work was divided into sections and let out to the Kurdish chiefs by contract, each section according to the number of his men on the job. It was laid out, supervised, and checked by the Sappers and the chief was paid at once on its completion ... Usual trouble of a contractor swindling his labour was eliminated, for these were the chief's own tribesmen ... The field fortifications covered a vast area both in width and depth, and in all resulted in over a million pounds finding their way into the pockets of these deserving people. As far as the army was concerned it was excellent value for money while at the same time freeing the troops for the more important work of training. It was the first chance the Kurds had of full employment at a time when the cost of living was rising fast. It was also sound propaganda for the Allied cause.[122]

Other British observers noted the enormous scale of defensive works being undertaken, and the local labour that it depended upon. Ann Lambton visited American installations at the port of Khorramshahr in Iran, including the truck assembly factory and the jetties:

> It is an impressive sight. Some 180 trucks are assembled daily. Some 25,000 local labourers are employed: Persians and Iraqis. These, together with some 25,000 employed by the AIOC will present a difficult problem if demobilization occurs. While the company is expanding its operations they are able to absorb some of the 'allied' labour which is already being laid off – even so there is likely to be some 15–20,000 to be dealt with eventually. If they are not returned to their place of recruitment, they are a potential irritant in the local situation and the permanent friction between Arabs and Persians, especially as many of them have arms (pilfered) in their possession.[123]

Employment opportunities were also created by the additional fuel requirements of the allied forces stationed in Iran and Iraq. New installations and pipelines were required. In May 1942 the British Embassy in Baghdad presented the Iraqi government with a *note verbale* stating that 'as an emergency military measure, the production of motor spirit, gas oil and fuel oil, has been arranged at the Iraqi Petroleum Company Kirkuk Plant, and a Pipe Line has been constructed between Kirkuk and Mosul. Thus a delivery of motor spirit and gas oil will be made available to the British military authorities and for civilian consumption through the Rafidain Oil Company.'[124] A new pipeline for military purposes was laid on the 52-mile stretch between Abadan and Basra, buried to a depth of 18 inches and laid alongside a new phone line. Pipelines were also laid from the Alwand refinery near Khanaqin to Naft Shah, and from Ahwaz to Andimeshk, one for benzene and kerosene, another for fuel oil. In July 1942 Cornwallis cabled his opposite number in Tehran, requesting that he inform the Iranian government that 'project Q9 is being operated at Army request. Kermanshah refinery is shut down and refined petrol is being pumped from Alwand Refinery Khanaqin direct to Kermanshah' for the benefit of the Tenth Army.[125] Extensive defensive measures were undertaken to protect this vital oil infrastructure, including the erection of splinter-proof walling around oil tanks at Abadan and elsewhere.

A large number of Polish troops served under British command in Iran and Iraq. The headquarters of what was known as the Polish Army in the East was at Khanaqin, a town on the main Baghdad–Tehran road, and most Polish forces were concentrated in the area. Thousands of Polish soldiers

and civilians had been released from Soviet labour camps in 1942 and transported to Iran; many died en route. Arriving in terrible physical condition,
surviving Polish soldiers were 'so embittered by the experience that they
would much preferred to have fought against the Russians than the Axis'.
The British were to re-form the soldiers into coherent and properly equipped
military units, which would bolster British forces defending the region and
provide the Polish government in exile with additional military resources.

Wearing one of his many hats, political adviser Wallace Lyon liaised
between the British and Polish armies and the local Iraqi people. Following
their poor treatment in the Soviet labour camps, things had improved
immeasurably for the Poles.[126] They were now properly paid, equipped and
receiving a ration one and a half times that of a British soldier. The Poles
had 'never seen so much food and cash' and splashed it around, 'holding out
a one dinar note equivalent to a pound for a local chicken worth a shilling',
contributing to price inflation. Lyon realized that if left unchecked this
could cause the cost of living to rocket, so he 'approached their general with
a suggestion for holding back some of their pay and reserving it for their
post-war welfare'. 'In their conduct with the local inhabitants they were
much more ruthless than the British troops, and consequently caused more
friction.'[127] The Polish soldiers also knew how to have a good time, Lyon
continued, and in 'their search for and consumption of alcohol they were
second to none, while in matters of culture they showed great interest and
artistic ability'.[128] They excelled at putting on shows and other entertainments, creating splendid props, programmes and costumes.

The East Persian Auxiliary Transport Service

Britain's initial attempt to supply the Soviet Union was the East Persian
Auxiliary Transport Service (EPATS). Clarmont Skrine helped establish
this supply route beginning in India and running via north-eastern Iran:

> Gunny-bags, jute, lead, shellac, rubber, tin, ferro-tungsten and other
> small-bulk war supplies were being sent from Karachi to railhead at Nok
> Kundi, eight hundred miles; thence a service of hired civilian lorries
> entitled the East Persian Auxiliary Transport Service (EPATS for short)
> and organized by a retired Indian Army colonel in the bus business in
> Rawalpindi would carry them to Meshed, seven hundred and fifty miles,
> and hand them over to the Russians for transport on their own trucks to

Ashkhabad on the Transcaspian Railway. The General Staff's target was 32,000 tons a month.[129]

This was an exciting opportunity for Skrine, entailing valuable war work on a logistical front teeming with activity. The Indian Army was having sections of the road repaired, from the India–Iran frontier to Mashhad and linking British military headquarters in Baghdad. Contracts had been issued to Iranian firms. The political difficulties involved in carrying large amounts of goods between British Balochistan and Iran for onward transit to the Soviet Union were formidable. 'Neither India Command nor Middle East Command had any troops within 500 miles of the road or any other visible means of impressing local opinion with the might of the Allies.' Iranian cooperation in recruiting and feeding local labour along the route and for protecting it therefore had to be secured by diplomatic means, and this was no easy task. The ruling class, as was to be the case for some considerable time, 'expected German victory and resented recent invasion ... Rebellious tribes, outlaws and Afghan raiders from across the frontier preyed on the traffic in collusion with the local gendarmerie, and scarcity of grain hampered road work.'[130]

The British were in a hurry to open the supply route but the work was behind schedule. Skrine identified transport, food and security as the three main problems on the route and 'bread and brigands' as the biggest problems facing the regional governor. The new supply route had not even reached Nok Kundi in Balochistan, close to the border between India and Iran. The Mashhad road had to be reconditioned on a large scale, and one of Skrine's tasks was to inspect the work of the Tenth Army's contractors undertaking it. 'Along the interminable vistas of rock-strewn desert north of Hormuk,' he wrote, 'thousands of peasants, most of them tribesmen from neighbouring Zabol and Afghan Sistan under their Sardars, were filling in pot-holes and clearing stones from the broad roadway', a striking manifestation of a world at war.[131] In this particular sector, one of the main contractors was an Armenian firm called Company Eighteen. It had no heavy lifting equipment and most of the men worked with primitive spades or their bare hands. Skrine considered them a ragged lot, 'and party after party of them complained of being underpaid, shelterless, without medical attention of any kind and, above all, inadequately rationed even with the adulterated and indigestible bread on which half of Persia's population were then living'.[132] Skrine questioned a company employee at Safidawa. ' "What can we do", he cried. The Finance officials at Zahedan won't allot us any wheat for our labourers. They say they haven't got any to spare, and anyway, the British have invaded the country, let them bring bread.'[133] Skrine sympathized with their plight: 'We, the Allies, were occupying their country and disrupting its economy, not the Germans. To us Hitler might be the villain of the piece, the traitor who had betrayed Western European civilization; to the Persians we were all, Allies and Germans alike, quarrelling among ourselves for the second time in a generation. Why should *they* suffer?'[134]

The Iranian Finance and Economic Ministry refused to part with wheat to feed the road labourers – they viewed it as an issue for the occupying forces to sort out. The Iranian people held Britain and the Soviets equally to blame for the lawlessness and scarcity that afflicted them. Conditions were very serious indeed, and Skrine noted the desperate need to feed local labour employed on military works, and to counter the impression that the allies were responsible for 'near-famine conditions'.[135] He wrote that British forces in his region had taken no wheat out, but had actually brought 72 tons in by sea and 3 tons overland from India. Theoretically this was purchased by the Iranian government 'but no one expected it would ever be paid for and the understanding was that agreed quantities would be sold at the current controlled price to Tenth Army contractors for their labour', under the supervision of the Royal Engineers. The sacks containing this wheat were marked in large Arabic letters 'India's wheat for the people of Iran'.

In Mashhad the British were generally unpopular, goodwill confined to the 'Berberis', a small community of Indian Army pensioners of the 106th Hazara Pioneers from the last war, and the Indian trading community which looked to the British consulate-general for protection. 'During our first year the Persian petty bourgeois and working class made no attempt to conceal their dislike of the British. Rude things were shouted at us in the streets, especially the picturesque covered bazaar . . . British wives were not served civilly in the shops . . . As for the upper class, only the Ali Mansours and a minority of the officials and professional people were really friendly.'[136] Skrine ascribed this anti-British sentiment to inflation, 'and the consequent catastrophic rise in the cost of living, for which the Allied occupation is blamed. Another is our known disapproval of Persian methods and standards; we are suspected of contemplating annexation or partition which, they fear, would be the doom of the vested interests which control public opinion. A third, of course, is our unholy alliance with Russia.'[137] 'One way to supplant Germany in the hearts of the Persians,' Skrine averred, 'is to show some signs of beginning to win the war.'[138]

British prestige rose slightly when the supply route began to operate vigorously. This came when the EPATS supply effort – 'never very successful' – ended in July 1942, operations being taken over by UKCC. This was an altogether more potent beast, harnessing Lend-Lease resources such as lorries from America, whereas EPATS had had to rely on vehicles bought second-hand in India. Earlier in 1942, military and civilian engineers of the Indian North-West Railway had re-laid the 140 miles of track between Nok Kundi and Zahedan just inside Iran, and in June the first train since 1931 arrived at the Iranian terminus with 1,300 tons of wheat for the government.

'A welcome sign of vigour' on the part of British Troops Persia and Iraq was the commencement of work on the construction of full-sized bomber aerodromes at Mirjawa, Zahedan and Kerman. An even better one was the order which the local UKCC buying agent, Joshua Pollock, received from Tenth Army headquarters in Baghdad for 87,000 sheepskin overcoats and 135,000 waistcoats of the type called on the Frontier 'poshteens', to be used by troops defending Iran's northern passes as the British prepared to withstand a German invasion should the Soviet front collapse.[139] This itself had significant side effects:

> The price of mutton slumped throughout Khorosan as sheep were massacred by the thousand and their skins brought in. When sufficient fleeces had been cured to make a start, Pollock hired every tailor within a hundred miles and before the end of the second week a factory with 1500 operatives was working at full swing ... a week later output had already reached 400 fleece overcoats and 800 waistcoats a day. Long before the order could be completed, however, the repulse of the Germans from Stalingrad removed the threat of a winter campaign in the Caucasus and the factory closed down. The work on the bomber aerodromes, on the other hand, went on for years.[140]

The rise in the cost of living was to be one of the most tangible of the war's impacts on the Iraqi and Iranian home fronts, which came to feature many of the elements familiar to European populations enduring the trials of war.

CHAPTER 11

War and the home front

Asked what his programme would be when he became Iranian prime minister, Ahmad Qavam picked up a piece of bread from his desk and replied, 'This is my program, if I can put bread of good quality in the hands of all Iranians other problems will be easy to solve'.[1] For most Iranians and Iraqis, quality of life deteriorated during the war. This deterioration was due to endemic factors such as poverty, poor harvests and the failings of government at national and local levels. It was also caused by exogenous, war-related factors such as shortages of food and other essential goods, inflation and a rising cost of living. These were stimulated by the presence of occupying forces competing for resources, the allied takeover of transport infrastructure and global factors such as decreasing food supplies and shipping shortages. Two allied organizations, the United Kingdom Commercial Corporation and the Middle East Supply Centre, took control of Iran's foreign trade, operating it according to allied, not Iranian, priorities. Foodstuffs could be brought to Iran only at the expense of aid shipments to the Soviet Union, which had undeniably greater strategic needs.[2] In Iran, the weakening of the state following the deposition of the shah placed an additional brake on government's capacity to care for its people, which it had never been good at doing anyway. Basics such as wheat, sugar and cotton goods became difficult to obtain; medicines were in even shorter supply than normal, and the automotive parts and tyres essential for running and maintaining vehicles, so important for food distribution, were scarce.

The food requirements of the people exercised the minds of both governments, as well as British agencies such as the Baghdad embassy and the Tehran legation, as well as the Middle East Supply Centre. This was because Britain was ultimately responsible for food security as the occupying power in Iraq and much of Iran. On New Year's Eve 1941, Sir Kinahan Cornwallis, British ambassador to Baghdad, wrote to his opposite number in Tehran, Sir Reader Bullard, saying that Iraq urgently needed 6,000 tons of wheat currently en route from India to Iran. The 'Iraqi Government and I are gravely concerned with the wheat shortage here,' he said, and the loan was 'essential to allay growing anxiety of Government and public which may well become panic if the delivery of wheat is delayed'.[3] At the same time, Iraq was expected to contribute to the war effort by producing cereals for the consumption of British forces, as well as the region's civilian population.[4] While the deleterious effects of war were felt by most people, as everywhere else in the world a small handful profited from extraordinary local and global conditions. Ann Lambton wrote that 'as a contrast to the vast mass of the people who live in abject poverty, there is a relatively small class of rich landowners and merchants. To these have been added small numbers of contractors who have made enormous profits during the war.'[5]

Shortages affected Iran most severely, and an unseemly blame game ensued as to who was responsible. The British blamed incompetent Iranian distribution, the Americans blamed the callous British as well as bungling Iranians and the Iranians blamed all three allies. There was some truth to the positions of all sides. The bottom line was that the allies were directly responsible for wheat shortages. Article 7 of the Treaty of Alliance that legitimized the occupation required Britain and the Soviet Union to protect the Iranian people against the 'privations and difficulties' of the war. But invasion and the shah's subsequent abdication destroyed Iran's old political and economic structures and failed to provide a viable replacement. The occupiers purchased or confiscated large amounts of Iranian food, and the food requirements of the 100,000-plus allied soldiers garrisoned and working in Iran were only partially met from outside. Tehran's major source of wheat was Azerbaijan, yet Soviet officials acquired 50 per cent of their grain needs from the province, allowing only 300 tons of Azerbaijani wheat to be shipped to Tehran from March 1942 to March 1943. In addition, Soviet occupation policies caused 200,000 Iranians to flee to Tehran, swelling its population and food needs by 37 per cent.[6]

Louis Dreyfus told Washington that the Iranian prime minister had spoken of the widespread dissatisfaction in the parliament regarding the manner in which Britain and the Soviet Union were carrying out their treaty with Iran: 'Members complain bitterly that Russians are taking their cattle, that Poles are being dumped in Iran, that the British are failing to provide food and are sending Iranian wheat to Iraq, that Russians are exploiting the situation in northern Iran, that the British are taking advantage of Iran in financial and other matters and that Iranians are being generally deceived and exploited.'[7] However, not everyone agreed with the harsh assessments of British motives and actions commonly evinced by people such as the American diplomat Dreyfus. Reader Bullard's letters and diplomatic correspondence present British authorities as less callous than they were often portrayed both at the time and in the subsequent historiography. What is more, contemporary files indicate that the British were less omnipotent than they have often been depicted subsequently. The diplomat Harold Eeman wrote that the Soviet occupation deprived Iran's more arid provinces – which were in the British zone – of their usual supply of cereals, shortages that were subsequently and predictably being blamed on the British authorities. 'This was grossly unfair,' Eeman wrote, 'since the British Army, apart from feeding its own troops, provided bread for thousands of Polish refugees from Russia living in camps near Tehran, and distributed flour to the Iranians themselves whenever actual famine threatened.'[8] George Kirk, in his history of the Middle East in the war, wrote that from the start of the Anglo-Soviet occupation of Iran, the Soviets 'incorporated the northern provinces of Persia within the "iron curtain" of their security system . . . They also appropriated the food resources of their zone, the most productive part of Persia, left the Western allies to provision the capital and the poorer southern provinces by importation, and then tried to exploit the resultant hardships for propaganda purposes.'[9] The British bore the burden of contumely, Kirk continued, and conspired in giving this impression because of their insistence on doing all possible to maintain the façade of allied unity. Kirk argued that the British should have done more to counter accusations, particularly from the Americans, of imperialism, and allocated more resources to putting the allied cause, especially the Anglo-American cause, to the local people.[10]

Inflation and the cost of living

'We receive strong indications of our increasing unpopularity in that country,' the new Resident Minister in the Middle East, Sir Richard Casey, told Winston Churchill. 'Inflation continues to be a cause of worry.' As consumer goods could not be imported, the Iranian government was being exhorted to increase taxes, raise loans for post-war development, stimulate savings, control prices and distribution and subsidize essential commodities.[11] But the simple fact was that the Iranian government had neither the will nor the capacity to effectively carry out any of these reforms. On 25 August 1943 Casey wrote that crops were 'generally good throughout the Middle East and cereal collection schemes functioning reasonably well save Persia (where nothing goes well)'.[12] The cost of cereals there were 'many times above pre-war levels.[13] The same was true in Iraq, where the cost of living rose fivefold during the war, 'hitting salaried employees, whether government officials or industrial workers, hardest'.[14] Even simple war news could impact the cost of living; when reports of Japan's entry into the conflict filtered through to northern Iraq, prices climbed, with markets reacting to fears that sea routes would be severed, leading to yet further reductions in imports. As a result, 'prices immediately soared to unprecedented heights', rising by 20 per cent in the Mosul bazaar.[15] At the same time the Iraqi government announced price controls for tea, sugar, coffee, wheat rice, barley and ghee. The wholesale price index, covering 57 commodities, 22 of them foodstuffs, rose in Iraq from 100 in August 1939 to 614 in January 1944.[16]

A memorandum on 'The economic situation in Iraq' prepared by Casey in 1942 reported that the Iraqi government was 'mainly preoccupied with economic difficulties resulting from the marked tendency towards inflation'. The cost of living was 'rising steadily, and currency circulation increasing at a rate which alarms the government ... Prices of essential commodities have risen on average by 200% to 300% since 1939.'[17] Currency in circulation rose from 4.7 million Iraqi dinars in August 1939 to 40.3 million in October 1944.[18] The attempts to fix maximum prices for essential goods had 'failed lamentably with sugar, which is being distributed on a ration basis', and flour was being subsidized. Other consumer goods such as tyres, cigarette papers, newsprint and alum were also brought under government control. The Commercial Secretary at the Baghdad embassy pointed to other factors: many farmers and merchants were benefiting from conditions and there was significant profiteering, while those on fixed incomes were suffering, with demand for labour exceeding supply.[19] Indicating inflationary trends, a January 1942 conference at the Iraqi Ministry of Finance set the rates paid for tobacco, of which there was a shortage: 'improved' special-quality tobacco had risen from 90 fils per kilo in 1940 to 200, while 'third'-quality had risen from 32 to 70 fils in the same period.[20]

What Daniel Silverfarb dubs 'the great inflation' in Iraq was caused primarily by British military expenditure.[21] Between 1941 and 1943 alone, the British spent £61.5 million on military tasks. Inflation was also caused by the decline in goods in circulation. Imports of items such as textiles and capital goods fell, and there was pressure on the Iraqi government to halt construction not essential for the war effort, causing a decline in house building.[22] Landowners benefited, however, due to a steep rise in agricultural prices.

In both Iran and Iraq, the massive allied expenditure on goods and services that unleashed a severe inflation was accompanied by speculation, hoarding and black-market operations. The Iranian currency, the rial, was devalued by more than 100 per cent.[23] Mathematically, the consequences were inevitable:

Allied purchases of Iranian goods and services cost them less than half price, and Iranian import of their products cost Iran more than twice as much as previously. The Iranian government was obliged to print money in order to extend credit to the Allies for their expenditures in Iran, to be paid back after the war ended. These policies led to rampant inflation and scarcity of goods, especially bread, but just avoided a famine.[24]

The consumer price index rose by 50 per cent per year in Iran.[25] The price index of the Iranian national bank, Bank Melli, rose from a base of 100 in 1937 to 193 in August 1941 and 331 in September 1942. For the same period, the cost-of-living index went up from 100 in 1937 to 209 in 1941 and 418 in 1942.

Allied demands caused the increase in the money supply and it was this, not the new exchange rate, that caused inflation.[26] Dreyfus offered his opinion on the causes of the Iranian currency crisis of October 1942, which was firmly centred on allied monthly war expenditure of about 400 million rials. Iranian note issue had increased from 1,550 million rials in August 1941 to 3 billion in October 1942.[27] It was now proposed to issue 2 billion additional rials for allied war needs and the Iranian wheat-purchasing programme. During the currency crisis a British brigade was placed on standby, and plans were drawn up to actually capture the central bank's premises.[28] Banknotes were failing to complete their normal cycle and return to the banks for reissue, instead being hoarded; a lack of confidence in the rial was causing Iranians 'to keep their money turning over by purchase of lands and goods rather than placing it in banks', and speculation by all classes had reached huge proportions.[29]

Food and hoarding

The spiralling price of cereals throughout the region 'encouraged landlords and merchants to profit from the export opportunities this offered. This not only added to the inflationary pressures within Iraq by creating scarcity, but, in some parts of the country, particularly in the Kurdish regions, created real hardship, amounting to starvation.'[30] In Iran, the British insisted repeatedly that only through a systematic campaign against hoarders would the food shortage be resolved. But the Iranian government feared the social consequences and refused to endorse official price increases and confined itself to coercion and the prosecution of hoarders. Hoarding was 'induced by the desire to benefit from starvation prices but also by the prevailing feeling of uncertainty as to the future.'[31] The 'progressive depreciation in purchasing power of local currency added to normal growers' tendency to hoard wheat and other cereals,' Casey told Churchill. People believe 'rightly that cereals represent better investments than notes – which can't be fully used anyway due to lack of imports because of shipping and internal transport difficulties.'[32]

The extraordinary circumstances of 1941 had had a calamitous effect on the wheat harvest, which declined by an estimated 30 per cent in 1941 and was 18 per cent below pre-war levels the following year. Yet before the war Iran had been a net exporter of grain, providing itself with a buffer in times of domestic shortages.[33] 'Unable and unwilling, out of domestic weakness, to impose its control over food distribution, the government chose to purchase large amounts of foreign grain.' In April 1942 Iran estimated its import needs at 160,000 tons of wheat through to the harvest of August 1943, but the British, who controlled shipping routes into Iran, set Iranian needs at 30,000 tons and agreed to ship 6,000 tons per month.[34] Shortages encouraged price inflation, putting what wheat was available beyond the reach of most of Tehran's population. Between 1939 and 1943 food prices increased an average of 555 per cent. The price of bread on Tehran's open market increased from 6 cents in January 1942 to $1 in May 1942. Iran also experienced a precipitate drop in imports due to the war, similar to those afflicting Iraq; overall, the value of goods imported into Iran in 1941 was only 44 per cent of the value registered for 1939.[35]

War caused food scarcity and exacerbated extant food-related problems in a country where many people lived in poverty and were malnourished, their condition often remarked upon by outsiders. Wallace Lyon wrote to the British ambassador in Baghdad saying that the economic state of the Kurdish areas was tragic, and that there was 'next to nothing between them and starvation'. Some 'people were emaciated, and their villages were devoid of medical services'.[36] Ann Lambton travelled to Bushire in 1944, an area where drought threatened food shortages, then to Shiraz. On the way she noticed the poor crops and 'was struck by the poverty of the people on the roadside and in general . . . The older people were in many cases emaciated and the children with swollen bellies . . . Eye diseases were common. Beggars were numerous. The people were dressed in rags; many of them almost naked'.[37] Australian journalist Alan Moorehead's impressions were similar: 'as a population, the people were in rags and the swollen bellies of the children I had seen in the villages showed how far famine and disease was spreading'.[38] General Slim wrote that the peasants were 'tragically poor, living too often on the starvation level'.[39] Commenting on the physical condition of Iranian army recruits in 1944, the British consul in Shiraz said it was very poor as 'the peasants have been underfed for years, and malaria is rampant'.[40]

A British political adviser reported similar scenes near Kirkuk:

The economic state of Zibar district, the Mergasar Mahiyah and Baradost Mehiyas is really tragic. These unfortunate people have literally nothing between them and starvation. The little corn sowing they had has been a complete failure and only a few villages which have irrigated patches have any hope of growing a summer cash crop of millet etc. Everywhere one sees people lying about in an emaciated condition. Their clothes spread out on the hedges to dry show more holes than cloth. They have not even the wherewithal to patch them. The population is fast dwindling[:] some are away harvesting in the plains, others have gone to Persia to try their luck . . . I consider their state is quite beyond the scope of mere charity.[41]

British political advisers in Iraq routinely recorded the conditions on the ground. Crops in the Diyala region of Iraq in August 1941, for instance, were 'largely a complete failure ... Price of wheat very high, figure not touched since aftermath of last war ... Famine conditions will probably prevail this winter in mountains'. Writing on the first day of the Anglo-Soviet invasion, one said that people in the Diyala area were 'preoccupied with the question of water ... and this year the position is aggravated by the fact that the customary border contacts have virtually ceased as a result of the present military position'.[42]

In Iran, it was a common sight to see impoverished people waiting beside roads and railways as allied road convoys and trains passed, in the hope of food, money or other bounty. British consul Clarmont Skrine wrote that the 'invaders were shocked by the grinding poverty of the peasantry, even by Indian standards ... The distribution of a sack of potatoes by our troops at one village through which they passed caused a desperate and pathetic scramble'.[43] Yet the same correspondent reported a day or two later that large stocks of grain had been found by the advancing troops and that local scarcities were 'evidently due to faulty distribution', a controversial version of cause and effect that the British insisted upon throughout the war.[44] This touched on one of the great controversies regarding the allied occupation of Iran – whether food scarcity was caused by the occupation itself, or by poor Iranian distribution of ample supplies:

> Bread riots had occurred at Kermanshah and Shiraz, and anti-British feeling ran high. The Allies were blamed for causing famine and upsetting Persia's economy and taking grain out of the country for the use of their armies elsewhere. In actual fact the opposite was the case. 13,500 tons of wheat had already, in November 1941, been delivered at Gulf ports and another 15,000 were on their way. In addition, India had promised to send 3,000 tons to Nok Kundi for East Persia.[45]

Hoarding and a pricy black market were as much part of the picture as the 'rations sold at the bread-shops to the impoverished bulk of the population'.[46] In 1942 the price of sugar in eastern Iran went up to about six times the price being asked at Quetta in India, and the labourers building the roads so that the East Persian Auxiliary Transport Service could take supplies from India to the Soviet Union complained bitterly to Skrine that they could not sweeten their tea.[47] For the British officials responsible for the supply line, there was a persistent dilemma: 'Which "carry" was the more urgent, gunny-bags and shellac for the Kremlin, or wheat for the road-labourers and the bread-queues at Zahedan and Khwash?'[48]

The issue of food and its distribution was a source of much animosity towards the occupiers – and of finger-wagging by the British, who constantly laid the blame for shortage at the door of hoarders and maladroit Iranian distribution arrangements. For their part, the Iranians pointed to the monopoly on imports exercised by the British and the Soviets and the extent to which the occupiers had taken over the transport infrastructure – including vehicles and tyres. They might also have pointed to the fact that it was the Anglo-Soviet invasion and subsequent regime change that had so weakened central government powers as to make food distribution even more of a challenge, especially when attempted in the face of local unrest and brigandage on the road and rail network. The Iranians were keen to ensure that America observed their plight, wishing to present themselves as hapless victims in need of protection, to the point that they would manufacture tales, or remain inactive in order to make a bad situation worse. For example, they might complain that the Soviets were denying them permission to move grain, when this was simply not true.[49]

The British remained stony-faced. Visiting Tehran from British military headquarters in Baghdad, the Countess of Ranfurly stayed in the legation compound. She met the minister, Sir Reader Bullard, who plied her with anecdotes and witticisms.' "The Persians are used to the wheat problem . . . they are bred on it" he said, smiling at his pun.'[50] He told Ranfurly that the problem was 'an age old thing that usually ends by a mob baking one of the millers in his own bread oven'. 'If supplies were brought in from outside it would make no difference,' Bullard continued airily: 'that would be hoarded too. If the ringleaders were rounded up another gang would take over immediately.'[51] Bullard's sally reflected standard British attitudes regarding Iranian society, and the familiar contention that food shortages were caused by Iranian inefficiency, leading to an insouciance that seemed to ignore the roles that occupation by foreign troops and the general war situation played in the matter. Nevertheless, it has to be said that Bullard and other British officials were much closer to the situation on the ground than anyone in Washington or Whitehall, or Dreyfus and the American legation, for that matter, which was very Tehran-centric, lacking the network of staff and contacts in the provinces that the British maintained. They were also closer to events than any subsequent historians, and so their reports and conclusions cannot lightly be dismissed. Bullard's correspondence reveals a genuine conviction that solutions to Iran's problems lay firmly in Iranian hands. 'It makes one sick,' he wrote, 'to think of the preventable misery here that a little honesty and diligence could prevent.'[52]

Though 'the odious Dreyfus' could appear anti-British and gullible, some of his countrymen shared this British exasperation with the Iranians, including Arthur Millspaugh, contracted by the Iranian government to overhaul its finances.[53] The Americans found it difficult to know quite what to believe or what to do; as Dreyfus put it, 'I am in a difficult position between intransigent British on the one hand and grasping Iranians on the other.'[54] Correspondence between the American legation in Tehran and the State Department in Washington shows that the Americans were concerned and critical about the apparently arrogant manner in which the British handled the Iranian government. They struggled to accept the British line that food shortages were largely down to Iranian hoarding and incompetence – even scrutinizing evidence that the British on occasions deliberately withheld food or medical supplies in order to influence Iranian government decision-making. The Iranians, naturally, hoped that by befriending the Americans they could pursue their own national agenda and relieve some of the pressure created by the stifling proximity of the British and the Soviets. What is more, they had some persuasive arguments to deploy; for example, why did the British, through the high-handed UKCC, decide how many trucks or tyres Iran received, when the lion's share was actually being provided by American Lend-Lease? This anomaly did not escape the attention of the Americans, either.

As we have seen, the occupation degraded the Iranian state's capacity to feed its people, as well as to protect them from lawlessness, and foreign monopolies over imports and internal transportation did little to serve Iranian needs. As Ann Lambton told the Parliamentary Labour Party's Middle East Group shortly after the end of the war, 'civilian traffic on the railway, never large, was reduced to a minimum; road transport, moreover, in the early part of the period under review was virtually monopolised by hiring by the UKCC for the transport of supplies to Russia. This seriously affected the economic life of the country, particularly in so far as the collection and distribution of foodstuffs was concerned.'[55] The food situation that developed was due in part to a failure to marshal extant stocks, made worse because the 'writ of the central government by this time no longer ran throughout the country.'[56] The lack of facilities made collection more difficult, and the Soviets disrupted the flow of food from the north. High prices in neighbouring countries encouraged smuggling, frontier control having virtually broken down after the invasion. 'The prevailing insecurity had, moreover, led to a failure to collect the harvest of 1941 to the full or to effect the normal sowings for 1942.'[57]

Trucks and tyres

The allies commandeered the Iranian rail network and contracted for one-half of Iran's publicly and privately owned lorries ('trucks' in American parlance), thereby removing over 75 per cent of food distribution capacity in the midst of the 1941 harvest. Lorries remaining in Iranian hands quickly became unusable because the allies restricted the importation of spare parts, especially tyres. In May 1942 the American legation gathered data regarding the supply situation and transmitted them to the State Department. There were 4,000 lorries operating in Iran at the time, with 1,500 more laid up for lack of tyres. This included all Iranian government and private lorries. UKCC had about half of the 4,000 under contract, and were expecting the arrival of a further 2,500 Lend-Lease lorries.[58] There were 600 buses on the road, 400 motorcycles and 3,000 passenger cars, with another 1,000 laid up. Given these figures, and allowing twelve tyres per truck per year, Dreyfus reckoned that UKCC's estimates regarding lorry and tyre requirements fairly reflected the level of demand and that the distribution it recommended would suffice for Iran's needs for the year, though distribution was a 'delicate and controversial point'. Tyre mortality in Iran was extraordinarily high due to bad roads, one estimate claiming that tyres that would last for 80,000 miles in American conditions would be worn out after 4,000 miles in Iran.[59]

Dreyfus believed that the food situation was getting worse because of transport problems. Exports had reduced to a trickle, and the running of supplies to the Soviet Union and other allied activities had brought about the 'appropriation of a considerable part of existing trucks'. So an acute stage had been reached, a consequence of which could be famine.[60] The UKCC stood its ground. Its position was that it 'has built a large and efficient transport organization which alone is capable of distributing and using trucks and tires efficiently'. Delivering direct to the Iranian government would be wasteful and harm the war effort, and if a parallel to the UKCC was set up by the Iranians it would lead to waste, destructive competition and overlapping. 'I feel the British are treating Iranians in a high-handed manner,' wrote Dreyfus, 'and that they are unfair in assuming Iranians are incapable of distributing tires equitably under foreign supervision.' The Iranian Finance Minister 'expressed great irritation at treatment being given Iran by the British', citing as an example a consignment of 3,000 tyres which arrived for Iran but were taken by the British military.[61]

While politicians and diplomats bickered, the effects on the ground were all too obvious. In July 1942 a British vice-consul toured Ram Hormuz, Sultanabad and Haftkel in the company of the consular liaison officer for southern Khuzestan, reporting that:

> About 200 tons grain had been collected in the Idareh-ye-Darai at Ram Hormuz but in spite of the urgent need of Ahwaz and other centres for grain, lorry transport could only be provided for about twenty tons. Almost all the privately owned lorries in Ahwaz are now working under contract for the British military authorities and the AIOC, who formerly helped out the Persian authorities in emergencies, have now pressing transport problems of their own to face. The Amnieh are attempting to round up Ram Hormuz' 400 camels, but the prospects are not bright.[62]

Camels represented a costly method of transporting grain, but there were other problems created by the war situation, specifically the breakdown of law and order that had followed the invasion. The 'general insecurity at the edge of the hills also tells against the wider use of animal transport' because of the prospect of ambush and robbery. Moreover, the action of the head of the Finance Department in Ram Hormuz 'in breaking into storehouses and taking over all the grain found has naturally raised a storm of protests that the grain taken included the landowners' "personal requirements" and seeds.'

On 20 July 1942 Dreyfus told the State Department that 'relations between the Iranian Government and UKCC over tires is reaching breaking point'. At a meeting attended by delegates of the Iranian Ministry of Finance and the UKCC, a senior Iranian official 'found it necessary in describing UKCC activities to use such expressions as abuse of confidence, dishonest, and unfair treatment. He took violent exception to what he called theft of tires by British.'[63] Dreyfus wrote that the:

> general British attitude in this and other matters is one of destructive criticism of Iranian competence and honesty rather than one of constructive suggestion, a condition of mind which has contributed in no small degree to British unpopularity here . . . I feel that due to UKCC obstruction and deception we are fiddling while Rome burns. Iranians are in a desperate position for road transport and will be unable to move crops without outside help.[64]

Dreyfus's dispatches to Washington in August 1942 illustrate the difficulties involved in ascertaining the truth regarding the food-supply situation. Dreyfus reported that the wheat situation was very serious, and famine likely. There were minor food riots in provincial towns and cavalry had 'been parading in Tehran to forestall riots here'. But on 26 August the diplomat said that he was 'doubtful there is a wheat shortage. The problem is primarily an internal one of collecting in rural areas and distributing to urban areas. Government has been delinquent in locating the wheat and making hoarders disgorge.' The 'crop in Azerbaijan is excellent and should help in supplying the urban centers with the 350,000 tons a year they need but it is not expected that the Soviets will permit the surplus to be shipped out'. Dreyfus recommended that America support the 'British stand and insist on Iran helping itself before relying on Allied imports'. Though the situation was serious, he did not accept that the blame lay entirely with the allies.

In October 1942 Dreyfus wrote that the recent Soviet demand for large quantities of American and British wheat 'brings out into open what has been known for some time – that Russians, British and Poles are buying up large quantities of Iran food products to detriment of local food situation ... It is becoming obvious that frantic Iranian appeals for wheat in recent months have been based on more than avarice or caprice.'[65] The press and public were deeply stirred, taking the general view that the 'Allies are pushing Iran into inflation and starvation ... Prices are soaring and poor classes can hardly afford to buy bread, their only staple. Profiteering is scandalous and Government has not taken corrective measures such as taxation and price control.' The British continued to blame the situation on hoarding, inefficient distribution and an inadequate transport system.[66] The Iranian view, according to Dreyfus, was that far from living up to their pledges, 'the Allies have pillaged the country to such an extent that a firm and inescapable rather than a vague promise must now be obtained. There is much to be said for the Iranian viewpoint for the country has been indeed pillaged of food and transport by the Allies.'[67]

The December 1942 riots

In December 1942, after a bad wheat harvest (caused in part by Soviet impressment of farm workers for its own labour gangs), a bread protest in Tehran overwhelmed the police and led to the occupation of the parliament, which required the call-up of the Iranian 2nd Division and saw allied troops deployed onto the streets. Thus began the infamous Tehran bread riots, the reaction to which illustrated the difficulty of disentangling whether domestic Iranian failings or the impact of war and occupation were the root cause of the people's suffering.

Famine conditions in poorer quarters caused popular indignation to rise to boiling point: a mob attacked the house of the prime minister, Ahmad Qavam, attempting to burn it down, and another demonstrated outside the parliament. Dreyfus wrote that 'several thousand persons including women and children have been demonstrating all day in front of Majlis crying, "You may kill us but we must have bread!"' Later that day the crowd was 'out of hand'; rioting 'developed on widespread and severe scale ... The shopping area is being looted by uncontrolled mobs.'[68]

Tehran was quieter the next day, and Dreyfus went to survey the damage. The business district was worst hit, some buildings gutted and little exposed glass left intact. The prime minister's residence had been sacked, the majlis broken into and damaged, several killed and many injured. A British battalion was on its way from Qom to be quartered at the race track, and would soon be parading through the streets. The British and the Soviets were saying that the violence was part of a German plot, though Dreyfus was not at all convinced that this was true. For their part, many Iranians believed the riots were inspired by the British or Soviets. The American consul's own assessment was that the riots had happened because people were desperate and bitter due to the food crisis, and the belief that their woes were caused by the invaders.

But Dreyfus soon changed his tune as he learned more. He reported that the shah had asked Qavam to resign, but that he had refused, bolstered by British support. Apparently the shah wanted to form a military government 'under his own domination', though British support for Qavam had prevented him from doing so. The British had spoken to the shah, giving him what amounted to an ultimatum: the military governor and police chief were to be removed from office; Qavam was to be asked to form a new government; the prime minister and others were to be compensated for damage to property caused by the riots; corrupt and pro-Axis officials were to be eliminated from the army; and there should be an inquiry into the causes of the riots. The shah was told that the British would 'not look with favour on the importation of wheat unless the government is favourable to the Allies.'[69]

Dreyfus's reports to Washington prompted Sumner Welles to meet with the British ambassador and read him extracts. He emphasized the State Department's grave concerns regarding the manner in which the British authorities in Iran had handled things. On the same day, Secretary of State Cordell Hull sent a message to Ambassador Winant in London, copied to the Foreign Office.[70] But as Dreyfus's continuing reports reveal, things were not as they seemed at first. The riots had in fact been staged, largely on the instigation of the shah, for domestic political reasons. The riot was 'planned, rehearsed, led and purchased'.[71] Some influential politicians wanted to get rid of Qavam, particularly a military clique headed by the shah. It seemed as if the shah was responsible for the demonstrations with 'the ultimate object of setting up a military government'.[72]

Subsequent historians have variously attributed the riots to food shortages, xenophobia, food hoarding, crop failure, allied occupation policies, political infighting, student dissatisfaction, inflation, insecurity, the post-Reza Shah re-emergence of street thugs and gangs, national humiliation resulting from the invasion and an absence of social responsibility. Though brief, the riots exacerbated allied tensions, influenced the course of Iranian history and helped drag America deeper into Iranian affairs. Food shortages in Tehran in late 1942 were not due to any acute and general scarcity, but to the failure of the transportation and distribution system. The allied presence increased demand, but famine would not have occurred if all other factors had remained the same. Allied policies and the ineptitude of the Iranian government so disrupted grain shipments that cities such as Tehran were forced to survive from day to day while supplies stacked up in grain-producing areas or were sold to meet Soviet and British needs. Grain distribution had depended on a fleet of lorries, a national rail system composed of a single railway line, the commanding presence of the despotic Reza Shah and the free movement of supplies inside of Iran. By September 1941, the allies had taken away all four.[73]

The riots 'marked the return of foreign troops to Tehran. They remained there until August 7, 1945, used by British and Soviet officials to influence Iranian politics, especially apparent during the oil concession crisis of December 1944.'[74] The riots increased intra-allied friction, and set America on a course of policy independence from Britain, convincing it that a strong commitment to state security was required in order to prevent Iran suffering internal collapse or foreign conquest. Iranians became increasingly anti-British and desirous of a greater American presence to offset the other two allies. Famine, or at least relative deprivation, though providing the necessary preconditions for the riots and perhaps inspiring some of its participants, was not alone responsible.[75] The riots revealed nationalistic reaction against foreign invaders, a popular reaction against an elitist, non-participative and largely inefficient political system, against the changes in the political economy begun by Reza Shah and against the deprivation resulting from the inability of the government to feed its people.

The Polish refugees

Adding to the burdens placed on Iran's resources at the most difficult time of the war, in 1942 it also became responsible for the accommodation and sustenance, with British assistance, of tens of thousands of Polish refugees. When the Soviets invaded Poland at the outbreak of the European war, 'an estimated 1.7 million civilians were forcibly expelled from their homes in the course of four mass deportations. Thrust at gunpoint into cattle trucks, they were transported to remote labour camps all over Siberia and Kazakhstan.'[76] When Germany invaded the Soviet Union in June 1941 their situation changed as Stalin, desperate for allies, undertook in the Polish–Soviet Military Agreement (14 August 1941) to release them. By 1942, as many as a half were dead. As well as placating his new British partners and wider world opinion, the German invasion also presented an opportunity for Stalin to rid himself of the remaining Polish prisoners scattered in labour camps across the Soviet Union. The plan was to transport men to Iran and from them to raise a new Polish 'army in exile', to be commanded by General Władysław Anders, who had himself been incarcerated in Lubyanka prison in Moscow. But thousands of women and children joined the exodus.

Reaching Iran required two phases, with most travelling by sea in overcrowded tankers and coal ships from Krasnovodsk (now Türkmenbaşy) in Turkmenistan to Bandar-e Pahlavi, and a smaller movement overland from Ashgabad to Mashhad. With many suffering from disease and malnutrition, thousands died during the exodus, too ill or feeble to complete the journey, and those who did arrive were in a terrible state. Helena Woloch, who had worked in forced labour camps in the Soviet Union, described how she and many others, 'Exhausted by hard labour, disease and starvation – barely recognizable as human beings … disembarked at the port of Bandar-e Pahlavi on the Caspian coast.'[77]

The first phase of the Polish exodus from the Soviet Union to Iran lasted from 24 March to 5 April 1942; the second, from 10 to 30 August 1942. In the first phase, 43,858 arrived at Bandar-e Pahlavi in Iran, of which 10,789 were civilians, including 3,100 children. The second phase involved 45,000 soldiers and 25,000 civilians. During this latter phase, 568 died at Bandar-e Pahlavi, and peak sickness figures saw 868 Poles in Iranian hospitals and 2,000 in the convalescent camp. Upon arrival, the refugees were deloused and disinfected and issued with clothes, and up to 100 vehicles driven by Armenians and Indians worked around the clock to transport them from the port.

The migration was chaotic. 'The British and Iranian authorities had not been told until very late that women and children would also be arriving, and were generally unprepared for the severity of malnutrition and disease the exiles were suffering. Typhus was the deadliest ailment. A makeshift camp comprising over 2,000 tents (provided by the Iranian army) was hastily erected along the shoreline.'[78] On 27 March 1942, London sent a telegram to the commander of Polish forces in the Soviet Union: 'British authorities are alarmed by the news that families are included in military transports . . . In view of the great food difficulties in Iran it is necessary to stop absolutely transport of families.'[79] But they kept on coming. Clarmont Skrine, British consul in the city of Mashhad, recalled the many Polish civilians who came through eastern Iran as they made their way south after escaping from the Soviet Union. They included 700 children separated in exile from their parents, 'a pathetic little army'.[80] They received special treatment from the locals and all were relieved when the maharaja of Nawanagar invited them to live in his Indian state.

Despite all the agonizing hardships, 'Iran stood as a beacon of freedom and hope.'[81] Arriving at Bandar-e Pahlavi, songs and prayers were offered for the refugees' deliverance. There, said Helena Woloch, 'we knelt down together in our thousands along the sandy shoreline to kiss the soil of Persia. We had escaped Siberia, and were free at last.' In Bandar-e Pahlavi, recalled Karol Huppert, 'we could see beautiful villas, people beautifully dressed and going in the boats for rides. Some even threw us oranges and other fruit. The difference between us and them was so much that I remember telling myself, "That is what paradise would be like".'[82] One Polish soldier described these momentous events thus: 'For us the summer of 1942 was the dawn of freedom.'[83]

A close bond between the Poles and their Iranian hosts developed, both nationalities finding affinity in their situation as smaller powers buffeted by great-power imperialism and aggression. Iranians made generous gifts of food and other supplies to the exiles, despite their own straitened circumstances. Polish troops punctiliously saluted Iranian officers, a sign of respect that the allied occupying forces were less forthcoming in showing.

The Iranian government considered them simply as people 'in transit'. Initially it was worried that the average Iranian, 'already reeling under occupation and wartime shortages, would suffer further with the presence of a large body of additional population'.[84] But soon the Iranians started cooperating in the provision of accommodation and medical attention. Looking after the desperate Poles also served as useful anti-Soviet propaganda. Though discouraged by the British, Bullard wrote that 'Russians can no longer upset Persian citizens by singing the glories of the Soviet Union, while Tehran is full of Poles who were starving in Russia and who admitted that Russians in the same circumstances were starving too'.[85]

The British consul in Isfahan reported in November 1942 that 'the sympathy at first felt by Isfahanis for the Polish children here, which now number nearly 2,000, has rather turned to dislike recently. The Poles' lack of comprehension of the value of money and their somewhat self-assertive habits have caused this. They are blamed too for the rapid rise in prices which is now taking place.'[86] But despite the difficulties experienced in accommodating them, the Polish forces were to form an important part of the order of battle of the British forces now massing in Iran and Iraq to withstand a German invasion. In order to coordinate them, the British prime minister decided that an entirely new command structure was called for.

CHAPTER 12

Churchill's new command

In late 1941, GHQ India 'war-gamed' German strategy for the Middle East. In the absence of hard intelligence as to German intentions, this detailed simulation was an informed estimate of what the Wehrmacht could and should do next. The concluding assessment was that the ultimate German objective was to advance into Iran and Iraq in order to obtain or destroy the oilfields and refineries. This was because 'total denial of these [to the British] might be decisive' and would dramatically boost Germany's war effort. 'All other longer-term objects,' it was concluded, 'must be subsidiary to this.'[1]

As the Eighth Army continued to labour against Rommel's forces in North Africa in 1942, defending the Middle East's outer shell, defensive cover for the Iran–Iraq region was provided by two weak armies: the Ninth Army, occupying Syria up to the Turkish border, and Quinan's Tenth Army, covering southern Iran and Iraq.[2] By August, a year on from the Anglo-Soviet invasion of Iran, the strategic picture had changed little. German forces in North Africa and the Soviet Union continued to threaten the security of Iran and Iraq, and this was a threat that Churchill's government could not ignore. The British seemed no closer to beating the Afrika Korps and its Italian allies than they had at any time since German forces first arrived in Libya back in February 1941. In fact, things seemed to be getting worse: June 1942 had witnessed the nadir of British fortunes when the imperial garrison at Tobruk in Libya surrendered as Rommel swept the British eastwards, dizzying news that Churchill received while in conference with Roosevelt at the White House. Rommel's advance had continued, stopped only by the Eighth Army's defensive success at the first Battle of El Alamein in July. Now, exhausted, both armies eyed each other across a scraggy patch of Egyptian desert, Rommel preparing for a final push that he hoped would take him to the Nile, the Suez Canal and the prizes beyond. The chance of a German thrust towards Iran via Turkey was also considered well within the bounds of possibility; in the Soviet Union, the southern wing of the invading Axis armies was pushing for the Caucasus.

German documents demonstrate that in the summer of 1942, preparation for future operations in the Iran–Iraq region was still very much in the minds of diplomats and regional experts. In July, with Axis troops on the cusp of victory in the Western Desert, Rashid Ali, the former prime minister of Iraq, told radio listeners across the Middle East that 'the hour of liberation has come'. A stock of over two million propaganda leaflets was readied for distribution. An Arabic broadcast declared: 'The hour of British doom has come ... unite and rise against the weakened British, proclaiming: "Long live the Grand Mufti, the leader of Arabism! Long live His Majesty, the beloved leader, Rashid Aly el-Kilani, and long live the valiant Iraqi Army, the liberator of the Arab nation!"'[3] In the same month, Rashid Ali spent two hours with Hitler at the Wolf's Lair, his Eastern Front headquarters in East Prussia, discussing cooperation with German forces when they moved into Iraq. Though his thoughts were clearly dominated by conquering the Soviet Union – the key to everything else – Hitler also had the Middle East in mind. Albert Speer recalled an evening with the Führer in August, sitting outside his lodge at the Werwolf headquarters at Vinnytsia in Ukraine. 'For a long time,' Hitler said:

> I have had everything prepared. As the next step we are going to advance south of the Caucasus and then help the rebels in Iran and Iraq against the English. Another thrust will be directed along the Caspian Sea toward Afghanistan and India. Then the English will run out of oil. In two years we'll be on the borders of India. Twenty to thirty elite German divisions will do. Then the British Empire will collapse. They've already lost Singapore to the Japanese. The English will have to look on impotently as their colonial empire falls to pieces ... By the end of 1943 we will pitch our tents in Tehran, in Baghdad, and on the Persian Gulf. Then the oil wells will at last be dry as far as the English are concerned.[4]

Hitler's eastward thinking was influenced by Japan's entry into the war in December 1941. In the most astonishing land-grab in the history of warfare, within six short months Japan had expunged the Western empires in South-east Asia and the Far East, penetrated deep into South Asia and extended its tentacles across the Indian Ocean. This threatened the sea lanes on which Britain depended for the movement of resources supporting the fighting in the Western Desert, for the conveyance of aid to the Soviet Union and for the extraction of oil from Abadan. Its eastern ally having joined battle, Germany descried new opportunities to press Britain in the Middle East, and also wanted to ensure its share of the spoils; it would not do to allow Japan to scoop them all. Coordinated action with Japan aimed against Britain offered the chance to seriously interdict or even sever its vital sea lanes in the Indian Ocean region, of which the Persian Gulf was an essential part.[5] 'The Germans in particular hoped that the Japanese would send submarines to cut the main lines of communication of the British mercantile marine leading from India to the Persian Gulf (to Iran) and from there to South Africa' and around the Cape.[6]

In July the German Foreign Minister Joachim von Ribbentrop met Hiroshi Oshima, Tokyo's man in Berlin, at Groß Steinort, the East Prussian village where he held meetings when staying at the Wolf's Lair. A note in the German archives from that meeting reads as follows:

> The success of the German summer offensive led Ribbentrop to suggest that the Russian powers of resistance had been broken ... Ribbentrop suggested that the Japanese navy move against British lines of communication in strength. He was convinced that Rommel would break British defences in Africa and that the German military would repulse any attempt by the British to land troops in the West in order to take the pressure off of Stalin. 'Two things are decisive for our conduct of the war; namely cutting off Russia from its supply lines in the North over the polar sea ... and second to seize Russian oil fields in the south and to cut off the flow of supplies from Iran' ... He further argued that the Axis were obligated to stop the fusion of American armaments potential with Soviet manpower reserves [hence his focus on severing the Iranian supply route].[7]

Disturbed by the state of affairs in the Middle East and Britain's apparent inability to beat the Germans no matter what advantage in men and material they possessed, Churchill decided it was time for a shake-up in the Middle East, and a scheduled visit to Stalin provided him with the opportunity to stop off in Cairo. Not only did the prime minister believe that a change of command was needed, but that the unwieldy Middle East Command should be split in two. A separate Persia and Iraq Command was required in order to give these two countries and their strategic resources the attention that their paramount importance demanded, and to allow the Commander-in-Chief Middle East to focus all his attention on beating Rommel. As things stood, Iran and Iraq were neither adequately protected or 'thought about'. Whatever happened in the Western Desert and the Mediterranean, the War Office thought, Britain needed 'sufficient resources left over to protect the Syria–Persia front'. The region 'required no protection so long as the Russians hold out. But if the Russians fall down, a serious threat will develop from the north by the late summer [of 1942]': 'From the purely military point of view, the retention of Iraq and Persia is perhaps more important to us than the retention of Egypt itself. This is so because the holding of these two countries is necessary for the protection of the oil at the head of the Persian Gulf. Without this oil we should be unable to carry on the war in the Indian Ocean [region].'[8] Iran and Iraq were paramount, a factor absent in most historical accounts, with their overbearing focus on the Western Desert and the defence of Egypt – which was actually an outworkings of the defence of Iran and Iraq.

Because of this, any final line of retreat had to encompass them. If the Soviets were defeated, wrote Major-General Kennedy, 'there is a poor prospect of holding the Middle East. We may then be reduced to defending the key points only. These are a) the oil supplies in the Persian Gulf, and b) Ceylon and such part of India as is necessary to security of Ceylon', vital because of its role in defending the Indian Ocean's sea lanes.[9] As well as underlining the central importance of the Iran–Iraq region, such assessments capture the extent of Britain's strategic overstretch as the war expanded, and the constant need to second-guess the enemy's moves and try to find the resources with which to meet them. 'We are faced,' Kennedy wrote, 'in a more acute form than ever before, with the problem of trying to do too much with too little. The dispersion, forced upon us, is worse than ever before ... Our fortunes, especially in the Middle East, are bound up, more than before, with the course of events on the Russian front.'[10] Given all of this, one of the biggest frustrations was the lack of clear intelligence regarding the situation in the Soviet Union, and the likelihood of its defeat. As Kennedy put it, the Eastern Front was 'wrapt [sic] in mystery.'[11]

The oil review, July 1942

The Chiefs of Staff and the War Cabinet were well aware of the arithmetic and geography of oil and war, and refreshed their collective memory in July

1942 as they studied a report prepared by the Oil Control Board, the 'apex of the wartime administrative machinery' for oil enjoying the status of a War Cabinet subcommittee.[12] Entitled 'Oil supplies in the East in the event of the destruction of the Persian oilfields', the report assumed German successes in the north and the loss of the Iraqi oilfields through scorched-earth action. 'Under present conditions we are counting upon Middle East sources for the following oil supplies for year ending 30 June 1943: Persian Gulf 11,558,000 tons; Haifa 1,923,000; Tripoli 145,000; and Suez 959,000 ... If Abadan, Haifa, and Tripoli are denied to us,' the report continued, the only alternative sources would be increased production from Bahrain, the Gulf of Mexico, Netherlands West Indies, or California. Assuming the maximum increase from Bahrain, this meant Britain would need 10,666,000 tons from these other, non-British controlled, sources.[13] 'This would add 200 to the number of tankers required to meet the present supply programme even after allowing for transference of bunkering from ports near to Abadan to ports near to the new sources of supply. If Bahrain also ceased to be available as a source of supply, a further seventy tankers would be needed.'[14]

Even if the necessary replacement supplies could be found from these sources, however, there would be difficulties over the supply of high-performance 100-octane aviation spirit. Abadan aviation spirit was vital to the Soviet Union and all Britain's eastern theatres of war. It was, according to the AIOC's official historian, the company's most significant contribution to the war effort.[15] It would also be extremely difficult, or impossible, to replace sufficient Admiralty fuel oil of the required specification.[16] The latter was 'in such increasing demand that it already presents a major problem'. Loss of supplies from Abadan 'would therefore be irreplaceable'.[17] Britain could not rely on the Americans: the country was stretched already and needed extra for American forces stationed in Britain. Consumption in Britain had 'already been cut several times and it has been generally accepted that the latest cut represented the utmost that could be achieved without adverse effect on our own war effort'. Large cuts had also been made in India, the dominions and the colonial empire.

Transport was the make-or-break issue. It was simply impossible to conjure an extra 270 ocean-going tankers, and losses were mounting (the Anglo-Iranian Oil Company had lost 46 per cent of its tanker fleet).[18] 'The cuts required to free this amount of tanker tonnage are impracticable and the Oil Control Board conclude that the loss of Abadan and Bahrain would be calamitous inasmuch as it would enforce a drastic reduction in our total war capacity, and probably the abandonment of some of our present fields of action.'[19] The implications of these figures were clear, the Oil Control Board stating that 'the conclusion from the foregoing is that it is of vital importance that there should be a maximum concentration on the military effort needed to safeguard the Persian oilfields'. To achieve this, the War Cabinet had to decide whether to put everything into the defence of Egypt in the hope that a large army would not be needed to defend Iran and Iraq, or to divide reinforcements between the two theatres, preparing to fight in both. 'The paramount importance of Abadan and the oilfields decided the issue,' wrote General Alan Brooke, Chief of the Imperial General Staff. It was this that bolstered Churchill's resolve to reorganize the command structure and build up the Empire's armed strength in Iran and Iraq.

Reinforcements: Iran and Iraq trump Egypt

Given the paramount importance of Iranian oil, the British war effort swung to a very large extent upon the security of Abadan. Its facilities expanding, its production increasing, Abadan was put on a war footing. There were barrage balloons and bomb shelters, even an enormous dummy refinery constructed a few miles away in order to deceive enemy reconnaissance. Employees performed civil defence and air raid precaution duties and the oil complex was militarized, partly in response to the insecurity that pertained in the surrounding rural areas. The rise in AIOC activity sucked in capital and labour, expenditure on facilities rising from £243,000 in 1941 to £7,006,000 in 1944.[20] Company employees and contractors in Iran rose commensurately from 48,000 Iranians, 1,700 Indians and 1,600 Britons in August 1939 to 60,000 Iranians, 2,500 Indians and 2,300 Britons in December 1945.[21] The AIOC's war-related initiatives could bring it into conflict with British military authorities – for example, its decision to kit out employees with khaki uniforms, and its predilection for approaching the Iranian military governor directly on military and security matters rather than going through the appropriate British channels. The company, according to historian Rasmus Christian Elling, sought to use the war situation to boost the quasi-colonial order in southern Iran on which its activities to a large extent depended.[22]

Meeting in London on 23 July 1942, the Chiefs of Staff discussed measures for the region's defence, especially that of Abadan. Brooke noted the meeting in his diary ('My birthday! 59! I don't feel like it!'): a 'difficult COS

[Chiefs of Staff Committee] at which we discussed the necessary measures to guard against German attacks through Persia on Abadan oil field should Russian resistance break'.[23] Six days later, the region was once again on the Chiefs of Staff's agenda, especially the relative importance of Egypt as opposed to Abadan. That evening, the prime minister sent for Brooke, and they spent an hour together in the garden of 10 Downing Street discussing India, Iran, Iraq and the Middle East.[24]

The Chiefs of Staff returned to the subject only days later, discussing reinforcements being diverted from General Auchinleck's Middle East Command to protect the oilfields. It assumed that he would be able to allot to the Iran–Iraq region the 51st and 56th infantry divisions, which he was about to receive from Britain, and an armoured division coming from America. Also, that the 5th Indian Division would be sent from India to Iraq and an option held to follow it up with the 2nd Division. If these reinforcements arrived, Iran and Iraq would have 'reasonable' defensive cover. To support the ground forces, 'requisite air forces should be available provided that delivery of US aircraft and arrival of US Air Corps units proceeds according to plan and providing intensive operations in the desert are not prolonged indefinitely'. It was assessed that the Gulf ports might come under German air attack by October. 'We are arranging for the completion of the anti-aircraft defences approved for the Basra–Abadan–Bahrein area, subject only to the immediate needs of the Nile Delta', currently at a critical juncture in the Desert War.

The Chiefs of Staff also reviewed the threat to Iran in the light of German successes on the Eastern Front: 'We realize that the Russian southern front may break this year. If it does and if we have taken no steps to deal with such a situation, there is little to prevent the enemy from advancing through Persia and reaching the Southern Persian oilfields'.[25] If the Soviet Union were defeated and Turkey acquiescent, 'the Axis may mount a very heavy attack from north and west against the Middle East position in spring 1943, which we would have difficulty in meeting. The situation however would be transformed if Rommel were decisively beaten and driven out of Tobruk or if "Bolero" shipping [ships used to build up American forces in Britain] were allotted to carry additional reinforcements'.[26]

'In making the decision to defend Abadan even if need be at the expense of Egypt', the War Cabinet distilled its thinking: 'The main purpose of our whole Middle East effort is to defend the sources of oil and its sea transport. If we lost Persia and Iraq, our position in Egypt would ultimately become untenable for military as well as economic reasons. Conversely, even were we forced to abandon Egypt, this should not necessarily involve the loss of Abadan.'[27] The problem was that the Iran–Iraq region was not receiving the priority in terms of defence that its status clearly required, partly because the situation in the Western Desert remained stubbornly unresolved, the decisive victory for which Churchill yearned proving elusive. In June 1942 the prime minister told Auchineck that considerable forces had been sent from Iraq to Libya (including the experienced 10th Indian Division) to reinforce the Eighth Army. He was struggling to make the troops go round, and was mindful of the need to anticipate a possible German attack through Anatolia or through the Caucasus towards Iran and Iraq.[28]

Churchill's desert sojourn

Due in Moscow for a summit with Stalin and Roosevelt's special representative, Churchill embarked for Cairo on 2 August 1942. Brooke was already on his way. Both men were gravely concerned about Middle East Command's defence of Egypt and its vital infrastructure, and its ability to protect the oil of Iran and Iraq. They had lost confidence in Auchinleck as Commander-in-Chief Middle East, frustrated that the Eighth Army was not performing better and worried by the fact that Rommel was only 60 miles from Alexandria. The embassy and military headquarters were busily burning their secret papers. Churchill wanted a new man at the helm, and the Eighth Army needed a new commander (General Neil Ritchie had been sacked and Auchinleck had temporarily taken over direct command).

Brooke conferred with the commanders of the three armed services in the Middle East on 4 August 1942. 'We discussed the relative importance of Egypt as opposed to Abadan and all agreed that the latter's importance was paramount.' Churchill had to convince sceptical colleagues to accept his plan to split Middle East Command in two. He opened his campaign by getting Brooke on side. On 6 August, the general wrote in his diary, 'An elated PM suddenly burst into my room whilst I was practically naked. Then went round after breakfast, and he made me sit on the sofa whilst he walked up and down. First of all he said that he had decided to split MEC in two. A Near East taking up to the Canal, and a Middle East for Syria, Palestine, Iran and Iraq.'[29] Churchill spent this day with Brooke and Smuts (having visited the Alamein positions the day before), making big decisions on personalities and the 'entire command in this vast theatre'.[30]

Having secured Brooke's support, as well as that of Smuts and Resident Minister Casey, Churchill sent his proposal to the War Cabinet, which immediately met to consider this far-reaching telegram, Reflex no. 35. The main argument for sticking with a *unified* command, articulated when the matter had last been discussed in December, was that 'since the Middle East might be attacked from Libya, Turkey or the Caucasus, all these fronts should be under one Commander, who could transfer his reserves as the situation demanded. Moreover, the air forces in the whole area had already been put under one Commander, and must so remain.' But now, in August 1942, 'the general feeling of the War Cabinet was that, while on balance they did not favour the suggested re-organization into two Commands, the case against the re-organization was neither so strong nor so clear-cut that they could properly oppose the views of those on the spot.'[31] Hardly a ringing endorsement of Churchill's recommendation, but it was enough for him to press on. Also on 6 August, Churchill decided on General Harold Alexander as Auchinleck's replacement, and Lieutenant-General William Gott as commander of the Eighth Army. But Gott was killed the following day when his plane was shot down while returning to Cairo, and so the Eighth Army went instead to Lieutenant-General Bernard Montgomery.

The two commands – Middle East and the proposed Persia and Iraq – were 'separated by 3–400 miles, with poor communications or a sea voyage . . . Both have entirely different bases of supply,' Churchill explained to Cabinet colleagues by telegram on the following day. Persia and Iraq were 'more naturally associated with India Command', and only removed from its purview because of the Japanese situation and the need to focus attention on Burma and Malaya. Churchill also said that there would be no difficulty maintaining a single air command over the whole region, and noted that both the Chief of the Imperial General Staff and Field Marshal Smuts supported the plan.[32] The present structure was 'far too diverse and expansive', and a fresh start was needed, along with 'vehement action to animate the whole of this vast but baffled and somewhat unhinged organization'.[33]

Brooke was summoned to Churchill's bedside in the early hours of 8 August to be told that the War Cabinet had 'rather reluctantly' agreed to the proposed separation.[34] Brooke subsequently claimed that, having studied the problem on the spot, he had reached the conclusion that the split was essential. 'Otherwise nothing adequate would be done to organize our defence in Persia in case the Germans got through the Caucasus. If Persia had been left under the Middle East Command or put under India, it would have been a Cinderella.'[35] That day,

Churchill wrote to Auchinleck, telling him of his sacking and offering him command of Persia and Iraq. He also informed Roosevelt.

Churchill and Stalin discussed the Iran–Iraq theatre during their Moscow meeting. At the Kremlin on 12 August the prime minister 'turned to the question of the Russian southern flank' and said that 'he and President Roosevelt had been turning over in their minds the question of helping in the defence of the Caspian Sea and the Caucasus': 'Nothing definite had been decided, but he and the President thought that if we could put a powerful Anglo-American air force in Northern Persia that would help both us and the Russians. The Caucasian Mountains and the neutrality of Turkey were matters of material importance to us in that they shielded the oil of Abadan, the loss of which would threaten our whole position in India and the Middle East.'[36] It was noted that at this point 'Stalin's interest flagged a little', as it usually did when the British talked down the 'second front' in western Europe and talked up other theatres of activity. But Churchill was off, expatiating at the grand strategic level. He told the Soviet leader how the 'battle of Egypt' needed to be won, and how Britain was 'trying to build up an army in Persia and Iraq and to make available an air force to support the Russians on the Caucasus front'. The prime minister concluded by asking how his idea appealed to Marshal Stalin, who replied that he was glad to accept, subject to agreement on certain points of detail. In tabling this offer, the British were motivated by the desire to protect oil supplies and the supply route to the Soviet Union.

The choice of commander

Having decided to create a new command, Churchill now had to work out who would lead it. The Tenth Army was currently commanded by Lieutenant-General Quinan who, 'it is agreed by all here, is not adequate to the task'. The Tenth Army would be to Persia and Iraq Command (PAIC) what the Eighth Army was to Middle East Command. It was agreed that Quinan had done an excellent job since taking command of imperial forces in Iran and Iraq fifteen months before, though he might not have appeared as an ideal fit as head of a new regional command, being renowned for attention to sub-unit detail and perhaps not suited to the political side of the commander-in-chief role.

Churchill proposed Auchinleck as the inaugural Commander-in-Chief Persia and Iraq, though not without reservation. Given that the general was to be removed from his position as Commander-in-Chief Middle East, Churchill said, the argument would be raised back in Britain that we were 'creating new posts for those who had failed to make good in their existing appointments'.[37] Addressing the War Cabinet through his deputy, Clement Attlee, Churchill said: 'I doubt the disasters would have occurred in the Western Desert if General Auchinleck had not been distracted by the divergent considerations of a too-widely extended front.'[38] Churchill had been angered by Auchinleck's phrase about not becoming 'immersed in the tactical problems of Libya' – revealing, in the prime minister's opinion, 'the false proportion engendered by extraneous responsibilities. It is in fact "the tactical problems of Libya" which dominate our immediate affairs.' On 8 August 1942 Attlee telegraphed Churchill: 'Your further telegram has not entirely removed our misgivings, either as to division of command, or as to Auchinleck's position.' The War Cabinet, however, was prepared to go along with his recommendations.[39] Churchill conferred with Auchinleck on 10 August, writing afterwards that the general was 'disinclined to accept', though the prime minister gave him a few days to ponder the offer.[40]

Further efforts were made to sell the idea to Auchinleck. The Resident Minister Middle East, Sir Richard Casey, told Churchill that he had had talks with the general. Casey had said that the new command would be independent but in its infancy would have to 'lean on' Middle East Command. For this and other reasons, the job really required someone who knew Iran and Iraq and also the inner workings of Middle East Command – someone like Auchinleck. 'Also I believe PAIC will have to deal with circumstances that are not much less than vital to our cause and that in consequence it is potentially an exceedingly important Command!' Casey told Auchinleck.[41] Auchinleck havered over whether or not to accept the role, which irritated Churchill still further. On 13 August he wrote that there was to be 'no bargaining'. 'I have made, with Cabinet approval, a high and honourable offer to Auchinleck and it is for him to settle whether he wishes to render further service to the Crown.'[42]

Ultimately Auchinleck refused the new appointment. He 'prefers retirement', wrote Brooke. 'I'm sure he is wrong – the Iraq–Persia front is the one place where he might restore his reputation as active operations are more than probable.'[43] Churchill was not so insensitive as to fail to understand what irked the man. Auchinleck, as Churchill told Attlee, was 'seriously upset by the turn of events', and clearly viewed charge of Persia and Iraq Command as a demotion.[44] Explaining Auchinleck's unwillingness to accept the position to the War Cabinet, Churchill added that the general did not think that PAIC 'was a very good arrangement. Second, his confidence in himself had suffered a severe shock as the result of his supersession' as Commander-in-Chief Middle East.[45]

Precious days were wasted waiting on Auchinleck's decision. After his visit to Moscow and an exhausting series of meetings with Stalin, the prime minister returned to Cairo after a stop-off at the British legation in Tehran. Here Churchill stayed not at the main legation but in the 'cool, quiet glades of the summer residence, high above the city'.[46] Developing his thinking regarding the new command, on 19 August he wrote to Attlee, Eden, Ismay and Roosevelt, explaining how he proposed to place on the southern flank of the Soviet armies a substantial British and later American force to strengthen the Soviet Union, and to form 'the advance shield of all our interests in Persia and Abadan, for moral effect of comradeship with the Russians'.[47]

On 21 August Churchill sent a secret telegram to the War Cabinet, arguing that the establishment of Persia and Iraq Command, the expansion of the Tenth Army and the strategic study of the growing danger from the Caucasus were urgent. 'Consequently a general must be appointed before I leave who will be responsible to HMG for taking all the decisions affecting Persia-Iraq area which would otherwise have been taken by General Alexander' as the new Commander-in-Chief Middle East. Britain would 'build up a separate command as quickly as possible . . . [The new commander-in-chief] will have allocated to him forthwith the principal elements out of which the Persia-Iraq Command and its HQ will be formed.'[48]

Clearly, on that particular day, both Brooke and Churchill had decided that immediate resolution was required. The prime minister reiterated the imperative need for a new and separate command, 'lightening the burden on General Alexander and beginning the expansion of the Tenth Army and large scale preparations to meet the enemy in Persia.' These matters, he said, 'cannot be delayed even for a single day. [Consequently] I have availed myself of Cabinet consent in principle and have appointed Wilson from tonight.'[49] On 21 August, therefore, General Sir Henry Maitland 'Jumbo' Wilson became the first Commander-in-Chief Persia and Iraq, and on the following day the new command was formally established. The War Cabinet met specially to discuss three telegrams sent from Churchill from the Western Desert which had been received during the night and which detailed what Brooke termed this 'step of great importance'.[50]

Wilson had been General Officer Commanding British Troops Egypt since before the war and had impressed in the early Western Desert fighting. He subsequently commanded the imperial forces in the abortive Greece

campaign, and as GOC British Forces Palestine and Trans-Jordan had over-
seen the successful operations in Lebanon and Syria. His nickname came
from his appearance: 'Tall, immensely fat, with kind little twinkly eyes, he
looks exactly like an elephant – an elephant standing on its hind legs.'[51]
Wilson recalled the circumstances of his appointment:

> The Prime Minister sent for me one evening and said he wanted me to
> go as Commander-in-Chief to a new command he was making in Persia
> and Iraq in view of the advance of the southern wing of the German
> armies towards Stalingrad and the Caucasus. He told me that he had
> previously offered the command to Auchinleck, who had refused it. The
> question of a separate command for Persia and Iraq had been a subject
> of discussion for quite a time in view of its distance from Cairo and the
> administrative problems arising from the Persian Gulf ports which had
> been under the commander of the Tenth Army (Quinan); the time had
> come, with the prospect of his army having an operational role in the
> near future, that he should be released from that responsibility.[52]

Wilson took with him Major-General Joseph Baillon of the Ninth Army
(the designation of British forces in Palestine and Trans-Jordan since
November 1941) as his Chief of Staff, 'and Selby who had been clearing out
Eritrea, as chief administrative officer'. Though Wilson assumed the position on 21 August, 'I was not allowed to leave Cairo until 7 September after
the defeat of Rommel's attempt to break through our position on the El
Alamein Line [he was commanding the Ninth Army, responsible for the
Nile Delta]. Then for the fourth time I left that city to take up a new assignment.'[53] Brooke wrote on 21 August that Churchill had 'produced a new
paper on the organization of PAIC', and that Wilson was delighted to accept
the command and 'get the show started'. He was soon holding a conference
at the British Embassy to address the manner in which America would join
the effort to supply the Soviets via Iran. 'It is imperative,' Brooke wrote, 'that
something should be done quickly as the Germans are pushing on into the
Caucasus rapidly. Our defences in Iraq–Persia are lamentably weak. Jumbo
Wilson will have an uphill task!'[54]

CHAPTER 13

'Jumbo' and the Germans

Following Churchill's decisive intervention, the business of forming Persia and Iraq Command (PAIC) commenced. It was up to Jumbo Wilson to get things moving quickly, to build on what had already been achieved under Quinan's command and to prepare a force that would grow to a strength of over 100,000 troops. In preparing to fight the Germans and improving the region's transport infrastructure and military establishment, Wilson was continuing work that had started as early as the spring of 1941. 'The vital network of signal lines for the control and maintenance of operations over so large an area had been planned and started by Tenth Army Headquarters which under the selfless, energetic and skilful leadership of General Quinan tackled that and many other formidable tasks.'[1]

Wilson's first task was to physically form a new headquarters in Baghdad – preparing the headquarters buildings, recruiting staff and transporting them and their equipment by land and by sea. There was then the small matter of mustering the requisite military resources – a planned total of nine army divisions and twenty squadrons of fighters and bombers – so that the command could perform the tasks that it had been created to undertake. PAIC officially opened on 15 September 1942. Arrangements were made, wrote Wilson, 'to convey staff and a good deal of office and signal equipment to Baghdad, most of it going in convoy across the Syrian desert'.[2] Wilson used his own journey from Cairo to the Iraqi capital to reconnoitre the terrain that he was charged with defending and to inspect the region's logistical infrastructure. He travelled via Aleppo to Mosul, where he stayed with the British consul, a man who had been imprisoned by the Iraqi army during the previous year's rebellion. Wilson then crossed the mountains of Kurdistan through the Rawandiz gorge and over the Iranian border before crossing back into Iraq to Kirkuk, where he stayed with Major-General Eric Miles, commanding officer of the 56th (London) Infantry Division, one of his new units.

Arriving in Baghdad on 23 September, Wilson was put up at the British Embassy on the banks of the Tigris by Sir Kinahan Cornwallis and his wife. Well over three-quarters of the 460 people who would form his headquarters staff had already been appointed. In order to liaise between the new command and its Middle East Command neighbour, Wilson left a brigadier and six staff officers in Cairo.[3] The memoirs of Hermione, Countess of Ranfurly, offer an insight into the rhythm and routine of PAIC headquarters. Making her own journey from Cairo, she had flown to RAF Habbaniya, apprehensively contemplating her new job on Wilson's staff while in the air. She was met on arrival by Mark Chapman-Walker, Wilson's military assistant. 'As we drove to Baghdad,' she wrote, 'he explained the situation regarding Persia–Iraq Command':

> Our position depends on the Russians; if they defeat the Germans on the Stalingrad front the chances of war in this Theatre will diminish; if they fail and the Germans come through the Caucasus we shall have a hard time holding them in the Paytak Pass which we have fortified. We have only two Corps, one British and one Indian, and it would take time to get reinforcements from India or the Middle East; we cannot ask for them till we really need them – manpower is short and shipping not available. If a disaster happened and the Germans forced our Paytak Line we have planned to 'scorched earth' Abadan ... our main task is to guard and develop the routes by which Allied aid is being sent from the Persian Gulf to Russia. This is not easy: Japanese submarines are thought to be operating in the Persian Gulf; pro-Axis elements are trying to stir up trouble amongst the tribes in Persia where there is already a good deal of unrest owing to inflation and a serious wheat shortage.[4]

All of this while travelling the 55 miles from the airbase to the capital city. 'As we drove through the outskirts of a poor little town I interrupted Mark to ask its name. "Baghdad", he said.'[5] Shortly afterwards, the vehicle 'drew up at a small villa surrounded by a sea of mud: our Headquarters'.[6] Here she met General Wilson's aide-de-camp, Francis Dorrien-Smith, who showed her where she would work. 'I am delighted with my office', which 'they have taken immense trouble over. It is a small room [containing] a map of the Caucasus and a tooth glass full of flowers.' There was a peep hole in the door giving on to Wilson's office – 'so that we don't barge in when he is busy or asleep.'[7] 'General Jumbo was sitting at his desk with his tin spectacles on the end of his nose,' she wrote, holding 'a fly swotter in one hand'. Ranfurly was invited to stay at the British Embassy until she could find lodgings, which she soon did, in Freya Stark's house.

As well as preparing to fight German forces if they invaded the region, and developing the supply line to the Soviet Union, challenges facing Wilson's new command included the provision of internal security and helping to move grain to feed civilians. Reflecting British preoccupations in the region, the first files Ranfurly was given to study were entitled 'Persia: Pro-German elements'; 'Defence'; 'Inflation'; 'Wheat'; 'Poles: Refugees'; 'Formation of "Polish Army in the East"'; 'Abadan: Defence'; 'Demolition'; 'Iraq Army, Rashid Ali: The Golden Square'; 'Quashquai: Tribes'; and 'Jap submarines in Persian Gulf'.

> I have to go to the office first to unlock the safe and desk drawers and type out the day's programme. Soon after eight thirty General Jumbo arrives – I always know when he is coming because the sentry on the front door stamps to attention. Then our day begins: orderlies in heavy boots clatter along the stone passages; telephones peal unceasingly – Francis draws wild fowl on his blotting paper while he answers them; Iraqi, Polish, Indian and British visitors arrive and salute – salute and depart. The General's bell keeps ringing for Mark who drafts all his telegrams; sometimes the buzzer calls for me to take down letters.[8]

For the Empire's forces to meet the threat of German invasion here, the lines of communication would need to bear the 2,000 tons of supplies that landed at Basra each day before being unloaded and carried in barges across the Shatt al-Arab, then reloaded onto railways at the Iranian ports. Foreseeing this, Auchinleck had built at Tanamu, opposite Basra, facilities linked to the railway, and ordered materials from India for a bridge of boats to provide road and rail access from Iraqi ports to Iranian railways and roads.[9] Indian sappers provided pontoons and in 4 days built the longest boat bridge in world, spanning 950 feet.[10] The long logistics chain linking the northern area of potential combat operations to the Gulf ports required the establishment of advanced workshops for the repair of tanks, guns and vehicles along with the creation of hospitals, convalescent depots and reinforcement camps. Wilson's construction programme included vast workshop spaces, though, even tapping local resources, the supply of skilled labour still fell short by 15,000 men.[11] Rest camps to give the troops a spell away from the intense summer heat were established at Kerend-e Gharb in the province of Kermanshah in Iran, and at Penjwin on the Iranian frontier of the Sulaymaniyah province. PAIC was supplied largely from India and relied on Indian military labour, administrative and communications support. In October 1942, for instance, India was providing engineer, signal and administrative units, as well as motor transport companies and labour battalions, and PAIC was to remain a considerable indentation on India's military resources for the rest of the war. Supplies for the Soviet Union would come from Britain and elsewhere from around the Empire, and on 9 October Churchill wrote to Stalin to inform him that 'we will send to you as soon as possible, by the Persian Gulf route, 150 Spitfires, with the equivalent of 50 more in the form of spares'.[12]

The simultaneous pursuit of PAIC's dual main tasks – preparing to face invasion and supplying the Soviet Union – was not always compatible. A far greater American commitment was thus required, given new urgency by the virtual cessation of the Arctic convoys. It was agreed that only the Americans were capable of providing the requisite increase in the load-bearing capacity of the Iranian supply route.[13] The American Service of Supply Iran Mission under Colonel Don Shingler began to focus exclusively on improving Iranian port facilities, rather than helping develop infrastructure in Iraq for the benefit of the Tenth Army. In June 1942 the mission was re-designated the Iran–Iraq Service Command, subordinate to the Cairo headquarters of US Army Forces in the Middle East. Shortly thereafter and reflecting its expansion and growing status, America's presence in the region was re-designated Persian Gulf Service Command. The word 'service' was soon dropped, as it was 'highly unpopular' among the troops of the command who 'felt they could detect in it an implication of general housework'.[14]

On 13 July 1942 Roosevelt's special envoy to Europe, W. Averell Harriman, had suggested to Harry Hopkins that America should offer to take over the Iranian railway in anticipation of the termination of the Arctic convoys. President Roosevelt endorsed this in a letter to Churchill on 16 July, in which he said that nothing should be omitted that would 'increase traffic through Persia'. He suggested that American railwaymen should take over the operation of the railway – 'they are first class at this sort of thing' – and asked the prime minister what he thought about this.[15] Churchill replied on 22 August. He wrote that traffic on the Trans-Iranian Railway was expected to reach 3,000 tons per day by the end of the year. The British government and local commanders, he added, were convinced that this could be doubled. This was 'to ensure an increase in Russian supplies while building up our forces which we must move into North Persia' to fight the Wehrmacht should it defeat the Red Army. To achieve this, additional railway personnel were required, as well as more rolling stock and technical equipment. Therefore, Churchill said, we 'welcome and accept your proposal' for a US Army takeover, which would include the improvement and operation of the ports at Bandar-e Shahpur, Khorramshahr and Umm Qasr in Iraq (this last newly built), to which the first American servicemen to arrive in theatre had already been assigned. They would also take over the operation of the railway in the British zone. The allocation of traffic, however, was to remain under the control of British military authorities 'for whom the railway is an essential channel of communications for operational purposes' for fighting the enemy.[16] The Americans would also operate an aircraft assembly plant at Abadan, two truck assembly plants at Andimeshk and ordnance repair and assembly centres at Umm Qasr.

In addition, it was agreed that the Americans should operate a truck fleet to supplement that of the UKCC. The president accepted these proposals, and on 25 August instructed the War Department to prepare a plan. Drawn up by the Strategic Logistics Division, it was ready by 4 September. The British would remain responsible for the ports of Abadan, Ahwaz and Basra and their existing road supply line. The new railway plan envisaged an additional 75 locomotives, 2,200 freight cars of 20 tons and 7,200 trucks averaging 7 tons. In September the combined American and British Chiefs of Staff endorsed this new mission for the US Army.

PAIC's composition and plans to fight the Germans

General Wilson's orders were clear and simple: '1) To secure at all costs from land and air attack the oil fields and oil installations of Persia and Iraq; 2) to ensure the transport from the Persian Gulf ports of supplies to Russia to the maximum extent possible without prejudicing my primary military task.'[17] Of course, the clarity and brevity of the orders belied the enormous challenges associated with their execution. It was considered 'more than probable' that the Iran–Iraq region would see fighting.[18] At the time of PAIC's foundation, Stalin had twenty-five divisions allocated for the defence of the Caucasus mountain line, but the Chiefs of Staff were 'by no means reassured'.[19] With Soviet capacity to resist seriously doubted in London and Washington, the Chiefs of Staff were determined that if the Soviets crumbled, then the Germans should be made to fight every inch of the way once they set foot in the Iran–Iraq region. This was Wilson's primary task.

Aside from the worrying prospect of major combat operations against the German army, other challenges included the initial lack of sufficient forces, the composite nature of those that were available and the difficult terrain and inadequate lines of communication stretching the 600 miles from the Gulf ports to the areas in which the fighting would likely take place. Those lines of communication had to bear the increasing weight of Anglo-American military aid to the Soviet Union as well as moving and supplying Wilson's fighting formations. There was an obvious tension between the two tasks.

PAIC was multinational in composition, consisting predominantly of men from India and Nepal – home of the men who formed the Indian Army's Gurkha regiments – as well as Britons and Poles. 'The Army in Persia and Iraq', as Churchill called the Tenth Army, would comprise one Indian armoured division and one British armoured brigade, two British and three Indian infantry divisions and the Polish Army of the East, comprising two infantry divisions and two tank brigades.[20] It grew rapidly to control three corps headquarters. In planning the deployment of the Tenth Army in order to meet the Germans, Wilson's challenge was to handle a rapidly assembled army in an unfamiliar theatre, and to prepare it to fight at very short notice. 'It is not generally realized,' he wrote, 'how vast is the difference between fighting a campaign with units and formations made up to establishment with modern equipment compared with having to operate with the shortages which confronted our commanders in the early days of the war when often one division had to be practically immobilized to allow another to operate.'[21]

Though the Tenth Army was expanding, few of its units were battle-hardened and fewer still were trained for mountain – as opposed to desert and jungle – fighting. Furthermore, many of its units were not fully kitted out. When Wilson took up the reins the only troops fit and ready to meet a German invasion were two Indian infantry divisions and an Indian armoured division. The two infantry divisions, the 6th and the 8th, were each a brigade down, and were below establishment and deficient in artillery, engineers and signals. The armoured division, the 31st, had no medium tanks, and all three were short of transport.[22] Nevertheless, at that stage, even if it had had more troops ready to fight, PAIC could not have maintained more than this force in northern Iran without substantial administrative reinforcements. By December 1942 the combined British and Indian forces in Iraq and Iran totalled six divisions and one independent brigade, plus the two Polish divisions.[23]

The 3rd Carpathian Division was the nucleus around which the Polish Army in the East was forming. As it assembled at Khanaqin in Iraq it had to be trained and equipped, though many of its men were still suffering from ill health engendered by their incarceration in Soviet labour camps.[24] On a visit to Iraq in October 1942, Sir Richard Casey, the Resident Minister Middle East, met General Władysław Anders, the Polish commander, and told Churchill of 'the very good impression of his Polish troops' he had formed. Anders was keen 'to secure the release of the estimated 60,000 Poles still languishing in Russian labour battalions'.[25] The Countess of Ranfurly met Anders on a visit to PAIC headquarters: 'his soldiers are slowly recovering from their terrible time in Stalin's camps: when they first arrived they were riddled with disease and practically starving'.[26] With surprising speed, they became an army, and at the end of August Anders had the pleasure of visiting Bandar-e Pahlavi and taking the salute as the 15,000 men of the 5th and 6th Polish divisions marched past.[27]

British and Indian divisions arrived in theatre to bring PAIC up to strength. The 5th British Division joined Wilson's command in the autumn of 1942, its soldiers unpleasantly surprised by the heat of the Persian Gulf as compared to that of India.[28] Heat was a life-threatening menace in this theatre. On advancing into Iraq in May 1941, Habforce troops had been subject to 'very strict water discipline' – men only drinking at halts on the order of an officer – and troops were ordered to wear sun helmets, 'a precaution which was never necessary in the Western Desert'.[29] The subaltern John Masters recalled a sailor rushing onto deck as his troopship approached Basra and throwing himself overboard, and one of his Gurkha soldiers dying from heatstroke as they marched to attack Habib Shawi while pushing the Iraqis back from Basra.[30]

Landing at Maqil, the port of Basra, the troops of the 5th Division were taken to Shaibah to be reunited with their vehicles. The next stage of the journey took them to the first staging camp at Ur, visiting the remains of Babylon, the troops frequently seeing mirages 'ranging from mountains and lakes to English Public Houses'.[31] They headed next to Lancer Camp south of

Baghdad and then on to Khanaqin, where they joined up with units that had made the journey from the Gulf by rail. Here they drove past 'miles and miles of Polish refugee camps'.[32] Crossing the border into Iran, the division's vehicles, numbered in their thousands, drove up the steep and winding Pai Tak Pass, 'a terrifying experience for the Division's drivers'.[33] They reached the garrison town of Kermanshah, where the whole division was reunited by 5 October. Here they focused on training – marching, company schemes and anti-tank and other weapons shooting. To avoid the worst of the winter, the division moved to the holy city of Qom. While stationed here, the famous gold dome of the shrine of Fatimah Masumeh was used as an aiming point by the artillery.

There were occasional deployments to show the flag or help temper unrest; the divisional artillery drove its guns through Hamadan, a detachment guarded PAIC GHQ in Baghdad and another guarded Tenth Army HQ at Sultanabad. The division's troops were also called in to keep the peace in Tehran, including battalions of the Northamptonshires, the Wiltshires and the Seaforth Highlanders. The Highlanders camped for a month in December on the Tehran racecourse at the time of the bread riots. The Soviet forces were generally aloof but, the divisional history records, were as susceptible to the regimental pipe band as the locals. The band would regularly lead the troops on route marches; on one occasion an Iranian army platoon attached itself to the column.[34] The highlight of Hogmanay 1942 was a dance in the racecourse totalisator hall, for which 120 Polish Auxiliary Territorial Service women were 'borrowed' as partners. While leave was permitted in Tehran, Qom was mostly out of bounds. There were occasional visits from entertainment troupes, including Terry-Thomas's 'You're Welcome' ENSA party, which visited Qom and other areas where imperial troops were concentrated. While stationed at Kermanshah, valued hospitality was to be found at Taq-e Bostan, 10 miles away, 'the little oasis of the British Colony of the oil company's pumping station. Here was hospitality indeed from a pleasant little outpost of empire.'[35]

The 5th Division was joined by other British and Indian infantry and armoured formations. In the event of German invasion, Wilson's intent was to meet the enemy as far north as possible and defeat it. He simply could not allow German armoured formations to penetrate beyond the mountains and reach the plains, where their armour would be effective and they could develop airstrips with which to bomb the southern oilfields. He was never going to have enough troops for static defence, so manoeuvrability was the key, and defences were prepared to support a mobile battlefront extending over a large area. The Chiefs of Staff, the War Office and GHQ Middle East estimated that the Germans might reach the River Araxes in northern Iran by October 1942. This was based on their assessment that in the short term the Germans 'best scenario' would see them capture Rostov and break the Soviets on the southern front. If this happened, 3–5 German divisions and 200–300 aircraft might be expected to advance into Iran from the direction of Astara and Tabriz in the first half of October.[36]

Wilson decided that the best defensive positions were to be found in the mountain passes of Chalus and Manjil, leading respectively from the Caspian coast to Tehran and Qazvin, and in the mountainous country around Mianeh astride the Tabriz–Tehran road. If the Germans avoided these routes, or advanced farther west, the mountains south of Sanandaj and the passes leading from Lake Urmia into northern Iraq would afford the British strong defensive positions. If all efforts in the north failed, Lieutenant-General Quinan had prepared a final defensive line farther south and west. German agents were active on the ground, and in collaboration with the leader of the Qashqai had already begun to develop airbases and were planning to link up with German forces when they had overcome Soviet resistance and were in a position to move towards Iran and Iraq.

British strategy for the defence of Iran, Iraq and the Gulf revolved around mountain warfare, most recently experienced by imperial forces during the campaign in Abyssinia (and to a limited extent during Slim's assault on the Pai Tak Pass). Fighting in mountainous regions offered the British, as the defenders, the advantage of making it difficult for the enemy to develop the airfields that the Luftwaffe would need in order to put the oilfields out of action. Between the open country about Qazvin, Tehran and Hamadan in the south and the River Araxes in the north, the only areas offering reasonable facilities for airfields were in the valley between Ardebil and Tabriz and around Lankaran on the Caspian coast. The British, therefore, needed to ensure possession of this region and its denial to the enemy. However, Wilson wrote, 'the forces I could maintain north of this important area were not strong enough to fight a successful battle if the Germans attacked in strength'. He therefore 'decided to fight the main defensive battle on the front line of the Elburz–Mianeh mountains'.[37] This line would be held and 'the intention was to send forward to the River Araxes whatever mobile force I could maintain to delay a German advance for as long as possible'.[38] Wilson's review of issues relating to time, distance and climate convinced him that he had to maintain the equivalent of one corps of two divisions just south-west of Qazvin and another corps at Khanaqin.[39] The probable 'Axis superiority in armour could be fully exploited to our disadvantage once the battle were to pass south of Kasvin'. Wilson thus wanted to concentrate his forces in areas where they would be certain of anticipating the Germans in the north.

In his pursuit of a 'balanced fighting force' capable of fighting German troops in early 1943, Wilson assigned III (British) Corps and XXI (Indian) Corps a British and an Indian division each, with extra divisions being added as they arrived. Together with the 31st Indian Armoured Division and the 10th Indian Motor Brigade, the two corps were placed under the command of the Tenth Army. Wilson retained the third corps, formed of a Polish division and two Indian brigades, under his personal command as a general reserve, integrating the British 7th Armoured Brigade with the Indian infantry. The defence of northern Iraq against German attack eastwards from Lake Urmia was entrusted to a Polish division and two divisions of the Iraqi army. Another major front from which a German attack might develop was through Anatolia, hence the extensive defensive work undertaken in the Mosul area and the retention here of forces adequate to meet an attack from up to five divisions.

In late 1942 most of the command's troops were in the highlands around Hamadan and Kermanshah, though Wilson intended to withdraw all forces to the railways for the winter to reduce the strain on transport and allow for refitting before the spring. The force maintained in Iran was reduced to one division and a motor brigade based at Qom and Andimeshk respectively. The rest of the troops moved to training locations in Iraq. Wilson was able to affect this change because, by the end of September 1942, the 'toughening of the Russian resistance to the German advance made a winter campaign in North Persia appear improbable'.[40] Even better news came when the final Battle of El Alamein in October and November, and its widely celebrated victory, further removed the German threat to the Iran–Iraq region. The timetable was moving inexorably in Wilson's favour.

In terms of air power, five RAF squadrons were dedicated to defending northern Iran and Iraq, a deceptively low figure. This was because the British were prepared to rapidly reinforce the theatre should the need arise. Preparations to make this practicable included stockpiling enough fuel, munitions and spare parts to support thirty-two squadrons for up to six months of combat operations. London's plans for PAIC envisaged the expansion of air forces in theatre to seventy-five squadrons by the end of September

1942 and eighty-eight by 31 December if necessary, an enormous air commitment. These figures included thirteen American squadrons by the end of September and twenty-four by 31 December. At the time of PAIC's creation, the government was also considering moving twenty squadrons to the southern Soviet Union from the Middle East if Rommel were decisively defeated. The scale of forces required depended entirely on the strategic situation, and whether or not the Soviets held the line against the Germans. Juggling an expanding range of commitments and available military resources, and having the region's infrastructure ready to sustain increasing force levels, was the key to imperial and allied defence of the region.

Though in the end British forces did not fight with the Soviets against the Germans, the fact that this was seriously considered is a point of more than passing interest, not least because it offers insights into what British decision-makers were having to contemplate and plan for at this crucial stage of the war. Planning to fight in this region was made more difficult by the fact that the Soviets were 'not prepared to accept joint planning, and permission had to be asked, and granted, to enter their zone'. Because of the Soviet Union's 'suspicious obstructiveness', Wilson observed, 'it was difficult to study the terrain which would be likely to be used in operations'.[41] Casey highlighted this difficulty in his correspondence with Churchill. He told the prime minister of Wilson's desire for an advanced base in the Soviet zone, but the lack of permission to develop it. The general was 'disturbed at complete absence of any contact with the Russians fighting in the Caucasus and with [the] general atmosphere of suspicion with which Russia regard us in Persia'.[42]

Casey described Wilson's dilemmas in a further report to Churchill. He could keep his forces at a level just suitable for internal security purposes, and focus on reinforcing the RAF – if he could be sure of the command's security from land and sea invasion until the spring of 1943. If this were the planning assumption, he could dedicate maximum transport for military aid to the Soviet Union. But if he were preparing to fight the Germans, they had to be stopped as far north as possible as the RAF would need landing grounds within easy range of the Caucasus. Given that the supply of Wilson's essential forward forces conflicted with Soviet supply needs, highest level representations were made to Moscow in order to get Stalin to agree to the requisite diversion of tonnage from military aid to supplying the Tenth Army as it prepared to fight.[43]

The delivery of aid was hampered by the slow arrival of locomotives, poor staff, a lack of experienced personnel and the dearth of cranes for dock work, which was a problem because lots of very heavy cargoes were arriving, such as steel plate and rails. There was then the slow development of the base depots on the railway network at Ahwaz and Andimeshk. Wilson found that he could not move construction stores fast enough without disrupting the flow of aid to the Soviet Union, and that he needed to clear Soviet goods stored on transit 'before our operations in Northern Persia begin'.

In other military preparations, Wilson needed to transfer hospitals and reserves now in Iraq and to pursue an 'extensive accommodation programme for those required to live and work in the notoriously bad climate of the base areas'. As if all of this was not enough to contend with, Wilson was subject to the frustrating withdrawal of resources that afflicted most British land, air and sea commanders throughout the war. As one theatre gained momentary priority because of major offensive or defensive operations, a neighbouring theatre would find itself denuded of resources. Thus in the summer of 1942, PAIC had lost 1,500 vehicles to Middle East Command to support operations in the Western Desert. They were, Wilson noted ruefully in October, yet to be replaced.[44] Similarly, the number of Indian troops in fighting formations in Iran and Iraq had fallen from 60,000 in April 1942 to 25,000 in August 1942, not least because units such as the 10th Indian Division had been rushed to North Africa.[45]

On 23 October 1942 Casey reported again to Churchill, this time on a recent eight-day visit to Iran. Regarding the situation still facing General Wilson, he wrote that 'his inability to get his troops forward into north-west Persia before the winter is, as you know, brought about by lack of cooperation on the part of the Russians, and by reasons of transport problems on the Persian line of communications, which will not yet carry adequate aid to Russia as well as the tonnage necessary to maintain substantial British forces in north Persia'. At that particular moment, the Tenth Army was focusing on training and reconnaissance of the ground on which it might have to fight.[46]

Scorched earth and special forces

As in Iraq, Britain had numerous pyrotechnic plans ready in case they needed to perform a scorched-earth retreat in Iran. In case the Germans did invade and looked like overwhelming Wilson's army, 'worst-case scenario' plans were devised. These involved the employment of special forces to conduct sabotage and behind-enemy-lines operations against an invading force, as well the destruction of essential lines of communication and infra-structure. If the British were going to lose their oil, they would do their level best to ensure that it was not scooped by the enemy. Wallace Lyon, political adviser for northern Iraq, one of the main regions threatened by German invasion, wrote that the north-east was experiencing significant turmoil because of the presence of large numbers of British, Indian and Polish troops. If the Germans then 'hammering away at Stalingrad' succeeded, 'there was practically nothing to stop them driving south through Persia to Iraq. Already the oil wells were being cemented and the plant prepared for demolition.'[47]

Other standard precautions were also being applied as part of the exten-sive British preparations to defend the region and deny its resources to the enemy. Special Operations Executive (SOE) were present on the ground, agents originally arriving to form sabotage teams though their main role became 'the covert production and dissemination of written and oral prop-aganda in an attempt to smear pro-German politicians, generate rumours, and inspire an anti-German spirit.'[48] Following the successful Iraq model, in 1942 it was decided to significantly extend SOE's operations in Iran. Gifts were judiciously disbursed in order to court friendship, and pro-British clubs, receptions and entertainments were quietly sponsored. Covert prop-aganda mostly involved oral propaganda and the spreading of rumours. The objective was to establish friendly relations and gain influence with important sections of society, such as young military officers, intellectual circles and local and national notables. These SOE activities in Iran were coordinated by Lieutenant-Colonel H.J. Underwood, political adviser to PAIC at Abadan.[49] In both Iran and Iraq, SOE aimed to gain influence for the British government and its representatives 'by using unacknowledge-able methods, of which bribery is only the mildest.'[50]

Deception activities were also initiated. 'A' Force Special Units were created in an attempt to fool enemy intelligence, and 'K' Detachment SAS Brigade, a phantom airborne force, was employed, as it had already been in the Western Desert. American special camouflage companies assisted in the work of constructing fake military units. Dummy tank units appeared in Iran under the guise of fictional Indian cavalry regiments such as '303 Indian Armoured Brigade', developed by Force 'X', raised originally in Iraq as a camouflage unit 'to manipulate and operate dummy tanks.'[51] A special workshop for the construction of dummy military vehicles and infrastruc-ture was created by the Tenth Army under Wilson, along with the 65th, 66th

and 67th cavalry regiments, for 'strategic deception as to our strength in
Iraq and Persia, and with a view to tactical deception in the event of active
operations'.[52] This was initially intended to cover the fact that the new
command had few armoured units actually under command, though the
situation changed from October 'in that real armoured units have material-
ized'. From the time of the battles of El Alamein, writes Sir Michael Howard,
'A' Force maintained 'a notional threat to Crete with the object of containing
Axis forces in the Aegean and Balkans and preventing the dispatch of reinforcements to Rommel and the opening of a new front in Iran and Turkey'.[53]

In September Wilson summoned to his headquarters in Baghdad Captain
Fitzroy Maclean, a rising star in the Special Air Service (SAS) regiment with
experience operating behind enemy lines in Libya:

> On my return from Kufra [a strategic oasis group in south-eastern
> Cyrenaica], I was ordered to proceed to G. H. Q. Persia and Iraq
> Command at Baghdad to discuss with the Commander-in-Chief,
> General Maitland Wilson, the possibility of raising a small force on
> S.A.S. lines to operate on enemy-occupied territory in Persia in the
> event of a German break through ... There was no time to be lost. I
> hurried down to the Canal Zone, collected a new jeep, some maps and a
> week's rations, some warm clothes and Guardsman Duncan, and set out
> post haste for Baghdad and points east.[54]

Maclean crossed the Suez Canal and the Sinai Desert, stopping on his
way at Gaza, Beersheba and Damascus, 'sleeping and eating by the roadside'.
Arriving in Baghdad, he reported as ordered to Wilson, 'a massive man'
combining 'a somewhat weighty manner with great alertness of intellect and
an altogether remarkable eye for country'.[55] (The Countess of Ranfurly
meanwhile had noted the arrival at PAIC HQ of 'a tall, angular young man
dressed in a kilt'.) Maclean had been brought to Iraq to recruit and raise an
SAS regiment from among the soldiery of Persia and Iraq Command, to be
'held in readiness for operations behind enemy lines if the Germans break
through the Caucasus'. Wilson gave Maclean authority to raise a force of
about 150 volunteers from troops under his command, to be known as M
Detachment SAS Regiment, directly responsible to Wilson. Maclean spent
the next few weeks 'touring British units in Persia, calling for volunteers and
at the same time making a reconnaissance of those parts of the country
which seemed most likely to furnish bases for irregular operations'.[56] There

was an abundance of volunteers due in large measure to the prolonged inactivity of the forces in Iran, and men were 'ready to give up rank and pay in return for the prospect of early action'.[57]

After recruiting his private army, whose members undertook an intensive training programme that featured parachuting and other methods of infiltration, Maclean toured areas of Iran from which he might mount operations against German invaders. In a jeep filled with food and petrol he visited Khanaqin, Kermanshah, Hamadan, Qazvin and Tehran. The mountainous regions provided ideal conditions for irregular operations. From Tehran he went north over the Elburz Range into the Soviet-occupied provinces of Gilan and Mazandaran on the shores of the Caspian, 'where the semi-tropical jungle offered excellent cover for guerrillas'. Then, it was westwards into Lorestan and south into the Dasht-e Kavir, 'the vast and largely unexplored Salt Desert stretching right across Central Persia':

> Here there were clearly possibilities of reproducing the conditions under which we had operated in the Western Desert. Aircraft could land, supplies could be dropped. There were excellent facilities for camouflage and lying up. Most important of all, the railway line, the main roads and Tehran itself were all within striking distance. Indeed the possibilities of making things hot for an occupying force were everywhere so good that it seemed to me incredible that the Germans had not tried something of the sort.[58]

Numerous other 'stay-behind' and scorched-earth plans were put in place in case the Germans arrived. Wallace Lyon was allowed to recruit four British officers to assist him and necessary local staff, as well as three specialists sent to him for training. They were specialists in the use of explosives, and 'in the event of the enemy driving over the Caucasus and occupying Iraq, would stay behind in command of guerrilla bands to disrupt their organization and lines of communication. While under my care they were to learn Kurdish and make friends with the tribal chiefs whose cooperation would be needed in the event of a British withdrawal'.[59]

German plans

Did German activities warrant the considerable investment of time and resources that the British put in to the defence of the Iran–Iraq region? The answer to this question is complicated by the fact that British endeavours reflected London's desire to seize the moment created by war and strengthen its position in a region of primary importance to the British Empire. British investment here also reflected the fact that they could afford to take no chances. Though opinion on likelihood varied, enough senior people thought that the German threat was real, because of the chance of German forces winning in North Africa and the Soviet Union. On the German side of the equation, efforts to take the Iran–Iraq region were piecemeal and uncoordinated. Propaganda was perhaps the strongest suit, other specific investments in Iran and Iraq amounting to the failed support for Rashid Ali's coup and the deployment of secret agents to Iran tasked with preparing the region for a German invasion – raising rebellion in the British rear to smooth their arrival, sabotaging their defences and preparing airstrips from which the Luftwaffe could attack. More indirectly because never actually deployed, the Germans also invested in the formation of an 'Arab legion' that would rally opponents of the British, in Iraq, Palestine and Syria.

There were other plans, too, to make good German objectives in the region. On 30 September 1942 Churchill sent a secret telegram to Stalin. Referring to Ultra he said that 'information from the source I used to warn you of the impending attack on Russia' had revealed that the Germans 'have already appointed an Admiral to take charge of naval operations in the Caspian. They have selected Makhach-Kala [in Dagestan] as their main naval base.' A force of about twenty submarines, minesweepers and torpedo boats was to be assembled and transported by rail from Mariupol [in Ukraine] to the Caspian 'as soon as they get a line open'. This latest development, Churchill opined, 'seems to make even more important the plan to reinforce you by about twenty squadrons of allied aircraft in the Caspian and Caucasus theatre'.[60]

For the Germans at this time, it was all about the big picture. Iran and Iraq, frankly, did not warrant maximum effort because they would simply fall to Germany once victory had been achieved elsewhere. At the time of PAIC's creation, confidence in this ultimate outcome remained high. Germany's allies in Iran and Iraq – and there were many of them, all wanting German help to rid them of the British or the Soviets, clear the Middle East of Jews or, in the case of Iran, help effect internal regime change or regional independence – still expected victory. Rashid Ali and the Grand Mufti were 'activated' for propaganda purposes. Keen to employ both men to foment rebellion, Germany nevertheless wanted to ensure that their activities aligned with the grand strategy, particularly the anticipated victory in the east:

The highlight of the propagandistic activities of the Grand Mufti and
Rashid Ali should comprise the call of both to the Arabian people for an
uprising against the English. The timing, most likely after the capture of
Tbilisi, will be determined by us. Both of them want to move in this
direction. An Iraqi government will be declared there. This appeal will
move the Arabian people to rebellion ... If a victorious German army
appears near the borders of the Arabian countries, there is no doubt that
the Arabian people will rise against England.[61]

Other German initiatives dedicated to the region included the formation
of Sonderstab F. Sonderstab F's instructions were provided by Hitler in his
Directive 30. Its mission was to support Rashid Ali and other Arab nationalists against the British. A Brandenburger Regiment (including ethnic Iranians
trained in Germany), a Luftwaffe component and a Foreign Office component were included, the latter led by Fritz Grobba. A key mission of General
Felmy's Sonderstab F, based in occupied Greece, was to raise, train and
deploy an Arab brigade. German-led, it comprised Arabs who had ended up
in German hands through capture or other means, including pro-German
students who had been studying in Germany, and would be expanded upon
deployment by nationalist volunteers from across the region. The selection
of recruits was carried out by the Grand Mufti and Rashid Ali in agreement
with the Foreign Office and the Oberkommando der Wehrmacht (OKW).
Fritz Grobba was also involved in the brigade's development. Sonderstab F
included a special desert mobile unit, which trained for deployment to Iran
in September 1942. Its intent was probably to conduct operations in the
Mosul oilfields region and to capture the pipeline to Abadan. Efforts were
made to contact Sheikh Mahmud in Iraq to seize and hold the Kirkuk
oilfields until German troops arrived that September.[62]

The intention was to deploy the unit as German forces arrived in the
region, to help stimulate rebellion and cause chaos for the defending British
forces and the forces of the Iranian and Iraqi states:

Regarding the deployment of the Arab volunteers after they enter Arab
lands, the Auswärtiges Amt [the Foreign Office], Sonderstab F, the Grand
Mufti and Gailani have together agreed that they will form the core of the
newly established Iraqi Arabian army. The members of Sonderstab F will
work as instructors in this army. The written formalization of these verbal
agreements, through the exchange of notes between Ribbentrop and

Ciana on the one hand and Gailani and the Grand Mufti on the other,
seems useful … There is a good chance that the largest portion of the
Iraqi army, four divisions prior to the Iraqi-English conflict, will join
Gailani and the Grand Mufti and that additionally the numerous volunteers from Syria and Palestine will flock to them.[63]

The Germans were also thinking ahead about the region's political landscape once the British had been defeated, and engaging with the Italians:
'There is agreement concerning the development of an Iraqi Government
under Gailani. The state reorganization of the other Arabian countries (Syria,
Lebanon, Palestine and Trans Jordan) will best happen through an agreement
between the the German and Italian government on the one hand and with
the Grand Mufti and Gailani, as well as other individual Arabian leaders, on
the other.'[64] Over-confidence, based on a belief in ultimate victory, characterized the discussions of the key protagonists, and unnecessary time and effort
was expended on smoothing relations between the Grand Mufti and Rashid
Ali, who vied for the position of 'top dog' while broadcasting their complaints
regarding Italian involvement in the Middle East's future, which was entirely
unwelcome but to which the Germans had agreed.[65]

The Qashqai and German agents

As with the Kurds of both Iran and Iraq, the Qashqai people saw in the war
and the breakdown of the Iranian state an historic opportunity to seize
confiscated lands and push for greater regional autonomy. Britain's official
line regarding the Qashqai, a largely nomadic community of ethnic Turkic
descent, was that it had no interest in their long-standing dispute with the
shah and the Iranian government. Britain's only interest was in the security
of the oilfields and the lines of communication, and the capture of German
agents and military personnel. Following the invasion and the shah's abdication, the rearmed Qashqai had left their settlements in Fars province and
moved quickly to reclaim former pasturelands. In October 1942 the government tried to disarm them, but after a few skirmishes the Iranian army
declared premature victory and ended the campaign. Clashes between
Qashqai forces and Iranian soldiers continued, the army losing 200 men
and as many as 1,000 soldiers surrendering along with 800 rifles and 63
machine-guns in a notorious battle at the village of Semirom, south of
Isfahan, in July 1943. This significant Qashqai victory led other tribes to

join them, forcing Tehran to offer a truce and begin negotiations. Peace was eventually restored through the mediation of Major-General W.A.K. Fraser, the former commander of 10th Indian Division, now serving as British military attaché to Iran. The Iranian government reluctantly agreed not to interfere in tribal territory, and left the chiefs in charge of the region's security. So, Nasir Khan, the primary sheikh of the Qashqai, became the effective ruler of a large tract of Iranian territory.

The Germans, meanwhile, encouraged the Qashqai to rise and to raid allied convoys and trains. They viewed an alliance with the Qashqai as a way of fomenting rebellion when the Wehrmacht arrived. As a symbol of his German connections, Khan was gifted a golden pistol from Hitler (King Ghazi of Iraq had been given a silver one). For their part, the British bought up food in areas where the Qashqai were unsubdued.

This was part of wider fifth-column preparation. The pro-German resistance movement of Iran had been created by nationalist Iranian politicians and army officers, most prominent among them General Zahedi. In January 1943 six Germans, including a wireless operator, were parachuted into Iran to join up with Franz Mayr, a Nazi agent. Two months later three more landed in the south-west to aid Berthold Schulze-Holthus, the German agent in Fars province who was advising the Qashqai regarding insurrection. He had previously operated from Tabriz, interacting with Azerbaijani nationalists. He was joined by three SS agents who brought with them bags of gold, explosives and letters from Berlin. General Zahedi (a future prime minister) was governor-general of Isfahan, and was identified by the British as the go-between for the Germans and the Qashqai. According to the British, plotting involved a cabinet minister, three members of parliament, eleven generals and many senior army officers, as well as Qashqai leaders.[66]

As what the British termed fifth-column activity increased, counter-intelligence officers had expanded operations against the German network. Thus was the 'extensive plot' instigated by Mayr and others discovered.[67] In August 1942, British counterintelligence officers captured one of the principal German agents along with a gold mine of information that led to the arrest by Iranian police of 170 suspected or proven collaborators and up to 40 army officers, parliamentary deputies and journalists. Mayr was nearly caught in Isfahan but escaped after being tipped off about the raid. British operations against German agents took place across the country, with known German activity in the south-east, for instance, prompting General

Wilson to send a detachment of irregular troops on an extensive mission throughout this area.[68] A detachment of Kurdish commandos was also sent to the Gulf on a four-month mission to investigate reports of German agents and weapons being landed by Japanese submarines.[69]

The latter months of 1942 was a crucial period, when outcomes for the Iran–Iraq region were being decided by battles in North Africa and the Soviet Union. A message informing Gruppe VI, responsible for all German covert operations in the region, that Mayr and Schulze-Holthus were preparing the ground in Iran for further exploitation 'provided speedy help was forthcoming', was received in August following a most circuitous journey via Tokyo. It was viewed as a 'ray of hope'. 'The importance of this independent activity', concluded a post-war British overview of German intelligence activities here, 'cannot be minimized when it is examined in the light of the general war situation in August 1942. The German armies were fighting in the foothills of the Caucasus and at the gates of Egypt. Had either army been able to break through, all the elements which precipitated the rapid fall of Norway, France and the Low Countries in 1940 were operative in Iran, the vital link between Russia and the Western Allies.'[70]

There were to be further arrests, the most prominent and celebrated of which was that of General Fazlollah Zahedi. Fitzroy Maclean received a signal instructing him to report at once to Wilson's Chief of Staff, Major-General Baillon, who had just arrived in Tehran from PAIC headquarters in Baghdad. He was waiting with Bullard at the British legation, and told Maclean that he had a job for him, explaining that German agents were active among the Qashqai and Bakhtiari (another Iranian tribe), and that they 'seemed likely to rise at any moment'. There was a mounting threat to the trans-Iranian supply route and discontent in Isfahan and other towns, largely caused by the hoarding of grain speculators. There was every chance that Iranian troops would side with rioters. Baillon outlined the 'sinister part being played by General Zahedi, commanding Iranian forces in Isfahan area'. He was known to be one of the worst grain-hoarders in the country, and 'it was believed that he was acting in cooperation with the tribal leaders and in touch with German agents living in the hills and through them reporting with German High Command in the Caucasus'.[71] Reports showed he was planning a rising against the allies, in which his troops and those of the Iranian general in the Soviet-occupied northern zone would take part, coinciding with an attack on the Tenth Army by German airborne troops, followed by a German offensive on the Caucasus front.

Altogether, it was a 'delicate situation', as British forces in Iran were spread thin. The nearest British troops to Isfahan were at Qom, 200 miles north. Maclean's task was to help 'nip the trouble in the bud, while avoiding a full-scale showdown'.[72] Baillon and Bullard told him that this would best be done by removing Zahedi, and left him to work out the details as to how this might be achieved. The only stipulations were that the general needed to be taken alive, and without creating a disturbance.

What transpired was Operation Pongo.[73] Maclean went to Isfahan for a reconnaissance. At the British consulate he was welcomed by the consul Charles Gault, a brace of partridge and a bottle of Shiraz. Following their repast, the two men took a stroll past Zahedi's house. Reconnaisance complete, Maclean's plan began to come together: posing as a brigadier, he would call on Zahedi, announcing himself as a senior staff officer from PAIC headquarters in Baghdad come to pay his respects, and then kidnap him. PAIC HQ, however, would not have a captain masquerading as a brigadier, so furnished a genuine colonel instead. Lieutenant-General Desmond Anderson, commander of III Corps and based at Qom, provided the platoon of Seaforth Highlanders, equipped with tommy-guns and hand grenades and commanded by Lieutenant Robertson, to help with the mission.

On 7 December 1942, Maclean and the borrowed colonel, Tarleton, accompanied by Gault as interpreter, called at Zahedi's house for a pre-arranged appointment. The telephone line had already been cut, and the Seaforths were concealed under tarpaulin in trucks parked nearby. Maclean knocked on the door; when Zahedi opened it Maclean greeted him, a Colt automatic pistol in hand. 'Everything worked smoothly and within ten minutes the General was being carried off under guard in a British military car for Sultanabad', escorted by Robertson.[74] Maclean remained behind to search Zahedi's house. He claimed to have found 'a collection of automatic weapons of German manufacture, a good deal of silk underwear, some opium, an illustrated register of the prostitutes of Isfahan and a large number of personal letters and papers'.[75] Included among them was a letter from someone styled the 'German Consul for South Persia'.

The German 'consul' in question, Franz Mayr, and Roman Gamotha had been the first SD agents to arrive in Iran in November 1940. Along with Schulze-Holthus, they were 'left to their own devices, without any ability to convince a largely disinterested Abwehr and SD in Berlin of the strategic importance of the region and of their need for support'.[76] The British military attaché, Lieutenant-Colonel H.J. Underwood, kept the German diaspora under surveillance, aided by SOE reports to Colonel 'Chokra' Wood's Combined Intelligence Centre Iraq (CICI) outfit in Baghdad.

In November 1942 Louis Dreyfus learned from the British of the extensive plot to seize power and commit sabotage in the event of German invasion. The 'alleged discovery,' wrote the suspicious Dreyfus, was due to the seizure of the Mayr documents. Dreyfus thought the British might have manufactured the plot as an excuse for the occupation of Tehran. This led to a meeting between the American ambassador Winant and Anthony Eden, who convinced the former that these suspicions were unfounded. Though CICI had not been involved in Operation Pongo, Zahedi was a prime target for them 'because he was deeply implicated in the activities of Franz Mayr and his Melliun Iran movement, on the basis of hard evidence acquired on 2 November 1942'.[77] Another reason for his arrest was his attitude towards the triple murder, on 3 August, of an Australian schoolboy, his medical-missionary father and a British agent, shot by Bakhtiari tribesmen. They had probably been paid to kill the agent on behalf of Zahedi as part of 'his personal vendetta against the staff of the Isfahan consulate'.[78] It was the view of Vice-Consul Isfahan, J.C.A. Johnson, that unless strong action were taken, other British people might well be targeted. After Zahedi's kidnap, CICI wrote that 'The removal of one of the main obstructions to British efforts to improve the economic conditions and security position in Isfahan is one of the most important security measures taken in Persia since the Allied occupation'.[79]

Dreyfus's inclination was to object to Operation Pongo, and his concerns percolated to Washington. The arrest of General Zahedi, he claimed, had aggravated the situation in Iran. The Iranian government, Dreyfus reported, said that the British had no right to make such an arrest, and the shah was reported to have said that 'If the British can do this to my country they can do anything'.[80] On the same day, Secretary of State Cordell Hull sent a message to Winant in London, copied to the Foreign Office. The British response was, essentially, an exhortation to calm down; Winant told the State Department that in British eyes Zahedi 'was considered so deeply and dangerously implicated in the plot organized by German agents that his arrest was considered urgently necessary'. The Foreign Office also claimed that 'the arrest passed off quite unnoticed by the public'.[81] There is little doubt that had the American military been in control of security in Iran, they would have done exactly what the British did.

The Mayr documents confirmed British intelligence's picture of German operations and the extensive fifth-column organization under the guise of the Melliun Iran political movement, involving civil servants, cabinet ministers, members of parliament, military officers including the Chief of the General Staff and General Yazdan Panah, head of the gendarmerie. Its plan was to rise up at the allotted moment along with the Iranian army.[82] Franz Mayr himself was now a fugitive, moving only under disguise, and adopting methods of subterfuge such as hiding messages in couriers' armpits beneath flesh-coloured condom scraps.[83]

Between August and September a spectacular series of arrests in the British zone, conducted with American cooperation, smashed Mayr's network in Iran. Compounding these blows was Germany's failure to achieve the expected victories in North Africa and the Soviet Union. A post-war British intelligence summary identified late 1942 as a crisis point for Germany's covert and intelligence operations across the Middle East, as well as for the German army. Gruppe VI C, responsible for the region, 'like the German High Command, had virtually staked everything on the success of these military operations.'[84]

The threat passes

As the Tenth Army continued to grow and defensive preparations burgeoned, 'the time factor kept improving in our favour', as Wilson put it. This was a crucial variable; the longer the enemy failed to appear, the stronger and better prepared Wilson's army became. But most importantly, when German forces suffered significant reverses in North Africa and the Soviet Union, the chance of them ever reaching Iran and Iraq evaporated. British victory in the Western Desert – and the Soviet counter-offensive in front of Stalingrad – changed everything; Britain would not have to fight the Germans in Iran and Iraq after all. Persia and Iraq Command lost its operational importance virtually overnight. Churchill wrote to Brooke on 1 December 1942 that 'the role of the Tenth Army is dependent upon the Russian defence of the Caucasus. Since we formed it in August a vast, favourable change has taken place, and it may be that before the end of the year all danger to Persia and Iraq will have rolled far to the westward.'[85] Given this possibility, Churchill's mind turned to using PAIC's forces to help Turkey, and he asked Wilson for a report 'showing how you could move four to six divisions of the Tenth Army westward into Syria and Turkey'.[86]

As well as keeping men fit, a major challenge for PAIC was sustaining the morale of its fighting troops. Though written with post-war hindsight, the historian of the 5th Division said that while serving under PAIC it was 'a real long-stop for Eighth Army in the Western Desert and for the Russian Armies in the Caucasus'.[87] The men constantly wondered when they were going to get to Egypt and Libya, where the 'real' war was taking place. The division's deployment to Iran and Iraq was 'a trying job with apparently no object in view except to sit and wait for the war to catch up'.[88] Yet, of course, there was an object, one that it was unlikely the men on the ground, even if they were aware of it, would appreciate. The object was to stand fast and ready lest the 'real' fighting in North Africa, or in the Soviet Union, ended in German victory. If it did, their turn would then come. Wars are not won by fighting alone; readying oneself to fight elsewhere if the main fighting fronts crumble is crucial too. As it happened, the men of the 5th Division eventually got what they wanted – a move to the North African theatre and a chance to be blooded against Axis tanks and soldiers. It was telling that they moved as soon as the Battle of Stalingrad had effectively put paid to any chance of the Germans invading Iran and Iraq from the north. As a result of this, General Wilson sent the 5th Division to Middle East Command. The Divisional Headquarters left Qom on 31 January 1943 – the very day on which German state radio announced the defeat at Stalingrad (the battle's formal ending would come on 2 February), following an airing of the solemn adagio from Bruckner's seventh symphony. The 5th Division was almost immediately followed by the 56th Division, and Wilson decided to 'regroup the remaining formations within the Command and issued orders for their location in the general area of Mosul–Kirkuk'.[89]

The Tenth Army was now able to release the greater part of its fighting units to join the campaign in North Africa. The Anglo-American 'Torch' landings the previous November had opened a new phase in the struggle to clear Axis forces out of Africa, and this was now reaching its culmination point.[90] General Alexander, Commander-in-Chief Middle East, informed Churchill of his plans for a mid-January offensive intended to reach Tripoli. Churchill searched for 'a source of further reinforcements, not only for North Africa but for a possible Turkish front', and asked the Chiefs of Staff to look at the scale of the Tenth Army under Persia and Iraq Command: 'With the German army no longer able to push beyond the Caucasus, the Tenth Army "can now be considered available in whole or in part for action in the Eastern Mediterranean or in Turkey".'[91]

In February Wilson left PAIC to replace Alexander as Commander-in-Chief Middle East. Both men were ascending the higher rungs of the command ladder together, Alexander having been appointed to command the new allied 18th Army Group under General Dwight Eisenhower's Allied Force Headquarters in North Africa and the Mediterranean. Leaving PAIC HQ in Baghdad, Wilson told Freya Stark that 'I had literally to eat my way out through farewell lunches and dinners'.[92] He was succeeded by Lieutenant-General Sir Henry Pownall, who learned of his new appointment on 13 March. He was another one of Britain's very well-travelled senior commanders. He had already served, in this war, as Chief of Staff to the British Expeditionary Force in France in 1940, Vice-Chief of the Imperial General Staff, Commander-in-Chief Far East, Chief of Staff to the American-British-Dutch-Australian Command and military commander Ceylon.

Pownall soon discovered that his new command was in the process of dismemberment, and that he would be left with only one Indian division and one Indian armoured division, and either two Polish divisions or another Indian division. As the German threat was receding from the Caucasus and North Africa, Persia and Iraq Command would be largely concerned with internal security.[93] The command had also been downgraded, and though it remained in existence, it now became subordinate to Middle East Command.[94]

The character of German covert activity in Iran changed with defeat in North Africa and the Soviet Union. German operational priorities became tactical, their 'general intent had become disruptive and destructive rather than preparatory (i.e. for invasion) and constructive'.[95] Pownall expected sabotage of the oil installations and lines of communication, and attempts to stir tribal risings among the Qashqai, Bakhtiari and Kurds. This is exactly what the Germans focused on. One significant British countermeasure was closing the port of Bushire to military supplies for the Soviet Union, so as to avoid the long mountain road by Shiraz and Isfahan through Qashqai country. Security Intelligence Middle East (SIME) and Combined Intelligence Centre Iraq and Persia kept a close watch on things. CICI was headquartered in Baghdad and run by Colonel E.K. 'Chokra' Wood. An offshoot of the Cairo outfit, it in turn had its own 'branch office' in Tehran, known variously as CICI Tehran or DSO (Defence Security Office) Persia, under Lieutenant-Colonel E.L. 'Joe' Spencer.[96] Excellent coordinated intelligence and security measures, together with the deception measures of 'A' Force, meant that 'the uncoordinated German, Italian, and Japanese espionage services were unable to obtain any useful information from the Middle East, despite the existence of disaffected, pro-Axis elements among the indigenous population'.[97] Britain's extensive intelligence network was highly effective, and by the end of the war DSO Persia had a card index of persons of interest containing 61,000 names.

Following the Anglo-Soviet invasion of Iran, the German agent Berthold Schulze-Holthus effectively became a tribal adviser rather than an active spy, offering tactical and legal advice to Nasir Khan.[98] Ultimately, though he proved to be rather good at it, this was futile: Berlin was not interested.[99] He was a trained military intelligence officer, deployed to gather intelligence and conduct espionage against the Soviet air force, not an agent of subversion and sabotage. What he was able to do to aid the German cause was disconnected from wider operational or strategic considerations. For example, with Khan's help, he was able to reconnoitre and prepare an aircraft runway and parachute landing ground at Farrashband, which was discovered by an RAF reconnaissance patrol in November 1942. Eventually, as the war swung against the Germans, the formerly pro-German Qashqai and Bakhtiari became less friendly to their cause. Nasir Khan was persuaded to trade the German agents for British support once it became clear that the allies would win the war. The Iranian officer who arrested Schulze-Holthus told him that 'even individual Germans are a potential danger, a stick of dynamite on two legs'.[100] In an extensive report on a visit to Nasir Khan, Charles Gault, British consul in Isfahan, described how he was accompanied by fifty armed horsemen as he journeyed into Qashqai country to Khan's summer camp at Chal Qafa.[101] In discussions, the Qashqai leader declaimed his passionate opposition to the Tehran government, and said that he was now waiting for the British to install a new one. His interest now lay with the British because they were the 'controlling power in the south and because of the Russian menace'. The British wanted him to enter mainstream politics; Khan boasted about how many people said he should become shah. His main foe, Gault was convinced, was the government in Tehran, which he hated. He was out for himself as a tribal leader, and was not pro-British, and had not really been pro-German. 'He took up with the Germans in 1941 because he thought his interests lay in doing that because they were clearly going to win the war and looked like clearing out the Pahlevi gang.' The German fifth-column movement had failed; in the north, the situation collapsed completely with the arrest of Mayr in August 1943, and in the south, Schulze-Holthus and the members of the Anton sabotage mission 'spent the following winter under virtual arrest in the tribes they had intended to exploit'.[102]

There remained plenty of jobs for the many thousands of troops who remained in the Tenth Army to perform. They supervised the continuing arrival of Polish refugees, many of whom joined the army. The human traffic in the region remained immense, between April and September 1943, for instance, 700,000 British Empire troops passed through the transit camp at Baghdad. In mid-1944, there were still about 100,000 Indian Army servicemen in the PAIC theatre, along with the 30,000 Americans of Persian Gulf Command (PGC).[103] The removal of the German threat meant that PAIC and PGC could focus unhindered on the delivery of millions of tons of military aid to the Soviet Union. It also meant that the oil upon which the British Empire depended would remain secure for the duration of the war.

While allied fortunes were improving throughout 1943, the war was very far from being won, and threats to Iran and Iraq remained. As one British consul wrote, 'every Persian without exception expects and looks forward to the arrival of the Germans to the Caucasus and to this town and district'.[104] Rashid Ali certainly wasn't giving up hope: in a radio broadcast on 20 January 1943 he said: 'I hereby declare … in the name of the Iraq people … Iraq remains in a state of war with the British.'[105] The Axis, he claimed, offered the best hope for 'freedom, independence, and unity' of the Arab peoples. In July 1943, the American legation chief in Tehran alerted Washington to the fact that Sir Reader Bullard had alleged 'that German parachutists have been dropped near Qum and have not been apprehended'. General Pownall had recently visited Iran in connection with this, and during his visit had told Colonel H. Norman Schwarzkopf, the American responsible for training the Iranian gendarmerie, 'in strictest confidence that he is considering recruiting a special Iranian force to be officered by the British to use as a striking force against tribes and to maintain security of supply lines'. The force 'would apparently be similar to the South Persia Rifles of the last war'.[106] Responding to this intelligence, the Secretary of State said that the department 'was inclined to think that such a move would be a mistake as it would present an invitation to the Soviets to create a similar force, a counterpart to the old Cossack Brigade. The best solution was to stick with building up the gendarmerie under American tutelage'.[107]

Notwithstanding this, there was no disguising the fact that the threat was greatly diminished, and confidence in ultimate allied victory ran strong. Political adviser Wallace Lyon registered the sudden change in tempo. He and his special officers were spending time among the Kurdish people, building extensive defensive positions and nurturing their contacts, and were 'very impressed with their work rate and their willingness to take on more work'. Defences in the Mosul area were extensive – in one sector alone 24 miles of anti-tank ditches were cut through solid rock:

> The field fortifications covered a vast area both in width and depth, and in all resulted in over a million pounds finding their way into the pockets of these deserving people. As far as the army was concerned it was excellent value for money while at the same time freeing the troops for the more important work of training. It was the first chance the Kurds had of full employment at a time when the cost of living was rising fast. It was also sound propaganda for the Allied cause ... But all of this intense activity came to a stop when the strategic situation changed. The Germans weren't coming through the Caucasus after all. They had been halted and resoundingly beaten by the Red Army, at Stalingrad and elsewhere.[108]

What followed in northern Iraq was a drawdown of forces as troops were moved to other, more active theatres of operations. They were replaced by a token force of Indian State Troops, and military work in the area ceased to be about preparing defences and began to focus on famine prevention. The troops that remained in Iran and Iraq manned the supply line to the Soviet Union, and provided necessary internal security.

In a footnote to those developments, in conversation with the shah in August 1943, Bullard told him about the arrest of the German agent Franz Mayr. The documents seized by the British, he was told, had given an accurate picture of the names and activities of all those mixed up in the plot involving German agents and Iranian anti-British and anti-government communities – 'a Who's Who of the Persian fifth column'.[109] Learning that the plot was also against him, not just the British, the shah was 'visibly alarmed'.[110] Mayr's capture and the documents found in his possession became a key element in Iran's subsequent declaration of war on Germany. Adrian O'Sullivan, a historian of intelligence and covert operations in wartime Iran and Iraq, writes that 'a robust defensive security-intelligence system, soundly conceived and efficiently run, succeeded in sustaining preventive measures which covered all aspects of potential offensive enemy movements and activities'. Into this 'solid wall of British determination,' he writes, German initiatives blundered. Germany's agents were 'ill-prepared, isolated, and fugitive from the start – with little realistic hope of survival'.[111]

CHAPTER 14

The Persian corridor

With the German threat to Iran and Iraq diminished to the point of inconsequence, the allies could now devote their attentions solely to the transport of military aid. Hundreds of barges clogged Iraq's waterways as imperial forces transported all manner of military goods northwards from the Shatt al-Arab, some of it destined for the British, Indian and Polish troops of Persia and Iraq Command, most of it bound for the Soviet war effort. On the commandeered railway network, meanwhile, hundreds of imported locomotives pulled enormous container cargoes of military supplies, while thousands of fighters and bombers flew from Abadan and the assembly factories to join the fight on the Eastern Front. Cecil Beaton, visiting Iran and Iraq for the Ministry of Information, saw 'phalanxes of newly arrived US bombers on the tarmac at Tehran, being readied to be flown to Russia', the rows of almost identical aircraft making 'a most imposing sight'.[1]

Thousands of American, British and Soviet jeeps and lorries appeared on the roads, together with thousands of requisitioned civilian lorries and buses. Convoy after convoy processed northwards from the Gulf ports, themselves in the process of being transformed, while far to the north the vehicles of the East Persian Auxiliary Transport Service wound their way from India to the Caspian Sea. Meeting an allied supply convoy on Iran's perilous roads was an experience not to be forgotten, and was often remarked upon in memoirs. 'To meet a UKCC [United Kingdom Commercial Corporation] convoy coming down a mountain road as one was going up,' wrote General Wilson, 'was a real nerve-shattering experi-ence'.[2] Driving from India to Baghdad, Freya Stark met British convoys all along the way, 'the military stream of help to Russia, that panted up from Karachi day and night: a river of metal flowed north across the wastes of the Persian borderland'.[3] Travelling from Baghdad in the car transporting the military bag to the Tehran legation, Hermione, Countess of Ranfurly, reached 'the hairpin bends of the well-fortified Paytak Pass' and 'was aston-ished by the size and beauty of the range'.[4] On the plain beyond, framed by snow mountains, lay Kermanshah. Here Ranfurly's car met a 'great convoy on the way to Russia'. On treacherous terrain, the driver kept in bottom gear, passing wrecked vehicles and gangs of Kurdish men laying gravel and clearing snow. Despite their caution, they blew a tyre before eventually arriving at Hamadan. On the final stretch to Tehran, they halted at a check-point at Qazvin which lay in the Soviet zone. 'Over the plain ahead of us a convoy, like a string of black beads, moved towards us': a line of over thirty trucks carrying supplies to the Soviets.[5]

The challenge of aiding the Soviet Union

British commanders were keen to ensure that Britain's achievements in developing and sustaining the trans-Iranian supply route before American help came on stream were duly acknowledged: 'In fairness to the personnel of the British Army,' wrote Wilson in his official dispatch concerning his period as Commander-in-Chief Persia and Iraq, 'I wish to place on record that the arrival of the United States Army to relieve has come at a time when much of the heavy work of preparation and development is at an end and about to show results'.[6]

The challenges involved in delivering aid were many. Distances were vast, shipping was at a premium, sea lanes were menaced by Axis warships and once aid had been landed, unloading cargoes and transporting goods overland required extensive and sophisticated infrastructure. Among the heaviest diversions of allied shipping from home supply and the transport of troops and equipment abroad was the scraping together of the aid convoys that sailed for the ports supplying the Soviet Union. In undertaking to shift supplies via the Persian Gulf and Iran, the British had taken on a formidable task. Basra was the only port in the area with any considerable capacity outside that on Abadan island, which was reserved for handling the products of the refinery. But the British needed nearly all of Basra's capacity for their own military purposes in theatre. The Iranian ports proper – Khorramshahr, Bandar-e Shahpur, Tanuma, Bushire and Ahwaz – lacked dock and handling facilities. The Iranian State Railway which ran northward from Bandar-e Shahpur to the Caspian was constructed on modern lines, but lacked rolling stock and was capable of carrying only 6,000 tons a month. Roads northwards from the ports were poor and un- developed. Then there were the problems of capacity; the British truck assembly plant at Bushire and aircraft assembly plant at Shaibah, for instance, were barely sufficient to meet the requirements of the British mili- tary forces in the region, with little spare capacity for helping to supply the Soviet Union.

There is no doubt that the troops of Persia and Iraq Command and its predecessor formations, and of America's Persian Gulf Command, achieved extraordinary feats of construction, transport and delivery. The ports needed to be expanded and new ones created; Basra, for instance, was developed and a new port built at Umm Qasr in September 1942.[7] Base depots and connected establishments were developed at Shaibah and an advance base at Musayyib. An 'extensive fleet' of inland watercraft were collected together and organized; railway communications extended and improved; and a 'comprehensive programme' of road construction and improvement got under way. Workshop and storage facilities were erected (over 1.25 million square feet of workshop space were required in the construction programme) and new hospitals were built; aerodromes were established and accommoda- tion for RAF repair and servicing work, and facilities for the storage of huge amounts of fuel and ammunition, were developed.

Given that Iran had no adequate harbour for the offloading of large quantities of military equipment, it was initially supplied from Maqil in Iraq. A new railway was built, and supplies began to be transported by barge to Kut, then by rail to Khanaqin, and then by road through Iran. Work was undertaken to develop the existing, inadequate Iranian ports, including Ahwaz, Bandar-e Shahpur and Khorramshahr. The British formed an Inland Water Transport branch, which grew into the largest centrally administered unit of PAIC, numbering 800 British officers and other ranks, and 12,000 soldiers and civilians of Indian and other nationalities. PAIC also undertook the improvement of the Trans-Iranian Railway. The Indian Army's 16th Line of Communications Column worked on aid to the Soviet Union from December 1942 to March 1944. It comprised a general company of the British Royal Army Service Corps, the Mysore General Purpose

Transport Company and the Jodhpur General Purpose Transport Company of the Royal Indian Army Service Corps, and eight other general purpose transport companies. It worked its convoys from Andimeshk to Khanaqin in Iraq and then to Tabriz. Here their loads were handed over at the Soviet railhead. The road from Khanaqin to Tabriz was 700 miles long and included 4 major mountain passes, the Pai Tak, Shah, Avey and Shibli passes.[8] Overstretch was the order of the day at this stage, with one company of the Indian Electrical and Mechanical Engineers, for instance, whose job it was to maintain 600 vehicles, actually maintaining 2,000 over 850 miles of road. In September 1942 there had been no civil trunk telephone or telegraphy facilities of use to the military, so independent military trunk lines had to be erected. By the end of the year about 500 miles of new iron pole routes had been constructed, and nearly 600 miles of poles erected on existing routes, together with 500 miles along the railway line and 500 miles of local networks. Other tasks included mapping the terrain for military and supply operations; by the end of 1942 Indian Field Survey companies had mapped nearly 100,000 square miles of land.[9] It was this British imperial effort of supply that the American troops, arriving in large numbers from late 1942, were intended to supercharge.

Allied vessels transporting supplies to the Soviet Union travelled along three ocean-spanning routes. The 'Persian corridor' stretched across the Indian Ocean to the ports of the Persian Gulf. Another traversed the North Sea and the Arctic from Britain, Iceland and North America to land supplies at Arkhangelsk and Murmansk. The third supply route bridged the Pacific from west-coast cities such as Los Angeles, San Francisco and Seattle to Vladivostok. At the time of the establishment of the first trans-Iranian route in 1941, German attacks on the Arctic convoys sailing to Murmansk were intensifying. Disasters on the Arctic route in 1942 led to its virtual closure (fewer than fifty ships made the run the following year). Thus 'what had hitherto been a minor aid route assumed paramount importance'.[10] Though considerably safer than the Arctic route, the sea lanes leading to and from the Gulf were haunted by enemy submarines and surface raiders. More distant acts of war could also hamper the development and utilization of the Persian corridor; on 16 June 1942, for example, the merchant ship *Kahuka*, bound from New York for Bandar-e Shahpur, was sunk by a German submarine 90 miles west of Grenada – 17 seamen lost their lives and a cargo of 7,480 tons of cranes, tractors and construction equipment destined for Iran was lost.

A drawback of the Persian Gulf–trans-Iranian supply route was that it was much longer by sea and land than the Arctic route: 12,000 miles by sea from America around the Cape of Good Hope. There was then an overland journey of over 600 miles from the Gulf ports to the Caspian Sea along the main highway from the port of Khorramshahr to Qazvin. The problems of distance were compounded by the limitations of the Iranian road and rail transport infrastructure and port facilities. Rail cargo started 'on a narrow-gauge railroad in Iraq and then switching to a standard-gauge railroad in Iran that followed a treacherous path through the Zagros [mountains]. After reaching Iran's central plateau, the line headed back north to Tabriz, where it was switched a third time to a Soviet-gauge railroad for the final leg.'[11] Goods delivered to the Iranian port of Khorramshahr, which was not linked to the Iranian railroad, had either to be moved across the desert to the first all-weather road at Dezful, or be transported by shallow boats up the Karun river to Ahwaz for transfer to the railroad. Goods were also delivered to Bandar-e Shahpur, the Gulf terminus of the 808-mile-long Trans-Iranian Raiway. The capacity of these ports to unload cargo was limited, as was the capacity of the road, rail and water transport systems to move it north towards the Soviet Union. In 1943, the turnaround shipping time for American ships sailing to Britain and back averaged 69.4 days; the comparable figure for the Persian Gulf was 241.7 days, scaled down to a still crippling 157.2 days once passage through the Mediterranean and Suez Canal reopened.[12] Similar restrictions pertained with regard to the Iranian rail network. Largely of German construction, the Iranian railway was an incredible feat of engineering, featuring 3,000 bridges, 231 tunnels and an altitude range of 7,400 feet. But it was severely limited in its ability to carry the envisaged amounts of aid to the Soviet Union. It was single-track and ran through deserts and mountains where water was sufficient for perhaps two trains a day. 'Most of its freight cars lacked brakes, its locomotives were without headlights, and neither were available in sufficient numbers.'[13]

Persian Gulf Command was a new type of command for the US Army – not at the forefront of the 'war of guns', but very much in the frontline of the war of military supply, 'an essential element of victory'.[14] Major General Donald H. Connolly assumed command on 1 October 1942. An engineer officer, he had directed the New Deal work relief construction programmes in Los Angeles during the Great Depression.[15] The command's insignia was designed to flatter and appease the Iranians: 'The red scimitar was taken from the Iranian flag representing the warlike ancient Persians. The white star was from the Kingdom of Iraq, representing the purity and religion of the Middle East, the green denoting the agriculture of Persia but also Islam.' PGC – rendered 'People Going Crazy' by the American serviceman and writer Joel Sayre and his fellow GIs – was a hotchpotch of 'railroaders, truckers, road builders, assemblers, dock-wallopers, and many others'. Basically, it was an army of civilians in uniform. On parade, Sayre wrote, PGC 'resembled a bunch of weary Texaco dealers more than it did the Coldstream Guards'.[16]

The first large contingent of American soldiers arrived in theatre in December 1942. A force of 5,500 men had left New York the previous month aboard the *West Point* bound for Khorramshahr. A second shipment of GIs sailed from San Francisco on the *Île de France* on 8 December, a third on the *Mauretania* in mid-January. PGC reached its maximum strength of 30,000 soldiers in August 1943, of whom 10 per cent were African-Americans, in accordance with War Department policy. Key initial projects included the expansion of the ports and development of road and rail communications, and the construction of vehicle assembly plants at Andimeshk and Khorramshahr where lorries for the Red Army were assembled from parts shipped from America. Upon first arrival, the troops were accommodated in British Army 'Bombay' tents, rather than the US Army's standard pyramidical ones, the British versions being considered excellent for hot weather shelter though not so good in the rain. Eventually, they would be accommodated in thirty-six specially constructed camps.

PGC's soldiers did not face enemy bombs and bullets, but service in Iran presented its own challenges to life, limb and comfort. Accidents were the most common cause of casualties. Between south-west Iran and the Soviet depots in the north, for example, there were 220 tunnels to be navigated – in one 163-mile section there were 133 tunnels totalling 47 miles in length. These unventilated tunnels filled with steam and often reached temperatures of 180 degrees Fahrenheit (82 degrees Celsius). There was then the ordeal of driving on unpaved and uneven roads, which caused a very high incidence of lower-back injuries to be recorded among allied service personnel, and the danger of driving on mountain roads featuring innumerable gorges and switchbacks. Between Khorramshahr and Andimeshk there was a 180-mile stretch of 'very nasty desert', and the road running through it contained over 10,000 bends of more than 30 degrees.[17] During the snow season of January to March 1944, First Sergeant Roland N. Kemp of 'F' Company, 334th Engineer (SS) Regiment, 'assumed the added responsibility of directing road traffic [and] furnishing information on road conditions from Khurramabad to Malayir'. This 'included the hazardous sections of highway, namely Zagheh and Rason Passes, relaying by telephone road conditions to MTS [Motor Transport Service] Headquarters in Khurramabad and Burujird and to District Headquarters and also to approaching convoys'.[18]

Private John F. Powers was awarded a Soldier's Medal for heroism for protecting government property, at great risk to his life, on the Iranian railway. Near Do-Kouh, he was acting as rear brakeman on an extreme gradient 'when twelve cars broke loose from the train and started moving backwards at ever-increasing speed. With the help of a native Iranian employee [Powers] remained at his post while moving cars were out of control for a distance of 15 miles until able to bring them under control with hand brakes'.[19] In another incident, a train pulling ten tankers of aviation fuel and eleven boxcars of ammunition and high explosives had just reached the summit of the Zagros mountains when the engine's throttle valve sheared. It was revving at peak engine output as it began the descent. Engineman Virgil E. Oakes activated the airbrakes, though only four cars possessed them. The train accelerated to 65 miles an hour, and stations up-line were told to clear the track. Due to Oakes's actions, the train was halted before it caused a collision.[20]

Rain, snowdrifts, dust storms and temperatures ranging from –25 to 120 degrees Fahrenheit (–31 to 49 degrees Celsius) were ordeals encountered by all allied troops in the theatre. Joel Sayre recorded temperatures of 140 degrees in the holds of ships being unloaded in Iranian and Iraqi ports – at midnight – and desert temperatures of 135 degrees. 'Iran could offer a Yank nothing,' wrote a browned-off GI. 'You can describe this country at its worst with two unpleasant words, heat and disease.'[21] Servicemen soon learned to tuck their dog tags into their breast pockets so as to prevent them heating up and burning their flesh. Tools and metal objects were sponged before they were handled. Yet the first American troops to arrive encountered pouring rain and muddy quagmires, the rainy season soon followed by baking temperatures and sand storms. There was also the cold. Lieutenant-General Arthur Smith recalled a convoy caught in a blizzard in northern Iran. 'When aid arrived, many of the drivers were found dead', frozen to death.[22]

The efforts of the first American troops to arrive in theatre were dedicated to preparing the ground for the expansion of American forces and their supply-line activities. It was all about infrastructure, and the logistical activities that it enabled. The first wave of ships brought in the material –

locomotives and rolling stock, construction equipment for port and rail expansion, management personnel – necessary to expand capacity before there was any prospect of fulfilling aid goals to the Soviets. Troops began setting up basic infrastructure and facilities that the envisaged size of PGC would require. This meant building barracks, medical centres, hospitals, heatstroke centres, mess halls and latrines. A new telephone system was installed, along with officers' quarters and service clubs. PGC was all about the steady performance of routine assignments by quartermaster troops 'who ran the depots and operated bakeries, laundries, water supply, refrigerated warehouses, and even ice cream plants'. There were also forty-four airstrips constructed.

Lieutenant William Hicks recorded the activities of 'F' Company, 334th Engineer SS Regiment. Landing at Khorramshahr on 11 December 1942, it was one of the first American units to arrive. The men immediately went into 'desert-type' tents at staging area, and soon began an intense period of construction work. They paved the docks and built roads, warehouses and mess halls. Working in the 'Permanent Troop Area', in its first 6 months the company built 10 250-man mess halls along with 78 barrack buildings, 14 washroom and latrine buildings, 14 prefabricated officer huts, a signal and message centre, a Post Exchange building, a Post Office building, a troop dispensary and a radio building. In the same six-month period, in the 'Truck Assembly Plant Area', where the parts of imported vehicles were put together in preparation for onward shipment to the Soviets, the company built five sheds, five 'native barracks', two executive bungalows and inspection ramps. In this period it also built a 1,250-man camp and facilities in the 'Russian village' and 'Russian Dump Area'. At Santab Jetty, it built two TG gear sheds, one port headquarters building, one port headquarters administrative building, one cold-storage building, two sorting sheds and also paved the jetty and built a hardstanding area. In the 'Faleyah Creek Area', the company provided filling for the wharf and conducted dredging operations. Finally, in this first six-month spell, at the Customs Yard 'F' Company undertook road works including grading, filling and maintaining all roads and streets in the Khorramshahr area.[23]

One of the new American camps was Road Camp Number 19, commonly known as Camp Zagheh, which opened on 5 September 1943. It was located in what the American military designated 'Desert District', 182 miles north of Dezful, 29 miles north of Camp Mario H. Pomato (named after the murdered GI, p. 224) on the trans-Iranian highway. The camp occupied over 8 acres at the top of the Zagheh Pass, an area of steep rocky hillsides with very little vegetation. Before the American soldiers arrived the area had been used by the local people for grazing sheep and cattle. What the Americans routinely termed 'native labour' was engaged for this work, the bulk of it the construction of Nissen huts and brick-built extensions. The latrines, water-purification building and camp generator buildings were constructed by military personnel from Beta-Pak panels.[24]

Camp Zagheh's water supply originated at 'a spring a mile north of camp and is purified by chlorination and filtration by means of a portable purification unit'. Pre-treated water was stored in a 1,500-gallon tank truck used for hauling and a 1,000-gallon redwood storage tank. Treated water was held in two 2,800-gallon Merang cells (self-sealing tanks, such as those used on B-26 bombers). The camp's rubbish disposal was by means of burning and periodic burial. 'Sewage disposal is by means of pits under the enlisted men's latrines and by septic tank and seepage pit for Officers' quarters.' Another camp, Camp White Rock, was opened on 20 July 1943 when 'F' Company had to move because of malarial conditions. It was located in the Desert District, 112 miles north of Dezful. Here, sewerage was dumped directly into a nearby river.[25] Like the construction and maintenance of the desert convoy route across Iraq earlier in the war, boosting Iran's capacity to shunt military hardware to the Soviet Union was all about the nitty-gritty of innumerable small but crucially interconnected logistical activities.

The work of Persian Gulf Command troops

Accommodation and facilities constructed, PGC could get down to business. Most units comprised specialist soldiers, though there were also 'general service' regiments, such as the 352nd Engineer General Service Regiment. In the second half of 1944 its six companies were deployed in different locations across Iran. 'A' Company was in the Desert District operating out of Quarry Camp, Kharkeh River Camp and Desert Camps 1 and 2. Its principal duty was the repair and maintenance of the Khorramshahr–Ahwaz highway. A detachment was stationed at Abadan airbase constructing a landing strip for Air Transport Command; 'B' Company meanwhile was at Desert Camp 37 in the Desert District working on road construction, airport construction and road maintenance; 'C' Company at Tehran operating a motor pool; 'D' Company at Shaur River Camp, Andimeshk, maintaining the highway from Kharkeh River Camp to Andimeshk; 'E' Company was in the mountains of

Tang-e Haft, maintaining the railroad and laying track; and 'F' Company was at the port of Khorramshahr, unloading cargo from ships and forwarding it by lorry to various installations.[26]

Other PGC specialist units included the 19th Field Hospital. One of its platoons was based at Ahwaz running a hospital accommodating sixty-four patients, over half of them suffering from neuro-psychiatric disorders.[27] There was the 788th Military Police Battalion, which patrolled the Ahwaz area, the Foley Hotel, 19th Field Hospital and the Camp Lowe area, which was in the vicinity of Ahwaz. It maintained roving patrols at all times, and a vice squad patrolled the brothel area every evening in the company of Baluchi soldiers from the British Indian Army. The 762nd Railway Diesel Shop Battalion specialized in assembling modified 1,000-horsepower ALCO RSD-1 diesel-electric locomotives – designed and built especially for the trans-Iranian supply line by the American Locomotive Company – along with thousands of freight cars.[28] Another specialist unit was the 3342nd Signal Service Battalion: its primary assignment was the 'installation, operation and maintenance of radio transmitting and receiving equipment, radio teletype operation of signal centers, and the handling of cryptographic devices in conjunction with code room activities. This called for the installation of low and high power radio transmitters with associated antenna equipment, radio receiving stations, and a complex system of radio teletype facilities throughout the area of the Persian Gulf Command.'[29]

The bulk of PGC's manpower formed specialist dock, rail and road units. Its battalions unloaded ships and improved port facilities at Abadan, Bandar-e Shahpur, Khorramshahr and Tanuma. For many of the command's soldiers, this was their reason for being. As the commanding officer of 663rd Port Company plainly put it, 'The permanent Mission of this Organization is to discharge United States and Russian War Supplies at a Port in the Persian Gulf Command.'[30] The congestion of stores at ports had been a major problem, and the inability to unload ships quickly enough led to a wasteful queue of allied merchant vessels waiting on the roads leading to the main ports. The Americans had come to Iran to support the British and increase the flow of war material, and they achieved this in an impressive manner. The British had averaged fifty-five days to get a ship berthed, unloaded and turned around. The Americans had it down to forty days by June 1943, and to eight a year later. PGC's port battalions became so efficient that, at its peak in 1944, Khorramshahr was the world's third-busiest port in terms of tonnage handled. Here there were two American port battalions, one white, the other comprised of African-Americans. Its pier could handle seven Liberty ships at once, each of which carried ten to fifteen trainloads of goods. There were cranes and 'tongs' for offloading material fastened to boom cables, which unloaded cargo from Liberty ships; meanwhile, to 'land the real whales, such as Sherman tanks and Diesel loco-motives, the ships would run up the nearby creek, where there were eighty-ton cranes among the palm trees along the shore.'[31] These enormous cranes for unloading the heaviest cargoes had been especially shipped in; the 'long piles that were needed for jetties in the extremely fluid coastal soils were spliced together from teak piling purchased in India.'[32]

Eugene Warren was a second lieutenant with the 482nd Port Battalion working at Bandar-e Shahpur, the main railhead for the Trans-Iranian line running north to the Caspian. When the Americans arrived it had only two berths, so three more were built, and 'cargo was unloaded directly onto rail-road cars for shipment to the Caspian Sea.'[33] Cargo was moved off the dock floors on flatcars pulled by little engines and in trucks towing huge trailers known as 'lowboys'. Many PGC soldiers were experts in stevedoring and lighterage (unloading by barge): 'The white boys and their officers were nearly all pros who had been in stevedoring and longshoring and lighterage on the Pacific Coast and in the Gulf of Mexico, but many of the colored boys had never even seen a ship before they got in the Army. There was a great rivalry between the two outfits over which could handle more tonnage.'[34] A flag was awarded for the leading battalion, an honour often won by the African-American unit. The men bet on the results, and prodi-gious feats were achieved, one company in a single 24-hour shift, for instance, taking off 980 tons of mixed freight.

Many PGC units were devoted to road construction and haulage. Substantial portions of the southernmost 172-mile stretch of the road to Andimeshk, for example, were completed in 1942, largely through the endeavours of the 1,325 African-American soldiers of the 352nd Engineer General Service Regiment. Construction projects were often frustrated by natural occurrences; in the spring of 1943, for instance, floods swept away two bridges and 8 miles of road, requiring the reconstruction of a 39-mile stretch.[35] In July 1944, 'F' Company of 334th Regiment had 'to send men back to White Rock Camp and open same in order to tear up approx. 11.2 miles of roadway in the section between waterfalls and tunnels. This was necessitated due to the failure of the British to properly maintain that portion of the highway.' In September 1943 the men of 'F' Company's two camps, Zagheh and White Rock, completed road construction assignments and reinforced the wearing surfaces of the curves, placing highway markers consisting of both signs and painted barrels to improve driving conditions on the many curves and bridges in this section. The company, its commanding officer wrote, had 'contributed considerably to the PGC mission of keeping supplies going steadily to Russia during the past Winter in spite of deep snows which required a well organized dispatch system to prevent congestion of trucks on the highway and, all too often, twenty four hour road patrols with snow plows and maintainers to remove the heavy drifts'.[36]

The main American lorry route, from Khorramshahr to Qazvin:

> was constantly under construction or repair. The British had made a valiant effort at road improvement with virtually no modern machinery to help them; they had done the work with men and donkeys – 67,000 men and 14,000 donkeys at the peak. But the Americans were equipped with road rollers, asphalt cookers and bulldozers, and they accomplished some remarkable feats of engineering such as a road able to take three lorries abreast across the 150 miles from Khorramshahr to Andimeshk.[37]

Floods in March 1943 damaged it so much that the road had to be done again.

Driving lorries on Iran's roads was not for the faint-hearted. Lieutenant William H. Bird commanded an American transportation unit made up of white officers and African-American enlisted men drawn from the Illinois National Guard. He recalled the 135-mile drive from Andimeshk to Khorramshahr, which was supposed to take 10 hours, but which with its 1,300 bends took 15 hours or more. The huge tractor-trailer lorries and the treacherous mountain roads overwhelmed the first batch of US Army Quartermaster drivers, whose experience had been limited to civilian jobs driving delivery trucks in Chicago. Road haulage in Iran was in need of specialist help, so the War Department contacted the Teamsters Union through the American Trucking Association and put out a call for volunteers for a 'secret mission'.[38] Over 1,000 volunteer professional heavy-duty truck drivers answered the call, arriving at the port of Khorramshahr, via Australia, with little idea of what lay in store for them. Lorries arrived in crates, were assembled by PGC, then loaded with cargo and driven north. As well as American drivers, Iranians were also employed, and by the end of 1944 PGC had trained over 7,500 local drivers.

The Motor Transport Service developed the road which ran roughly parallel to the railway line to Qazvin, 90 miles north of Tehran. Bulldozers and tons of asphalt rebuilt and smoothed the road, raising it 2 feet off the desert floor in the process and making it wide enough for three lorries to run abreast. Sometimes work had to be redone when sections of new road were wiped away by floods. The Motor Transport Service operated a block system along Iran's roads, which meant that when a loaded lorry reached a block terminal it was handed over by one driver to another. The first driver then returned to the home base with an empty lorry after a meal and a night's sleep at one of the waystations erected along the road. The roads were patrolled by wrecking crews and repair crews in order to respond speedily to accidents and breakdowns; PGC's ordnance depot at Andimeshk was a 'minor Detroit', boasting every conceivable kind of equipment for the maintenance of vehicles.[39] American and British engineers jointly constructed a new road from Andimeshk to Qazvin. The 334th Engineer Special Service Regiment, augmented by Iranian civilian workers, 'converted the extant road between Andimeshk and Malayer into a highway adequate for truck convoys' and also built a 240,000-gallon reservoir near Andimeshk.[40]

Allied forces employed hundreds of thousands of Iranians; PGC alone 'always had 50,000 or more Iranians working for it', in a variety of functions.[41] This included some rather unusual forms of employment, such as Captain Joseph Petersen's 'anti-malaria army of 2,000 small boys armed with flit guns'. Thousands of Iranian civilians played a role in the war effort, building roads, driving lorries and working as mechanics at the truck assembly plants, at Andimeshk and Khorramshahr, built on the desert floor by General Motors, where lorries for the Red Army were assembled from parts shipped from America. The mainstay was the Cased Motor Truck or 'CMT', Studebaker US6 lorries being the most common, of which the factories could turn out more than 100 a day. PGC recruited civilian experts to work in these assembly plants, though enticing them away from civilian jobs could present a challenge. Nevertheless, in early 1942, over 200 arrived from aircraft companies such as Douglas in order to help train the army for the job. Wanting them to have as many comforts as possible, three chefs from New York hotels – the Edison, the Waldorf-Astoria and the New Yorker – were 'bribed' by the army into service. The Andimeshk plant, run by Captain Kack Schoo, was operated by 116 American soldiers and 2,710 (mostly Iranian) civilians. Taken together, 'the two plants employed over five thousand of these poor, helpless citizens of Backward Races,' wrote Sayre ironically, 'and they were so shiftless and unteachable that they could do no better than learn how to turn out trucks at the rate of one every five minutes'.[42]

Iran's railways were improved with the construction of more than 200 tunnels and new trunk lines to the ports. The first American railroad troops to arrive in Iran were the men of the 711th Engineer Railway Battalion, the first railroad operating battalion formed by America during the war. PGC's rail terminal was Tehran, its truck terminal was Qazvin, 90 miles north-west of the capital along a 'spine-grinding road'.[43] Outside Qazvin, 435th Engineer Dump Truck Company worked supply depots located next to Soviet troops at Camp Stalingrad. Black GIs transferred goods to them and, according to Supply Sergeant Clifford B. Cole, they 'encountered less discrimination here than back home'.[44]

The allies steadily improving the load-bearing capacity of the Iranian railway. At the outset, the British had hoped to raise the railway's capacity from 200 to 2,000 tons a day. In its last two years of military operation it was delivering on average 3,397 tons per day and during its peak month – July 1944 – it delivered 7,520 tons of equipment every day. The physical strain on the rails was immense: 'In America the steel rails used on main-line tracks weigh a hundred and ten or more pounds per yard; in Iran the seventy-five pound rails of soft German iron whimpered beneath the tremendous loads of Sherman tanks, ammunition, explosives, heavy construction materials, food, clothing, and medicines that had to travel north night and day'.[45] For the railwaymen, the worst transport hazard was the topography:

> It is some six hundred miles from Khorramshahr to Tehran, the end of our supply route by rail. After crossing a hundred and eighty miles of desert to Andimeshk, the trains had to climb fearsome mountains rising to seven thousand feet. With the enormously increasing loads, it became very difficult for the little locomotives to get up the grades. Major Worthington Smith, an old-timer from the Northern Pacific, who commanded the mountain run, would often rush out a whole company of his men to throw sand on the tracks by hand.[46]

Gerald Harbaugh had been working for Norfolk and Western Railroad in the Crewe workshops at the time of Pearl Harbor. He volunteered and underwent combat engineer training, and was told that the army was in desperate need of trained railroaders. He was assigned as a locomotive machinist to 'A' Company, 754th Railway Shop Battalion, 3rd Military

Railway Service, destined for PGC.[47] The battalion activated on 15 October 1942, comprising 625 officers and men, and trained at Camp Claiborne, Louisiana. Leaving America, the unit entrained for Richmond, California, embarking on the converted ocean liner *Mauretania* on 13 January 1943. The ship refuelled at Pearl Harbor, docked at Wellington in New Zealand and Fremantle in Australia, and arrived at Bombay on 19 February. Here the unit boarded the British India Steam Company ship *Rohna*, anchoring at Bahrain on 28 February and Khorramshahr on 2 March. The battalion transferred to Tehran to Camp Atterbury, named in honour of Brigadier General W.W. Atterbury, former president of the Pennsylvania Railroad, who had served as chief of the Military Railway Service for the American Expeditionary Force in the First World War.

The battalion assumed responsibility for the Tehran shops, PGC's principal locomotive and car repair facility. By March 1943 there were 40 American-built steam locomotives in service, 143 British and 57 German. These were later supplemented by about 60 diesel locomotives and nearly 100 Japanese-built Mikado locos, as well as some other types. The total number of locomotives reached about 570, and there were about 8,000 railcars for cargo and passengers.[48] All required routine maintenance. Harbaugh's battalion established a foundry in order to manufacture its own spare parts, such as brake shoes, and items for other units, such as boxing rings, flagpoles, refrigerators and foot lockers (as well as denture castings and dental tools for the army hospitals).

Ezra Scott, a warrant officer in the 3410th Ordnance Medium Automotive Maintenance Company, also arrived aboard SS *Rohna*. His unit's task was to maintain vehicles working on the supply line from the port to Tehran. Having moved up country to Camp Atterbury, near a British camp, Scott's unit then moved across Tehran to the Queen's Stables 'where we set up a permanent camp area'. When the detachment moved to Hamadan to set up another maintenance shop area, contact was established with a nearby Polish refugee camp through the Hamadan Red Cross chapter and a local merchant named Isaac Urshan. Among other things, the Poles undertook to do the Americans' laundry.[49]

Another specialist PGC task was the assembly of aircraft, which after testing were handed over to the Soviets. Before the construction of the aircraft assembly plant at Abadan, which assembled between 300 and 400 airframes a month, the US Air Force flew Douglas A-20 Havoc bombers across the Atlantic and via Africa to Iran. On arrival, they were serviced, the white

American military star was painted Soviet red and they were then taken over by Soviet pilots and flown north. PGC's aircraft assembly plants built A-20s, Bell P-39 Airacobras, North American AT-6 Texans and B-25 Mitchells and Curtiss P-40 Warhawks. The largest crates offloaded on Iran's docks, 10 by 38 feet long, carried a P-40 or the wing of a P-39 complete with landing gear.

Captain Francis Sheppard, a PGC test pilot, was recommended for the Distinguished Flying Cross by his commanding officer at Abadan airbase. Between 1 August 1943 and 1 February 1944 Sheppard flew 371 test flights without accident.

> These flights were made in P-39, P-40 and A-20 type aircraft. All of these flights, except those made in the A-20 type, were made in aircraft newly assembled which had never before been flown. This test work was carried out under extremely adverse conditions. Continual summer temperatures of over 170 degrees Fahrenheit [76 degrees Celsius], together with frequent sand storms of an intensity unknown in North America, which blow up with little or no warning, causing zero visibility to heights in excess of 12,000 feet on the airport, add to the other ever present hazards of such flights.[50]

In a single month Sheppard flew ninety-eight different aircraft on original test flights. Documents in the American archives also record the exploits of Captain Bernard Seitzinger, who would go 'into a power dive' and practise dog-fighting by flying in pursuit of ducks, crows, hawks, 'or any bird he could find as he put the aircraft through its paces before it was handed over to the Russians'. 'Once he dogfought a transport plane which turned out, unfortunately, to be carrying a visiting General.' Of the 14,834 American aircraft sent to the Soviets under Lend-Lease, 4,874 went through Iran.

Soldiers' complaints

Maintaining morale was a real challenge for commanders in Iran. An extensive survey in the American archives offers a fascinating glimpse of the issues that affected the lives of soldiers serving in the Iran–Iraq theatre. Conducted in 1944, the survey reveals that the biggest gripe among enlisted men concerned officer incompetence and discrimination favouring officers over enlisted men. Complaints regarding food and messing facilities were also prominent, as were objections to the fact that towns and places of entertainment were usually 'off limits' for enlisted men. Iran's remoteness from the main theatres of combat preyed on the minds of some soldiers, while others struggled to adjust to military life: 'I feel like a lost person. I came here with good patriotic intentions, good ideas of the US Army but have found it the exact opposite of what I expected. I have no responsibility, I have lost all ambition all initiative and all mannerisms of good speech.'[51] Another soldier wrote: 'PGSC is no dam good. They treat the Soldiers up in Teheran like Kings and down here they treat us like convicks.' Some soldiers were unhappy with everything: 'How about better chow get rid of native workers, they only steal. Why can officers do so little, and get away with it?' wrote one.

Lieutenant Colonel Lars Steinert spent ten months as chief of surgical services at 21st Station Hospital, Khorramshahr, a fully equipped 500-bed hospital (even bigger was 113th General Hospital at Ahwaz, with 1,000 beds). Returning to America in May 1944, he was highly critical of PGC's medical set-up, claiming that its hospitals were 'tremendously overstaffed, for the amount of work they do': 'I handled more cases in one month at Fort Bliss, Texas, than I did in the entire ten months at Khorramashahr ... It used to irk my colleagues and me a great deal to read newspaper articles telling of the Army's great need for doctors and nurses, while we were wasting away both physically and mentally in the 140-degree temperatures of Iran.'[52] Steinert went on to make some rather astonishing claims:

> more than sixty per cent of men working in the labor battalions have bad eyesight. I sometimes wonder how many of the cases of crushed skulls have resulted simply because the men did not see what hit them ... We had 6 or 7 cases of serious conjunctivitis among the labor battalions. These men, sightless in one eye, wore glass substitutes which cracked under the intense 140-degree heat, resulting in infection of the conjunctival sac. Infection spread to the good eye and caused total blindness.

He also wrote that 'there was a lack of proper nutritious food, and facilities for preparing what we had, up to November, 1943, when the condition did improve with a few shipments of frozen meat'. He corroborated the accusations of the ordinary soldier; there was a 'great expenditure of money for luxurious quarters and facilities for officers, very little is done for the enlisted men'.

Food was a common cause for complaint among the soldiery, a matter of immediate, daily concern for men whose lives were dominated by demanding, routine work and who did not have the option of sourcing and preparing their own meals. 'I am very tired of all the canned food we are getting here and believe we should have fresh meats and vegetables', was a typical response. 'Another thing is the chow', wrote one soldier:

> What in the name of God, do you think we guys have anyway. Cast iron stomachs? I would like to see you after a six month dose of spam and vienna sausage (hot dogs to you) ... There are endless streams of United Nations boats coming into this port and never yet have I seen so much as one single pork chop swing over the side. Aid to Russia is really swell. But how about some fresh meat aid to a de-hydrated GI? Come on Brass hats wake up.

Fresh meat, or rather the lack of it, was a big issue. Soldiers of the 334th Engineer Regiment were unable to observe Thanksgiving in 1944 because of a lack of turkey, which was deemed very bad for morale.[53] 'Why do we have so much Hash-Spam etc. when canned pork and chicken goes right through to Russia?', asked another soldier. 'If the US can supply Russia with that it sure as hell should be able to supply the American Troops with it at least once in a while.' There was then just the general blandness of mess fare. 'Can't the cooks flavor the food a little?' asked another, either sardonically or in a spirit of genuine enquiry.

On the subject of fresh meat, Lieutenant Colonel Norberg said:

> Regulations forbade the purchase and use of native-grown cattle by Army mess officers in Iran. British troops nearby were using the meat with no serious consequences, and we had ample facilities for slaughtering and refrigerating it. We also had sufficient vets for inspecting the meat. But we were forced to subsist on a diet of Spam and what game or fowl we could shoot in the area. The reason given for this order was that the Army did not want to appear to be taking meat from the natives. This was ridiculous, as the natives were eager to sell their livestock and did a great deal of business with the British.[54]

American soldiers also complained about the provision for entertainments. 'The practice of putting every decent night club "out of bounds" causes much resentment among EM [enlisted men].' These types of complaints were often linked to gripes about officers and the presence of

nurses in Iran: 'This post is a play ground for the officers and nerses [*sic*].'
One soldier wrote a list of 'suggested improvements': '1. Bus service to
Ahwaz; 2. Open a few taverns in Ahwaz for the Enlisted Men; 3. Dating
facilities with the Red Cross Girls for the Enlisted Men; 4. I don't believe the
officers should do their love making in public places with nurses. Its [*sic*] a
great moral [*sic*] buster for the Enlisted Men.'

Unfair privileges for officers, as perceived by the enlisted men, provoked
heated comment: 'This whole camp is as undemocratic as Hitler. I'll be glad
when I leave this hell hole behind me,' wrote one soldier. Another commented
that 'in my estimation and I think I'm also talking for the rest of the boys,
this camp is very close to a concentration camp'. The apparent 'availability'
of female nurses, to the officers but not to men, was a common grudge:

> The arrival of female nurses, allowed to associate with the officers,
> increased even more the resentment of the men. All men feel, rightly or
> wrongly, that the chief purpose of the nurses overseas is to provide
> sexual intercourse for the officers. In this case it may be that the conduct
> of the few has blackened the reputation of the many, but it is also equally
> possible that the chief function of the nurse is as a prostitute. At any
> event, the adoption of such an attitude by the men shows clearly just
> how great is their animosity toward the officers.

Another man wrote that enlisted men 'can dance with Polish girls at rare
dances, but can't develop further as Polish camp off limits. Meanwhile
officers have nurses and a beautiful officers club.' One respondent wrote:

> On the whole, Officers are pampered too much as big babies. Officers
> tend to class distinction as in British Army. Enlisted men do all the work,
> Officers receive credit. Officers monopolise everything, enlisted men
> get what's left. WAACS [Women's Auxiliary Army Corps], enlisted, are
> now allowed to go with officers. Why not let Nurses go with enlisted
> men, which they would rather do. We are not dogs! Also, the officers tell
> the white men that if they were half as good as the negroes they would
> be good outfits.

Another man wrote that 'Foreign soil is no place for a bunch of GI glamour
girls who openly protest that the hospital takes too much of their time from
entertaining the officers of the Command'. 'In general,' concluded another,

'the enlisted men of the PGSC are getting a royal screwing, while the officers are getting all the gravy.'[55]

Some American soldiers wished for more opportunities to experience Iranian culture and to go sight-seeing: 'Being stationed in the Middle East, there are towns near our encampment that would interest myself and my buddies greatly . . . We will probably never be lucky enough to ever get here again. So why not give a soldier a break and relieve the monotony of camp life. Don't say it can't be done. It can and you damn well know it.' Another soldier wrote: 'A fine service could be rendered the men of this command, if an opportunity was given to visit the historical and religious spots of this part of the world. Civilization had its beginnings here and it has many interesting placed that we should be given the opportunity to visit.'

Entertainments, leisure activities and home comforts were essential aspects of a soldier's life. At Camp Lowe, softball, baseball, volleyball and boxing were all popular, and matches attracted crowds of several thousand servicemen. Teams in PGC leagues included the Atterbury All Stars, the Camp Atterbury Streamers, the Andimeshk Raiders, the Khorramshahr Dolphins and the Ahwaz Sandhogs. In terms of musical and stage entertainment, Camp Lowe boasted the thirteen-strong Camp Lowe Dance Orchestra, 'The Chow Hounds', a regular schedule of motion pictures, and stage shows such as the 'Iranian Railwaymen's Show', the British Entertainments National Service Association's 'Arabian Nights' and a 'GI show of coloured troops from Bandar Shapur'. As part of the soldiers' survey, respondents were asked the question 'Do you have any criticisms of the stage shows you have seen?' Sixty-four per cent replied 'No', 15 per cent objected to the 'lack of talent', 13 per cent to the 'low type of humour or too many dirty jokes', and 18 per cent had other criticisms, most of which were that shows were too short or did not feature enough 'girls'. Sir Reader Bullard in Tehran, meanwhile, was impressed by the spiritual songs sometimes sung by African-American troops at Anglican services.[56]

American and British soldiers saw little of each other professionally or socially. Where they did, it was in remote districts where they had posts near each other; 'they would visit our movies, we would drink their ale'. PGC also entered teams in the PAIC football league. In Tehran, the Brigade of Gurkhas' bagpipe band was esteemed. There were visits from USO (United Services Organization) Troupe 99, featuring Gene Emerald MC, a guitar-playing baritone and 'comedy pantomimist', Basil Fomeen, a Russian-American accordion player, Joe Tershay, a magician of Syrian descent and Jack Cavanaugh, a lasso performer.

As elsewhere in the world, American bases were envied for their facilities and luxury comestibles. The Coca-Cola ration was a bottle per man a day, and ice cream was so important that when its sale in the Post Exchange at Camp Lowe was 'curtailed due to overheating of freezing unit', a special 'desert cooler' was quickly installed in order to remedy the situation. In March 1945 a new wing of the Camp Lowe Service Club was opened and repair to the old parts completed following storm damage. The new wing included a games room with four ping-pong tables and an American Red Cross snack bar. In the old building, the lobby was redecorated, lighting fixtures re-arranged and the library remodelled. New curtains and stage lighting equipment were installed in the 'Madison Square Garden Theater'. The region supported a weekly Special Service newspaper, *The Ahwazian*.[57] Movies were shown on four nights a week at the Camp Lowe Outdoor Theater and elsewhere. In March 1945 there had been 3 enlisted men's dances at the Foley Hotel, each attended by over 500 GIs and guests, prominent among them young Polish women. Camp Lowe also had a swimming pool.[58]

More cerebral and esoteric pursuits included the 'Camera Club of the Gulf District' and Persian language classes.[59] Bingo was organized in conjunction with the Red Cross, and there were organized hunting trips. A dedicated PGC radio station broadcast from Tehran, and the survey revealed that the most listened to shows were 'Hello America', 'Command Performance', the BBC Overseas Service, Jack Benny, Bob Hope and Fred Allen. Other radio shows included 'Showtime', 'Concert Hall' and 'PGC Hit Parade'. The survey also revealed that the most popular types of books were recent bestsellers, mystery and detective stories and books addressing the problems of the post-war world.

In December 1943, Brigadier General Donald P. Booth took over as Commander PGC. Leaving the post, his predecessor Major General Connolly drove through 5 miles of allied troops drawn up at 'present arms'. British and American efforts along the Persian corridor were matched by extensive activity in the Soviet zone, in order to take the Anglo-American war material and move it onwards to the fighting fronts where it was urgently required.

Accounts written by Soviet officers and translated by the American military in the 1980s offer insights into this huge Soviet undertaking. Enormous supply centres were formed in the rear areas behind the front line in order to build up supplies of war material, food and fodder to support troop movements and operations. Between August and September 1941 the State Defence Committee brought all rear services into one administrative organization. In this region, the Transcaucasus Centre Depot at Baku was linked to Iran, and a transloading base was developed at the port of Pahlavi to receive and dispatch Anglo-American freight throughout the Transcaucasus Military District and to the Stalingrad sector. With the movement of supplies in the Transcaucasus extremely difficult, and given the need also to evacuate the wounded, it was decided to make more use of the waterways of the Caspian and the Volga.[60] Goods delivered into the Soviet zone by the Anglo-Americans were then taken by Soviet transport headquarters in Iran to the border towns of Astara, Dzulfa and Kizyl-Atrek. To expedite delivery, some of the material was taken to the Iranian port of Pahlavi for onward shipment to Baku and Makhachkala. The road from Tehran to Pahlavi was widened. Pahlavi's facilities had to be greatly improved; its approaches were too shallow for the Soviet ships, so a 3-kilometre-long channel had to be excavated from the seabed. Warehouses and living quarters had to be constructed, with all requisite construction material imported from the Soviet Union. Sent to inspect the progress being made in August 1942, Colonel S.N. Skryabin, a Soviet logistics officer, wrote that 'On the shore an enormous construction site was going up. At it there was the unceasing chatter of jack hammers, the crunch of the dredger buckets, the clank of bulldozer tracks, the roar of engines, the deafening blows of the pneumatic hammers driving in the pilings and the piercing whistle of the launches.'[61]

It was vital to unclog the road network. Two road companies were sent to Iran and an extensive network of support facilities was developed, including a food, rest and refuelling station on the western outskirts of Tehran for drivers proceeding to Djulfa, capable of servicing 500 people per day. Similar facilities were developed at Astara, Julfa and Mengil, each of which could serve 700 people per day; the facility at Qazvin could serve 1,000.[62] The Qazvin–Astara–Baku road was reconstructed and covered with asphalt in 1944. Moving along these roads were the 2,034 vehicles of two separate regiments, and the 3,000 vehicles of the 287th, 520th, 528th, 572nd and 586th motor transport battalions.[63] Taken together, the work of American, British, Indian and Soviet forces represented an enormous effort to connect allied industry and supplies with the battlefronts. But while the mechanics of aid delivery became smoother as the war progressed through 1943 and into 1944, and the capacity of the Iranian transport network grew exponentially, intra-allied cooperation in the political sphere was increasingly threatened by major political differences.

CHAPTER 15

An allied battleground

The last two years of the Second World War saw the allies at loggerheads in the Iran–Iraq theatre. The drama of the period 1940–41, when the region was threatened by external and internal military challengers, leading to a spate of brisk campaigns, had passed. So, too, had the strategic danger of 1942, once Axis forces had been evicted from Africa and the Battle of Stalingrad had extinguished the threat of German invasion. The Germans had long shot their bolt and missed the great opportunities that had opened up before them early in the conflict. As Fritz Grobba told an Arab delegation to Berlin, the tragedy for nationalists like Rashid Ali and the Grand Mufti was that while Germany 'truly feels sympathy for the Arabs', it 'neither can nor wants to support them with arms'.[1]

Grobba lamented this failure. He was convinced that the Arab nationalist movement was essentially pro-German and ready and willing to forge a proper alliance, though Germany's capacity to take up this opportunity was 'clouded by German anti-Semitism and racial approaches', and the predilection of 'Hitler's enemies in the Foreign Office' who 'worked against any expanding of the war to the Middle East'.[2] Germany, the diplomat fervently believed, should have supported Arab nationalism much more strongly and shown far less deference to Italian ambitions, and worked harder to use uprisings to gain entry into Iraq and Syria in order to wreak havoc with allied interests. In the end, Grobba wrote, 'the Arab movement made more concerted attempts to exploit Germany than did Germany to exploit the Arab movement'.[3] Thus Germany fell by the wayside in the race for the Middle East long before the war ended. A special report on German policy in the Middle East under the Nazis was prepared for the US Army in the 1950s, compiled with the involvement of former senior German officers and diplomats. It stated that 'an effective Middle Eastern policy requires experienced experts with insider knowledge based on their knowledge of regional languages, developed and ready means of intervention, and a well-placed secret service'.[4] While Germany had long possessed the first of these requirements, it failed to provide the second and its efforts in the third domain were, the report concluded in hindsight, risible.

From 1943 on, the allies were able to concentrate, in as unhindered a manner as is possible during a world war, on developing the supply route connecting British and predominantly American factories to the Soviet Union. Something of a wartime normalcy also came to settle over the internal affairs of Iran and Iraq in this latter period, too, as both states stabilized following invasion, grew used to occupation and overcame the worst of the home front crises that had beset the region in the earlier period. Though regional separatism was an issue that would not go away before the end of the war, some of the most pressing problems associated with food supply in 1941–42 were being remedied. In Iran, 1943 was a better year, and in 1944 'a good harvest combined with better methods of collection to enable the authorities to establish a reserve of grain unprecedented, it is believed, in Persian history'.[5]

The last two years of war also witnessed the manifestation of growing rivalries among the three occupying powers, reflecting their wider competing national interests and attempts to shape the post-war world. It is telling that in this period, there was virtually no focus at all on fighting the Germans, and considerably more on intra-allied rivalries. As an example, when the American Office of Strategic Services (OSS) first deployed agents to Iran – without, it is interesting to note, telling the British – 'Germany was no longer a factor for OSS, and German intentions merited no consideration whatsoever'.[6] In line with the character of the allied presence in Iran in 1943–45, their priorities instead were the interpretation of internal politics and the study of Soviet activities and of what the Americans perceived to be British interference in Iranian politics and its efforts to dominate post-war markets. Having come late to the region, America now needed to draw its own lines in the sand and make decisions about how it intended to act to pursue its interests here, and the extent to which it would work to contest the activities of other powers as they attempted to do the same thing.

Mohammad Reza Shah Pahlavi's declaration of war against the Axis powers, issued by royal decree on 9 September 1943, was supported by seventy-three out of seventy-seven deputies in the majlis. A parliamentary statement from Prime Minister Ali Soheili cited German attempts to incite tribal uprisings against the government as the reason, along with the deployment of agents such as Franz Mayr and Berthold Schulze-Holthus to sabotage lines of communication and create an espionage network.[7] The declaration was viewed favourably by the allies and, in response, the American legation in Tehran was elevated to full embassy status, as was the British legation. Louis Dreyfus left Tehran as the last minister plenipotentiary and was replaced by Leland Morris in 1944, America's first ambassador to Iran, who would himself be replaced by Wallace Smith Murray in early 1945.[8] President Roosevelt acknowledged the reasons for the change. These included the declaration of war and also Iran's support for the ideas of the Atlantic Charter and the United Nations. He also wanted to acknowledge the 'difficulties and suffering which Iran has experienced in making available her transport system, by means of which huge quantities of military supplies have been and are being moved to Russia.'[9] The legation's upgrade was also stimulated by America's realization that it was going to have to take a keen interest in Iran's affairs when the war ended, as it transmogrified from an area of peripheral American interest into a theatre of intense Cold War rivalry and, just as importantly, of competition between American and British visions of the post-war world.

Iran was the one place on earth where large numbers of soldiers from the three major allied powers operated alongside each other. There were tens of thousands of Soviet troops in the north, and tens of thousands of American and British soldiers in the south. As the threat of fighting receded from the region, Iran became a battleground of another kind. Britain retained its historic suspicion of Moscow's agenda, and sought to forward its own, which amounted to a restatement of its long-standing economic and strategic interests in the Middle East for the sake of oil, lines of communication and the defence of India. For their part, the Soviets viewed both America and Britain as unwelcome challengers while grudgingly welcoming the military aid that they delivered, desiring territory, resources and the lines of communication running through Iraq, and the region's continued utility as a buffer zone. The Americans, meanwhile, looked askance at British policy, particularly what they considered to be its old-fashioned imperialist taint, and resolved to oppose the Soviet Union's regional ambitions and instead to develop Iran as a model of American-sponsored nation-building.

To broaden Christopher Thorne's description of the Anglo-American alliance against Japan, in Iran the 'Big Three' powers showed themselves to be 'allies of a kind'.[10] While their alliance bore the hallmarks of war-winning excellence, so united were they in prioritizing the defeat of Hitler's Germany, agreeing on how the world would be remade after the final victory was quite another matter. The Soviets were becoming more assertive; the war was forcing a phenomenal quickening of the sinews of American power; and the ongoing eclipse of the old European powers, Britain included, would thrust both America and the Soviet Union to the centre stage of global affairs. For its part, the war represented the apogee of British power and influence in Iran, while unleashing the forces that would cause this power and influence to wane.

While the historical record has focused on the growth of rivalry between the Soviet Union on the one hand and the Western allies on the other, in this region the clash between America and Britain was just as significant. The historian Simon Davis has proposed a new interpretation of intra-allied relations in the Persian Gulf region during the war and immediately after it. It is one in which America sought to supplant or distance itself from British economic, political and military policies, rather than supporting or validating them, in spite of contemporary and historical rhetoric regarding Anglo-American solidarity. In effect, a new American 'informal empire' was evolving alongside Britain's extant empire and in competition with its 'neo imperial' designs, and for its own regeneration.[11] The British optimistically anticipated a return to a familiar world divided into the rulers and the ruled, and hoped to co-opt America in a British-led post-war Middle Eastern order. America, on the other hand, looking from the outside in, could see the signs of British decline, and pondered how to manage it. At the same time, it beheld the rise of Soviet power, which was almost certain to conflict with America's own determination to fashion a new world order in its own image. British diplomats and politicians were not blind to the changes taking place about them, and understood that they faced new challenges in securing their interests, and that these came from America as well as the Soviet Union.[12]

Sir Richard Casey, the Resident Minister Middle East, told Churchill that Iran was 'undoubtedly our biggest short-range political problem and a major long-range one'. Inflation was 'very acute', he said, and the general situation 'menacing'. The government was 'feeble', the press hostile to Britain, and Russian influence was increasing.[13]

America in Iran

America's economic might, represented by the Lend-Lease elixir now coursing through its allies' veins, as well as its beefed-up physical presence, represented by the troops of PGC, trailed political power in its wake. This became more than usually significant when President Roosevelt identified Iran as a shop window for the world he hoped to build from the ruins of war. Having visited Iran for the Tehran conference in late 1943, the president came to view it as a testing ground for the ideas embodied by the Atlantic Charter and the United Nations. America's post-war idyll would be based upon strong and viable independent nation-states – as opposed to colonies and 'spheres of influence' – that were friendly towards America's internationalist goals and practitioners of open-door economics. Iran's situation, buffeted between two imperial powers, also awoke in Washington an urge to rescue a weak, flawed state from the clutches of ruthless great powers. The chief of the State Department's Near East Division wrote that Iran was 'passing through a serious crisis as a result of the British and Russian occupation, [and] is turning to the United States in its hour of need'.[14] America's Iran policy was based on institution-building aimed at helping the country develop its own capabilities so that it could look after itself and resist foreign interference.

The problem with all of this was that the British and the Russians did not share America's vision of the post-war world. Neither did many of the Iranian elite, who applauded the intent but frowned upon the internal reforms required to achieve it. When it came to instituting the reforms that the Americans (and British) thought were necessary in order to make the Iranian state viable, Iranians resisted and came to resent the interference. The limits of Iranian ambitions and the Iranian state's inability to bear the weight of American expectations caused friction. While the Iranian elite continued to welcome as much American involvement as possible as a counterweight to British and Soviet importunities, it did not have its heart in the transformative agenda that the Americans prescribed. Iranians had no desire to become pawns in a new great-power game, nor did they wish to seriously forward the ideas of democracy that America espoused and to which the shah paid lip-service.

America's vision for the future was further sullied by the prosaic ambiguities created by its alliance with Britain and the Soviet Union inside Iran – which looked to many like the growing presence of a new imperialist power, deploying troops, taking things over and inclined to bully and nag.

The three powers clearly disagreed; the Americans thought Britain looked on Iran as a satrapy, and both of the Western powers believed that Moscow had designs on Iranian territory and resources which would persist beyond the end of the war, when the occupation, according to treaty, was due to end. For their part, the Soviets feared that America wanted Iran to become a satellite of the emerging Western world order. They were all, of course, correct.

American diplomats in Tehran were seriously concerned that the circumstances of war were encouraging Britain and the Soviet Union to take over the Iranian state, because of their historic involvement, their wartime needs and the Iranian government's incapacity, which had 'become both a reason and an excuse for direct intervention by the Russian and British authorities in Iranian political matters. At the present moment, no Iranian Cabinet can survive without the direct support of the Allied powers.' Of longer term concern were Soviet activities in northern Iran:

> We should be fully alive to the character of the present Russian occupa-
> tion of the northern provinces. In Azerbaijan [province], the Soviet
> authorities have greatly restricted the operations of the Iranian civil
> authorities and have virtually immobilized the small Iranian military
> forces which they reluctantly permitted to return to the area. They have
> alternately encouraged and discouraged the restive Kurds, always a
> thorn in the flesh of the local government. More important still, they
> have been so successful in propagandizing the population that our
> Consul at Tabriz has reported that a soviet could be established over-
> night in Azerbaijan if the Russians gave the word.[15]

The State Department's early 1943 document 'American policy in Iran' drew attention to the 'largely Turkish-speaking population whose cultural ties with Soviet Transcaucasia and Turkish Kurdistan are almost as strong as those with the rest of Iran ... It is also the most important grain-producing area of Iran and would be a welcome addition to the food resources of Transcaucasia.'[16] It was noted how suspicious the Soviet Union was of its allies, and how it was attempting to weaken British influence by leaving Britain to bear the brunt of Iran's economic problems. The Soviets were also trying to take control of Iranian arms plants and factories. The document considered the possibility of Anglo-Soviet rivalry breaking out in an accen-tuated form, a danger that was 'greatly increased' by the presence of large numbers of troops and the weakness of the Iranian government. 'If events are allowed to run their course unchecked, it seems likely that either Russia or Great Britain, or both, will be led to take action which will seriously abridge, if not destroy, effective Iranian independence. That such action would be contrary to the principles of the Atlantic Charter is obvious.'[17]

The best way towards realizing America's vision was 'to strengthen Iran as much as possible so it can stand on its own two feet'. Thinking of the post-war world, the policy document considered how to break out of a situation in which Iran was dominated by rival external powers. It was suggested, perhaps naïvely, that America as a 'disinterested' power could eliminate the dispute. 'It seems hardly possible that either could suspect the United States of having imperialistic designs in a country so far removed from us and where we could never hope to employ military force against an adjacent Great Power.'[18] It might have seemed hardly possible to the Americans, but it was in fact easy for the British and especially the Soviets to suspect American motivation, ascribing it to a desire to muscle in on Iran and the Gulf region for American political and economic ends.

America dispatched a number of missions to reorganize, train and strengthen key Iranian state institutions. Some historians have seen the missions as early moves in a Cold War game. But the initiative arose from 'anti-British concerns that unwittingly provoked Soviet counteraction and future cold war confrontation by advancing development through American oil exploration up to the Iranian–Soviet border.'[19] Iran convinced America that it deserved reconstructive military, civil and economic aid, under what Roosevelt dubbed 'an unselfish American policy'.[20] Initially, there was something of a groundswell in favour of the American missions that came to provide it; 'government, people and the press are clamouring for American advisers and our prestige has reached a peak'.[21] But not all Iranians welcomed this invited intervention, and some had distinctly different agendas from those the Americans thought they had signed up to. For numerous reasons, foreign advisers were 'opposed, disliked or suspected by those who were supposed to cooperate with them'.[22]

Identifying America as the only power that was both acceptable and capable of providing the levels of assistance required, Iran asked for American experts and advisers to reform or reconstruct key ministries of state, from the army to the treasury. There was no doubt that Iran needed such reform, and the British supported the missions. Louis Dreyfus believed that this was at least partly motivated by a British desire to see the Americans fail in the process. Britain's bid for American support in Iran, he cautioned Washington, 'may well be an attempt to bolster their own declining prestige'.[23] The British would 'support the adviser program, though perhaps to allow us enough rope to hang ourselves'. Dreyfus also believed that the British were prepared to 'use us as a buffer against the Soviets'.[24]

But Dreyfus's assessment was wide of the mark. While the British certainly exhibited some schadenfreude when the missions stumbled, they did support them, clearly assessing that without the kind of reforms the Americans proposed, the Iranian state would fail, which would lead inevitably to unwanted great-power competition and hinder the prosecution of the war. The situation was critical, in the opinion of British consul Clarmont Skrine. The government faced economic chaos which could lead to revolution, or the alternative of 'foreign tutelage'. Skrine summarized the problems facing the country and its rulers. The cost of living had risen enormously because of the war and inflation was 'plainly getting out of control; Persia felt small and weak, in danger of being ground to powder between the millstones of global war; she needed a protector, and who better filled the bill than the richest and industrially most powerful nation on earth, a nation, moreover, guiltless of imperialism and colonialism and all the other sins that blackened the faces of Britain and other possible protectors'.[25]

The American missions sought to reform key sectors of the Iranian state infrastructure and economy. To deal with the problem of haulage racketeering, a Road Transport Administration was set up to control the use of lorries and issue of tyres. A military mission under Major General Clarence Ridley advised the Ministry of War. The Iranian prime minister 'stated he wishes to have a complete American military mission to reorganize and train the Army which is demoralized, inefficient, depleted in materials and almost disintegrated as a result of the invasion of the country'.[26] American experts also advised on police administration, irrigation, agricultural education and public health. By far the most successful mission was that of Colonel H. Norman Schwarzkopf, a former chief of the New Jersey State Police who had led the investigation into the kidnapping of Charles Lindbergh's son, and who was the father of 'Stormin' Norman, of later Gulf War fame. Renowned as 'a gang-smasher', Schwarzkopf was sent to Iran to reorganize the gendarmerie and improve security on the all-important road network, reorganizing and retraining a force of 20,000 men under a US Army mandate.[27] The force trained by Schwarzkopf would later be instrumental in suppressing autonomous movements in Azerbaijan and Kurdistan.[28]

The main American mission was undoubtedly that responsible for financial reconstruction. Arthur Millspaugh, who had led an economic mission to Iran in the 1920s, was appointed administrator-general of finance by the Iranian parliament in 1942 in an attempt to rejuvenate the country's economy. The Americans believed that the mission existed to help improve Iran's economy, whereas 'Iranians seem to want it to stay more for political purposes of having the US as a buffer'.[29] Dreyfus detected a 'deeprooted and concerted campaign against our advisers' on the part of the Iranians. 'This springs undoubtedly from corrupt and selfish political elements in the Majlis who stand to lose personally with the institution of the kind of regime our advisers contemplate'.[30] Under Millspaugh's direction an income tax was levied via the Full Powers Law of May 1943 for the collection of grain and the equitable distribution of bread and the 'monopoly commodities'. This was resented by the wealthy: Millspaugh encountered opposition from landowners, merchants, speculators and the possessing classes in general, because he threatened to attack their interests. There was also very strong opposition from military and court circles because he wished to bring the army budget under the control of the Ministry of Finance. Deputies in the parliament opposed his income tax bill, which took six months and much modification to pass, requiring a threat of resignation from Millspaugh in order to do so. The finance mission in particular became a source of irritation in relations between Tehran and Washington. Its insistence, for example, on decreasing the military budget caused a rift with the shah, to whom the army was dear. Furthermore, the missions generally 'eroded the image of the US as a benevolent third power'.[31] In his book *Americans in Persia*, published just after the war, Millspaugh was to express the opinion that the Iranians were incapable of independent self-government.[32]

The potential implication of America's increasing involvement in Iranian affairs was not lost on the State Department. Wallace Smith Murray, Assistant Secretary of State and the future ambassador to Iran, wrote that the 'obvious fact is that we shall soon be in a position of actually "running" Iran through an impressive body of American advisers eagerly sought by the Iranian Government and urgently recommended by the British Government'.[33] Dreyfus believed that American advisers faced 'a colossal task, in organizing or reorganizing demoralized services, in overcoming inherent Iranian jealousies and suspicions, in by-passing bureaucrats, in withstanding the complaints of unreasonable politicians and in keeping their balance in the midst of chaos'.[34] The American missions provided ammunition for its enemies and those who sought an Iran free of foreign interference. The communist Tudeh Party pointed to American meddling in Iranian affairs and thrived on the discontent caused by the government's reform failures, while they also helped strengthen the nationalist politician Mohammad Mossadegh's claim that Iran would never be free until all external interference had been expunged.

American suspicions and British reactions

The nature of British economic activities in Iran, and the manner in which they were conducted, continued to rile the Americans. Diplomats on the ground as well as State Department officials believed that through the agency of the United Kingdom Commercial Corporation and the Middle East Supply Centre (MESC) Britain had a near monopoly on the Iranian economy. This, they contended, was bad for Iran and contrary to American interests. Given this, association with these British agencies and British policies damaged America's reputation and its ability to pursue its own goals. Legation chief Louis Dreyfus regretted that America had found it necessary 'to associate ourselves in this country with a MESC program based on compulsion and monopoly'.[35] He was also unable to see why Britain should get the credit for disbursing Lend-Lease aid from America to Iran. 'On the other hand I do not have confidence in the ability or honesty of Iranian government to make equitable distribution.' He summarized the situation regarding the fraught issue of tyre supplies, on which thousands of words were expended across hundreds of communiqués, thus: 'UKCC is insisting on obtaining a monopoly on import and distribution of tires, trucks, and spare parts in order to control all road transport. This coupled with control of other imports through MESC and British control of railways would complete their strangle hold on Iranian economy'.[36] According to Major General Patrick Hurley, the UKCC had become the 'handling agent and middle man' for Lend-Lease. 'It is a fact, however, that Britain is furnishing lend lease material to other nations at a time when she is being sustained in her war effort by American lend lease ... The least we should demand is that we be permitted to do our own giving.'[37]

The British needed to respond to mounting American criticism regarding their conduct in Iran, no matter how irksome they found it. In July 1943 Anthony Eden wrote that in 'view of difficulties recently arisen in our relations with the United States representatives in the Middle East it has been suggested that a memorandum should be prepared setting forth our general policy in the Middle East for communication to the US government'. The hope, the Foreign Secretary told the War Cabinet, was 'that by discussing matters with complete frankness at a high level something may be done to mitigate the disagreements which have recently arisen and to coordinate British and American policy'.[38] It was difficult to say at present, Eden continued, 'just what considerations are uppermost in the mind of the American government so far as the Middle East is concerned'. They already had an interest in the oil of the Persian Gulf, 'and they possibly suspect the existence of oil in hitherto undeveloped parts of Saudi Arabia'. It was surmised that American oil resources would 'in a few years be insufficient, and if so this explains an increasing American interest in the oil of the Persian Gulf . . . the pressure the Americans have brought to bear is another indication of their new interest in the Persian Gulf now that American ships go there constantly and that American troops are in Iraq and Persia'.[39]

As regards Iran, Eden's memorandum continued:

the Americans last year accused us of handling the Persians in a manner likely to make the task of the American adviser more difficult and to prejudice the position of the Allies there. They thought that we were bringing unjustifiable pressure to bear on the Persian Government, and they objected to our arrest of General Zahidi, Military Governor of Isfahan, for complicity in a pro-Axis plot. We had little difficulty in explaining our policy to the State Department, but co-operation with the Americans in Persia has not always gone smoothly and their Minister there seems, in spite of all efforts to gain his confidence, to harbour suspicions of our real intentions, or at least to question the wisdom of our policy. These doubts are unquestionably reflected in the State Department.

One of the American prejudices we have got to overcome is the feeling that Britain has exploited the Middle Eastern territories for her own imperialist ends and has retarded political progress contrary to the wishes of the inhabitants. Seeing that we have done more than any other Power to further Arab freedom and to develop the countries of the Middle East, this seems a particularly unfortunate misapprehension.[40]

The 'unfriendly attitude' of Wallace Smith Murray at the State Department, whose remit included India as well as the Middle East, was noted by the Foreign Secretary. 'We have had positive proof of his hostility in connexion with Persia, and it seems preferable that there should be frank discussion rather than continual latent ill-feeling.' In conclusion, Britain welcomed America in the region. 'But we must somehow ensure that the US influence is not used against our own in an area where our vital interests are so closely affected.'[41] Eden tabled a draft memorandum on British policy in the Middle East written specifically for American consumption and in anticipation of the formation of the United Nations, aiming to justify Britain's approach and diminish Washington's growing criticism of it.

Further evidence of America's growing presence in this region, so long the exclusive preserve of the British and the Soviets, was their appointment of a minister to Kabul, who had recently 'intervened in an unhelpful way in negotiations' regarding enemy activity. Fielding American criticisms of British imperial policy became a major effort during the war, identified as a critical activity by the Colonial Office, causing clashes between Churchill and Roosevelt over India and leading, among other things, to the dispatch of the British administrator Lord Hailey on a tour of America in an attempt to 'educate' opinion regarding the supposedly enlightened and progressive nature of British imperialism.

A reflection of the differences between American and British representatives on the ground in Iran is to be found in the attitudes of American servicemen toward their British peers revealed in the aforementioned US Army survey. Three-quarters of the respondents believed that the Americans were contributing more to winning the war than the other allies. Of the remaining quarter, the vast majority thought the Soviets were contributing most, 'England' hardly at all. While 60 per cent thought that they, the Americans, were working harder than the other allied soldiers, 30 per cent picked the Soviet soldier as the hardest worker and only 10 per cent 'picked the English'. 'The Russians are greatly admired as fighters but the English are not ... The English are rated considerably below the Germans and only slightly above the Japanese as fighters.' A staggering 44 per cent of respondents 'disagrees or doubts that England is doing as good a job as possible' or that she can 'take it on the chin and come back for more'. Very few had similar doubts about the Soviets.[42]

American soldiers felt little affinity towards their allies, and saw them as potential rivals:

Less than half the men feel that the English can be depended upon to cooperate with us after the war (as against three fifths who have faith in

French cooperation). But less than one third extend that confidence to the Russians ... Mistrust of our major Allies is so great among our soldiers that less than half say they <u>disagree</u> with the statement that Russia may turn on us when Germany is defeated. Scarcely three quarters disagree with the same statement about England. Over one third say we will fight Russia or England in the next 25 years ... Despite this greater mistrust of the Russians as compared with the English, the soldiers express far more friendliness for the Russians than for the English. Positive dislike of the English is extensive.[43]

Three-quarters of the men surveyed said that there was 'ill feeling between Americans and English. Only 1 in 4 says the same thing about Americans and Russians.' Two-thirds believed that the English did not 'go out of their way to help the Americans and show them a good time'. Half of the men said that they 'did not like the English', whereas only one in seven men said they disliked the Russians. This was intriguing, and potentially worrying. What is more, it was clear that increased contact with British soldiers tended to increase dislike for them. 'The effect of acquaintance and contact with the Russians apparently is exactly opposite to that of acquaintance and contact with the English.' When asked the question 'Which country is contributing most to winning the war?', 74 per cent answered America, 24 per cent Russia, but only 1 per cent Britain, putting it on a par with China.[44] While only so much can be read into this, it is if nothing else an interesting reflection on the attitudes of soldiers serving in this unusual theatre.

Parliamentary elections and the shah

However American policy might diverge from that of Britain, and whatever the post-war future might hold, it is important to remember that the British were the primary movers and shakers in the British zone of Iran during the war, and uncontested masters of Iraq. They were deeply engaged in Iranian political affairs, not because they particularly wanted to be, but because without their involvement, things would likely go awry, to the detriment of the war effort and the security of Britain's vital interests. Trying to prop up the Iranian state and temper its more feckless excesses was necessary, and it was for this reason that the British supported the American missions and their institution-building ambitions – and got involved in electoral politics.

National elections were a key feature of the post-invasion political landscape in Iran. Some British officials viewed the phenomenon with scepticism – 'the idea of "elections" in wild tribal country like Persian Baluchistan is grotesque', wrote a consul. 'The issue is bound to be contested on tribal lines: the Baluch are highly inflammable.'[45] Nevertheless, getting the best people into parliament, which along with the shah and the court was a key pillar of Iranian politics, was obviously a sensible policy to pursue. The 1943 parliamentary elections demonstrated the extent of British political influence in Iran, the efforts of Iranians to involve the British in their political affairs and British attitudes to Iranian people and politics. British officials collected information at a prodigious rate and had an extensive information and intelligence network; sources allowed them, for example, to know what the deputies of Azerbaijan province had discussed with the prime minister when they met, and the consular network generated comprehensive pen portraits of political candidates, detailing their strengths and weaknesses. Lengthy descriptions of all the political parties were composed, and the British legation drew up a list of parliamentary candidates who met with British approval and who might, therefore, benefit from British support during the election campaign.

Assessing the limits of Britain's power in Iranian affairs served to reveal its extent. Writing to the consul in Kermanshah, and later the consul in Tabriz, Minister Reader Bullard told them that it 'is of course quite impossible for us to eliminate all undesirable candidates and we must therefore concentrate on supporting the election of the least undesirable candidates in addition to any candidates of good character whom we may be able to encourage to stand as representatives of progress and reform'.[46] Britain's entanglement in Iranian affairs allowed opponents to seek to make political capital. For example, a memorandum recorded that a parliamentary candidate named Nabakht had been:

> telling everyone that the British Legation have instructed their consul at Shiraz that he, Nabakht, must on no account be elected to the coming majlis. This is of course more or less true: it is a pity it has got out but consuls have to take some action and so it all gets known. We must face up to this in many places in Iran: our enemies will get hold of our lists of approved candidates and will tell the world, especially the Russians.[47]

The British bemoaned the ineffectiveness of the central government, which obliged them, they believed, to maintain this level of involvement. If only a 'responsible' minister of the interior were appointed, the legation claimed, 'we could stop working through consuls and confine ourselves to getting the Minister of the Interior to pull whatever strings he can in favour of our approved candidates ... We are always up against the fundamental difficulty that we are interfering in matters which technically we ought not to touch, and without having any means of enforcing our wishes.'[48]

The shah meanwhile lamented the difficulty of getting competent officials into post, and the parliamentary opposition said that 'unless Government and officials took strong measures against big landowners and merchants who hold up wheat, not only might there be serious discontent now, but it might lead to justified revolt later'. The shah agreed.[49] This was a key stimulus of British involvement in Iranian political affairs: though of course motivated by self-interest, it happened that British interests would be furthered if the Iranian state became competent enough to enact social and economic reforms leading to a healthier and happier population. The British were even prepared to support candidates from the Soviet-leaning, communist Tudeh Party, because it pursued a reform agenda that would at least encourage the Iranian elite to get its act together and devise reforms, rather than face the alternative of continued ineptitude and possible state disintegration which would impede the pursuit of British war aims.[50]

In a telegram to Bullard, Anthony Eden bluntly summarized the ineluctable logic behind British electoral interference: 'So long as the war lasts we are clearly entitled to use our influence to prevent the election of elements which are directly associated with the enemy ... You should also consider what can be done to ensure that the Americans do not misunderstand our motives and realise that our sole intention is to use our influence in the interests of good government.'[51] Bullard and the consular network needed no encouragement, deeply involved in local and national politics as they already were. As the British minister wrote to Charles Gault, consul in Isfahan, 'I have no objection to your letting the Governor-General know that you and I both advised Sarem-al-Daula to let Fidakar obtain one of the Majlis seats for Isfahan ... I told the Prime Minister that I had given Sarem-al-Daula this advice, and that I did so because I thought it less dangerous to let a man of advanced opinion into the Majlis than to leave the workmen of Isfahan with no weapon but the strike and the street demonstration.'[52] Another typical example of British involvement in electoral politics is revealed in a telegram sent to A.S. Calvert, the consul at Kermanshah: 'Fuzuni has been told,' wrote legation official McCann, 'that we raise no objection to his standing for the

Majlis ... He seems well-disposed towards us, as well he may be, at any rate for the present, for he hopes we will get some of his lands back for him.'[53]

Britain continued to base its policy on the survival of the monarchy, with numerous caveats. 'I do not think,' wrote Eden:

we should adopt too rigid an attitude regarding the Shah's influence in political affairs. The present confusion in Persian politics does not augur well for the continued independence of the country in the political conditions that seem likely to emerge from this war. On the other hand, the Shah can and does have a long-term interest in an independent Persia, which is also our interest. As he must know this quite well, he is a natural ally for us if we play our cards rightly and are able to keep him on the right lines. This means that our policy towards him should be one of friendly guidance and constructive criticism.[54]

Indicating the extent of Britain's power in Iran, an internal legation survey in mid-1943 posed the question 'Do we wish to retain the shah?' Officials were asked to furnish answers to questions such as 'What are his qualities and defects?' and 'Is he pro or anti British?' Answers included that he was 'Keen, patriotic, kind natured but easily swayed and very susceptible to surroundings. Violently anti-Brit in sentiment tho not in policy.' Another official averred that he was 'determined to seize the power that his father had'. It was airily claimed by another respondent that the new shah 'possesses the defects of character of all Persians in an oriental country where honest men can hardly exist', and that 'in the circumstance he can hardly do anything else but throw in his lot with the British'. Extending his answer to the rest of the royal household, one official opined that the British should try and get the queen 'to do more good works and pay less attention to clothes'. Efforts should be made to 'marry off' the sisters and send them abroad. The old queen, now the queen mother, Tadj ol-Molouk, 'will I fear never forgive us though we might try talking to her'.[55] The British legation kept up quite a campaign to try to curb royal expenditure and encourage abstemious habits and household economies. Minister Bullard was determined that they set a suitably parsimonious example, and in September 1943 admonished a consul as he prepared for the shah's visit to Mashhad. The consul, clearly hoping to entertain in some style, had asked for a dozen bottles of whisky, a dozen of liqueur brandy, ten of assorted liqueurs and five dozen of champagne. Recoiling at the expense, Bullard told him that he should serve 'good local wine and tolerable spirits'.[56]

Problems with the Soviets

Even after the Anglo-Soviet invasion and occupation, Britain found that sending military aid to the Soviet Union was hampered by restricted access to the Soviet zone in the north. Royal Engineers officers, for example, had difficulty gaining access to the Soviet zone for the maintenance and construction of the Qazvin–Tehran road, even though, as the army acerbically observed, the work was 'at request of MOSCOW.' And while the Soviets were at that moment seeking British permission to export dates from Bushire in the British zone, they 'do NOT cease to interfere with British Army local purchases in their zone'.[57] It was the same for the Americans. Major General Donald Connolly, PGC commander, had 'difficulties in obtaining Russian permission to establish service stations and accommodations for convoy drivers in Soviet zone'. Because of this he was dumping war supplies at Qazvin 'until his reasonable demands are met,' Dreyfus reported to Washington.[58] Soviet encroachment on the British zone was partly motivated by the desire to purvey the idea of a better, prosperous future for all as a way of stirring criticism of the Iranian government for Soviet ends.

One of the reasons for Soviet animosity towards the Americans was the fact that they had not been formally notified of the arrival of their troops. The Americans felt that the British should have told 'their' ally about the deployment of American troops – after all, it came as a result of a British Army request for American technical units to improve communications. In conversations with the Soviets, Dreyfus had stressed that there were no combat forces included among their number. But, as was the case in other theatres of war, the habitually abrasive Soviets chose to take offence, and to seek to profit from the situation. But they had always been very clear that they did not want any form of American presence anywhere in Iran, so their reaction was hardly surprising. Efforts had been made to smooth things out. On 4 May 1943 Sir Reader Bullard showed Dreyfus a telegram from the British Foreign Office to the British ambassador in Moscow, Sir Archibald Kerr. It informed 'the Soviet Government that the British had thought no formal notification of the fact of Americans taking over the operation of the southern section of the Trans-Iranian Railway was necessary under the Tripartite Pact because Americans were not a separate command but were to operate the railway as part of the British Persia and Iraq command'.[59] Kerr was instructed to express the hope that in the light of this explanation the Soviet government would notify the Iranian government that it had no objection to American operations. But the Soviets remained concerned about the aims and role of American forces in Iran. As well as being annoyed by their arrival, they opposed the programme of appointing American advisers to the Iranian government; to them, it looked like a build-up towards permanent occupation.

From 1943 onwards, the correspondence between the American legation in Tehran and the State Department in Washington charts a shifting focus as concern regarding Soviet intentions grew. The attention of American diplomats migrated from what the British were (or were not) doing, to what the Soviets were up to. They were 'already engaged in political activities inconsistent with the terms of occupation' – stimulating and sponsoring anti-Tehran and pro-Soviet political movements, some of them secessionist – and were clearly using Iranian resources for their own ends. Dreyfus gave the example of a canning plant at Shaki that the Soviets had taken over. Eighty per cent of its output was to be taken to the Soviet Union: the Iranians had been reluctant to sign the contract but did so 'to appease the Russians who are pressing on other and more objectionable questions'.[60] In a 1944 memorandum entitled 'Soviet exploitation of Iran', Harold Minor of the State Department's Division of Middle East Affairs raised concerns regarding Soviet trade agreements with Iran which granted Moscow very favourable terms for obtaining products such as small arms, rice and cotton piece goods.[61]

The British believed that the Soviets routinely spread anti-British rumours, and were aware that they disseminated their communist and separatist message. The consul in Isfahan, for example, reported that his Russian counterpart was taking a special interest in the Armenians of Jolfa. There had been a special showing of an Armenian-language film about Lenin's life, a present from the Soviets to their Armenian 'brothers'. The Armenian community was apparently 'very flattered by this attention'. There was even a play performed in Jolfa in the Armenian language about the collection of funds for a Soviet tank regiment manned by Armenians.[62] The Soviets also published booklets in Azerbaijani praising the Red Army, urging the celebration of Kurdish culture and encouraging the people to throw off Tehran's yoke.

Though the Germans had been drummed out of Iran, the Nazi propaganda machine was quick to capitalize on the inroads into Iranian politics and society being made by the allies. Broadcasts emphasizing rivalries between American and British commanders in the field, and the deleterious effects of occupation, must have resonated with people experiencing the hardships associated with foreign occupation. Such broadcasts also considered the ideological pretensions of the allies. Discussing the offer of 'democracy and justice for all nations', one announcer asked his listeners to consider two examples. '[L]ook at the condition of India', he said, 'instead of a rule of democracy a rule of stagnation, misery and starvation prevails.' Contrast that with Iran: 'instead of recognising the sovereignty of Iran, the allies are trying to be big bullies and have taken control of the Persian railway and other means of communication.'[63] A subsequent broadcast contrasted the happiness of the people of the Balkan states now they were under German patronage, and the desire of the nefarious British to divide them for the benefit of the Soviet Union.[64]

German broadcasts dwelled on the Soviet Union's imperial ambitions in the Middle East, its designs on Medina and Mecca and its aim of 'extending [its] sphere of influence in Iran and the Arab countries. Americans want the same kind of exploitation, specially oil.' Another broadcast claimed that 'when Americans saw their own oil supplies being exhausted they decided to look elsewhere, and began to exert pressure on the Persian Government.'[65] Intra-allied discord was a consistent theme, gaining greater prominence as the war progressed: 'The Russians want to secure their position against the British and Americans who intend to double-cross them in the long run. Now Persia realises the plight in which the British have landed them by inviting the Bolshevik hordes to overrun their country . . . American concessions will be very beneficial to the Jews and Armenians, who will be able to fill their pockets at Persian expense.'[66] Since most Middle Eastern countries had 'become centres for Allied military forces they are faced with great economic difficulties', the German propagandists observed.

> In countries occupied by the Allies three causes are contributing to the rapid dwindling of the population – famine due to looting by the Allies and their inability to ship foodstuffs; lack of security due to Allied inability to maintain order; epidemics due to undernourishment and Allied inability to send medical supplies. But the Allies are not satisfied with all that. They exploit the people and their natural resources and grow rich on the proceeds of their robbery.[67]

US civil–military relations and the Hurley–Roosevelt exchange

In addition to their difficulties with the British, Iranians and Soviets, the Americans had problems of their own. These stemmed from the fact that the military, from the War Department in Washington down to the head of Persian Gulf Command, had a much narrower understanding of their role in Iran than that envisioned for them by the State Department, which was in favour of a form of American influence-building. The US Army and War Department refused to get involved. Secretary of State Cordell Hull wrote to President Roosevelt on 16 August 1943 saying that the political and economic situation in Iran was 'critical and may dissolve into chaos at any moment', and urged that the State Department's policy be more actively pursued. To do this, the War Department needed to come into line; at present, 'the general commanding sticks strictly to his orders about trans-porting supplies [and] he does not feel free to cooperate, even informally, with the efforts of American civilian representatives and agencies to solve the numerous, pressing, internal problems of Iran'.[68] The army, however, stuck to its guns, responding to diplomatic requests by insisting that it 'had no military function other than developing and operating transportation and port facilities'.[69]

The State Department eventually took the matter to the commander-in-chief himself. 'As you know,' Acting Secretary of State Edward Stettinius Jr told President Roosevelt on 29 October 1943, 'the situation in Iran is crit-ical. I think it would be desirable, in certain contingencies, to make use of Major General Patrick Hurley for a short period on a special mission to Tehran.' He suggested that he could be sent as the president's personal representative with the rank of ambassador, describing him as 'persona grata to the Russians' and therefore able to engender 'greater cooperation with them and also help coordinate activities of our own agencies'. This letter was returned with an addendum from the president which read: 'ERS [Stettinius] OK FDR.' In the wake of this correspondence, Stettinius wrote to the American minister in Egypt saying that Hurley should be informed that the president wanted him to undertake a special mission to Iran, as an ambassador with the temporary rank of major general.

Hurley was a colourful character. He had served as Secretary for War from 1929 to 1933, and had already undertaken a range of missions in the Second World War, such as examining the chances of relieving troops in the Bataan peninsula on behalf of George Marshall, and visiting Australia to arrange supplies and transport for forces evacuating the Philippines. He had visited China, New Zealand and the Soviet Union on behalf of the president (and was later to become ambassador to China). He was a confirmed Anglophobe, and believed that Britain was a malign influence in world affairs, and that British and Soviet policies had brought poverty to Iran.

Just as a correspondence on Iran was developing between Hurley and Roosevelt, the president had occasion to visit the country in person, to take part, along with Churchill and Stalin, in the Tehran conference in late November and early December of 1943.[70] It was to be one of the war's show-piece heads-of-state conferences, at which important decisions were made about the future conduct of the war, such as the launch of the Anglo-American invasion of Western Europe, and the shape of the post-war world. Roosevelt's visit to the Iranian capital, and a meeting with Major General Hurley during it, sparked an important exchange of letters.[71] The stimulus was a conversation between the two men at Tehran airport as the president waited to fly home. During the course of their conversation, Roosevelt outlined to Hurley 'a tentative basis for American policy in Iran which could be a template for relations with all less favoured associate nations'. On the strength of their discussion, Hurley composed an eleven-page letter to Roosevelt, which the president subsequently endorsed and sent around Washington.[72]

The president's vision, Hurley wrote, was of a free and independent nation in which the Iranian people had 'an opportunity to enjoy the rights of man as set forth in the Constitution'. Iran as a backward country could be a real 'project' for the American policy of bringing 'independent nations along in a selfless way'. This required two things: the removal of external imperialism, and within Iran 'a government based on the consent of the governed and a system of free enterprise which will enable the nation to develop its resources primarily for the benefit of its own people'. This would entail freedom of press and speech, freedom from want and equality of opportunity. So far, so visionary. To accomplish this, America would furnish Iran with expert advisers in any or all of the fields of government, invited and paid for by the Iranian government. Hurley continued:

> Modern history of this country shows it to have been dominated by a powerful and greedy minority. The people have also been subjected to foreign exploitation and monopoly. This plan of nation building may be improved through our experience of Iran and may become the criterion for the relations of the United States towards all the nations which are now suffering from the evils of greedy minorities, monopolies, aggression and imperialism . . . The American people, single-mindedly devoted to independence and liberty, are fighting today not to save the imperial-

isms of other nations nor to create an imperialism of our own but rather to bestow upon the world the benevolent principles of the Atlantic Charter and the Four Freedoms.[73]

Hurley then summarized the major obstacles to the achievement of the American vision: 'In all the nations I have visited, I have been told, usually by British and Americans, that the principles of imperialism already have succumbed to the principles of democracy. From my own observations, however, I must say that if imperialism is dead, it seems very reluctant to lie down.' America needed to bring its British ally to heel, and remedy the problematic nature of America's presence in Iran. In writing about this Hurley showed prescience regarding Britain's decline:

> Britain can be sustained as a first class power but to warrant this support from the American people she must accept the principles of liberty and democracy and discard the principles of oppressive imperialism ... I think it important that we understand that since our troops entered Iran on the invitation of the British, without advance notice to the Government of Iran, it was natural for the Iranians to look upon us as a British instrumentality. In addition to this the United Kingdom Commercial Corporation has been attempting, and to a considerable degree, succeeding in establishing a complete trade monopoly in Iran.[74]

Hurley explained that the Soviets viewed the Americans as instruments of Britain. 'In my opinion Britain and Russia aspire to control Iran after the war, not jointly but separately', Britain for the oil and trade monopoly, the Soviet Union for access to a warm-water port. But Britain's power was waning even before the war; the country, wrote Hurley, 'no longer possesses within herself the essentials of power needed to maintain her traditional role as the dominant influence in the Middle East area'. Problematically, in Hurley's opinion, 'antipathy towards Britain has caused a growth first of pro-Nazi and now of pro-Soviet sentiment'. American prestige was decreasing 'without any parallel benefit to British prestige'. He discerned a 'growing feeling among British officials that the US has ambitions to become a colonial power'. He noted that there had been extensive Axis propaganda to the effect that the Americans intended to take over the British Empire. Given all of this, the president needed to exercise firm leadership.

The president's reaction to this letter was all-important. He could have politely responded while shelving it. But he did not. On 12 January 1944, he wrote a memorandum for the Secretary of State, enclosing the 'very long letter from Pat Hurley'. Rather than distancing himself from its robust content, Roosevelt confirmed that 'it is in general along the lines of my talk with him'. In his letter the president wrote:

> Iran is definitely a very, very backward nation. It consists really of a series of tribes and 99% of the population is, in effect, in bondage to the other 1%. The 99% do not own their land and cannot keep their own production or convert it into money or property . . . I was rather thrilled with the idea of using Iran as an example of what we could do by an unselfish American policy. We could not take on a more difficult nation than Iran. I would like, however, to have a try at it. The real difficulty is to get the right kind of American experts who would be loyal to their ideals, not fight among themselves and be absolutely honest financially . . . If we could get this policy started, it would become permanent if it succeeded as we hope during the first five or ten years.[75]

Roosevelt agreed with Hurley 'that the whole Lend-Lease Administration should take complete control of the distribution of our own Lend-Lease supplies in the Middle East'. Iran had become an American project. But it remained a British and a Soviet one, too.

The intensification of allied competition

The reaction of the British and the Soviet Union to the situation in Iran was due to the 'initiatives of the Iranians as well as to any preconceived policy of great power confrontation or global expansion. Domestic crises within Iran attracted great power intervention and anticipated the ensuing Cold War struggle.'[76] Iranian statesmen worked the national strategy of 'positive equilibrium' and 'laboured to intensify differences' between the British and Soviets and enmesh the Americans as arbitrators and protectors.'[77] Convinced that the Atlantic Charter principles and America's history of non-intervention made it a trustworthy partner, they continued to seek to engage it as a buffer. Government and interest groups used allies as protectors and promoters of internal power struggles, through which the monarchy was able to regain its supremacy and, ultimately, Iran was able to secure its independence and territorial integrity.[78] Hasan Arfa, a wartime Chief of Staff of the Iranian army, wrote that 'Our policy was to bring as many Americans as possible to Iran to be witnesses of the Soviet political encroachment and by their presence act as a deterrent for the more open violations of our independence'.[79] Key to this strategy was the supply of a constant feed of information to American diplomats regarding Soviet transgressions. Complaint after complaint was lodged, helping convince Dreyfus and his team that the Soviets represented a genuine danger to Iran's independence. The Iranians would even embellish their stories for effect, claiming for example that the Soviets had denied Iran access to the Soviet zone to prevent a Kurdish uprising in 1942. But the Soviets had agreed and granted permission for 500 security personnel to enter. The Iranians had then said that this was not enough, and demanded access for 1,500 personnel; the Soviets agreed to this too, and so the Iranians raised the figure to 5,000, all part of a game intended to cast the Soviets in a poor light in American eyes.[80]

The decisive event in determining the battle lines between America and the Soviet Union in Iran occurred in October 1944. Active Soviet aggression and interference up until this point had been limited. The catalyst was the Iranian government's announcement of its decision to postpone all negotiations on oil concessions until after the war, with the oil crisis that followed becoming the catalyst for American–Soviet confrontation.

In 1943, American companies were invited to seek agreement on an oil concession. The Iranian government warned that it might damage allied unity, but American companies and the American government jumped at the opportunity. The invitation included prospecting in the north of the country, despite long-standing Soviet warnings regarding their 'prior rights' to northern oil.

The Iranian government had initially been considering offers from American Standard Vacuum, Sinclair Oil and British Shell for a concession in the south. But then the Soviets came in. In September 1944 Sergey Kavtaradze, Soviet Commissar for Foreign Affairs, arrived in Tehran demanding a concession for oil and other minerals covering almost all of northern Iran. Stricken by panic, the government's reaction appeared not to treat the Soviet proposal as fairly as those of the Western companies. The Iranians had begun the episode by asking for proposals, and yet here, in typical fashion, were the Soviets, refusing merely to propose and instead asking for an up-front agreement in principle. Parliament united in opposition to the Soviet demand, and found an unsatisfactory way out of the situation by cancelling all oil discussions until the war had ended. The Soviets felt thwarted and humiliated: Moscow's reaction was severe, unleashing a barrage of anti-government propaganda, much of it directed through the Tudeh Party.

The Tudeh Party had been formed after the shah's abdication with the tacit approval of the occupying powers and became Iran's first popular mass movement. It consisted of intellectuals persecuted under the shah who admired European democracies and favoured collaboration with the allies.[81]

> The party began to attract the young and progressive, the educated, and the intellectuals because of its modern, democratic and popular ideals, the large number of reputable Marxist and non-Marxist individuals in its leadership and among its cadres, and the growing popularity of the Soviet Union towards which it was clearly (but not yet slavishly) inclined. But – perhaps most important of all – it provided channels for airing and publishing modern European ideas, and a home for those who talked, wrote and read about them.[82]

The party came out openly in support of the Soviet Union, and became subject to Soviet policy. The only practical response to its demands, from a British point of view, was to strenuously advocate that the shah, his government and parliament work towards similar reform goals. But the Iranian elite was incapable of inaugurating such reforms. Nevertheless, the British pressed for them; Bullard, for example, advised Prime Minister Soheili to protect the rights of industrial workers and increase cultivators' share of produce, as well as setting a limit to the size of individual estates. The British were not averse to Tudeh deputies in parliament given their aims and the chance that they might shock the elite into action. This was also a way for the British to try to distance themselves from their association in the public's eye with the forces of reaction.

But, to the chagrin of the British and the Americans, the Tudeh Party had become increasingly and overtly communist, and at its first party congress in August 1944 the leadership was captured by Marxists. This enabled it to become a vehicle for the Soviet Union's policies within Iran, with telling effect. For example, when the Iranian government rejected the Soviet's proposed oil concession in 1944, the Tudeh Party demonstrated against the decision, exposing the party as a Soviet mouthpiece. Tudeh organized targeted rallies, supported by Soviet military police, against the prime minister, whom they wanted to depose in order to restore their prestige. 'Demonstrators' were bussed around, with Soviet tanks and troops in attendance. A Tudeh press campaign against the Iranian government and 'imperialistic greed' followed, and the Soviet Union broke off contact with the Iranian government, causing the prime minister to resign.[83]

Throughout the war, Moscow kept a close eye on Iranian political affairs and surveyed attitudes towards the Soviet Union. The news agency TASS received reports from Tehran, and Morse code dispatches reported 'provocative' attacks on the Soviet Union in the Iranian press. Certain newspapers, it was asserted, 'have finally overstepped all bounds and are trying to outdo each other in slanderous and provocative attacks on the USSR'. Soviet-sponsored media hit back, declaring that 'the Soviet Government is sacrificing the lives of its citizens for the freedom of small nations' such as Iran.[84] Of particular interest to Moscow was Iranian reaction to its demands for oil concessions. Mohammad Mossadegh's vehement speech against the Soviet 'offer' was reported, as was a national newspaper's assertion that there should be no oil concession 'so long as foreign troops remain on Persia's territory'. The *Raad* newspaper was 'endeavouring to impress upon its readers that Persia is now under threat of losing her independence. *Raad* makes the provocative appeal: "People of Persia, be ready for everything: appeal for God's help!"'[85] Since early in the war, the Soviets had clearly stated their objections to American concessions anywhere in Iran. What the oil crisis did was make America come out strongly in support of Iran, and decisively harden its anti-Soviet stance.

The allies' takeover, and their involvement in so many intimate matters of state, augmented the calls for genuine independence and democracy heard across the country since the overthrow of Reza Shah's autocratic regime:

It was understood that democracy was not possible without full independence, and the latter would not be possible as long as the Iranian government and politics were manipulated by foreign concessionaries and their governments. For a short period it looked as if the Tudeh party would be the organizer and standard-bearer of the Popular Movement. But it fell to Mussadiq [Mossadegh] and the National Front to continue the struggle for independence without, and democracy within, the country.[86]

The invasion had opened a new chapter in the career of Mohammad Mossadegh. From 1928 he had completely withdrawn from the social and political scene, behaving as an internal émigré, 'a rebel in silence'.[87] In 1940 the old shah had had him incarcerated in a medieval desert citadel at Mashhad, where he attempted suicide. Released under the new regime and elected the first Tehran deputy in the fourteenth parliament, he had been vehemently opposed to the Soviet bid for an oil concession, because it could only inhibit the achievement of full independence. He became a voluble critic of the allied presence, and his primary political goal was the nationalization of the oil industry as the basis for proper independence.[88]

But while Mossadegh was to play a crucial role in Iran's post-war future, the immediate problem facing the country in the final stages of the war was the manner in which the three allies would exit, and the ways in which they would seek to stay on.

CHAPTER 16

War's end

The shah, wrote Lieutenant-Colonel Gilbert Pybus, assistant British military attaché in Tehran, 'longs for this war to be over and for all foreigners to go and leave Persia for the Persians.'[1] Iranians yearned for a post-war world free from the exactions of external powers. The Iranian elite continued to seek American assistance in achieving this as the war drew towards its conclusion. In an interview, the shah told *News Chronicle* correspondent Stuart Emeny that, Iran had 'no great propaganda bureau':

> If we had, your people and the world might be more interested in my country, more willing to understand our point of view at the Peace Conference [that would follow the war] – not that we have any additional territorial claims; we ask only for our independence ... We shall need our sterling and dollar balances of some £20,000,000 but that will probably be insufficient for all the reforms we are planning. But just as we have to enable you to finance your military commitments in Persia by giving rials for sterling, we shall expect to receive financial assistance from you after the war.

The shah added with a smile: 'Of course, if Britain goes on spending at her present rate, perhaps you may require a loan from us' – a telling reference to the parlous state of the British economy caused by the war.[2]

The shah was not the only one to find Britain's financial position amusing; 'There is no need to fear British bankruptcy after the war,' jibed a German

Persian language broadcast. 'The British are bankrupt already.'³ The state of the British exchequer was to contribute to significant shifts in the regional balance of power. A pyrrhic victory when it came, the end of the war hastened British decline just as it accelerated America's and the Soviet Union's rise to superpower status. Though Britain was to remain active in Iran and Iraq into the post-war era, the war represented the the high water-mark of its power in the region, and its position became increasingly chimerical.⁴

Even as the noose tightened around Germany's neck, Persian-language propaganda broadcasts continued to emanate from the village of Zeesen near Berlin: though the German threat to the region had entirely disappeared, the voice remained. Reflecting Germany's encirclement, broadcasts gave prominence to tales of terror weapons such as the V-bomb which would supposedly spearhead a revival of German military fortunes. Churchill's demand for unconditional surrender was mocked, and German resolve to 'stand firm' emphasized. The British and Americans were lambasted for 'taking advantage of Germany's concentration on the Eastern Front to save European civilization'.⁵

German broadcasts in the war's terminal months derided the United Nations, arguing that it threatened the rights of small states rather than secured them: 'the Allies intend to trample on the rights of small nations'.⁶ The Soviet Union was portrayed as a particularly dangerous imperialist power in the latter stages of the war, 'taking advantage of Britain's weakness' in pursuit of its desire to establish its exclusive position in northern Iran 'and proceed later to the Persian Gulf and the Indian frontier, thus becoming the absolute ruler in the Middle East'.⁷ Broadcasts discussed Soviet meddling in Iranian politics and its oil demands as a pretext for occupation.⁸ Stalin intended to 'penetrate into Iran, annex that country and gain an outlet to the Persian Gulf', and the Soviets planned to create a breakaway 'Kurdistan Soviet Republic'.⁹ 'Soviet agents, mostly Armenians, have for some time been distributing arms and ammunition to the Kurds of those countries and instructing them to rise against the Iranian Government and fight regular troops.' They hoped to give the Red Army an excuse to 'maintain order'.¹⁰ Many of these assertions were not far wide of the mark. Germany's surrender on 7 May 1945 was marked in Iran by a Red Army parade, supporters of the Tudeh Party driving up and down in open trucks waving Soviet, Iranian and even British flags lent by the consulate.

Extraordinary levels of British military and political activity had occurred in Iran and Iraq during the war. The campaigns Britain fought, and the logistical activity it planned and executed, were integral to the functioning of the system of imperial defence and the waging of war, for Britain, the Empire and the allies. While counterfactual history never proved a thing, it is possible to assess the impact of events and likely alternative scenarios. The Anglo-Iraqi war of May 1941 was a turning point, and it is no exaggeration to say that defeat could have cost Britain its position in the region, especially if Germany had capitalized on the opportunity the war presented. In the end, it was 'a distraction that proved little more than vexatious,' wrote Lord Ismay, 'but which might have had disastrous consequences.'[11] 'If we had lost it,' wrote Freya Stark, 'Hitler's pincer movement could have succeeded, and oil, our access to India, and our desert strategy would have shown in a new and very unpleasant light.'[12] The loss of the region's oil would have been catastrophic for Britain and, in turn, the allies. Questioning General Wavell's stolid reluctance to act in Iraq in April 1941, Elie Kedourie points out that there is good reason to believe that, had the Germans gained the initiative, another Rommel could have been found to do 'behind' Middle East Command's Cairo headquarters what Rommel himself was doing in front of it.[13]

British campaigns in Iran, Iraq and Syria shored up the allied position in a vital region. The campaigns facilitated the conversion of Iran, and to a lesser but important extent, Iraq, into a highly effective highway connecting the combined industrial might of America and Britain to Soviet fighting fronts. All three operations were typical of the workings of the system of imperial defence and the 'British way' of warfare. They displayed, all at once, the fruits of extant planning, opportunism and improvisation, joint air, land and sea operations, effective strategic decision-making and direction, the initiative of subordinate commanders such as Joe Kinstone, Ouvry Roberts, William Slim and Reggie Smart, the combination of British, Indian, colonial and locally recruited forces and the fundamental importance of sea power. Lieutenant-General Edward Quinan, responsible for conducting these campaigns as the in-theatre commander, deserves more than a 'forgotten general' epithet in the annals of the war. His time at the helm amply demonstrated that 'sideshow' campaigns, the movement of military resources and preparing for what might happen, are as much a part of success in war as major combat operations themselves. Knighted in June 1942, Quinan was promoted full general. On leaving Baghdad to make way for General Wilson, he took charge of India Command's North West Army.

Persia and Iraq Command was a manifestation of imperial vision and strategic sound sense. It was created on a shoestring given the many clamant calls on British resources, at a time when major operations looked as if they might well take place in the Iran–Iraq region. Looking forward from the vantage point of 1941–42, no one knew that events elsewhere would prevent it from becoming a kinetic war zone. In the crucial months before the Battle of El Alamein and German reverses on the Eastern Front, preparing to fight here was as important for Britain as its activity in any theatre beyond Britain and the Atlantic. On balance, it is probably a good job that General Wilson's defensive plans were not put to the test by a German invasion.

Major-General Kennedy's quotidian work at the War Office reflected the scale of the British war effort, and the ceaseless struggle to match available resources to actual and potential enemy initiatives. To illustrate the point, on 14 August 1941, as Kennedy worked on plans for the imminent invasion of Iran, he was also preparing plans for operations in the Canaries, Malaya and Spitzbergen, as well as the further reinforcement of Singapore. Here lay the fundamental conundrum of imperial defence in a war against enemies who were so powerful and so widely spread: the problem was 'to decide how far we can strengthen our position in the Indian Ocean and in the Far East without weakening ourselves unduly at home and in the Middle East'.[14] It was a question of robbing Peter to pay Paul – but Paul kept coming back for more. Given this situation, Kennedy understood that patience was a virtue, and that *not losing* in the most strategically important regions was the key to ultimate victory. Though the idea might have brought colour to the cheeks of the notoriously impatient prime minister, the secret was to 'hold our own and gradually harbour our resources which were slowly growing'.[15] 'It is unfortunate,' Kennedy continued, 'that so much time is required for the development of the full power of the British Empire and of America. But this has to be accepted. And we must find consolation in the fact that it is the last battle that counts.'[16]

In addressing these strategic dilemmas, particularly the question of the relative balance of commitments to the Middle East, the Indian Ocean region and the Far East, Kennedy summed up British thinking at the time:

We were still quite uncertain of the outcome of the campaign in Russia. Would the Russians stand up to the German attacks, which were certain to be renewed when the snows melted in the spring? Or would they collapse? We had to bear in mind this second possibility. If it came to pass, could we hold the Middle East, with its garrison depleted, against German attacks through Turkey and Iraq and Persia? Could we defend the oilfields in the Persian Gulf without which our fleet could not operate in Eastern Waters? Could we prevent a junction of the Germans and the Japanese on the shores of the Indian Ocean? And would we have to face, once more, the possibility of a German attempt to invade the British Isles?[17]

In the end, through a combination of resolute action, the dexterous management of risk, sound judgement, good fortune and the activities of allies and enemies alike, the British got it right. Despite the associated anguish and long-term damage to the British Empire, it was the correct decision to prioritize the Mediterranean and Middle East above the defence of the Far East and Pacific. Resources that could have gone to defend Malaya and Singapore went instead to the Soviet Union via Iran, but like the decision to embrace American economic and military power, hitching Britain's fortunes to the success or failure of Soviet resistance to Hitler was part of a war-winning formula. So, too, were the military campaigns in places such as Iran, Iraq, Madagascar and Syria, which effectively nipped enemy threats in the bud and guaranteed Britain's position in regions that it needed to control.

Nevertheless, Simon Davis makes the important point that threats to British interests in the Iran–Iraq region, and efforts to meet them, need to be considered alongside two other important variables. The first is that Britain took advantage of the circumstances thrown up by war to round out its historic position in the Iran–Iraq region and to advance its imperial interests in both countries. The second point is the severe limitations of German and Italian interest and activity in the region, as remarkable in its own way as British vulnerability.[18] Adrian O'Sullivan's pioneering work on German activities in Iran and Iraq demonstrates how poorly utilized were the German resources deployed to the region. He points to the 'resounding dysfunction' of the relationship between the Abwehr and the SD, general ineptitude and failure to cultivate requisite indigenous support.[19] Germany's Iran policy lacked 'unified strategy, well-directed policy, or clearly formed operational priorities'. It was characterized by a lack of inter-service cooperation and the failure to recruit suitable personnel, and was entirely thwarted by the robust and sustained response of the allies.[20] Ultimately, German relations with the region were to prove to be 'replete with misunderstandings and failed expectations', though this should not diminish appreciation of the fact that, at the time, they appeared full of promise.[21]

Winding down the Persian corridor

British initiative as well as British sea power enabled the creation of the 'trans-Iranian highway', for some time primarily a British-run affair with expanding American participation following the formation of Persian Gulf Command. It is as important to acknowledge this foundation as it is to recognize how subsequent American involvement supercharged the operation. The figures speak for themselves. Between early 1942 and September 1945 America provided a total of 409,526 lorries to the Soviet Union, amounting to an estimated 2 years and 7 months-worth of Soviet pre-war production. Nearly 45 per cent of the Lend-Lease lorries reached the Soviets through the Persian corridor and 88 per cent of these were assembled in truck assembly plants in Iran run by PAIC and PGC ordnance units. Of the 14,834 American aircraft sent to the Soviets under Lend-Lease, 4,874 went through Iran, 4,000 arriving in crates, the remainder flown in direct by Air Transport Command from Brazil, across the Atlantic to West Africa and on to Abadan and Basra. Such enormous assembly, construction and maintenance activity had a major impact on local communities as 'the industrialization of the desert spread outward from Basra and Abadan in all directions'.[22] This was what war-winning logistics looked like close up, and 'by doing what it did', PGC 'helped earn this country precious time to prepare and saved an incalculable number of American lives, and it should be credited with a colossal assist in the destruction of a large part of the German Army'.[23]

Once fully operational, the Persian Gulf trans-Iranian route delivered more aid to the Soviet Union than the better-known Arctic route. The latter delivered 23 per cent of total American aid to Moscow, the 'Persian corridor' 27 per cent. The remaining 50 per cent traversed the route from America's west coast to Vladivostok, supplemented by the Alaska–Siberia air route, but was confined to *non-military* supplies. Altogether about 7,900,000 tons of allied shipborne cargo were delivered into the Persian corridor, mostly for the Soviets, but with substantial amounts going also to Persia and Iraq Command and the Iranian government. In October 1941, as the British began operating the trans-Iranian supply route, Iran's railways had been capable of carrying 6,000 tons per month; 2 years later, the figure stood at 175,000 tons. This extraordinary logistical feat was achieved by massively upgrading the region's port, rail and road infrastructure, the importation of thousands of lorries, locomotives and rail cars and the labour of tens of thousands of allied soldiers and Iranian and Iraqi civilians.[24] 'Port and shipping experts were brought in to assess, recommend, and take charge ... Sophisticated operational logistics were introduced to coordinate, schedule and route traffic flows through the ports and upcountry. To add the necessary transport capacity, the allies built out harbour installations and shipped in locomotives, rolling stock, river craft, and trucks.'[25] The Anglo-American powers met and surpassed the commitments made to their ally, a signal achievement of intra-allied supply and cooperation.

The Persian corridor fell into disuse as the war moved decisively in the allies' favour in 1945. As Axis forces were rolled back towards the German heartland, more-direct supply routes between the Western powers and the Soviet Union once more became usable. By September 1944, for example, the Soviets had regained complete control of the northern shores of the Black Sea, 'and it was apparent that great economies in both US military shipping and Soviet rail transportation could be affected by shifting the lines of supply from the Persian Gulf' to shorter routes. The Turkish government agreed to allow passage of the Dardanelles, and the British agreed to provide convoy escort for ships transiting the Aegean.[26] Shipments to the Soviet Union via the Black Sea duly began in January 1945. Truck assembly plants were rushed from Iran to Odessa, and this new, more direct route soon supplanted the Iranian one.

Increasingly, the activities of PAIC and PGC were confined to cleaning up the backlog of supplies in hand, transporting oil from the Abadan refinery to the Soviet zone and liquidating facilities, though some remained intact as an insurance against a sudden reversal in allied fortunes. All manner of materials were dismantled, packed up and shipped to the Soviet Union when the new supply lines opened, such as port cranes and railway equipment, including 792 10-ton trucks and over 3,000 railcars delivered before VE Day.[27] As an example of the work involved in winding down, 'C' Company, 762nd Railway Diesel Shop Battalion found itself at Camp Lowe near Ahwaz in May 1945. Hailing from Erie, Kansas City, New York and Pittsburgh, its troops dismantled and repaired railway cars and prepared them for removal from Iran. Over the course of a single month, they dismantled 454 cars and readied them for shipment, along with 200 20-ton low-side gondolas, 210 40-ton box cars and 44 50-ton war flats. 'Due to the intense heat and high percentage of iron parts necessary to handle,' the commanding officer wrote, 'this was exceptionally good progress.'[28]

The effects of the material delivered were significant, though remain difficult to quantify. The start of the Soviet Union's war-winning offensives relied on vehicles delivered by British and American forces through Iran. As the serviceman Joel Sayre put it in his 1945 account of PGC's activities, 'The world was amazed by the Red Army's mobility two summers ago, when that offensive which never stopped began; contributing mightily to that mobility were a hundred and forty-three thousand American vehicles assembled and delivered by the PGC – trucks, command cars, jeeps, weapons carriers, halftrucks, wreckers, rolling shops, ambulances, and even fire engines.'[29]

Around five million tons of supplies were transported overland via Iran. This amounted to perhaps little more than 7 per cent of the total supplies – *all*, not just Lend-Lease – consumed by the Soviets during the war, but the Soviet historian Alexander Orlov writes that 'supplies received during 1941 and 1942 amounted to closer to 90 per cent of what some front line units had to fight with'.[30] David Glantz argues that without it the war might have taken twelve to eighteen months longer for the allies to win, and it has been estimated that aid delivered through the Persian corridor amounted to enough to supply sixty Red Army combat divisions.

Looking to the post-war future

While the war reaffirmed America's belief in free international trade, Britain sought to round out its imperial position in the Middle East, to protect vital national strategic and economic interests and to head off Arab nationalism, proclaiming regional development as the key.[31] But while the British favoured a continuation of Middle East Supply Centre-style controls and trade barriers, the Americans pushed for a free-market approach in an international environment scourged of exclusive spheres of influence. The Foreign Office had little choice but to acquiesce in the termination of the Middle East Supply Centre in November 1945.

Looking to the future, and despite their mutual differences, both America and Britain worried about Soviet intentions in the region as the war drew to a close. Building the Iranian state's capacity to stand on its own two feet and providing a sound post-war development strategy 'would eliminate the need or excuse for the establishment of any sort of "protectorate"', but might require a lingering Anglo-American presence.[32] This policy was articulated in a State Department memorandum as early January 1943. The president had instructed the department to examine trusteeship schemes here and in other parts of the world to stabilize unsettled regions and provide for open-door access. Roosevelt wanted a free port and internationalized rail access in Iran.[33] Inevitably, America's vision of a free and independent Iran in a post-war United Nations world was at odds with Soviet ambitions. 'Our experts on Soviet Russia are most dubious,' wrote Murray at the State Department, 'that Russia would be interested, at least for the present, in an international trusteeship or would participate in it in the genuine manner intended by the President':

> The British, moreover, would doubtless raise strenuous objections. Britain's policy for a hundred years has been to prevent Russia or any other great power from establishing itself on the Persian Gulf, and there is no indication that British policy has changed in this respect. There is, in fact, sound reason for the continuation of this policy. If we proceed on the assumption that the continuance of the British Empire in some reasonable strength is in the strategic interests of the United States (and I understand the strategists of the War Department proceed on this assumption), it is necessary to protect the vital communications of the Empire between Europe and the Far East.[34]

Fearing that the Soviets would not honour the agreement with Iran and evacuate their forces from the northern provinces on the conclusion of hostilities, on 15 January 1945 Churchill told Roosevelt that they needed to discuss the future of Iran. The prime minister said that it would be 'something of a test case' regarding Soviet intentions in the post-war world.[35] Roosevelt was thinking along similar lines, mulling a 'trusteeship' arrangement whereby the allied powers would assume supervision of parts of Iran, including the railway and a 'free' port. This would give the Soviets access to the Gulf, a long-standing Kremlin ambition. But there remained, the State Department noted, 'certain difficulties' with an idea redolent of the worldview associated with the end of the previous world war.

> No matter how drawn up or proposed, the plan would appear to Iran, and doubtless to the world, as a thinly disguised cover for power politics and old-world-imperialism. Iranians are highly suspicious of foreign

influence in the country and would unquestionably resent any extension of foreign control there. The railway, built by their own strenuous
efforts at a cost of some $150,000,000, without foreign borrowing, is a
source of especial and intense patriotic pride. The Department's judgement is that the trusteeship could only be imposed on Iran, a sovereign,
allied nation, by force of arms.[36]

In proposing to turn parts of Iran, to all intents and purposes, into a United
Nations 'mandate', the Americans risked being hoist by their own petard.

With Germany and Italy prostrate, the allied occupation was due to end
in accordance with the treaty signed after the Anglo-Soviet invasion. But as
the Western allies feared, getting the Soviets to honour its terms was problematic. The Americans wanted to keep some 'caretaker' forces in Iran
because of their suspicions regarding the Soviets, and in June 1945 there
were still 11,000 American troops present, including 3,000 guarding fixed
installations and moveable equipment.[37] Some of the troops were required
for ongoing operations against Japan, which depended on a global logistics
chain that embraced Iran. For example, Ambassador Murray explained to
the State Department that 'we must keep an estimated 1500 at Abadan
airfield so long as that is needed for transit of military aircraft to and from
Far East'.[38] But on 19 September Persian Gulf Command headquarters was
transferred to Khorramshahr, and in a 'few days [the] only US troops in
Tehran will be security detachments, Liquidation Commission personnel
and Air Transport Command'.[39] Total American strength in Iran would fall
to 4,000 by 1 November 1945.[40]

The British were pulling their troops out of Iran too. Gerald Pybus, now
promoted to full colonel and British military attaché, told the Americans that
the schedule of British troop evacuations from Tehran had been completed in
mid-September, only seventy-five officers and men remaining in the capital.[41]
Brigadier Rupert Lochner, who had commanded the 18th Indian Infantry
Brigade during the Anglo-Soviet invasion, was now in command of all British
troops in Iran. He informed his colleagues at PGC that 'all British troops will
be withdrawn to points as far away as Hamadan, Kermanshah, and Andimeshk
within [the] immediate future', and that he expected that 'all 18,000 British
troops may soon leave country entirely going possibly to Iraq'.[42] The problem
was that there remained an estimated '75,000 Soviet troops in [the] north',
compared to what would soon amount to no more than 5,000 British and a
similar number of non-combatant Americans in the south.

By this stage, the Iranian government had dropped all pretence and appealed to America for direct military intervention to stop Soviet aggression.[43] Unrest in the provinces of Azerbaijan and Kurdistan as the war was drawing to a close was encouraged though not created by the Soviets. It led Tehran to initiate military measures to restore control and order, which the Soviets said threatened the security of their forces in Iran. The declaration of autonomous republics in Azerbaijan and Kurdistan in late 1945 had domestic roots, but the Soviets had nurtured them, spending the previous four years claiming basic rights for northern minorities. They had sought to capitalize on the war situation to extend their buffer zone deep into Iranian sovereign territory and press aggressively for oil concessions. They stimulated and nurtured the northern separatist movements and refused to leave when the war ended, and the People's Republic of Azerbaijan was declared, as well as the Republic of Mahabad. Azerbaijani and Kurdish forces, armed and trained by the Soviets, fought the Iranian army as Iran struggled to reclaim its sovereign territory.

Blame attached to the inept Iranian government, which signally failed to respond to the demands of minority groups and used the Soviet presence as an excuse for doing nothing to remedy age-old internal problems. In doing so, it sought to enlist American aid, which was forthcoming. Eventually, American statements in support of an Iranian–Soviet oil agreement in April 1946 allowed Moscow a face-saving way out and ended their refusal to withdraw their forces. They were out by the following month, the strategy of 'positive equilibrium' paying off for the Iranians once again. The American historian Stephen McFarland claims that these crises stemmed from Iranian initiative and not from a preconceived Soviet–American policy of confrontation.[44]

With America assuming a leading role in Iranian affairs and Britain on the wane, the CIA offered percipient insights into Iran's strategic importance, and internal challenges, two years after the war ended: 'The strategic importance of Iran lies in its geographical position in the Middle East bridge connecting Europe, Africa, and Asia, its consequent position with regard to lines of communications of other powers, and its oil resources. If Iran came under the control of a hostile power, the independence of other countries in the Middle East would be threatened, and the interests of the US would thus be jeopardized throughout the entire area.'[45] The voice might well have been a British one, at any time since the nineteenth century. The same applied to America's assessment of the Soviet threat:

The Soviet Union views Iran not only as a possible base for an attack against the USSR and particularly against its vital Caucasus oilfields, but also as a Soviet base for political penetration and possible military operations against areas of vital importance to the security of the Western Powers. If the USSR occupied or dominated Iran, it would: (a) gain control of the oil resources now exploited by the Anglo-Iranian Oil Company; (b) threaten the oil fields in nearby Iraq, Kuwait, Saudi Arabia, and Bahrain; (c) acquire additional bases for carrying on subversive activities or actual attack against Turkey, Iraq, Afghanistan, India, and Pakistan; (d) control continental air routes to Iran, threaten those crossing Turkey, Iraq, the Arabian Peninsula, and the Persian Gulf, and menace shipping in the Persian Gulf; (e) undermine the will of all Middle Eastern countries to resist aggression; and (f) acquire a base 800 miles nearer than any held at present to potential British-US lines of defense in Africa and the Indian Ocean area.[46]

The problem was that the Iranian state remained a poor foundation for the type of nation-building envisioned by the Americans. Assessing the current political situation, the CIA asserted that 'though technically a constitutional monarchy, Iran is an oligarchy. Control of parliament and predominant influence in the affairs of the country are in the hands of wealthy landowners and merchants, army generals, and tribal leaders. Great mass of the people is largely illiterate and politically impotent.' The country's ruling groups were 'united in fear' of the Soviet Union, and with declining British power in the Middle East were turning more to America for support. But the continued failures of the Iranian government 'to rectify critical internal conditions is seriously jeopardizing stability. Widespread corruption by civil and military officials and their discriminatory policies against tribal groups are alienating the major population elements whose support is essential to resisting Soviet demands.' The economic and social reforms long promised were still yet to be delivered.

Unsettled in Mauritius, the deposed Reza Shah Pahlavi moved to South Africa, where he died in exile in 1944. He had 'had little if any interest,' wrote Murray of the US State Department, 'in bettering living and health conditions among his unhappy people. A brutal, avaricious, and inscrutable despot in his later years, his fall from power when the country was occupied in 1941 by British and Soviet forces and his death later in exile were regretted by no one.'[47] But they were regretted by at least one person, his son,

Mohammad Reza Shah Pahlavi. 'In spite of outward protestations', wrote Ann Lambton of the new shah, he 'never really forgave the British for the fall of his father, and this secret resentment was an important influence in deciding his subsequent actions'.[48] Ruling groups united in fear of the Soviets and increasingly turned to America for support. But American diplomats noted that under the new shah the 'continued failure of government to rectify critical internal conditions is seriously jeopardizing stability. Widespread corruption by civil and military officials and their discriminatory policies against tribal groups are alienating the major population elements whose support is essential to resisting Soviet demands.'[49] It was because of this that the American missions met with such limited success and were unable to generate the type of reforms that would have helped Iran become a better governed, and therefore more prosperous and secure, nation.

Nevertheless, as the war drew to its conclusion, Iranian policy and increasingly nationalist political trends dragged America in. Before the war, American contact with Iran had been largely confined to individuals, who usually left a good impression, and characterized by general deference to Britain as the main external power in the country. The American government showed little interest even when PGC stood up and American involvement in the country entered a new phase. What had captured Washington's attention was Soviet policy, especially in Azerbaijan, and the subsequent perception that a highly aggressive Soviet Union wanted a communist government in Tehran.[50]

The consequences for Iran and Iraq

Though ostensibly independent nation-states, at the end of the war both Iran and Iraq were occupied semi-colonies at the mercy of the 'Big Three'. The invasions of 1941 left political scars as democratic values supposedly being championed were ignored. The governments of both countries were too inefficient, too weak and too corrupt to deliver the internal reforms that might have sparked economic development, and were preoccupied with suppressing demands for autonomy in key regions, thus stifling the prospects of greater national unity. Iran's internal security forces had collapsed, semi-autonomous conditions prevailed in the provinces and the administrative machinery of government had been severely disrupted. The ruling elites of both countries completely neglected the welfare of the common people, and the circumstances of war had made things even worse. The cost of living rose astronomically and people went hungry. Transportation systems were disrupted, severely so in Iran, and allied interference penetrated from the national to the local level. 'Although Allied troops spent large sums of money in Iran temporarily increasing the number (and profits) of bazaaris, at war's end, cheap Western goods flooded the market causing bankruptcies among artisans and bazaar shopkeepers.'[51] Importation led to the closure of factories, and the employment boom caused by the demands of allied occupation ended with the war. Addressing the Parliamentary Labour Party's Middle East Group shortly after the war had ended, Ann Lambton said:

> Road and railway activity gave, it is true, temporary employment to many thousands of labourers, but it is not by any means clear whether a greatly expanded road and railway system will be an asset to Persia in the post war years; the upkeep of the system should it be either beyond her needs or nor in accordance with them – and it must be remembered that expansion was carried out to meet allied war needs, not Persian needs – may prove a social incubus rather than a social asset.[52]

As the shah's power diminished in Iran, the political fortunes of Mohammad Mossadegh rose. Having returned to parliament, he led the National Front of Iran. He came to prominence advocating the need to secure genuine independence by ending the grip of external powers, killing off foreign concessions and repatriating the lion's share of the profits derived from Iranian oil through the nationalization of the Anglo-Iranian Oil Company. This put him on a collision course with the British, and led to a joint CIA and MI6 plot, involving fake 'communist' demonstrators, that removed him in 1953 and led to the return of the shah, who had fled the country, and a favourable deal for Anglo-Iranian Oil. Thereafter, Reza Pahlavi remained on the throne until the Iranian Revolution of 1979.

Iran's contemporary sensitivity to foreign interference and pressure is rooted in its history of external invasion and influence, not least during the Second World War when each of the 'Big Three' allies intervened so robustly in its affairs. Among other things this deepened the widespread belief in British manipulation behind almost everything; the Iranian historian Homa Katouzian writes that in the minds of many Iranians, the British 'masterfully – magically – plotted and executed some of the minutest happenings regarding the least important issues in Iranian society.'[53] But remaining vestiges of British influence in Iran were disappearing, the consular service, for example, abolished in 1952 by a government tired of its interference.

As for Iraq, the defeat of May 1941 led to a period of re-colonization and a fatal weakening of parliamentary democracy. The end of the war found the Iraqi government conducting military operations against Mullah Mustafa Barzani, who had led a Kurdish separatist movement since 1943. 'Heavy-handed neo-colonial intervention intended to keep Iraq in the Western orbit ironically helped push it, later on, in the 1950s, toward precisely the authoritarian populism, in the form of the Communist and Ba'ath Parties, that London had sought to forestall.'[54] Britain maintained its position in Iraq because the ruling elite felt threatened by the Soviet Union and because Britain still needed to protect the region's oil and maintain military facilities, and wanted to continue to exercise leadership in the Middle East. It retained its military bases, which meant that their unpopularity did not ebb; they propped up a ruling elite that did little for its people, but could find no other viable collaborators. In 1946 Vic Smith was posted to the 19th Indian Infantry Brigade, still sporting the pink elephant shoulder flash of Persia and Iraq Command. In August the brigade sailed from Karachi to the Shatt al-Arab. They were joined in Basra by thousands of vehicles and formed a recovery unit and a light aid detachment at Shaibah. At the time there were still about 20,000 imperial troops in Iraq. 'All modernizing units, brand new equipment, the cruiser HMS *Glasgow* in the harbour, with a frigate beside it, and at least one squadron of rocket-firing Tempests based in Egypt at a moment's notice,' Smith wrote. Their tasks included convoying ex-Afrika Korps prisoners of war, but their real purpose was to provide a defensive screen in a region that it was feared the Soviets might attack.[55]

At the end of the war the British encouraged democratization and social reform, but this policy ran into trouble because rather than providing a viable alternative base for collaboration, those influenced by democratic ideas tended to want to break with the ruling elite and sever Iraq's links with Britain. The elite was also keen to retain the British link because they feared domestic unrest along with secessionism in Iran and Turkey and the Iraqi communist party (both Soviet-sponsored). They also stuck with Britain because they did not want an association with America on account of its pro-Jewish policies, though naturally continued to be galled by Britain's record in Palestine and its failure to prevent the foundation of the state of Israel.[56] Long into the post-war period the Iraqi military remained disaffected following its 1941 defeat and subsequent purge, thus making the regime even weaker and perpetuating the fundamental problems at the heart of Iraq's uneasy relationship with Britain since the aftermath of the First World War. For its part, restored by British arms in 1941, the Hashemite monarchy's subsequent Anglophilia 'helps explain why the Royal family became isolated from Iraqis',[57] having lost its 'nationalist credentials' when it became 'wholly subservient to Britain' following the crisis of April and May 1941.[58]

As elsewhere in the world, despite the outward appearance of strength in 1945, time was running out for the British, and the post-war world was to be one of increasing nationalism and independence, and the retreat of colonialism. The Anglo-Iraqi Treaty was due to expire in 1957 and a rising tide of nationalism was making things difficult throughout the Middle East. In Iraq, the British encountered the challenges of declining empire. They felt obliged to remain, to protect the oil, maintain air communications with the East and to provide a defensive screen across a region that it was feared the Soviets might attack. But with the world changing so quickly and Britain enervated by war, it might have been better to have followed Clement Attlee's preferred policy of gracefully withdrawing from 'lead nation' status in the Middle East, shifting Britain's position away from military bases and treaties to less obtrusive economic relationships with friendly, independent regimes. But imperial powers seldom plot their own demise. As Daniel Silverfarb remarks, 'by remaining too long in places where they were not wanted, the British ensured that when their withdrawal came it would be ignominious'.[59] So it was to prove. Attlee was overruled, and Britain's position in the Middle East was to be precipitously diminished by the aftermath of the 1953 Iran episode, Nasserism, the Suez crisis of 1956 and the Iraqi revolution of 1958. During the course of this revolution, the wartime regent Prince Abdulillah and King Faisal II were machine-gunned along with other members of the royal family in a palace courtyard, the body of the former mutilated and strung up, that of the latter suspended from a lamp-post. Nuri as-Said, in his fourteenth term as prime minister, was murdered and buried the following day, but his corpse was dug up, mutilated, run over repeatedly by municipal buses and dragged through the streets.

Legacies of the Second World War in the Iran–Iraq region can be traced through the modern histories of both nations, in physical objects and the built environment, and in less tangible ways.

For instance, nearly 3,000 Polish refugees died and were buried in Iran, mostly perishing from typhus. Tehran's Doulab cemetery alone accommodates nearly 2,000 graves in a section subsequently purchased by the Polish government. The name Darius would become a common Polish boys' name.

At Chartwell, Winston Churchill's mansion in Kent, a framed German iron cross hangs on a wall. It had belonged to Franz Mayr, the influential German agent deployed to Iran and captured by the British in August 1943. The decoration had been presented to Churchill later that year in Tehran by men of the Combined Intelligence Centre Iraq and Persia, on the occasion of his birthday on 30 November. After Churchill, Roosevelt and Stalin had congregated in Iran for what became known as the Tehran conference, they too left a trace: prominent streets in Tehran were named after them. Yet, reflecting the vastly altered political landscape of post-revolutionary Iran, the street named for the British prime minister, on which the British Embassy stood, was renamed Bobby Sands Street in honour of the Irish Republican Army hunger striker soon after his death in the Maze prison in 1979.

Back in 1943, prior to the conference Stalin had made a courtesy call on the shah, though he insisted on using his own guards when he did so.[60] But neither Churchill nor Roosevelt did, with the American president subsequently, and rather lamely, sending a framed photograph of himself.[61] Roosevelt was informed that the shah and his government were 'bitterly disappointed and even felt humiliated that you were unable to make a return call upon the Shah and receive the hospitality and the honor which he was eager to accord to you. The chagrin of the Iranians is all the more poignant because Marshal Stalin took special pains to call upon the Shah.'[62]

Revealing the realities of power, Iran was simply the backdrop for a meeting of the war's main protagonists, an inconvenient compromise venue given Stalin's unwillingness to travel farther away from his capital and his country. It is important that history does not mirror this meeting by simply alighting on Iran and Iraq in order to reference a couple of 'sideshow' campaigns or remark on global logistics and the start of the Cold War, treating it, along with so many other regions, as a minor stage in the story of 'our' war. The persistent habit of telling the story of history's most pervasive conflict with little thought for the people and countries in which the action took place must be overcome, if we are to create new histories of the conflict.

History is written with hindsight, which dictates what is remembered and what is forgotten. It is also written, especially when it comes to war, with an eye for action and drama. Like moths to a flame, historians, novelists and film producers return time and again to the bright lights of battle, and to 'turning point' moments only discernible when complex sequences of events are unravelled backwards. But for those living life forwards during the Second World War, there was no hindsight, and no crystal ball to reveal the stepping stones to victory. Iran and Iraq deserve due integration into our understanding of the war, as do other regions important to its outcome and deeply affected by it, though not the scene of the big battles, and remote from the heartlands of the main belligerents.

ENDNOTES

Abbreviations

BBCMSA   BBC Monitoring Service Archive
CAC   Churchill Archives Centre
CIA   Central Intelligence Agency
FRUS   Foreign Relations of the United States
IWM   Imperial War Museum
LHCMA   Liddell Hart Centre for Military Archives
MECA   Middle East Centre Archive
NARA   National Archives and Records Administration
TNA   The National Archives

Preface and acknowledgements

1. Together with the project's Postdoctoral Research Fellow, Gajendra Singh, Yasmin and I edited *An Imperial World at War*, which brought together a selection of the papers presented at the project's main conference event held at Kellogg College, Oxford, in 2013.

Introduction

1. Central Office of Information, War Office, *PAIFORCE: The Official Story of the Persia and Iraq Command, 1941–1946* (London: HMSO, 1948), p. 2. This is a peerless contemporary description of the work of the British and Indian armies in the region. Nearly 900,000 imperial troops had served in Mesopotamia during the First World War, 100,000 of them becoming casualties. Variations of the description of the Persian Gulf and Shatt al-Arab as 'the arsehole of the world' were ubiquitous at the time. Deployed there in April 1941, the Gurkha officer John Masters wrote: 'Mr Hopkins, President Roosevelt's special envoy, went to Iraq a little while later and remarked to a British general, "The Persian Gulf is the arsehole of the world, and Basra is about eighty miles up it". It was to this exact spot that we were now to be sent, a form of military enema ... We threw away the Jungle Warfare pamphlets and began a search for the Desert Warfare series.' John Masters, *The Road Past Mandalay* (London: Companion Book Club, 1961), p. 22. On Basra, see also Peter Coats, *Of Generals and Gardens: The Autobiography of Peter Coats* (London: Weidenfeld and Nicolson, 1976). Baghdad routinely came in for similar stick from Britons with unrealistic expectations and very tinted cultural lenses. See the baleful initial impressions of the Countess of Ranfurly, discussed in chapter 13, note 5. Noël Coward thought it looked fascinating from the air, conforming to *Arabian Nights*-style romantic images, but horrid once on the ground; see Noël Coward, *Middle East Diary* (London: William Heinemann, 1944), p. 65. Harold Eeman, the Belgian diplomat accredited to

Tehran during the war, wrote that 'I could not think much of a city that turns its back on its only asset – the river. For noise, dirt, and squalor, the main street of Baghdad, running parallel to the Tigris, hidden behind a screen of shabby buildings, is hard to beat.' Harold Eeman, *Clouds Over the Sun: Memories of a Diplomat, 1942–1958* (London: Robert Hale, 1981), p. 48.

2. Martin Wilmington reminds us that before the war, 'the "Middle East" as spoken of today had been in practically nobody's lexicon or map of political geography'. The term was 'not generally in use until somebody in London contrived the term in 1939 as a convenient geographic reference for a military command to be set up in Cairo with a small staff under General Wavell ... Before then the term had been infrequently and inconsistently applied to designate either the Levant States or the area made up by Iran, Iraq, and Afghanistan.' Martin Wilmington, *The Middle East Supply Centre* (Albany, NY: SUNY Press, 1971), p. 2. Compton Mackenzie, a critic of Middle East Command's failure to take the Iran–Iraq region seriously enough, wrote that the 'command might be called Mideast, but the vital strategic importance of the true Middle East to the whole future course of the war did not seem to have been fully appreciated'. Compton Mackenzie, *Eastern Epic*, vol. 1: *September 1939–March 1943 – Defence* (London: Chatto and Windus, 1951), p. 89. For his part, Churchill wrote that he had 'always thought that the name "Middle East" for Egypt, the Levant, Syria and Turkey was ill-chosen. This was the Near East. Persia and Iraq were the Middle East.' Churchill, *The Second World War* (London: Cassell, 1948–54), vol. 4, p. 415.

3. The Suez Canal was popularly described as the British Empire's Clapham Junction, or, following Anthony Eden, as its 'swing-door'.

4. John Heaney ['Surfield'], 'Indian Surveyors in Paiforce', *Journal of the United Services Institution of India and Pakistan*, vol. 78, no. 331 (April 1948), pp. 153–62, p. 158. Heaney, writing here under the penname 'Surfield', became surveyor-general of India in 1946. His papers are held by the Centre of South Asian Studies, Cambridge. Box 7 contains a Xerox copy of his memoir, 'The Winding Trail', which covers his wartime work in Iran and Iraq.

5. Among other references, see Steven Trent Smith, 'Off the Rails', *World War II*, vol. 31, no. 1 (May 2016) and and Frank Schubert, 'The Persian Gulf Command: Lifeline to the Soviet Union', in Barry Fowle (ed.), *Builders and Fighters: US Army Engineers in World War II* (Fort Belvoir, VA: US Army Corps of Engineers Office of History, 1992), pp. 305–15; chapter online at http://www.parstimes.com/history/persian_gulf_command.pdf (accessed 15 December 2017).

6. I am very grateful to Simon Davis for the reflections on the big 'so whats?' that his probing questions and suggestions prompted.

1 Iran, Iraq and the great powers

1. Coats, *Of Generals and Gardens*, p. 107. Captain Coats was Wavell's aide-de-camp. This was a 'very dicey run' – the aircraft, which had sent repeated signals for help, managed to limp into Lydda.

2. Arthur Smith, 'PAIFORCE', *Household Brigade Magazine* (autumn 1945), pp. 110–12.

3. Freya Stark, *Dust in the Lion's Paw: Autobiography 1939–1946* (London: John Murray, 1961), p. 147.

4. For an excellent introduction, see Gordon Pirie, *Air Empire: British Imperial Aviation, 1919–1939* (Manchester University Press, 2009).

5. See Ken Delve, *The Desert Air Force in World War Two: Air Power in the Western Desert, 1940–1942* (Barnsley: Pen and Sword, 2017).

6. Robert Lyman, *Iraq 1941: The Battles for Basra, Habbaniya, Fallujah, and Baghdad* (Oxford: Osprey, 2006), p. 7. Daniel Silverfarb, *The Twilight of British Ascendancy in the Middle East: A Case Study of Iraq, 1941–1950* (New York: St Martin's Press, 1994), p. 21.

7. MECA: GB165-0349, 'From Pillar to Post', the family and autobiography of George Tod.

8. Central Office of Information, *PAIFORCE*, p. 5.

9. On propaganda, there are numerous excellent works, including Jeffrey Herf, *Nazi Propaganda for the Arab World* (New Haven, CT: Yale University Press, 2010) and David Motadel, *Islam and Nazi Germany's War* (Cambridge, MA: Harvard University Press, 2014). On the lineage of German policy in the region, see Wolfgang Schwanitz,' "The Jinnee and the Magic Bottle": Fritz Grobba and German Middle Eastern Policy, 1900–1945', in Wolfgang Schwanitz (ed.), *Germany and the Middle East, 1871–1945* (Princeton, NJ: Markus Wiener, 2004), pp. 87–117.

10. For an overview, see Renate Dieterich, 'Germany's Relations with Iraq and Transjordan from the Weimar Republic to the End of the Second World War', *Middle Eastern Studies*, vol. 41, no. 4 (July 2005), pp. 463–79.

11. Throughout the period Britain 'tended to overestimate the influence these [Axis] programmes actually had'. Ibid., p. 466.

12. See Geoffrey Warner, *Iraq and Syria 1941* (Cranbury, NJ: Associated University Press, 1979), p. 81, for Woermann's appreciation of the value of Iran–Iraq to the British, and its potential value to Germany.

13. NARA, German Military Documents Section, EDS/Misc/6, Box 12/15.
14. Adrian O'Sullivan, 'German Covert Initiatives and British Intelligence in Persia (Iran), 1939-1945', PhD thesis (University of South Africa, 2012) p. 33.
15. Ibid.
16. Printed Records of the German Foreign Office: Fragmentary Records of Miscellaneous Reich Ministries and Offices, 1919-1945: No. 8. Miscellaneous German Records Collection (Part II), Rolls: 67-88; No. 90. Miscellaneous German Records Collection (Part IV), Serial: EAP 3-k-10 Roll: 0294, 1st Frame: 0000182; Serial: EAP 3-1-1a Roll: 0294, 1st Frame: 0000258; Box no. 21. Records of the Deutsches Ausland-Institut, Stuttgart: Part II: The General Records: Serial: 738 Roll: 520, Provenance: Deutsches Ausland-Institut Item: DAI 835, 1st Frame: 5284748; Box no. 33 (Iran, Irak, Indien, Isld. I u. II), Serial: 761 Roll: 543, Provenance: Deutsches Ausland-Institut Item: DAI 902, 1st Frame: 5314659; Folder no. 12, H2/I, Serial: 776 Rolls: 558-9 Provenance: Deutsches Ausland-Institut, Item: DAI 941, 1st Frame: 5334282. Records of Reich ministries contain items relating to the Iranian railway system, including 'The Railways of Persia', a copy of *The Railway Gazette* detailing the region's railway system and reports on the Iranian road network prepared by the Kiel-based Institute for World Economics in 1940. The German Foreign Institute in Stuttgart, responsible for collating intelligence on German nationals overseas, gathered material on political conditions in the Near East and the economic development of Iran. Its files contain documents on Iraq's relations with the Arab world; Iraqi-German relations; Iraqi politics and economics; and Iraqi relations with Britain. It reported on German 'cultural work' in Tabriz; German-Iranian economic collaboration; the treatment of Germans in Iran; reports from Germans returning home from Iran; and Iranian economic development. There was also data on Soviet encroachment in northern Iran, British policies in Iran and Iraq and the oil resources of both countries.
17. 'The Great Game' is a common description of the political and diplomatic rivalry between Britain and Russia/the Soviet Union in Central Asia, and the activities of the personnel – soldiers, diplomats and spies – who played it, popularized by Rudyard Kipling's *Kim*. For a standard work on the subject, see Peter Hopkirk, *The Great Game: On Secret Service in High Asia* (London: John Murray, 1992).
18. For an overview of military operations, see Frederick Moberly, *Operations in Persia, 1914-1919* and Touraj Atabaki (ed.), *Iran and the First World War: Battleground of the Great Powers* (London: I.B. Tauris, 2006).
19. Andrew Scott Cooper, *The Fall of Heaven: The Pahlavis and the Final Days of Imperial Iran* (New York: Henry Holt, 2016), p. 44.
20. An attitude still discernible in the twenty-first century. Witness press coverage at the time of the Iranian seizure of a party of British Marines in 2007. This well-known perspective – that the wily British are behind everything – is lampooned in the famous Iranian novel by Iraj Pezeshkzad, *My Uncle Napoleon*, published in 1973 and set during the wartime occupation of Iran by allied forces.
21. Fakhreddin Azimi, *Iran: The Crisis of Democracy from the Exile of Reza Shah to the Fall of Musaddiq – 1941-1953* (London: I.B. Tauris, 2009), p. 1.
22. Ibid., p. 61.
23. De Gaury, *Traces of Travel Brought Home from Abroad* (London: Quartet Books, 1983), pp. 110-11. British visitors to Baghdad, by contrast, tended to focus on its perceived squalor. Gerald de Gaury reminds us that, until the British created the state of Iraq, Baghdad had not been a true capital for nearly seven centuries, the city described in the 1920s as 'an ancient oriental hive ... nearly oblivious of the Western world' ('or, indeed, of distant parts of its own new kingdom'), with a road cut through it on the insistence of the German high command in the First World War for military supply purposes. By the late 1930s, much building and road-making was under way, heralding the appearance of glass-fronted shops, cinemas, cabarets and modern-style baths. The old city ramparts and its gates had been torn down. Gerald de Gaury, *Three Kings in Baghdad: The Tragedy of Iraq's Monarchy* (London: I.B. Tauris, 2008), pp. 3, 26, 29 and 96-7.
24. Eeman, *Clouds Over the Sun*, p. 12.
25. Eve Curie, *Journey Among Warriors* (New York: Doubleday, Doran and Co., 1943), p. 100.
26. Homa Katouzian, *Mussadiq and the Struggle for Power in Iran* (London: I.B. Tauris, 1999), p. 34.
27. Clarmont Skrine, *World War in Iran* (London: Constable and Company, 1962), p. 174.
28. John Colville, *The Fringes of Power: Downing Street Diaries, 1939-1955* (London: Hodder and Stoughton, 1985), preface, p. 14 and p. 21.
29. Durham University Special Collections, Ann Lambton Papers, 57/5 typed notes.
30. Katouzian, *Mussadiq and the Struggle for Power*, p. 36.
31. Mansour Bonakdarian, 'US-Iranian Relations, 1911-1951', in Amanat Abbas and Magnus T. Bernhardsson (eds), *US-Middle East Historical Encounters* (Tallahassee: University Press of Florida, 2007), pp. 9-25, p. 15.
32. Katouzian, *Mussadiq and the Struggle for Power*, p. 37.

33. Reader Bullard, *Letters from Tehran: A British Ambassador in World War Two Persia*, ed. E.C. Hodgkin (London: I.B. Tauris, 1991), p. 20.

34. Ehsan Yarshater, 'Persia or Iran, Persian or Farsi', *Iranian Studies*, vol. 22, no. 1 (1989); reproduced in part online at http://www.iranchamber.com/geography/articles/persia_became_iran.php (accessed 15 December 2017). Churchill requested the use of 'Persia' for the duration of the war. While this would of course have appealed to the sentimentalist prime minister's overdeveloped sense of historical and indeed imperial nostalgia, it was not primarily a mark of nefarious orientalism. On 2 August 1941 he told Anthony Eden that 'Persia' should be used in all correspondence in order to avoid 'dangerous confusion'. Bullard, British minister in Tehran, wrote that the army found the confusion between 'Iran' and 'Iraq' in written documents a problem, so insisted on 'Persia'. See Bullard, *Letters from Tehran*, diary entry, 6 October 1941, p. 84 and footnote. Officers and men of British military units were duly ordered to call Iran 'Persia'. J.D. Summers, 'Into Persia', *Household Brigade Magazine* (summer 1942), pp. 49–53. Of course, many British diplomats, politicians and officers had never *stopped* calling it 'Persia'.

35. See M. Reza Ghods, 'Iranian Nationalism and Reza Shah', *Middle Eastern Studies*, vol. 27, no. 1 (1991), pp. 35–45.

36. Youssef Aboul-Enein and Basil Aboul-Enein, *The Secret War for the Middle East: The Influence of Axis and Allied Intelligence Operations during World War Two* (Annapolis, MD: Naval Institute Press, 2013), p. 104.

37. Berthold Schulze-Holthus, *Daybreak in Iran: A Story of the German Intelligence Service*, trans. Mervyn Savill (London: Staples Press, 1954), p. 21.

38. Soviet reply to the German draft proposal, 26 November 1940. See 'Hitler and Molotov Meetings, Official Transcripts', online at http://www.worldfuturefund.org/wffmaster/Reading/Germany/Hitler-Molotov%20Meetings.htm (accessed 15 December 2017).

39. Steven Ward, *Immortal: A Military History of Iran and its Armed Forces* (Washington, DC: Georgetown University Press, 2009), p. 152.

40. 'Iran in World War Two', *Changing the Times*, online at http://www.changingthetimes.net/resources/iran_in_world_war_two.htm (accessed 22 January 2018).

41. FRUS, Engert to Secretary of State, 3 October 1939.

42. FRUS, Engert to Secretary of State, 17 October 1939.

43. FRUS, Engert to Secretary of State, 4 January 1940.

44. Ibid.

45. TNA, CAB 65/57, Meeting of ministers held in Lord Halifax's room at the Foreign Office, 8 February 1940.

46. TNA, CAB 66/5/46, War Cabinet: Hostilities with Russia: Attitude of Iran, report by the Chiefs of Staff Committee, 23 February 1940. See also CAB 65/5/35, War Cabinet: Conclusions, 7 February 1940 regarding request via military attaché for aircraft.

47. TNA, CAB 66/6/46.

48. FRUS, Engert to Secretary of State, 5 May 1940.

49. Ibid.

50. FRUS, Engert to Secretary of State, 4 January 1940.

51. See Sean McMeekin, *The Berlin–Baghdad Express: The Ottoman Empire and Germany's Bid for World Power, 1898–1918* (London: Allen Lane, 2010).

52. The early years of the RAF and the Iraq mandate were intertwined, Iraq becoming one of the first parts of the world where the air force became the main service responsible for 'imperial policing'. See David Omissi, *Air Power and Colonial Control: The Royal Air Force, 1919–1939* (Manchester University Press, 1990), and David Killingray, ' "A Swift Agent of Government": Air Power in British Colonial Africa, 1916–1939', *Journal of African History*, vol. 25, no. 4 (October 1984), pp. 429–44.

53. The dynasty's overthrow in 1958 led to the dictatorship of Saddam Hussein.

54. De Gaury, *Three Kings*, p. 31.

55. Ibid., p. 1. De Gaury spent most of his life in Iraq as a soldier, intelligence officer and friend of the royal family.

56. Ibid., p. 21. For a fascinating Iraqi perspective on the presence of the RAF in Iraq, from the 1920s until the early decades of the twenty-first century, and British interference and violence, see Robert Young, *Postcolonialism: A Very Short Introduction* (Oxford: Oxford University Press, 2003), pp. 32–44.

57. Quoted in D.K. Fieldhouse (ed.), *Kurds, Arabs, and Britons: The Memoir of Wallace Lyon in Iraq, 1918–1944* (London: I.B. Tauris, 2002), p. 23.

58. Warner, *Iraq and Syria*, p. 19.

59. Ibid., p. 108.

60. Silverfarb, *The Twilight*, p. 121.

61. De Gaury, *Three Kings*, p. 76.

62. Fieldhouse (ed.), *Kurds, Arabs, and Britons*, p. 99.
63. See Silverfarb, *The Twilight*, chapter 3, 'The British Airbases'. BOAC was formed in 1940 following the merger of British Airways and Imperial Airways.
64. This Cabinet-ranking office had been created in 1936 to oversee British rearmament. It was superseded in May 1940 when Prime Minister Churchill made himself 'Minister of Defence'.
65. TNA, CAB 24/282, Cabinet: Strategic importance of Egypt and the Arab countries of the Middle East: Note by Minister for Co-ordination of Defence, 16 January 1939.
66. See Hiroshi Shimizu, 'Anglo-Japanese Competition in the Textile Trade in the Inter-war Period: A Case Study of Iraq, 1932–1941', *Middle Eastern Studies*, vol. 20, no. 3 (July 1984), pp. 259–89.
67. The inspector-general, though technically a servant of the Iraqi state, wearing Iraqi uniform and paid by the Iraqi government, was a representative and agent of Britain. On his recommendation in 1944 the army was reduced by two divisions. The position offered significant influence over appointments and dismissals, conditions for enlisted men and the conduct military exercises. Silverfarb, *The Twilight*, p. 108.
68. Juan Cole, 'Iraq in 1939: British Alliance or Nationalist Neutrality towards the Axis?', *Britain and the World*, vol. 5, no. 2 (2012), pp. 204–22, p. 215.
69. Stark, *Dust in the Lion's Paw*, p. 83.
70. Emile Marmorstein, 'Fritz Grobba', *Middle Eastern Studies*, vol. 23, no. 3 (1987), pp. 376–8. See also Francis Nicosia, 'Fritz Grobba and the Middle East Policy of the Third Reich', in Edward Ingram (ed.), *National and International Politics in the Middle East: Essays in Honour of Elie Kedourie* (London: Frank Cass, 1986).
71. Dieterich, 'Germany's Relations'.
72. Hayyim J. Cohen, 'The Anti-Jewish "Farhūd" in Baghdad 1941', *Middle Eastern Studies*, vol. 3, no. 1 (October 1966), pp. 2–17 .
73. Dieterich, 'Germany's Relations'. Though the Germans claimed no colonial ambitions, if the Axis had triumphed the Middle East would have been parcelled out between Germany and Italy as colonies and spheres of influence. Older empires would have given way to new, more ruinous ones. While it is widely acknowledged that interest in Nazism was fundamentally motivated by the desire to win support for their own nationalist causes, opinions differ on the extent to which those involved were aware of the ultimate logic of Nazism as regards attitudes to race. Some claim that they imperfectly understood the racist heart of Nazism and were beguiled by Germany's rise and its potential, others that it was fully understood and rejected. Peter Wein, *Iraqi Arab Nationalism: Authoritarianism, Totalitarianism, and Pro-Fascist Inclinations, 1932–1942* (London: Routledge, 2006).
74. FRUS, Knabenshue to Secretary of State, 14 November 1940.
75. Avad al-Qazzaz, 'The Iraqi-British War of 1941: A Review Article', *International Journal of Middle East Studies*, vol. 7, no. 4 (October 1976), pp. 591–6, p. 594.
76. Joseph Nevo, 'Al-Hajj Amin and the British in World War II', *Middle Eastern Studies*, vol. 20, no. 1 (January 1984), pp. 3–16.
77. Aboul-Enein and Aboul-Enein, *The Secret War*, p. xi.
78. TNA, FO 371/24568.
79. Nevo, 'Al Hajj Amin'. Exile, to an island fastness or the Savoy Hotel, had befallen many enemies of the British Empire, including Abdullah, Sultan of Perak, Cetshwayo, King of the Zulus, Khalid bin Barghash, Sultan of Zanzibar, Napoleon, Emperor of France, Mutesa, Kabaka of Buganda, Arabi Pasha, Egyptian nationalist and, soon, Reza Pahlavi, Shah of Iran. For some years I've thought about writing a book on this subject, but recently learned that there is no need, with the forthcoming publication of Robert Aldrich, *Banished Potentates: Dethroning and Exiling Indigenous Monarchs under British and French Colonial Rule, 1915–1955* (Manchester: Manchester University Press, 2018).
80. Schubert, 'The Persian Gulf Command', p. 306.
81. For an overview, see Bonakdarian, 'US–Iranian Relations'.
82. Camron Michael Amin, 'An Iranian in New York: 'Abbas Mas'udi's Description of the Non-Iranian on the Eve of the Cold War', in Kamran Scott Aghaie and Ashfin Marashi (eds), *Rethinking Iranian Nationalism and Modernity* (Austin: University of Texas Press, 2014), p. 170.
83. Bonakdarian, 'US–Iran Relations', p. 11.
84. On this intriguing historical whodunit, and diametrically opposed British and Iraqi constructions of historical truth, see Matthew Elliot, 'The Death of King Ghazi: Iraqi Politics, Britain, and Kuwait in 1939', *Contemporary British History*, vol. 10, no. 3 (1996), pp. 63–81. See also Matthew Elliot, *'Independent Iraq': British Influence from 1941 to 1958* (London: I.B. Tauris, 1996).
85. De Gaury, *Three Kings*, p. 53.
86. Philip Mansel, 'Preface: The Lost Kingdom', in de Gaury, *Three Kings*, p. 4.
87. Alan de Lacy Rush, 'Introduction', in de Gaury, *Three Kings*, p. 9.

88. Reeva Spector Simon, *Iraq Between Two World Wars: The Militarist Origins of Tyranny* (New York: Columbia University Press, 2004).
89. Cole, 'Iraq in 1939', p. 209. De Gaury's account offers an alternative scenario, claiming that Ghazi was furious when the radio malfunctioned during his favourite programme. He jumped into a sports car and rushed to the summer palace on the Ramadi road to catch the end of it. Crossing a railway track, he lost control and the car hit a telegraph pole. A compensation of £20,000 was voted to his widow. See Kwasi Kwarteng, 'Iraq: Oil and Power', in his *Ghosts of Empire: Britain's Legacies in the Modern World* (London: Bloomsbury, 2011), which offers useful insights on this incident and 1930s and 1940s Anglo-Iraqi relations, including references to the 'more English than the English' Abdulillah (who replaced Ghazi), with his Rolls-Royces and foxhounds, the Casuals cricket club and the expatriate Alwiyah Club in Baghdad.
90. Cole, 'Iraq in 1939', p. 209.
91. *Sydney Morning Herald*, 6 April 1939.
92. *Ottawa Evening Journal*, 4 April 1939.
93. Cole, 'Iraq in 1939', p. 211.
94. Mansel 'Preface', in de Gaury, *Three Kings*, p. 3. Faisal II had a British nanny, governor and tutor, and would also go to Harrow, enjoying it much more than Ghazi.
95. See Silverfarb, *Britain's Informal Empire in the Middle East: A Case Study of Iraq, 1929–1941* (Oxford: Oxford University Press: 1986), chapter 11, 'The Deterioration of Anglo-Iraqi Relations: Phase One, September 1939–October 1940'.
96. MECA. Stewart Perowne, Public Relations Section, Baghdad Embassy, to Elizabeth, 28 August 1942.
97. TNA, CAB 67/6/49, 'The Arab states and Palestine', 12 June 1940.
98. It allowed a maximum of 75,000 more Jewish immigrants over five years, placed strict restrictions on land sales to Jews and recommended the appointment of Palestinians to head government departments, as well as the creation of an independent Palestinian state within a decade. This was seen as ending official British sponsorship of a Jewish national home in Palestine.
99. Cole, 'Iraq in 1939', p. 212.
100. FRUS, Knabenshue to Secretary of State, 12 November 1940.

2 Defending Iran and Iraq

1. John Kennedy, *The Business of War: The War Journal of Major-General Sir John Kennedy* (London: Hutchinson, 1957), p. 63.
2. TNA, CAB 66/11/42, War Cabinet: Future Strategy, appreciation by COS Committee, 4 September 1940.
3. Ibid.
4. Ibid.
5. TNA, AIR 23/673, Heron Plan: Arrangements for the movement of troops from India to Egypt via Iraq, 26 August 1939. Heron had other avian partners: Emu was a plan for the reinforcement of Singapore, Wren for Burma.
6. Ibid., War Office secret cypher to Egypt, India, Iraq, and Palestine, 24 July 1939.
7. TNA, AIR 23/673.
8. This meant that the division's equipment would be 'tactically loaded' aboard the transports, ensuring that it could disembark in a state of fighting readiness. Fighting vehicles, machine-guns and those that operated them, for example, would emerge first from the holds rather than the tents and the mess silver. A conference in India in March 1940 focused on assisting Iraq, and was preceded by a reconnaissance of the all-important Basra base area led by Major-General Noel Beresford-Peirse of the 4th Indian Division.
9. TNA, AIR 23/5901. War period: Reinforcement of Iraq and AIOC area, notes on Lobster administrative plan, April 1940.
10. Ibid., 5 August 1939.
11. TNA, AIR 23/673.
12. TNA, AIR 23/667, Joint plan for the defence of Iraq and British lines of communication between Persian Gulf and Trans-Jordan, Air Headquarters British Forces in Iraq to No. 1 ACC, 15 June 1940.
13. John Frost, *A Drop Too Many* (Barnsley: Pen and Sword, 2008).
14. In September 1939 Britain's air strength in Iraq comprised the fourteen Blenheim bombers of 30 Squadron and 55 Squadron, and 84 Squadron's nineteen Blenheims. There were eight Aircraft Storage Unit airframes, and fifteen more were in crates at Basra awaiting assembly, with a further ten due to arrive shortly.
15. Frost, *A Drop Too Many*, p. 2. Frost was a keen huntsman, and became master of the Royal Exodus Hunt, its hounds kennelled at Habbaniya. When he was transferred there to help guard the base, he

enjoyed good winter hunting, chasing mainly jackal living among tamarisk coverts along the river banks or among the wadis leading up to the plateau overlooking the airbase. At Christmas, they took the hounds to Baghdad, a great social occasion attended by the regent, Abdulillah, and his bodyguard.
16. Somerset de Chair's account of the campaigns in Iraq and Syria offers excellent descriptions of the experience of military traffic traversing Iraq. See Somerset de Chair, *The Golden Carpet* (London: Faber and Faber, 1945).
17. Masters, *The Road Past Mandalay*, p. 47. Masters' account offers a description of his work as a junior line of communication officer at GS3 level.
18. TNA, AIR 23/673, notes on Lobster administrative plan; cypher message from 'Mideast' to 'Armindia', 31 May 1940.
19. TNA, CAB 66/2/24, War Cabinet: Appreciation by the Chiefs of Staff Committee of the situation created by the Russo-German agreement, 9 October 1939.
20. TNA, CAB 66/3/48, War Cabinet: Review of military policy in the Middle East, Chiefs of Staff, 5 December 1939.
21. TNA, AIR 23/667.
22. TNA, AIR 23/5901.
23. TNA, CAB 65/5/14, War Cabinet 14 (40) conclusions, 15 January 1940.
24. TNA, AIR 23/667, Headquarters RAF Middle East, Cairo to Air Headquarters British Forces in Iraq, 9 May 1940.
25. Ibid., Headquarters RAF Middle East intelligence branch, 8 May 1940.
26. TNA, AIR 23/5901, Joint Planning Staff paper, number 12, 'Defence in Iraq'.
27. See Patrick Osborn, *Operation Pike: Britain Versus the Soviet Union, 1939–1941* (Westport, CT: Greenwood, 2000).
28. TNA, CAB 66/6/21, War Cabinet: Military implications of hostilities with Russia in 1940, Chiefs of Staff report.
29. TNA, CAB 66/6/46.
30. Ibid.
31. Ibid., Baggallay minute, 9 February 1940.
32. TNA, AIR 23/667, Headquarters RAF Middle East intelligence branch, 8 May 1940. The RAF had had a base in Mosul until recently. But the RAF withdrew from there before the war, and from RAF Hinaidi on the outskirts of Baghdad, as part of concessions to Iraqi nationalists, to dampen friction. Instead, bases were to be in less populated areas such as Habbaniya and Shaibah. Hinaidi was renamed Rashid airbase.
33. TNA, CAB 66/9/10, War Cabinet: Dispatch of troops to Iraq, memorandum by the Chiefs of Staff, 29 June 1940.
34. TNA, AIR 23/5901, Air Headquarters Middle East, internal correspondence, 2 October 1940.
35. Dill Papers, 3/2/1, Dill to Wavell, 3 July 1940.
36. TNA, AIR 23/5901, Air Headquarters Middle East, internal correspondence, 2 October 1940.
37. Ibid.
38. TNA, AIR 23/667, most secret cypher from MICE to Trooper, Army India, Air Officer Commanding Iraq, 16 May 1940. Notes prepared for AOC Iraq ahead of his meeting with Iraqi General Staff, 13 May 1940.
39. Ibid., notes from Air Officer Commanding Iraq in connection with the conference with the Iraqi General Staff to be held in Baghdad, from Air Headquarters Iraq, 4 May 1940. The Iraqi regime had ambitions to absorb the part of south-west Iran that they called 'Arabistan', as well as Kuwait. See Silverfarb, *Britain's Informal Empire*, 'The Struggle for Kuwait'. See also Daniel Silverfarb, 'The British Government and the Question of Umm Qasr, 1938–1945', *Asian and African Studies*, vol. 16, no. 2 (July 1982), pp. 215–38. The Iraqis were concerned about a possible invasion from Iran, and a border dispute concerning the Shatt al-Arab persisted. There were also fears that the Turks might try to reclaim territory lost with the demise of the Ottoman Empire.
40. See 'The Supply of Arms' and 'The Supply of Credit' in Silverfarb, *Britain's Informal Empire*.
41. TNA, CAB 65/7/62, War Cabinet, 167 (40) conclusions, 15 June 1940.

3 Towards the Iraqi coup

1. Silverfarb's work and that of scholars such as Reeva Spector Simon and Peter Wein offer copious detail.
2. Charles Tripp, *A History of Iraq* (Cambridge: Cambridge University Press, 2002), p. 101.
3. 'They failed, however, to influence the troops in outstations', Waterhouse added. TNA, FO 624/26, British Embassy Baghdad: British Forces: Reports, Waterhouse to Cornwallis, 7 July 1941.
4. TNA, FO 624/26, British Embassy Baghdad: Military Mission: Inspector-General.

5. De Gaury, *Traces of Travel*, p. 110.
6. TNA, CAB 66/8/35, War Cabinet: Internal security in Iraq, memorandum by the Chiefs of Staff Committee, 14 June 1940.
7. Ibid.
8. It worked the other way, too; remarking upon a rare British success, the American consul in Baghdad noted that British and Greek victories against the Italians, together with 'Turkish demarche', were 'deciding factors in averting a serious crisis between Britain and Iraq' as 1940 drew to a close. FRUS, Knabenshue to Secretary of State 3 January 1941.
9. TNA, CAB 67/6/49, War Cabinet: The Arab states and Palestine, memorandum for Secretary of State for Foreign Affairs, 12 June 1940.
10. Mackenzie, *Eastern Epic*, p. 75.
11. FRUS, Knabenshue to Secretary of State, 29 August 1940.
12. Silverfarb, *Britain's Informal Empire*, p. 62.
13. FRUS, Knabenshue to Secretary of State, 28 June 1940. On the proposed deal regarding Palestine, see Knabenshue to Secretary of State, 29 December 1940.
14. FRUS, Knabenshue to Secretary of State, 29 May 1940.
15. TNA, CAB 65/8/1, War Cabinet, 189 (40) conclusions of meeting, 1 July 1940.
16. TNA, CAB 66/9/10, War Cabinet: Dispatch of troops to Iraq: memorandum by the Chiefs of Staff, 29 June 1940.
17. Ibid.
18. The commander of the Arab Legion, Glubb Pasha, castigated 'tactless British officers ... ignorant of Arabic and [who] refer to the Arabs as "wogs" ... Such persons breed intense race hatred.' Their 'inevitable ignorance of Arab mentality and customs often produce intense frustration and dislike'. In a correspondence viewed by the British ambassador in Iraq and the British High Commissioner for Palestine, Sir Harold MacMichael, Waterhouse hit back, having taken 'great offence'. In his six years in Iraq, Waterhouse claimed, the British had not been 'tactless' and did not refer to the Iraqis as 'wogs'. 'All officers and other ranks on arrival', he stated, presumably unaware that his words might be construed as lending credence to Glubb's charges, 'are warned by me of the importance of tact and forbearance in dealing with the mingled ignorance, conceit, and childishness of the average Iraqi officer'. TNA, FO 624/26, British Embassy Baghdad, British Forces: Reports on operations of Habforce from General Clark, Waterhouse to Cornwallis, 7 July 1941.
19. TNA, CAB 65/7/62, War Cabinet, 167 (40) conclusions, 15 June 1940.
20. TNA, AIR 23/5901.
21. TNA, CAB 66/9/10.
22. See Michael Cohen, *Britain's Moment in Palestine: Retrospect and Perspectives, 1917–1948* (London: Routledge, 2014), p. 367.
23. See Nevo, 'Al-Hajj Amin'.
24. FRUS, Knabenshue to Secretary of State, 2 December 1940.
25. Sean Govan. 'Pawns, Provocateurs, and Parasites: Great Britain and German Fifth Column Movements in Europe and the Middle East, 1934–1941', PhD thesis (University of Birmingham, 2016), chapter 5, 'Gilded with Axis Gold'.
26. Silverfarb, *The Twilight*, p. 114.
27. LHCMA, Brooke-Popham Papers, 6/2/2, Brooke-Popham to Dill, Chief of the Imperial General Staff, 15 November 1940. Brooke-Popham had met Air Vice-Marshal Smart and embassy officials at Habbaniya.
28. See Silverfarb, *The Twilight*, chapter 12, 'The deterioration of Anglo-Iraqi Relations: Phase One, November 1940–May 1941'.
29. Tripp, *A History of Iraq*, p. 102.
30. TNA, CAB 66/13/11, War Cabinet: An advance by the enemy through the Balkans and Syria to the Middle East, report by the COS, 1 November 1940.
31. Ibid.
32. FRUS, Hull to Knabenshue, 3 December 1940.
33. Ibid.
34. De Gaury, *Three Kings*, p. 116.
35. FRUS, Knabenshue to Secretary of State, 8 January 1941.
36. Ibid. On applications for dollar exchange see TNA, CAB, War Cabinet, 18 (41) conclusions, 17 February 1941.
37. The Italians had been defeated during the British Operation Compass offensive.
38. Mackenzie, *Eastern Epic*.
39. TNA, CAB 65/17/18, War Cabinet, 18 (41) conclusions, 17 February 1941.
40. Based on Silverfarb, *Britain's Informal Empire*.

41. TNA, AIR 23/668, Joint plan for the defence of Iraq and the British line of communication between the Persian Gulf and Trans-Jordan, Office of the Chief of the Iraqi General Staff to Waterhouse, 18 March 1941.
42. TNA, FO 371/27064, Air Headquarters Iraq to Air Ministry, quoted in Govan, 'Pawns, Parasites, and Provocateurs'.
43. FRUS, Knabenshue to Secretary of State, 25 March 1941.
44. Simon, *Iraq Between the Two World Wars*, p. 136.
45. De Gaury, *Three Kings*, p. 118.
46. FRUS, Knabenshue to Secretary of State, 2 April 1941.
47. Avon Papers, Eden to Churchill, 6 May 1941. In this private communication, Eden asked Churchill to defend the Foreign Office in a debate in parliament on 7 May. The department had been charged with not knowing what was going on and being unfit to meet the war situation. Eden offered Iraq as an example of the Foreign Office knowing 'only too well what was going on', stating that it had asked as early as May 1940 for troops to be sent 'as being the only effective method in their judgement to meet the situation. We quite accepted, of course, that troops were not then available'.
48. Tripp, *A History of Iraq*, p. 103.
49. FRUS, Knabenshue to Secretary of State, 3 April 1941.
50. Cornwallis had been a prominent presence in Iraq until the mid-1930s, and the British community there had lobbied for his return as the situation deteriorated. He had arrived in Iraq with Faisal I, at his request, and stayed on as adviser in the Ministry of the Interior.
51. Ronald Lewin, *The Chief: Field Marshal Lord Wavell, Commander-in-Chief and Viceroy, 1939–1947* (London: Hutchinson, 1980), p. 136.
52. Ibid.
53. Tripp, *A History of Iraq*, p. 103. Faisal was kept under guard in Iraq.
54. Mackenzie, *Eastern Epic*, p. 89.
55. Tripp, *A History of Iraq*, p. 104.
56. Mackenzie, *Eastern Epic*, p. 90.
57. Ibid.
58. Ibid., p. 77.
59. Ibid., p. 91.
60. Ibid., p. 89.
61. Elie Kedourie, 'Wavell and Iraq, April–May 1941', *Middle Eastern Studies*, vol. 2, no. 4 (1966), pp. 373–86.
62. Mackenzie, *Eastern Epic*, p. 91.
63. TNA, CAB 65/18/19, War Cabinet, 40 (41) conclusions, 14 April 1941. See also TNA, CAB 65/18/21, War Cabinet, 42 (41) conclusions, 21 April 1941.
64. Srinath Raghavan, *India's War: The Making of Modern South Asia, 1939–1945* (London: Penguin, 2016), p. 132.
65. Kennedy, *The Business of War*, p. 103.
66. Lyman, *Iraq 1941*, p. 29.
67. Ibid., p. 31.
68. Avon Papers, PM personal minute to Eden, 20 April 1941.
69. FRUS, Knabenshue to Secretary of State, 19 April 1941.
70. Ibid.
71. Ibid.
72. Silverfarb, *Britain's Informal Empire*, p. 129.
73. FRUS, Knabenshue to Secretary of State, 29 April 1941.
74. TNA, FO 624/26, British Embassy Baghdad: British Forces: Reports, Cornwallis to Wilson, 7 July 1941.
75. FRUS, Knabenshue to Secretary of State, 30 April 1941.
76. Silverfarb, *Britain's Informal Empire*, p. 129.
77. Ibid., p. 130.

4 Iraq goes to war

1. CAC, Churchill Papers, CHUR 4/201A-C, 14 March 1950.
2. The other was RAF Shaibah near Basra. See the excellent RAF Habbaniya Association website online at https://www.habbaniya.org (accessed 15 December 2017).
3. See the description of Habbaniya, in Philip Guedalla, *Middle East 1940–42: A Study in Air Power* (London: Hodder and Stoughton, 1944), pp. 138–9.
4. Cecil Beaton, *Near East* (London: B.T. Batsford, 1943), p. 102. The well-known photographer worked for the Ministry of Information, and visited both Iran and Iraq. While staying at the airbase,

he met the crews of American Liberator bombers who were using it for operational purposes. The archives show that the braying, orientalist tones (notable even in the context of those prevalent at the time) of his descriptions of Tehran and the royal family stimulated anger and ridicule among the British diplomatic community in Iran.

5. De Chair, *The Golden Carpet*, p. 51.
6. Beaton, *Near East*, p. 103. While Habbaniya was not best positioned, Hinaidi would have been much more of a problem to defend. The RAF had also once had an airbase at Mosul.
7. De Gaury, who accompanied him on these flights as interpreter, memorably described the view of Baghdad as their aircraft took off as 'a khaki jigsaw in the desert'. See de Gaury, *Three Kings*, p. 82. Habbaniya's location was also part of a compromise between the British and Iraqi governments. The RAF bases were to be out of urban sight, west of the Euphrates, and the levies were to be kept only as guards. Habbaniya was considered attractive partly because it could be reinforced from Palestine, and because the lake allowed for shooting, fishing, sailing and bathing. Silverfarb, *Britain's Informal Empire*, pp. 29–30.
8. H.G. Smart, 'Report of Operations in Baghdad Area – 2 May to 31 May 1941', AOC RAF Iraq Air Commodore (Acting AVM) H.G. Smart to the AOC-i-C Middle East.
9. FRUS, Knabeshue to Secretary of State, 30 April 1941.
10. Smart, 'Report of Operations in Baghdad Area'.
11. TNA, AIR 23/667, Notes by Air Officer Commanding Iraq on the situation in Iran in relation to the proposal for sending a brigade to reinforce in certain eventualities.
12. H.G. Smart, 'Report of Operations in Baghdad Area'.
13. This is often quoted, though I have yet to find a definitive source.
14. Lyman, *Iraq 1941*, p. 43.
15. Colin Dunford Wood, 'A Story of War', diary entry 3 May 1941. Colin's son James has created a website featuring all of his father's 600-plus diary entries covering his service across several continents with the RAF. The website also contains images of the 'C' Squadron Historical Record, written by Dunford and Pilot Officer Alan Haig; online at https://storyofwar.com (accessed 15 December 2017).
16. TNA, CAB 66/16/23. War Cabinet weekly resumé, no. 88, 1–8 May 1941.
17. The Iraqis also bombed their own forces at Ramadi by mistake. See Smart's account in 'Report of Operations in Baghdad Area'.
18. Simon, *Iraq Between the Two World Wars*, p. 142.
19. Ibid., p. 143.
20. BBCMSA, M90, BBC Mayfair CT, Baghdad in Arabic and English for the Arab world.
21. Ibid., Baghdad English news commentary for Near East, 3 May 1941.
22. Ibid., Broadcast in Italian for Italy from Baghdad, 3 May 1941.
23. FRUS, Knabenshue to Secretary of State, 4 May 1941.
24. Ibid.
25. Lyman, *Iraq 1941*, p. 44.
26. Ibid.
27. Ibid., p. 43.
28. Mike Dudgeon, 'No. 4 SFTS and Raschid Ali's War: Iraq 1941', *RAF Historical Society Journal*, vol. 48 (2010), pp. 39–57.
29. Lyman, *Iraq 1941*, p. 48.
30. Stark, *Dust in the Lion's Paw*.
31. Lyman, *Iraq 1941*, p. 48.
32. BBCMSA, M90, Baghdad in German for Germany, 4 May 1941.
33. Ibid.
34. Ibid.
35. Ibid.
36. Beaton, *Near East*, p. 106.
37. TNA, CAB 65/18/26, War Cabinet, 47 (41) conclusions, 5 May 1941.
38. LHCMA, Alanbrooke Papers, 6/2/4, telegram, 5 May 1941. Dill was replaced as CIGS by Alan Brooke on Christmas Day 1941. Wavell favoured 'carrying the baby' analogies. On being appointed ABDA commander, he wrote: 'I've heard of carrying the baby but this is twins.' Dill's reply, 6 May 1941. Though Wavell accepted command in Iraq reluctantly ('I have always hated this commitment'), when he returned it to India Command in mid-June, he expressed some reluctance, mainly because he believed that 'their method may cause trouble in the Arab world'. Dill Papers, 3/2/5, Wavell to Dill, 15 June 1941.
39. Kedourie, 'Wavell', p. 382.
40. Hastings Lionel Ismay, *The Memoirs of General the Lord Ismay* (London: Heinemann, 1960), pp. 205–6.

41. Coats, *Of Generals and Gardens*, p. 106.
42. Kedourie, 'Wavell'.
43. Ibid., p. 376. Writing in March 1941, he gave an example: when licences had been permitted for shipwrecked Jewish refugees to land in Palestine, Wavell had sent a telegram predicting widespread disaster in the region caused by Arab resistance.
44. Quoted in Harold Raugh, *Wavell in the Middle East 1939–1941: A Study in Generalship* (London: Brassey's, 1993), p. 220.
45. Ibid.
46. Mackenzie, *Eastern Epic*, p. 97.
47. Ibid., p. 99.
48. BBC World War Two People's Archive, Article ID A2008108, testimony of Flight Lieutenant Maurice Skeet, commanding the Habbaniya Communications Flight. Among its many tasks, the Communications Flight also supplied troops on the Fallujah plain with water and medical supplies.
49. Dunford Wood, 'A Story of War', diary entry 6 May 1941.
50. Lyman, *Iraq 1941*, p. 50.
51. Ibid., p. 51.
52. Mackenzie, *Eastern Epic*, p. 96.
53. Smart, 'Report of Operations in Baghdad Area'.
54. Lyman, *Iraq 1941*, p. 52.
55. Beaton, *Near East*, p. 104.
56. Smart, 'Report of Operations in Baghdad Area'.
57. Hellmuth Felmy and Walter Warlimont, *German Exploitation of Arab Nationalist Movements in World War II* (Washington, DC: Historical Division, Headquarters, United States Army, Europe, Foreign Military Studies Branch, 1954), online at http://www.allworldwars.com/German-Exploitation-of-Arab-Nationalist-Movements-in-World-War-II.html (accessed 5 January 2018).
58. Stark, *Dust in the Lion's Paw*, p. 96.
59. Ibid.
60. BBCMSA, M90, Baghdad in Arabic for the Arab world, 8 May 1941.
61. Ibid.
62. Iraqi desert police had recently seized Rutbah fort and been joined by the guerrillas led by Fawzi al-Qawuqji. These forces had attacked a British road survey party on 1 May. Clark ordered the mechanized squadron of the Trans-Jordan Frontier Force to repossess the fort. But its men refused, believing they were beyond contract operating outside of Trans-Jordan, and not keen on fighting fellow Arabs. They were marched back to H3 and disarmed.
63. Lyman, *Iraq 1941*, p. 56.
64. Born in Calcutta in 1885, Quinan was a scion of the Indian Army and had learned his trade in France and Mesopotamia in the First World War, and commanded forces fighting the Faqir of Ipi in Waziristan in the 1930s. (He also penned the official history of the 1919 Afghan campaign.) Quinan represented a type of British soldier relatively common at the time, a man whose career had been spent east of Suez and who was of Britain but rarely in it. Central Office of Information, *PAIFORCE*, p. 32.
65. Ibid. See also *The Times* obituary, 15 November 1960.
66. Lewin, *The Chief*, p. 137.
67. J.D. Summers, 'Nine Weeks in the Desert: An Account of the Adventures of the Household Cavalry Regiment in Iraq and Syria', *Household Brigade Magazine* (spring 1942), pp. 9–13.
68. Lyman, *Iraq 1941*, p. 57.
69. See Humphrey Wyndham, *The Household Cavalry at War: First Household Cavalry Regiment* (Aldershot: Gale and Polden, 1952).
70. Ibid., p. 61.
71. De Chair, *The Golden Carpet*, p. 28.
72. Ibid., p. 47.
73. Ibid. p. 48.
74. TNA, CAB 66/16/25, War Cabinet weekly resumé, no. 89, 8–15 May 1941.

5 Fallujah and the advance on Baghdad

1. TNA, CAB 66/16/25, War Cabinet weekly resumé, no. 89, 8–15 May 1941.
2. LHCMA, Dill Papers, 3/2/5. In the same letter, Dill asked when India Command could take back responsibility for the region, and told Auchinleck in confidence that Churchill had lost confidence in Wavell – 'if he ever had any'.
3. Avon Papers, AP20/8/767.

4. NARA, NAI 195959, Churchill to Roosevelt, 14 May 1941. Churchill also told Roosevelt that one of the conditions for peace with Germany, brought to Britain by Rudolf Hess, was the evacuation of Iraq. Churchill, *The Second World War*, vol. 3, p. 46.
5. BBCMSA, M90, Mayfair CT, Baghdad in Arabic and English for the Arab world.
6. Tripp, *A History of Iraq*, p. 105.
7. FRUS, MacMurray to Secretary of State, 13 May 1941.
8. Avon Papers, Eden to Churchill, 5 May 1941.
9. TNA, CAB 66/16/25, War Cabinet weekly resumé, no. 89, 8–15 May 1941.
10. NARA, German Military Document Section, EDS/Misc/6, Box 12/15, 'Axis Activities in Syria and Iraq 1939–41', produced by Enemy Document Section, Historical Branch, Cabinet Office, London, June 1951.
11. Ibid.
12. Lyman, *Iraq 1941*, p. 67.
13. Ibid., p. 65. The official War Office history – Central Office of Information, *PAIFORCE* – claims that it was a shot from an Iraqi rifleman that killed von Blomberg, striking him in the neck. Compton Mackenzie's account claims that a bullet from a rifle salute killed him, as Rashid Ali and his ministers stood on the runway waiting to greet him. General Felmy states that his death was caused by anti-aircraft fire. Fritz Grobba, meanwhile, insisted that he was killed by a stray bullet from a British fighter engaged in a dogfight with an Iraqi machine over the capital. See Mackenzie, *Eastern Epic*; Felmy and Warliamont, *German Exploitation*; and Warner, *Iraq and Syria*, p. 106.
14. Dieterich, 'German Relations'.
15. TNA, FO 624/26, British Embassy Baghdad: Oil: German mission, Cornwallis to Eden, 3 July 1941. Includes copy of letter to the ambassador from the director of the Government Chemical Laboratory, Baghdad, dated 21 June 1941, regarding activities of German petroleum experts during their May visit. Also sent to AIOC and Combined Intelligence Centre Cairo. Reeva Simon claims that the Germans needed to refine their own aviation fuel because stockpiles had not been adequately prepared. Simon, *Iraq Between the Two World Wars*.
16. Lyman, *Iraq 1941*, p. 63.
17. Ibid., p. 64.
18. Ibid., p. 68.
19. Avon Papers, Eden to Churchill, 19 May 1941.
20. Fieldhouse (ed.), *Kurds, Arabs, and Britons*, p. 213.
21. FRUS, Knabenshue to Secretary of State, 4 May 1941.
22. Masters, *The Road Past Mandalay*, p. 72.
23. See Stark, *Dust in the Lion's Paw*, chapter 7, 'Baghdad: The Siege of the Embassy'.
24. Ibid., p. 102.
25. TNA, FO 624/26: British Embassy Baghdad: Political Situation: Treaty. This was standard procedure, and the same thing had happened in Berbera in August 1940 before the British evacuated. The siege led to other destruction, too; the following month, the Second Secretary was searching for the Iraqi Naturalization Law amidst 'the confused pile of Library books which Defence HQ recklessly and improvidently (and I might say criminally) saw fit to dump pell-mell in the ball room during May'. TNA, FO 624/26, British Embassy Baghdad: British Forces: Incidents.
26. Stark, *Dust in the Lion's Paw*, p. 89.
27. Ibid., p. 94.
28. Ibid., p. 90.
29. Ibid., p. 89.
30. Ibid., p. 93.
31. Ibid., p. 92.
32. Ibid., p. 94.
33. Ibid., p. 94.
34. Ibid., pp. 95–6.
35. Ibid., p. 99.
36. Ibid., p. 102.
37. FRUS, Knabenshue to Secretary of State, 5 June 1941.
38. Smart, 'Report of Operations in Baghdad Area'.
39. Lyman, *Iraq 1941*, p. 69.
40. TNA, CAB 66/16/25, War Cabinet weekly resumé, no. 89, 8–15 May 1941.
41. Ibid.
42. Ibid.
43. The Assyrian RAF Levies website contains excellent information on the Iraq campaign and some harrowing photographs. See http://assyrianlevies.info (accessed 15 December 2017).

44. LHCMA, *Basrah Times*.
45. Stark, *Dust in the Lion's Paw*.
46. Smart, 'Report of Operations in Baghdad Area'.
47. TNA, FO 624/25, British Embassy Baghdad: British Force, Air HQ D'Albiac to Cornwallis 26 June 1941. After the Anglo-Iraqi war, there were repercussions; the success of the Assyrians against Iraqis had been 'very galling to Iraqi self-respect, and they are now apparently trying to get own back on Assyrians'. Ambassador Cornwallis noted that 'feelings against them are strong'.
48. De Chair, *The Golden Carpet*, p. 69.
49. Hitler's Directive 30, reproduced in Churchill, *The Second World War*, vol. 3, p. 234.
50. TNA, CAB 66/16/40, War Cabinet weekly resumé, no. 91, 2–29 May 1941.
51. Stark, *Dust in the Lion's Paw*.
52. W.J. Laurie, 'With the Household Cavalry Regiment in Iraq and Persia', *Household Brigade Magazine* (autumn 1942), pp. 86–8. See Glubb's response to de Chair, *The Golden Carpet*, in the book's appendix.
53. Coats, *Of Gardening and Generals*.
54. Ibid.
55. De Chair claims that at Khan Nuqta he tried an Iraqi headquarters telephone. To his surprise, it was answered, and he told the answering voice that the position was surrounded by British forces, including tanks. A patrol of the 3rd Division was ordered to investigate. De Chair, *The Golden Carpet*, p. 69.
56. TNA, AIR 23/5938, 'Coup d'état April 1941 operational summaries Iraq Command'.
57. Stark, *Dust in the Lion's Paw*, p. 112.
58. Smart, 'Report of Operations in Baghdad Area'.
59. De Chair, *The Golden Carpet*, pp. 102–4. The armistice terms are described on p. 107.
60. De Gaury, *Three Kings*, p. 128.
61. FRUS, Knabenshue to Secretary of State, 31 May 1941.
62. Stark, *Dust in the Lion's Paw*, p. 112.
63. Ibid., p. 116.
64. Durham University Special Collections, J.G.S. Macphail Personal Papers, SAD, 764/6/1-45, CGH, c/o Base Post Depot, Basra, 17 July 1941.
65. De Chair, *The Golden Carpet*, p. 108.
66. Stark, *Dust in the Lion's Paw*, p. 113.
67. De Chair, *The Golden Carpet*, p. 174.
68. It has been suggested that the Iraqi gunners *deliberately* avoided hitting Habbaniya's essential infrastructure. See Fieldhouse (ed.), *Kurds, Arabs, and Britons*, p. 106.
69. Aboul-Enein and Aboul-Enein, *The Secret War*, p. 200.
70. Ibid., p. 201.
71. Dieterich, 'Germany's Relations', p. 469.
72. NARA, German Military Document Section, EDS/Misc/6, Box 12/15, 'Axis Activities in Syria and Iraq 1939–41', produced by Enemy Document Section, Historical Branch, Cabinet Office, London, June 1951.
73. LHCMA, 6/2/13, Major-General Sir Hastings Ismay to Air Chief Marshal Brooke-Popham, 15 June 1941.
74. Henry Pownall, *Chief of Staff: The Diaries of Lieutenant-General Sir Henry Pownall*, vol. 2: *1940–1944*, ed. Brian Bond (London: Leo Cooper, 1974), diary entry 3 June 1941, p. 18.
75. Franz Halder, 'Foreword' in Felmy and Warlimont, *German Exploitation*. General Warlimont directed the Planning Branch of the Wehrmacht High Command. This important document, which, with Fritz Grobba's 1957 addition following his release from Soviet imprisonment, runs to 300 pages, is about German exploitation of Arab nationalism during the war, and known as document MS# P-207. It was prepared for the Historical Division of the US Army Europe. See Schwanitz, ' "The Jinnee and the Magic Bottle" '.
76. Halder, 'Foreword' in Felmy and Warlimont, *German Exploitation*.
77. Fieldhouse (ed.), *Kurds, Arabs, and Britons*, p. 32.
78. Tripp, *A History of Iraq*, p. 105.
79. Simon, *Iraq Between the Two World Wars*, p. 144.
80. Silverfarb, *Britain's Informal Empire*, p. 134.
81. Ibid., p. 136.
82. Ibid., p. 137.
83. Ismay, *The Memoirs*, p. 206.
84. Ibid., pp. 206–7.
85. Lyman, *Iraq 1941*, p. 68.
86. Quoted in Schwanitz, ' "The Jinnee in the Magic Bottle" ', p. 98.
87. Ibid., p. 109.

88. Silverfarb, *Britain's Informal Empire*, p. 133.
89. Ibid., p. 134.
90. Cole, 'Iraq in 1939', p. 222.
91. William Ready Division of Archives and Research Collections, McMaster University, Hamilton, Ontario, John Connell Papers, Box 9, FSA-Wavell, Connell to Ismay, 16 August 1961. Connell also says that he believes he demonstrated conclusively in John Connell, *Auchinleck: A Critical Biography* (London: Cassell, 1959), that the impetus had come from Amery, Auchinleck and Linlithgow.
92. William Ready Division of Archives and Research Collections, McMaster University, Hamilton, Ontario, John Connell Papers, Box 9, FSA-Wavell, Ismay to Connell, 21 August 1961.
93. Dill Papers, 3/2/5, Wavell to Dill, 15 June 1941. Given the weak forces under Clark's command when the armistice was called, Wavell did not agree with those who believed that the armistice terms were not severe enough.
94. See Cohen, 'The Anti-Jewish "Farhūd"'.
95. Stark, *Dust in the Lion's Paw*, p. 114.
96. See Sarah Ehrlich, 'Farhud memories: Baghdad's 1941 slaughter of the Jews', BBC Middle East (1 July 2011), online at http://www.bbc.co.uk/news/world-middle-east-13610702 (accessed 15 December 2017).
97. TNA, CAB FO 624/25, British Embassy Baghdad: British officials, political advisers part 2, Major V.H.J. Dodson to Cornwallis, 19 August 1941.
98. Cohen, 'The Anti-Jewish "Farhūd"'.
99. TNA, 624/25, Situation Reports (political officers), Political Adviser Central Area report, 3 December 1941.

6 Mopping up and de-Nazification

1. Kedourie, 'Wavell', p. 578.
2. Central Office of Information, *PAIFORCE*.
3. See W. Averell Harriman and Elie Abel, *Special Envoy to Churchill and Stalin, 1941–1946* (London: Random House, 1975). In the following month Harriman negotiated the Lend-Lease agreement with the Soviet Union and also attended the Atlantic Charter meeting between Churchill and Roosevelt at Placentia Bay off the British dominion of Newfoundland. At this meeting, the two leaders came to an understanding regarding Iran, though Roosevelt was hardly enlightened as to British intentions beyond the most general level. Harriman was a key architect of American policy regarding the Soviet Union; he attended the allied conferences in Moscow (1942), Tehran (1943) and Yalta (1945), and served as US ambassador to Moscow from 1943, and to London from 1946.
4. Warner, *Iraq and Syria*, p. 161.
5. Ibid., p. 162.
6. Silverfarb, *The Twilight*, chapter 2, 'The Destruction of Iraq'.
7. Private correspondence, Chris Snelling to A. Jackson, December 2017.
8. Ibid., p. 25.
9. Mahmood al-Durrah claims that in its aftermath, the British and the pro-British government aimed to weaken it further, dismissing 2,879 officers. The draft was ignored, so the army was reduced by between a half and a third of its 1941 level, and cut from four to three divisions. Al-Qazzaz, 'The Iraqi-British War of 1941'. The levies expanded from 1,250 to around 10,000. See 'The Levies' in Silverfarb, *Britain's Informal Empire*, p. 54. Eight hundred levies, mostly Assyrian, had participated in a distinguished manner in the attack on Fallujah. According to Silverfarb, Assyrians specially trained as paratroopers fought bravely against German armoured units in combat at Arnhem in 1944 (ibid., p. 55). In April 1942, and in recognition of its loyal support during the Anglo-Iraqi war, Air Headquarters Iraq recommended that their name be changed to RAF Levies (Iraq), and that other ranks of the unit should wear the red eagle shoulder badge as worn by RAF airmen in khaki drill (TNA, AIR 2/4846, The Iraq Levies). The unit's primary duty would remain the defence of RAF aerodromes in the country. The proposal gained support, but possible difficulties were identified, and the proposal was put before the Foreign Office (ibid., minutes 4 April 1942, 7 April 1942). On 17 April 1942, a minute declared that while the shoulder flashes were a good idea, the name 'on no account should be changed from Iraq Levies – keeping this is fundamental to the legal sanction for the force in Iraq'. In May 1942 the Air Officer Commanding Iraq sought permission to employ the levies outside of the country. Prime Minister Nuri as-Said agreed verbally, adding that those levies so employed were not to be called Iraq Levies. As lots of them were to be employed outside of Iraq, the AOC asked the Air Ministry that all levies recruited over the original Anglo-Iraq Treaty force of 1,500 should be called RAF Levies. The Iraqi prime minister said that he had no problem with this proposal, as long as the British did not officially approach his government about the matter. While the British had his verbal agreement to this

as a war measure, he explained that any official action to do with the change of title would put him in an embarrassing position vis-à-vis his government. Subsequently, an official GHQ Middle East press release recorded that the Iraq Levies, who had 'played so notable a part in the successful Iraq campaign of May last year, have been presented with the red eagle badge of the RAF.' The presentation was made at a ceremonial parade of the levies by Air Vice-Marshal Hugh Champion de Crespigny, Air Officer Commanding Iraq, and 2,000 levies took part in the parade (TNA, AIR 2/4846, GHQ ME telegram. Also see press handout 31 May 1942).

10. TNA, FO 624/25, British Embassy Baghdad: Burials.
11. TNA, FO 624/26, British Embassy Baghdad: Foreigners: Internment.
12. TNA, FO 624/26, British Embassy Baghdad: RAF claims.
13. De Chair, *The Golden Carpet*, p. 51.
14. TNA, 624/28, British Embassy Baghdad: Looting claims.
15. FRUS, Wilson to Secretary of State, 12 May 1943.
16. TNA, FO 624/26, British Embassy Baghdad: RAF claims, 20 July 1941.
17. Ibid., 29 November 1941.
18. TNA, FO 624/26, RAF claims.
19. Ibid.
20. TNA, FO 624/27, British Embassy Baghdad: Foreigners: Looting.
21. TNA, FO 624/28, British Embassy Baghdad, February 1942.
22. TNA, CAB 65/18/35, Conclusions of War Cabinet meeting, 2 June 1941.
23. De Chair, *The Golden Carpet*, p. 119.
24. In his response to de Chair's book, which de Chair printed as an appendix, Glubb wrote: 'The British of course always knew that we were going to win the war, but at the time of these operations every Arab was perfectly convinced that Britain was finished forever, and that it could only be a question of weeks before Germany took over Arabia.' *The Golden Carpet*, p. 214.
25. Ibid., pp. 132–4.
26. Ibid., p. 141.
27. TNA, AIR 23/5854, diary of events.
28. Also on 18 June control for Iran and Iraq passed once again from Middle East Command to India Command, and Quinan was appointed overall command on the ground. His force became known as British Troops Iraq or Iraq Force, and from 21 June 1941, Iraq Command.
29. Masters, *The Road Past Mandalay*, p. 38.
30. De Chair, *The Golden Carpet*.
31. William Slim, *Unofficial History* (Barnsley: Pen and Sword, 2008). De Chair and Masters' accounts record their experiences during the invasion of Syria from Iraq.
32. Slim, *Unofficial History*, p. 103.
33. See 'Major-General A. H. J. Snelling: A Short Biography', at http://www.alexandra-palace-lodge.co.uk/images/army_snelling/SNELLING-Major-General-Arthur-Hugh-Jay.pdf (accessed 22 January 2018).
34. Slim, *Unofficial History*, p. 103.
35. TNA, AIR 23/5938, cypher message, 12 June 1941, Daily Operational Summary 42.
36. LHCMA, John Crumb Papers. The brigade headquarters established itself in Baghdad on 2 October 1941.
37. FRUS, Knabenshue to Secretary of State, 5 June 1941.
38. TNA, CAB 66/17/2, War Cabinet weekly resumé, no. 93, 5–12 June 1941.
39. TNA, FO 624/26, British Embassy Baghdad: UK–Iraq joint defence: Senior Naval Officer Persian Gulf, Basra, 19 July 1941, CICI Paper no. 17.
40. Ibid.
41. Stark, *Dust in the Lion's Paw*, p. 133.
42. Ibid., p. 119.
43. O'Sullivan, 'German Covert Initiatives'.
44. Tripp, *A History of Iraq*, p. 110.
45. Simon, *Iraq Between the Two World Wars*, p. 154.
46. TNA, Political Adviser Central Area, 30 November 1941.
47. TNA, FO, 624/25, British Embassy Baghdad: British officials: Political officers, part 2, 19 August 1941.
48. Fieldhouse (ed.), *Kurds, Arabs, and Britons*, p. 109.
49. Alan de Lacy Rush, 'Introduction', in de Gaury, *Three Kings*, p. 13.
50. Silverfarb, *The Twilight*, p. 17.
51. TNA, 624/25, Situation reports (political officers), part 2, Central Area, 7 December 1941.
52. Silverfarb, *The Twilight*, p. 17.
53. TNA, 624/27, British Embassy Baghdad: Mosul: Situation, Subhi to Cornwallis, 30 May 1942.
54. TNA, 624/26, British Embassy Baghdad: Iranians, letter to ambassador, 16 October 1941.

55. TNA, FO 624/27, British Embassy Baghdad: Censorship organization, C.R. Grice, 4 April 1942.
56. Ibid.
57. The military had its own intelligence officers, known as area liaison officers.
58. TNA, FO 624/25, Cornwallis, 'The political advisory staff'.
59. Ibid., British Embassy Baghdad, British officials: Political officers (part 2), CICI, 7 June 1941.
60. Fieldhouse (ed.), *Kurds, Arabs and Britons*, p. 219.
61. Ibid.
62. TNA, FO 624/25, Situation reports (political officers), Northern Area, 23 September 1941.
63. TNA, FO 624/25, Political Adviser Central Area, 30 November 1941.
64. Ibid., 21 September 1941.
65. Ibid., Political Adviser Northern Area, 10 September 1941.
66. Ibid.
67. Ibid.
68. Ibid.
69. Ibid.
70. Ibid., Political Adviser Central Area, 26 September 1941.
71. Ibid.
72. Ibid., Political Adviser Northern Area, 26 August 1941.
73. Ibid., Political Adviser Central Area, 28 August 1941.
74. Ibid., Political Adviser Central Area, 2 September 1941.
75. TNA, FO 624/27, British Embassy Baghdad: Mosul: Situation.
76. TNA, FO 624/25, Political Adviser Central Area, 30 July 1941.
77. Ibid.
78. TNA, FO 624/27, 1 April 1942.
79. TNA, FO 624/25, Political Adviser Central Area, 23 November 1941.
80. Ibid., Political Adviser Northern Area, 6 December 1941.
81. Ibid., 10 November 1941.
82. Ibid., 10 November 1941 and Political Adviser Central Area, 14 August 1941.
83. Ibid., Political Adviser Central Area, 16 November 1941.
84. Ibid., Political Adviser Northern Area, 20 October 1941.
85. Ibid.
86. TNA, FO 624/25, Situation reports (political officers), Northern Area, 23 September 1941.
87. TNA, FO 624/26, British Embassy Baghdad: Public Relations Section Basra, Stewart Perowne, Public Relations Attaché, Baghdad Embassy, 20 November 1941.
88. TNA, FO 626/26, British Embassy Baghdad: Public Relations.
89. TNA, FO 624/26, British Embassy Baghdad: German murder plot. An 'agent of standing' had made a report concerning attempts on the lives of Nuri, Abdulillah, regent of Iraq, and Ibn Saud, king of Saudi Arabia.
90. British Embassy Baghdad: Situation reports (political officers), part 2, Political Adviser Central Area, 7 December 1941.
91. Ibid., 21 September 1941.
92. TNA, FO 624/26, British Embassy Baghdad: Communism, 17 December 1941.
93. MECA, Public Relations Section, British Embassy Baghdad.

7 Barbarossa and Iran

1. Richard Leighton and Robert Coakley, *Global Logistics and Strategy, 1940–1943* (Washington, DC: US Army Center of Military History, 1995, first published 1955), p. 97.
2. Hopkins attended the Atlantic Charter meeting and subsequent allied conferences in Cairo (1943), Casablanca (1943), Tehran (1943) and Yalta (1945), and was administrator of the Lend-Lease programme.
3. F. Eshragi, 'The Anglo-Soviet Occupation of Iran: August 1941', *Middle Eastern Studies*, vol. 20, no. 1 (1984), pp. 27–52, p. 28.
4. Ibid., p. 27.
5. TNA, FO 624/28, British Embassy Baghdad: Iran: Kurds. Foreign Office to Baghdad, 19 January 1942.
6. Ibid.
7. Hansard, vol. 373, House of Commons debate, 15 July 1941.
8. Quoted in Simon Rigge, *War in the Outposts* (Chicago, IL: Time-Life Books, 1980), p. 76.
9. BBCMSA, M89, Germany in Hindustani and Persian, Persian for the Near East, 22 June 1941.
10. Kennedy, *The Business of War*, p. 154.
11. Katouzian, *Mussadiq and the Struggle for Power*, p. 37.

12. FRUS, Dreyfus to Secretary of State, 28 June 1941.
13. TNA, FO 371/27230, 9 July 1941, quoted in Govan, 'Pawns, Provocateurs and Parasites', p. 95.
14. Bullard, *Letters from Tehran*, p. 31.
15. Skrine, *World War in Iran*, p. 76.
16. TNA, AIR 23/676, 'Iraq Command Operation No. 23/1941', 8 August 1941.
17. Eshragi, 'The Anglo-Soviet Occupation', p. 44.
18. Kaveh Farrokh, *Iran at War, 1500–1958* (Oxford: Osprey, 2011).
19. Stark, *Dust in the Lion's Paw*, pp. 85 and 86.
20. FRUS, Dreyfus to Secretary of State, 19 August 1941.
21. Continuing the inter-command exchange that had hampered Britain's intervention in Iraq four months earlier, responsibility for the Iran–Iraq region had been returned to India Command on 18 June. The Government of India even asked London for 'control of policy in respect of Iraq and Persia'. They were told that control of all policy must remain in London, at the Foreign Office, and Eden wrote to Churchill to reinforce this point. Avon Papers, Eden to Churchill, 15 August 1941.
22. Quoted in Churchill, *The Second World War*, vol. 3, p. 424.
23. TNA, CAB 65/19/4, War Cabinet conclusions, 10 July 1941.
24. Ibid., cipher telegram War Office to C-in-C India, cc C-in-C Middle East, 30 July 1941.
25. Kennedy, *The Business of War*, p. 156.
26. Ibid.
27. Eshragi, 'The Anglo-Soviet Invasion', p. 34.
28. Witness at the same time the reluctance to invade Thailand, which, if it had occurred, would have better enabled Malaya Command to resist the Japanese landings of December 1941.
29. Joan Beaumont, 'Great Britain and the Rights of Neutral Countries: The Case of Iran, 1941', *Journal of Contemporary History*, vol. 16, no. 1 (1981), pp. 213–28.
30. Pownall, *Chief of Staff*, p. 38.
31. Ivan Maisky, *The Maisky Diaries: Red Ambassador to the Court of St James's, 1932–1943*, ed. Gabriel Gorodetsky (New Haven, CT: Yale University Press, 2015), p. 373.
32. Ibid., p. 374.
33. TNA, FO 248/1405, telegram, 19 July 1941.
34. TNA, CAB 65/19/12, War Cabinet conclusions, 31 July 1941, minute 5, confidential annex.
35. Summers, 'Into Persia'.
36. Ibid.
37. Ibid.
38. H.O. Dovey, 'The Eighth Assignment, 1941–1942', *Intelligence and National Security*, vol. 11, no. 4 (October 1996), pp. 672–95.
39. Slim, *Unofficial History*, 'Persian Patterns'.
40. Ibid., p. 179.
41. Ibid., p. 181.
42. TNA, CAB 95/4, War Cabinet: Persia (Iran), minutes of meeting, 4 August 1941.
43. Ibid.
44. Nevertheless, the Foreign Office was adamant that Britain should not attempt to wield an economic weapon unless it had an adequate military one to hand as well, in case it failed. 'It would be highly dangerous even to begin economic pressure,' wrote Eden, 'until we were militarily in a position to do this … we must not move diplomatically ahead of our military strength or we shall court disaster'. Avon Papers, Eden to Churchill, 22 July 1941.
45. Eshragi, 'The Immediate Aftermath', p. 339. The BBC criticised the Shah's 'Nazilike government'.
46. Annabelle Sreberny and Massoumeh Torfeh, *Persian Service: The BBC and British Interests in Iran* (London: I.B. Tauris, 2014), p. 40.
47. Ibid., p. 40-1, quoting FO 371/211/34/4902.
48. FRUS, Dreyfus to Secretary of State, 29 July 1941.
49. Ibid., 21 August 1941.
50. Ibid.
51. Pownall, *Chief of Staff*, diary entry 8 August 1941, p. 35.
52. Eshragi, 'The Anglo-Soviet Occupation of Iran', p. 45.
53. FRUS, Dreyfus to Secretary of State, 21/8/41.
54. Abbas Milani, *The Shah* (London: Palgrave Macmillan, 2011), p. 77.
55. FRUS, Dreyfus to Secretary of State, 22 August 1941.
56. Schulze-Holthus, *Daybreak in Iran*, pp. 56-7.
57. FRUS, Dreyfus to Secretary of State, 21 August 1941.
58. Pownall, *Chief of Staff*, p. 38.
59. Kennedy, *The Business of War*, p. 163.
60. Ibid.

61. TNA FO 624/26, British Embassy Baghdad: Iran: Operations: Soviet mission.
62. CAC, CHAR 20/36/8 1–31 August 1941, PM's printed personal minutes.
63. Ibid.
64. FRUS, Sumner Wells memorandum of conversation with minister of Iran, 25 August 1941.
65. FRUS, Murray to Secretary of State, 26 August 1941.
66. FRUS, Hull to minister of Iran, 27 August 1941.

8 Anglo-Soviet invasion

1. Colville, *The Fringes of Power*, p. 430.
2. Masters, *The Road Past Mandalay*, p. 62.
3. John Harvey (ed.), *The War Diaries of Oliver Harvey, 1941–1945* (London: William Collins, 1978), p. 36.
4. O'Sullivan, 'German Covert Initiatives', p. 40.
5. F. Eshragi, 'The Immediate Aftermath of Anglo-Soviet Occupation of Iran, 1941', *Middle Eastern Studies*, vol. 20, no. 3 (1984), pp. 324–51, p. 325.
6. Skrine, *World War in Iran*.
7. TNA, AIR 23/676, 'Iraq Command Operation Order No 23/1941', 8 August 1941.
8. Slim, *Unofficial History*.
9. TNA, AIR 23.5854, Secret report by AVM J. H. D'Albiac on RAF operations in conjunction with the Royal Navy and Army in Iran between 25 and 28 August 1941.
10. TNA, AIR 23/676, Iraq Command operation order no. 23/1941, 8 August 1941.
11. TNA, AIR 23/676, appendix M, operational order no. 1/1941, RAF Basra Wing HQ, Thomson to OC RAF Station Shaibah, all squadron commanders, and Force Commander 8th Indian Division.
12. TNA, AIR 23/676, Iraq Command operation order no. 23/1941, 8 August 1941. D'Albiac, Air Officer Commanding Iraq, laid down some restrictions for Thomson's squadrons: '84 Squadron may be called upon to carry out operations (bombing or reconnaissance) in direct support of the military operations in Khuzestan but may not be employed on strategic operations outside the area of military operations without the specific authority of Air Headquarters. If this squadron is required to undertake bombing operations in close support of troops, the greatest care is to be taken that targets are accurately specified and pilots kept fully informed as to position of our own troops.' He also stipulated that bombing should be restricted to 'definite and recognizable objectives' and that ground strafing should be restricted entirely to enemy occupied aerodromes'. This was because in the southern area there were 'no trained army cooperation or close support squadrons … and neither the fighter nor the bomber personnel had the training to recognize our own troops or to deal with various signs and symbols employed in close support of the Army'.
13. G.A. Titterton, *The Royal Navy and the Mediterranean*, vol. 2, *November 1940–December 1941* (London: Frank Cass, 2002), pp. 156–8.
14. Ward, *Immortal*, p. 1.
15. Schulze-Holthus, *Daybreak in Iran*. The German intelligence system was built on independent channels of information and reporting, and the individual struggle to impress superiors. Schulze-Holthus's superior was sceptical about his mission. The Foreign Office had cold feet, he said, the SS officer Ettel, Germany's representative in Tehran, 'will spike your guns', and the SD's Mayr and Gamotha would be competitors. Ibid., p. 9.
16. BBCMSA, BBC Mayfair Tehran Arabic for Arab world, 24 August 1941.
17. 'Bridge to Victory' (excerpt from Robert Burgener's *On Borrowed Wings* documentary), *The Iranian* (3 November 1997); online at https://iranian.com/History/Nov97/WWII/index.html (accessed 5 January 2018).
18. Ibid.
19. Raghavan, *India's War*, p. 149.
20. CIA archives, 'AMT VI of the RHSA, Gruppe VI C', Counter Intelligence War Room London, situation report 8, CIA Archives, RG263, Box 3, German intelligence service.
21. Schulze-Holthus, *Daybreak in Iran*, p. 57.
22. Farrokh, *Iran at War*, p. 270.
23. Eshragi, 'The Immediate Aftermath', p. 326.
24. Avon Papers, H.J. Seymour, Foreign Office, to Churchill, 31 August 1941.
25. Alan Moorehead, *A Year of Battle* (London: Hamish Hamilton, 1943), p. 32.
26. NARA, German Military Documents Section, EDS, Misc/6, Box 12/15, 'Axis Activities in Syria and Iraq 1939–41'.
27. TNA, AIR 23/5854, diary of events.
28. Ibid.

29. Ibid.
30. Ibid.
31. For the Iranian order of battle, see Eshragi, 'The Immediate Aftermath', p. 325.
32. Farrokh, *Iran at War*.
33. Summers, 'Into Persia'.
34. Slim, *Unofficial History*, p. 182.
35. Ibid., p. 183.
36. Ibid., p. 184.
37. Masters, *The Road Past Mandalay*, p. 61.
38. Slim, *Unofficial History*, p. 184.
39. BBCMSA, M90, Mayfair in Arabic for the Arab world, 25 August 1941.
40. BBCMSA, M90, Mayfair Tehran in Arabic for the Arab world, 27 August 1941.
41. Roosevelt Papers, diplomatic correspondence, box 40. The shah's appeal to the president was spread across five RCA (Radio Corporation of America) radiogram message sheets.
42. Cooper, *The Fall of Heaven*, p. 60.
43. TNA, AIR 23/5854, diary of events.
44. Ibid.
45. Moorehead, *A Year of Battle*, p. 27.
46. Ibid., p. 28.
47. Ibid., p. 29.
48. Ibid.
49. Ibid., p. 30.
50. Ibid., p. 33.
51. TNA, AIR 23/5854, diary of events.
52. Slim, *Unofficial History*, p. 185.
53. Summers, 'Into Persia'.
54. Ibid.
55. Slim, *Unofficial History*, p. 185.
56. Ibid., p. 186. In the southern sector, Alan Moorehead had observed boxes of new Iranian army Bren guns marked 'Skoda Works, Czechoslovakia'. Moorehead, *A Year of Battle*, p. 32.
57. Slim, *Unofficial History*, p. 187.
58. Ibid.
59. Summers, 'Into Persia'.
60. Slim, *Unofficial History*, p. 192.
61. Ibid., p. 194.
62. Moorehead, *A Year of Battle*, p. 35.
63. Slim, *Unofficial History*, p. 221.
64. The easy victory even earned Wavell, who had directed the campaign from Simla, some respite from Churchill. On 27 August the prime minister cabled to say that he 'entirely agree[d] with you coming over on duty for consultation as Commander-in-Chief India and consider visit to be invaluable. Pray however do not go beyond Cairo till the situation in Persia can be measured by us as well as by you.' CAC CHAR 20/42A/24, Churchill to Wavell, 27 August 1941. On 30 August he signalled: 'So glad the Persian adventure has prospered. Deeply interested in your [Iranian] railway projects which are being sedulously examined here.' CHAR 20/42A/38.
65. Summers, 'Into Persia'.
66. BBCMSA, M90, Tehran, Persian for Persia, 28 August 1941.
67. Ibid., 31 August 1941.
68. Ward, *Immortal*, p. 150.
69. Homa Katouzian, *Iran: A Beginner's Guide* (London: Oneworld, 2013), p. 114.
70. Eshragi, 'The Immediate Aftermath', p. 326.
71. Roosevelt Papers, Whitehouse to His Imperial Majesty Reza Pahlavi, 2 September 1941.
72. Ibid., Hull to Roosevelt, 17 September 1941. Dreyfus had been summoned by the shah and asked to convey to Roosevelt his thanks for his 'friendly telegrams'.
73. Colville, *The Fringes of Power*, p. 430.
74. Quoted in David Carlton, *Churchill and the Soviet Union* (Manchester University Press, 2000), p. 87.
75. Maisky, *The Maisky Diaries*.
76. Kennedy, *The Business of War*, p. 163.
77. Special Service Division, United States Army Services of Supply. *Pocket Guide to Iran* (Washington, DC: US Army War and Navy Departments, 1943), p. 7.
78. Masters, *The Road Past Mandalay*.
79. Tooze, *The Wages of Destruction*, p. 402.
80. Curie, *Journey Among Warriors*, chapter 6, 'Teheran: A Center of War Communications', pp. 99–100.

9 Abdication and occupation

1. CAC, CHAR 20/36/8, 1–31 August 1941, PM's printed personal minutes.
2. Ibid.
3. CAC, CHAR 20/43/39.
4. Eshragi, 'The Immediate Aftermath', p. 329.
5. CAC, CHAR 20/36/9, PM's printed personal minutes.
6. Ibid., CHAR 20/42A/54-55.
7. Ibid., CHAR 20/42B/187.
8. Aboul-Enein and Aboul-Enein, *The Secret War*, p. 106.
9. Skrine, *World War in Iran*, p. 81.
10. Ibid.
11. Avon Papers, Eden to Churchill, 9 September 1941. Eden wrote: 'Personally I consider the Persian affair to have been a neat piece of joint military and diplomatic action. In its way it is a minor classic!'
12. Ibid., Churchill to Alexander Cadogan, Foreign Office, 2 September 1941.
13. Ibid., Churchill to Eden, 6 September 1941. On 25 September, Churchill pressed Eden regarding the Grand Mufti, who was known to be in the Japanese legation. Churchill was anxious to get his surrender and avoid him slipping away. Ibid., Churchill to Eden, 25 September 1941.
14. Bullard, *Letters from Tehran*, 3 September 1941, p. 76.
15. BBCMSA, M90. Ali Mansur had resigned the office on 27 August.
16. Ibid.
17. BBCMSA, M90, BBC Mayfair Tehran in Persian for Iran, 11 September 1941.
18. Milani, *The Shah*, p. 79.
19. Ward, *Immortal*, p. 168.
20. Shaul Bakhash, 'Britain and the Abdication of Reza Shah', *Middle Eastern Studies*, vol. 52, no. 2 (2016), pp. 318–34.
21. TNA, CAB 65/23/17, War Cabinet conclusions, confidential annex, 16 September 1941.
22. Ibid.
23. Azimi, *Iran*, p. 36.
24. Milani, *The Shah*, p. 80.
25. Slim, *Unofficial History*, p. 203.
26. Ibid.
27. Ibid., p. 205.
28. Summers, 'Into Persia'.
29. Ibid.
30. BBCMSA, M90, Mayfair Persian for Iran, 18 September 1941.
31. Ibid.
32. Ibid., 20 September 1941.
33. Summers, 'Into Persia'.
34. Slim, *Unofficial History*, p. 238.
35. TNA, FO 248/1414, Internal situation Kermanshah, 29 April 1942. British propaganda was considered 'a bit of a joke' by the Iranians consulted, boasting about low casualties while still apparently losing the war. It was thought that the Japanese would do more damage to British interests than Germany had, and that India would rebel.
36. Summers, 'Into Persia'.
37. Slim, *Unofficial History*, p. 238.
38. BBCMSA, M90, BBC Mayfair Persian for Iran, 18 September 1941.
39. Ibid., BBC Mayfair CT, 16 October 1941.
40. Summers, 'Into Persia'.
41. Eshragi, 'The Immediate Aftermath'.
42. O'Sullivan, 'German Covert Initiatives', p. 250.
43. Katouzian, *Musaddiq and the Struggle for Power*, p. xiii.
44. Ibid., p. 34.
45. Azimi, *Iran*, p. 5.
46. Ibid., p. 37.
47. Katouzian, *Musaddiq and the Struggle for Power*, p. 37.
48. Annabelle Sreberny and Massoumeh Torfeh, 'The BBC Persian Service, 1941–1979', *Historical Journal of Film, Radio and Television*, vol. 28, no. 4 (October 2008), pp. 515–35, p. 519.
49. Azimi, *Iran*, p. 37.
50. Sreberny and Torfeh, *Persian Service*, p. 34.
51. Skrine, *World War in Iran*, p. 121.

52. TNA, FO 248/1426, Shah Mohamed Reza. For Bullard's shifting attitude towards the shah, see Bakhash, 'Britain and the Abdication'.
53. De Gaury, *Traces of Travel*, p. 111.
54. Skrine accompanied the ex-imperial family on their journey into exile and offers an account in *World War in Iran*. The exile is also covered in Milani, *The Shah*. Sir Bede Clifford, Governor of Mauritius, writes about his stay on the island in his autobiography, *Proconsul: Being Incidents in the Life and Career of the Honourable Sir Bede Clifford* (London: Evans Brothers, 1964).
55. Ervand Abrahamian, *Iran Between Two Revolutions* (Princeton University Press, 1982), p. 165.
56. Cooper, *The Fall of Heaven*, p. 61.
57. Katouzian, *Iran*, p. 48.
58. BBCMSA, M90, BBC Mayfair Persian for Iran, 18 September 1941.
59. Ibid.
60. Ibid.
61. Katouzian, *Iran*, pp. 29–30.
62. Durham University Special Collections, Lambton Papers, 57/5.
63. Ibid.
64. Katouzian, *Iran*, pp. 43–4.
65. BBCMSA, M90, BBC Mayfair Persian for Iran, 7 October 1941.
66. Ibid., M90, Tehran Arabic for the Arab world, 13 November 1941.
67. TNA, FO 248/1406, HM Minister's interviews with Shah Muhammad Reza.
68. Ibid., minute, 20 December 1941.
69. TNA, FO 248/1406, HM Minister's interviews with Shah Muhammad Reza.
70. Ibid., interview with shah, 8 December 1941.
71. Ibid.
72. Ibid., Holman to Foreign Office, 6 June 1942.
73. Ibid.
74. FO 248/1407 10 April 1942.
75. Katouzian, *Iran*, p. xiii.
76. Ibid., p. 121.
77. Durham University Special Collections, Lambton Papers, 57/5.
78. Ibid., 57/10, Lecture for Chatham House, 1945.
79. Katouzian, *Iran*, p. 115.
80. FRUS, Dreyfus to Secretary of State, 28 September 1941. In the same dispatch, Dreyfus reported a Soviet Persian-language newspaper, *Thoughts of the People*, which had referred to the high prices pertaining in Iran, and asked 'when will the people stop living impoverished lives and begin to live like human beings?', an attempt to undermine the authority of the Tehran government.
81. Eshragi, 'The Immediate Aftermath', p. 339.
82. TNA, FO 248/1416, Tribal lands.
83. Katouzian, *Iran*, p. 122.
84. Azimi, *Iran*, p. 57.
85. HM Minister, 24 July 1943.
86. TNA, FO 248/1410, Internal situation, Azerbaijan, 16 March 1942. Bullard to Eden, English translation.
87. Durham University Special Collections, Lambton Papers.
88. TNA, FO 248/1410, Tabriz to Tehran, 17 January 1942.
89. Azimi, *Iran*, p. 43.
90. Ibid.
91. TNA, FO 248/1412, Internal situation Kurdistan, 10 November 1942.
92. Ibid. Copy of petition from Hian bin Shanuuf, Chief of Dris tribes of Manyuhi to Consul HMG Khorramshahr.
93. TNA, FO 624/25, Situation reports (political officers), British Embassy Baghdad: Political officers, Holt to Dowson, 25 October 1941.
94. TNA, FO 248/1404, Internal political situation.
95. Ibid.
96. Ibid.
97. TNA, FO 248/1412, Internal situation Kurdistan.
98. TNA, FO 248/1405, Kurdish situation.
99. Ibid.
100. Slim, *Unofficial History*.
101. Ibid.
102. Summers, 'Into Persia'.
103. TNA, FO 248/1405, Holman to Bullard, 7 September 1941.

104. Summers, 'Into Persia'.
105. TNA, FO 248/1405, 20 July 1941.
106. Fieldhouse (ed.), *Kurds, Arabs and Britons*, pp. 220–1.
107. TNA, FO 624/25, Assistant Political Adviser Southern Area, report no. 11, 16 December 1941.
108. Ibid., Political Adviser Northern Area, 10 September 1941.
109. Ibid., 23 September 1941.
110. TNA, FO 248/1405, Unrest in Kurdistan, memorandum from Consul Kermanshah, 18 September 1941.
111. Ibid. Minister's telegram, 14 October 1941.
112. TNA, FO 248/1408, Tehran legation, Internal situation Kurdistan, Bullard telegram to Foreign Office, 6 February 1942.
113. TNA, FO 248/1433, Internal situation Kermanshah, Operations in Kurdistan by Persian Forces, British military attaché Tehran to Consul-General Tabriz, 26 September 1944.
114. TNA, FO 624/28, British Embassy Baghdaad: Iran: Kurds, Foreign Office to Baghdad, 19 January 1942. This file contains a great deal of material on Kurdish affairs, grievances, government actions, reports on Soviet actions and British military reports and minutes.
115. TNA, FO 248/1410, cipher, 21 January 1942.
116. Ibid., Ankara to Foreign Office, Tehran legation, 14 January 1942.
117. FRUS, Dreyfus to Secretary of State, 1 May 1942.
118. Azimi, *Iran*, p. 55.
119. There is a mass of detail on British imperial efforts in the official War Office book *PAIFORCE*, and contemporary publications such as E.R. Yarham, 'The Trans-Persian Railway', *Royal United Services Institute Journal*, vol. 87, no. 545 (1942), pp. 44–50.
120. Henry Maitland Wilson, 'Despatch on the Persia and Iraq Command Covering the Period 21 August 1942 to 17 February 1943', *London Gazette* (1946), pp. 4,333–40.
121. Silverfarb, *The Twilight*, p. 13.
122. Wilson, 'Despatch on the Persia and Iraq Command'.
123. Dudley Clarke, *The Eleventh at War: Being the Story of the XIth Hussars (Prince Albert's Own) Through the Years 1939–1945* (London: Michael Joseph, 1952), p. 235.
124. Like many of the soldiers who served in Iran and Iraq, the men of Masters' battalion soon got their wish. While Masters himself was ordered to leave the battalion and attend the Imperial Staff College at Quetta, 'in the Desert my battalion, and the rest of the brigade, disappeared on 6 June 1942 in the Battle of the Cauldron, overwhelmed by German panzers'. Masters, *The Road Past Mandalay*. The same fate awaited other units serving in the Iran–Iraq region at this time; less than two weeks after Masters' Gurkha battalion was destroyed, the 20th Indian Infantry Brigade, part of Slim's 10th Division while in Iraq, was overrun and largely wiped out at Gambat during the same German offensive.
125. Maisky, *The Maisky Diaries*, p. 381.
126. Skrine, *World War in Iran*, p. 88.
127. TNA, CAB 66/19/45, War Cabinet: Relations with Russia, memorandum by the Secretary of State for Foreign Affairs, 15 November 1941.
128. Ibid., Cripps to Eden, 23 October 1941.
129. Ibid., Cripps to Eden, 23 October 1941.
130. Ibid., Eden to Cripps, 25 October 1941.
131. Ibid., Cripps to Eden, 25 October 1941.
132. Ibid., Eden to Cripps, 28 October 1941.
133. Ibid., Eden to Cripps, 1 November 1941.
134. FRUS, US chargé, memorandum of conversation, 10 October 1941.
135. FRUS, Dreyfus to Secretary of State, 28 September 1941.
136. Rigge, *War in the Outposts*, p. 77.
137. Ibid.
138. Ward, *Immortal*.
139. T.H. Vail Motter, *United States Army in World War II: The Middle East Theater – The Persian Corridor and Aid to Russia* (Washington: US Army Center of Military History, 1952).
140. Schubert, 'The Persian Gulf Command', p. 306.
141. Masters, *The Road Past Mandalay*.
142. Rigge, *War in the Outposts*, p. 80.
143. Curie, *Journey Among Warriors*, p. 103.

10 The consequences of occupation

1. Hermione, Countess of Ranfurly, *To War with Whitaker: Wartime Diaries of the Countess of Ranfurly, 1939–1945* (London: Mandarin, 1995), diary entry 5 January 1942.

NOTES to pp. 208-216

383

2. TNA, FO 624/25, Political Adviser Central Area, 4 September 1941.
3. Ibid., 30 November 1941.
4. TNA, FO 624/25, Situation reports (political officers), Northern Area report, 6 December 1941.
5. Ibid., 10 November 1941.
6. Ibid., British Embassy Baghdad: British forces, Cornwallis to His Excellency Seiyid Ali Jaudet-a-Aiyubi, 23 July 1941.
7. Ibid., Situation reports, Political Adviser Northern Area, 31 October 1941.
8. Ibid., 20 October 1941.
9. TNA, FO 624/25, Situation reports (political officers), Northern Area, 6 December 1941.
10. TNA, FO 624/25, Political Adviser Central Area, 3 December 1941.
11. Ibid., Political Adviser Northern Area, 20 October 1941.
12. Skrine, *World War in Iran*.
13. When Skrine received official visitors in Mashhad, usually from British troops or the Indian Army, most made a bee-line for the bazaars in search of karakul coats and turquoise jewellery, cheap Leica cameras, poshteen overcoats, Turcoman rugs and hams cured by Armenian experts.
14. Skrine, *World War in Iran*.
15. Special Service Division, United States Army Services of Supply, *A Short Guide to Iraq* (Washington, DC: US Army War and Navy Departments, 1943).
16. Special Service Division, *Pocket Guide to Iran*.
17. Special Service Division, *A Short Guide to Iraq*, p. 1.
18. For a fascinating expansion of this theme in a different theatre of war, see Judith Bennett, *Natives and Exotics: World War Two and Environment in the Southern Pacific* (Honolulu, HI: University of Hawaii Press, 2009).
19. Special Service Division, *Pocket Guide to Iran*, p. 6.
20. Ibid., p. 8.
21. Special Service Division, *A Short Guide to Iraq*, p. 5.
22. Ibid., p. 17.
23. Ibid., p. 11.
24. Special Service Division, *Pocket Guide to Iran*, p. 6.
25. NARA, Interviews with PGC officers returned on SS *Anne Bradstreet* on 2 May 1944 at HRPE, Newport News, VA: Lieutenant Colonel Ernest Norberg, formerly commander of Camp Park, Hamadan, Iran.
26. TNA, FO 624/25, Political Adviser Central Area, 1 November 1941.
27. Ibid.
28. Ibid., Political Adviser Central Area, 8 August 1941 and 24 November 1941.
29. Ibid., Political Adviser Central Area, 8 August 1941. Over 400 Polish and 100 other British Empire troops were commemorated here too.
30. Printed Records of the German Foreign Office.
31. TNA, FO 248/1414, Internal situation Kermanshah, Consul Khorramshahr to British legation, 14 April 1942.
32. See the picture in Rigge, *War in the Outposts*, p. 95, showing a long line of Iranian workers beside a dock being individually searched by a small boy, under the gaze of an armed American military policeman.
33. Adrian O'Sullivan, 'Joe Spencer's Ratcatchers: British Security Intelligence in Occupied Persia', *Asian Affairs*, vol. 48, no. 2 (2017), pp. 296–312, p. 297.
34. Ibid., p. 297.
35. Rigge, *War in the Outposts*, p. 92–3.
36. Kamran Dadkhah, 'The Iranian Economy during the Second World War: The Devaluation Controversy', *Middle Eastern Studies*, vol. 37, no. 2 (April 2001), pp. 181–98, p. 192.
37. TNA, FO 248/1418, Internal situation Khuzistan, Khorramshahr to Tehran, 26 August 1943.
38. FO 624/25, Political Adviser Central Area, 30 November 1941.
39. See the picture of such a search in Rigge, *War in the Outposts*, p. 94.
40. Fieldhouse (ed.), *Kurds, Arabs, and Britons*, p. 222.
41. RAF Habbaniya had its own kennel of hunting dogs, the Royal Exodus Hunt.
42. De Chair, *The Golden Carpet*.
43. See Ezra Scott, 'My Time in the Persian Gulf Command, 1943–1945', *Pars Times* (n.d.); online at www.parstimes.com/travel/iran/memoirs_persian_gulf_command.html (accessed 12 December 2017).
44. Frost, *A Drop Too Many*, p. 6.
45. TNA, FO 624/25, Political Adviser Central Area, 21 August 1941.
46. Srinath Raghavan, *India's War: The Making of Modern South Asia, 1939–1945* (London: Penguin, 2016).

47. Ibid., Political Adviser Northern Area, 10 September 1941.
48. Ibid., Political Adviser Central Area, 26 September 1941.
49. Ibid., 23 November 1941.
50. TNA, FO 799/11, Isfahan diaries, allied liaison officer Hamadan telegram to military attaché, 3 July 1942.
51. TNA, FO 624/25, Political Adviser Northern Area, 10 August 1941.
52. Ibid., 22 August 1941.
53. TNA, FO 624/25, Political Adviser Central Area, 14 December 1941.
54. TNA, FO 799/11, Isfahan diaries, 1–15 March 1942.
55. TNA, FO 624/25, Political Adviser Northern Area, 24 November 1941.
56. Masters, *The Road Past Mandalay*, p. 40.
57. FRUS, Dreyfus to Secretary of State, 10 June 1943.
58. Ibid., 24 June 1943.
59. TNA, FO 248/1412, Internal situation Kurdistan, 13 June 1942.
60. Ibid.
61. For examples, see TNA, FO 799/12, Shiraz diaries.
62. TNA, FO 799/9, Military: Control of civil disturbances.
63. Wilson, 'Despatch on the Persia and Iraq Command', p. 4336.
64. Fieldhouse (ed.), *Kurds, Arabs and Britons*, p. 222.
65. Bullard, *Letters from Tehran*, pp. 186–7.
66. Ward, *Immortal*, p. 177.
67. TNA, FO 248/1433, Internal situation Kermanshah, British Embassy to Imperial Ministry of Foreign Affairs, 23 May 1944. Legation upgraded to embassy in early 1944.
68. TNA, FO 248/1414, Internal situation Kermansh, I.F.L. Fyman to J.G. Baillie, Consul, Ahwaz, 8/4/42.
69. TNA, FO 624/25, Political Adviser Northern Area, 20 October1941.
70. Ibid., Political Adviser Central Area, 26 September 1941.
71. Ibid., Political Adviser Central Area, 1 November 1941.
72. Ibid., Political Adviser Northern Area, 21 December 1941.
73. Ibid., British Embassy Baghdad: British Forces: Incidents, 31 December 1941.
74. Ibid., Political Adviser Central Area, 18 December 1941 and 16 November 1941.
75. Ibid., 26 September 1941.
76. Rigge, *War in the Outposts*, p. 94.
77. TNA, FO 248/1418, Internal situation Khuzistan.
78. Ibid., HM Consul Khorramshahr to HM Minister Tehran, 8 November 1943.
79. Schubert, 'The Persian Gulf Command', p. 309.
80. FRUS, Berle to Murray, 10 January 1942.
81. Ibid., Dreyfus to Secretary of State, 13 March 1942.
82. TNA, FO 624/26, British Embassy Baghdad: British Forces: Indian, Embassy to Force Headquarters Baghdad West, 7 November 1941.
83. Ibid., Embassy to Force Headquarters, Baghdad West, 2 December 1941.
84. Ibid., Deportation of S.M. Rafique.
85. TNA, FO 624/25, Political Adviser Central Area, September 1941.
86. TNA, FO 624/26, British Embassy Baghdad: British Forces: Incidents, Embassy *note verbale* to Iraqi Ministry of Foreign Affairs, 19 December 1941.
87. Ibid., Ministry of Foreign Affairs to British Embassy, 4 December 1941.
88. Ibid., 8 November 1941 and FO 624/25, Political Adviser Northern Area, 20 October 1941.
89. TNA, FO 624/26, British Embassy Baghdad: British Forces: Incidents, Ministry of Foreign Affairs to British Embassy, 25 October 1941.
90. Ibid., Basra consulate to Embassy, 8 September 1941.
91. Bullard, *Letters from Tehran*, p. 76. Letter to Foreign Office, 23 September 1941. British railwaymen in Tehran asked the minister if the swastika could be removed from the German legation for fear that it would incite attempts to smash it up.
92. FRUS, 9 March 1943.
93. FRUS, Prime Minister's note cited in Dreyfus to Secretary of State, 23 August 1943.
94. Ibid., Dreyfus to Secretary of State, 26 June 1943.
95. FRUS, Dreyfus to Secretary of State.
96. Eeman, *Clouds Over the Sun*, p. 33.
97. TNA, FO 624/25, Political Adviser Central Area, 30 November 1941.
98. Ibid., 28 August 1941.
99. Ibid., British Embassy Baghdad: British Forces: Incidents, 26 September 1941.

100. Ibid., Political Adviser Central Area to ambassador, 8 December 1941.
101. Ibid., testament of Pilot Officer Charles Rash, 37 Squadron, attached Shaibah. Sworn statement, 6 June 1941.
102. Ibid., 15 July 1941.
103. Ibid., sworn statement, 6 June 1941.
104. Ibid., intelligence, regarding murder of Blackhall, 14 July 1941.
105. Ibid., Ministry of Foreign Affairs to ambassador, 28 September 1941.
106. Ibid.
107. Silverfarb, *The Twilight*, p. 95.
108. TNA, FO 624/25, Political Adviser Southern Area, 30 September 1941.
109. Ibid., Political Adviser Central Area, 26 September 1941.
110. Ibid.
111. Ibid., Political Adviser Northern Area, diary of Major Kinoch, 13–19 December 1941.
112. Ibid., Political Adviser Northern Area, 17 December 1941.
113. Ibid., 31 October 1941.
114. Ibid., 26 August 1941.
115. Ibid., 23 September 1941.
116. Ibid., 24 November 1941.
117. Ibid., 17 December 1941.
118. Ibid.
119. Ibid., 10 November 1941.
120. TNA, FO 624/27, BEB: Mosul: situation. 'A report on Mosul: The general situation', by P. Mason, 1 July 1942.
121. TNA, FO 624/25, Situation reports (political officers), Northern Area, 10 November 1941.
122. Fieldhouse (ed.), *Kurds, Arabs, and Britons*, pp. 222–3.
123. Durham University Special Collections, Lambton Papers, 16/37.
124. TNA, FO 624/28, British Embassy Baghdad: Oil: Pipelines.
125. Ibid.
126. Fieldhouse (ed.), *Kurds, Arabs, and Britons*, p. 211.
127. Ibid., p. 221.
128. Ibid.
129. Skrine, *World War in Iran*, p. 89.
130. Ibid.
131. Ibid., p. 97.
132. Ibid.
133. Ibid., p. 98.
134. Ibid.
135. Ibid., p. 117.
136. Ibid., p. 128.
137. Ibid.
138. Ibid., p. 129.
139. Ibid., p. 150.
140. Ibid., pp. 150–1.

11 War and the home front

1. FRUS, Dreyfus to Secretary of State, 5 August 1942.
2. See Dadkhah, 'The Iranian Economy'.
3. TNA, FO 624/26, Cornwallis to Bullard, 31 December 1941.
4. See Daniel Silverfarb, 'Britain and Iraqi Barley during the Second World War', *Middle Eastern Studies*, vol. 31, no. 3 (June 1995), pp. 524–32.
5. Durham University Special Collections, Lambton Papers, 57/5.
6. The preceding paragraph is based on Stephen McFarland, 'Anatomy of an Iranian Political Crowd: The Tehran Bread Riot of December 1942', *International Journal of Middle East Studies*, vol. 17, no. 1 (February 1985), pp. 51–65.
7. FRUS, Dreyfus to Secretary of State, 7 April 1942.
8. Eeman, *Clouds Over the Sun*, pp. 32–3.
9. George Kirk, *Survey of International Affairs 1939–1946: The Middle East in the War* (Oxford: Oxford University Press, 1952), p. 26.
10. Ibid., p. 466.
11. CAC, CHAR 20/108/69-71.

12. CAC, CHAR 20/117/83-86.a.
13. TNA, CAB 66/44/22, War Cabinet: Memorandum by Chancellor of the Exchequer, 17 December 1943.
14. Tripp, *A History of Iraq*, p. 116.
15. TNA, FO 624/25, Political Adviser Central Area, 17 December 1941.
16. See Silverfarb, *The Twilight*, chapter 3, 'The Great Inflation'.
17. TNA, FO 624/28, British Embassy Baghdad: Middle East Cabinet Minister, Casey, 'The Economic Situation in Iraq', 1942.
18. Silverfarb, *The Twilight*, p. 31.
19. TNA, FO 624/28, British Embassy Baghdad: Middle East Cabinet Minister, Walker, Commercial Secretary.
20. TNA, FO 624/28, BEB: Tobacco, Ministry of the Interior, Iraq, 1 October 1942, to Political Adviser Northern Area.
21. The British government also purchased large quantities of Iraqi barley and dates to feed other parts of the Middle East.
22. Silverfarb, *The Twilight*, p. 35.
23. Katouzian, *Iran*, p. 122.
24. Ibid., p. 123.
25. Dadkhah, 'The Iranian Economy'.
26. The post-occupation devaluation under Finance Minister Hassam Naficy remains hotly debated. The British sold pounds to Bank Melli in return for rials, and the Soviets earned rials for the goods they promised to sell to Iran.
27. FRUS, Dreyfus to Secretary of State, 19 November 1942.
28. Wilson, 'Despatch on the Persia and Iraq Command', p. 4,336.
29. FRUS, Dreyfus to Secretary of State, 18 November 1942.
30. Tripp, *A History of Iraq*, p. 116.
31. Lambton Papers, 48/11, Lecture notes: 'Problems Facing Persia', paper read to Middle East Group of Parliamentary Labour Party, 13 March 1946.
32. CAC, CHAR 20/81/92-94, personal telegrams.
33. McFarland, 'Anatomy of an Iranian Political Crowd'.
34. Ibid., p. 53.
35. Dadkhah, 'The Iranian Economy'.
36. Lyon to Cornwallis, 19 June 1941 and 4 January 1944 reproduced in Fieldhouse (ed.), *Kurds, Arabs, and Britons*.
37. Lambton Papers, 16/37.
38. Moorehead, *A Year of Battle*, p. 38.
39. Slim, *Unofficial History*, p. 202.
40. TNA, FO 248/1436, Majlis elections, 30 January 1944.
41. MECA, Political Adviser Northern Area, 19 June 1942.
42. Ibid., 26 August 1941.
43. Skrine, *World War in Iran*, p. 79.
44. Ibid.
45. Ibid., p. 94.
46. Ibid., p. 95.
47. Ibid., p. 174.
48. Ibid., p. 94.
49. Stephen McFarland, 'A Peripheral View of the Origins of the Cold War: The Crises in Iran, 1941-47', *Diplomatic History*, vol. 4, no. 4 (October 1980), pp. 333-52.
50. Ranfurly, *To War with Whitaker*, p. 164.
51. Ibid., pp. 164-5.
52. Bullard, *Letters from Tehran*, p. 154.
53. This is Adrian O'Sullivan's memorable epithet for the American consul-general.
54. FRUS, Dreyfus to Secretary of State, 25 June 1942.
55. Lambton Papers, 48/11, Lecture notes, 'Problems Facing Persia'.
56. Ibid.
57. Ibid.
58. FRUS, Dreyfus to Hull, 10 May 1942.
59. Rigge, *War in the Outposts*, p. 85.
60. FRUS, Verbal notice, Washington, 19 June 1942.
61. FRUS, Dreyfus to Secretary of State, 7 July 1942.
62. TNA, FO 248/1412, Internal situation Kurdistan.
63. FRUS, Dreyfus to Secretary of State, 20 July 1942.
64. Ibid.

65. FRUS, Dreyfus to Secretary of State, 23 October 1942.
66. Ibid., 24 October 1942.
67. Ibid., 9 November 1942.
68. Ibid., 8 December 1942.
69. Ibid., 9 November 1942.
70. FRUS, Hull to Winant to Foreign Office, 11 December 1942.
71. McFarland, 'Anatomy of an Iranian Political Crowd', p. 61.
72. FRUS, Dreyfus to Secretary of State, 13 December 1942.
73. McFarland, 'Anatomy of an Iranian Political Crowd', pp. 52–3.
74. Ibid., p. 61.
75. Ibid.
76. See Ryszard Antolak, 'Iran and the Polish Exodus from Russia 1942', *Pars Times* (n.d.); online at http://www.parstimes.com/history/polish_refugees/exodus_russia.html (accessed 12 December 2017).
77. Antolak, 'Iran and the Polish Exodus'.
78. David Meyler, 'Polish Exodus: The Unlikely Iranian-Polish Alliance in World War II', Avalanche Press (October 2015); online at http://www.avalanchepress.com/PolishExodus.php (accessed 12 December 2017).
79. Anuradha Bhattacharjee, *The Second Homeland: Polish Refugees in India* (New Delhi: Sage, 2012), p. 153.
80. Skrine, *World War in Iran*.
81. Antolak, 'Iran and the Polish Exodus'.
82. Quoted in Bhattacharjee, *The Second Homeland*, p. 162.
83. Rigge, *War in the Outposts*, p. 82.
84. Bhattacharjee, *The Second Homeland*, p. 155.
85. Ibid.
86. TNA, FO 799/11, Isfahan diaries.

12 Churchill's new command

1. TNA, WO 106/3078, 12 October 1941, quoted in O'Sullivan, 'German Covert Initiatives', p. 239.
2. Clarke, *The Eleventh at War*, 'Interlude in Persia and Iraq'.
3. Herf, *Nazi Propaganda for the Arab World*, p. 125.
4. Taken from Speer's diaries, quoted in O'Sullivan, 'German Covert Initiatives', pp. 236–7.
5. See Ashley Jackson, *Of Islands, Ports, and Sea Lanes: Africa and the Indian Ocean in the Second World War* (Solihull: Helion, 2018).
6. Printed Records of the German Foreign Office, Serie E, Band 03, Iraq, Nr. 3926, June 1942.
7. Ibid., Nr. 68.7, and Serie E, Band 03, Nr. 7610, July 1942.
8. Kennedy, *The Business of War*, p. 219.
9. Ibid., p. 220.
10. Ibid.
11. Ibid., p. 148.
12. J.H. Bamberg, *The History of the British Petroleum Company*, vol. 2: *The Anglo Iranian Years, 1928–1954* (Cambridge: Cambridge University Press, 1994), p. 209. See ibid., chapter 8, 'War, 1939–1945' and chapter 9, 'Transition in Iran, 1939–1947'; TNA, CAB, 66/27/18, War Cabinet: Oil supplies in the East in the event of the destruction of the Persian oilfields, 21 July 1942; see also D.J. Payton-Smith, *Oil: A Study of War-time Policy and Administration* (London: HMSO, 1971).
13. TNA, CAB, 66/27/18, War Cabinet: Oil supplies in the East.
14. Ibid.
15. Bamberg, *The History of the British Petroleum Company*, p. 205.
16. TNA, CAB 66/27/15, War Cabinet: Review of the situation in the Middle East, note by secretary of the War Cabinet, 2 August 1942, Annex II: Middle East oil position.
17. TNA, CAB 66/27/18, War Cabinet: Oil supplies in the East.
18. Bamberg, *The History of the British Petroleum Company*, p. 216. There was also a significant change in the destination of Iran's oil; shipments to Europe stopped in 1940, and to Britain in 1941, supplies to the Mediterranean area fell dramatically between 1940 and 1943 (Italy's entry and exit from the war), while supplies to eastern markets, including Africa, Australian, Burma, Ceylon, Egypt and India, rose dramatically. Allied occupation of Iran and Iraq caused local consumption to rise dramatically (doubling between 1938 and 1943), and Admiralty consumption remained constant. The changing pattern was influenced by sea routes and the loss of alternative supplies in Burma and the East Indies. See Bamberg, *The History of the British Petroleum Company*, table 8.3, p. 220.
19. TNA, CAB 66/27/15, War Cabinet: Review of the situation in the Middle East.

20. Bamberg, *The History of the British Petroleum Company*, p. 241.
21. Ibid., table 9.6, p. 247.
22. See Rasmus Christian Elling, 'The World's Biggest Refinery and the Second World War: Khuzestan, Oil, and Security', conference paper, International Conference on the Comparative Social Histories of Labour in the Oil Industry, International Institute of Social History in Amsterdam (June 2014).
23. Field Marshal Lord Alanbrooke, *War Diaries, 1939–1945*, ed. Alex Danchev and Daniel Todman (London: Weidenfeld and Nicolson, 2002), p. 284.
24. Ibid., p. 286.
25. TNA, CAB 66/27/15, War Cabinet: Review of the situation in the Middle East.
26. Ibid.
27. Ibid.
28. Churchill, *The Second World War*, vol. 4, p. 326.
29. Alanbrooke, *War Diaries*.
30. Churchill, *The Second World War*, vol. 4, p. 415.
31. TNA, CAB 65/31/13, War Cabinet conclusions, 7 August 1942, minute 1, confidential annex.
32. Ibid., Reflex telegram, 7 August 1942.
33. Churchill, *The Second World War*, vol. 4, pp. 416–17.
34. The Resident Minister Middle East, Sir Oliver Lyttelton, believed that the 'argument for unified command appears to me to be overwhelming'. See CAC, CHAR 20/47/104, Cairo to Foreign Office. Major-General Kennedy agreed. See Kennedy, *The Business of War*, p. 259.
35. Ibid., p. 266.
36. TNA, CAB 66/28/3, War Cabinet: USSR: prime minister's visit to Moscow, 7 August 1942 telegram.
37. TNA, CAB 65/31/13, WM (42) 108th conclusions, 7 August 1942, minute 1, confidential annex, Mideast to Air Ministry (Reflex 35), PM to deputy PM.
38. TNA, CAB 65/31/13, War Cabinet conclusions, 7/8/42, minute 1, confidential annex, Mideast to Air Ministry (Reflex 35), PM to deputy PM.
39. TNA, CAB 65/31/13, WM (42) 108th conclusions, 7/8/42, minute 1, confidential annex, Mideast to Air Ministry (Reflex 35) 8/8/42, deputy PM to PM.
40. Churchill, *The Second World War*, vol. 4, p. 423. Churchill to Ismay, 10 August 1942.
41. CAC, CHAR 20/79A/8.
42. CAC, CHAR 20/79A/20-21.
43. Alanbrooke, *War Diaries*, diary entry 8 August 1942.
44. CAC, CHAR 20/87/49-50.
45. TNA, CAB 65/31/20, War Cabinet conclusions, 25 August 1942, minute 2, confidential annex.
46. Churchill, *The Second World War*, vol. 4, p. 449.
47. Ibid., pp. 459–60.
48. From Mideast to Air Ministry Reflex (176 21 August 1942 – a secret cypher telegram from Churchill): CAB 65/31/19, WM (42) 116th conclusions confidential annex 22 August 1942, appendix A – record of decisions taken at meeting held at GHQME 21 August.
49. CAC, CHAR 20/87/67.
50. TNA, CAB 65/31/19, WM (42) 116th conclusions confidential annex 22 August 1942, Reflex telegrams 175, 176 and 177 ; also see Alanbrooke, *War Diaries*, p. 314.
51. Ranfurly, *To War with Whitaker*.
52. Henry Maitland Wilson, *Eight Years Overseas, 1939–1947* (London: Hutchinson, 1950), p. 134.
53. Ibid. Churchill wrote to Roosevelt on 22 August telling him that Wilson was responsible for the defence of Cairo. Churchill, *The Second World War*, vol. 4, p. 469.
54. Alanbrooke, *War Diaries*, pp. 310–11.

13 'Jumbo' and the Germans

1. Mackenzie, *Eastern Epic*, p. 592.
2. Wilson, *Eight Years Overseas*.
3. CAC, CHAR 20/80/8-10, Casey to Churchill, 10 September 1942.
4. Ranfurly, *To War with Whitaker*, p. 155.
5. Ranfurly's impressions of Baghdad serve to illustrate a theme encountered in many diaries and memoirs written by Britons who happened to be stationed in, or visitors to, Baghdad and Tehran. A long way from home and in a strange place, Ranfurly's first impressions of Baghdad probably reflected her mood:

Under a leaden sky Baghdad has a dismal appearance; the one-storeyed houses that straggle along both sides of the Tigris are brown as the river itself; the narrow streets are lined with shabby shops – some of them mere hovels; and the land is flat. The Embassy stands on the edge of the Tigris. This evening a dead camel floated past the windows. Save for my lacquered fingernails and the General's red tabs, there seems to be no colour here.

Just a week later and she had changed her tune: 'Have learned to love this town which has a mulled beauty all of its own. Kingfishers live in the riverbanks; painted boats lie beneath the latticed windows that overhang the river; there are parrots in the grain shop near the bridge.' Each day she would go to the racecourse before breakfast or during the lunch break. 'Then I ride out into the desert or canter along the bund under silver gum trees to cross the Tigris by the Bridge of Boats and explore the streets of Mu'addham where brass door knockers, fashioned like Fatima's hand with elegant cuffs, gleam on the old doors.' Ranfurly worked from five until eight in the evening, and then dined in establishments such as the Sinbad Hotel, the Tigris Palace or the Zia, 'where Uncle Elie plies you with walnuts and Jesus the barman mixes cocktails called Desert Dreams'. She might then go on to 'one of the antiquated cinemas – little red plush boxes or the Opera House where Poles give brilliant performances'. There were two main clubs in Baghdad, the Alwiyah and the British Club. The first allowed ladies to enter, had tennis courts and was a general social club. The latter had two snooker tables and a good bar. The streets, she wrote, 'are crowded with Indian, Iraqi, Polish, and British troops'.

6. Ibid., pp. 155–6.
7. Ibid., p. 156.
8. Ibid., p. 157.
9. Mackenzie, *Eastern Epic*.
10. Ibid.
11. Ibid.
12. Churchill, *The Second World War*, vol. 4, p. 519.
13. Leighton and Coakley, *Global Logistics and Strategy, 1940–43*, chapter 21, 'The Long Road to Russia'.
14. Joel Sayre, *Persian Gulf Command: Some Marvels on the Road to Kazvin* (New York: Random House, 1945), p. 109.
15. CAC, CHAR 20/78/15.
16. CAC, CHAR 20/79A/52-53.
17. See Wilson, 'Despatch on the Persia and Iraq Command' and Wilson, *Eight Years Overseas*.
18. Wilson, 'Despatch on the Persia and Iraq Command'.
19. Ibid.
20. TNA, CAB 66/30/34, Army strengths: Directive by Minister of Defence, 1 November 1942.
21. Wilson, *Eight Years Overseas*, p. xi.
22. Wilson, 'Despatch on the Persia and Iraq Command'. Britain's overall army manpower situation at this time was set out in Churchill's directive of 1 November 1942 relating to British, dominion, Indian and colonial divisions. There were at that moment thirty-three divisions, five of them under orders for overseas operations. What the prime minister called the 'Army of the Nile' comprised twelve divisions, the 'Army of Persia and Iraq' nine. Garrisons in Africa and elsewhere comprised a further nine divisions, and the 'Army of India' twenty. TNA, CAB 66/31/19, War Cabinet: Manpower, memo by Lord President of the Council, 20 November 1942.
23. Wilson to Casey, 3/12/42, quoted in Silverfarb, *The Twilight*, p. 13.
24. CAC, CHAR 20/80/8-10, Casey to Churchill, 10 September 1942.
25. CAC, CHAR 20/81/92-94, personal telegrams.
26. Ranfurly, *To War with Whitaker*, pp. 170–1.
27. Meyler, 'Polish Exodus'.
28. George Aris, *The Fifth British Division, 1939 to 1945: Being an Account of the Journey and Battles of Reserve Division in Europe, Africa, and Asia* (London: The Fifth British Division Benevolent Fund, 1959), chapter 7, 'Autumn and Winter in Persia, 1942–3'.
29. Wyndham, *The Household Cavalry at War*, pp. 22–3.
30. Masters, *The Road Past Mandalay*.
31. Aris, *The Fifth British Division*, p. 86.
32. Ibid.
33. Ibid., p. 87.
34. Ibid., p. 90.
35. Ibid., p. 88.
36. TNA, CAB 66/27/15, War Cabinet: Review of the situation in the Middle East, 2 August 1942.
37. Wilson, *Eight Years Overseas*, p. 137.
38. Wilson, 'Despatch on the Persia and Iraq Command'.

39. CAC, CHAR 20/80/101-103, Casey to Air Ministry and PAIC, 27 September 1942.
40. Mackenzie, *Eastern Epic*, p. 593.
41. Wilson, *Eight Years Overseas*.
42. CAC, CHAR 20/80/24-26, Casey to Churchill, 11 September 1942.
43. CAC, CHAR 20/80/101-103, Casey to Air Ministry and PAIC, 27 September 1942.
44. CAC, CHAR 20/81/80-84, Casey to Churchill, 20 October 1942.
45. Alexander Wilson, 'The Indian Army in Africa and the Eastern Mediterranean, 1939–1943', PhD thesis (King's College London, 2018).
46. CAC, CHAR 20/81/92-94, personal telegrams.
47. Fieldhouse (ed.), *Kurds, Arabs, and Britons*, p. 211.
48. O'Sullivan, 'German Covert Initiatives', p. 273.
49. LHCMA, Taylor Papers, 1/2, January to February 1943: Report by DFA to director of finance on the Tehran accounts, 16 March 1942; report on Baghdad accounts, 16 March 1943. Also, Taylor Papers, 4/5, Memos, January 1944: report on activities of SOE field forces in Syria, Palestine, and Iraq.
50. Ibid.
51. TNA, WO 169/24869, War diary no. 14: 'A' Force permanent record file: Development of 'A' Force Special Units.
52. Ibid., GHQ Persia and Iraq Command, Major-General Baillon, 26 October 1942.
53. Michael Howard, *Strategic Deception in the Second World War: British Intelligence Operations Against the German High Command* (London: Norton, 1996), p. 85.
54. Fitzroy Maclean, *Eastern Approaches* (London: Jonathan Cape, 1949), chapter 7, 'A Passage to Persia'.
55. Ibid., p. 264.
56. Ibid., p. 265.
57. Ibid.
58. Ibid.
59. Fieldhouse (ed.), *Kurds, Arabs, and Britons*, p. 219.
60. CAC, CHAR 20/80/115-116, personal telegrams.
61. Printed Records of the German Foreign Office, Nr. 253 30, 'The Political Preparations for the German Advance to the Arabian Countries', May 1942.
62. O'Sullivan, 'German Covert Operations'.
63. Printed Records of the German Foreign Office, Nr. 253 30, 'The Political Preparations for the German Advance to the Arabian Countries', May 1942.
64. Ibid., Serie E, Band 02, Nr. 253, 30 May 1942.
65. Ibid., Serie E, Band 03, Nr. 11720, 20 July 1942.
66. TNA, FO 799/9, Dacoutry, military, control of civil disturbances, diary no. 4 of Naik Hakim Khan Isfahan. He reported that 'Nasir Khan, the leading Qashgai Sardar, and his brother Khosrow are encouraging lawlessness and disorder in the hope that this will enable them to recover property confiscated by the late Shah'. He also reported on German propaganda in Isfahan.
67. Wilson, 'Despatch on the Persia and Iraq Command', p. 4,336.
68. Ibid.
69. O'Sullivan, 'Joe Spencer's Ratcatchers', p. 306.
70. CIA Archives, 'AMT VI of the RHSA, Gruppe VI C', Counter Intelligence War Room London, situation report 8, RG263, Box 3, German intelligence service.
71. Maclean, *Eastern Approaches*.
72. Ibid., p. 266.
73. See O'Sullivan, 'German Covert Initiatives'.
74. TNA, FO 799/11, Gault cited in Isfahan diaries, 1–15 December 1942.
75. Maclean, *Eastern Approaches*, p. 274.
76. O'Sullivan, 'German Covert Initiatives', p. 38.
77. Ibid., p. 266.
78. Ibid., note 110.
79. Ibid., p. 267.
80. FRUS, Dreyfus to Secretary of State, 8 December 1942.
81. FRUS, Winant to Secretary of State, 12 December 1942.
82. Suleyman Seydi, 'Intelligence and Counter-Intelligence Activities in Iran in WW2', *Middle Eastern Studies*, vol. 46, no. 5 (September 2010), pp. 733–52.
83. O'Sullivan, 'German Covert Initiatives', p. 202, note 31. See Joe Spencer's (head of British secret intelligence in Iran) excellent profile of Mayr on pp. 214–15.
84. CIA Archives, 'AMT VI of the RHSA, Gruppe VI C', Counter Intelligence War Room London, situation report 8, RG263, Box 3, German intelligence service.
85. Churchill, *The Second World War*, vol. 4, p. 807.
86. Ibid.

87. Aris, *The Fifth British Division*, p. 89.
88. Ibid., p. 91.
89. Wilson, *Eight Years Overseas*.
90. Churchill and the Chiefs of Staff, together with their American colleagues, were also at this time making plans for the invasion of both Western and Southern Europe once Africa had been cleared. These would first see fruition with the launch of Operation Husky, the invasion of Sicily, in July.
91. Churchill to Ismay for Chiefs of Staff, 5 January 1943, reproduced in Churchill, *The Second World War*, vol. 4, p. 823.
92. Stark, *Dust in the Lion's Paw*, p. 160.
93. Pownall, *Chief of Staff*, pp. 101–2.
94. Churchill, *The Second World War*, vol. 4, p. 827, Churchill to Chiefs of Staff, 21 January 1943.
95. Sullivan, 'German Covert Initiatives', p. 240.
96. See O'Sullivan, 'Joe Spencer's Ratcatchers'. Spencer was awarded the DSO for arresting Mayr at gunpoint in dangerous circumstances. See also Seydi, 'Intelligence and Counter-Intelligence Activities in Iran during the Second World War'.
97. O'Sullivan, 'German Covert Initiatives', p. 242.
98. Ibid., p. 105.
99. Ibid., p. 49.
100. Schulze-Holthus, *Daybreak in Iran*, p. 81.
101. TNA, FO, untraced reference, C. Gault to Tehran, 3 August 1944.
102. CIA Archives, 'AMT VI of the RHSA, Gruppe VI C', Counter Intelligence War Room London, situation report 8, RG263, Box 3, German intelligence service.
103. Churchill, 14 July 1944, 'Analysis of the Worldwide Indian Army and British Army in India'. There were 2.67 million men in the Indian Army, of whom 260,000 were 'white personnel'.
104. Azimi, *Iran*, p. 43.
105. Herf, *Nazi Propaganda for the Arab World*, p. 163.
106. FRUS, Dreyfus to Secretary of State, 21 July 1943.
107. FRUS, Secretary of State to Dreyfus, 29 July 1943.
108. Fieldhouse (ed.), *Kurds, Arabs, and Britons*, p. 223.
109. Kirk, *The Middle East at War*, p. 157.
110. TNA, FO 248/146, note of conversation between Bullard and the shah, 19 August 1943.
111. 'In operational terms', writes O'Sullivan:

> apart from sending a few radio messages to Berlin, they achieved nothing. The stories told after the war by Paul Leverkuehn and Berthold Schulze-Holthus of German agents tying up thousands of British troops are a nonsense; the truth is that by the latter half of 1943 the British only had a few battalions of fighting forces in Persia, having transferred most PAIFORCE units to the Italian campaign or returned them to India. Clearly, the strategic deception perpetrated by Dudley Clarke's 'A' Force which greatly inflated the number of British and Indian troops deployed as part of Tenth Army in Persia had its effect and continued to be believed by the Germans even after the war.

O'Sullivan, 'German Covert Initiatives', p. 264. The PAIFORCE Tenth Army deception operation was part of Clarke's highly successful Middle East order-of-battle deception codenamed Cascade, which was initiated in March 1942, fully implemented by July 1942, and terminated in February 1944. Dovey, 'The Eighth Assignment, 1941–1942'.

14 The Persian corridor

1. Beaton, *Near East*, p. 99. When Beaton was taken to see the latest consignment of RAF aircraft being handed over to the Soviets, Soviet soldiers took umbrage, called the police and took the film from his camera. The photographer failed to endear himself to British officials, one consul writing: 'Cecil Beaton arrived here unexpectedly by plane on June 8 42, left on 9th to take pictures for Ministry of Information ... It is incredible how these press gentlemen [*sic*] abuse the facilities which we are at pains to provide for them.' See FO TNA 248/1426, Shah Mohamed Reza. Pictures in Beaton's *Near East* of RAF Iraq Levies and members of the Iranian and Iraqi royal family are memorable.
2. Wilson, *Eight Years Overseas*, p. 140.
3. Stark, *Dust in the Lion's Paw*, p. 147.
4. Ranfurly, *To War with Whitaker*, p. 61.
5. Ibid., p. 62.
6. Wilson, 'Despatch on the Persia and Iraq Command', p. 4,339.
7. Silverfarb, *The Twilight*.

8. Mackenzie, *Eastern Epic*, p. 592.
9. Armstrong, 'The Tenth Army', pp. 233–4.
10. Michael Miller, 'Sea Transport', in Michael Geyer and Adam Tooze (eds), *The Cambridge History of the Second World War*, vol. 3: *Total War: Economy, Society, and Culture* (Cambridge: Cambridge University Press, 2015), p. 177.
11. Ward, *Immortal*, p. 175.
12. Miller, 'Sea Transport', pp. 177–8.
13. Ibid.
14. Motter, *United States Army in World War II*.
15. Schubert, 'The Persian Gulf Command', p. 307.
16. Sayre, *Persian Gulf Command*, p. 5.
17. Ibid., p. 14.
18. NARA, commendation recommendation, 24 September 1944.
19. NARA, commendation recommendation, 8 August 1943.
20. Trent Smith, 'Off the Rails'.
21. NARA.
22. Smith, 'PAIFORCE'.
23. NARA, Headquarters, 'F' Company, 334th Engineer SS Regiment, Camp No. 19 Iran, 4 December 1944, historical overview from 1942 by Lieutenant Hicks, acting commander.
24. NARA, Headquarters, 'F' Company, 334th Engineer SS Regiment, Camp No. 19 Iran, completion report road camp 19, 4 December 1944.
25. NARA, detachment 'F' Company, 334th Engineer SS Regiment, Camp No. 20, completion report road camp 20, 4 December 1944.
26. NARA, Headquarters, 352nd Engineer General Service Regiment, historical report, July to December 1944.
27. NARA, Headquarters, 2nd Platoon, Ahwaz, 3 March 1945, historical report.
28. Trent Smith, 'Off the Rails'.
29. NARA, Meritorious service unit plaque awarded to HQ Company 3342nd Signal Service Battalion.
30. Schubert, 'The Persian Gulf Command', p. 313.
31. Sayre, *Persian Gulf Command*, p. 123.
32. Schubert, 'The Persian Gulf Command', p. 313.
33. Eugene Warren, 'Bandar Shahpur (Now Bandar Khomeini) – World War II – Persian Gulf Command', *Pars Times* (n.d.); online at www.parstimes.com/travel/iran/bandar_shahpur.html (accessed 12 December 2017).
34. Sayre, *Persian Gulf Command*, pp. 123–4.
35. Christopher Buckley, *Five Ventures: Iraq–Syria–Persia–Madagascar–Dodecanese* (London: HMSO, 1954).
36. NARA, 'F' Company historical report, September 1944.
37. Rigge, *War in the Outposts*, pp. 84–5.
38. 'Bridge to Victory', *The Iranian*.
39. Sayre, *Persian Gulf Command*, p. 105.
40. Schubert, 'The Persian Gulf Command', p. 310.
41. Sayre, *Persian Gulf Command*, p. 67.
42. Ibid., pp. 126–7.
43. Ibid., p. 9.
44. Smith, 'Off the Rails', p. 66.
45. Sayre, *Persian Gulf Command*, p. 100.
46. Ibid., pp. 100–1. 3rd Military Railway Service comprised 711th Railway Operating Battalion, 702nd Railway Grand Division, 730th Railway Operating Battalion, 754th Shop Battalion and 762nd Shop Battalion.
47. Greg Eanes, *A Railroader in World War II: Gerald Harbaugh and the 3rd Military Railway Service* (The Eanes Group, 2015).
48. Ibid., pp. 35–6.
49. Scott, 'My Time in the Persian Gulf Command, 1943–1945'.
50. NARA.
51. NARA, Confidential: Supplement to survey of soldier opinion no. 3, Persian Gulf Service Command, US Army forces in the Middle East, October–November 1942, report prepared under the direction of the US Army Information Office by staff of the Research Branch, Morale Services Division, US Army services forces, War Department, 28 January 1944.
52. NARA, interviews with PGC officers returned on SS *Anne Bradstreet* on 2 May 1944 at HRPE, Newport News, VA.

53. NARA, Headquarters 'F' Company, 334th Engineer SS Regiment, Camp No. 19, Iran, completion report, 4 December 1944.
54. NARA, Interviews with PGC officers returned on SS *Anne Bradstreet* on 2 May 1944 at HRPE, Newport News, VA: Lieutenant Colonel Ernest Norberg, formerly commander of Camp Park, Hamadan, Iran.
55. NARA, Confidential: Supplement to survey of soldier opinion no. 3, 28 January 1944.
56. Bullard, *Letters from Tehran*, p. 173.
57. Persia and Iraq Command, and its predecessor formations, maintained a range of publications for service personnel, including *Trunk Call*, the PAIC weekly (copies available at the Imperial War Museum, reference E9302) and a range of newsletters (Imperial War Museum, reference E07/4337). Individual units stationed in Iran and Iraq also published their own material, such as *Ahead*, the journal of 7 Base Depot, Royal Army Ordnance Corps, at RAF Shaibah (Imperial War Museumm reference E96/16).
58. NARA, Headquarters Camp Lowe, historical report, March 1945, men of 711th Rail Operating Battalion and 762nd Railway Shop Battalion.
59. NARA, Headquarters Camp Lowe, Gulf District, PGC, historical reports, 1944.
60. Russian Military Archives Service. S.N. Skryabin, 'Establishment of Center Supply Depots in the Great Patriotic War', *Voyenno Istoricheskiv Zhurnal [Journal of Military History]*, vol. 10 (October 1986). Translated by the American military's Broadcast Information Service.
61. Ibid.
62. Russian Military Archives Service. L. Zorin and I. Kargin, 'Organization of Road Transport of Military Cargoes in Iran', *Voyenno Istoricheskiv Zhurnal [Journal of Military History]*, vol. 4 (October 1977).
63. Ibid. This account is at great pains to make the point that the Anglo-American aid was not very important, that the British and Americans did not fulfil their obligations to the Soviet Union to the agreed extent and that the material they supplied was often deficient or obsolescent.

15 An allied battleground

1. David Yisraeli, 'The Third Reich and Palestine', *Middle Eastern Studies*, vol. 7, no. 3 (October 1971), pp. 343–53.
2. Schwanitz, ' "The Jinnee and the Magic Bottle" ', p. 98.
3. Ibid., p. 99.
4. Ibid., p. 106.
5. Durham University Special Collections, Lambton Papers, 48/11, Lecture notes: 'Problems facing Persia', Paper read to Middle East Group of Parliamentary Labour Party, 13 March 1946.
6. O'Sullivan, 'German Covert Initiatives', p. 259. There were a few late flourishes, such as the German parachute expedition to Iraq in November 1944, its mission to train and arm bands to fight Jews in Iraq and Palestine. It was rapidly broken up. See CIA Archives, 'AMT VI of the RHSA, Gruppe VI C', Counter Intelligence War Room London, situation report 8, RG263, Box 3, German intelligence service.
7. FRUS, Dreyfus to Secretary of State.
8. FRUS, Secretary of State Hull memorandum for Roosevelt, 22 March 1943.
9. Roosevelt Papers, memorandum, 22 December 1943.
10. Christopher Thorne, *Allies of a Kind: The United States, Britain, and the War Against Japan, 1941–1945* (Oxford: Oxford University Press, 1978).
11. Simon Davis, *Contested Space: Anglo-American Relations in the Persian Gulf, 1939–1947* (Leiden: Brill, 2011).
12. As with the general story of British decolonization, almost as remarkable as the precipitate decline of British power – obvious with hindsight – is the sanguinity with which British policymakers faced the future, confident in Britain's capacity to remain a global power.
13. CAC, CHAR 20/110/82-84.
14. FRUS, chief of Near East Department, 10 January 1942.
15. FRUS, State Department memorandum, 'American policy in Iran', by John Jernegan of the Division of Near Eastern Affairs, 23/143.
16. Ibid.
17. Ibid.
18. Ibid.
19. Simon Davis, 'The Middle East and World War Two', in Thomas Zeiler (ed.), *A Companion to World War II*, vol. 1 (Chichester: Wiley-Blackwell, 2013).
20. Ibid.

21. FRUS, Dreyfus to Secretary of State, 9 June 1942.
22. Azimi, *Iran*, p. 86.
23. FRUS, Dreyfus to Secretary of State, 13 March 1942.
24. Ibid.
25. Skrine, *World War in Iran*, p. 171.
26. FRUS, Dreyfus to Secretary of State, 14 August 1942.
27. Skrine, *World War in Iran*, p. 170.
28. Anthony Toth, 'Tribes and Tribulations: Bedouin Losses in the Saudi and Iraqi Struggles over Kuwait's Frontiers, 1921–1943', *British Journal of Middle East Studies*, vol. 32, no. 2 (November 2005), pp. 145–67.
29. FRUS, Hull memorandum, 13 October 1943.
30. FRUS, Dreyfus to Secretary of State, 14 April 1943.
31. Bonakdarian, 'US–Iranian Relations', p. 17.
32. Ibid., p. 19.
33. FRUS, Murray memorandum, 3 August 1942.
34. FRUS, Dreyfus to Secretary of State, 4 March 1943.
35. Ibid., 14 April 1943.
36. Ibid.
37. FRUS, Hurley to Roosevelt, 21 December 1943.
38. TNA, CAB 66/39/1, War Cabinet: British policy in the Middle East, memorandum by the Secretary of State for Foreign Affairs, 12 July 1943. This document outlined British policy towards each country in the Gulf region.
39. Ibid.
40. Ibid.
41. Ibid.
42. NARA, Confidential: Supplement to survey of soldier opinion no. 3, Persian Gulf Service Command, US Army forces in the Middle East, October–November 1942, report prepared under the direction of the US Army Information Office by staff of the Research Branch, Morale Services Division, US Army services forces, War Department, 28 January 1944.
43. Ibid.
44. Ibid.
45. TNA, FO 248/1436, Majlis elections, Consul-General Mashhad to Tehran, 6 May 1944.
46. TNA, FO 248/1428, Majlis elections, secret, HM Minister Tehran to Kermanshah, 8 July 1943.
47. Ibid., Majlis elections, memorandum, 3 July 1943.
48. Ibid.
49. TNA, FO 248/1406, HM Minister's interview with Shah Muhammad Reza, 26 July 1942, dispatch to Foreign Office.
50. Azimi, *Iran*.
51. TNA, FO 248/1428, Majlis elections, Secretary of State to Tehran, 22 March 1943.
52. Ibid., 4 September 1943.
53. Ibid., 25 August 1943.
54. Ibid., Foreign Office to Tehran, 1 August 1943.
55. TNA, FO 248/1426, Shah Mohamed Reza, 5 July 1943.
56. Ibid., Bullard, 19 September 1943.
57. TNA, FO 248/1421, PAIC HQ to British military attaché Tehran, 7 May 1943.
58. FRUS, Dreyfus to Secretary of State, 20 March 1943.
59. FRUS, Dreyfus to Secretary of State, 4 May 1943.
60. FRUS, Dreyfus to Secretary of State, 9 January 1942.
61. FRUS, Minor memorandum, 14 February 44.
62. TNA, FO 248/1421, 30 May 1943.
63. BBCMSA, E89, Germany in Hindustani and Persian, German overseas service in Persian, 25 October 1943.
64. Ibid., 27 October 1943.
65. Ibid., 9 October 1944.
66. Ibid.
67. Ibid., 10 October 1944.
68. FRUS, Hull to Roosevelt, 16 August 1943. See also Assistant Secretary of State Berle to Admiral William Leahy, Chief of Staff to the Commander-in-Chief of the Army and the Navy, 15 August 1943.
69. FRUS, War Department to State Department, 20 October 1943.
70. CHAR 20/121/109-12, Roosevelt to Churchill, 2 August 1943. This contains the tetchy correspondence between Roosevelt and Stalin regarding the location of the conference. The Soviet leader did not want

to go to any of the places Roosevelt suggested, but Tehran was possible. Stalin's reason was that he needed daily contact with his high command. At one point Roosevelt wrote, 'I am deeply disappointed in your message', saying that he could not conduct the business of American government easily from Tehran. 'I regret to say that as head of the Nation, it is impossible for me to go to a place when I cannot fulfil my constitutional obligations.' Roosevelt said that he could 'make one last practical suggestion' – Basra, 600 miles away for Stalin, 6,000 for Roosevelt, he pointed out. But Tehran it was to be.

71. FRUS, Dreyfus to Secretary of State, 10 December 1943. The allied declaration on Iran signed on 1 December received an 'enthusiastic' reception, some press excerpts even adopting an 'almost rhapsodic tone'. 'Apparently there is genuine rejoicing even though the mass is probably unaware of the declaration and too preoccupied with the quest for bread to give it much attention.'
72. Roosevelt Papers, Diplomatic correspondence, box 40.
73. Ibid.
74. Ibid.
75. Ibid.
76. McFarland, 'A Peripheral View of the Origins of the Cold War'.
77. Ibid., p. 334.
78. Ibid., p. 336.
79. Ibid., p. 337.
80. Ibid., p. 338.
81. Azimi, *Iran*, p. 40.
82. Katouzian, *Musaddiq and the Struggle for Power*, p. 49.
83. BBCMSA, M91, Near East, including Egypt, Iran, Leban, Sudan and Palestine.
84. Ibid.
85. Ibid.
86. Katouzian, *Musaddiq and the Struggle for Power*, p. 43.
87. Ibid., p. 32.
88. Ibid., p. 53.

16 War's end

1. TNA, FO 248/1421, Shah Mohamed Reza, 30 May 1943.
2. Emeny was a senior correspondent on the *Chronicle*, killed along with Orde Wingate in an air crash in India in March 1944.
3. BBCMSA, E89, Germany in Hindustani and Persian, 7 November 1944.
4. This is a key argument in Davis, *Contested Space*.
5. BBCMSA, E89, Germany in Hindustani and Persian, 19 and 28 January 1945 and 1 April 1945.
6. Ibid., 11 October 1944.
7. Ibid., 1 November 1944.
8. Ibid., 3, 7, 14 and 18 November 1944.
9. Ibid., 21 November 1944 and 23 November 1944.
10. Ibid., 23 November 1944.
11. Ismay, *The Memoirs*, pp. 205–7.
12. Stark, *Dust in the Lion's Paw*, p. 76.
13. Kedourie, 'Wavell'.
14. Kennedy, *The Business of War*, p. 188.
15. Ibid.
16. Ibid., p. 189.
17. Ibid.
18. Personal communication from Simon Davis, 2017.
19. O'Sullivan, 'German Covert Initiatives', p. 294.
20. Ibid., p. 294.
21. Ibid., p. 463.
22. Rigge, *War in the Outposts*, p. 84.
23. Sayre, *Persian Gulf Command*, pp. 5–6.
24. Ward, *Immortal*.
25. Miller, 'Sea Transport'.
26. Leighton and Coakley, *Global Logistics*.
27. Ibid.
28. NARA, HQ Company, 762nd Railway Shop Battalion, Camp Lowe, historical report, May 1945.
29. Sayre, *Persian Gulf Command*, p. 7.
30. 'Bridge to Victory', *The Iranian*.

31. Nathan Godfried, 'Economic Development and Regionalism: United States Foreign Relations in the Middle East, 1942–1945', *Journal of Contemporary History*, vol. 22, no. 3 (July 1987), pp. 481–500.
32. FRUS, Murray, 11 February 1943.
33. William Roger Louis, *Imperialism at Bay: The United States and the Decolonization of the British Empire, 1941–1945* (New York: Oxford University Press, 1978), pp. 449–50.
34. FRUS, Murray, 14 September 1945.
35. CAC, CHAR 20/10/113-14.
36. FRUS, Acting Secretary of State to President, 11 January 1945.
37. FRUS, Murray to Secretary of State, 19 June 1945.
38. Ibid.
39. Ibid., 19 September 1945.
40. Ibid., 21 September 1945.
41. Ibid., 14 September 1945.
42. Ibid., 19 September 1945.
43. McFarland, 'A Peripheral View', p. 343.
44. Ibid., p. 351.
45. NARA, CIA, 'The Current Situation in Iran', ORE 48, 20 October 1947.
46. Ibid.
47. FRUS, Murray to Secretary of State, 26 June 1945.
48. Lambton Papers, 62/8.
49. NARA, CIA, 'The Current Situation in Iran', ORE 48, 20 October 1947.
50. Richard Cottam, 'The United States, Iran, and the Cold War', *Iranian Studies*, vol. 3, no. 1 (winter 1970), pp. 2–22.
51. Lisa Reynolds Wolfe, 'Cold War in Iran: The Politics of Oil', Cold War Studies blog (15 February 2011); online at https://coldwarstudies.com/2011/02/15/cold-war-in-iran-the-politics-of-oil (accessed 17 December 2017).
52. Durham University Special Collections, Lambton Papers, 48/11, Lecture notes, 'Problems Facing Persia', read to the Parliamentary Labour Party's Middle East Group, 13 March 1946.
53. Katouzian, *Iran*, p. xx.
54. Cole, 'Iraq in 1939', p. 221.
55. Arthur Smith, 'Pink Elephants on the Road to Baghdad', *MV Magazine*, nos 2 and 3 (1996).
56. Silverfarb, *The Twilight*. For an eloquent statement on Iraqi anti-Zionism written in 1944, see MECA, Mohammad Fadhel Jamali, 'Experiences in Arab Affairs 1943–1958'.
57. Silverfarb, *The Twilight*.
58. Alan de Lacy Rush, 'Introduction', in de Gaury, *Three Kings*, p. 11.
59. Silverfarb, *The Twilight*, p. 234.
60. See Kelly Bell, 'Operation Long Jump: Hitler's Attempted Triple Play', *World at War*, vol. 7 (August–September 2009), pp. 21–8. It was reported that Iranians felt 'mortified over the report that there had been a plot against the lives of the three distinguished statesmen meeting in Tehran'. Roosevelt Papers, memorandum to president, 23 December 1943. 'The Iranian Minister in Washington pleads for some special mention in your Friday radio address'. Roosevelt to Pat Hurley via State Department 10 January 1944: Regarding Iranian perturbation about plot reports: 'I wish you would explain to the Foreign Minister that there was never any question of suspicion about any Iranian, but that the report of threatened violence involved German agents who were believed to have entered Iran without authority. As you know, my move from the American Legation was made primarily in order not to expose any of the conferees to the risk of attack by Axis agents while coming to visit me'.
61. Roosevelt Papers, shah to president, 6 December 1943. The shah wrote 'thanks for the framed photo your minister delivered before your departure from Tehran'. He said that it was 'a very good likeness', and that the friendship of the American people was 'very precious to us'.
62. Ibid., memorandum to Roosevelt, 23 December 1943.

SOURCES AND BIBLIOGRAPHY

Primary sources

Avon Papers, Special Collections, University of Birmingham.
BBC Monitoring Service Archive (BBCMSA), temporarily held at the Imperial War Museum, Duxford.
Central Intelligence Agency (CIA) Archives.
Churchill Archives Centre (CAC), Cambridge.
Durham University Special Collections, Ann Lambton Papers.
Foreign Relations of the United States (FRUS), Diplomatic Papers.
Franklin D. Roosevelt Papers, Franklin D. Roosevelt Library, Hyde Park, New York, USA.
Imperial War Museum (IWM).
John Connell Papers, William Ready Division of Archives and Research Collections, McMaster University, Hamilton, Ontario, Canada.
Liddell Hart Centre for Military Archives (LHCMA), King's College London, including:
   Alanbrooke Papers, GB0099 KCLMA Brooke AF.
   Brooke-Popham Papers, GB0099 KCLMA Brooke-Popham.
   Dill Papers, GB0099 KCLMA Dill.
   Pownall Papers, GB0099 KCLMA Pownall.
   George Taylor Papers.
Middle East Centre Archive (MECA), St Antony's College, Oxford.
National Archives and Records Administration (NARA), Washington, USA.
Printed Records of the German Foreign Office: on behalf of the author, Dr Oliver Haller prepared an extensive report on the location of sources relating to Iran and Iraq during the Second World War.
Russian Military Studies Archive, Barrington Library, Cranfield University, Defence Academy of the United Kingdom.
The National Archives (TNA).

Secondary sources

Aboul-Enein, Youssef and Basil Aboul-Enein. *The Secret War for the Middle East: The Influence of Axis and Allied Intelligence Operations during World War Two* (Annapolis, MD: Naval Institute Press, 2013).
Abrahamian, Ervand. *A History of Modern Iran* (Cambridge: Cambridge University Press, 2008).
——*Iran Between Two Revolutions* (Princeton University Press, 1982).
Ahmad, Shikara. *Iraqi Politics 1921–1941: The Interaction between Domestic Politics and Foreign Policy* (London: Laam, 1987).
Alanbrooke, Field Marshal Lord. *War Diaries, 1939–1945*, ed. Alex Danchev and Daniel Todman (London: Weidenfeld and Nicolson, 2002).

Antolak, Ryszard. 'Iran and the Polish Exodus from Russia 1942', *Pars Times* (n.d.); online at http://www.
parstimes.com/history/polish_refugees/exodus_russia.html (accessed 12 December 2017).

Aris, George. *The Fifth British Division, 1939 to 1945: Being an Account of the Journey and Battles of
Reserve Division in Europe, Africa, and Asia* (London: The Fifth British Division Benevolent Fund,
1959).

Armstrong, W.J. 'The Tenth Army in Iran', *Army Quarterly*, vol. 52, no. 2 (1946), pp. 226–35.

Atabaki, Touraj (ed.). *Iran and the First World War: Battleground of the Great Powers* (London: I.B.
Tauris, 2006).

——*Iran in the 20th Century: Historiography and Political Culture* (London: I.B. Tauris, 2009).

Auchinleck, Claude. 'Operations in the Middle East from 5 July 1941–31 October 1941', *London Gazette*
(1946), pp. 4,215–30.

——'Operations in the Middle East from 1 November 1941–15 August 1942', *London Gazette* (1948),
pp. 309–400.

Azimi, Fakhreddin. *Iran: The Crisis of Democracy from the Exile of Reza Shah to the Fall of Musaddiq –
1941–1953* (London: I.B. Tauris, 2009).

Baker, Robert. *Oil, Blood and Sand* (New York: Appleton-Century, 1942).

Bakhash, Shaul. 'Britain and the Abdication of Reza Shah', *Middle Eastern Studies*, vol. 52, no. 2 (2016),
pp. 318–34.

Bamberg, J.H. *The History of the British Petroleum Company*, vol. 2: *The Anglo Iranian Years, 1928–1954*
(Cambridge: Cambridge University Press, 1994).

Bari, Carole. 'The Jewish Refugee from Arab Countries: An Examination of Legal Rights – A Case Study
of the Human Rights Violations of Iraqi Jews', *Fordham International Law Journal*, vol. 26, no. 3
(2002), pp. 656–720.

Barua, Pradeep. 'Strategies and Doctrines of Imperial Defence: Britain and India, 1919–45', *Journal of
Imperial and Commonwealth History*, vol. 25, no. 2 (May 1997), pp. 240–66.

Beaton, Cecil. *Near East* (London: B.T. Batsford, 1943).

Beaumont, Joan. 'Great Britain and the Rights of Neutral Countries: The Case of Iran, 1941', *Journal of
Contemporary History*, vol. 16, no. 1 (1981), pp. 213–28.

Beck, Lois. *The Qashqa'i of Iran* (New Haven, CT: Yale University Press, 1986).

Bell, Kelly. 'Operation Long Jump: Hitler's Attempted Triple Play', *World at War*, vol. 7 (August–
September 2009), pp. 21–8.

Bennett, Judith. *Natives and Exotics: World War Two and Environment in the Southern Pacific* (Honolulu,
HI: University of Hawaii Press, 2009).

Bharier, Julian. *Economic Development in Iran, 1900–1970* (London: Oxford University Press, 1971).

Bhattacharjee, Anuradha. *The Second Homeland: Polish Refugees in India* (New Delhi: Sage, 2012).

Bill, James. *The Eagle and the Lion: The Tragedy of American–Iranian Relations* (New Haven, CT: Yale
University Press, 1988).

Blake, Kristin. *The US–Soviet Confrontation in Iran, 1945–1962* (Lanham, MD: University Press of
America, 2009).

Bonakdarian, Mansour. 'US–Iranian Relations, 1911–1951', in Amanat Abbas and Magnus T. Bernhardsson
(eds), *US–Middle East Historical Encounters* (Tallahassee: University Press of Florida, 2007), pp. 9–25.

Bonine, Michael and Nikki Keddie (eds). *Continuity and Change in Modern Iran* (Albany, NY: SUNY
Press, 1981).

Brady, John. *Eastern Encounters: Memoirs of the Decade, 1937–46* (Braunton: Merlin Books, 1992).

Bryson, Thomas. *Seeds of Mideast Crisis: The United States' Diplomatic Role in the Middle East during
World War Two* (Jefferson, NC: McFarland and Co., 1981).

Buckley, Christopher. *Five Ventures: Iraq–Syria–Persia–Madagascar–Dodecanese* (London: HMSO,
1954).

Buhite, Russell. *Patrick J. Hurley and American Foreign Policy* (New York: Cornell University Press,
1973).

Bullard, Reader. *The Camels Must Go: An Autobiography* (London: Faber and Faber, 1961).

——*Letters from Tehran: A British Ambassador in World War Two Persia*, ed. E.C. Hodgkin (London:
I.B. Tauris, 1991).

Bykofsky, Joseph and Harold Larson. *The Transportation Corps: Operations Overseas* (Washington, DC:
US Army Center of Military History, 1954).

Carley, Michael Jabara. '"A Situation of Delicacy and Danger": Anglo-Soviet Relations, August 1939 to
March 1940', *Contemporary European History*, vol. 8, no. 2 (July 1999), pp. 175–208.

Carlton, David. *Churchill and the Soviet Union* (Manchester University Press, 2000).

Central Office of Information, War Office, *PAIFORCE: The Official Story of the Persia and Iraq
Command, 1941–1946* (London: HMSO, 1948).

Churchill, Winston. *The Second World War*, 6 vols (London: Cassell, 1948–54).

Clarke, Dudley. *The Eleventh at War: Being the Story of the XIth Hussars (Prince Albert's Own) Through the Years 1939–1945* (London: Michael Joseph, 1952).

Clifford, Bede. *Proconsul: Being Incidents in the Life and Career of the Honourable Sir Bede Clifford* (London: Evans Brothers, 1964).

Coakley, Robert. 'The Persian Corridor as a Route for Aid to the USSR', in Kent Roberts Greenfield (ed.), *Command Decisions* (New York: Harcourt, Brace and Company, 1959), pp. 225–54.

Coats, Peter. *Of Generals and Gardens: The Autobiography of Peter Coats* (London: Weidenfeld and Nicolson, 1976).

Cohen, Hayyim J. 'The Anti-Jewish "Farhūd" in Baghdad 1941', *Middle Eastern Studies*, vol. 3, no. 1 (October 1966), pp. 2–17.

Cohen, Michael. *Britain's Moment in Palestine: Retrospect and Perspectives, 1917–1948* (London: Routledge, 2014).

Cohen, Michael and Martin Kolinsky (eds). *Britain and the Middle East in the 1930s: Security Problems, 1935–1939* (London: Frank Cass, 1992).

——*Demise of the British Empire in the Middle East: Britain's Response to Nationalist Movements, 1943–1955* (London: Frank Cass, 1998).

Cole, Juan. 'Iraq in 1939: British Alliance or Nationalist Neutrality towards the Axis?', *Britain and the World*, vol. 5, no. 2 (2012), pp. 204–22.

Colville, John. *The Fringes of Power: Downing Street Diaries, 1939–1955* (London: Hodder and Stoughton, 1985).

Connell, John. *Auchinleck: A Critical Biography* (London: Cassell, 1959).

——*Wavell: Scholar and Soldier – to June 1941* (London: Collins, 1964).

Cooper, Andrew Scott. *The Fall of Heaven: The Pahlavis and the Final Days of Imperial Iran* (New York: Henry Holt, 2016).

Cottam, Richard. 'The United States, Iran, and the Cold War', *Iranian Studies*, vol. 3, no. 1 (winter 1970), pp. 2–22.

Coward, Noël. *Future Indefinite* (London: Methuen, 2004).

——*Middle East Diary* (London: William Heinemann, 1944).

Cronin, Stephanie. *Soldiers, Shahs, and Subalterns in Iran: Opposition, Protest and Revolt, 1921–1941* (London: Palgrave Macmillan, 2010).

Cull, Nicholas. 'Selling Peace: The Origins, Promotion and Fate of the Anglo-American New Order during the Second World War', *Diplomacy and Statecraft*, vol. 7, no. 1 (March 1996), pp. 1–28.

Curie, Eve. *Journey Among Warriors* (New York: Doubleday, Doran, and Co., 1943).

Dadkhah, Kamran. 'The Iranian Economy during the Second World War: The Devaluation Controversy', *Middle Eastern Studies*, vol. 37, no. 2 (April 2001), pp. 181–98.

Dalziel, Nigel. *The Penguin Historical Atlas of the British Empire* (London: Penguin Books, 2006).

Daneshvar, Simin. *Savushun: A Novel about Modern Iran* (Washington, DC: Mage Publishers, 1990).

Davis, Simon. ' "A Projected New Trusteeship"? American Internationalism, British Imperialism, and the Reconstruction of Iran, 1938–1947', *Diplomacy and Statecraft*, vol. 17 (2006), pp. 31–72.

——*Contested Space: Anglo-American Relations in the Persian Gulf, 1939–1947* (Leiden: Brill, 2011).

——'The Middle East and World War II', in Thomas Zeiler (ed.), *A Companion to World War II*, vol. 1 (Chichester: Wiley-Blackwell, 2013), pp. 278–95.

Davison, Roderic H. 'Where is the Middle East?' *Foreign Affairs*, vol. 38, no. 4 (July 1960), pp. 665–75.

Dawisha, Adeed. 'Democratic Attitudes and Practices in Iraq, 1921–1958', *Middle East Journal*, vol. 59, no. 1 (January 2005), pp. 11–30.

de Chair, Somerset. *The Golden Carpet* (London: Faber and Faber, 1945).

de Gaury, Gerald. *Three Kings in Baghdad: The Tragedy of Iraq's Monarchy* (London: I.B. Tauris, 2008).

——*Traces of Travel Brought Home from Abroad* (London: Quartet Books, 1983).

Delve, Ken. *The Desert Air Force in World War Two: Air Power in the Western Desert, 1940–1942* (Barnsley: Pen and Sword, 2017).

DeNovo, John. 'The Culbertson Economic Mission and Anglo-American Tension in the Middle East', *Journal of American History*, vol. 63 (March 1977), pp. 913–36.

Deringil, Selim. *Turkish Foreign Policy During the Second World War: An Active Neutrality* (Cambridge: Cambridge University Press, 1989).

Diba, Farhad. *Mohammed Mossadegh: A Political Biography* (London: Croom Helm, 1986).

Dieterich, Renate. 'Germany's Relations with Iraq and Transjordan from the Weimar Republic to the End of the Second World War', *Middle Eastern Studies*, vol. 41, no. 4 (July 2005), pp. 463–79.

Dodge, Toby. 'The British Mandate in Iraq, 1914–1932', *The Middle East Online, Series 2: Iraq, 1914–1974* (Reading: Thomson Learning EMEA Ltd, 2006).

Dovey, H.O. 'The Eighth Assignment, 1941–1942', *Intelligence and National Security*, vol. 11, no. 4 (October 1996), pp. 672–95.

——'The Middle East Intelligence Centre', *Intelligence and National Security*, vol. 4, no. 4 (1989), pp. 800–12.

Dudgeon, A.G. *Hidden Victory: The Battle of Habbaniya, May 1941* (Stroud: Tempus Publishing, 2000).

Dudgeon, Mike. 'No. 4 SFTS and Raschid Ali's War: Iraq 1941', *RAF Historical Society Journal*, vol. 48 (2010), pp. 39–57.

Eeman, Harold. *Clouds Over the Sun: Memories of a Diplomat, 1942–1958* (London: Robert Hale, 1981).

Elling, Rasmus Christian. 'The World's Biggest Refinery and the Second World War: Khuzestan, Oil, and Security', conference paper, International Conference on the Comparative Social Histories of Labour in the Oil Industry, the International Institute of Social History in Amsterdam (June 2014).

Elliot, Matthew. 'The Death of King Ghazi: Iraqi Politics, Britain, and Kuwait in 1939', *Contemporary British History*, vol. 10 (1996), pp. 63–81.

——'*Independent Iraq*': The Monarchy and British Influence, 1941–1958 (London: I.B. Tauris, 1996).

Elpeleg, Zvi. *The Grand Mufti: Haj Amin al-Husseini, Founder of the Palestinian National Movement* (London: Routledge, 1993).

Eppel, Michael. 'The Elite, the Effendiya, and the Growth of Nationalism and Pan-Arabism in Hashemite Iraq, 1921–1958', *International Journal of Middle Eastern Studies*, vol. 30 (February 1998), pp. 227–50.

Eshragi, F. 'The Anglo-Soviet Occupation of Iran: August 1941', *Middle Eastern Studies*, vol. 20, no. 1 (1984), pp. 27–52.

——'The Immediate Aftermath of Anglo-Soviet Occupation of Iran, 1941', *Middle Eastern Studies*, vol. 20, no. 3 (1984), pp. 324–51.

Farrokh, Kaveh. *Iran at War, 1500–1958* (Oxford: Osprey, 2011).

Fawcett, Louise. *Iran and the Cold War: The Azerbaijan Crisis of 1946* (Cambridge: Cambridge University Press, 1992).

Felmy, Hellmuth and Walter Warlimont. *German Exploitation of Arab Nationalist Movements in World War II* (Washington, DC: Historical Division, Headquarters, United States Army, Europe, Foreign Military Studies Branch, 1954).

Fieldhouse, D.K. (ed.). *Kurds, Arabs, and Britons: The Memoir of Wallace Lyon in Iraq, 1918–1944* (London: I.B. Tauris, 2002).

——*Western Imperialism in the Middle East, 1914–1958* (Oxford: Oxford University Press, 2006).

Fort, Adrian. *Archibald Wavell: The Life and Times of an Imperial Servant* (London: Jonathan Cape, 2009).

Frost, John. *A Drop Too Many* (Barnsley: Pen and Sword, 2008).

Gasiorowski, Mark. *US Foreign Policy and the Shah: Building a Client State in Iran* (Ithaca, NY: Cornell University Press, 1991).

Gheissari, Ali. 'Persia', in I.C.B. Dear and M.R.D. Foot (eds), *Oxford Companion to the Second World War* (Oxford: Oxford University Press, 1995), pp. 874–5.

Ghods, Reza. 'Iranian Nationalism and Reza Shah', *Middle Eastern Studies*, vol. 27, no. 1 (1991), pp. 35–45.

Golan, Galia. *Soviet Policies in the Middle East: From World War Two to Gorbachev* (Cambridge: Cambridge University Press, 1990).

Goren, Haim (ed.). *Germany and the Middle East: Past, Present, and Future* (Jerusalem: Hebrew University Press, 2003).

Govan, Sean. 'Pawns, Provocateurs, and Parasites: Great Britain and German Fifth Column Movements in Europe and the Middle East, 1934–1941', PhD thesis (University of Birmingham, 2016).

Graham, A. 'The Iraq Levies at Habbaniya', *Army Quarterly*, vol. 44, no. 2 (1942), pp. 249–55.

Guedalla, Philip. *Middle East 1940–42: A Study in Air Power* (London: Hodder and Stoughton, 1944).

Hamdi, Walid. *Rashid Ali al-Gailani: The Nationalist Movement in Iraq, 1939–1941* (London: Darf, 1987).

Harriman, W. Averell and Elie Abel. *Special Envoy to Churchill and Stalin, 1941–1946* (London: Random House, 1975).

Harvey, John (ed.). *The War Diaries of Oliver Harvey, 1941–1945* (London: William Collins, 1978).

Haslani, Jamil. *At the Dawn of the Cold War: The Soviet–American Crisis over Iranian Azerbaijan, 1941–1946* (Lanham, MD: Rowman and Littlefield, 2006).

Heaney, John ['Surfield']. 'Indian Surveyors in Paiforce', *Journal of the United Services Institution of India and Pakistan*, vol. 78, no. 331 (April 1948), pp. 153–62.

Herf, Jeffrey. *Nazi Propaganda for the Arab World* (New Haven, CT: Yale University Press, 2010).

Hinsley, Harry. *British Intelligence in the Second World War* (Cambridge: Cambridge University Press, 1990).

Hirszowicz, Łukasz. *The Third Reich and the Arab East* (University of Toronto Press, 1966).

Hopkirk, Peter. *The Great Game: On Secret Service in High Asia* (London: John Murray, 1992).

Howard, Michael. *Strategic Deception in the Second World War: British Intelligence Operations Against the German High Command* (London: Norton, 1995).

Ismay, Hastings Lionel. *The Memoirs of General the Lord Ismay* (London: Heinemann, 1960).

Jackson, Ashley. *The British Empire and the Second World War* (London: Continuum, 2006).

——*Of Islands, Ports, and Sea Lanes: Africa and the Indian Ocean in the Second World War* (Solihull: Helion, 2018).

Jackson, Ashley, Yasmin Khan and Gajendra Singh (eds). *An Imperial World at War: Aspects of the British Empire's War Experience, 1939–1945* (London: Routledge, 2016).

James, Barrie. *Hitler's Gulf War: The Fight for Iraq, 1941* (Barnsley: Pen and Sword, 2009).

Johnson, Danny. 'The Persian Gulf Command and Lend-Lease Mission to the Soviet Union during World War Two', National Museum of the United States Army (28 June 2016); online at https://army-history.org/the-persian-gulf-command-and-the-lend-lease-mission-to-the-soviet-union-during-world-war-ii (accessed 14 December 2017).

Katouzian, Homa. *Iran: A Beginner's Guide* (London: Oneworld, 2013).

——*Mussadiq and the Struggle for Power in Iran* (London: I.B. Tauris, 1999).

Kedourie, Elie. 'The Sack of Basra and the Farhud in Baghdad', in Kedourie, *Arabic Political Memoirs and Other Studies* (London: Frank Cass, 1974), pp. 283–314.

——'Wavell and Iraq, April–May 1941', *Middle Eastern Studies*, vol. 2, no. 4 (1966), pp. 373–86.

Keen, B.A. *The Agricultural Development of the Middle East* (London: HMSO, 1946).

Kennedy, John. *The Business of War: The War Journal of Major-General Sir John Kennedy* (London: Hutchinson, 1957).

Kent, John. *British Imperial Strategy and the Origins of the Cold War* (Leicester University Press, 1993).

Khadduri, Majid. 'General Nuri's Flirtation with the Axis Powers', *Middle East Journal*, vol. 16, no. 3 (summer 1962), pp. 328–36.

Killingray, David. ' "A Swift Agent of Government": Air Power in British Colonial Africa, 1916–1939', *Journal of African History*, vol. 25, no. 4 (1984), pp. 429–44.

Kimball, Warren. *Forged in War: Churchill, Roosevelt, and the Second World War* (New York: William Morrow, 1997).

——'Lend-Lease and the Open Door: The Temptation of British Opulence, 1937–1942', *Political Science Quarterly*, vol. 86, no. 2 (June 1971), pp. 232–59.

Kirk, George. *Survey of International Affairs 1939–1946: The Middle East in the War* (Oxford: Oxford University Press, 1952).

Kolinsky, Martin. *Britain's War in the Middle East: Strategy and Diplomacy, 1936–1942* (Basingstoke: Macmillan, 1999).

Kozhanov, Nikolay. 'Pretexts and Reasons for the Allied Invasion of Iran', *Iranian Studies*, vol. 45, no. 4 (2012), pp. 479–97.

Kurowski, Franz. *The Brandenburger Commandos: Germany's Elite Warrior Spies in World War II* (Mechanicsburg, PA: Stackpole Books, 2005).

Kwarteng, Kwasi. *Ghosts of Empire: Britain's Legacies in the Modern World* (London: Bloomsbury, 2012).

Laurie, W.J. 'With the Household Cavalry Regiment in Iraq and Persia', *Household Brigade Magazine* (autumn 1942), pp. 86–8.

Leighton, Richard and Robert Coakley. *Global Logistics and Strategy, 1940–1943* (Washington, DC: US Army Center of Military History, 1995, first published 1955).

——*Global Logistics and Strategy, 1943–1945* (Washington, DC: US Army Center of Military History, 1967).

Lenczowski, George. *Russia and the West in Iran, 1918–1948: A Study in Big-Power Rivalry* (Ithaca, NY: Cornell University Press, 1949).

Lewin, Ronald. *The Chief: Field Marshal Lord Wavell, Commander-in-Chief and Viceroy, 1939–1947* (London: Hutchinson, 1980).

Lohbeck, Don. *Patrick Hurley* (Chicago, IL: Henry Regnery, 1956).

Louis, William Roger. *Imperialism at Bay: The United States and the Decolonization of the British Empire, 1941–1945* (New York: Oxford University Press, 1978).

Lucas, James. *Kommando: German Special Forces of World War Two* (Barnsley: Frontline Books, 2014).

Lyman, Robert. *First Victory: Britain's Forgotten Struggle in the Middle East, 1941* (London: Constable, 2006).

——*Iraq 1941: The Battles for Basra, Habbaniya, Fallujah, and Baghdad* (Oxford: Osprey, 2006).

Lytle, Mark. *The Origins of the Iranian–American Alliance, 1941–1953* (New York: Holmes and Meier, 1987).

MacDonald, Callum. 'Radio Bari: Italian Wireless Propaganda in the Middle East and British Countermeasures, 1934–1938', *Middle Eastern Studies*, vol. 13, no. 2 (May 1977), pp. 195–207.

Mackenzie, Compton. *All Over the Place: Fifty Thousand Miles by Sea, Air, Road, and Rail* (London: Chatto and Windus, 1948).

——*Eastern Epic*, vol. 1: *September 1939–March 1943 – Defence* (London: Chatto and Windus, 1951).

Maclean, Fitzroy. *Eastern Approaches* (London: Jonathan Cape, 1949).

Macris, Jeffrey. 'The Persian Gulf Theater in World War II', *Journal of Middle East and Africa*, vol. 1 (2010), pp. 97–107.

Magenheimer, Heinz. *Hitler's War: Germany's Key Strategic Decisions, 1940–45 – Could Germany Have Won World War Two?* (London: Weidenfeld and Nicolson, 1999).

Maisky, Ivan. *The Maisky Diaries: Red Ambassador to the Court of St James's, 1932–1943*, ed. Gabriel Gorodetsky (New Haven, CT: Yale University Press, 2015).

Majd, Mohammad Gholi. *Iran Under Allied Occupation in World War II: The Bridge to Victory* (Lanham, MD: University Press of America, 2016).

Marmorstein, Emile. 'Fritz Grobba', *Middle Eastern Studies*, vol. 23, no. 3 (1987), pp. 376–8.

Masters, John. *The Road Past Mandalay* (London: Companion Book Club, 1961).

McFarland, Stephen. 'A Peripheral View of the Origins of the Cold War: The Crises in Iran, 1941–47', *Diplomatic History*, vol. 4, no. 4 (October 1980), pp. 333–52.

——'Anatomy of an Iranian Political Crowd: The Tehran Bread Riot of December 1942', *International Journal of Middle East Studies*, vol. 17, no. 1 (February 1985), pp. 51–65.

McMeekin, Sean. *The Berlin–Baghdad Express: The Ottoman Empire and Germany's Bid for World Power, 1898–1918* (London: Allen Lane, 2010).

Meyler, David. 'Polish Exodus: The Unlikely Iranian-Polish Alliance in World War II', Avalanche Press (October 2015); online at http://www.avalanchepress.com/PolishExodus.php (accessed 12 December 2017).

Milani, Abbas. *The Shah* (London: Palgrave Macmillan, 2011).

Miller, Michael. 'Sea Transport', in Michael Geyer and Adam Tooze (eds), *The Cambridge History of the Second World War*, vol. 3: *Total War: Economy, Society, and Culture* (Cambridge: Cambridge University Press, 2015), pp. 174–95.

Millspaugh, Arthur C. *Americans in Persia: A Clinic for the New Internationalism* (Washington, DC: Brookings Institute, 1946).

Moberly, Frederick. *Operations in Persia, 1914–1919* (London: HMSO, 1987).

Monroe, Elizabeth. *Britain's Moment in the Middle East, 1914–1956* (London: Chatto and Windus, 1963).

Moorehead, Alan. *A Year of Battle* (London: Hamish Hamilton, 1943).

Morris, Christopher. 'The RAF Armoured Car Companies in Iraq (Mostly) 1921–1947', *RAF Historical Society Journal*, vol. 48 (2010), pp. 20–38.

Motadel, David. *Islam and Nazi Germany's War* (Cambridge, MA: Harvard University Press, 2014).

Motter, T.H. Vail. *United States Army in World War II: The Middle East Theater – The Persian Corridor and Aid to Russia* (Washington: US Army Center of Military History, 1952).

Nevo, Joseph. 'Al-Hajj Amin and the British in World War II', *Middle Eastern Studies*, vol. 20, no. 1 (January 1984), pp. 3–16.

Nicosia, Francis. 'Fritz Grobba and the Middle East Policy of the Third Reich', in Edward Ingram (ed.), *National and International Politics in the Middle East: Essays in Honour of Elie Kedourie* (London: Frank Cass, 1986), pp. 206–28.

——*Nazi Germany and the Arab World* (Cambridge: Cambridge University Press, 2014).

——*The Third Reich and the Palestine Question* (Austin, TX: University of Texas Press, 1985).

Omissi, David. *Air Power and Colonial Control: The Royal Air Force, 1919–1939* (Manchester University Press, 1990).

Osborn, Patrick. *Operation Pike: Britain Versus the Soviet Union, 1939–1941* (Westport, CT: Greenwood Press, 2000).

O'Sullivan, Adrian. *Espionage and Counterintelligence in Occupied Persia (Iran): The Success of the Allied Secret Services, 1941–45* (Basingstoke: Palgrave Macmillan, 2015).

——'German Covert Initiatives and British Intelligence in Persia (Iran), 1939–1945', PhD thesis (University of South Africa, 2012).

——'Joe Spencer's Ratcatchers: British Security Intelligence in Occupied Persia', *Asian Affairs*, vol. 48, no. 2 (2017), pp. 296–312.

——*Nazi Secret Warfare in Occupied Persia (Iran): The Failure of the German Intelligence Services, 1939–1945* (Basingstoke: Palgrave Macmillan, 2014).

Pahlavi, Mohammad Reza Shah. *Mission for My Country* (London: Hutchinson, 1961).

Pal, Dharm. *Campaign in Western Asia*, vol. 5 of *Official History of the Indian Armed Forces in World War Two*, ed. Bisheshwar Prasad (Calcutta: Combined Inter-Services Historical Section, 1957).

Payton-Smith, D.J. *Oil: A Study of War-time Policy and Administration* (London: HMSO, 1971).

Pezeshkzad, Iraj. *My Uncle Napoleon* (Washington, DC: Mage Publishers, 1996).

Piotrowski, Tadeusz (ed.). *The Polish Deportees of World War Two: Recollection of Movement to the Soviet Union and Dispersal Throughout the World* (Jefferson, NC: McFarland, 2004).

Pirie, Gordon. *Air Empire: British Imperial Civil Aviation, 1919–1939* (Manchester University Press, 2009).

Pitt, Barrie. *Churchill and the Generals* (Barnsley: Pen and Sword, 2004).

Playfair, I.S.O. et al. *The Mediterranean and Middle East* (London: HMSO, 1954–87).

Pownall, Henry. *Chief of Staff: The Diaries of Lieutenant-General Sir Henry Pownall*, vol. 2: *1940–1944*, ed. Brian Bond (London: Leo Cooper, 1974).

al-Qazzaz, Ayad. 'The Iraqi-British War of 1941: A Review Article', *International Journal of Middle East Studies*, vol. 7, no. 4 (October 1976), pp. 591–6.

Raghavan, Srinath. *India's War: The Making of Modern South Asia, 1939–1945* (London: Penguin, 2016).

Ragsdale, Bernard. '"A Railroader Goes to War": The Personal WWII Diary of PFC Herbert Bernard Ragsdale, 1942–1945 – The Iranian State Railway' (1996–2012); online at http://www.ww2diary.com/isr.html (accessed 13 December 2012).

Ranfurly, Hermione, Countess of. *To War with Whitaker* (London: Mandarin, 1995).

Raugh, Harold. *Wavell in the Middle East 1939–1941: A Study in Generalship* (London: Brassey's, 1993).

Reynolds, David, A.O. Chubarian and Warren F. Kimball (eds). *Allies at War: The Soviet, American and British Experience, 1939–1945* (Basingstoke: Palgrave Macmillan, 1994).

Rezun, Miron. *The Iranian Crisis of 1941: The Actors: Britain, Germany, and the Soviet Union* (Cologne: Böhlau Verlag, 1982).

——*The Soviet Union and Iran: Soviet Policy in Iran from the Beginning of the Pahlavi Dynasty until the Soviet Invasion in 1941* (Geneva: Institut Universitaire des Hautes Études Internationales, 1981).

Richardson, Charles. 'French Plans for Allied Attacks on the Caucasus Oil Fields, January–April 1940', *French Historical Studies*, vol. 8, no. 1 (spring 1973), pp. 130–56.

Rigge, Simon. *War in the Outposts* (Chicago, IL: Time-Life Books, 1980).

Roberts, Geoffrey. 'Ideology, Calculation and Improvisation: Spheres of Influence and Soviet Foreign Policy, 1939–1945', *Review of International Studies*, vol. 25, no. 4 (October 1999), pp. 655–73.

Rosenblatt, Naomi. 'Oil and the Eastern Front: US Foreign and Military Policy in Iran, 1941–1945', Undergraduate Humanities Forum 2008–09: Change (University of Pennsylvania, 2009).

Rowan-Robinson, H. 'Lessons from the Levant', *Army Quarterly*, XLIII (October 1941 and January 1942), pp. 73–9.

Rubin, Barry. 'American Perceptions and Great Power Politics in the Middle East, 1941–1947', PhD thesis (Georgetown University, 1978).

——*The Great Powers in the Middle East, 1941–1947: The Road to the Cold War* (London: Frank Cass, 1980).

——*Paved with Good Intentions: The American Experience and Iran* (Oxford: Oxford University Press, 1980).

Rusterholtz, Wallace. 'The History of the Motor Transport Service, Persian Gulf Command, United States Army', PhD thesis (State University of New York, Buffalo, 1949).

al-Sabbagh, Salah al-Din. *Mudhakkirati* (Damascus, Syria: n.p., 1956).

Sarners, Harvey. *General Anders and the Soldiers of the Second Polish Corps* (Toronto: Brunswick, 1997).

Sayre, Joel. *Persian Gulf Command: Some Marvels on the Road to Kazvin* (New York: Random House, 1945).

Schmider, Klaus. 'The Mediterranean in 1940–1941: Crossroads of Lost Opportunities?', *War and Society*, vol. 15, no. 2 (1997), pp. 19–41.

Schreiber, Gerhard, Bernd Stegemann and Detlef Vogel, *Germany and the Second World War*, vol. 3, *The Mediterranean, South-East Europe, and North Africa 1939–1941*, trans. Dean S. McMurry, Ewald Osers and Louise Wilmott (Oxford: Clarendon Press, 1995).

Schubert, Frank. 'The Persian Gulf Command: Lifeline to the Soviet Union', in Barry Fowle (ed.), *Builders and Fighters: US Army Engineers in World War II* (Fort Belvoir, VA: US Army Corps of Engineers Office of History, 1992), pp. 305–15; chapter online at http://www.parstimes.com/history/persian_gulf_command.pdf (accessed 15 December 2017).

Schulze-Holthus, Berthold. *Daybreak in Iran: A Story of the German Intelligence Service*, trans. Mervyn Savill (London: Staples Press, 1954).

Schwanitz, Wolfgang (ed.). *Germany and the Middle East, 1871–1945* (Princeton, NJ: Markus Wiener, 2004).

Schwarz, Jordan. *Liberal: Adolf A. Berle and the Vision of an American Era* (New York: Macmillan, 1987).

Scott, Ezra. 'My Time in the Persian Gulf Command, 1943–1945', *Pars Times* (n.d.); online at www.parstimes.com/travel/iran/memoirs_persian_gulf_command.html (accessed 12 December 2017).

Seydi, Suleyman. 'Intelligence and Counter-Intelligence Activities in Iran in WW2', *Middle Eastern Studies*, vol. 46, no. 5 (September 2010), pp. 733–52.

Sherwen, Douglas. *The Persian Corridor: The Little-known Story of the Signal Corps in the Middle East During World War II* (New York: Exposition Press, 1979).

Shimizu, Hiroshi. 'Anglo-Japanese Competition in the Textile Trade in the Inter-war Period: A Case Study of Iraq, 1932–1941', *Middle Eastern Studies*, vol. 20, no. 3 (July 1984), pp. 259–89.

Silverfarb, Daniel. 'Britain and Iraqi Barley during the Second World War', *Middle Eastern Studies*, vol. 31, no. 3 (June 1995), p. 524–32.

——*Britain's Informal Empire in the Middle East: A Case Study of Iraq, 1929–1941* (Oxford: Oxford University Press, 1986).

——'The British Government and the Question of Umm Qasr, 1938–1945', *Asian and African Studies*, vol. 16, no. 2 (July 1982), pp. 215–38.

——*The Twilight of British Ascendancy in the Middle East: A Case Study of Iraq, 1941–1950* (New York: St Martin's Press, 1994).

Simon, Reeva Spector. *Iraq Between the Two World Wars: The Militarist Origins of Tyranny* (New York: Columbia University Press, 2004).

Skrine, Clarmont. 'Assignment to Mauritius', *Blackwood's Magazine*, vol. 275, no. 1,660 (February 1954), pp. 143–57.

——*World War in Iran* (London: Constable and Company, 1962).

Slim, William. *Unofficial History* (Barnsley: Pen and Sword, 2008).

Sluglett, Peter. *Britain in Iraq: Contriving King and Country* (London: I.B. Tauris, 2007).

Smart, H.G. 'Report of Operations in Baghdad Area: 2 May to 31 May 1941', AOC RAF Iraq Air Commodore (Acting AVM) H.G. Smart to the AOC-i-C Middle East, 'The Battle for Habbaniya – The Forgotten War', RAF History, online at http://archive.li/2NdXC (accessed 22 January 2018).

Smith, Arthur. 'PAIFORCE', *Household Brigade Magazine* (autumn 1945), pp. 110–12.

Smith, Vic. 'Pink Elephants on the Road to Baghdad', *MV Magazine*, nos 2 and 3 (1996).

Smyth, Howard M. et al. (eds). *Documents on German Foreign Policy 1918–1945*, vol. 8: *The War Years, June 23–December 11, 1941* (Washington, DC: US GPO, 1954), online at http://www.ibiblio.org/pha/policy/pre-war/1918-00-00a.pdf (accessed 13 December 2017).

el-Solh, Raghid. *Britain's Two Wars with Iraq* (Reading: Ithaca Press, 1996).

Special Service Division, United States Army Services of Supply. *Instructions for American Servicemen in Iran during World War II* (North Charleston, SC: CreateSpace, 2012).

——*Pocket Guide to Iran* (Washington, DC: US Army War and Navy Departments, 1943).

——*A Short Guide to Iraq* (Washington, DC: US Army War and Navy Departments, 1943).

Sreberny, Annabelle and Massoumeh Torfeh. 'The BBC Persian Service, 1941–1979', *Historical Journal of Film, Radio and Television*, vol. 28, no. 4 (October 2008), pp. 515–35.

——*Persian Service: The BBC and British Interests in Iran* (London: I.B. Tauris, 2014).

Stark, Freya. *Dust in the Lion's Paw: Autobiography 1939–1946* (London: John Murray, 1961).

Stewart, Richard. *Sunrise at Abadan: The British and Soviet Invasion of Iran, 1941* (New York: Praeger, 1988).

Stoff, Michael. 'The Anglo-American Oil Agreement and the Wartime Search for Foreign Oil Policy', *Business History Review*, vol. 55, no. 1 (spring 1981), pp. 59–74.

Stoler, Mark. *The Politics of the Second Front: American Military Planning and Diplomacy in Coalition Warfare, 1941–1943* (London: Greenwood, 1977).

Summers, J.D. 'Into Persia', *Household Brigade Magazine* (summer 1942), pp. 49–53.

——'Nine Weeks in the Desert: An Account of the Adventures of the Household Cavalry Regiment in Iraq and Syria', *Household Brigade Magazine* (spring 1942), pp. 9–13.

Tamkin, Nicholas. *Britain, Turkey and the Soviet Union, 1940–45: Strategy, Diplomacy and Intelligence in the Eastern Mediterranean* (Basingstoke: Palgrave, 2009).

Tarbush, Mohammad. *The Role of the Military in Politics: A Case Study of Iraq to 1941* (London: Keegan Paul International, 1982).

Thorne, Christopher. *Allies of a Kind: The United States, Britain, and the War Against Japan, 1941–1945* (Oxford: Oxford University Press, 1978).

Thorpe, James. 'The United States and the 1940–41 Anglo-Iraqi Crisis: American Policy in Transition', *Middle East Journal*, vol. 25, no. 1 (winter 1971), pp. 79–89.

Titterton, G.A. *The Royal Navy and the Mediterranean*, vol. 2: *November 1940–December 1941* (London: Frank Cass, 2002).

Toprani, Anand. 'Germany's Answer to Standard Oil: The Continental Oil Company and Nazi Grand Strategy, 1940–1942', *Journal of Strategic Studies*, vol. 37, nos 6–7 (December 2014), pp. 949–73.

Toth, Anthony. 'Tribes and Tribulations: Bedouin Losses in the Saudi and Iraqi Struggles over Kuwait's Frontiers, 1921–1943', *British Journal of Middle East Studies*, vol. 32, no. 2 (November 2005), pp. 145–67.

Tooze, Adam. *The Wages of Destruction: The Making and Breaking of the Nazi Economy* (London: Penguin, 2007).

Trent Smith, Steven. 'Off the Rails', *World War II*, vol. 31, no. 1 (May 2016), online at http://www.historynet.com/the-battle-before-the-battle.htm (accessed 22 January 2018).

Tripp, Charles. *A History of Iraq* (Cambridge: Cambridge University Press, 2002).

Ward, Steven. *Immortal: A Military History of Iran and its Armed Forces* (Washington, DC: Georgetown University Press, 2009).

Warlimont, Walter. 'The Decision in the Mediterranean 1942', in H. Jacobsen and J. Rohwer (eds), *The Decisive Battles of World War Two: The German View* (New York: Putnam Publishing Group, 1965).

Warner, Geoffrey. *Iraq and Syria, 1941* (Cranbury, NJ: Associated University Presses, 1979).

Warren, Eugene. 'Bandar Shahpur (Now Bandar Khomeini) – World War II – Persian Gulf Command', *Pars Times* (n.d.); online at www.parstimes.com/travel/iran/bandar_shahpur.html (accessed 12 December 2017).

Weber, Frank. *The Evasive Neutral: Germany, Britain, and the Quest for a Turkish Alliance in the Second World War* (Columbia: University of Missouri Press, 1979).

Weeks, Albert. *Stalin's Other War: Soviet Grand Strategy, 1939–1941* (Lanham, MD: Rowman and Littlefield, 2002).

Weinberg, Gerhard. *A World at Arms: A Global History of World War II* (Cambridge: Cambridge University Press, 1995).

White, Donald. 'The Nature of World Power in American History: An Evaluation at the End of World War Two', *Diplomatic History*, vol. 11, no. 3 (July 1987), pp. 181–202.

Wien, Peter. *Iraqi Arab Nationalism: Authoritarian, Totalitarian and Pro-Fascist Inclinations, 1932–1941* (London: Routledge, 2007).

Williams, Manuela. 'Mussolini's Secret War in the Mediterranean and the Middle East: Italian Intelligence and the British Response', *Intelligence and National Security*, vol. 22, no. 6 (2007), pp. 881–904.

Wilmington, Martin. *The Middle East Supply Center* (Albany, NY: SUNY Press, 1971).

Wilson, Alexander. 'The Indian Army in Africa and the Eastern Mediterranean, 1939–1943', PhD thesis (King's College London, 2018).

Wilson, Henry Maitland. 'Despatch on the Persia and Iraq Command Covering the Period 21 August 1942 to 17 February 1943', *London Gazette* (1946), pp. 4,333–40.

——*Eight Years Overseas, 1939–1947* (London: Hutchinson, 1950).

Wright, Denis. *The English among the Persians during the Qajar Period, 1787–1921* (London: Heinemann, 1977).

Wyndham, Humphrey. *The Household Cavalry at War: First Household Cavalry Regiment* (Aldershot: Gale and Polden, 1952).

Yarham, E.R. 'The Trans-Persian Railway', *Royal United Services Institute Journal*, vol. 87, no. 545 (1942), pp. 44–50.

Yisraeli, David. 'The Third Reich and Palestine', *Middle Eastern Studies*, vol. 7, no. 3 (October 1971), pp. 343–53.

Young, Robert. *Postcolonialism: A Very Short Introduction* (Oxford: Oxford University Press, 2003).

Zamir, Meir. *The Secret Anglo-French War in the Middle East: Intelligence and Decolonization, 1940–1948* (London: Routledge, 2014).

Films

British Film Institute

672358, *British News*, No. 54, 1941: 'British pinch out Iraqi revolt'; 'The advance into Syria'.

672473, *British News*, No. 72, 1941: 'Empire and Soviet forces meet in Iran'.

Imperial War Museum

AYY 215/2 War Office Film Unit (WOFU), 'Supplies to Russia': Royal Engineers loading goods from ships onto trains at Ahwaz and Bandar Shahpur.

AYY 215/3 WOFU: American Dodge trucks at Andimeshk being handed over to Soviet troops.

AYY 215/4 WOFU, the Duke of Gloucester's visit to Baghdad: inspecting Tenth Army with General Quinan, 1942; arriving at the British Embassy; inspecting a guard of honour consisting of Punjabis and the 9th Gurkhas; Duke of Cornwall's Light Infantry band plays; the Duke of Gloucester leaves the embassy to inspect the 26th Corps of Signals and also the 24th Combined General Hospital wards; shots of Indian nurses; HRH inspects the 3/8th Punjabi Regiment, the 2/10th Gurkhas and the 21st Brigade HQ and decorates Indian troops for gallantry; inspection of Royal Indian Army Ordnance Corps workshops; HRH receiving guests at a British Embassy reception together with Sir Kinahan and Lady Cornwallis.

AYY 215/6, 1942: Brigadier Sir Godfrey Rhodes, Director of Transport, Iran, with Iranian and Soviet colleagues; a car carrying a Japanese diplomat leaves the Japanese Embassy in Tehran on the morning of the rupture of Iranian–Japanese relations; locomotives at the head of a supply train with an Indian troop convoy; the supply train travelling through Iran.

AYY 215/7 WOFU: New Polish forces in Iran and Iraq.

AYY 220/1 WOFU: the Duke of Gloucester in Basra and Tehran, May 1942.

AYY 344/2 WOFU, Britain versus Poland football match, Baghdad, 1943: General Anders, General Wilson, the Iraqi regent and Ambassador Cornwallis in attendance; England team included players from Burnley, Chesterfield, Crystal Palace, Leeds United, Liverpool and Tottenham Hotspur.

AYY 396/7/1 WOFU, 'Wheat for Persia'.

AYY 396/11 WOFU: Russian Spitfires being worked on by 119 Maintenance Unit, RAF Shaibah.

AYY 396/12 WOFU, 'Planes to Russia': US Army Air Force base at Abadan; all three allies working together.

CVN 232: *The Road to Russia: The Story of PAIFOR.*

INR 58, *Indian News Parade*, No. 58, 1944: 'Iranian interest in Indian culture'.

Ministry of Information MOI FLM 507, 508, 509: Ministry of Information films of British and Soviet forces.

Ministry of Information 2012-10-27: Ministry of Information film about the Iranian supply route; three large format leather bound albums with affixed prints, a mixture of official and private and ephemera denoting the service of Lieutenant Peter Hopkinson, a cameraman with No. 1 Army Film and Photographic Unit; the album 'Persia' gives coverage of Hopkinson's time in Iran while his unit made the Ministry of Information film *Via Persia* about the journey supplies made to get through to the Soviet Union.

NMV 645, *Movietone News*, 16 October 1941, British and Soviet forces meet in Iran: 'Indian troops pass through Kermanshah before meeting Soviet troops near Qazvin'; 'Russian officer fires Very light now that allied front stretches from Arctic to Libya'; 'All is quiet in Tehran after departure of the Germans'; 'Eagle emblem outside empty German embassy'.

WPN 29, *War Picture News*, 20 October 1941, Iran: Aerial and street scenes of Tehran; commentary on the strategic importance of the country and the need to oust German influence; pictures of Iranian women with children strapped to their backs; the new shah; British infantry guarding the pipelines and refinery at Abadan; views of the refinery; British machine-gun defences; British and Soviet troops meeting at Qazvin; Australian troops embarking on a ship on the Shatt al-Arab; a convoy of British Crossley armoured cars in an Iranian town; British and Indian troops inspecting a Soviet T-26 tank and mingling with tank crew, who then inspect British 15cwt Morris Commercial lorries; a meal and toasts shared by imperial and Soviet troops, including Major-General Slim and Brigadier Aizlewood.

Other

Allies Meet in Iran, Pathé.

Boy King of Irak and *Axis Agents Leave Iran*, Movietone: the second of the two *Boy King of Irak* films shows Faisal II and the regent inspecting British military positions, handling Bren guns and wireless equipment, and inspecting a Sikh guard of honour.

More News Pictures from Iran, Pathé.

Occupation Troops in Iran, Pathé.

Poles in Persia, Pathé.

The Big Three in Teheran, Pathé.

The Occupation of Iran, Gaumont.

The War in Iraq, Pathé.

With British Forces in Iraq, Pathé.

And finally . . .

As ever, the manuscript has had the final word. Viewed too late for inclusion, but nevertheless worthy of mention here, are these wonderful Imperial War Museum documents:

K88/219, *Services Guide to Iraq.* This is the British equivalent to the American guides discussed in the book.

K79/3533, *Iraq.* A comprehensive handbook issued to British Officers.

K11/1491, *Baghdad to Beirut.* For troops travelling along the trans-desert line of communication when going on leave.

INDEX